AF333068

INTEGRATION AND INNOVATION ORIENT TO E-SOCIETY VOLUME 2

IFIP – The International Federation for Information Processing

IFIP was founded in 1960 under the auspices of UNESCO, following the First World Computer Congress held in Paris the previous year. An umbrella organization for societies working in information processing, IFIP's aim is two-fold: to support information processing within its member countries and to encourage technology transfer to developing nations. As its mission statement clearly states,

> *IFIP's mission is to be the leading, truly international, apolitical organization which encourages and assists in the development, exploitation and application of information technology for the benefit of all people.*

IFIP is a non-profitmaking organization, run almost solely by 2500 volunteers. It operates through a number of technical committees, which organize events and publications. IFIP's events range from an international congress to local seminars, but the most important are:

• The IFIP World Computer Congress, held every second year;
• Open conferences;
• Working conferences.

The flagship event is the IFIP World Computer Congress, at which both invited and contributed papers are presented. Contributed papers are rigorously refereed and the rejection rate is high.

As with the Congress, participation in the open conferences is open to all and papers may be invited or submitted. Again, submitted papers are stringently refereed.

The working conferences are structured differently. They are usually run by a working group and attendance is small and by invitation only. Their purpose is to create an atmosphere conducive to innovation and development. Refereeing is less rigorous and papers are subjected to extensive group discussion.

Publications arising from IFIP events vary. The papers presented at the IFIP World Computer Congress and at open conferences are published as conference proceedings, while the results of the working conferences are often published as collections of selected and edited papers.

Any national society whose primary activity is in information may apply to become a full member of IFIP, although full membership is restricted to one society per country. Full members are entitled to vote at the annual General Assembly, National societies preferring a less committed involvement may apply for associate or corresponding membership. Associate members enjoy the same benefits as full members, but without voting rights. Corresponding members are not represented in IFIP bodies. Affiliated membership is open to non-national societies, and individual and honorary membership schemes are also offered.

INTEGRATION AND INNOVATION ORIENT TO E-SOCIETY VOLUME 2

Seventh IFIP International Conference on e-Business, e-Services, and e-Society (I3E2007), October 10-12, Wuhan, China

Edited by

Weijun Wang
HuaZhong Normal University, China

Yanhui Li
HuaZhong Normal University, China

Zhao Duan
HuaZhong Normal University, China

Li Yan
HuaZhong Normal University, China

Hongxiu Li
Turku School of Economics, Finland

Xiaoxi Yang
HuaZhong Normal University, China

 Springer

Library of Congress Control Number: 2007

Integration and Innovation Orient to E-Society, Volume 2

Edited by W. Wang, Y. Li, Z. Duan, L. Yan, H. Li, and X. Yang

   p.   cm. (IFIP International Federation for Information Processing, a Springer Series in Computer Science)

  ISSN: 1571-5736 / 1861-2288 (Internet)
  ISBN: 978-0-387-75493-2
  eISBN: 978-0-387-75494-9
Printed on acid-free paper

Printed in the United States of America.

9 8 7 6 5 4 3 2 1
springer.com

Table of Contents
Volume 2

Conference Chair's Message

Organizing Committee

Program Committee

External Reviewers

e-Service Track

CONFERENCE CHAIR'S MESSAGE

This volume contains the papers presented at I3E2007, the seventh IFIP International Conference on e-Business/Commerce, e-Services and e-Society, which was held in Wuhan from 10-12 October 2007. The conference was sponsored by IFIP TC6/WG6.11 in co-operation with TC8, TC9, TC11, and TC6/WG 6.4.

The scope of six past I3E conferences was on e-Commerce, e-Business, and e-Government. It is changed to "e-Business, e-Services and e-Society" this time, which is not only a diction modification, but also represents the upcoming trends of integration and innovation in the growing areas of e-Business/Commerce, e-Services and e-Society. Modern Service Science based on e-Services is developing as a discipline in all over the world, which would undoubtedly improve the research and application of e-Commerce and e-Society. It really shows the integration and innovation of multidisciplinary research and application in e-Business/Commerce, e-Learning, e-Tourism, e-Government, e-Health, e-Payment, etc. All of these construct the base and bricks of the e-Society.

A total of 460 papers were submitted and 149 papers were accepted through double-blind reviewing, the submissions came from 20 different countries, and it is the first time for I3E to attract big attentions of so many Chinese scholars. We believe more and more Chinese authors will participate in the future activities of I3E.

I would like to express my sincere thanks to the many people that made this volume and the I3E2007 conference in Wuhan possible. The first thank you goes to Reima Suomi, co-chair of the IFIP WG6.11 and Executive Liason, who visited my university in 2005, encouraged me to attend the I3E2006 conference and trusts us to hold the I3E2007 in Wuhan. He has spent much time to discuss issues with us and answer our detailed questions on how to organize the conference. The next goes to Winfried Lamersdorf and Wojciech Cellary, co-chairs of the IFIP WG6.11. They have put forward many good suggestions to our team in preparing for the conference and this book. The third goes to Lefkada Papacharalambous and Narciso Cerpa, program co-chairs. The detailed help was always available from them. And total reviewers have paid great contribution for improving the quality of the already high-quality submitted papers. This conference would not have been possible without your huge support. Thank you very much, all of you.

I also would like to thank my leaders and several colleagues in HuaZhong Normal University. Our president, Ming Ma, vice-president, Zhongkai Yang and Dean, Xuedong Wang pay hight attention to this conference as a core academic activity in the university's and our department's portfolio. Dr.Yanhui Li, Zhao Duan and Li Yan have spent much time and paid much contribution works to edit book and perpare the conference. Our staff Yangai Cai, Tian Jie, Xiaoli Chi and postgraduated students Xiaoxi Yang and Jing Sun took care of the administration of the conference.

Special thanks go to our support institutes: Ministry of Education of People's Republic of China, Ministry of Commerce of People's Republic of China, Ministry of Information Industry of People's Republic of China, National Natural Science Foundation of China, Wang-Kuangchen

Education Foundation and HuaZhong Normal University.

Finally, I want to thank all the contributors to this book and the conference, as well as the I3E2007 conference participants. Because the quality and success of the IFIP I3E2007 was based on the sound work of all the committee members, reviewers and participants.

Weijun Wang
I3E2007 Wuhan Conference Chair

Organizing Committee

Honorary General Chair

Ming Ma, *Huazhong Normal University, Wuhan, China*

General Chair

Zongkai Yang, *Huazhong Normal University, Wuhan, China*
Xuedong Wang, *Huazhong Normal University, Wuhan, China*

Conference Chair

Weijun Wang, *Huazhong Normal University, Wuhan, China*

Program Co-Chairs

Narciso Cerpa, *University of Talca, Chile*
Lefkada Papacharalambous, *TEL of Halkida, Greece*

Liaison Chairs:

Executive Liason: *Reima Suomi, Turku School of Economics, Finland*
Europe: Volker Tschammer, *FhG FOKUS, Germany*
North America: Ranjan Kini, *Indiana University Northwest, USA*
South America: Manuel J.Mendes, *Unisantos, Brazil*
Asia-Pacific: Katina Michael, *University of Wollongong, Australia*

Members of Organizing Committee

Zhihao Chen, *Zhongnan University of Economics and Law, China*
Weiguo Deng, *South China Normal University, China*
Xiaozhao Deng, *Southwest University, China*
Tingting He, *Huazhong Normal University, China*
Jinyi Hong, *Ministry of Information Industry, China*
Yisheng Lan, *Shanghai University of Finance & Economics, China*
Hongxin Li, *Dongbei University of Finance & Economics, China*
Jun Liu, *Beijing Jiaotong University, China*
Qingtang Liu, *Huazhong Normal University, China*
Tenghong Liu, *Zhongnan University of Economics and Law, China*
Yezheng Liu, *HeFei University of Technology, China*
Yong Liu, *ZhengZhou Institute of Aeronautical Industry Managent, China*
Zhenyu Liu, *Xiamen University, China*
Haiqun Ma, *Heilongjiang University, China*

Shihua Ma, *Huazhong University of Science & Technology, China*
Weidong Meng, *Chongqing University, China*
Guihua Nie, *Wuhan University of Technology, China*
Zheng Qin, *Tsinghua University, China*
Yongzhong Sha, *Lanzhou University, China*
Xiaobai Sheng, *Nanjing Audit University, China*
Jinping Shi, *Hubei University, China*
Ling Song, *China Electronic Commerce Association, China*
Yuanfang Song, *Central University of Finance and Economics, China*
Baowen Sun, *Renmin University of China,, China*
Binyong Tang,*Donghua University, China*
Xinpei Wang, *Ministry of Commerce of the People's Republic of China, China*
Yuefen Wang, *Nanjing University of Science & Technology, China*
Yan Wu, *Ministry of Education, China*
Kang Xie, *Sun Yat-Sen University, China*
Yangqun Xie, *Anhui University, China*
Kuanhai Zhan, *South West Univesity of Finance & Economics, China*
Ning Zhang, *Beijing University, China*
Liyi Zhang, *Wuhan University, China*
Bangwei Zhao, *Xidian University, China*
Chengling Zhao, *Huazhong Normal University, China*
Shuangyi Zheng *South-Central University For Nationalities, China*

Local Arrangement Committee

Yanhui Li, *Huazhong Normal University, China, Chair*
Zhao Duan, *Huazhong Normal University, China*
Li Yan, *Huazhong Normal University, China*
Xiaoxi Yang, *Huazhong Normal University, China*
Jing Sun, *Huazhong Normal University, China*

Program Committee

Americo Nobre Amorim, *Ufpe/FIR, Brazil*

Melanie Bicking, *Universität Koblenz-Landau, Germany*

Regis Cabral, *University of Umeå, Sweden*

Wojciech Cellary, *The Poznan University of Economics, Poland*

Narciso Cerpa, *Universidad de Talca, Chile*

Deren Chen, *Zhe Jiang University, China*

Jin Chen, *School of Business, China*

Kok-Wai Chew, *Multimedia University, Malaysia*

Dirk Deschoolmeester, *Universität Ghent, Belgium*

Motohisa Funabashi, *Hitachi, Japan*

Rüdiger Grimm, *Universität Koblenz-Landau, Germany*

J. Felix Hampe, *University of Koblenz-Landau, Germany*

Farouk Kamoun, *Campus Universitaire Manouba, Tunis*

Dipak Khakhar, *Lund University, Institute for Informatics, Sweden*

Kos Koen, *Parktown Business School of Entrepreneurship, South Africa*

Dimitri Konstantas, *University of Geneva, Switzerland*

Irene Krebs, *Brandenburgische Technische Universität, Cottbus, Germany*

Winfried Lamersdorf, *Universität Hamburg, Fachbereich Informatik, Germany*

Gang Li, *Wuhan University, China*

Qi Li, *Xi'an Jiaotong University, China*

Yijun Li, *Harbing Institute of Technology, China*

Hongxiu Li, *Turku School of Economics, Finland*

Tingjie Lv, *Beijing University of Posts and Telecommunications, China*

Manuel Mendes, *CENPRA and Uni Santos, Brazil*

Zoran Milosevic, *Deontik, Australia*

Harri Oinas-Kukkonen, *University of Oulu, Finland*

Lefkada Papacharalambous, *TEI of Halkida, Greece*

Spyridon Papastergiou, *University of Pireus, Greece*

Despina Polemi, *University of Pireaus, Greece*

Kai Rannenberg, *T-Mobile Stiftungsprofessur für m-Commerce, Frankfurt, Germany*

Reinhard Riedl, *Universität Zürich, Switzerland*

Santosh Shrivastava, *Newcastle University, UK*

Katarina Stanoevska-Slabeva, *Universität St. Gallen, Switzerland*

Reima Suomi, *Turku School of Economics, Finland*

Paula Swatman, *University of South Australia, Australia*

Roland Traunmüller, *Universität Linz, Austria*

Aphrodite Tsalgatidou, *NTUA Athen, Greece*

Hans Weigand, *Tilburg University, Netherlands*

Rolf T. Wigand, *University of Arkansas at Little Rock, USA*

Maria Wimmer, *Universität Koblenz-Landau, Germany*

Kyoko Yamori, *Waseda University, Japan*

Deli Yang, *DaLian University of Technology, China*

Shanlin Yang, *HeFei University of Technology, China*
Jinglong Zhang, *Huazhong University of Technology and Sciences, China*
Jing Zhao, *China University of Geosciences, China*
Daoli Zhu, *Fu Dan University, China*
Hans-Dieter Zimmermann, *Swiss Institute for Information Research, Switzerland*

Measuring the performance of G2G services in Iran

Behrouz Zarei[1], Maryam Safdari[2]
1 Management School, University of Tehran, Tehran, Iran,
E-mail: bzarei@ut.ac.ir
2 London School of Economics, University of London,
E-mail:maryam.safdari@gmail.com

Abstract. To highlight the growth of e-government and the importance of its services it is essential to evaluate the performance of the service delivery to customers. Research indicates that traditional performance indexes are not suitable for this evaluation; moreover, it is noticeable that the e-government services are intangible and invisible. Among different e-government services, measurement of quality government to government (G2G) services has been less attractive for researchers while crucial for government policy-makers. This calls for a better understanding of the specific needs of users of these services in order to provide appropriate type and level of services that meets those needs. In this paper, the performance of the G2G services is measured in the Iranian context. For this purpose, SERVQUAL, which is a well-known method for assessing service quality, is employed. This study proposes and tests a five-factor of SERVQUAL instrument to explain user satisfaction and gap analysis, between expectations and perceptions of its customers, consisting thirty ministries and main governmental organizations. Based on a Chi-square test, factor analysis, gap analysis and correlations, it is concluded the gap between expectations and perceptions of G2G customers is significant and customer satisfaction of G2G services is at low level.

1   Introduction

Government organizations usually rely on other government agencies information to deliver services. This makes the electronic interactions crucial for effective inter-organizational business processes management in the government, known as Government-to-Government (G2G). G2G is normally accessed via a government's intranet or private networks and may utilize some of the components of G2C and G2B services but generally require more direct access to databases and applications.

Please use the following format when citing this chapter:

Zarei, B., Safdari, M., 2007, in IFIP International Federation for Information Processing, Volume 252, Integration and Innovation Orient to E-Society Volume 2, eds. Wang, W., (Boston: Springer), pp. 1-8.

There are many studies on e-government concept and its services, some have emphasized on service evaluation and their influence on the country.

G-to-G system of Iran revolves around three axes: needs, problems, and possibilities/ facilities. *Needs* was defined as the top factor in shaping the electronic administration of Iran's government. The notion of Government Electronic Administration (GEA) was the result of the president's offices need for collecting information from government agencies as well as the agencies' need for classified and access to the information at various levels. The need for GEA was due to many *problems* including inefficient management and also the need for expertise in the process of decision making as well as enhancing the productivity of scarce resources. Lack of various technological infrastructure as well as managerial, cultural and financial limitations were effective in changing the concept of electronic government into GEA [2] in Iran.

The type of assumed e-government services in some agencies and organizations are not qualified enough and they lead to many new problems. Therefore, e-government in Iran is conceptually a way to a new level of performance aiming at reducing the operations cycle time, offering prompt, quality, inexpensive services to demanding citizens as well as catering for the needs of officials who are not satisfied with the existing systems. Iranians GEA and Lenk and Trannmullers' model are somehow similar in establishing the type of e-government [1]. Although, both concentrate on the process and coordination of e-government development, they ignore the interaction of e-government with three major issues: e-business, knowledge and citizen requirements.

Always there exists an important question: why should service quality be measured? Measurement allows for comparison before and after changes, for the location of quality related problems and for the establishment of clear standards for service delivery. Edvardsen [3] state that, in their experience, the starting point in developing quality in services is analysis and measurement. The SERVQUAL approach, which is studied in this paper, is the most common method for measuring service quality. SERVQUAL as the most often used approach for measuring service quality has been to compare customers' expectations before a service encounter and their perceptions of the actual service delivered [4]. The SERVQUAL instrument has been the predominant method used to measure consumers' perceptions of service quality. It has five generic dimensions or factors and are stated as follows [5]:

(1) *Tangibles*. Physical facilities, equipment and appearance of personnel.

(2) *Reliability*. Ability to perform the promised service dependably and accurately.

(3) *Responsiveness*. Willingness to help customers and provide prompt service.

(4) *Assurance* (including competence, courtesy, credibility and security). Knowledge and courtesy of employees and their ability to inspire trust and confidence.

(5) *Empathy* (including access, communication, understanding the customer). Caring and individualized attention that the firm provides to its customers.

SERVQUAL is a survey instrument based on extensive research. In particular, it measures what the customer expects from the organization in relation to these dimensions against what the customer perceives the organization performs along these dimensions, this is of major importance in selecting SERVQUAL among existing instruments for this study because it can make clear the horizon of customer satisfaction and also significant difference between ideal and real conditions. This instrument is well proven and widely recognized. In addition, it identifies and understand where service gaps exist within the organization and between the organization and its customers prioritize those gaps in terms of relative impact on quality of service identify the reasons for the existence of those gaps develop a program of activities to close those gaps implement an appropriate set of processes to continuously review and refine customer service quality.

The primary objective of this study is to use SERVQUAL instrument in order to ascertain any actual or perceived gaps between customer expectations and perceptions of the service offered. It is also attempted to point out how management of service improvement can become more logical and integrated with respect to the prioritized service quality dimensions and their affections on increasing/decreasing service quality gaps. In the following, the model of service quality gaps and the SERVQUAL methodology is demonstrated and an example is presented to pinpoint the application of the SERVQUAL approach. Then, after a discussion, major conclusions are derived.

2   Research methodology

The concept of measuring the difference between expectations and perceptions in the form of the SERVQUAL gap score proved very useful for assessing levels of service quality. Parasuraman *et al.* [6,7,8,9], argue that, with minor modification, SERVQUAL can be adapted to any service organisation. They further argue that information on service quality gaps can help managers diagnose where performance improvement can best be targeted. The largest negative gaps, combined with assessment of where expectations are highest, facilitate prioritisation of performance improvement... Equally, if gap scores in some aspects of service do turn out to be positive, implying expectations are actually not just being met but exceeded, then this allows managers to review whether they may be "over-supplying" this particular feature of the service and whether there is potential for re-deployment of resources into features which are underperforming. Therefore, the first research question is:

There is a gap between expectations and perceptions of e-government services, or in better words, expectations are greater than performance

Service quality can thus be defined as the difference between customer expectations of service and perceived service. If expectations are greater than performance, then perceived quality is less than satisfactory and hence customer dissatisfaction occurs.

The measurement of service quality can provide specific data that can be used in quality management; hence, service organizations would be able to monitor and maintain quality service. Assessing service quality and better understanding how various dimensions affect overall service quality would enable organizations to efficiently design the service delivery process. By identifying strengths and weaknesses pertaining to the dimensions of service quality organizations can better allocate resources to provide better service and ultimately better service to external customers. And finally the last research question is:

Dimensions of questionnaire are independent of each other

This evaluation has been focused on G2G sector and also, this will let us know if the organizations are satisfied with the given service quality of e-government plan? Among existing ministries and organizations some of them which are directly government- related organizations were the best choice.

Table1. List of ministries and organizations

Ministries	governmental organization
Science, Research &Technology	Environment Protection Organization
Crusade of Agriculture	Atomic Energy Organization
Islamic guidance and culture	Central Bank
Labor and Social Affairs	Physical Education Organization
Commerce	Management & Planning
Cooperative	Parliament
Energy	TV Radio
Foreign Affairs	Tax organization
Health and medical education	
Housing and Urban Development	
Industries and Mines	
Justice	
Economic and Property1	
Economic and Property2	
Oil	
Post, Telephones & Telegraphs1	
Post, Telephones & Telegraphs2	
Roads and Transport	
Country	
Welfare & Social Affaires	
Education	
Education 2	

3   Research finding

The mean, median, maximum, minimum, standard deviation was measured for all the questions. The minimum expectation for Question 1 is 5, while for most other questions as shown in the above table this figure is 1. However, the value for maximum expectation and perception was a constant 7 for all the questions shown in the table.

Table2. Descriptive statistics on questions

Question	Expectations					Perceptions				
	Mean	Median	Std.D	Min	Max	Mean	Median	Std.D	Min	Max
1	6.63	7.00	.615	5	7	3.83	3.00	1.84	1	7
2	5.20	5.00	1.73	1	7	4.17	4.50	1.72	1	7
3	4.47	4.00	1.13	2	7	2.97	2.00	1.93	1	7
4	5.97	7.00	1.60	1	7	4.17	5.00	1.85	1	7
Tangibles	Mean:16.53; Median:17.50; Std.D:8.37; Max: 5; Min: 40									
5	6.47	7.00	1.07	2	7	3.53	3.00	2.08	1	7
6	6.47	7.00	1.10	2	7	4.13	4.00	1.94	1	7
7	5.90	6.00	1.21	3	7	3.63	3.50	1.95	1	7
9	2.97	2.00	2.14	1	7	4.23	5.00	2.11	1	7
Reliability	Mean:26.60; Median:27.50; Std.D:10.16; Max: 10; Min: 50									
8	6.33	7.00	1.09	2	7	3.50	3.00	1.96	1	7
10	6.27	7.00	1.23	3	7	3.47	3.00	2.03	1	7
11	6.00	7.00	1.33	2	7	3.50	3.00	2.01	1	7
12	6.10	7.00	1.21	3	7	3.73	4.00	1.53	1	7
13	5.40	6.00	2.04	1	7	3.90	3.50	2.02	1	7
Responsiveness	Mean:21.17; Median:20.00; Std.D:8.77; Max: 10; Min: 50									
14	6.27	7.00	1.20	3	7	4.47	5.00	1.77	1	7
15	6.20	6.50	1.09	2	7	4.23	4.50	1.83	1	7
16	5.83	6.50	1.59	1	7	4.33	4.00	1.80	1	7
17	6.47	7.00	1.00	3	7	4.77	5.00	1.59	1	7
Assurance	Mean:22.50; Median:20.00; Std.D:7.16; Max: 10; Min: 40									
18	5.10	6.00	1.76	1	7	3.50	3.00	1.83	1	7
19	5.87	6.00	1.59	1	7	3.83	3.00	1.84	1	7
20	4.33	5.00	1.88	1	7	3.47	3.50	1.73	1	7
21	6.03	6.50	1.27	3	7	3.83	3.50	1.98	1	7
22	6.23	6.00	.927	3	7	4.53	5.00	1.77	1	7
Empathy	Mean:12.37; Median:10.00; Std.D:5.86; Max: 4; Min: 20									

In order to evaluate the user satisfaction, similar tests for each question is designed, each test has two hypotheses:

H_0: *Gap between expectation and perception is significant.*

H_1: *Gap between expectation and perception is not significant.*

Measured statistic for this test has chi-square distribution. In line with measured value for each statistic, all questions should be analyzed one by one. According to measured P-value of each question, if P-value is less than .05, H_0 will be rejected in meaningful level of .95 and so H_1 will be accepted. Also if P-value is larger than .05, H_0 will be accepted in meaningful level of .95 and H_1 has been rejected. If H_0 is accepted, it means that there is no relationship between expectations and performance of respected organizations. In other words, user expectations and perceptions are independent as well as users of G2G services are dissatisfied. In the case that H_1 is accepted, user expectations and perceptions are dependent and lead to user satisfaction.

Shortly, it is worth noting that each question with P-value less than .05 includes user satisfaction and each question with P-value larger than .05 entails to user dissatisfaction.

Table3. Respondents' satisfaction or dissatisfaction of G2G services in Iran.

Satisfaction and Dissatisfaction of ICT services users				
question	Chi-square	P-Value	Test result (H_0)	Descriptions
1	11.75	.46	accepted	User dissatisfaction
2	22.91	.81	accepted	User dissatisfaction
3	23.46	.26	accepted	User dissatisfaction
4	45.26	.03	rejected	User satisfaction
5	17.98	.45	accepted	User dissatisfaction
6	16.96	.85	accepted	User dissatisfaction
7	15.98	.88	accepted	User dissatisfaction
8	10.99	.89	accepted	User dissatisfaction
9	37.57	.39	accepted	User dissatisfaction
10	21.68	.59	accepted	User dissatisfaction
11	24.64	.74	accepted	User dissatisfaction
12	16.85	.89	accepted	User dissatisfaction
13	42.06	.22	accepted	User dissatisfaction
14	26.35	.33	accepted	User dissatisfaction
15	17.09	.51	accepted	User dissatisfaction
16	29.81	.47	accepted	User dissatisfaction
17	27.67	.06	accepted	User dissatisfaction
18	45.01	.14	accepted	User dissatisfaction
19	17.11	.97	accepted	User dissatisfaction
20	34.27	.27	accepted	User dissatisfaction
21	13.93	.73	accepted	User dissatisfaction
22	19.92	.70	accepted	User dissatisfaction

Factor analysis categorized these questions into five components as shown in Table 1. Bold figures in each column represent the significant values in constituting the respective components. Questions 8, 10, 11, 12 and 13, which are in the component, presents Responsiveness feature of the SERVQUAL survey. Among these questions, question 8, providing services in promised time, has the lowest importance level in the G2G users' view. Also question 12, willing to help customer, is not important for the G2G users due to their significant inter-organizational transactions and less face-to-face communication. In the G2G context, most relevant concepts in the Responsiveness feature are giving prompt service to customer, telling customers exactly when the services will be performed, and never be too busy to respond to customers' request as demonstrated in questions 11, 10 and 13 respectively. The content of these questions in the G2G context is very similar to information dissemination.

Questions 14, 15, 16 and 17 in the second component are related to Assurance feature in SERVQUAL. Question 15, customers feeling safe in their transaction, can be ignored because of its insignificant impact and the rests are close to Confidence and Knowledge concept in the G2G context. Courteous and respectful behavior to operators inspires confidence and creates an ideal place for their transactions with those sectors.

Third component represents questions 1, 2, 3 and 4 and is related to the first feature of SERVQUAL, Tangibility. Analyzing the results indicates that question 3 compared to others in this group is insignificant. Based on the G2G concept, such as avoiding advertisement, contents of questions 4 and 2 underline Facing of ICT sector.

Questions 5, 6, 7 and 9 in the forth component are related to Reliability feature in SERVQUAL. According to the results, 9th question, error-free records, and question 6, showing interest in solving problems, can be omitted because of the negative value and insignificant role, respectively. The concept of the remaining questions is Time Management with respect to the G2G services.

Fifth feature of the SERVQUAL, Empathy, are entailed in questions 18, 19, 20, 21 and 22. According to the values in Table 1 all of the questions in this group except for 18, individual attention to customers, have insignificant role in the viewpoint of the G2G users and so, they can be ignored. This feature can be specified into Individual attention. These five new features introduce a new reversion of SERVQUAL that is customized for G2G services.

4   Conclusion

This study measuring customer satisfaction and difference between expectations and perceptions of customers for finding existing gap according to SERVQUAL model. Although no attempt was made at replication, the author borrowed from earlier studies, relying to a great extent on the service quality literature.

The results of this study suggested that e-government services organizations focus on five major elements (Tangible, Reliability, Responsiveness, Assurance and Empathy) if providing customer satisfaction is to be underscored in their strategic vision. Reliability strategy is important because ICT service users expect the performance of these organizations has been acceptable and customers have been satisfied at first time.

In today dynamic environment of information availability, Reliability does not mean only the performance in offering services but, rather includes a variety of other above factors that, the customers consider in order for their satisfaction to be met. Consequently, e-government agencies must continuously monitor the electronic information environment to provide customer-focused services. This is not suggested that the role of the government should be passive, reacting only to the demands placed on it. Government actually can play proactive role by forging partnership relationships with their electronic parts which offers these services and decreasing bureaucratic process in organizations and developing a variety of information and services access options for themselves and their customers that meet cost and efficiency criteria.

Since it is superior and capable to other models, SERVQUAL model has been selected for evaluation of quality in G2G services in Iran among 30 ministries and major governmental organizations. Generally, assessment results indicated that governmental operators were not absolutely satisfied with most of the 22 questions. Lowest level of performance was related to question 5. Also, highest level of quality services was related to question 9.

Factor analysis recognized different dimensions and confirmed claim of investigators based on that SERVQUAL dimensions are not appropriate for all kinds of services. For means of environment of execution questionnaire in particular governmental organizations and G2G services, factor analysis identified new five dimensions called Information, Confidence and safety, Facing of ICT sector, Time commitment and Empathy.

References:

1. Lenk, K., and Traunmuller, R.. Presentation at the IFIP WG 8.5, Working Conference on Advances in Electronic Government, 2000, February.

2. Hossein Sharifi, Behrouz Zarei., "An adaptive approach for implementing e-government in I.R. Iran", Journal of Government Information, 2004, 30, 600–619.

3. Edvardsen, B., Tomasson, B. and Ovretveit, J., Quality of Service: Making it Really Work, McGraw-Hill, New York, NY, 1994.

4. Lewis, R.C. and Booms, B.H., "The marketing aspects of service quality", in Berry, L.,Shostack, G. and Upah, G. (eds), Emerging Perspectives on Services Marketing, American Marketing Association, Chicago, IL,1983, 99-107.

5. Van Iwaarden, J., van der Wiele, T., Ball, L., and Millen, R., "Applying SERVQUAL to web sites: An exploratory study", International Journal of Quality & Reliability Management, 2003, Vol.20, No.8, 919-935.

6. Parasuraman, A., Zeithaml, V.A. and Berry, L.L., "SERVQUAL: a multi-item scale for measuring consumer perceptions of the service quality", Journal of Retailing, 1988, Vol. 64, No. 1, 12- 40.

7. Parasuraman, A., Zeithaml, V.A. and Berry, L.L., "Refinement and reassessment of the SERVQUAL scale|", Journal of Retailing, 1991, Vol. 67, 420-450.

8. Parasuraman, A., Zeithaml, V.A. and Berry, L.L., "Research note: more on improving service quality measurement", Journal of Retailing, 1993, Vol. 69, No. 1, 140-147.

9. Parasuraman, A., Zeithaml, V.A. and Berry, L.L., "Reassessment of expectations as a comparison standard in measuring service quality: implications for future research", Journal of Marketing, 1994, Vol. 58, 111-124.

The Study on the Architecture of Public knowledge Service Platform Based on Collaborative Innovation

Chang ping Hu, Min Zhang, Fei Xiang
Center for the Studies of Information Resources of Wuhan University,
Wuhan,430072,China, sxzhangm@yahoo.com.cn

Abstract. The knowledge service platform is seen as the vital intermediaries in innovation cycle, and for users to locate, exchange and acquire knowledge in a systematic way. It is increasingly recognizing the powerful role that knowledge service platform provide in building a national innovation capacity. The knowledge service platforms in the China's national innovation system, mostly based on the digital libraries, are supported and constructed by diverse departments and systems. These platforms disperse in construction, have respective division and orientation. However, along with the development of information technology and the revolution of innovation model, the requirements for the reconstruction of knowledge service platform in innovation system are brought forward. In this paper, we analyze the resources integration framework of the existing public service platform, and put forward the architecture of the public knowledge service platform based on collaborative innovation; we also discuss its concrete implementation.

1 Introduction

The knowledge service platform，an important part of the national innovation system, is seen as the vital intermediaries in innovation cycle, and for users to locate, exchange and acquire knowledge in a systematic way, with a view to development of new products, processes and services. It is increasingly recognizing the powerful role that knowledge service platform provide in building a national innovation capacity[1].The knowledge service platforms in the China's national innovation system, mostly based on the digital libraries, are supported and constructed by diverse departments and systems. These platforms disperse in construction, have respective division and orientation. However, along with the development of information technology and the revolution of innovation model as well as the change

Please use the following format when citing this chapter:

Hu, C. P., Zhang, M., Xiang, F., 2007, in IFIP International Federation for Information Processing, Volume 252, Integration and Innovation Orient to E-Society Volume 2, eds. Wang, W., (Boston: Springer), pp. 9-17.

of international information environment, the development model of knowledge service platform according to the system construction and the department organization receives challenges coming from various aspects, the requirements for the reconstruction of knowledge service platform in innovation system are brought forward.

Given this background，this paper mainly discusses the construction and development strategy of public knowledge service platform based on the collaborative innovation. Section two analyzes the driving mechanism of the innovation service platform and explores the influence of the new innovation paradigm and technology environment. Section three introduces Hubei province Science and Technology information sharing service platform as a case to illustrate the practice of the service sharing platform based on the information integration, and points out its shortage of knowledge collaboration. Section four we set up a framework of public knowledge service platform base on collaborative innovation, expound its construction and implementation. Finally we give some possible avenues for further research.

2   The driving mechanism of knowledge service platform in national innovation system

Nowadays, the innovation way has been undergone great changes. The new innovation model springs up continually such as open innovation, online innovation, distributed innovation and connected innovation [2-4]. Innovation development puts greater emphasis on interaction and collaboration of the service platform. The knowledge service platform, as an important intermediary in the whole process of the innovative chain, provides knowledge and information service for innovative system factors (government, educational and research institution, enterprise, etc.), facilitating resource sharing and behavior interaction among the factors and realizing the collaborative innovation effect.

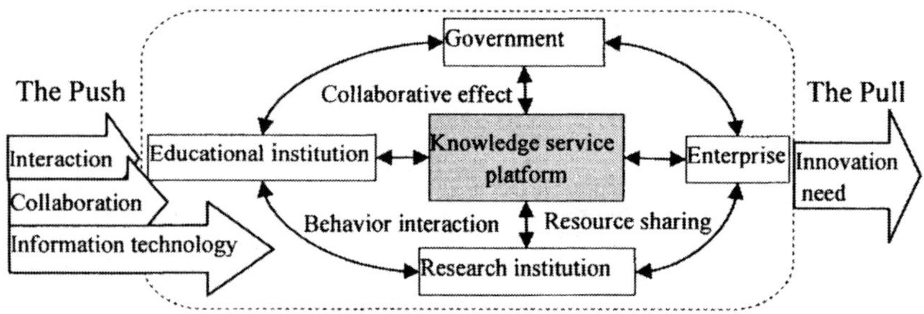

Fig. 1. The driving mechanism of knowledge service platform in national innovation system

• Innovation requires the development of new relationships among and between businesses, government, education and research organizations, workers and society in general. Above all, it requires a culture of collaboration, a symbiotic relationship between research and commercialization [5].

• The innovation process relies heavily on groups collaboration across institutions and time zones, sharing data, complementary expertise, ideas, so requires a closer integration among the innovative resource, activities and personnel. At the same time it requires that the service platform can promote coupling and interaction in all links of innovation chain to enhance the whole system innovation ability.

• Under the distributed, heterogeneous and dynamic changes environment, knowledge service platform are aiming on a transition from an integrated, centrally controlled system to a dynamic configurable federation of services and information collections. This transition is inspired by new technology trends and developments, which includes technologies like Web services and the Grid as well as the success of new paradigms like Peer-to-Peer Network and Service oriented Architectures.

3   Practice of Knowledge service platform based on information resource integration and its shortage of knowledge cooperation

In recent years，China has constructed the sharing service platform including National Science and Technology Library（NSTL）presided by Ministry of Science and Technology of the People's Republic of China[6], China Academic Library and Information System (CALIS) presided by Ministry of Education[7], regional and national sharing platform of literature and information resource with the National Library of China at the core[8], National Science Library of Chinese Academy of Sciences (NSL)[9], and so on. These platforms promoted national innovation development greatly. Nevertheless, the platforms developed by various sectors work in their own ways and information can't manage in unity. In the course of constructing innovational nation, collaborative innovation emphasizes on closer cooperation and mutual integration, so strategic request of reconstruction of knowledge platform across industries and systems is brought forward.

Hubei Science and Technology information sharing service platform is the service sharing platform across system. It is supported by Hubei Academy of Scientific and Technical Information，which has integrated four information systems including high education, Chinese Academy of Sciences, science and technology information and public libraries[10]. In 2005, Hubei Academy of Scientific and Technical Information realized the integration between education network and science and technology network through the interconnection between Changjiang Technology and Economy Information Network and China Education and Research Network.. The successful integration between Changjiang Technology and Economy Information Network and Huazhong center of CALIS (The Library of Wuhan University) realized the retrieval on the unified platform, realized the synchronous transmission of science and technology literature and information through the seamless interconnection project cooperated with NSTL as well(see figure 2). The service pattern of the platform includes regional service station pattern, commissioned service pattern, database service pattern and end-user service pattern.

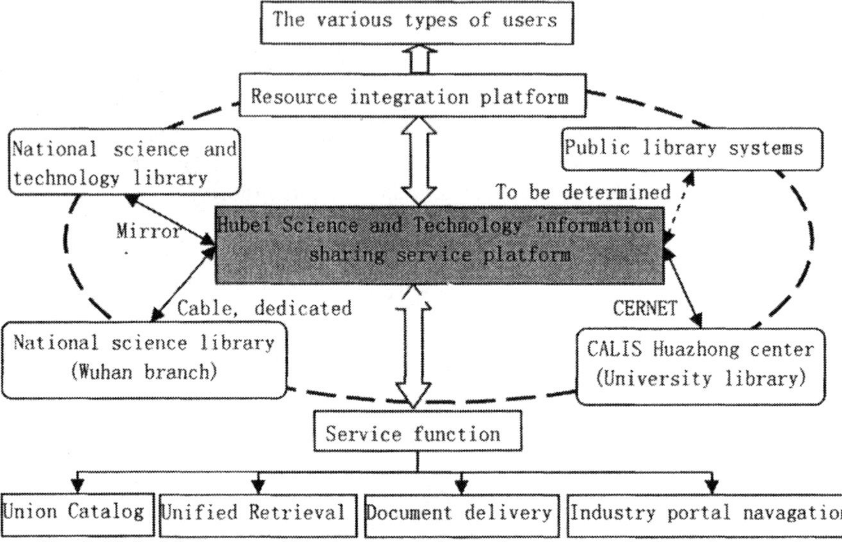

Fig. 2. Hubei Science and Technology information sharing platform framework

Hubei Science and Technology information sharing platform is the typical representative of innovative service platform based on information resource integration, which has already realized resource integration and service sharing across the space-time and systems to some degree. However the existing platform still has inadequate in knowledge collaboration:

• the platform has low efficiency of human resources and can't organize the innovational team according to the task need, so well as support the work of the cooperation team.

• the utilization efficiency of knowledge is not high enough and the research focuses on the information transmission and information management, not on the knowledge, can't promote the increment of knowledge in the cooperation course.

• From the angle of the technology, the present platform is based on the physical interconnection. The resource offering and service sharing are static. It doesn't offer the framework of resource and service sharing among multi-organizations and can't realize the large-scale resource and service sharing. Besides, the cost of the system is high while the efficiency is low.

4   Construction and Implementation of the knowledge service platform based on the collaborative innovation

In order to satisfy the demand of the collaborative innovation, As figure 3 shows, we construct the public knowledge service platform, which can be divided into three layers: physical layer, logical layer and user layer. The physical layer mainly consists of various kinds of distributed repositories（including publicly funded digital repositories，Industry Information platforms，business information platforms, etc.）.These distributed and heterogeneous digital repositories provide the material for dynamic configuration of services and information collections. On the basis of the physical level，the logical layer realizes the centralized resource allocation and mediation，as well as dynamic deployment service. The user layer provides the knowledge access based on the innovation demand for the different user.

The architecture of Collaboration innovation-oriented public knowledge service platform reflects the following three characteristics:

 • The resources choice is decided by the users' innovation demands and the standard which user own defines to；

 • Knowledge service platform provide dynamic service through integration of distributed resource；

 • The knowledge service process is base on the Virtual organization (VO) mechanism.

Now through the functions and processes of the public knowledge service platform we explain its realization to support collaborative innovation.

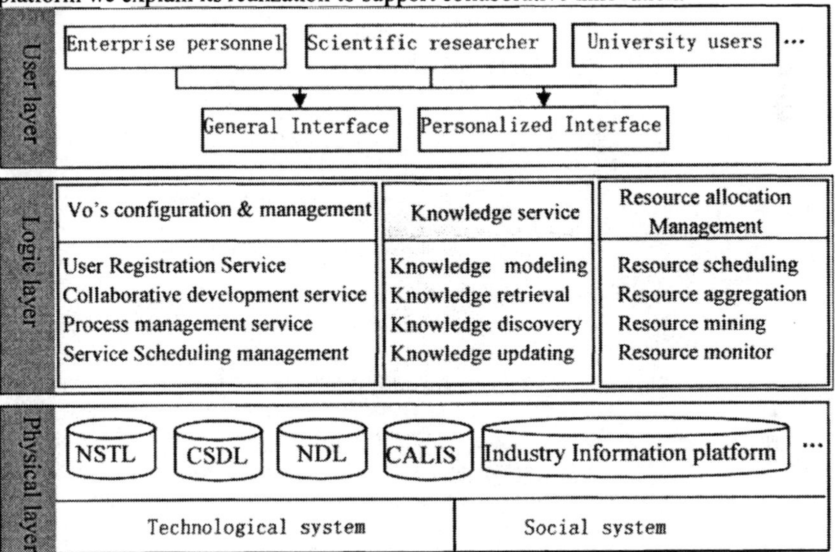

Fig. 3. the Architecture of the Public knowledge service platform based on collaborative innovation

4.1   VO's creation and execution based on Service-Oriented Architecture

Following the development of knowledge globalization, the technology innovation across profession and discipline pervades all over the world, Virtual organization (VO) and Virtual enterprises and so on appear one after another. VO integrates the unique advantages of diverse organizations through resources sharing and risk pooling to boost innovation. With providing the VO's configuration and the task management mechanism, the knowledge service platform we constructed will facilitate the integration of innovation resources 、 innovation personnel and innovation activities.

Considering the technical feasibility, We realize the creation of virtual organizations and operations management based on SOA （Service-Oriented Architecture）.SOA is a kind of software development architecture suitable for the changing environment, which can carry on the distributional deployment, the combination and the use for the loose coupling application module according to the demand[11-12]. Web service based on SOA describes three roles and three basic operations (sees figure 4).Three roles are service provider, service requester and service broker; three basic operation are publish, find and bind respectively.

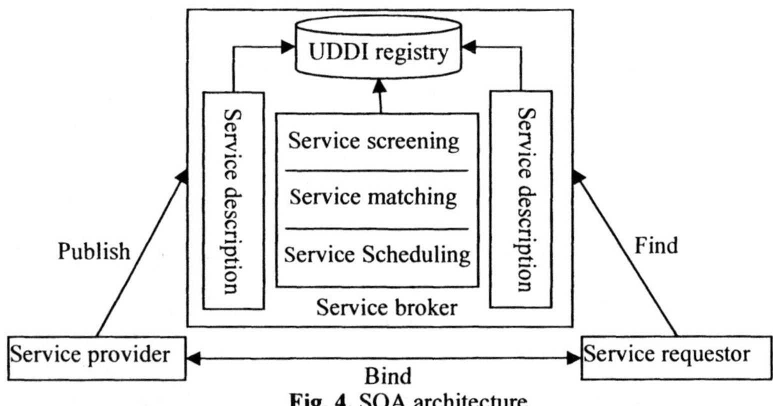

Fig. 4. SOA architecture

Based on SOA architecture, Innovation main bodies release the innovation information through registry module, meanwhile inquiry relevant information which have been registered, and use certain appraisal mechanism to Choose the appropriate partner and set up the virtual organization. The virtual innovation organization integrates several services to complete a specific innovation project. After the completion of the project, registry members cancel their functions, and withdraw from alliance. As a result, the entire dynamic VO declares on the dissolution.

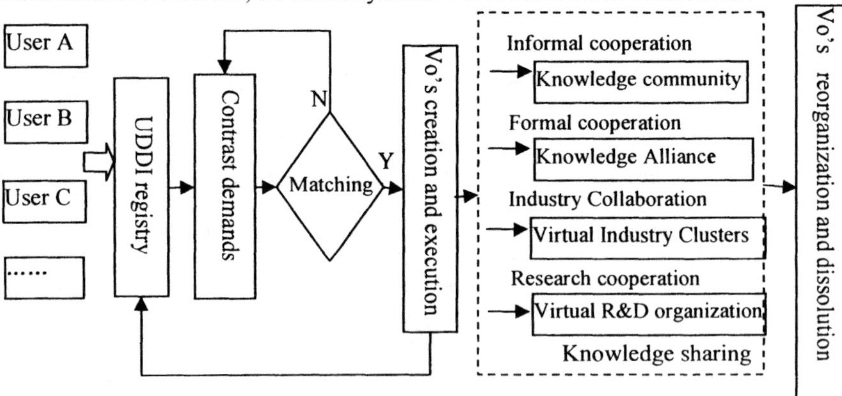

Fig. 5. VO's creation and execution

4.2   task-driven resource allocation and coordination services

In the operation of VO, task management module is used to realize the dynamic dispatch and assignment of the innovation project or task, in the mean time manage task operation condition in order to optimize the resource allocation. Decomposes the task and distributes each member of virtual organization, then discoveries the knowledge unit in the light of each business activity, and unifies the knowledge unit and the specific business process so as to establish mapping relations. Extracts the knowledge from distributional repository and completes the process from knowledge representation, organization, retrieval and knowledge innovation.

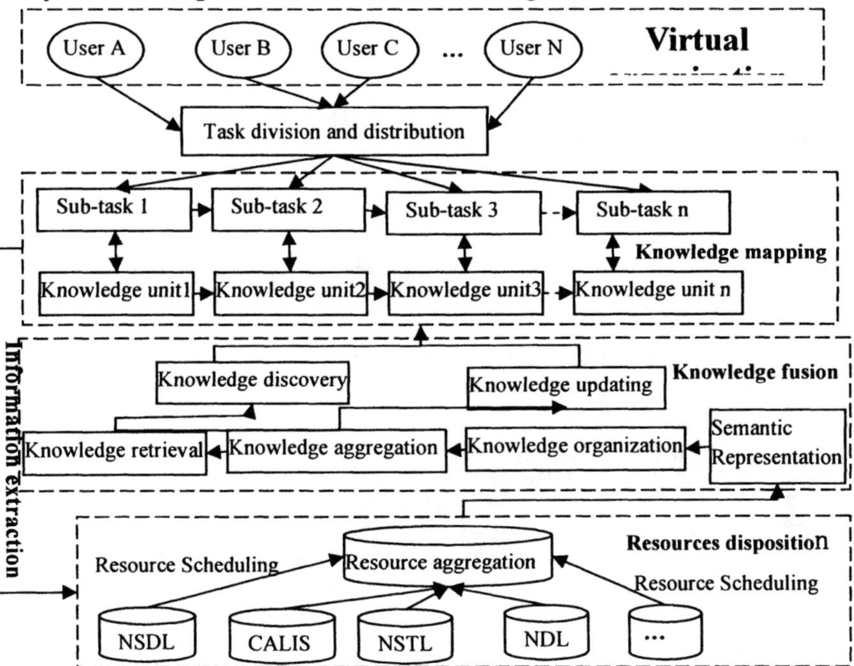

Fig. 6. task-driven process of knowledge service platform

5   Conclusion

Although innovation itself is a continuous process for producing new ideas, productions, services and tools, The operation of innovation is highly environment-dependent or platform-dependent. The innovation knowledge must be transferred through the integrated information infrastructure; the consummation of innovation chain as well as the optimized disposition of innovation resources also must be supported by the information infrastructure, therefore, the research of knowledge service platform has become a vital issue which need to be resolved urgently in the process of construction of innovational nation.

On the basis of the analysis of resources integration framework of the existing public service platform, we put forward the architecture of the public knowledge service platform based on the collaborative innovation, and analyze its concrete implementation. But we now only proposed the prototype design thought, on the foundation of collaboration scenario proposed in this article, In the next step of research work, we will further study on the realization details based on collaborative mechanism, such as: communication, data storage management, conflicts scheduling, and so on.

Acknowledgments

This paper is one of research results of project "The research on the institution of information service and the system of information guarantee in the construction of innovative nation" (number 06&ZD031) funded by National Philosophy and Social Science foundation of China.

References

1. J. Howard, "Knowledge exchange networks in Australia's innovation system: overview and strategic analysis", *A report to department of Education, Science and Training. Canberra: Howard Partners.* 2005,6,p1-3

2. B. Kogut, and A. Turcanu, "The emergence of E-innovation: insights from open source software development", A working paper of the refined H. Jones Center, The Wharton School, University of Pennsylvania, 1999,p30

3. M. Sawhney, and E. Prandelli, "Communities of creation: managing distributed innovation in turbulent markets", *California Management Review*, summer, VOL.43, NO.4, pp.24-54, 2000

4. B. Wu, J.E. Chen, "innovation: a new innovation platform based on the internet", *Engineering Management Conference*, 2005. *Proceedings 2005 IEEE International* , Vol.2 ,p519-523

5. United States. Council on Competitiveness. 2004. Innovate America: Thriving in a World of Challenge and Change, National Innovative Initiative Report. 2004, p2-26.

6. National Science and Technology Library (April 20, 2007); http://www.nstl.gov.cn/index.html

7. http://www.calis.edu.cn/calisnew/

8. National Library of China (April 20, 2007);http://www.nlc.gov.cn

9. National science Library, Chinese Academy of Sciences (April 20, 2007); http://www.las.ac.cn/

10. Hubei Science Technology Library (April 20, 2007); http://www.hbstl.org.cn/index.jsp

11. Y.E. Yu, Y. Shi, W.Z. LI, "Research of SOA and Its System Building", *Application Research of Computers*,2, p32-34(2005).

12. Q. Chen, J. Shen, Y.Q. Dong, "Building a collaborative Manufacturing System on an Extensible SOA-based Platform", *Proceedings of the 10th International Conference on Computer Supported Cooperative Work in Design,* p1-6(2006).

Wiki-based Knowledge Sharing in A Knowledge-Intensive Organization

Changping Hu, Yang Zhao, Xueqin Zhao
Wuhan University, Center for Studies of Information Resources
430072, Wuhan, P.R. China , zyaxjlgg_0813@hotmail.com
WWW home page: http://www.csir.whu.edu.cn/

Abstract. Knowledge sharing is the core of knowledge management. For a knowledge-intensive organization, knowledge sharing plays a very important role in organizational knowledge integration and innovation. However, as many knowledge-intensive organizations do not have good knowledge-sharing platforms and advanced methods, it is very difficult for them to achieve knowledge sharing effectively. Wiki is a kind of new software of knowledge sharing, generated along with the development of web 2.0. It can effectively help organizations achieve internal knowledge sharing. From the necessity and validity of knowledge sharing inside a knowledge-intensive organization, this article discusses the important role of Wiki for knowledge sharing combined the characteristics of it, on the basis of which studies the implementation of Wiki-based knowledge sharing in a knowledge-intensive organization.

1 Introduction

In contemporary society of knowledge economy, knowledge is playing an increasingly important role. For the knowledge-intensive organizations (KIO) such as universities and high-tech enterprises, knowledge has been regarded as their own important strategic resource and the key factor of representing organizational core competence. To an organization, internal knowledge sharing is more important than knowledge sharing between organizations. It's the crux of improving organizational performance and core competence. Knowledge sharing within an organization makes the knowledge of individual or group in the organization transformed into the knowledge of the whole organization. Sequentially the staff can fully and efficiently utilize these knowledge resources which the organization has already owned to

Please use the following format when citing this chapter:

Hu, C., Zhao, Y., Zhao, X., 2007, in IFIP International Federation for Information Processing, Volume 252, Integration and Innovation Orient to E-Society Volume 2, eds. Wang, W., (Boston: Springer), pp. 18-25.

create value for the organization. However, many organizations lack nicer platform of knowledge sharing and the support of advanced technology in actual operation. As a result, it obstructs the smooth realization of knowledge sharing inside the organization. With the rapid development of network technology, especially as the era of web 2.0 arrives, a series of advanced knowledge sharing software and technologies are generated. This offers a new opportunity for knowledge sharing inside a KIO. Wiki [1] is one of the important application software in web 2.0. It's a hyper text system, which supports community-oriented collaborative composition and also includes a set of assistant tools that support this collaboration. Compared with other hyper text systems such as BBS or Blog, Wiki is more open and collaborative. Anyone can edit and manage its content, and can also create new knowledge with the collaboration of community members. Thus Wiki can better help a KIO achieve internal knowledge sharing and promote organizational knowledge innovation.

This paper is organized as follows: Section 2 discusses the challenges of knowledge sharing in a KIO at present. Section 3 describes the important role of Wiki for knowledge sharing in an organization. The implementation of Wiki-based knowledge sharing in a KIO is presented in Section 4. Section 5 concludes the paper and presents some future work for research.

2   Challenges

2.1   Knowledge Sharing Necessity

In many knowledge-intensive organizations, most of the knowledge is fragmentary, scattered among different employees' minds, and is difficult to play an effective role when the organization solves practical problems. Knowledge sharing provides efficient approaches for the exchanges and communications between staffs. It can help the organization achieve the transfer and integration of individual knowledge, and make the scattered knowledge resources pooled to organizational knowledge assets which can create value, and improve the effectiveness of organizational knowledge resources. Through knowledge sharing, a staff's personal knowledge can be grasped by other staffs within the organization. This expands the scope of organizational internal knowledge owners, thereby avoids the loss of organizational knowledge resources resulting from personnel flow, and provides fully guarantee for the stable operation of the organization [2]. Therefore, knowledge sharing plays a very important role in promoting the integration of organizational internal knowledge resources and the level of the whole organizational knowledge.

2.2   Knowledge Sharing Validity

The effective implementation of knowledge sharing still depends on the strong support of a variety of factors in the practical applications. First, the organization needs to possess complete infrastructures and advanced knowledge-sharing models and establish a good platform. Secondly, it also needs good organizational culture and a complete organizational system, so that an ideal atmosphere can be created for knowledge sharing [3]. However, there are still several restraining factors in these aspects for a great many organizations at present. On one hand, a lack of effective knowledge sharing equipments and advanced technologies in some organizations influences on the efficiency of knowledge sharing to a certain extent. On the other hand, there are many differences from knowledge-sharing values between some organizations and their staffs. And there is a lack of sufficient trust in knowledge sharing between staffs. So, many staffs are often unwilling to share knowledge on their own initiative out of selfish interests.

3   A Wiki-based Approach to Knowledge Sharing in A KIO

3.1   Providing Knowledge Sharing Platform

At present, many organizations establish their own internal LAN and hope to achieve internal knowledge sharing better through the instantaneity and diversity of network communication. But network itself is obviously not enough for knowledge sharing. The organization still needs knowledge management and knowledge sharing systems with full functions to achieve ideal effect of knowledge sharing together combined with some advanced groupware technologies and coordinated software. Consequently, it's very necessary that organizations apply Wiki technology to achieve internal knowledge sharing based on LAN. Considering the staffs, Wiki is a completely open platform for the exchange of ideas, in which anybody inside the knowledge-intensive organization can express their views, discuss with others at any time and carry out brain storming better. Meanwhile, the communications among staffs is no longer limited in a single department. It can span borders of departments to establish different communities and complete a certain organizational task together such as drafting a scheme of product promotion or an organizational development strategy through mutual cooperation and knowledge sharing among community members. In addition, it further reinforces the mutual trust and collective consciousness among staffs during the process of mutual cooperation and effectively strengthens the organizational cohesion.

3.2   Promoting Tacit Knowledge Transformation

Knowledge can be divided into explicit knowledge and tacit knowledge according to different forms. Explicit knowledge is easily expressed, definite and carried by materials and it can be spread by the normal linguistic way between organizational members, while tacit knowledge is implicit experiential knowledge, which exists in the minds of staffs or in the corporate culture [4]. It's difficult to describe in words accurately and to be learned or used by others. In a knowledge-intensive organization, most of knowledge is tacit knowledge, the unutterable trait of which causes objective obstacles for the inside knowledge communication. So that internal knowledge sharing is unachievable. The traditional solution is to transform tacit knowledge into easily diffused explicit knowledge through coding, face to face communication, personnel rotation and so on. But these ways usually take up a lot of manpower, materials and financial resources, so they are not the best ways of achieving knowledge sharing for the organization. The advent of Wiki offers a more advanced way to solve this problem. As Wiki supports multiple formats of document types and is easy to operate, staffs can express the unutterable tacit knowledge vividly on Wiki according to the need at any time through the issuance of pictures, animation, video and so on. Therefore, other members can understand and learn the knowledge more visually so as to achieve knowledge sharing within the organization.

3.3   Enhancing Spiritual Motivation

As the society develops, the hierarchy of needs of people is improved continuously. The staffs not only desire for material rewards but also hope to receive social acknowledge and establish self-worth. Accordingly, while the KIO is encouraging its staff to share knowledge, it should attach great importance to meeting staff's spiritual needs. Wiki provides the organization with a knowledge-sharing platform of resource co-construction. It allows any staff to modify, delete and create its pages, and maintain the web site together [5]. Thus every staff of the organization can contribute to the smooth realization of internal knowledge sharing. Their sense of accomplishment is increased and their passion and enthusiasm of participating in knowledge sharing are stimulated better. Moreover, the staffs quickly establish personal reputation while contributing their own knowledge via Wiki. The more valuable knowledge who contributes, the more respect and admiration one can obtain from others. Based on this, the organization can still name the new knowledge concepts that the staffs create after the name of one labor or one team. This improves the popularity of knowledge contributors and enhances spiritual stimulation for contributors through the fast spread of network while people are learning and utilizing the knowledge.

3.4   Reducing Knowledge Sharing Risks

Organizational achievements of knowledge are collective intelligence gathering. If they aren't protected well but imitated or filched by others, it will be a terrible blow to the enthusiasm of staffs in knowledge sharing and knowledge innovation and also a tremendous loss to the whole organization. Therefore organizations must take effective measures to protect them. Though Wiki is an open knowledge-sharing platform, on which everyone can edit the knowledge content, it also provides the version resuming function at the same time, namely organizations can recover pre-edited version and previous content. So this can avoid man-made destruction availably. Moreover, the staff's IP address will be automatically recorded by the system when they landed on the Wiki site. Once the maintainers discover a suspicious IP address, they can prohibit it from visiting the site in time. Meanwhile, organizations can also set the scope of IP addresses and the jurisdiction of editing web pages, and only allow their own staff to land on Wiki to share knowledge. Accordingly, organizational internal achievements of knowledge get effectively protected.

4   The Implementation of Wiki-based Knowledge Sharing in A KIO

The SECI[6]model put forward by a Japanese scholar Nonaka Yujiro describes the transformation process of knowledge formats and indicates the essential of knowledge sharing within an organization reasonably, as shown in Fig. 1.

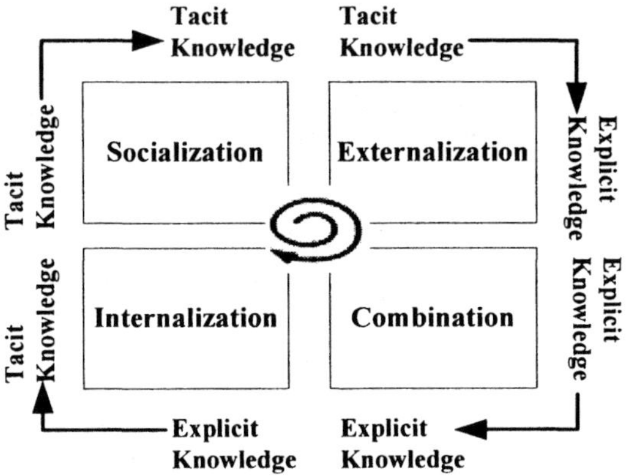

Fig.1. SECI model of knowledge sharing

In this model, knowledge sharing is divided into four processes, namely socialization, externalization, combination and internalization. By the four processes, knowledge transforms among the four states from individual tacit knowledge to organizational tacit knowledge, organizational explicit knowledge and individual explicit knowledge to achieve internal knowledge sharing. On the platform of knowledge sharing based on Wiki, knowledge externalization, combination and internalization can be fully realized by the functions of Wiki, while knowledge socialization that is a civilizing process means transforming tacit knowledge into tacit knowledge and needs to be completed through mutual observations, learning, and constant practices between staffs. Therefore, the process of knowledge sharing inside a KIO based on Wiki is mainly to achieve mutual transformation among states of individual tacit knowledge, individual explicit knowledge and organizational explicit knowledge, as shown in Fig.2.

Fig.2. The process of knowledge sharing in a KIO based on Wiki

4.1   Individual Tacit Knowledge to Individual Explicit Knowledge

This is the externalization of tacit knowledge and also the difficulty of knowledge sharing inside a knowledge-intensive organization. In an organization, personal tacit knowledge of staffs means mostly individual skills, know-hows and experiences which are closely connected with organizational specific situation and difficult to specify, express and imitate [7]. In the ordinary course of events, the staffs in an organization usually externalize a part of tacit knowledge either consciously or unconsciously with practical acts in their everyday life. Then they absorb this externalized knowledge consciously or unconsciously each other by constant contact and influence in the long years of working together, accordingly realize knowledge sharing to some extent. But in this case, the externalized tacit knowledge of staffs is quite limited. Furthermore, other staffs often need to have a certain understanding of the knowledge contributors' background (such as personal preferences, work habits, attitude, etc.), then they can fully understand and grasp the externalized explicit knowledge. Thereby, it takes a long time to achieve the transformation from tacit knowledge to explicit commonly. While on the platform of knowledge sharing based on Wiki, this transformation process of knowledge forms is entirely based on the conscious and voluntary knowledge-sharing behaviors of staffs. Thus it can increase the efficiency and quality of tacit knowledge transformation. Staffs can record some instantaneous thoughts in their own minds on Wiki in everyday work at any moment [8].

4.2   Individual Explicit Knowledge to Organizational Explicit Knowledge

Staffs will get a complete understanding and cognition of knowledge structures of each other after the first phase of transforming personal tacit knowledge into explicit knowledge. Based on this, staffs who have similar interests in a certain knowledge field of the organization will gradually come together and form a community via Wiki, then discuss the problems of this knowledge field together. During their discussion, each community member can put forward his/her own views on the topic of mutual concern, while others can edit and modify the content of Wiki pages at any moment to have a denotative and connotative complement and improvement for these perspectives about explicit knowledge issued by other people [9]. Finally they can reach a meeting of minds in the whole community and form integral knowledge achievements till the same topic is discussed very fully and deeply [10]. In this process, the explicit knowledge of each community member is transformed into that of group sharing via constant accumulation and fusion. Meanwhile, this promotes the generation of new knowledge, and makes the effect of knowledge sharing namely 1+1>2 achieved.

4.3   Organizational Explicit Knowledge to Individual Tacit Knowledge

This is the internalization of explicit knowledge. When personal explicit knowledge of staffs is transformed into that of the organization, it becomes the sharing resource of the whole organization. Other staffs can login Wiki site to browse the sharing knowledge, and can also query desirable knowledge directly by the search engine within the site. After staffs capture the organizational explicit knowledge, they gradually apply it in personal daily work by their constant learning, experience and practice, and make it become their own skills and know-hows. They transform organizational explicit knowledge into individual tacit knowledge, and perfect their own knowledge system further.

4.4   The Spiral Elevation of Knowledge Sharing

Through the three above-mentioned phases of knowledge form transformation, the KIO achieves internal knowledge sharing based on Wiki. Subsequently, staffs will utilize the tacit knowledge acquired from knowledge sharing to solve practical problems. Meanwhile, they will also produce new ideas according to their practical work experience, and then continue to express these new experiences and thoughts through the Wiki platform. Personal tacit knowledge is transformed into personal explicit knowledge. Accordingly, a new round of knowledge-sharing process will begin. The difference is that staffs have already basically cleared about the knowledge system of the organization and have nailed down the specific organizational needs of knowledge resource through the previous knowledge-sharing process. As a result, the knowledge contributed by staffs will be more valuable for the organization in the new knowledge-sharing process. After numerous rounds of knowledge-sharing cycles, the organizational knowledge resources are complemented and improved continuously[11].The whole performance and knowledge innovation competence of the organization both are advanced at very fast speed. Therefore, Wiki-based knowledge sharing in a knowledge-intensive organization is a spiral process.

5   Conclusions

At present, the application of Wiki for knowledge sharing in a knowledge-intensive organization has only just begun, and there are many problems to be further researched and considered. For instance, how to better motivate the staff to share their knowledge voluntarily, how to avoid the credit risks between the staff, and so on. However, it's convinced that various applications of Wiki in a KIO will be gradually matured with people's constant understanding and deep research of Wiki, which will play a more active role in promoting the growth and sustainable development of a knowledge-intensive organization.

Acknowledgment

The research reported in this paper is supported by the project Research on Knowledge Information Service System of Innovation-Oriented Country (Project No. 06JZD0032) sponsored by Key Project of Philosophy and Social Sciences Research, Education of Ministry of P.R.China.

References

1. Sander, Knowledge management by wikis, (May 10, 2007); http://www.wikipedia.org/
2. Chen Lihua and Xu Jianchu, Wiki: the platform of collaborative work and knowledge sharing in the network age, *China Information Herald* , no.1,2005(1), pp. 51–54.
3. Using a Wiki for knowledge sharing and SQL Server database documentation, (March 19, 2007); http://www.codeproject.com/asp/wiki.asp.
4. Song Jianyuan and Chen Jin, Research on the sharing approaches and organizational culture of enterprise tacit knowledge, *Technology Economy,* no.4, 2005, pp. 27–29.
5. Sebastian Schaffert, IkeWiki: A SemanticWiki for Collaborative Knowledge Management, (May 7, 2007); http://www.bibsonomy.org/bibtex/.
6. Gua Hongying and Li Feng, Wiki technology and application, *Oil-Gasfield Surface Engineering* ,vol.24 ,no.6, 2005, pp. 53–54.
7. Fan Pingjun, On the Barriers And Cures In Organizational Knowledge Sharing, Scientific Management Research, vol.21, no.6, 2003, pp. 93–95.
8. Jennifer Gonzalez-Reinhart, Wiki and the Wiki *Way: Beyond a Knowledge Management Solution*(May 19, 2002); http://www.kmcenter.org.
9. Wiki-one of New Internet Applications, (April 20, 2007); http://digi.it.sohu.com/s2005.
10. An enterprise applys Wiki: are you ready, (April 16, 2007); http://blog.beyond-future.com.
11. ZhangLL, Li J, Shi Y, Study on improving efficiency of knowledge sharing in knowledge-intensive organization, *1st International Workshop on Internet and Network Economics*, DEC 15-17, 2005,pp.816-825.

Web 2.0 Applications in China

Dongsheng Zhai [1], Chen Liu [2]
School of Economics and Management, Beijing University of
Technology, Beijing, China, 100022
1 zhaidongsheng@bjut.edu.cn
2 bill1130@gmail.com

Abstract. Since 2005, the term Web 2.0 has gradually become a hot topic on the Internet. Web 2.0 lets users create web contents as distinct from webmasters or web coders. Web 2.0 has come to our work, our life and even has become an indispensable part of our web-life. Its applications have already been widespread in many fields on the Internet. So far, China has about 137 million netizens [1], therefore its Web 2.0 market is so attractive that many sources of venture capital flow into the Chinese Web 2.0 market and there are also a lot of new Web 2.0 companies in China. However, the development of Web 2.0 in China is accompanied by some problems and obstacles. In this paper, we will mainly discuss Web 2.0 applications in China, with their current problems and future development trends.

1   Introduction

Web development can be classified in terms of four drivers: First driver: email exchange (Group support: FTP server and email list) in the 1980's. Second driver: passive web pages (Electronic & image publishing, access to remote services) in the 1990's. Third driver: P2P (Communities of exchange of music, movies, files, etc) in the late 1990's. Fourth driver: Blogs (Universe of syndicated diaries) in the 2000's. The Blog is also the main application representative of Web 2.0.

The creator of World Wide Web (WWW), Tim Berners-Lee [2] once talked about WWW: "There was a second part of the dream… we could then use computers to help us analyze it, make sense of what we' re doing, where we individually fit in, and how we can better work together." As a matter of fact, Web 2.0 has become more and more similar to what he said.

Since 2005, Web 2.0 has become a buzzword on the Internet. A great number of Web 2.0 applications appeared suddenly in a short time, Blog, Wiki, RSS and so on. In particular, the search engine giant Google developed several innovative Web 2.0

applications at this time, such as Google Maps and Google Mail. Almost every netizen was attracted by the colorful and personalized interfaces, various and useful functions and more interactive approaches with the Web from those applications. In a sense, Google promoted the influence and development of Web 2.0. Therefore, more Web 2.0 applications and Web 2.0 companies emerged. The core spirit of Web 2.0 is: Open, Shared, Communication and Growing-up together, which has been an inspiration to everyone.

China has a large number of netizens. Therefore, many sources of venture capital poured into Chinese Web 2.0 market at the beginning of Web 2.0 development. Certainly, many Web 2.0 companies in China started their dreams at that time. Almost everyone wants to be the second Flickr or YouTube, two famous Web 2.0 websites recently bought by Yahoo and Google respectively, but the ideal is often contrary to the reality. A very small number of them gain success from Web 2.0.

The rest of the paper is organized as follows. In section 2, we will briefly introduce some concepts of Web 2.0. Section 3 discusses Web 2.0 applications in China, including its history, current problems and future development trends. Section 4 is the conclusion.

2 Web 2.0

2.1   What is Web 2.0?

The concept of Web 2.0 was presented during a conference brainstorming session between O'Reilly [3] and MediaLive International in October 2004. Later, by the efforts of Tim O'Reilly and his partners, the Web 2.0 Conference was held to continue discussions further. Today, there are about 4.1 million hyperlinks relevant to Web 2.0 in Google.com.

In order to understand what Web 2.0 is, we firstly should learn what Web 1.0 is. Web between 1993 and 2003 is regarded as Web 1.0, and the Web since 2003 is so-called Web 2.0. Web 1.0 are mostly HTML pages viewed through a Web browser, while Web 2.0 are web pages, plus a lot of other "content" shared over the web, with more interactivity. This is more like an application than a "page". Users may create the contents of web rather than just web coders. They are no longer restricted within the fixed and rigid pages' contents without any users' interaction. In other words, users' participation is the core of Web 2.0.

Jim Cuene analyzed the differences between Web 1.0 and Web 2.0 incisively in his speech "Web 2.0: Is it a whole new Internet?" [4].

Table 9. The differences between Web 1.0 and Web 2.0 presented by Jim Cuene

Web 1.0		Web 2.0
"Read"	Mode	"Write" & Contribute
"Page"	Primary Unit of content	"Post / record"
"static"	State	"dynamic"

Web browser	Viewed through…	Browsers, RSS Readers, anything
"Client Server"	Architecture	"Web Services"
Web Coders	Content Created by…	Everyone
"geeks"	Domain of…	"mass amateurization"

We can say Web 2.0 is the symbol of the second revolution and release of web technology. Of course, Web 2.0 also provides us with more creative and personalized web applications.

In conclusion, Web 2.0 is not just a simple update of Web 1.0, but brings great innovation in technology and creative notions in people's minds.

2.2   Main technology of Web 2.0 – Ajax

When we refer to Web 2.0 technologies, we have to mention AJAX, one of core technologies of Web 2.0. AJAX is an acronym for Asynchronous JavaScript and XML. It isn't a new technology, but a combination of certain technologies in order to realize their respective function under the collaboration.

As Jesse James Garrett [5] (the presenter of Ajax) explained, Ajax includes following aspects:

- standard-based presentation using XHTML and CSS
- dynamic display and interaction using the Document Object Model
- data interchange and manipulation using XML and XSLT
- asynchronous data retrieval using XMLHttpRequest
- And Javascript binding everything together

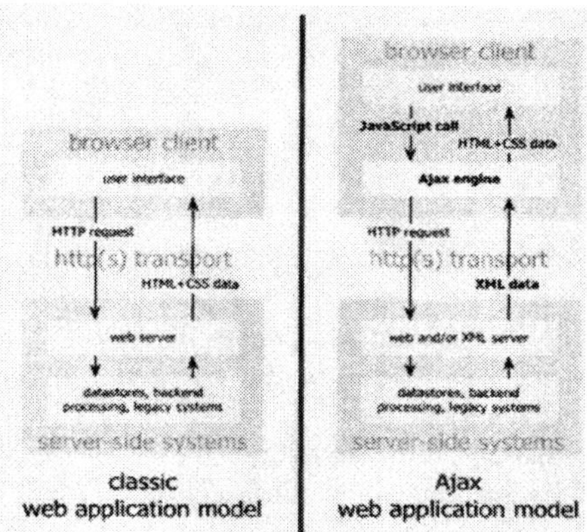

Fig. 9. Comparison of classic and Ajax web application model

From the pictures above, a traditional web application is always submitted from the client browser to the server, the server returns the new pages and these pages display in the browser again, which mean that each data travel needs to update the browser pages.

Ajax application changes this pattern. The Ajax Engine written in Javascript takes on the middle-level tasks in the Ajax application. When users submit data to the server, Ajax is responsible for collecting data and sending them to the server by Http Request (XMLHttpRequest). It returns XML after processing in the server. The Ajax Engine processes XML in order to display XHTML and CSS data in the users' interfaces and update the corresponding parts of the presentation, rather than refreshing the entire pages, so it avoids unnecessary data travel and only necessary data are transmitted in the necessary time between browser and server.

Because Ajax undertakes the tasks of communication with the server, it makes possible that web browsing and interactions between applications are processed in asynchronous mode. The asynchronous mode allows users never to be faced up with blank screen and so users can't continue their own jobs until the processing of the server is completed. Ajax technology lets web applications have similar users' experiences with desktop applications and improves the usability of web applications. In a sense, we can say that it produces the most distinct advantage and improvement between Web 1.0 and Web 2.0.

2.3   Some Web 2.0 Applications

Blog

Blog is the abbreviation for "Web Blog". It is a personal log in chronological order, updated at regular intervals as users wish. Users can put their own pictures, diaries, and even ideas on their Blogs, which can be scanned by other people. Visitors are allowed to leave comments for the authors [6-8].

Wikipedia

This is an online encyclopedia, created and supported by its users. In the latest data report issued by comScore Networks, a marketing research company, Wikipedia has become one of the top 10 hot websites in the United States, which exceeds the New York Times and Apple. While in the worldwide, Wikipedia has already been one of the top 10 hot websites for a long time.

RSS

RSS means Really Simple Syndication, which is a format of description and synchronization of website contents. It provides a technical platform for transmitting information rapidly. As long as you are subscribed to the contents of certain web pages you need in the RSS reader, the latest updated contents will be sent to your RSS reader in time. Then you may look at them in the RSS reader directly instead of turning to the pages and refreshing them by yourself.

SNS

SNS stands for Social Network Software. In terms of the Six Degrees of Separation Theory, we can know each person throughout the world only by knowing six persons directly. Therefore, SNS is exactly an effective way to expand one's circle of friends.

Tag

In short, Tag allows us to name something on the Internet, such as photos, diaries, with meaningful names. It permits systems to search the results in a natural way appropriate to each user.

3   Web 2.0 applications in China

3.1   The history of Web 2.0 applications in China

As the biggest developing country, China has attracted many sources of venture capital in various markets. According to statistics, the total number of netizens in China has reached 137 million nowadays. Therefore, Internet is also a "battle" for them. The most significant characteristic for Web 2.0 is users' participation. Internet is not the Internet as it was 10 years ago. It allows users to design modes, contents and other aspects of the web. In China, there exists some successful Web 2.0 websites, such as Mop.com and Douban.com. They are the leading strength of Web 2.0 in China. Users may taste Web 2.0 and learn more about Web 2.0 from these websites.

As for Web 2.0 applications, such as Blog, have been gradually given more attentions since 2002. Fang Xingdong and Wang Junxiu set the Chinese name of Blog as "Bo Ke". In August, 2002, they created the first Chinese Blog website, that is, www.blogchina.com. Since 2005, Blog application in China has developed rapidly. In terms of data issued by CNNIC in July, 2006 [9], among the netizens in China, Blog users are 17.5 million, active Blog users are 7.7 million and Blog readers are 75 million. In contrast, the number of netizens in America who read Blog is about 57 million, which occupies 37% of the netizens in America [10].

Compared with Blog, the development of Wiki in China is rather slow. Although there are some Wiki websites, such as www.wikicn.com and www.wikilib.com, their impacts and the number of users are limited. In China, RSS application started in March, 2004. Many websites, such as China Blog, XinHua Net and Sina, published their own RSS Aggregation News services and developed RSS readers. At present, most News websites have provided RSS services, which are also embedded in Blog.. Users can gain great conveniences from RSS. As for Tag and SNS, several websites provide such applications. However, to some extent their influences are limited and Chinese netizens know little about them in general. Compared with China, the proportion of netizens in America who use Tag is about 30%. MySpace, the biggest SNS website in America, was bought by Murdoch with 850 million dollars in 2005 and its click rate has already exceeded Yahoo and Google now.

3.2   The current problems of Web 2.0 applications in China

Compared with the situation in 2005, tremendous changes have occurred in Chinese Web 2.0 market nowadays. The turnings of venture capital, the reducing of the staff and the closing down of some Web 2.0 companies are also the harmful factors for the development of Web 2.0 industry in China.

In China, there are so many Web 2.0 companies providing parallel applications and services that the creativeness and individuation of web pages and the quality of services can't be ensured and satisfied. For example, many websites provide Blog services, but their services are almost the same and haven't any innovation, which can't attract most netizens to access the same function and service of different websites. It may not be good that many people do the same thing.

Yahoo recently bought Flickr, while Google acquired YouTube with 1.65 billion dollars. Both Flickr and YouTube are Web 2.0 companies. By providing personalized contents, friendly users' experiences and innovative services, they have millions of registered users around the world. In China, thousands of Web 2.0 companies appeared in 2005, but in the Web 2.0 wave of China, the winners like Flickr and YouTube are extremely the few. Many new web companies paste the label of Web 2.0 on themselves in order to attract more users and more sources of venture capital. However, unfortunately, many of them go bankrupt after a short time. There are a lot of reasons for that. Perhaps, the most important factor is that those companies only focus on the presentations of Web 2.0 and claim themselves to be Web 2.0 websites by just providing some Web 2.0 applications. In fact, they don't really know the true essence of Web 2.0. Web 2.0 is more like an idea or a concept. The main principle of Web 2.0 is users' participation. That is, companies should have the idea that users are the creator of web contents. Therefore they should make efforts to provide really open environments for users' interaction and let them easily enjoy the advantages and conveniences of Web 2.0. However, many companies try hard to gain business chances firstly and only focus on temporary profits. Providing services for users is just a mask for them. Sometimes, they may hurt the users for the sake of their own temporary profits.

Compared with America, China has some disadvantages in Web 2.0. For example, although China has about 137 million netizens, the popularity of netizens in China stands at less than 10%, while the popularity of netizens in America is more than 70%. Furthermore, the principle of Web 2.0 is users' participation, so higher requirements to netizens are needed. However, most of Chinese netizens are preliminary and less-educated. Besides, the success of Web 2.0 companies in America, such as YouTube, partly attributes to wise and brave venture capital. Those sources of venture capital give Web 2.0 more and more supports. Therefore they also promote the healthy and steady development of Web 2.0 in America. On the contrary, in China many sources of venture capital lack courage and insight and they are easily prone to follow others. On the other hand, Web 2.0 has something with economy and culture in society. For example, the popularity of camera equipments in China is far less than in America. Hence, some video-share companies, such as YouTube, may succeed in America, while in China such companies may encounter much more obstacles and difficulties.

3.3 The development trends of Web 2.0

Although there are many problems and obstacles for the development of Web 2.0 in China, some sources of venture capital still flow into certain Web 2.0 companies. For example, Mop.com gained about 48 million dollars from American Venture Capital Corporation and General Atlantic last year. After that, Sequoia Capital, Redpoint Ventures and Highland Capital Management Corporation invested 25 million dollars in Qihoo, a company specialized in Blog search. In conclusion, Web 2.0 market in China is still attractive to venture capital, but they are more rational than ever before.

Web 2.0 emphasizes users' interaction, because the service object of Internet should be users not webmasters or web coders. That is, let the users, the receiver of contents in the web, become the creator and provider of contents at the same time.

Because only the users know the contents what they really want to gain exactly from the web.

The Long Tail Theory [11] put emphasis on the pursuit of so-called long tail. As for Web 2.0, "the long tail" is that the better personalized services you provide, the more likely you succeed. Web 2.0 has many advantages over Web 1.0 and it offers a large scope of profits. The key is whether you can grasp them. Only by paying more attentions to users' requirements and providing more attractive and personalized services, Chinese Web 2.0 companies can exist longer and make more profits. It is an extremely good advantage that China has a great number of netizens. The current problem is how to attract them to access Web 2.0 websites and let them enjoy in those websites. Some websites, such as Sina.com, Mop.com and Douban.com have exploited the road for us. They provide good Web 2.0 applications with friendly users' experiences and really open environments for users' interaction. Therefore, as long as other companies can understand the true essence of Web 2.0, learn much more valuable things from those good examples and create their own predominances, they may win the users and the Web 2.0 market. Maybe the next YouTube or Flickr will be in China in the near future.

4   Conclusion

We have experienced the Internet bubble a few years ago, while we are facing up with a new era of web or just another Internet bubble. Web 2.0 has brought us with many creative technologies and personalized web applications. User's participation is the main principle of Web 2.0. Users become the creator of web contents instead of webmasters or web coders. As for Web 2.0 companies in China, Web 2.0 is not only an opportunity, but also a challenge. Although there are many problems and obstacles during the development of Web 2.0 in China, Chinese netizens and Web 2.0 companies are still making efforts in this road. Whether they can gain a result of win-win is depending on their endeavors and contributions in the future.

References

1. China Internet Network Information Center(CNNIC), China Internet Development Statistics Report, January 23, 2007
2. Hak Lae Kim, Towards the Semantic Web 2.0, 2005
3. Tim O'Reilly, What is Web 2.0: Design Patterns and Business Models for the Next Generation of Software, September 30, 2005
4. Jim Cuene, Web 2.0: Is it a whole new internet ?, May 18, 2005
5. Jesse James Garrett, Ajax: A New Approach to Web Applications, February 18, 2005
6. Tang Dailu, The transformation of Internet: Web 2.0 ideas and design, January 1, 2007
7. David Best, Web 2.0: Next Big Thing or Next Big Internet Bubble ?, January 11, 2006

8. Win Treese, Web 2.0: Web 2.0: Is it really different?, June, 2006
9. China Internet Network Information Center(CNNIC), 2006 Chinese Blog
    Survey Report, September 23, 2006
10. Pew Internet & American Life Project, Bloggers-A portrait of the internet's new
    storytellers, July 19, 2006
11. Chris Anderson, *The Long Tail* (China CITIC Press, December, 2006)

On the Standardization of Semantic Web Services-based Network Monitoring Operations

Chengling Zhao[1] , Ziheng Liu[2] , Yanfeng Wang[2]
The Department of Information Techonlogy, HuaZhong Normal University;
Wuhan, China,lzh20201@yahoo.com.cn,lzh20201@sohu.com,
yanfengwang123@sohu.com

Abstract. Web services have become an emerging XML-based approach in network management. And the combination of Web services and Semantic Web, in other words, Semantic Web services, make it possible to add semantic manners to services and automate network monitoring.This paper focuses on the standardization of network monitoring operations from the Semantic Web services' point of view. During this course, we especially take into account the problems about parameter transmission and operation granularity, and present the considerations about these problems in detail.

1 Introduction

Over many years, the Simple Network Management Protocol (SNMP) has become the most commonly used management protocol in IP network. However, these days, more focus is put on the XML-based approaches. And as one of the emerging XML-based standards, Web services have been used in the network management. On the other hand, Semantic Web, known as the "Next Generation Internet", makes it possible to add semantic manners to services. Thus in this way, Semantic Web services can possibly automate network management.

Several studies have focused on the use of Web services in network management [1-3]. Additionally, a few researches have paid attention to the function of Semantic Web, especially Ontology, in network management [4,5].

However, few studies have turn to the potential of Semantic Web services in network monitoring. And our study just focuses on the use of Semantic Web services in the network monitoring operation instead of monitoring information. The goal of this paper is then to explain how standardization of monitoring operation can be achieved for Semantic Web services by the means of semantic markup languages for Web services, such as OWL-S in our study.

The organization of the paper is as follows. We will firstly present Semantic Web services background in Section 2, which is followed by Section 3 about the needs and the markup languages for standardization of network monitoring operations. With the OWL-S, we standardize Semantic Web services-based monitoring operations in Section 5, taking into account the parameter transmission and the operation granularity. We will conclude with Section 5, which gives a summary of this paper.

2 Background

2.1Web services and SOA

Web services is developed and standardized by the World Wide Web Consortium (W3C), which gives the following definition [6]: "A Web service is a software system designed to support interoperable machine-to-machine interaction over a network. It has an interface described in a machine-processable format (specifically WSDL). Other systems interact with the Web service in a manner prescribed by its description using SOAP-messages, typically conveyed using HTTP with an XML serialization in conjunction with other Web-related standards".

The word "services" in Web services refers to a Service-Oriented Architecture (SOA) [7]. In fact, SOA is a recent development in distributed computing, in which applications call functionality from other applications over a network. In an SOA, functionality is "published" on a network where two important capabilities are also provided – "discovery", the ability to find the functionality, and "binding", the ability to connect the functionality. So when considering a SOA, these three parts must be take into account, which are briefly presented as "publish", "find", and "bind".

In the Web services Architecture, three important roles are Web service provider, Web service requester, and Web service register, which correspond to the "publish", "find", and "bind" aspects of a SOA.

2.2 Semantic Web

As the "Next Generation Internet", the Semantic Web is a vision of the new architecture for the World Wide Web, characterized by the machine-accessible formal semantics added into traditional Web content.

As Tim Berners-Lee has presented, the Semantic Web is not a separate Web but an extension of the current one, in which information is given well-defined meaning, better enabling computers and people to work in cooperation [8]. The Semantic Web architecture put forward by Tim Berners-Lee in the academe is depicted in Fig. 1.

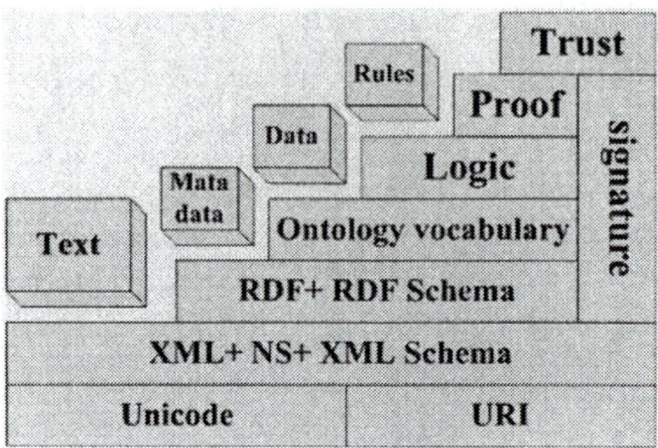

Fig 1. Semantic Web architecture

2.3 Semantic Web services

Semantic Web Services, as a new research paradigm, is generally defined as the augmentation of Web Service descriptions through Semantic Web annotations, to facilitate the higher automation of service discovery, composition, invocation, and monitoring in an open, unregulated, and often chaotic environment (that is, the Web) [9].

In fact, Semantic Web services represent an important step toward a new vision of the Semantic Web applied to Web services, in terms of utilizing, managing, and creating semantic markup languages for services.

Some experts have argued that, the relationship between the Semantic Web and the current Web Service architecture depends on your viewpoint [9]. In the near term, the deployment of Web Services may be critical, and Semantic Web techniques can enhance the current service architecture. In the long run, however, the Semantic Web vision itself may become more interesting, with Web Services offering an ubiquitous infrastructure on which to build the next generation of deployed multi-agent systems.

3 Standardization for network monitoring

3.1 The needs

In order to easily use Semantic Web services for network monitoring, there should be agreement on the monitoring information and operations. In other words, there is a need for standardization of information and operations.

Since standardization of information is a very broad subject and it is not directly related to Semantic Web services, we will abstract from it and just assume we have certain monitoring information defined in a MIB, such as in SNMP. The focus here will be on standardization of network monitoring operations.

3.2 The markup languages

As for the standardization of network monitoring operations, an appropriate markup language is in great demand.

WSDL (Web Services Description Language) [10,11] only provides a mechanism to describe a Web service in a modular manner. This means that a WSDL document can be used jus in the case that the services are not automated.

But considering the semantic manners added into the Web services, we need a markup language particularly for Semantic Web services. As is shown in Fig. 2, we can see that XML, RDF and Ontology are three main layers for describing the semantics of Web information. However, RDF and RDF Schema, as well as XML and XML Schema, are not strong enough to express various resources and reason automatically. This has pushed the development of Ontology languages, from DAML (DARPA Agent Markup Language) [12] and OIL (Ontology Inference Layer) [13], to DAML + OIL (DARPA Agent Markup Language + Ontology Inference Layer) [14], and recently to OWL (Web Ontology Language) [14]. And OWL-S [16], an application of OWL, in particular, has evolved into a semantic markup language for Web services.

4 Semantic Web Services-based network monitoring operations

For standardization, we must consider two significant problems: parameter transmission and operation granularity.

4.1 Parameter transmission

Since OWL does not provide for the use of variables, there is no way to state in a class definition that one of the class properties is referenced elsewhere by a variable name, which makes the parameter transmission rather harder.

However, the use of parameter binding in a process definition will enable a specialized OWL-S process reasoner to use this information to determine which properties should have "the same value" in any coherent instance of the process being defined. In the notation of parameter binding, an instance of the class VALUEOF, with properties at Process and the Parameter denotes the object (value) of the specified parameter of the specified process.

On the other hand, parameters can also be combined and/or serialized in such a way, that the parameters are not described in the Service Model class. Merely their serialization is described in the class Input, a subclass of the class Parameter. Thus in this way, the input parameter is transmitted in data flow. This can be seen as lightweight parameter transparency.

An advantage of transparency is that monitoring information is abstracted from the process level, so the structure of information can change without having to modify the operation part. Since the transparent parameters are serialized in an XML structure, it can be contained in a class whose value is a string type. On both the manager and agent side, a generic XML parser can then be used to extract the parameters from the class.

4.2 Operation granularity

In this study we have focused on the ifTable, which is part of the Interfaces Group MIB (IF-MIB) [17]. The ifTable contains data objects related to the state of all network interfaces available in the system on which the agent runs.

Using the ifTable, we have determined 4 distinct data retrieval schemes, each resulting in a different network monitoring agent. All granularities will be able to retrieve any data object from the ifTable; the distinction is that the structure and amount of data objects that are retrieved varies.

The first granularity is to retrieve all data objects separately. Our Semantic Web service that retrieves a single data object at a time is called GetIfCell.

The second granularity is to retrieve an entire row of data objects at a time, thus transmitting all available information on a single network interface. The Semantic Web service that retrieves a single row of data objects at a time is called GetIfRow.

The third granularity we have investigated is to retrieve an entire column of data objects at a time, thus transmitting the same piece of information for all network interfaces. The Web service that handles one column at a time will be called GetIfColumn.

The last granularity is to retrieve all data objects in the ifTable in a single operation. The Semantic Web service that retrieves all data objects in the ifTable at once is GetIfTable.

Then we can get a containment hierarchy of these four operations as a tree from relatively coarser operations to relatively finer operations. The containment tree is shown in Fig. 2.

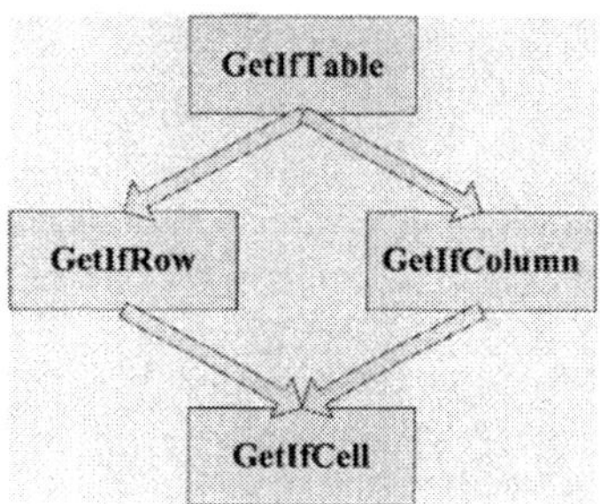

Fig 2. Containment tree of the four operations

5 Conclusions

In summary, standardizing Semantic Web services-based network monitoring operations can be done by the help of a semantic markup language for Web services, such as the OWL-S adopted in our study.

In the course of standardizing network monitoring operations, two important problems must be taken into account: parameter transmission and operation granularity. Parameter transmission can be achieved in OWL-S by the notation of parameter binding in the form of data flow, and the choice between non-transparent parameters and transparent parameters. As for the operation granularity, we take the IfTable for example and give four operations of different granularities, and argue that the choice for a certain operation granularity will be a tradeoff between simplicity and expressiveness.

The work presented here is part of ongoing research. We strongly encourage interested parties to react and comment on the discussed issues.

References

1. G. Pavlou, P. Flegkas, S. Gouveris, A. Liotta, On Management Technologies and the Potential of Web Services, *IEEE Communication Magazine* (July 2004), pp. 58-66.

2. J. Sloten, A. Pras, M. Sinderen, On the Standardisation of Web service management operations, Proc. 10th Open European Summer School (EUNICE 2004) and IFIP WG 6.3 Workshop(June 2004), pp. 143-150.

3. T. Drevers, R. Meent, A. Pras, Prototyping Web Services based Network Monitoring, Proc. 10th Open European Summer School (EUNICE 2004) and IFIP WG 6.3 Workshop(June 2004)pp. 135-142.

4. JE. López de Vergara, VA. Villagrá, JI. Asensio, B. Julio, Ontologies: Giving Semantics to Network Management Models, *IEEE Network, special issue on Network Management*, 17(3)(May/June 2003)pp. 15-21.

5. JE. López de Vergara, VA. Villagrá, B. Julio , Applying the Web Ontology Language to management information definitions, *IEEE Communications Magazine*, 42(7)(July 2004)pp. 68-74

6. W3C, Web services Architecture (8 August 2003), *W3C Working Draft* (August 2003):http://www.w3.org/TR/2003/WD-ws-arch-20030808/\#whatis,

7. Service-Oriented Architecture (SOA), http://www.service-architecture.com/.

8. T. Berners-Lee et al, The Semantic Web, *Scientific American*, 2001, 284(5), pp. 34-43..

9. T. Payne, O. Lassila, Semantic Web Services, *IEEE Intelligent Systems*, 19(4), (July/August 2004), pp. 14-15.

10. W3C, Web Services Description Language (WSDL) Version 2.0 Part 1: Core Language, *W3C Working Draft* (August 2005): http://www.w3.org/TR/2005/WD-wsdl20-20050803,

11. Web Services Description Language (WSDL) Version 2.0 Part 2: Message Exchange Patterns, *W3C Working Draft*,(March 2004) :http ://www. w3.org/ TR/ 2004 /WD-wsdl20 - patterns-20040326,

12..M.Dean DARPA AgentMarkup Language(DAML) http://www.daml.org/2001/04/ssd-md/Overview.html.

13. OIL (Ontology Inference Layer), http://www.ontoknowledge.org/oil/.

14. T. Berners-Lee et al, DAML + OIL (DARPA Agent Markup Language + Ontology Inference Layer), http://www.daml.org/2001/03/daml+oil-index.html.

15. W3C, OWL--Web Ontology Language Overview, *W3C Recommendation*, (February 2004)http://www.w3.org/TR/2004/REC-owl-features-20040210/.

16. W3C, OWL-S: Semantic Markup for Services, *W3C Member Submission*(November 2004): http://www.w3.org/Submission/2004/SUBM-OWL-S-20041122/,

17. K. McCloghrie, F. Kastenholz, The Interfaces Group MIB, *IETF RFC* 1902, June 2000.

Antecedents for Building Trust in Professional e-Services

Dieter Fink
Edith Cowan University, Perth, Australia
d.fink@ecu.edu.au

Abstract. Professional service providers are exploiting the web to deliver e-services to a larger but also more diverse client base. This has increased the need for building trust between them and their clients and within the firm itself. In this paper the antecedents of trust are identified and matched against strategies that public accounting practices could adopt to build trust. Eleven antecedents for external relationships ranging from trustworthiness to benevolence are identified. A key strategy is to display information about the firm's expertise, standards and clients on the website. Trust for internal relationships range from the individual to inter-firm alliances and largely rely on providing technological (Internet) support and information about the firm's vision and values.

1   Introduction

The question of trust has occupied our minds for many decades. In 1958 Morton Deutsch wrote, "The significance of the phenomenon of trust and suspicion in human life is attested to not only by past preoccupations but also by current problems." (p. 265) Today we can categorise as a 'current problem' the trust or lack of it associated with doing business on the Web. In this paper we will again examine the concept of trust and apply it to the environment and needs of Public Accounting (PA) practices endeavouring to offer e-services on the World Wide Web (Web).

The Web offers PA firms the potential to advise clients through electronic communication channels rather than in face-to-face meetings in the traditional office environment. The Web has the capability of providing continuous service by offering access to information around the clock and globe in multiple languages. Furthermore, it can do this in a static or interactive mode. The former is suitable for the provision of intelligence (information) services while the latter supports consulting and counselling types of services. A Web site can also contain links to other Web sites and thereby facilitate relationship networking and inter-firm alliances.

Please use the following format when citing this chapter:

Fink, D., 2007, in IFIP International Federation for Information Processing, Volume 252, Integration and Innovation Orient to E-Society Volume 2, eds. Wang, W., (Boston: Springer), pp. 41-49.

A closer examination of the characteristics of PA e-services readily establishes the need for trust. The following are some examples. First, there is the principle that diversity results in less reliance on interpersonal similarity, common background and experience (Mayer et al, 1995). Diversity is a key feature of the many disparate types of PA clients who can be found all over the world. Second, with e-services, clients can choose from a wide range of service providers available anywhere in the world. Furthermore, PA firms can form strategic alliances with other firms to overcome their deficiencies (e.g. intelligence sharing) or exploit market opportunities beyond their means by becoming a bigger virtual organization. The diversity of opportunities for e-services increases the need for trust

2   Underlying Assumptions for Trust

In an attempt to provide suitable definitions for trust, one needs to establish the underlying assumptions from which they can be developed. According to Tyler and Kramer (1996), trust can be viewed from an instrumentalist and non-instrumentalist perspective. The instrumentalist model reflects rational behaviour while the non-instrumentalist model applies to social relationships. If one accepts that e-service is essentially about maximizing one's business opportunities, then the instrumentalist model appears to best meet the requirements of e-service. Furthermore, people behave rationally and "people's decisions about whether to cooperate – for example, their willingness to trust others – are based on their estimates of the probability that others will reciprocate that cooperation." (Tyler and Kramer, 1996, p. 10)

The instrumentalist model focuses on the efforts of self-interested individuals to achieve optimum outcomes in interactions with others along two principles. First, trust is a calculation of the likelihood of future co-operation (Williamson, 1993, referenced in Tyler and Kramer, 1996). "As trust declines, people are increasingly unwilling to take risks, demand greater protection against the possibility of betrayal, and increasingly insist on costly sanction mechanisms to defend their interests." (Tyler and Kramer, 1996, p. 4)   Should trust decline in long term relationships between service provider and client, transaction costs increase because of the need for self-protective actions.

Second, trust is determined by the 'reputational' market and the 'shadow of the future' (Axelrod, 1984, referenced in Tyler and Kramer, 1996). In other words, unsatisfactory performance by a service provider will lead to a decline in the provider's reputation and cast a shadow over future dealings between client and the provider. With the growth in the size of the market the effectiveness of the reputational market declines as service providers and clients can now be more physically apart. As stated earlier, the Web has enabled PA practices to attract clients from anywhere in the world.

The instrumentalist perspective of trust has two implications for e-services. One, risk assessment is critical to doing business on the Web and hence increasing attention is being given to measures to minimise risk exposure. The anonymity offered by the Web provides scope for unethical and criminal behaviour. Requirements such as professional accreditation in the PA sector ensure that clients' interests and rights are being protected. Two, e-service has seen a tremendous growth in market size (its spans the globe) and hence has reduced the effect of the 'reputational market'. However, at the same time, its is easy to communicate dissatisfaction with services received over the web and it is therefore critical that the PA practice operates professionally at all times or suffer the loss of clients.

3   Building Trust with Clients

Figure 1 provides a schematic overview of the main characteristics of a PA practice. The practice is made up of professionals who operate as individuals or as teams in providing services to their clients. Before being able to practice their profession, a PA has to undergo extensive education, typically at a university, to acquire the necessary knowledge and skills in accounting and related fields such as auditing, finance, taxation. When joining a firm, the novice PA gains experience under the supervision of an already qualified PA. Knowledge, skill and experience are all required to become a qualified PA. The levels of expertise required are laid down in the standards produced by the sectors professional body. It also provides guidelines on professional conduct of its members. Since individual firms may not have all of the necessary expertise required by its clients, they often form alliances with other firms in a network of PA practices.

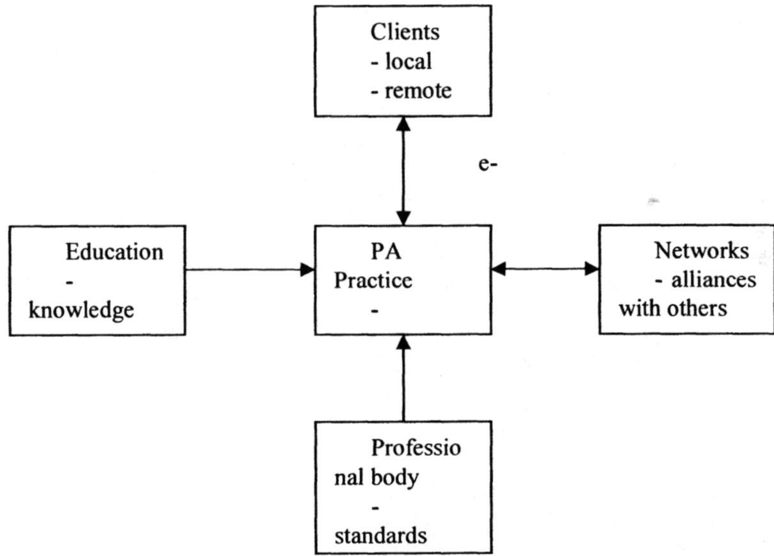

Figure 1 Schematic of Public Accounting Practice

As indicated earlier in the paper, trust is essential to establishing successful e-services because of the great diversity that now exists. However, to operationalise the meaning of trust is difficult because there have been numerous attempts to define and provide meaning to trust and no 'global' definition or complete acceptance of relevant antecedents for trust exist. Butler (1991, p. 647, cited in Hosmer, 1995) commented that "there is no agreement as to what these trust conditions are, and there is no instrument for measuring an exhaustive set of them." Instead, "Several terms have been used synonymously with trust, and this has obfuscated the nature of trust." (Mayer at al, 1995, p. 712) Below is an outline of the antecedents (conditions and determinants) that have been associated with trust (Fink, 2000) and how they may be relevant to PA e-services.

3.1   Trustworthiness

Trust is most often linked with trustworthiness. According to Deutsch (1958), trust exists when the trustworthy person is aware of being trusted and he/she is somehow bound by the trust invested in him/her. The person is 'responsible' for the trust of another. Motivation to be responsible, according to Deutsch (1958), can come from a positive sentiment towards the other and wanting the other one's goal to be realised, a fear of punishment if one is not responsible, and when one's internalised values makes one responsible. In the PA sector, internalised values (those of a PA) are generated through education and training while irresponsible behaviour would be penalised by the professional body. In the online environment, these aspects should be clearly articulated on the firm's website.

3.2   Integrity

"The relationship between integrity and trust involves the trustor's perception that the trustee adheres to a set of principles that the trustor finds acceptable." (Mayer et al, 1995, p. 719) In PA, guiding principles form a significant role. First, they are reflected in the education the PA undertakes. Second, various standards are developed by the profession itself and they are continually refined in response to the changing environment. A high level of initial education (at university) combined with ongoing adherence to up-to-date standards through continuous professional education should ensure that the client can rely on the integrity of performance of the service provider. Again, this information should be displayed on the website.

3.3   Ability

"Ability is that group of skills, competencies, and characteristics that enable a party to have influence within some specific domain" (Mayer et al, 1995, p. 717). It is reflected in the capacity of the PA practice to show that it understand the needs of the client and is able to offer solutions to problems. Demonstrating this competence has to be carried out in a persuasive manner since there is an expectation of technically competent role performances from the PAs involved. However, the difficulty is that most clients are unable to critically evaluate the competencies of specialists, such as PAs. An effective way to demonstrate ability online is to display testimonials provided by clients on the website.

3.4   Reliability

Hart and Saunders (1997) outlined the role of reliability, which they perceive as consistency between what a firm says and does. Reliability reinforces and strengthens co-operation and high levels of co-operation reinforce trust. Barber (1983, referenced in Hosmer, 1995) relates this to expectation of the persistence and fulfilment of the natural and existing social order. In other words, a person would expect the world to continue without discontinuous change. In PA, reliability is taken for granted since the execution of a service has to be in accordance with current standards. For example, the service provider cannot deviate from existing taxation laws when offering taxation advice. By providing information about the PA firm's ability to comply with laws, etc, increases the perception of reliability.

3.5   Confidence

A number of researchers have equated trust and confidence or implied that trust was synonymously with confidence (Hosmer, 1995, referencing Deutsch, 1958; Zand, 1972; Golembiewski and McConkie, 1975). However, the distinction of trust and confidence depends on perceptions. A useful approach is to link the two concepts with risk. Luhmann (1988, referenced in Mayer et al, 1995) associated trust with risk while confidence is not associated with risk. One can illustrate this distinction as follows. If a client chooses to accept advice from the service provider without seeking the opinion of another PA, he/she is ignoring risk and one could argue that the person is in a situation of confidence. On the other hand if the client chooses the advice of one in preference to others because of an assessment of the respective levels of risk the situation can be defined as one of trust. One way to increase confidence is to publish the size and complexity of the client base that already uses e-services.

3.6   Co-operation

Trust and co-operation are often used synonymously although one can co-operate with someone who is not trusted. According to Powell (1996) trust increases in co-operative situations through routinising contact between parties, reducing errors, and allowing for adjustment in the relations. Yearly audit work carried out by PAs demonstrate clearly the requirement for trust; both client and provider want to ensure correct annual reporting, standards require diligent compliance from the auditor, and it is difficult and costly for the client to change auditors in an ad hoc manner because of the need to bring the incoming auditor 'up to speed'. To maintain maximum co-operation, it may be necessary to complement online with regular physical contact.

3.7   Predictability

The distinction between predictability and trust is ambiguous. Mayer et al (1995) held the view that trust goes beyond predictability. "To equate the two is to suggest that a party who can be expected to consistently ignore the needs of others and act in a self-interested fashion is therefore trusted" (p. 714). In other words, trust needs more than predictability since self-interest for example would causes a lack of trust. In PA, predictability is governed by the expected behaviour of the service provider. The client can expect that the provider performs his/her role by strictly adhering to the profession's codified conduct guidelines and responsibilities. Again, providing information about this on the website will increase trust in e-services.

3.8   Dependence

Trust can be viewed as the reliance on another person under conditions of dependence and risk. Dependence is experienced when outcomes are contingent on the trustworthy or untrustworthy behaviours of another while risk is determined by the experience of negative outcomes from the other person's untrustworthy behaviour (Kipnes, 1996). Dependence on the actions of others will vary by task, the situation and the person. In PA, the client very much depends on the provider giving the best advice based on the provider's advanced knowledge and experiences. The website should provide information on the credentials of the service provider, i.e. qualifications and experiences.

3.9   Openness

Hart and Saunders (1997) defined openness as the willingness to listen to new ideas and share rather than withhold information. This behaviour reinforces trust by reducing the probability that the service provider will behave opportunistically. PA often act in a pro-active manner, informing their clients of new developments and opportunities that may benefit them. However, such openness should be practised to the advantage of all clients rather than selected ones. It is therefore important that PA firms make information and advice accessible to all clients via their website.

3.10   Caring

Openness as outlined above is linked with the concept of caring. According to Hart and Saunders (1997) caring is demonstrated by goal compatibility, "the unequivocal representation that both firms share similar, not conflicting, goals" (p. 35). In PA, both parties seek success; the provider by increasing levels of services and hence fees and the client by using the advice or information provided to improve business or professional outcomes. Caring, being a human trait, is re-enforced through human contact such as through regular provider-client get-togethers.

3.11   Benevolence

"Benevolence is the extent to which a trustee is believed to want to do good to the *trustor*, aside from an egocentric profit motive. Benevolence suggests that the trustee has some specific attachment to the trustor." (Mayer et al, 1995, p. 718) In PA, the client-provider relationship is often build over a long period and both parties get to know each other very well. Since some of the old clients may not wish to make use of e-services, it would be necessary for the provider to also continue to offer previous face-to-face services to show that the client's best interests are being looked after.

4   Building Trust within the PA Practice

As outlined earlier, a PA practice operates at different levels, namely the individual, the team, the firm and as a network with other practices. At the individual level Creed and Miles (1996, p. 33) concluded that "trust is build by trusting". This is akin to approaches used in recognised professions and highest levels of skilled artisans. "When the 'master' professional treats the apprentice as a colleague from the beginning, he or she is taking a risk in the hope that such trust will both elicit greater trustworthiness and will be returned." (Creed and Miles, 1996, p. 33) PA firms should therefore provide employees with the necessary technological support to develop into competent PAs. For example, they should be provided with Internet access to be able to carry out environmental scanning without being concerned with the misuse of the technology.

At the team level, trust needs to be part of modern self-managing teams. Trust is generated by putting teams through exercises to build awareness of common responsibilities and fostering the skills needed for self-governance. A good example is an audit team that works together in applying professional audit techniques when examining the client's financial accounts. Each team member has an important role to play in establishing the audit opinion on various systems and sub-systems they are responsible for. In the online environment, this can be achieved by linking professionals through group support systems on an intra- or extranet.

At the firm level, management should "begin the process of activating dormant preferences for cooperation" (Creed and Miles, 1996, p. 33). This means that practice views employment relationships as social as well as economic exchanges. Handy (1995) suggested that their vision and mission statements emphasise the need for learning, bonding and leadership to enhance trust. The firm's intranet would be a suitable media to display the firm's vision and values that guide professional conduct.

Collaborative networks depend on minimal transaction costs for their responsiveness and efficiency. The existence of high levels of trust allows a reduction in transaction costs (Creed and Miles, 1996). Extended business groups often share historical experiences, obligations and advantages of group membership. In Japan they are called *keiretsu* (meaning societies of business) where "the large networks of producers look like complex, extended families, organized either in a cobweb-like fashion or a vast holding company with financial institutions at the apex" (Powell, 1996, p. 58). They apply the principles of obligation and reciprocity in their business dealings to generate trust. Internet technology provides the means to bring partners closer effectively (e.g. quick responses and turnaround) and efficiently (e.g. reduced transaction costs).

5   Conclusion

This paper has attempted to identify the antecedents of trust and applied the various perspectives to the nature of pubic accounting. Once the conditions and determinants of trust for e-services are know, PA firms will be able to maximize trust through adopting the strategies identified in this paper. They are summarized in Table 1. Due to the word restrictions of the paper the list of actions is not comprehensive and others could be identified. However, it provides good examples on what the PA practice may able to achieve in developing increasing levels of trust, both with their clients and within the practice itself.

Table 1: Antecedents and Strategies

Antecedents	Strategies
Trust with clients	
Trustworthiness	Display information on website about professional training and standards
Integrity	Display information on website about continuous training and adherence to professional standards
Ability	Display client testimonials on website
Reliability	Display information on website about compliance with laws and regulations
Confidence	Display on website information about size and complexity of client base
Co-operation	Complement online service with regular physical meetings
Predictability	Display information on website requirement to adhere to professional standards and behaviour
Dependence	Display information on website about provider's credentials, i.e. qualifications and experiences
Openness	Ensure that information on website is accessible to clients
Caring	Arrange for regular get-togethers with clients
Benevolence	Continue to offer face-to-face services in addition to online services
Trust within practice	
Individual	Provide technology (Internet) access for personal development
Team	Provide intranet support to link team members
Firm	Display information in website about firm's vision and values
Alliance	Link partners through Internet to for efficiency and effectiveness

The consequences of ignoring, or worse loosing trust, can be severe. Within interpersonal networks, such as the one between service provider and client, trust and distrust have opposite effects, their influence is not symmetrical. Trust builds incrementally, but distrust has a more dramatic 'catastrophic' quality. Thus while we cautiously develop trust with each other, often over a lengthy period of time, a sudden, unexpected and unpleasant development can destroy the relationship. Should one of the parties have cause to loose trust in the other party it may be impossible to re-establish it.

References

1. Axelrod R. (1984) *The Evolution of Cooperation, Basic Books*, New York.

2. Barber B. (1983) *The Logic and Limits of Trust*, Rutgers University Press, New Brunswick, NJ.

3. Butler J.K. (1991) "Toward Understanding and Measuring Conditions of Trust: Evolution of a Conditions of Trust Inventory", *Journal of Management*, 17(3), 643-663.

4. Creed W.E. and Miles R.E. (1996) "Trust in Organizations A Conceptual Framework Linking Organizational Forms, Managerial Philosophies, and the Opportunity Costs of Controls", in Kramer R.M. and Tyler T.R. (Eds.) *Trust in Organizations - Frontiers of Theory and Research, Sage Publications, London.*

5. Deutsch M. (1958) "Trust and Suspicion", *Conflict Resolution,* 2(4), 265-279.

Fink D. (2000) "Developing Trust for E-Commerce" in Janczewski L. (ed) Internet and Intranet Security Management: *Risks and Solutions, Idea Group Publishing*, London.

6. Golembiewski R.T. and McConkie M. (1975) "The Centrality of Interpersonal Trust in Group Processes" in Cooper C.L. (Ed.) *Theories of Group Processes*, Wiley, New York, 131-185.

7. Handy C. (1995) "Trust and the Virtual Organization", *Harvard Business Review,* May-June, 40-50.

8. Hart P. and Saunders C. (1997) "Power and Trust: Critical Factors in the Adoption and Use of Electronic Data Interchange", *Organization Science,* 8(1), 23-42.

9. Hosmer L.T. (1995) "Trust: The Connecting Link between Organizational Theory and Philosophical Ethics", *Academy of Management Review,* 20(2), 379-403.

10. Kipnis D. (1996) "Trust and Technology" in Kramer R.M. and Tyler T.R. (Eds.) *Trust in Organizations - Frontiers of Theory and Research*, Sage Publications, London.

11. Luhmann N. (1988) "Familiarity, Confidence, Trust: Problems and Alternatives" in Gambetta D.G. (Ed.) Trust, Basil Blackwell, New York, 94-107.

12. Mayer R.C., Davis J.H. and Schoorman F.D. (1995) "An Integrative Model of Organizational Trust", *Academy of Management Review,* 20(3), 709-734.

13. Powell W.W. (1996) "Trust-Based Forms of Governance" in Kramer R.M. and Tyler T.R. (Eds.) Trust in Organizations - Frontiers of Theory and Research, Sage Publications, London.

14. Tyler T.R. and Kramer R.M. (1996) "Whither Trust?", in Kramer R.M. and Tyler T.R. (Eds.) *Trust in Organizations - Frontiers of Theory and Research*, Sage Publications, London.

15. Williamson O.E. (1993) "Calculativeness, Trust, and Economic Organization", Journal of Law and Economics, 34, 453-502.Zand D.E. (1972) "Trust and Managerial Problem Solving", *Administrative Science Quarterly,* 17, 229-239.

Service-Oriented Software Testing Platform[*]

Fagui Liu[1], Chunwei Luo[1]
School of Computer Science and Engineering, South China University of
Technology
510640 Guangzhou, Guangdong, P.R. China
fgliu@scut.edu.cn, lcwiron@163.com

Abstract. Software testing is an important quality guarantee for software. It is
an indispensable stage in software life cycle. After the analysis into the idea of
the service-oriented systems, this paper tries to integrate service-oriented
thinking with software testing to propose a service-oriented software platform
to solve the limitations that exist in actual software testing tools, such as
costliness, heterogeneity, lack of expansibility, single function, and so on.
Service-oriented software testing platform (SOSTP) adopting a distributed
structure separates testing client and server. Logical function of testing
services is completed on the server end. It can integrate existing software
testing tools, and provide corresponding testing services to the clients. The
biggest characteristic of SOSTP is the dynamic deployment of testing service,
which enables users to customize testing services dynamically. This platform
has high extensity and transparency.

1   Introduction

Software testing is an important assurance of software quality. It is an indispensable
stage in the software life cycle.

Corresponding to different phases of development, there is different software
testing technology. According to the technique, testing technology can be divided
into three categories: system structure testing, system function tests and unit testing
[1].

So far, many automated testing tools have already emerged, such as Purify [2],
Rational Robot, TestBed, CodeTEST, RTInsight, Logiscope, Cantata++, VectorCast
and so on. These tools have covered many aspects of static testing and dynamic

Please use the following format when citing this chapter:

Liu, F., Luo, C., 2007, in IFIP International Federation for Information Processing, Volume 252, Integration and
Innovation Orient to E-Society Volume 2, eds. Wang, W., (Boston: Springer), pp. 50-59.

testing. In allusion to different project operating platform and language development environment, these tools have different development edition.

However, there are some common limitations:

1. The testing tool is comparatively expensive while many software developers cannot bear.
2. The testing tool is too huge, while testing personnel only use partial functions.
3. The single testing tool cannot fully meet testing personnel's demand, so that testing personnel have to purchase many testing tools.
4. Heterogeneity of different programming language causes non-universality of the testing tool.
5. The heterogeneity of the software platform also causes the heterogeneity of the testing tools.
6. Due to the poor performance of many development machines, it is difficult to run some large-scale testing tools.

Therefore, software testing becomes one of the hottest research fields. A lot of scholars have done a lot of research and proposed different software testing tools framework.

SUN Chang-ai [3], LIU Chao, etc. proposed component-based software testing tools integration framework. These components are compatible with CORBA. The framework is scalable. Users can meet their own needs by selecting and reusing software testing function components.

DONG Lei [4] and LU Qiang proposed the distributed software testing platform. The platform adopts client/server architecture. The software testing logic function is concentrated on the server, which effectively lowers the complexity to deploy the testing tool.

However, if the function provided by different testing tool is taken as a kind of service, it is plausible to seek the corresponding service when a testing request is proposed.

Based on this idea, this article attempts to combine the thought of Service-oriented with the software testing, thus proposes a Service-oriented software testing platform.

Service-oriented software testing platform adopts distributed structure. It separates the testing client end and the server end. Logical function of the testing service is completed at the server end. This platform can integrate the existing software testing tools, and provide the corresponding testing service to requesters for testing. The biggest characteristic is that provider of testing service can expanding services to the platform dynamically which empowers users to customize testing services dynamically. This platform has high extensity and transparency.

In the second chapter, the correlative work about the software test framework is presented. In the third chapter, service-oriented software testing framework is proposed and specified.

2   Related Technique

2.1   SOA and Software Testing Platform

Essentially , SOA (Service-oriented Architecture) is a collection of services. Services communicate with each other (these communications can be a simple data transfer or coordination between two or more services.). The so-called service is a function that is precise in definition, well-formed in packaging, independent from the surrounding environment and the state of other services. SOA is a newly developed method emerging from software development in recent years. It is a common method of framework design [5].

Service-Oriented Architecture is a component model. It links different functional units (called services) of the application through well-defined interfaces and protocols. Interface is neutrally defined, independent of platform, systems and languages in format of XML. Through these well-formed interfaces and contracts, all services of SOA interact in a unified and common approach. Moreover, the neutral definition of interface lowers the coupling between the services. The entire application structure will not be affected by the changes of the single individual internal structure [6]. Services call each other through service description.

In the course of development, software testing framework gradually absorbs many software engineering ideas to break through the traditional software testing platform model. How to combine the current upswing SOA idea with software testing platform to solve the mentioned problems of software testing tools is a practical and promising research topic. A service-oriented software testing platform aims to provide an integrated testing environment with multi-function, high scalability and high degree of automation. Therefore, the software testing platform should have some flexibility for users to customize platform functions on their demand, to expand new features, to integrate new tools and to lower development costs.

We can design a service-oriented software platform by the idea of Service Software Bus (SSB). In essence, the main bus architecture is to connect all the functional components to a public mutual communication structural component in a common way. Then the service-oriented software testing platform provides a layer of soft bus structure for users under the interactive interfaces. In this way, if other functional testing components interact with the test platform under the pre-defined interface standard, it can be integrated into the platform, when any other functional testing components attempt to expand to the software testing platform.

2.2   Eclipse Open Source Framework

Eclipse is a software framework followed OSGi (Open Service Gateway Initiative) standard [7], an excellent integrated development environment.

It is a complete and open infrastructure development platform. Graphic tools and other functions can be integrated to the development environment through the

Eclipse-defined interface standards in the form of plug-in, thereby expanding the functions of Eclipse itself. Eclipse can be convenient to expand on the basis of that it provides a concept Extension Point which is similar to the soft-Bus, see Fig. . Platform Runtime is the whole basis of the Eclipse framework. All other components are treated as plug-ins to expand. The basic Eclipse SDK has already included a basic set of development tools, and help system, other tools needed can be customized to and integrated into the platform framework by users. To facilitate the users, Eclipse also provides a PDE (Plug-in Development environment) [8] dedicating to the Eclipse plug-in development. Programs can be developed steadily and rapidly with PDE extension module of Eclipse.

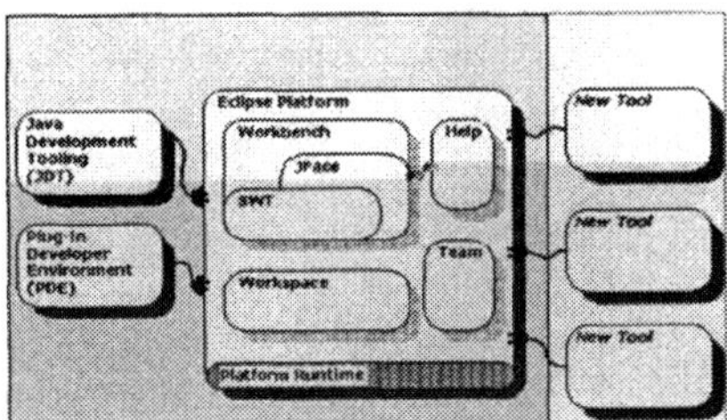

Fig. 1. Eclipse Architecture [9]

3   Service-Oriented Software Testing Platform

3.1   Framework of Service-Oriented Software Testing Platform

As shown in Fig. , the entire framework of Service-oriented software testing platform is made up of client and server components., which will be described in the next two sections.

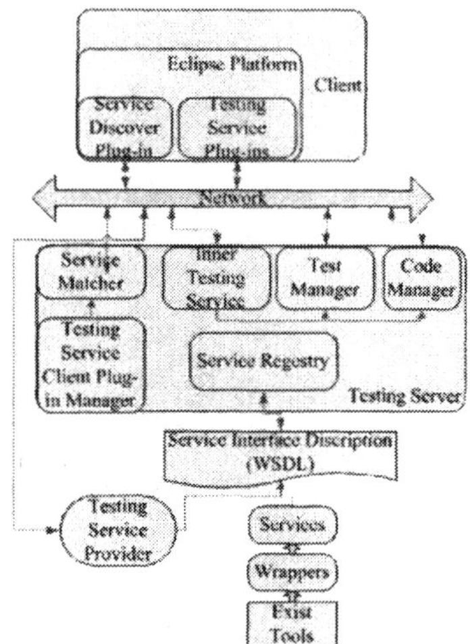

Fig. 2. Framework of Service-Oriented Software Testing Platform

One characteristic of the Service-oriented software testing platform is that testing services can be dynamically located and customized. At client, users can use testing services through customizing testing services. Based on the service-oriented idea, the testing module can be reused and eliminates heterogeneity of platforms. The entire platform is distributed, multi-tier, therefore the testing service concurrent use can be achieved easily.

3.2   Client Design

We implement the design of client of SOA-based software testing platform expediently by using the Eclipse framework and Eclipse plug-in mechanism.

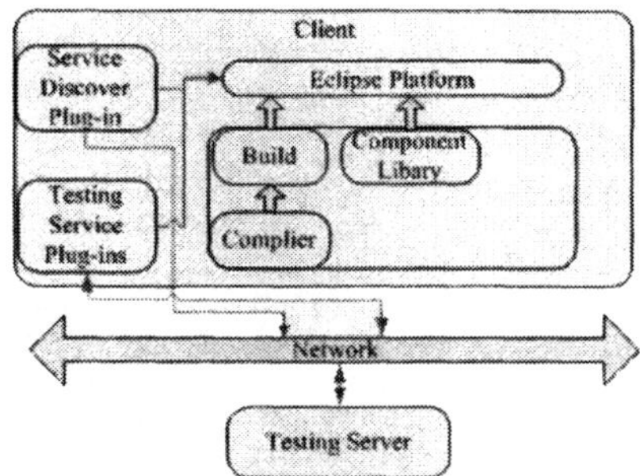

Fig. 3. Design of Software Testing Platform Client

From Fig. we can see that the client framework is implemented by the Eclipse framework, while soft bus is implemented by Eclipse framework. The low coupling between testing service module and the existing of the soft bus reduced the coupling between testing service and platform, which means testing services module can be added or deleted to the platform at any time.

Service Discover Plug-in is a plug-in that integrates into the client platform. Use of this plug-in user can search and customize the testing service at their demand.

Testing Service Plug-ins is also called Client Plug-in, plug-ins used in the client. They bind with customized services. They are developed by service providers. They are provided to services requester. By collaborating with testing services, they help users to generate test cases, submit test scripts, show test results and so on.

3.3   Server Design

The server of testing platform proposed by this paper includes Services Registry, Testing Services Client Plug-in Manager, Services Matcher, Inner Services, Test Manager and Code Manager.

Service Registry is used to provide registry interface to testing services provider. Testing services have to accord to certain criterion to register into the platform. Testing services use WSDL to describe its interface. Each service need provide the corresponding Client Plug-in. Testing services can be divided into several types: The first one is the testing services developed by us, which we call Inner Services. The second one is to use wrapper to package the existing testing tools as services and register to the server. In this way, other testing tools are able to be integrated to the platform. The third one is testing services provided by third party.

Testing Services Client Plug-in Manager is a component used to manage the Client Plug-in when service providers register services, and provide Client Plug-in to users when service is customized.

Service Matcher is designed for the users to discover services. Service Matcher matches the services which are registered according to the user's request description and displays the suited service to users for customization.

Inner Services are testing services integrated in the platform. It need use Code Manager for code management and Test Manager for the management of testing case and results.

3.4   Model of Testing Services

This paper presents the service-oriented software testing platform. Therefore, the testing service model is a very important part. In order to meet service-oriented idea, testing service should have uniform model requested by the testing platform. Only in this way, the testing platform can achieves transparency and scalability. As shown in Fig. , testing service model is made up of service components and client plug-in. They are closely bundled. They can communicate and do logic control through networks. Service component includes Transaction Control, Waiting List Manager, Code Manager, Test Manager, Test Script Manager, Test Execute and testing services interface description.

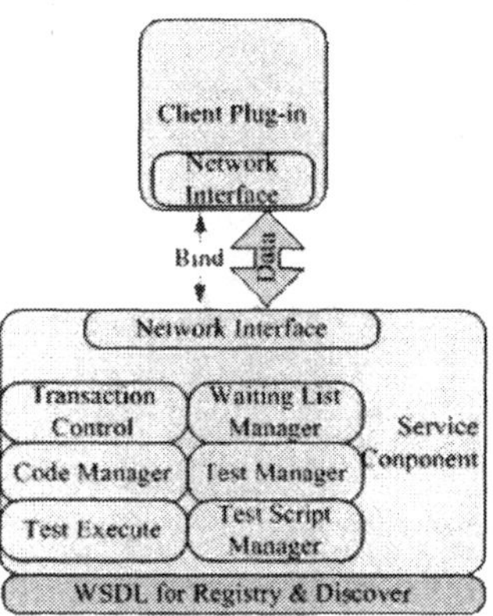

Fig. 4. Model of Testing Service

3.5   Registration of Testing Services

How the Service registration process integrates services to the platform is shown in Fig. .

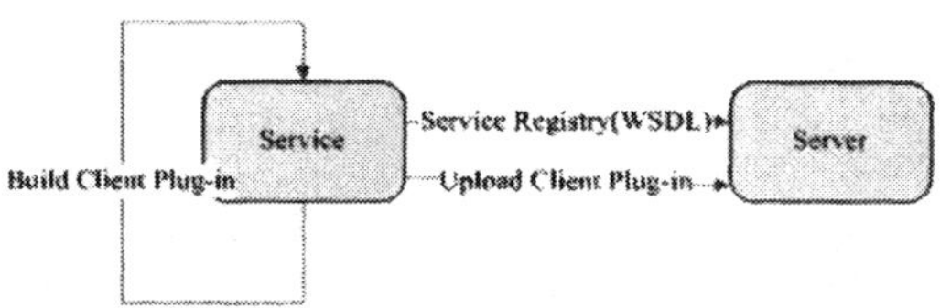

Fig. 5. Registration of Testing Service

In the platform that proposed by this paper, the registration process is as follows:
1. According to the work flow of testing service, service providers develop the Client Plug-in (compatible with the Eclipse Plug-in).
2. Use WSDL to describe the service interface, and register to the server of the platform.

Service providers upload the Client Plug-in of testing services. Test server uses Testing Service Client Plug-in Manager to manage the plug-in. It is provided to users when services are customized.

3.6   Request of Software Testing

In this section, we do not describe the software testing process of a testing technique, which is not the focus of this paper. We describe how the user gets testing services and the process of using the testing service.

Users can use the Service Discover Plug-in to search for required testing services dynamically and customize testing services.

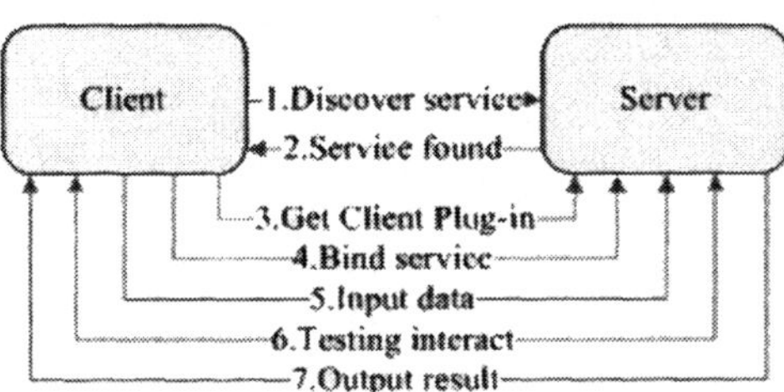

Fig. 6. Testing Process

As shown in Fig. , the software testing process is as follows:
1. Clients use the Service Discovery Plug-in to search the needed services.
2. Server returns the suited service to Client.
3. Client customizes the service and gets the Client Plug-in.
4. Client integrates the Client plug-in into the test environment of client, and use the Client plug-in to bundle with service.
5. According to the testing, the Client inputs the testing data required for.
6. During the testing process, client and testing services interact and collaborate.
7. Upon completion of the testing, the client receives test results.

4   Conclusion and Further Study

SOA based Software testing platform can meet testing needs in different circumstances. If we follow the unified soft-bus standard, both various service and third party implement can be integrated into testing platform conveniently. Adopting Eclipse Framework as a soft-bus standard, users can make a completely personalized software testing platform, according to themselves' needs.

Service-oriented software testing platform can resolve the limitations of the current software testing tools properly. Utilization of this platform can integrate existing software testing tools, and provide testing function in the form of services. It makes these testing functional components reusable. Service-oriented software testing platform can reduce the complexity of the testing software. The service-oriented characteristic makes testers focus on software development, which can reduce the cost of constructing a testing environment effectively. Testers can customize needful testing service when software needs to be tested.

For some test that needs to use the source code, there is a problem that if test service providers can provide the assurance of safety or not.

Further work is how to reinforce the security of service-oriented software testing platform.

Acknowledgments

This research is supported by Guangdong Province Key Field Breakthrough (2005A10208005 & Department of Information Industry 2004-2005).

References

1. William E. Perry, *Effective Methods for Software Testing Second Edition* (China Machine Press, China, 2004).

2. L.B Zhao, X. Wang, and H.T ZHAO, Software test and its supporting tools, Technology & Economy in Areas of Communications (TEAC), No.2, 102-103 (2006)

3. C.A Sun, C. Liu, M.Z Jin, and M. Zhang, Architecture Framework for Software Test Tool, Proceedings of the 36th International Conference on Technology of Object-Oriented Languages and Systems, 2000, TOOLS-Asia 2000, 40-47

4. L. Dong, and Q. Lu, "The design and implementation of distributed software test platform", *Journal of Suzhou Vocational University*, 17(1), 90-93 (2006)

5. IBM corporation, Service Oriented Architecture and Web services (2002); http://www-306.ibm.com/software/solutions/webservices/

6. Rick Robinson, Understand Enterprise Service Bus Scene and Solutions in Service-Oriented Architecture (July, 2004); http://www-306.ibm.com

7. OSGI Alliance, OSGI Service Platform Specification (October 10, 2005); http://www.osgi.org/

8. Eclipse Foundation Inc., Eclipse PDE API Specification (2004); http://www.eclipse.org/pde/

9.   Eclipse Foundation Inc., Eclipse Platform Architecture (2004);
http://help.eclipse.org/help30/index.jsp?topic=/org.eclipse.pde.doc.user/reference/api/overvie
w-summary.html

A Research Study on Externalization of Tacit Knowledge Based on Web2.0

Gang Li 1, Kun Lu 2

1 Wuhan University, School of Information Management, E-mail :imiswhu@yahoo.com.cn

2 Wuhan University, School of Information Management, E-mail: ghostk.student@gmail.com

Abstract. In this era of knowledge economy, knowledge management, the key point of which is externalization of tacit knowledge, has been drawing more and more attention. By using the new concepts and tools emerging after Web 2.0 this paper provides a conceptual model to externalize and utilize of tacit knowledge on the basis of analysis and cogitation of difficult key issues during the process of externalization.

1 Introduction

The era of internet is characterized with knowledge explosion, last half century during which people have created more knowledge than ever before has witnessed the flourish in the human civilization. More and more knowledge is being created at a fast pace. There are two kinds of knowledge which are explicit knowledge and implicit knowledge. The explicit knowledge is knowledge that has been or can be articulated, codified, and stored in certain media and can be readily transmitted to others while implicit knowledge also called tacit knowledge is knowledge that people carry in their minds and is, therefore, difficult to access. Often, people are not aware of the knowledge they possess or how it can be valuable to others, just as Michael Polanyi said "we know more than we can tell" Tacit knowledge accounting for the major part of the repository of human knowledge is often gained through the experience of individual or organization, thus, it is extremely personal knowledge which is difficult for sharing or utilization. In virtue of the new concepts and tools emerging after Web2.0 this paper provides a conceptual model for utilization of tacit knowledge based on analysis and cogitation of the difficult key issues during the process of externalization of tacit knowledge.

2 An Analysis of Externalization of Tacit Knowledge

In the past people have placed much emphasis on explicit knowledge but ignored the importance of tacit knowledge. Actually, tacit knowledge often turns out to be the most valuable knowledge in an organization, the research on tacit

Please use the following format when citing this chapter:

Li, G., Lu, K., 2007, in IFIP International Federation for Information Processing, Volume 252, Integration and Innovation Orient to E-Society Volume 2, eds. Wang, W., (Boston: Springer), pp. 60-67.

knowledge can not only help to exploit and utilize the human's knowledge to larger extend but better extract knowledge from people, which is conducive to knowledge share. Since more and more researchers began to realize the importance of tacit knowledge, the transformation between explicit knowledge and tacit knowledge aroused increasing attention. Some researchers maintain that tacit knowledge can not be transformed into explicit knowledge, the psychologists Wagner and Sternberg are the supporters of this theory while some other researchers think the transformation between two kinds of knowledge is available, and this is typically supported by the SECI model provided by Nonaka which named the transformation from tacit knowledge to explicit knowledge externalization. This paper holds the opinion that tacit knowledge can be transformed into explicit knowledge, and the process of transformation is universal, however, the transformation seldom happens due to the characteristics of tacit knowledge. As a result, the major of tacit knowledge still exists in human's brains and is hard to share and utilize.

2.1   Obstacles of Externalization

In the previous part we have discussed the possibility and importance of the externalization of tacit knowledge. And in this section, this paper will analyze the obstacles which prevent the externalization:
➤   Tacit knowledge is difficult to articulate

Tacit knowledge is difficult to articulate. It comes from the practical experience of people, and thus it is extremely individual knowledge. It is this intrinsic character of tacit knowledge that makes the externalization process so difficult.
➤   Barrier in the subjective intention

Knowledge management encourages knowledge share which is altruism behavior. Notwithstanding, people pay prices to gain knowledge so as to take advantages over other competitors. They will certainly think that knowledge is power. Thinking of their self-interest, people are resistant to share knowledge with others. This is the barrier in the subjective intention.
➤   Lack of platform and environment

Tacit knowledge is intangible. Sometimes it is the inspiration fleeting across our mind. And if there is no available platform to record this ephemeral knowledge resource it may well hides again. Unfortunately, many organizations are lack of this kind of platform which is convenient to grasp and record the ephemeral knowledge and able to provide an access to the share of tacit knowledge.
➤   Lack of insurance mechanism of credit

Knowledge share requires credit without which nobody would be willing to share and communicate knowledge with others. When the concept of credit is established, people will believe each other, staff are willing to contribute their knowledge and all of them will benefit. When this share action becomes common regulations, one will maximize the use value of knowledge and build his reputation by offering his knowledge to others. However, this insurance mechanism is still imperfect which restrains staff's activity to share knowledge.

3   An Analysis of Web2.0 and Its Tools

3.1   An Analysis of Web2.0

The concept of "web 2.0" began with a conference brainstorming session between O'Reilly and MediaLive International. Like many important concepts, Web 2.0 doesn't have a hard boundary, but rather, a gravitational core. That is to say we can not exactly define what is web 2.0 but we tell whether a web product belongs to it. We can formulate the sense of Web 2.0 by examples:

Table 1: what is Web 2.0

Web 1.0		Web 2.0
DoubleClick	-->	Google AdSense
Ofoto	-->	Flickr
Akamai	-->	BitTorrent
mp3.com	-->	Napster
Britannica Online	-->	Wikipedia
personal websites	-->	Blogging
evite	-->	upcoming.org and EVDB
domain name speculation	-->	search engine optimization
page views	-->	cost per click
screen scraping	-->	web services
publishing	-->	Participation
content management systems	-->	Wikis
directories (taxonomy)	-->	tagging ("folksonomy")
stickiness	-->	Syndication

Generally speaking, Web2.0 is an outcome of the integration of new technology and concepts. It is a new application on the internet which appreciates all kinds of new understanding for internet, such as the web as platform, using the wisdom of crowds, long tail and so on. If a web service is based on these new understandings, then it is web 2.0 service. The transformation from web 1.0 to web 2.0 includes transformations from absolutely "reading" to "writing", from passively accepting to positive creating the information on internet. With respect to the fundamental element, the web page is for Web1.0 and the publishing or recording information on the internet for Web2.0; With respect to mechanism, the "Client Server" is for Web1.0 and the "Web Services" for Web2.0; In the environment of Web2.0 the web authors expand from experts to common users. Web2.0 emphasizes two core aspects, one is microcontent, the other is user. The microcontent is all the data created by users, no matter how trivial it is. For example, a web log, comments, pictures, bookmarks, favorite music lists, new friends and so on. All the microcontent is fraught with our work, everyday life and study, and it makes as much sense, if not more, as those formal documentations such as papers, books and journals do in the aspects of importance, amount and effects. On the other hand, Web2.0 gives identity to its user. In the era of Web1.0, users are not identified; it is an abstract representative of crowds. When it comes to Web2.0, web users are embodied and given to identifications just as our real world. These users will no longer feel they are the standers-by, which is conducive to arouse their sense of ownership and encourage them to contribute their wisdom.

3.2   An Analysis of Web2.0 Tools

It is determined by the intrinsic characters of Web2.0 that we can use it for the externalization of tacit knowledge in an organization. The following paragraphs will analyze three typical tools of Web2.0---Blog, RSS and Wikipedia in order to illustrate the advantages and feasibility of using Web2.0 tools to externalize and utilize tacit knowledge.

3.2.1 Blog

Blog is a web log system which is based on the microcontent concept. Usually we call the blog users bloggers. Bloggers can get access and create links to each other, they make comments to others blog and communicate their ideas. In virtue of co-linking, visiting others' blog or being visited by others, commenting and communicating, a certain social web is established among these bloggers which is called blogosphere. The reasons why choosing blog as tools for externalization are explained as follows:

➢ As a typical application of Web 2.0, blog is different from personal home page in many aspects. Firstly, personal home page requires more technology knowledge and costs than a blog. A blogger can easily install a blog without any payment or technological knowledge about web such as HTML. Secondly, the primary goal of the personal home page is to provide a platform to display web users. Thus, a personal home page does more in displaying rather than communicating. However, blog is used to communicate which lays more attentions on knowledge accumulation, share and communication. And it focuses on the content rather than appearance, which makes it as a personal knowledge management system.

➢ Blog is based on the concept of microcontent. Compared with traditional formal documentation, blog has its advantages in flexibility and convenience which is extremely beneficial for externalize staff's tacit knowledge step by step. Therefore, blog can do a better job than other traditional documentation does in exploiting tacit knowledge which is hard to express and easy to slip away from our minds. Moreover, in the era of knowledge economy, knowledge are widely scattered among various people from different industries. Some of them may be specializing in research, whose knowledge is more systematic. They are more likely to give out a complete theoretical system via formal documentations such as books, papers and periodicals. Since in most situations, knowledge is mastered by those who are not specialists, they may have some trivial ideas or scattered knowledge which is unable to be published and conveyed by formal documentation. And blog is effective for recording and collecting these knowledge fractions which may cover a plethora of knowledge.

➢ As a web service, blog is maintained by the BSP(blog service provider), which is free for its users. We don't have to think of how it works, but just use it to satisfy our needs. Being transplanted into the Web 2.0 concept, blog service is designed to most major part of crowds. It is a fool-proof application that is easy to manipulate and popularize.

➢ Blog is not only technique tool but also social channel. It may seem like a trivial piece of functionality now, but it was effectively the device that turned web logs from an ease-of-publishing phenomenon into a conversational mass of overlapping communities. For the first time it became relatively easy to gesture directly at a highly specific post on someone else's site and talk about it. Discussion emerged, chat emerged. And – as a result – friendships emerged or became more entrenched. Finally, a new social web blogosphere established and endow it with certain social attributes facilitating knowledge sparkle.

3.2.2 RSS

RSS was born in 1997 out of the confluence of Dave Winer's "Really Simple Syndication" technology, used to push out blog updates, and Netscape's "Rich Site Summary", which allowed users to create custom Netscape home pages with regularly updated data flows. Netscape lost its interest in this field, and the technology was carried forward by blogging pioneer Userland, Winer's company. In the current crop of applications, we see, though, the heritage of both parents. Nowadays, we use RSS to aggregate information across different sites. Via RSS someone would be able to link not just to a page, but to subscribe to it with notification every time that page changes. The following figure demonstrates how RSS works:

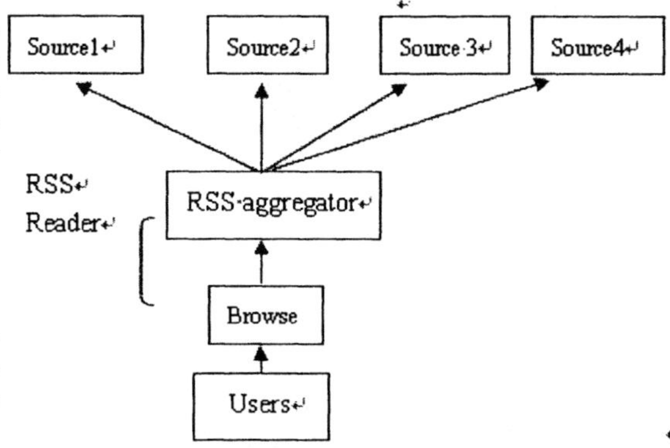

Fig.1: Mechanism of RSS

As the above figure shows, RSS can collect information from different sites and then reorganize them. RSS can also notice the update of sites and provide latest information for its users. On the other hand, users can choose and subscribe whatever they are interested in RSS reader. By virtue of RSS, web users can enjoy various information sources from different sites from only one window that is RSS reader.

3.2.3 Wikipedia

Wikipedia is also a typical application of Web 2.0; it is a free and open collaborative encyclopedia project. In the wikipedia every entry can be added by any web user and edited by any other, which is fully based on the application of Eric Raymond's dictum that "with enough eyeballs, all bugs are shallow". It is the freedom and equality, trust and self-discipline, collaboration and share make up of the core value of wikipedia, a new type of encyclopedia facing the common crowds rather than elites. This kind of encyclopedia is efficient when apply to accumulate and deposit knowledge since it accepts any different view and encourage discussion which is conducive to self-improvement.

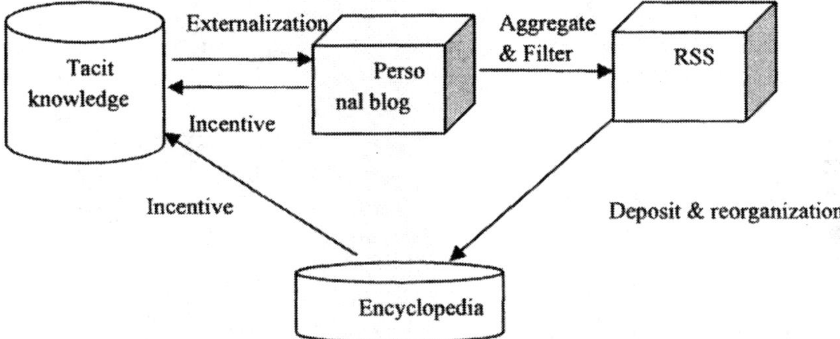

Fig.2: Conceptual model for externalization and utilization of tacit knowledge

4   A Conceptual Model for Externalization and Utilization of Tacit Knowledge

In the former part, we have analyzed web 2.0 and its tools. In this section we would like to give a conceptual model for externalization and utilization of tacit knowledge in virtue of the tools and concepts mentioned before. The figure below demonstrates my conceptual model of using web 2.0 for externalization and utilization of tacit knowledge:

4.1   Externalization

As is clearly demonstrated in the former paragraphs, blog, a typical Web2.0 application based on microcontent concept, has its natural advantages in externalizing personal tacit knowledge .In order to make full use of blog to externalize people's tacit knowledge in an organization we should first establish a personal blog system, and then encourage everyone to write blog and contribute his knowledge especially those with close relevance with his field. Make full use of blog's advantages to externalize more tacit knowledge in the organization and record it in the blog system.

4.2   Aggregate & Filter

Blog has its advantages in flexibility. However, on the other hand, knowledge externalized by blog system often appears to be so fragmentary and in low quality that we can hardly use them efficiently. Thus, we need to use RSS to aggregate all the knowledge fractions together, filter the low quality information and provide all valuable knowledge for users in a RSS reader. By aggregating and filtering, we make the knowledge externalized from blog system easier to utilize.

4.3   Deposit & Reorganize

By using blog to externalization and RSS to aggregate and filter, we can get some high quality knowledge resources coming from the staff of organization which is closely relevant to survival and development of organization. And the externalized tacit knowledge is vital for an organization's core competency. Some of the knowledge may be real time knowledge which is valuable in a short time. Some others may be of long term value which can be deposited for the further use in future. Therefore, it is necessary to build an organization encyclopedia based on the concept of wikipedia.

We can extract important or long term valuable knowledge from the knowledge in RSS by further analyzing and evaluating. Then we need to reorganize this knowledge in order to make them better organized. By accumulation and deposit of this knowledge we will get a valuable knowledge repository in the organization fraught with various important, valuable and high quality knowledge. Moreover, all knowledge in the organization encyclopedia is highly relevant with the field of this organization, which generates the individual encyclopedia. And just like the wikipedia, this organization encyclopedia is also a free and open one, every staff can make comments about any entry and we can modify the entry if the comment is reasonable.

4.4   Incentives

To realize knowledge share within an organization, one needs not only some useful tools but to institute some regulations to catalyze this process. By establish incentive mechanism we can ensure credit of knowledge share, eliminate negative emotions preventing staff from contributing his knowledge, and enforce potential effects of organizational culture.

➤   Quantitive incentive:

An organization should institute a serial of quantitive incentives to quantify the contribution of each staff in knowledge share. For example, how many blogs does one write in a month, how many visitors have browsed a certain blog, how many times is a blog cited by others or how many entries has one contributed to organization encyclopedia. Then corresponding reward should be provided to encourage one's contribution so as to construct a good environment for knowledge share.

➤   Culture incentive:

The organizational culture is the view of core value in an organization. It is potential behavior regulations which restrain every person in this organization. It is essential to build an organizational culture which is conducive to encourage its staff to contribute and share their knowledge. Establish a common conscious that being proud with contributing knowledge and respect those who make contributions.

5   Summary

In this era of knowledge economy, more and more organizations began to take steps for knowledge management and utilization. If an organization wants to take precedence over others in today's intensive competition, it should handle the tacit knowledge well. This paper begins with analysis of tacit knowledge and its externalization, provides a measure for externalization and utilization of tacit knowledge in virtue of the concepts and applications of Web2.0.

Acknowledgements

The research reported in this paper is supported by the project Research on Competitive Intelligence Based on Knowledge Organization (Project No. 05JJD870159) sponsored by Key Project of Key Institution in Humane and Social Science Research, Education of Ministry of P.R. China.

References

1. Wikipedia(April 9,2007); http://en.wikipedia.org/wiki/Explicit_knowledge

2. Polanyi M. *Personal Knowledge* [M], Chicago: the University of Chicago Press, 1958, 13-15

3. Wagner R K, Sternberg R J. Practical in Intelligence in Real World Pursuits: The Role of Tacit Knowledge. *Journal of Personality and Social Psychology,* 1985(49).436-458..

4. Nonaka I. A dynamic theory of organizational knowledge creation. *Organization Science.* 1994,5(1).14-36.

5. Tim O'Reilly. What is Web2.0 (March10,2007) ; http://www.oreillynet.com/pub/a/oreilly/tim/news/2005/09/30/what-is-web-20.html

Application of Electronic Business in Safe Accident Prevention and Control on Coalface

Guozhi Lu[1], Jianquan Tang [2], Chunhui Yao[3] and Lei Yang[1]

1College of Economics and Management, Shandong University of Science and Technology 579 Qianwangang Road Qingdao Economic and Technological Development Zone Shandong, 266510, P.R.China
LGZ2050@163.com

2 Institute of Resource and Environment Engineering, Shandong University of Science and Technology579 Qianwangang Road Qingdao Economic and Technological Development Zone Shandong, 266510, P.R.China

3 Geoinfomation Science & Engineering College, Shandong University of Science and Technology579 Qianwangang Road Qingdao Economic and Technological Development Zone Shandong, 266510, P.R.China

Abstract: In this paper, by analyzing the coal mine safety accident of present stage, the author has come to a conclusion that the safe accidents on coalface accounting for a lot of coal mine safety accident, and has brought forward the cause leading to this phenomenon. Then, through the discussion about "Overlying Strata Movement Law", this author has suggested that Electronic Business can be used for the coal mine to prevent and control safe accident on coalface, and has given out the operating pattern of Electronic Business innovatively. This conclusions are most instructive to Chinese coal mine in managing safe accident on coalface and innovative for application of Electronic Business in coal mine safety.

1   Introduction

In recent years, the Chinese coal mine casualty accident is very serious, accidents such as roof caving, water inrush, coal bump that caused by extraction (coalface advances) frequently happen. The gas explosions or water inrush accidents causing more than 10 workers to death had appears in the local mine and state-owned coal mines many times, these accidents frequently threaten the safety production of coal mine, at the same time affect the developing image of China mine industry [1].

Please use the following format when citing this chapter:

Lu, G., Tang, J., Yao, C., Yang, L., 2007, in IFIP International Federation for Information Processing, Volume 252, Integration and Innovation Orient to E-Society Volume 2, eds. Wang, W., (Boston: Springer), pp. 68-74.

At present, great progress has been made on the safe mining theory of coalface, but since the coal mining is busy and strenuous, safety mining condition is complex and changeful, the new theory and knowledge on coal safety mining can not apply to coal mine safety production practice effectively. In this paper, the operating mechanism of Electronic Business was introduced in detail at first, and coal mine safety exploiting theory was extended and taken as foothold to push Chinese coal mine safety production to a new stage.

2. Current Situation of China Coal Mine Safety Production and Causes of Accident

2.1   Review of history data

From 2002 ~ 2005 [2], coal mine safety accident death toll decreases year by year, from 6971 deaths of 2002 dropping down to 5986 people of 2005. But coal production rises up step by step from 1.45 billion tons of 2002 to 2.16 billion tons of 2005. In 2002 the death rate of million tons coal is 5.13, but in 2005, the death rate of million tons coal comes down to 2.84. These three indexes can perceive Chinese coal mine safety production is developing to a fine situation.

But in recent years, the increasing of coal mining depth and the changing of geology conditions do not lead to the big change of the occurrence numbers of large-scale accident and the super-huge type accident, but one accident death toll rise to some extent. 58 super-huge type safety accidents occurred in 2005, 1739 people died, average accident death toll at every time is about 30 people, but 55 super-huge type accidents occurred in 2002, death 1137 people happened, average about 20 people.

2.2   Analysis of coal mine safety accidents

By analyzing the proportion of coal mine safety accident of coal mine from 2002 to 2005, we can find that roof accident death toll and gas accident death toll accounting for 70% ~ 75% of total death toll, and the following conclusions can be reached.

Firstly, the coal mine safety production circumstance is making a turn for the better day by day;

Secondly, coal mine safety accident population death toll is dropping down, but a super-huge type accident death toll rise to some extent;

Thirdly, the accident caused by people is coming down;

Fourthly, the prevention and control about safe accident on coalface such as the gas explosion, roof caving, water inrush, and coal bump does not make a breakthrough;

Fifthly, the safe accident happened in excavating procedure takes up bigger specific gravity in coal mine safety accident.

2.3   Key factor of solving Chinese coal mine safety situation

By the end of 2005, more than 24,800 coal mines got Coal mine safety system of state license for the manufacture in China[2], in order to improve the current situation of Chinese coal mine safe production, the following two aspects must be focused:

Firstly, pay close attention to the problem studying of the key and core factors effecting coal mine excavates face safe production, try to find breakthrough from theory and application;

Secondly, strengthen knowledge updating about preventing and control of coal mine safety, explore new approach of technology transfer.

3. Key Theory of Coal Mine Safety Mining ——"Overlying Strata Movement Law"

3.1   Outline of Overlying Strata Movement Law

During advancing of coalface or stope, the coal body is mined out, the overburden strata above the stoped out area and the coal body around the face change regularly, this change of the overburden strata above the gob and the coal body around the coal face is called "Overlying Strata Movement Law" [3].

3.2   Content of Overlying Strata Movement Law

Firstly, the height of roof caving strata above the gob (immediate roof for short, there is no force transfer between the strata), the first time span of roof caving (the step distance of immediate roof first fall).

The height of rupture roof on the roof fall strata (main roof for short, there is force transfer between the strata), the first time step distance of cliff, period rupture step distance.

The regularly alteration of overlying strata lead to stress's distribution again, form stress elevate area (be called high stress area for short) and stress reduce area (be called low stress area for short) [4];

The range of overlying strata strenuous moving (caving or rupture) when the length of face is definite.

3.3   Relationship between Overlying Strata Movement Law and safe accident on coal face

Safe accident on excavate face such as roof accident on the face (roof strides over fall, roof fall and so on), gas accident (gas density exceed limitation), bump accident, water accident of roof and floor have relation with "Overlying Strata

Movement Law ", it is direct incentive of all kinds of accident[5]. So estimate the rule of strata changing can prevent and control safe accident on Excavate Face.

3.4   Existing problems on application of "Overlying Strata Movement Law"

Although "Overlying Strata Movement Law" has stronger directive function to safe accident on the excavate face, but nowadays this theory is not approved and is extended broadly, there is several following aspect:

Coal mine geology condition of China are tremendous difference, the different seam in the same mineral area, the different mining area in the same seam， even the different section in the same mining area may have quit different geology condition, therefore un-discriminatingly applying mechanically identical calculation condition be complete wrong. This is the ultimate reason why "Overlying Strata Movement Law" do not having universal extending.

There are a lot of coal mine in China, and the employee's quality differ at any rate, it is impossible to accept this theory completely and fast. This is the objective reason why "Overlying Strata Movement Law" do not having universal extending.

At present, because of the economy benefit occupies leading factor position in coal mine, facing strenuous production mission and austerity situation of safe production, the manager is tired and do not have any more time and energy to learn modern knowledge and experience. This is the subjective reason why "Overlying Strata Movement Law" do not having universal extending.

4. Electronic Business Operation of "Forecast and Control the Safety Accident on Coalface"

4.1   Advantages of Electronic Business in Extending "Overlying Strata Movement Law"

There are broad sense and narrow sense about Electronic Business, the broad sense Electronic Business meanings making use of IT to reform traditional business affairs process, communication mode electronically, reach the purpose of data transmission and information communicating [6]. There are several following advantage in using Electronic Business to resolve safe accident problem on excavate face:

Electronic Business can realize distant real time communication, this can solve the real problem of coal mine numerous, distributes broad, have poor transport facilities in China.

Electronic Business can realize online services in time, by calculating the scene data, couples back result, can resolve the problem of the scene personnel is low quality, busy and lacks experience and so on.

Electronic Business can realize great capacity for data memory, can contact the all-direction mining experts, accumulate more practical experience and provide forceful technology hold for preventing and control the coal mine safety accident.

4.2   Operating pattern of Electronic Business

The Electronic Business operation pattern of "Forecast and control the safety accident on coal mine excavate face" is commonweal and service and abides by the principle of "serving as guiding , technology support as core, improves coal mine excavate face safety as purpose " .

Manage pattern: commonweal and service;

Manage idea: transfer blind, passive traditional safety manage pattern to initiative, scientific modern safety manage pattern.

Serve object: manager, chief engineer and employees of Chinese coal mine, especially all kinds of technician working at scene.

Manage target: make Chinese coal mine safety information platform, structure Chinese coal mine safety large scale system.

4.3   Operating framework of Electronic Business

The operating framework of Electronic Business sees Figure 1.

The portal (Electronic Business website of coal mine safety) provides an Electronic Business platform of forecast and controlling coal mine excavating face safe accident. Through this platform, can announce the new theory about coal mine safety manages, sum up coal mine safety managerial experience, provide the interface to input the scene data, use intelligence computer system to provide situation of safe production, decision suggestion, and scheme of prevent and control accident to every user by the web.

Submit static information means the user submit the inherence information of a fixed face. This part information is: fundamental parameter information of face (includes the trend long of face, the incline long of face, obliquity, relative coordinate etc.); borehole post shape picture of the area where face located (includes: anti-press intensity, anti-pull intensity and so on); contour of seam bottom; plane disposal chart of face. Trough this information can draw the outline of relative stratum, geology condition and space-time relation.
The static state data is to describe the geology form of face location mainly, it is that all basis of accidents forecast and controlling.

Submit dynamic data since stratum geologic structure is multifarious, even if different section of the same stope there is very distant difference condition in geology also. Because of the gap of drilling and inaccuracy of stratum geology parametric, the Overlying Strata Movement Law may change a lot in the excavate face push forward process. Therefore must use relative instrument to observe and measure the press of roadway and face incessantly, calculate in time, adjust relative parameter of the model [7], to make the mathematic model of Overlying Strata Movement Law fit actual model step by step, achieve the purpose of provide reliable decision support information to the scene.

Backstage information platform the information platform behind the website has two composition parts mainly: the first part is decision support intelligence analysis system of coal mine safety and high-effect production, this system can provide automatic information analysis on the base of given information, give reasonable suggestion about some problem in the mining process; the second part is the coal mine expert serves system, the simulation result made by computer can not be the ultimate basis, the result should feed back to expert regiment, and the expert regiment make the finally decision to ascertain accuracy of decision information.

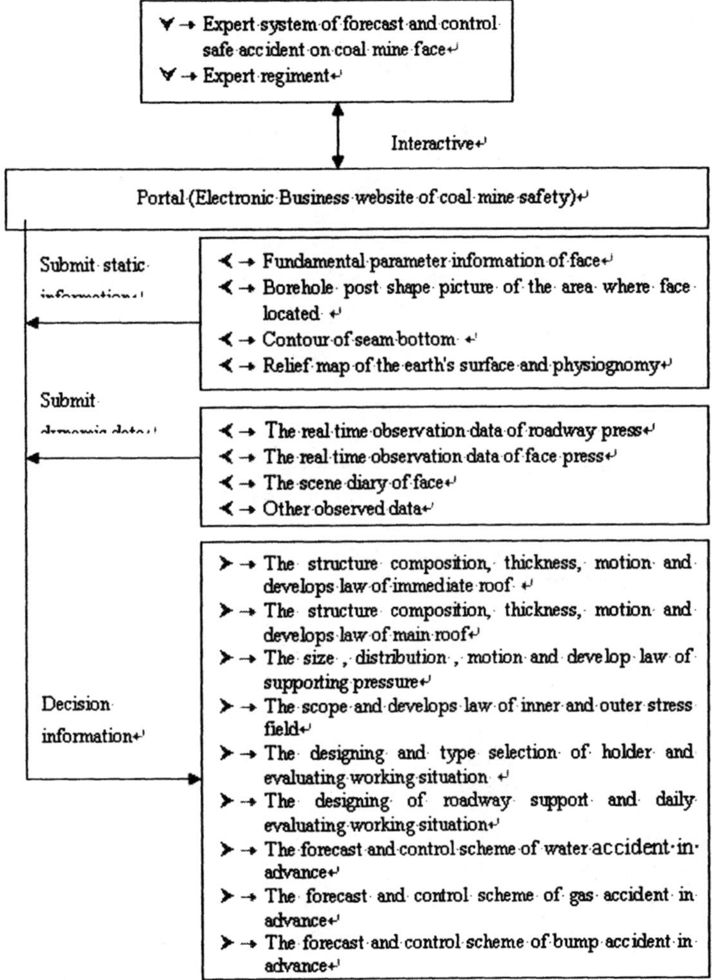

Figure 1 The Electronic Business structure in Safe Accident Prevention and Control on Coalface

Decision-making supports information to forecasting and control the safe accident on excavate face, the Electronic Business platform should provides scene worker some parameters, such as the structure composition, thickness, motion and develop law of immediate roof; the structure composition, thickness, motion and develop law of main roof; the size, distribution, motion and develop law of support press; the scope and develops law of inner and outer stress field; the designing and type selection of holder and evaluating working situation; the designing of roadway support and daily evaluating working situation; the forecast and control scheme of water accident in advance; the forecast and control scheme of gas accident in advance; the forecast and control scheme of bump accident in advance, etc.

5 Conclusions and Expectations

Safety and high-effect production of coal mine is a great event being to concern Chinese economy, politics, Electronic Business is a new and developing commerce operating pattern, it has practical significant to combine these two aspects.

The "Overlying Strata Movement Law" has guiding significance to prevent and control safe accident on excavate face, and the Electronic Business pattern mentioned in this text has feasibility and maneuverability, this pattern has vast application prospect and extensibility value.

References

1. W.J. Zhang, Z.Q. Song, "Present Situation and Direction of the Study on Severe Disasters in Coalmines", Journal of Shandong University of Science and Technology, No.1, (2006), pp. 5-8.

2. "The Eleventh Five Plan For of Coalmine Safety Science and Technology", (State Administrator of Work Safety, State Administrator of coal Mine Safety, BeiJing,2006), pp. 1-3.

3. Z.Q. Song, *The Information Of Strata In Severe Disasters In Coalmines*, The Press Of Coal Industry, BeiJing, 2003, p. 12.

4. Z.Q. Song, G.Z. Lu, "A New Algorithm for Calculating the Distribution of Face Abutment Pressure", Journal of Shandong University of Science and Technology, No.1, (2006), pp. 1-4.

5. Z.Q. Song, G.Z. Lu, "Forecast and Prevention of Rockburst for Colliery and Its Motivity Information System", Journal of Shandong University of Science and Technology, No.4, (2006), pp. 1-4.

6. G.Z. Lu, The New native of all kinds of accident. Edition Of The E-Business Conspectus, (The Press Of Peking University, BeiJing, 2005), p. 3.

7. G.Z. Lu, "Study of Combined Observation Scheme about Coal Mine Stress", Rock and Mechanics, 2006(Supp), pp. 319-321.

Fulfillment of HTTP Authentication Based on Alcatel OmniSwitch 9700

Hefu Liu

Center of Network and Education Technology, Huazhong Normal
University, Wuhan, Hubei, China

Abstract. This paper provides a way of HTTP authentication On Alcatel OmniSwitch 9700. Authenticated VLANs control user access to network resources based on VLAN assignment and user authentication. The user can be authenticated through the switch via any standard Web browser software. Web browser client displays the username and password prompts. Then a way for HTML forms can be given to pass HTTP authentication data when it's submitted. A radius server will provide a database of user information that the switch checks whenever it tries to authenticate through the switch. Before or after authentication, the client can get an address from a Dhcp server.

1   Introduction

A VLAN (virtual local area network) is a collection of nodes that are grouped together in a single broadcast domain based on something other than physical location. A LAN in turn often connects to other LANs, and to the Internet or some other WAN. Authenticated VLANs control user access to network resources based on VLAN assignment and log-in process, and the process is sometimes called user authentication [4]. The type of security is device authentication, which is set up through the use of port-binding VLAN static port assignment.

On Alcatel OmniSwitch 9700, it can be realized that web browser clients authenticate through the switch via any standard Web browser software, which is based on AVLAN(Authenticated VLAN). Web browser client displays the username and password prompts. Then a way for HTML forms can be given to pass HTTP authentication data when it's submitted. So the implementation of HTTP authentication is simple and safe.

Please use the following format when citing this chapter:

Liu, H., 2007, in IFIP International Federation for Information Processing, Volume 252, Integration and Innovation Orient to E-Society Volume 2, eds. Wang, W., (Boston: Springer), pp. 75-80.

2   HTTP Authenticated Network Overview

An authenticated network involves several components as shown in this illustration.

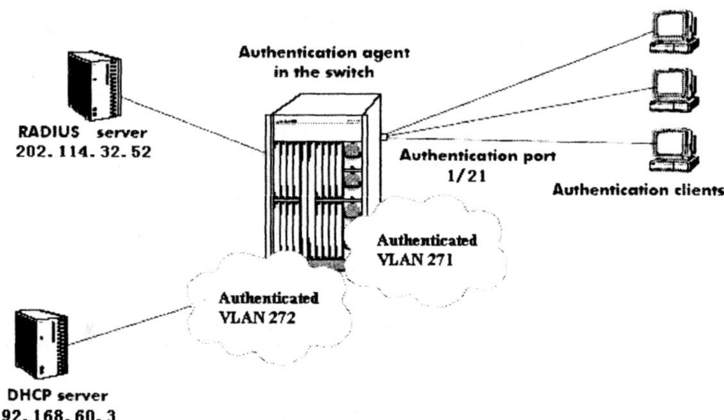

Fig. 1. HTTP Authenticated Network Components

This Fig.1 describes all of these components in detail. A brief overview of the components is given here:

RADIUS server—A RADIUS server must be configured in the network. The server contains a database of user information that the switch checks whenever a user tries to authenticate through the switch. The external server may also be used for authenticated switch access.

DHCP server—Web browser clients may get IP addresses via a DHCP server prior to authenticating or after authentication in order to move into a different VLAN. When multiple authenticated VLANs are configured, after the client authenticates the client must automatically issue a DHCP release/renew request in order to be moved into the correct VLAN.

Authentication port—At least one mobile port must be configured on the switch as an authentication port. This is the physical port through which authentication clients are attached to the switch.

Authentication clients—Authentication clients login through the switch to get access to authenticated VLANs.

Authenticated VLANs—Authenticated VLAN 272 is used to make the client get IP address before authentication, and after authentication ,the client will be moved into another VLAN 271.

Authentication agent in the switch—Authentication is enabled when the server(s) and the server authority mode is specified on the switch.

Configure a DNS name on the switch. A Domain Name Server (DNS) name may be configured so that Web browser clients may enter a URL on the browser command line instead of an authentication IP address. A Domain Name Server must be set up in the network for resolving the name to the authentication IP address. There may be multiple authentication IP addresses on the switch (if multiple authenticated VLANs are set up); however, there is only one authentication DNS path or host name. When the client enters the DNS path, the switch determines the IP authentication address based on the client's IP address, and the browser authentication page is displayed. A DNS name must be configured so that users may enter a URL rather than an IP address in the browser command line.

Typically the client address is provided by DHCP. DHCP also supplies DNS IP addresses to the client. The DHCP server must be configured with DNS addresses that correspond to the authenticated VLANs.

Normally, authentication clients cannot traffic in the default VLAN, so authentication clients do not belong to any VLAN when they connect to the switch. Even if DHCP relay is enabled, the DHCP discovery process cannot take place. To address this issue, a DHCP gateway address must be configured so that the DHCP relay "knows" which router port address to use for serving initial IP addresses.

When the client authenticates, the client is moved into the allowed VLAN based on VLAN information sent from an authentication server (single mode authority) or based on VLAN information configured directly on the switch (multiple mode authority).

After authentication a client may be moved into a VLAN in which the client's current IP address does not correspond. This will happen if the DHCP gateway address for assigning initial IP addresses is the router port of an authenticated VLAN to which the client does not belong. In this case, clients will automatically send DHCP release/renew requests to get an address in the authenticated VLAN to which they have access; DHCP relay must be enabled so that the request can be forwarded to the appropriate VLAN.

3   RADIUS Server Attributes

3.1 Introduction

RADIUS servers and RADIUS accounting servers are configured with particular attributes defined in RFC2138 and RFC 2139, respectively [4]. These attributes carry specific authentication, authorization, and configuration details about RADIUS requests to and replies from the server. This section describes the attributes and how to configure them on the server. The Standard RADIUS server attributes 1–39 and 60–63 are hardly supported by the Alcatel RADIUS client in the switch. However , attribute 26 is for vendor-specific information and is able to do these, and the standard attributes supported for RADIUS accounting servers of   HTTP AUTHENTICATION.

3.2 Vendor-Specific Attributes for RADIUS

The Alcatel RADIUS client supports attribute 26, which includes a vendor ID and some additional subattributes called subtypes[3]. The vendor ID and the subtypes collectively are called Vendor Specific Attributes (VSAs). Alcatel, through partnering arrangements, has included these VSAs in some vendors'RADIUS server configurations. The attribute subtypes are defined in the server's dictionary file. If you are using single authority the first VSA subtype, **Alcatel-Auth-Group**, must be defined on the server for each authenticated VLAN.Alcatel's vendor ID is 800 (SMI Network Management Private Enterprise Code).

The following are necessary VSAs for RADIUS servers [1]:

Number	RADIUS VSA	Type	Description
1	Alcatel-Auth-Group	integer	The authenticated VLAN number. The only protocol associated with this attribute is Ethernet II. If other protocols are required, use the protocol attribute instead.
2	Alcatel-Slot-Port	string	Slot(s)/port(s) valid for the user.
3	Alcatel-Time-of-Day	string	The time of day valid for the user to authenticate.
4	Alcatel-Client-IP-Addr	address	The IP address used for Telnet only.
5	Alcatel-Group-Desc	string	Description of the authenticated VLAN.
6	Alcatel-Port-Desc	string	Description of the port.
7	Not Defined	Not Defined	Not Defined
8	Alcatel-Auth-Group-Protocol	string	The protocol associated with the VLAN. Must be configured for access to other protocols. Values include: IP_E2, IP_SNAP, IPX_E2, IPX_NOV,IPX_LLC, IPX_SNAP.
9	Alcatel-Asa-Access	string	Specifies that the user has access to the switch. The only valid value is all
10	Alcatel-End-User-Profile	string	Specifies the name of an end-user profile associated

3.3 Preparations For Web Browser Authentication Client

Web browser clients authenticate through the switch via any standard Web browser software (Netscape Navigator or Internet Explorer).

   • **Make sure a standard browser is available on the client station**. No specialized client software is required.

   • **Provide an IP address for the client**. Web browser clients require an address prior to thentication. The address may be statically assigned if the authentication network is set up in single authority mode with one authenticated VLAN. The address may be assigned dynamically if a DHCP server is located in the network. DHCP is required in networks with multiple authenticated VLANs.

3.4 Fulfillment of HTTP Authentication

Before you perform HTTP authentication, you must have access to the Radius server and the Dhcp server form your switch.

First we must create two vlans such as vlan 271 and vlan 272,which are named radius and dhcprad.

Step 1 vlan 271 enable name radius

Step 2 vlan 272 enable name dhcprad

Step 3 ip interface radius address 202.114.39.1 mask 255.255.255.248 vlan 271

Step 4 ip interface dhcprad address 192.168.60.1 mask 255.255.255.0 vlan 272

Now ,Create and enable at least one mobile authenticated port. The port must be in VLAN 272.

Step 5 vlan 272 port default 1/21

Step 6 vlan port mobile 1/21

Step 7 vlan port 1/21 authenticate enable

After vlan authentication is set up the enable status, the switch will automatically create an authentication IP address based on this router port address (in this example, the address would be 192.168.60.253). The authentication address is configurable.

Step 8 vlan 271 authentication enable

Step 9 vlan 272 authentication enable

Set up a path to a DHCP server if users will be getting IP addresses from DHCP. The IP helper address is the IP address of the DHCP server; the AVLAN default DHCP address is the address of any router port configured on the VLAN. The DHCP server address is 192.168.60.3. The DHCP gateway address is 192.168.60.1.

Step 10 ip helper address 192.168.60.3

Step 11 aaa avlan default dhcp 192.168.60.1

Configure the switch to communicate with the authentication servers.

Step 12 aaa radius-server rad1 host 202.114.32.52 key testkey auth-port 1812 acct-port 1813

Enable authentication by specifying the authentication mode (single mode or multiple mode) and the server. Use the RADIUS or LDAP server name(s) configured in step 12.

Step 13 aaa authentication vlan single-mode rad1

At last, connect the PC you will be using to test to the appropriate slot and port configured above, bring up a web browser and enter the appropriate authentication address as the URL,https://192.168.60.253, and then enter the appropriate username and password when prompted.

4   Conclusion

The paper describes a simple HTTP Authentication mechanism that could be used in the B/S architecture.HTTP Authentication offers lots of advantages:

- It's simple to implement and no hassle to use, and clients love it.

- It carries no baggage unlike cookies.
- We can use HTTP Digest which is pretty secure and is easy to be understood.

So here we have discussed HTTP authentication method on Alcatel OmniSwitch 9700, there is no need for HTTP authentication to be shunned.

References

1. Alcatel Enterprise Data Training Course 9006-OmiSwitch Boot Camp
2. C. Rigney, A. Rubens, W. Simpson and S. Willens， "Remote Authentication Dial In User Service (RADIUS)", *RFC 2138*， April 1997.
3. http://www.freeradius.org/rfc/
4. http://www.ietf.org/rfc/

On the Potential of Web Services in Network Management

ZiHeng Liu[1] ,Yu Bai[2],YouQing Wan[3]
1 The Department of Information Techonlogy, HuaZhong Normal
University; Wuhan, China,lzh20201@yahoo.com.cn
2 The Department of Information Management, HuaZhong Normal
University; Wuhan, China,baiyu926@sohu.com
3 The Deaprtment of Management, WuHan University of
Technology,youqingwan123@sohu.com

Abstract. These days, Web services, which are based on XML and consist of several XML-related technologies, have been emerging as a promising technology, and it seems that Web services may be used in the field of network management. In this paper, we examine Web services as a XML-based approach to network management. Since Web services are a Service-Oriented Architecture (SOA) more than just a set of technologies, it could be used in XML-based network management, not only at the technology level, but also at the architecture level, which has many remarkable advantages and may be more effective in network management along with the concepts of Peer-to-Peer and Point-to-Point, in order to make a better use of its capability. Correspondingly, two models are presented to further demonstrate the potential of Web services in XML-based network management.

1 Introduction

Since network management research and standardization started in the late 1980s, there still has been no such a framework and technology that satisfies the general needs of network management. Recently, more attention is paid to XML-based approaches, and in particular, as a standard based on XML, Web services seem to be appropriate for network management.

Some organizations have participated in the research of using Web services in network management, such as the Organization for the Advancement of Structured Information Standards (OASIS) and the Network Management Research Group (NMRG) of the Internet Research Task Force (IRTF). In addition, several researchers have also studied the standardizations and prototypes for applying Web

Please use the following format when citing this chapter:

Liu, Z., Bai, Y., Wan, Y., 2007, in IFIP International Federation for Information Processing, Volume 252, Integration and Innovation Orient to E-Society Volume 2, eds. Wang, W., (Boston: Springer), pp. 81-87.

services to network management [1], [2]. But only few investigators have ever considered its potential in management [3].

In most studies, the real potential of Web services in XML-based network management has rarely been discussed. However, as a XML-based standardization, Web services have many advantages offered by XML and its related technologies, all of which facilitate its use in XML-based network management. What is more, since Web services is a Service-Oriented Architecture (SOA) more than a set of technology, a study at the architecture level may seem more effective than just at the technology level, in order to make full use of its capability. The aim of this paper is then to provide the advantages of Web services in network management from XML's point of view, and based on the current development of XML-based network management, to apply Web services at the architecture level more than just at the technology level.

The organization of this paper is as follows. First, a brief introduction of XML and Web services will be offered in Section 2, with an emphasis on the architecture. Section 3 will describe the advantages of Web services in network management, focusing on the benefits offered by XML-related technologies, including Web Services Description Language (WSDL) and Simple Object Access Protocol (SOAP). Sequentially in Section 4, we will discuss XML-based network management using Web services not only at the technology level but also at the architecture level, and two corresponding models will then be given. In addition, the benefits from the latter one are analyzed in detail. Finally, we conclude our work and discuss future work in Section 5.

2 Preliminaries

Nowadays, generic Internet technologies such as XML are being adopted to manage network resources. Thus in this background, XML-based network management, which applies XML technologies to network management, has been regarded as an alternative to existing network management. Extensible Markup Language (XML) is a meta-markup language standardized by the World Wide Web Consortium (W3C) for document exchange in the web. XML is now a standard that is supported and accepted by thousands of vendors as well as a lot of related technologies and tools.

Under this background, Web services have also been emerging as a promising Internet-oriented technology and architecture for network management [4]. A number of widely adopted Web services technologies are now available, such as Simple Object Access Protocol (SOAP) [5] [6] [7], Web Services Description [8] [9] [10] [11], and Universal Description Discovery, and Integration (UDDI) [12].

The word "services" in Web services refers to a Service-Oriented Architecture (SOA). In an SOA, functionality is "published" on a network where two important capabilities are also provided – "discovery", the ability to find the functionality, and "binding", the ability to connect the functionality. So when considering a SOA, these three parts must be take into account, which are briefly presented as "publish", "find", and "bind".

The concept of a SOA is not new, for service-oriented architectures have been used for years. However, what is relatively new is the emergence of Web services-based SOAs. In a Web services-based SOA, three important roles are Web service provider, Web service requester, and Web service register, which correspond to the "publish", "find", and "bind" aspects of a SOA.

3 The advantage of Web service in XML-based network management

As one of the emerging standards based upon XML, Web services are a generic technology and the use of standard XML protocols or technologies makes Web services platform-, programming language-, and vendor-independent. The support of XML technologies, such as WSDL and SOAP, provides the capability for the standardizations of management information definition and access, which are very important in network management.

3.1 Standardization of management information definition by WSDL

A Web service is described in a WSDL document. In order to easily use Web services for network management, standardization of management information definition is needed. On the other hand, with the mechanism provided by WSDL to describe a Web service in a modular manner using the elements <import> and <include>, modularization can be achieved.

With regard to the division of WSDL documents, some attempts have been done. The Universal Description, Description, Integration (UDDI) Technical Committee recommends "two separate WSDL definitions" containing an interface part and an implementation part. With WSDL import mechanism, Reference [1] suggests "three separate WSDL definitions" containing an abstract part:
- messages and interfaces (the **what** part) and two concrete parts:
- a binding (the **how** part)
- a service (the **where** part)

In our study, we propose the latter one, for it seems more reasonable according to the functionalities of each element.

3.2 Standardization of management information access by SOAP over HTTP

According to related specifications, SOAP focuses on the basic forms of transporting messages, regardless of the transfer protocol. Since SOAP messages and transfer protocols are strictly separated from each other, SOAP has the capability of combining with any transfer protocol. Considering the common usability and practicability, and the fact that most applications are transmitted through HTTP, the combination of SOAP messages and HTTP is undoubtedly the most practical and widely used means to implement the interconnections between services.

Thus in this way, SOAP over HTTP, which supports its own Remote Procedure Calls (RPC) interfaces, becomes a natural application protocol for network management and this default transport scheme provides a standardization of management information access.

4   XML-based network management using Web services

XML-based network management systems have become more and more popular these days, for it applies XML technologies to network management. However, these systems differ much in the extent of using the XML technologies. Most of these systems just use a few simple XML technologies, while some do make a better use of the XML technologies, such as the system presented in [13].

As to current attempts to use Web services in XML-based network management, the usage level of Web services must be taken into account. Since Web services are a SOA more than a set of XML-based technologies, it is reasonable to distinguish the XML-based network management using Web services at two levels: the technology level and the architecture level. Recent studies focus more on the technology level, but in order to make a better use of Web services-based SOA, it seems to be more appropriate to focus on the architecture level.

4.1   At the technology level

Web services technologies, such as WSDL and SOAP over HTTP, are now used in XML-based network management. Using them carefully can provide high-level operations to deal with complicated management problems, such as configuration management and device management, etc. Figure 1 illustrates a manager-agent model of XML-based network management using Web services at the technology level

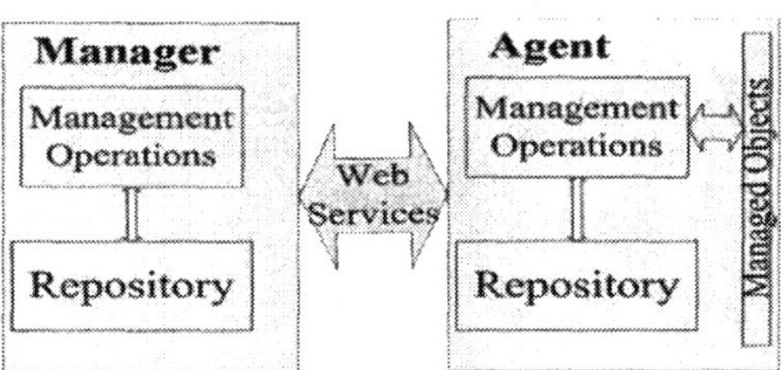

Figure 1. A common model at the technology level

As is shown in Figure 1, either the manager or the agent is composed of two modules: Management Operations, and a Repository, which contains RPC operation WSDL document. The Web Services module usually contains the SOAP engine, including the HTTP server/client, which provides SOAP APIs for initiating a bidirectional connection. The manager can access the Web service on the agent through SOAP over HTTP (or another lower network protocol), which enables the system to support network management. After the manager encapsulates the request message with SOAP, it is sent to the agent through HTTP. When receiving the request, the agent parses it, executes the corresponding service and returns the result to the manager still with SOAP over HTTP.

4.2   At the architecture level

Figure 1 just extends the manager-agent model for network management by the means of Web services technologies. However, in a distributed environment, or more exactly over a network, a number of managers and agents exist.

Bear in mind that, SOA and Web services are not just abstract concepts, but are real approaches to solving network management problems. A Web services-based SOA is essentially a collection of services. These services communicate with each other. The communication can involve either simple data passing or it could involve two or more services coordinating some activity, when some means of connecting services to each other is needed. Thus in this case, we could make a better use of the Web services-based SOA.

As a seamless integration of XML-based network management and Web services-based SOA, Figure 2 illustrates a common model at the architecture level, in which each entity can act as either an **agent** role (*a Web service provider*) or a **manager** role (*a Web service requester*), or both.

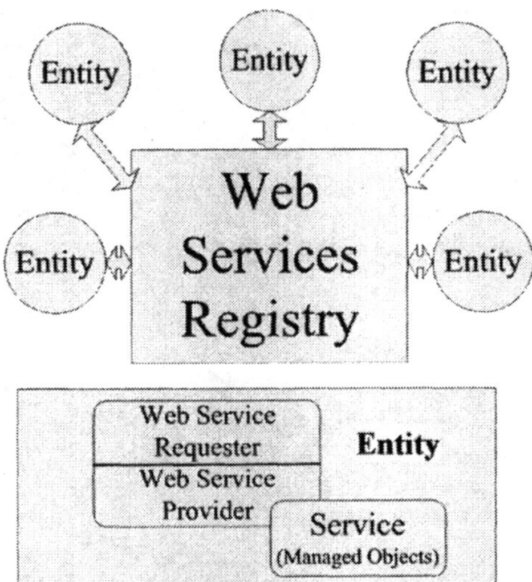

Figure 2. A common model at the architecture level

As is shown in Figure 2, two main components in the model are the Entity and, the Web Services Registry, which can be a private one for a particular network management task. The use of entities based on the Web services-based SOA, in fact, utilizes the concepts of Peer-to-Peer and Point-to-Point.

What makes peer-to-peer systems interesting is that they are totally distributed and all nodes are symmetric. On the other hand, point-to-point networks consist of many connections between individual pairs of machines, in contrast to broadcast networks. The concepts of Peer-to-Peer and Point-to-Point are essentially the same: the former one demonstrates the communication style, while the latter one reveals the link means. With the very use of these two concepts, the working flow of this model is as follows.

First of all, these entities, each of which acts as a Web service provider in this model, register their own services of some managed objects to the Web Services Registry. When another entity, acting as a Web service requester, wants to acquire the information of one or more managed objects provided by one entity, it just needs to connect the Web Services Registry to get the access information to that entity, the procedure of which is based on the Web services and the peer-to-peer communication. To accomplish the point-to-point link, the entity can acquire the service through SOAP over HTTP or another transfer protocol.

In the following, the main advantages of this model will be discussed in detail.

First of all, a management process in OSI-SM architecture can be configured to act in either the agent role or the manager role, or both roles. However, in SNMP network management systems and existing XML-based network management systems, both of which have been widely used, a management process can only be configured to act in either role but never both. Therefore, the use of Web services can bring XML-based network management closer to OSI-SM, which is so far the strongest network management architecture that supports all the essential features in any management framework.

Additionally, Web services-based SOA can largely and effectively improve the current network management systems. On the one hand, one primary feature of Web services-based SOA is scalability, which can properly solve this problem in network management. Since services in an SOA are loosely coupled, applications that use these services tend to scale easily and certainly, more easily than applications in a tightly coupled environment. On the other hand, the flexibility of Web services-based SOA, which is provided by the loosely coupled, document-based, asynchronous nature of services, allows applications to be flexible, and easy to evolve with changing network management requirements.

5   Conclusions and further work

This paper discusses issues on the potential of Web services in the field of network management, and provides two models of XML-based network management using Web services at the technology level as well as at the architecture level, focusing more on the latter one, which has several remarkable advantages and makes a better use of Web services recur to the concepts of Peer-to-Peer and Point-to-Point.

Our study indicates that in XML-based network management, using Web services at the architecture level would be better than that at the technology level.

Further work is needed to implement XML-based network management systems using Web services at these two different levels, and performance tests are also needed in order to validate our point of view. In addition, considering the capability of Web services in coordinating network management, we also plan to design and implement a practical XML-based collaborative network management system in the future.

References

1. J. Sloten, A. Pras, M. Sinderen, "On the Standardisation of Web service management operations", *Proc. 10th Open European Summer School (EUNICE 2004) and IFIP WG 6.3 Workshop* (June 2004), pp. 143-150.

2. T. Drevers, R. Meent, A. Pras, "Prototyping Web Services based Network Monitoring", *Proc. 10th Open European Summer School (EUNICE 2004) and IFIP WG 6.3 Workshop*(June 2004), pp. 135-142.

3. G. Pavlou, P. Flegkas, S. Gouveris, A. Liotta, "On Management Technologies and the Potential of Web Services", *IEEE Communication Magazine*(July 2004), pp. 58-66.

4. J. Schonwalder, A. Pras, J.P. Martin-Flatin, "On the Future of Internet Management Technologies", *IEEE Communications Magazine*(October 2003), pp. 90-97.

5. W3C, "SOAP Version 1.2 Part 0: Primer", *W3C Recommendation*, April 2007.

6. W3C, "SOAP Version 1.2 Part 1: Message Framework", *W3C Recommendation*(April 2007).

7. W3C, "SOAP Version 1.2 Part 2: Adjuncts", *W3C Recommendation*(April 2007).

8. W3C, "Web Services Description Language (WSDL) Version 2.0 Part 0: Primer",
W3C Proposed Recommendation(May 2007).

9. W3C, "Web Services Description Language (WSDL) Version 2.0 Part 1: Core Language",
W3C Proposed Recommendation(May 2007).

10. W3C, "Web Services Description Language (WSDL) Version 2.0 Part 2: Message Exchange Patterns", *W3C Working Draf*(March 2004).

11. W3C, "Web Services Description Language (WSDL) Version 2.0 Part 3: Bindings", *W3C Working Draf*(August 2004).

12. UDDI Spec TC, "UDDI Version 3.0.2 UDDI Spec Technical Committee Draft", *UDDI Spec Technical Committee Draft*(October 2004).

13. M. Choi, W. Hong, H. Ju, "XML-Based Network Management for IP Network", *ETRI Journal*, Volume 25(Number 6, December 2003), pp. 445-463.

A conceptual model of public medical service system based-on cell phone mobile platform

Hongjiao Fu[1], Yue Zhao[1]
1 Department of Economic Information Management, School of Information,
Renmin University of China, Beijing 100872, P.R. China
{zhao.yue, fuhj}@ruc.edu.cn

Abstract. In recent years, cell phones have played an increasingly important role in rapidly-developing global telecommunication services. At present, mobile business develops very fast. However, the development in other mobile service fields, such as public service, mobile medical service, etc, is still in its infant stage. Drawing on the experience of the 'doctor workstation project' which is cooperated by Renmin University of China and Norway Fredskorps Corporation, this paper discusses the research and implementation of the Doctor Workstation System based on cell phone mobile platform. From the practice of the Doctor Workstation System, the paper advances a conceptual model of public medical service system based-on cell phone mobile platform.

1   Research Background

Along with the revolution of global information technology and the vigorous development of mobile communication technology, cell phones have played an increasingly important role in rapidly-developing global telecommunication services. Consequently, mobile services are fast becoming an integral part of people's life. At present, mobile business, which is one of typical representative form of mobile services, develops very fast. Pertinent data show that in recent years development of mobile business will produce a leap in quality. It is estimated that the value brought by global mobile business will exceed 0.2 billion US dollars in 2007[1].

However, the development in other mobile service fields, such as public service, mobile medical service, mobile government affairs, etc, is still in its infant stage. Their application scope and depth remain very limited. The knowledge and acceptance of these services by the public are extremely low.

Drawing on the experience of the 'doctor workstation project' which is cooperated by Renmin University of China and Norway Fredskorps Corporation, this paper discusses the research and implementation of the Doctor Workstation System

---

based on cell phone mobile platform. From the practice of the Doctor Workstation System, the paper advances a conceptual model of public medical service system based-on cell phone mobile platform.

2 Introduction to doctor workstation system based-on cell phone mobile platform

2.1 Introduction to doctor workstation project

Two operation parties of this project are our University and Norges Fredskorps Corporation. Our goal is to establish an integrated doctor workstation system which consists of two parts: traditional web browser and doctor workstation system based-on cell phone mobile platform which is the key point of the paper.

Now whether in developing or developed countries, doctor workstation system based-on information technology all has different degree application. However, among them, most systems are based-on traditional browser. Although this kind of systems have high technology maturity and users are very familiar with them, this way of implementation which is unitary and influenced largely by equipment limitation already cannot adapt demands of every aspects in today when mobile services, mobile application develop very fast and mobile demand are very high. Under this situation, we put forward doctor workstation system based-on cell phone mobile platform which will effectively make full use of flexibility and convenience of cell phone mobile platform to overcome shackles of traditional doctor workstation system and provide medical service to doctors at all times and places[1,2].

2.2 Doctor workstation system based-on cell phone mobile platform

2.2.1 The function of system

The prominent characteristics of doctor workstation system based-on cell phone mobile platform are flexibility and convenience, however, the limitations of cell phones, such as processing capacity of CPU, storage capacity, space of main memory and interactive ability, restrict implementation of system function to a great extent. In short, with regard to doctor workstation system based-on cell phone mobile platform, we cannot expect and do not need to pursue integrity of system function. We will realize function modules which are suitable for cell phone mobile platform through which doctors can complete their work with high efficiency.

After logging in the system by cell phone, the doctor can do the following works:

(1) Case inquiring

Through connecting distant database, users will inquire related case data within their authorities, and then the system will transfer the inquired result back to cell phone platform to the doctors. So doctors will not limited by the space and time, they can inquire cases and know the situation of their patients at any time and places. They also can revise or delete case information and input information of new cases, which extremely increases efficiency and saves human resources. The procedures of case inquiring are shown in Fig. 1.

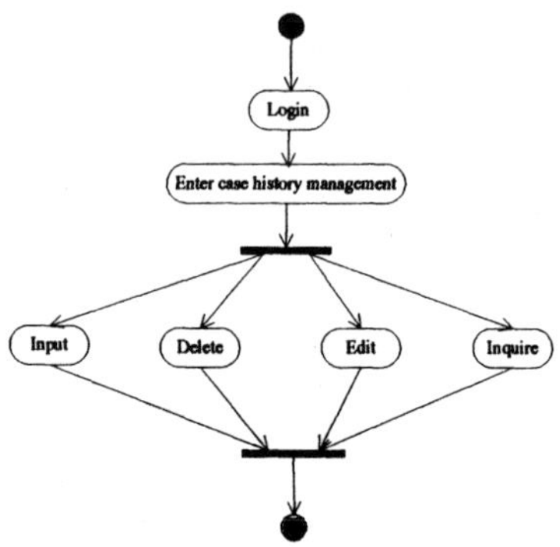

Fig. 1. The procedure of case inquiring

(2) Consultation management

Consultation management is the most distinguishing featured function module in the system, which realizes the function of inter-consultation about cases and patient's conditions between doctors. The system adopted sending–receiving mechanism which is similar to a simple email system to realize this function. Consultation between the doctors is created, distributed and processed similarly to the way of email.

- **Creating consultation**

The doctor logs in the system, enters consultation management interface and creates a new consultation. After the doctor finishes filling in consultation information, he can lead in cases information and medical images related to this consultation as attachments, for example, related X-Ray image, etc. The process of creating a new consultation is shown in Fig. 2.

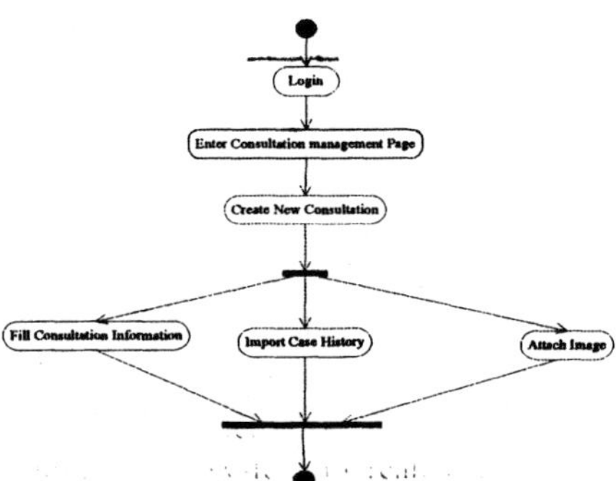

Fig. 2. The process of creating a new consultation

- **Distributing consultation**

After creating a new consultation, distributing consultation can be made. There are two types of distributing consultation: (1) point-to-point. On the premise of having a clear target, the system will transfer the consultation in the way of point-to-point, which means directly sending the consultation to the receiver who asked for it. For example, a difficult and complicated case of illness can be sent to an expert in this field to ask for advice. (2) mass-distributing. In some cases, the user does not have a clear consultation target, but need a mass line and listening to more useful opinions from the experts. In this case, we can use the way of mass-distributing. We can select a series of experts and send them the consultation to obtain more opinions.

In the way of mass-distributing, the system also supports a special way called "public consultation", i.e. we don't select persons specially designated for a post when creating a consultation, but mark this consultation as a public consultation in this field. In this way, all users in this field can browse current public consultations by checking public consultation column and choose questions they interested.

- **Responding consultation**

After receiving consultation information from other users, the user can respond by the system. As to the consultation in the way of point-to-point, obviously the way of response is aimed at single user. As to the consultation in the way of mass-distributing, two ways of response can be selected. One is to send the response directly to the sender, which is similar to the way of point-to-point. Another one is to send the response oriented towards the public, in which all users who concern this consultation topic can see related condition of discussion, and which will take effect of knowledge exchanging and sharing.

(3) Image processing

In the information of cases, it is more probable to contain image information, for example, X-ray photographs, Nuclear Magnetic Resonance (NMR) photographs, etc, so the system should have basic functions of image processing.

The basic functions of image processing realized by the system include: function of zooming whole or partial image, function of marking image comparison, and function of trimming, etc.

(4) Multi-language support

In order to facilitate system's international application and dissemination in the future, the system supports multi-language operation. Users can select one language when they log in.

2.2.2 The architecture of system

In general, this system is composed of two parts, a J2ME-based portal and a J2EE-based application server [2-4]. The architecture of system is shown in Fig. 3.

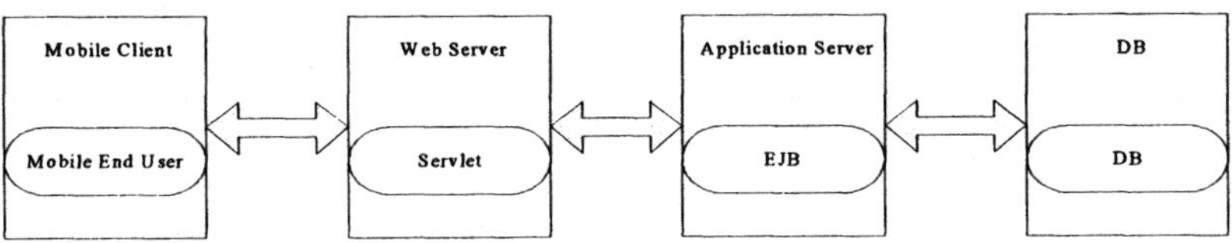

Fig. 3. The architecture of system

The web server is responsible for handling the request of the end user. The web server receives the request from the end user and sends it to the application server. The EJB container is responsible for interacting with database and it handles most of the application logic. We make full use of the benefits of the EJB container, for example, the support for the transaction management, the data persistency and the guarantee for high security level.

2.2.3 The communication mechanism of system

(1) The way of communication

Considering the CPU capacity and the support way of communication of mobile devices, we choose the widely used lightweight HTTP protocol as the way of communication.

(2) Data format

In order to release the network transfer pressure, save the storage space and reduce the transfer delay, we choose the binary as the format of the data [2].

(3) The security of communication

Because the J2EE application server and the J2ME platform both support the SHTTP based on the SSL, we can transfer the data in encrypt to communicate with server.

2.2.4 The features of system

Firstly, the most important advantage of the system is flexibility [3, 5]. Doctor workstation system based-on cell phone mobile platform could be accessed by the doctor ubiquitously, which breaks the limitation of space and time. This is one of the crucial factors for the service quality of the doctor workstation system and this is also the core concept of the mobile services which embodies the value of the system.

Secondly, the support of multi-language which is also one of the important items for the system usability makes the system easy for international application and dissemination in the future.

3 A conceptual model of public medical service system based-on cell phone mobile platform

By taking an example of corporation project of our University and Norway Fredskorps Corporation, the paper discussed doctor workstation system based-on cell phone mobile platform and its functions and the system architecture.

Today, with the high speed development of the mobile application and mobile service, every walk of life will consider whether this industry could serve in mobile way as one of the important factors of the service quality, which is more important in medical service industry.

Currently, the information technology has widely used in the medical service industry and its application has already come to a certain level, for example, the application of the management information system in the hospital. We believe that with the high speed development of the mobile application and service, it is certain that the mobile application will widely be used in the medical service industry [6, 7].

Now we will discuss the conceptual model of public medical service system based-on cell phone mobile platform specifically.

3.1   The characteristic of the system

3.1.1 Agility
Agility is the essential and distinguishing characteristic of the system and the reason why a mobile application exists [8].

(1)The easy acquirement of the application and the compatibility of the client software

The end user could get the application software easily by the way of web download, mobile device based GPRS download and so on.

The client software should have strong compatibility and not rely on special mobile devices and operating systems. The mainly used operating systems in the mobile device now are Symbian, Windows CE and Linux which three are now sharing the market. So the client software should have these three versions at least.

(2) Usability of the system

This is mainly concerned with the human-computer interaction, for example, the Graphical User Interface (GUI), the response delay time and so on. We will not discuss further on this.

3.1.2 The open interface
The prevalence of the mobile application is an inevitable trend and it will be widely used in every face of life. This requires us be well prepared for the cosmically forthcoming application in the future. In order to establish an integrated mobile service system, the system should have open interface for the future connection with other systems, for example, the data interface with the bank, human resources management department and supervision departments, etc.

3.1.3 Security
It is obvious that the system security is very important, because there are lots of personal privacy and secrecy data. Beside the security measures we usually take, we must pay more attention to the danger of data filched when the data is transferred between the database and mobile device.

In the security area, we should guarantee the following facts: (1) the resources of the system can't be accessed without authorization; (2) the user can't access the resources of the system that are not included in his authorization; (3) make sure that the resource of the system can't be filched during the data transformation; (4) well prepared for the disaster backup.

We are going to take the measures that integrate the information technology and the management rules. The information technologies used include the identity validate, the software fire-wall, and the data encryption; the management rules include the proper assigning of the access authorization, the data restore and backup, and auditing the system periodically.

3.1.4 Internationalization
The system should have the function of internationalization and could easily switch to different versions between different languages and custom. Moreover, we should use the international standard for the specialty term, which makes it easy for the future international communication, for example, we should use the International Classification of Diseases version 10 (ICD10) as the only identity of the diseases.

3.2   Conceptual model of the system of public medical service system based-on cell phone mobile platform

The conceptual model of the system of public medical service system based-on cell phone mobile platform we put forward is shown in Fig. 4. We will describe every module of the model as follow [8-10]: (1) The patients communicate with the doctor by the system to inquire about their illness and update the doctor's advice. (2) The patients finish the payment through the interface with the bank. (3) The patients make appointment with the doctor through the medicine treatment interface. (4) The patients purchase the medicine from the medicine vendor through the medicine seller interface. (5) The doctors make consultations with each other by the mobile device. (6) The doctor can inquire the records of cases and update them by the mobile device. (7) The functional department could supervise the behaviors of the related parts to avoid illegal operation and could also inspect the plague and make warnings and take measures in time.

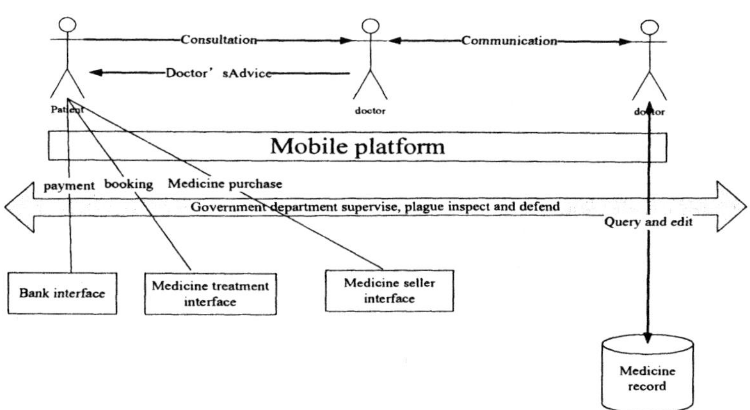

Fig. 4. The conceptual model of the system of public medical service system based-on cell phone mobile platform

The working mechanism of the model indicates the following two features: (1) The strong interactive communication ability: The model not only integrates the old systems but builds an agile platform for the communication of the users including the doctors and patients. They could make the communications easily through the system. We even could integrate the instant messaging system into our platform to maximize the communion feature of the system. This is not only about the cost and the efficiency but concerns the quality of the health and the life. (2) Coordinate management: This model integrates the bank, medical treatment and the medicine seller system which could be managed coordinately. This feature avoids the emergence of the information gaps and the information isolated. Mean while, the government department could handle the supervision responsibility simply through this model which saves lots of human resource and time.

4 Summary

This paper discusses the system architecture, functions and benefits of the doctor workstation based-on cell phone mobile platform. And then we put forward a conceptual model of the system of public medical service system based-on cell phone mobile platform, and illustrate its characteristic.

We believe that, with the fast development of the mobile application, public medical service system based-on cell phone mobile platform will gradually come into practice in the near future.

Reference

1. C.X. Fan and J.W. Zou, "Research and design for a mobile application integrated delivery platform", *Journal of Beijing University of Posts and Telecommunications* ,27, 202-206 (2004).

2. P. Tarasewich, "Designing mobile commerce applications", *Communications of the ACM* , 46(12), 57-60(2003).

3. C. Ryan and A. Gonsalves, "The effect of context and application type on mobile usability: an empirical study", *Proceedings of the Twenty-eighth Australasian conference on Computer Science*,115-124(2005).

4. D. Narayanan, J. Flinn, and M. Satyanarayanan, Using history to improve mobile application adaptation, *Third IEEE Workshop on Mobile Computing Systems and Applications* ,61-66(2000).

5. P. Abrahamsson, A.Hanhineva, H. Hulkko, T. Ihme, J. Jaalinoja, M. Korkala, J. Koskela, P. Kyllonen and O. Salo, "Mobile-D: an agile approach for mobile application development", *Companion to the 19th annual ACM SIGPLAN conference on Object-oriented programming systems, languages, and applications,* 174–175(2004) .

6. T. Zrimec, "A content-based retrieval system for medical images", *Proceedings of 2002 7th International Conference on Control, Automation, Robotics and Vision* ,180-185(2002).

7. Y.F. Chen, H. Huang, J.R. John, S. Jora, S.Reibman and A.B. Wei, "Personalized multimedia services using a mobile service platform", *Proceedings of 2002 IEEE Wireless Communications and Networking Conference* ,918- 925(2002).

8. G.A. Bolvary and S. Kis, "Computer based information/advisory/alert system for the Hungarian healthcare professionals", *Biomedical Engineering Days, Proceedings of the 1992 International* , 134- 136(1992).

9. N. Houssos, A. Alonistioti, L. Merakos, M. Dillinger and M. Fahrmair, "Advanced adaptability and profile management framework for the support of flexible mobile service provision", *Wireless Communications, IEEE [see also IEEE Personal Communications]*,52-61(2003).

10. A. Pfitzmann, B. Pfitzmann and M. Schunter, "Trusting mobile user devices and security modules", *Computer*,30(2), 61-68(1997).

An Integrated Model in E-Government Based on Semantic Web, Web Service and Intelligent Agent

Hongtao Zhu [1], Fangli Su [2]

1 Department of Information Science, Zhengzhou Institute of
Aeronautical Industry Management
Zhengzhou, China, Postcode: 450015
pds_zhht@126.com

2 Department of Information Science, Zhengzhou Institute of
Aeronautical Industry Management
Zhengzhou, China, Postcode: 450015
suli_2000@163.com

Abstract. One urgent problem in E-government service is to improve service efficiency through breaking information islands while constructing integrated service systems. Web Service provides a set of standards for the provision of functionality over the Web, and Web Service descriptions are pure syntactic instead of semantic content. Semantic Web provides interoperability from syntactic level to semantic one not only for human users but also for software agents. Semantic Web and Intelligent Agent are highly complementary, and the existing technologies have made their unification quite feasible, which brings about a good opportunity to the development of E-government. Based on Semantic Web and Intelligent Agent technologies an integrated service model of E-government is suggested in this paper.

1 Introduction

E-Government applications often require affording united information through integrating resources from all kinds of sources, or combining a few component software systems from the same or different institutions and organizations into one distributed software system. To the end user, the whole system should be felt like one single service system [1]. Nowadays most E-Government services are usually offered directly by different government organizations, or by the-third-partner information service provider (ISP). Because of relying on different basic technologies, they do not have an interface for software system integration. This

Please use the following format when citing this chapter:

Zhu, H., Su, F., 2007, in IFIP International Federation for Information Processing, Volume 252, Integration and Innovation Orient to E-Society Volume 2, eds. Wang, W., (Boston: Springer), pp. 96-102.

makes it difficult to communicate, to share and to integrate information for the institutions, and also the end user. On the other hand, most of E-government information on the internet can't be understood and processed by computer automatically but only by human beings. The degree of automation and intelligence is rather low, which slows the velocity of information circulation and results in low efficiency of E-government services. Sufficient E-government applications should be an architecture that can be used to automate the routine petition process which includes analyses of users and their queries, information retrieval, integration of searching results [2], and so on. In this article the authors suggest an integrated service model of E-government based on Semantic Web and Intelligent Agent technologies, which is indispensable during constructing sharing systems of E-government.

There are four sections in this paper. In section 1, the present condition of E-government is introduced briefly. In section 2, the feasibility of combination of Semantic Web, Web Service and Intelligent Agent is discussed while explaining their features and functions. In section 3, the authors propose an integrated model of E-government services and illustrate its framework. In section 4, a conclusion is given.

2 Technologies related

2.1 Semantic Web

According to the World Wide Web Consortium (W3C), who defines the Semantic Web as "The Semantic Web provides a common framework that allows data to be shared and reused across application, enterprise, and community boundaries" [3], the Semantic Web is about two things. First, it is about common formats for integration and combination of data drawn from diverse sources, where on the original Web mainly concentrated on the interchange of documents. Second, it is about a language for recording how the data relates to real world objects. That allows a person, or a machine, to start off in one database, and then move through an unending set of databases which are connected not by wires but by being about the same thing. Its frame is like a layered cake [4] (See Fig.1).

At present the above three layers (logic, Proof, and Trust) in Fig.1 are still under discussion, the other four layers are widely used in many fields, even if some key technologies are rather less stable.

It is obvious that Semantic Web allows computers to track links and facilitate the integration of information from many different sources. So the Semantic Web initiative aims to resolve sharing problems from the information perspective. There exist many problems in present E-government Service system that could be settled by Semantic Web.

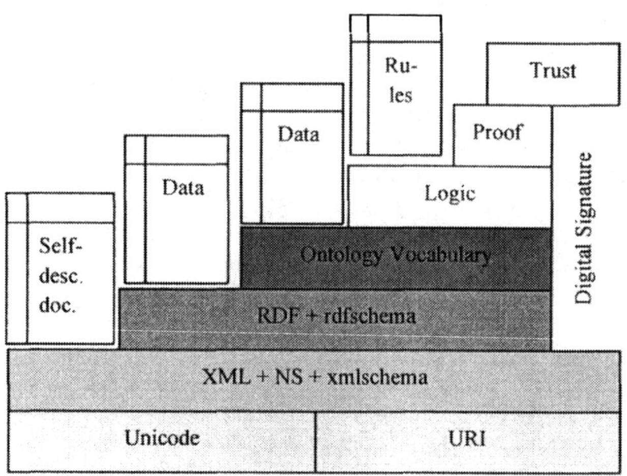

Fig. 1. The frame of Semantic Web

2.2   Supplementary of Semantic Web and Web Service

Web Service provides a set of standards for the provision of functionality over the Web: the specification of the SOAP (Simple Object Access Protocol) as a standard for transmitting messages, the WSDL (Web Services Description Language) as a standard for describing interfaces provides platform-independent access to back-end functionality, and the UDDI (Universal Description, Discovery and Integration) as a standard for describing, promulgating and integrating services. These standards are the core of Web Service. Together, the Web infrastructure and Web Service descriptions have the functions of reducing the cost and time of integrating applications and integrating distributed information, because with the Web Service there is no need to build customized communication lines, to implement proprietary messaging protocols, and to interpret the information from different government respective department [5].

However, Web Service descriptions are usually syntactic instead of semantic content, which leads to necessity of much man-intervention when to decide whether it offers the desired functionality. Furthermore, if E-government services have different interaction styles or use different terms for the description of the data formats and functionality, there will be no way of cooperating.

The improvement of efficiency in the use of Web Service can be attained if it is combined with Semantic Web technology. The common goal of Semantic Web and Web Service is to create automatic and intelligent services and E-government processing infrastructure by using web contents which can be understood by both people and computers. Therefore, the realization of function supplementary is one kind of natural choice, with which service providers and end users enable dynamically to locate partners they want, and to promote cooperation with them.

2.3   Integration of Intelligent Agent and Semantic Web

Nowadays, although there has not been a single universally accepted definition, the term "Agent" is widely used by many experts working in related areas, especially in the fields of computer science and artificial intelligence (AI). In computer science, an Intelligent Agent (IA) is generally a software agent that assists users and will act on their behalf, in performing non-repetitive computer-related tasks [6]. It has multitudinous merits, such as independency, openness, and so on. It is usually used in the system which is open, distributed, and logic. Just as what Michael Wooldridge and Nick Jennings wrote in their article [7], now we can feel that Intelligent Agent has been a key technology as computing systems become ever more distributed, interconnected, and open. In current web environments, the ability of agents to autonomously understand , to cooperate, coordinate, and negotiate with others, and to respond flexibly and intelligently to dynamic and unpredictable situations will lead to more convenience for users. While Intelligent Agent accomplishing various tasks, it is rather important to estimate and comprehend semantic environment exactly. Semantic Web has provided favorable environment for Intelligent Agent. If end users hope to access distributed web information through Intelligent Agent, Ontology Vocabulary, one part of Semantic Web, must be used. Higher grade applications of Intelligent Agent will connect web information with related knowledge and rules, and then achieve useful information from the web. The integration of Intelligent Agent technology and ontologies——Semantic Web, could significantly affect the use of web services and the ability to extend programs to perform tasks for users more efficiently and with less human intervention [8].

3   E-government Service Integrated Model Based on Semantic Web, Web Service and Intelligent Agent

In this section, the authors propose an E-government Service Integrated Model based on the technologies of Semantic Web, Web Service and Intelligent Agent (See Fig.2).

The model can associate all levels of government information system and provide services for end users with unified interface. From the point of theory, the model makes the semantic content of web resources (including information and services) more clear and perfect and enables computers to understand more exactly. With this model the distributed information or service with different description-format can be processed more automatically and intelligently. With the aid of SOAP, UDDI and WSDL, we can unify Semantic Web and Web Service to realize loose coupling among E-government services. The colligation of Semantic Web and Intelligence Agent reduces human-intervention and facilitate the realization of automation.

It is evident that our integrated model architecture may be divided into four levels, namely: (I) E-government Resource Providers Level, which provides all kinds

of information or services that may be described with different formats; (II)
Mediation Level, which supports the communication of G2G and G2C with the aid
of the DAML-S/Matchmaker [9], agent and ontologies; (III) Interaction Level, which

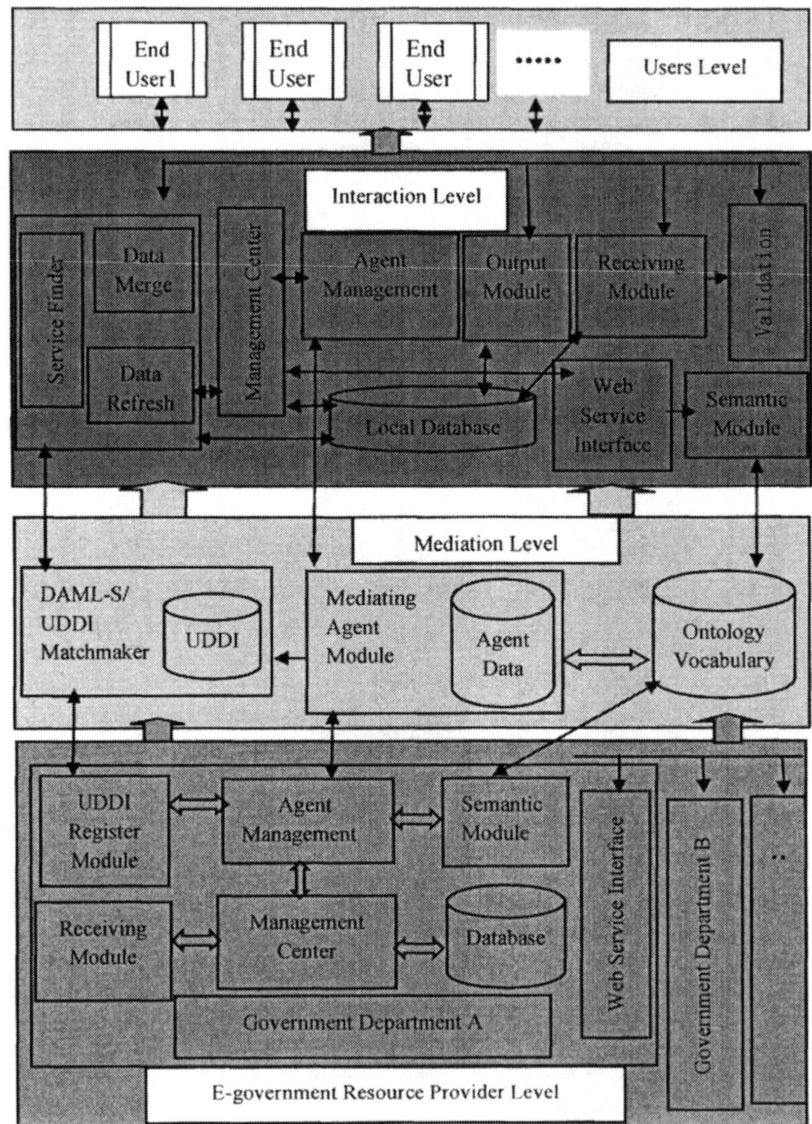

Fig.2. E-government Service Integrated Model

provides suitable information or services for end users with the right forms. (IV) Users Level, which provides interface system. Every Level has several modules which implement some specific functions. Another point that should be noticed is that every level except the fourth one in this model has its own Intelligent Agent. There are three kinds of agents in all: intelligent user agents, E-government local information agents and mediation agents. Information that all the agents hold has specific semantic meaning so that cooperation is done well among the agents in order to achieve certain service.

In the following sub-sections we describe in detail all these components. E-government Resource Providers Level is the bases of the whole model, which may operate on different servers because they may not be from the same government department. There are a few modules as following. They seal their information or services they provide with UDDI Register Module, and then register in it after giving descriptions with DAML-S. Furthermore, they usually provide the catalog of government information or their services items. Receiving Module is in chare of receiving, register, modify and delete user's query record. Web Service Interface Module provides foreign interface while displaying government information or services lists. Semantic Module is used to assure semantic unification between interior system and exterior system and to afford semantic aids to other modules. Agent Management Module manages to interior agents and their information exchange with foreign agents (such as mediation query agent). Management Center harmonizes interactions of all the modules and intervenes with the process if it is necessary.

Mediation Level includes DAML-S/Matchmaker, Mediation Agent database and Ontology. DAML-S/Matchmaker is a frame of Semantic Web Service register and discovery based on DAML-S. It can implement bidirectional information match. Mediation Agent Module is responsible to harmonize end user agent and E-government local agent. Ontology provides sharing concept model which includes a vocabulary with semantic relations.

Interaction Level acts as a bridge that connecting G2G or G2C. Validation Module is used to know user's qualification. Output Module is responsible to transfer classified information or service information to users' interface. Furthermore, the provided content can be changed dynamically according to users' need. Receiving Module collects and registers users query and then transfers them to E-government Providers. Web Service Interface Module integrates the catalog of E-government resources or service information, and then stores them in local database. Service Finder Module can seek the new provided information in UDDI, afterward, put the results into the local database. Functions of Semantic Module and Agent Management Module in this level are similar as those in E-government Service Providers Level mentioned above. The content of intercommunion in the whole system is transferred to the end users through Users Level.

Contrast to the other model related, this E-government integrated model has following distinct merits at least:
- Distributional Application
- Platform Irrelevant
- High Integration of Different-structured Government Information
- E-government One Station Service

> Resources and Services Sharing and Cooperation

4   Conclusion

Present E-government solutions often require a costly and custom hardware and software infrastructure for both department of cooperating partners and end users. Furthermore, the lack of formal and unified descriptions of services offered by organizations hampers automation in the location and usage of services required to perform a Government information or services access activity. In this paper the authors discuss the feasibility of integration of several technologies, including Semantic Web, Web Service and Intelligent Agent, after analyzing their own features. And then a new E-government integrated model is brought forward. This model provides a framework for the integration and sharing of distributed and different-structured E-government resources. It enables seamless E-government services integration through formal descriptions, maximal decoupling of components, and strong intelligent cooperating support. However, realization of some technical details should be further researched, which is our next work recently.

References

1. J. Korhonen, L. Pajunen and J. Puustjärvi, "Requirements for Using Agent-Based Automation in Distributed E-Government Applications", *R. Traunmüller (Ed.): EGOV*, LNCS 2739,157-160 (2003).
2. R. Traunmüller and M. Wimmer, Directions in E-Government: Processes, Portals, Knowledge, Proceedings of the 12th International Workshop on Database and Expert Systems Applications (*IEEE Computer Society*, Washington, DC, 2001), 313-317.
3. W3C, "Semantic Web" (April 25, 2007). http://www.w3.org/2001/sw.
4. R. Klischewski, "Semantic Web for E-Government",*R. Traunmüller* (Ed.): EGOV, LNCS 2739, 288-295 (2003).
5. G. Alonso, F. Casati, H. Kuno and V. Machiraju, "Web Services: Concepts, Architecture and Applications", Springer Verlag, Berlin , 123-149(2004).
6. Wikipedia, " Intelligent agent "(July 8, 2007). http://en.wikipedia.org/wiki/Intelligent_agent.
7. M. Wooldridge and N. Jennings, "Intelligent Agent: Theory and practice", *Knowledge Engineering Review* 10 (2), 115-152 (1995).
8. J. Hendler, "Agents and the Semantic Web", *IEEE Intelligent Systems*, March/April, 30-37 (2001). http://oopsla.snu.ac.kr/~jnkim/pdf/IS_2.pdf.
9. S. Katia, P. Massimo, A. Anupriya and S. Naveen, "Automated discovery, interaction and composition of Semantic Web Services", *Web Semantics* 1 (1), 27-46 (2003).

Electronic Commerce in Tourism in China: B2B or B2C?

Hongxiu Li[1], and Reima Suomi[2]

1   Information Systmes Instutute, Turku School of Economics
Turku Center for Computer Science
Joukahaisenkatu 3-5 B, 20520 Turku, Finland
Hongxiu.li@tse.fi

2   Information Systmes Instutute, Turku School of Economics
Rehtorinpellonkatu 3, 20500 Turku, Finland
Reima.suomi@tse.fi

Abstract. E-commerce has significantly changed the distribution channels of travel products in the world including China. Online channels are growing important in travel service distribution. In China tourism industry has been developed rapidly with the economic development, more and more international travel service providers are trying to expand their Chinese market through the Internet. This paper sheds lights on the e-commerce development models in China for international travel service providers. It explores the current e-tourism in China from the three different participants in the value chain in tourism industry - consumer, travel agent and travel service provider. The paper also identifies the barriers in B2C arena in international outbound travel market, and discusses the possible approaches for international travel service providers to develop their e-commerce in the huge Chinese market. The results in this study reveal that international travel service providers should focus on B2B model to expand their electronic market in China. B2C development in tourism largely depends on the change of Chinese customers' behavior and the change of international tourism regulations. The findings of the study are expected to assist international travel service providers to understand current e-tourism in China and to support their planning for future e-commerce development in China.

1 Introduction

With the Internet as a commercial medium, new ways of conducting business have developed in almost every sector. In the travel and tourism industry, new and

Please use the following format when citing this chapter:

Li, H., Suomi, R., 2007, in IFIP International Federation for Information Processing, Volume 252, Integration and Innovation Orient to E-Society Volume 2, eds. Wang, W., (Boston: Springer), pp. 103-112.

efficient Internet business models, including both B2B and B2C, have gained a strong foothold. The Internet has a tremendous impact on today's travel and tourism industry on both domestic travel and international travel, and the travel industry is ranked as the prime sector in e-commerce [1]. In the past several years, online transactions in the travel and tourism industry are continuously growing with the proliferation of e-commerce [2]. With these changes, customers' behavior is also changing, which is different in nature from the behavior of traditional customers due to the unique characteristics of the Internet and the interaction of technology and culture [3]. Customers are using both online and offline channels to book travel services.

In China tourism industry has been developed rapidly with the economic development, especially in international travel, which has attracted international travel service providers to develop their market in the huge Chinese market through the Internet. Some researches have been conducted on the e-commerce benefits, consumer behavior, evaluation of websites in travel industry in China, but the e-commerce development model in tourism industry in China, especially for international travel service providers around the world, has not been explored.

This paper attempts to investigate current e-commerce development in tourism industry in China and aims to find the proper e-commerce development model in China for international travel service providers. It explores the current electronic tourism (E-tourism) in China from the consumer, travel agent and travel service provider perspectives. This paper also identifies the barriers in B2C arena in international outbound travel market and discusses the possible approach for international travel service providers to develop their e-commerce in the huge Chinese market. This study has been completed based on interviews and survey conducted both in China and Europe. The findings of the study are expected to assist international travel service providers to understand current e-tourism in China and to support their planning for future e-commerce development in China.

2 Background

2.1 Value chain in tourism in China

The typical value chain in tourism consists of four components: travel service provider, travel operator, travel agent and traveler. The travel services provided by travel service providers can be distributed by the joint operation of travel operator and travel agent, or just by travel agent to traveler (See Figure 1) [4]. On the intermediary level, normally the travel operator plays the role as a wholesaler of travel service in the value chain, which integrates a number of different travel services and offers them as a packaged service to travel agent, since many travel services are composed of various services provided by different travel service providers. The travel agent is the retailer of travel service in the value chain, which tie prospective travelers and service providers together by handling the information flow among the different participants in the value chain, and selling the information to travelers [5].The value chain is based on the cooperation among travel service provider, travel operator and travel agent with the help of Global Distribution Systems (GDS). In China on the traditional value chain the intermediary function of travel operator is weaker compared to that of travel agent, and most travel agents have taken the responsibilities of the travel operators [6].

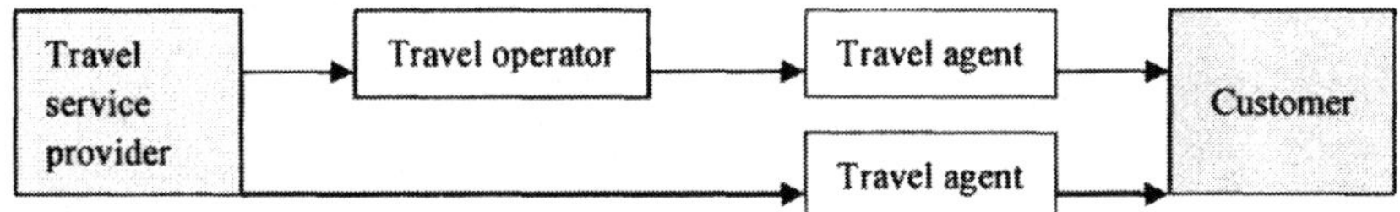

Figure 1. Traditional value chain in tourism

The last decade has witnessed the increased internationalization of the tourism industry because of the proliferation of e-commerce. All the participants in the traditional value chain in travel industry have been forced to seek global business strategies in order to generate a sustainable competitive advantage.

The travel service providers have adopted the Internet to offer online travel services to customers, including travel service searching and travel service booking (See Figure 2), which has been the responsibilities of the travel agents in the traditional value chain [7]. This is defined as the B2C e-commerce model. Benjamin and Wigand (1995) have hypothesized the disintermediation prediction from a cost-based perspective. There appears to be strong economic incentives for both travel service providers and customers to drive intermediaries (travel operator and travel agencies) out of the tourism value chain – for travel service providers to reduce transactional cost and for customers to get a reduced price. Further, the travel service provider can dominate the price and quality of their services, which can reduce the uncertainties of consumers [8,9].

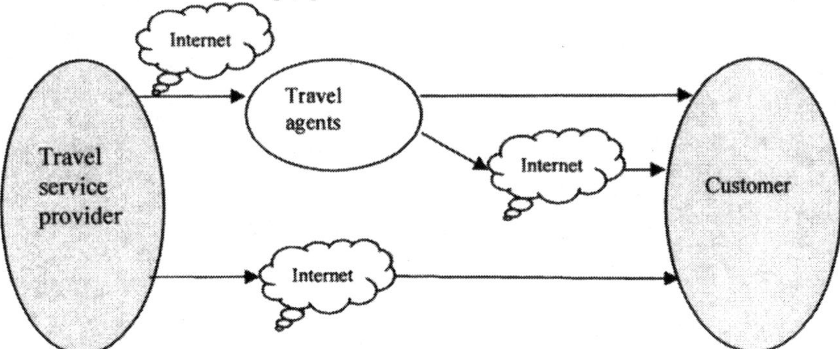

Figure 2. Combined Value Chain in tourism in e-commerce times

The disintermediation argument focuses primarily on the cost of intermediation, and the values that can be added by intermediaries are ignored. Sargar et al (1995) state that intermediaries should not be seen as pure transaction cost minimizing actors. They often add value to transactions by providing intensive services [10].

Travel agents have also used the Internet to develop differentiated value proposition and to reinforce their intermediary position in the tourism value chain. Travel agents are still the intermediaries in tourism value chain combined with the Internet (See Figure 2) [11]. The cooperation between travel service providers and travel agents based on Internet is the B2B business model in e-commerce.

In E-tourism, both B2B and B2C models have offered great opportunities for international travel service providers to promote their travel service to customers directly or indirectly through the Internet. The Internet has typically helped travel service providers and travel agents out of the spatial and temporal limitation in business.

2.2   E-tourism in China

China's tourism industry has developed quickly in the past 20 years. In China since 1999 the government has put effort on further pushing tourism development by establishing three "Golden weeks" holidays, which has impelled both the domestic and international tourism development in China. According to the statistics of China National Tourism Administration (CNTA), since 2001 there is great increase on the number of outbound travelers and inbounds travelers. In 2006 the amount of outbound travels in China has arrived at 34.52 million (See Table 1). CNTA expects that in 2020 there will be about 210 to 300 million inbound tourists and 100 million outbound departures in China. World Tourism Organization (UNWTO) also predicts that China's tourism industry will take up to 8.6 percent of world market share and become the world's top tourism industry by 2020. The outbound travelers from China will be the main source of international travelers in the world [12]. The great growth in outbound travel market in China has attracted international travel service providers around the world to promote their services in the huge Chinese market for more business profits.

Table 1. The numbers of outbound travelers in China from 2001 to 2006
M: Million

	2001	2002	2003	2004	2005	2006
Outbound	12M	16.6M	20.22M	28.5M	31.02M	34.52M

Source: CNTA

In the past several years the e-commerce market in China has expanded rapidly with the increase of the population of Internet users in China. According to the survey conducted by China Internet Network Information Center (CNNIC), the number of Internet users in China has reached 137 million, and the number of websites has arrived at 843 thousand until the end of 2006. The Internet users in China are mainly under 35 years old, and they often use the Internet to search information, read news and receive/send e-mails [13]. With the e-commerce expansion, the value of e-commerce is also growing in China. According to the survey conducted by China Market Information Centre (CCID), in China the revenue generated in e-commerce has arrived at $137.5 billion in 2006 with an increase rate of 52% [14].

The e-commerce development and the expansion of electronic market in China bring both challenges and opportunities for travel organizations in tourism industry in the world. Although the Internet has become an important travel service delivery channel, e-tourism in China is still at its initial stage [3]. In China, travel organizations have moved more and more activities and services online to attract more customers and guide their activities [6]. But only around 8.6% of Internet users are using the Internet to book travel service [13]. Under the high profitability pressure some online travel agencies have to combine both offline and online service delivery to keep competitive in the market, for example Elong.com and Ctrip.com. Chinese customers still rely more on the traditional intermediary – travel agencies to book travel service. The electronic market in tourism is still not so good compared to some other developed countries [6]. In 2006 the Chinese government has started the Golden Tourism project, which aims at pushing e-tourism development in China.

3   Method

This research aims to explore the issue on the e-commerce development model in China for international travel service providers. Since the study is focusing on the e-commerce development model in tourism in China, which is involved in both the supply side and the customer side. In this study both qualitative and quantitative approaches are adopted. The study issue is investigated based on the data collected form the three different participants in the combined value chain in tourism in e-commerce times: travel service provider, travel agent and customer.

In this study interviews were conducted to explore the perceptions of e-commerce development model on both travel service providers and travel agents perspectives. Some qualitative data were collected from interviews conducted in 9 companies - 1 travel service provider and 8 travel agencies. The travel service provider is an international airline company in Europe, and the 8 travel agencies are big international travel agencies in Beijing, Shanghai, Guangzhou and Shanghai in China, which have cooperation with the international airline company.

Totally 15 interviews were conducted - 6 in the international airline company and 9 in travel agencies (See Table 2). Among the 6 interviewees in the international airlines, three of them are sales managers in China, one is the manager of the e-commerce department, one is the manager of the revenue and pricing department, and one is the project director of the e-commerce department. Among the 9 interviewees in the tour agencies, 4 of them are general managers or deputy general managers, and 5 of them are sales department managers or directors.

Table 2. Formal Interviews

	Number of companies	Number of interviewees
International airlines	1	6
Travel agencies in China	8	9

We compiled two different lists of questions depending on the different investigated two interviewee groups – one list for the interviewees from the international airlines and the other for the interviewees from travel agencies. Structured interviews were conducted in both groups. Before interviews, all the interviewees were informed of the interviewed topics in advance in order to make sure that they know about e-commerce in tourism and can offer some valuable data for this research. The interviewees were asked to express their perceptions of e-commerce development model in tourism in China. Every interview lasted around 1 hour.

In order to investigate customer's attitude towards online travel service booking in the B2C model, a quantitative survey was conducted in this study. In the survey a questionnaire was developed to collect empirical data. We chose some passengers of the interviewed international airlines in our study to investigate the customer perceptions of online travel service booking. The passengers were asked to report on their current use of the Internet to book travel service or search travel information, and their future intentions on online travel service booking. The survey was conducted by the airline company onboard. In the study totally 190 copies were received, and 169 copies are usable.

4 Data analysis

4.1 Travel service provider perspective

The e-commerce development in China was discussed with the interviewees from the international airlines, which helps to understand the travel service providers' perceptions on e-commerce development models in China. The Chinese customers of the international airlines are mainly group traveler, and individually customers take a small share in the Chinese market. Clearly all the interviewees agreed that for the international airline company its e-commerce in China is just at the beginning, and it still depends on the travel agencies and their sales offices in China to promote flight tickets though they have adopted e-commerce in their ticket sales. As regards to their e-commerce development models, the two interviewees from the e-commerce department stated that in China the international airlines is focusing on B2B business at the beginning and B2C is developed as well, but currently B2C is not their focus in China, since its B2C business in China has not achieved improvement compared to its B2B business. It is quite different from that in Europe. In fact in Europe its B2C business has performed very well. They agreed that there are barriers for their B2C development in China. The main barrier is the restricted visa regulations. Chinese citizens traveling to Europe for leisure should be in travel groups. They agreed that the Chinese customers' behavior and the e-commerce development in tourism industry in China is quite different from that in Europe. Chinese customers prefer group travel to DIY travel, and groups keep the main tourism model in China. They states that its e-commerce should be developed based on the nature of the Chinese market. Currently, the travel agencies are its main ticket sales channel in China. Thus currently good cooperation with travel agencies based on the B2B business will be more important for its business in Chinese market.

4.2   Travel agents perspective

Travel agents, mainly travel agencies, are always important intermediaries in the value chain of tourism. Nowadays, travel agencies have adopted both B2B and B2C in their e-commerce development, which tie the travel service providers and customers. Travel agencies conduct business transaction with customers directly or through the Internet, which makes them know better about the customer behavior in tourism. According to the discussion with the interviewees from different travel agencies, they have some similar ideas on e-tourism development in China. They agree that in China travelers are mainly group travelers, especially in the outbound travel market, and the travelers are mainly between 25-40 years old. Travel agencies in China are still the main intermediaries of travel service providers, especially the international travel service providers in the world. The 8 travel agencies have already conducted good B2B cooperation with different travel service providers around the world, including airlines, hotels and so on, which brings them convenience and save their time in working. The 8 travel agencies promote their travel services provided by travel service providers through both traditional channels and the Internet. Individual customer in their business is less than group customer in both domestic and international tourism. At present, 7 travel agencies focuses their e-commerce mainly on B2B, and only 1 travel agency is going to focus on both of them.

In the discussion the interviewees illustrated their barriers in developing B2C in international travel service in China. Among the interviewees, 6 of them agreed that restricted visa regulation is the main barrier, which is similar to the opinions of the interviewees from the international airlines, and 4 of them stated that language is another obstacle. Most of the Chinese travelers are not good at English. The Chinese customers are not willing to get into trouble in their trip out of China. They prefer to go with travel groups in their outbound trip with more insurance of their trip. They also mentioned that the language barrier will disappear gradually with the enhanced internationalization in China.

4.3   Customer perspective

The customers are investigated on their online travel service booking experience, online travel service searching and online booking for future travel service in the B2C arena. Among the 169 respondents, most of them (97.2 %) are Internet-users. And 99 of them have booked travel service online, accounting for 58.8% of all the respondents. As regards to travel information search, based on means comparison, travel agencies are ranked as the most important travel information searching channel and the Internet is not so important. (See Table 3).

For their future travel service booking, travel agencies are still more important than the Internet, 45.6% of the respondents are intended to use travel agency to book travel service and 33.1% of them will use the Internet to book their future trips. The investigated results on online bookers and potential online bookers are much higher than the results released by CNNIC.

Table 3. Travel information search channel

	Mean	Std. Deviation
Travel agency	1.99	1.322
Friends	2.04	1.145
Experience, habit	2.29	1.486
Internet	2.31	1.316
Advertisement	3.24	1.522

5   Discussion and conclusion

Travel industry is quite fit for e-commerce and the Internet because of its information-intensive nature. But in China e-tourism is still in its initial stage, which is different from that in Europe and in America, since the Chinese customers' behavior and the e-commerce development condition in China is different. The research findings in this study reveal that in China B2B business model will be popular than B2C in both the domestic and international travel market. In the international travel market, the B2C business model has been impeded by the language barrier from customers and the visa regulations from destinations countries. Though international travel service providers are eager to catch the opportunities that the Internet bring to them to expand their B2C market as in Europe or in America, it seems they have no power to solve the barrier of visa regulations.

According to the customers' perception, travel agencies keep the main intermediaries in tourism in China, though the Internet has become an important travel service booking channel. Travel agencies take the combined business model to offer travel services to customer – through both the traditional offline and the popular online service. The intensive travel services offered by travel agencies in the combined business model are not what travel service providers can offer to customers through their direct online sales. The results in the study state that half of the investigated customers will still book travel services from travel agencies, which is much higher than that of the Internet bookers for future trip. The results from customer survey are in consistent with the results from the interviews in travel agencies. At present the group travelers are the main customers of travel agencies. The share of online travel service booking from individual customers is less than the share of group travelers in traditional offline channels. The role of travel agency as the middleman in travel value chain will keep important.

In addition according to the results of the study, the age of the main outbound travelers in China are quite similar to the age of the main Internet users in China. It implies that in the future with the change of the international tourism regulations B2C should have its great potential in e-tourism since the main outbound travelers are also the main Internet users in China.

Based on the discussion we can arrived at the conclusion that e-commerce in China has a great potential for international travel service providers, currently international travel service providers, who are developing or planning to develop their e-commerce in China should mainly focus on B2B to expand their electronic market in China. B2C model development largely depends on the change of Chinese customers' behavior and the change of international tourism regulations. Appropriate e-tourism strategies based on the e-tourism condition in China can help international travel service providers to expand their Chinese market successfully.

The primary limitation of the study is that the empirical data collected is based on a small size of respondent, which is used to represent the general perceptions of customers in China with a large size of population. This study has provided an in-depth knowledge about the e-tourism development in China, and offered some valuable guideline for both international travel service providers around the world. Future study should take into consideration of the factors that affect the adoption of booking travel online in China.

Reference

1. V.C.S. Heung, "Barriers to Implementing E-commerce in the Travel Industry: A Practical Perspective", *Hospitality Management* 22(2003), 111-118 (2003).
2. H. Werthner, and F. Ricci, "E-commerce and Tourism", *Communications of the ACM* 47(12), 101-105 (2004).
3. L. Li, and D. Buhalis, "E-commerce in China: The Case of Travel", *International Journal of Information Management* 26(2006), 153-166 (2006)
4. M. Kaukal, W. Hopken, and H. Werthner, "An Approach to Enable Interoperability in Electronic Tourism Market", In : *Proceedings of International Conference of Information Systems (ECIS 2000)*. Vienna, Austria, 1104-1111(2002).
5. B. Anckar, and P. Walder, "Destination Maui? An Exploratory Assessment of the Efficacy of Self-Booking in Travel", *Electronic Market* 10(2), 110-119 (2000).
6. Jie Lu, and Zi Lu, "Development, Distribution and Evaluation of Online Tourism Services in China", *Electronic Commerce Research* 4(2004), 221-239 (2004).
7. C. Wynne, and P. Berthon, "The Impact of the Internet on the Distribution Value Chain: The Case of the South African Tourism Industry", *International Marketing Review* 18(4), 420-431 (2001).
8. R. Benjamin, and R. Wigand, "Electronic Markets and Virtual Value Chain on the Information Superhighway", *Sloan Management Review* 36(2), 62-72 (1995).
9. G.M. Giaglis, K. Stefan, and R.M. O'Keefe, "The role of Intermediaries in Electronic Marketplaces: Developing a Contingency Model", *Information System Journal* 12(2002), 231-246 (2002).
10. M.B. Sarkar, B. Butler, and C. Steinfield, "Intermediaries and Cybermediaries: A Continuing Role for Mediating Players in the Electronic Marketplace", *Journal of Computer Mediated Communications* 1(3), http://jcmc.huji.ac.il/vol1/issue3/sarkar.html
11. K. Stefan, and R.A. Teubner, "Web-based Procurement New Roles for Intermediaries", *Information Systems Frontier* 2(1), 19-30 (2000).
12. Outbound Travel Development in China, http://www.cnta.gov.cn/news_detail/newsshow.asp?id=A20075101738546353446
13. China Internet Network Information Center (CNNIC), The 19th Statistical Survey of Internet Development in China, http://www.cnnic.net.cn/uploadfiles/pdf/2007/1/23/113114.pdf

14. China Market Information Center (CCID). The Report of Internet Development
    in China 2007, http://market.ccidnet.com/pub/report/show_12636.html

Customer's Perceptions and Intentions on Online Travel Service Delivery: An Empirical Study in China

Hongxiu Li[1], and Reima Suomi[2]

1   Information Systmes Instutute, Turku School of Economics
Turku Center for Computer Science
Joukahaisenkatu 3-5 B, 20520 Turku, Finland
Hongxiu.li@tse.fi

2   Information Systmes Instutute, Turku School of Economics
Rehtorinpellonkatu 3, 20500 Turku, Finland
Reima.suomi@tse.fi

Abstract. With the wide adoption of e-commerce in travel and tourism industry, the Internet has become an important travel service delivery channel, and traditional travel agency has been under severe disintermediation threat. This paper reports on a survey conducted to explore the Chinese consumer's current usage of the Internet as the channel to search travel information and to book travel services. It also investigates customer's future intentions on using the Internet to book travel services. This paper aims to examine whether there are difference between different consumer segments in terms of gender and age, and to find the hypothesis of disintermediation or intermediation in travel industry. The results indicates that online travel service delivery has grown as a popular direct distribution channel in travel industry, but more of the customers still turn to the traditional travel agencies, which support both the disintermediation and intermediation in travel industry. The results also reveal that online travel services provided by travel service providers still need to be improved since the number of online bookers is declined. This paper concludes by discussing the limitation of this study and highlighting areas for the future research in online travel service field.

1   Introduction

The rapid advance in information technology (IT) and the proliferation of technology-based systems, especially the Internet, are leading fundamental changes

Please use the following format when citing this chapter:

Li, H., Suomi, R., 2007, in IFIP International Federation for Information Processing, Volume 252, Integration and Innovation Orient to E-Society Volume 2, eds. Wang, W., (Boston: Springer), pp. 113-122.

in how companies are performing business and interacting with customers [1-3]. Electronic commerce (e-commerce) has become an important business model with these great changes. In fact, travel and tourism industry has been particularly affected by the great advancement and the wide application of e-commerce in business, especially the way travel organizations deliver their travel products to the market and the customers [4-6]. The Internet, as a universal and interactive communication means, has resulted in great changes of customer's behavior and attitude. Consumers can conduct travel information searching and travel service booking online. They shifted from the traditional offline channels to online channels. Online travel service reservation has constituted one of the largest and fastest growing segments of e-commerce in B2C arena [7,8]. The Internet has become a new intermediary in travel industry and the traditional travel agencies or tour operators are threatened to be replaced by the Internet.

This paper is to examine the issue of the Internet as a travel service delivery channel and the issue of disintermediation or intermediation in travel and tourism industry. It explores these important issues building both on previous researches and empirical data collected in airline industry. The purpose of this study is to contribute toward an improved understanding of the current usage of the Internet as a travel information searching and travel service booking channel. This paper aims to examine whether there are difference between different consumer segments in terms of gender and age. This study is also to investigate the customer's future intentions on booking travel services online. This paper concludes by discussing the limitation of this study and highlighting areas for the future research in online travel service field.

2   Background

2.1   Disintermediation in travel industry

Malone et al (1987) first introduce the threatened intermediation or disintermediation hypothesis. They argue that the role of the traditional retailers, distributors, brokers, and other middlemen will be eliminated or reduced in business transaction between the producers and the customers [9]. In the context of Web, it comes to signify the disappearance of different intermediaries or middlemen and the creation of enhanced online sales – customers deal directly with service or product providers on the Internet [10]. Studies on disintermediation in the Internet and e-commerce field provide quite contradictory predictions about the impact both e-commerce and the Internet would have on intermediaries. Some suggest that the Internet and e-commerce would create efficiencies and lower transaction cost with fast and better service by eliminating the need for intermediaries in business transaction [10-12]. While some researchers raise criticism on the threatened disintermediation hypothesis. Evans and Würster (1997) argue that e-commerce requires a new creation of partnership for all the participants in the value chain [13]. Bailey and Bakos (1997, 1998) suggest that the need for intermediaries is not likely to be eliminated. Though some traditional roles of intermediaries may become less important as a result of advance in IT, some new types of electronic intermediaries and new version of traditional intermediaries will appear in the electronic market because of the various needs for outsourcing services in e-commerce [14-16].

With the wide adoption of e-commerce in travel and tourism industry, the traditional travel agency has been under severe disintermediation threat. More and more travel service providers are conducting travel service distribution online without dependence on traditional intermediaries of travel agencies and without commissions paid to travel agents. Travel service providers allow their customers to access to their online booking system to book travel service directly [17,18]. Various studies have shown the direct fit of the Internet and travel products [6,7,19,20]. Travel and tourism industry is assumed to experience disintermediation on a large scale because of e-commerce. Thus, the traditional principle intermediary, tour agencies, in the travel distribution chain throughout the world are under threat of disintermediation [7,17,21,22]. Clemons et al. (2002) illustrate the following three reasons for disintermediation in travel industry: travel agencies' focus on the interest of themselves and customers, but not on the interests of travel service providers, travel agencies having strong power on information control in the distribution channel, and the Internet taking the place of travel agencies as a low cost distribution channel [23].

As discussed above, some tourism researchers state that the traditional distribution system could be threatened by disintermediation because of the Internet as a cheaper distribution channel. Others, however, argue that although the volume of online travel distribution keeps increasing, some travelers still rely on the traditional travel agencies for customized and professional services or human touch, and disintermediation can be avoided by re-intermediation in travel industry [24].

2.2   Electronic travel service delivery

The increased penetration of online service and home computing has resulted in more consumers' home-shopping. Consumers are able to search travel information through websites, to engage in the subsequent decision-making process, and to purchase travel services without leaving home. The Internet has greatly affected consumers' behavior, which makes it available for travel service suppliers to sell their products to consumers directly and omit the traditional travel retailer – travel agency [25]. With the change of consumers' behavior, travel service providers are implementing online travel service distribution to customers. As the travel industry is largely information-driven, the Internet has been considered ideally suited as a medium for travel service delivery [26], and it is hardly surprising that online travel services have developed into one of the largest e-commerce domains [23].

Online travel service delivery helps travel service providers to establish direct promotion to targeted potential customers and send them tailor-made information at the appropriate time. On the travel service provider perspective, they can gain channel control in the market by this way without dependence on traditional travel agencies. In addition, minimizing cost and maximizing marketing effectiveness can be achieved. Travel service providers can also obtain a broad customer base, understand customers' needs better, and offer customized service to customers in online distribution [27].

Customers' switch from offline channels to online channels is related to their perceptions on online channels. On customer perspective, online travel service delivery offers them more benefits compared to traditional offline channels. Convenience, time saving and cheaper price are the most common motivations for customers to book travel service online [28]. Customers can search travel information online easily, including travel information, price information and so on. Online channels dramatically reduce customer's searching effort on travel information, including both searching time and searching costs. In addition, online channels offer customers with more information to support their decision based on their comparison of different travel products and prices. All these activities, including travel information searching, travel service booking, payment and service delivery, can be conducted online by customers without face-to-face meeting, and customized service according to their demand can be possible [29].

Indications in studies are that at present though online travel service delivery is growing in tourism, sales through traditional travel agents have accounted for a large percent of travel industry [25]. As Chircu et al (2001) and Gupta (2004) state that online travel service booking does not have the same appeal for travelers, despite numerous travel service providers have made effort to implement online direct sales to customers. Customers may have difficulties with online booking involving the significant complexity of travel service, for example, multiple destinations, international travel, travel involving mixed air carrier arrangements and so on, and channel risks to switch to online travel service delivery is also an obstacle for customers to adopt online channels in travel service distribution [28,30]

3   Method

In this study we conducted a consumer survey in airline industry to explore the general public's perceptions on online travel service distribution and their future intentions on travel service booking. In the survey a questionnaire was developed to collect empirical data. The investigated objects in this study are the Chinese passengers of an international airline company. Copies of the questionnaire were distributed to passengers onboard. Totally 190 copies were received in the survey, and 169 copies are usable.

The questionnaire includes some questions based on background studies and secondary research. At the beginning a brief narrative introduction of the study and an explanation of the purpose on the questionnaire are provided. Respondents are asked to indicate their current and perceived future use of online travel service booking. Some questions are demographic-related and others are related to travel service delivery, including online booking experience, travel information searching channels, and future intentions on travel service booking.

The empirical data was analyzed using SPSS14.0 program. In the survey respondents were clustered on the basis of their responses to some questions on their gender, age, Internet use and online booking experiences, and these groups were then related to the scales on their current travel searching channel, their current use of online travel service booking, and their future intentions on travel service delivery.

4   Data analysis

4.1   The current usage of the Internet in travel information searching and travel service booking

Of the respondents in the questionnaire, 104 (61.5%) are males, and 65 (38.5%) are females, and 97.2 % are Internet-users, only 2.8% of the respondents have never used Internet. As regards online travel service booking experience, 58.8% of them reported that they had purchased travel service online, and 41.2% had not. The data revealed that there are significant difference between groups with different gender (Chi-square: 9.639/df 1, Sig. = .002) and in different ages (Chi-square: 94.377/df 5, Sig. = .000) on the variable of online travel booking experience. The male respondents had adopted online travel service booking more extensively than the female respondents (See Table 1). The respondents in 26-35 ages group has the greatest online booking experience, and the respondents in 55-65 age group has the least (see Table 2). The results are in consistent with the current condition of Internet use in China. In China males use the Internet more than female, and the young generation between 18-35 years old is the main Internet users in China [31].

Table 1. Online travel service booking experience of respondents by gender

	Total Resp.	Gender	
		Male	Female
Online experience	58.6 (99)	36.1 (61)	22.5 (38)

Table 2. Online travel service booking experience of respondents by ages

	Total Resp.	Age				
		18-25	26-35	36-45	46-55	55-65
Online experience	58.6 (99)	18.3 (31)	23.1 (39)	8.9 (15)	6.5 (11)	1.8 (3)

Note: All values are illustrated in the following way Percentage (Number of respondent).

The survey also empirically investigated the customer's current travel information searching channels. The respondents are instructed to express their preference of travel information searching channels on a five point scale where one represents most important channel and 5 represents the least important channel. According to the means comparison, the data implies that travel agency is still the most popular channel to search travel information and advertisement has lost its power in travel product promotion. Surprisingly, even friends, experiences and habits are more important than the Internet (See Table 3). That can partly be explained by the fact that most Chinese rely strongly on their experiences and good social relationship in their life. The statistical tests for difference between means reported that there are no significant differences between female and male respondents, or between the respondents in different ages on the perception of travel information searching channels (See Tables 3 and 4).

Table 3. Reported perception of travel information searching channels by gender

	All Resp.	Male	Gender Female	Sig. (2-tailed)
Travel agency	1.99	1.91	2.18	.331
Friends	2.04	2.20	2.77	.104
Experience, habit	2.29	2.51	1.94	.360
Internet	2.31	2.09	2.78	.038
Advertisement	3.24	3.13	3.52	.082

Table 4. Reported perception of travel information searching channels by ages

	All Resp.	18-25	26-35	Age 36-45	46-55	55-65	Sig. ANOVA
Travel agency	1.99	2.38	2.12	1.75	1.67	1.00	.547
Friends	2.04	1.88	2.32	1.82	2.00	1.00	.496
Experience, habit	2.29	2.15	2.37	2.27	2.36	1.50	.364
Internet	2.31	2.60	2.28	2.40	1.70	-	.501
Advertisement	3.24	3.67	2.92	3.44	3.17	3.00	.823

4.2   Customer's future intentions on travel service booking

To investigate customers' future intentions on travel service booking is also one of the main objectives of this study. All the respondents were asked to report on their intended ticket booking channel selection in related to their future trip, including booking channel, payment method and ticket delivery.

Table 5. Reported future ticket book channels

	All Resp.	Use of Internet Non-user	User	Online booking experience Non-booker	Booker
Travel agency	45.6	1.2	44.4	21.3	24.3
Internet	33.1	.6	32.5	9.4	23.7
Airline office	14.8	-	14.8	6.5	8.3
Others	6.6	-	6.6	3.0	3.6

The results reveal that the dominant ticket booking channels are travel agencies and the Internet. Among the respondents, 45.6% of them reported they primarily will use travel agency to book travel service. Even a large part of the Internet users

(44.4%) and online bookers (24.3%) will not use the Internet (See Table 5). And 33.1% of the respondents will use the Internet to book their future trips, most of them are Internet-users (32.5%) and online bookers (23.7%) (See Table 5).

The respondents reported on their payment methods of ticket booking for their future trip. Online payment and pay in cash are the dominant methods. Among the respondents, 43.8% of them reported they primarily will pay online. Most of them are Internet users (43.3%) and online bookers (29.0%) (See Table 6). Still 31.4% of the respondents will pay in cash, including some Internet-users (29.6%) and online bookers (18.4%) (See Table 6). These findings are in line with the report from China Internet Network Information Center (CNNIC). In China pay in cash is still preferred by customers though online payment is getting more and more popular than before [31].

Table 6. Reported payment method in future ticket booking

	All Resp.	Use of Internet		Online booking experience	
		Non-user	User	Non-booker	Booker
Online payment	43.8	.5	43.3	14.8	29.0
Bank transfer	23.7	-	23.7	16.6	7.1
In cash	31.4	1.8	29.6	13.0	18.4
With a check	1.1	-	1.1	.5	.6

The respondents were asked to report on their likely ticket delivery channels as well. More than half of the respondents (63.3%) will use e-ticket. Most of them are Internet users (62.8%) and online bookers (41.2 %) (See Table 7). Some Internet users and online bookers still will use paper tickets delivered by post or picked up by them (See Table 7).

Table 7. Reported ticket delivery in future ticket booking

	All Resp.	Use of Internet		Online booking experience	
		Non-user	User	Non-booker	Booker
E-ticket	63.3	.5	62.8	22.1	41.2
Paper ticket by post	11.3	-	11.3	2.4	8.9
Paper ticket picked up in person from ticket office	25.4	1.1	24.3	16.5	8.9

5   Discussion and conclusion

Travel industry has been quite fit with the new interactive media – the Internet, and has developed as the main sector in e-commerce field [23,26]. The results in this study support the view since nearly half of the respondents have used the Internet to book travel services and still about one third of the respondents will use the Internet to book travel services for their future trip. But the current use of online travel service booking is not equally spread in the groups of different gender and age, and online booking services still need to be improved. Since there is a decline in the numbers of respondents who are intended to book travel service online, and even some online bookers are not complete e-commerce adopters. Some online bookers will not pay online, but turn to pay in cash or in other ways, and some of them will not accept e-ticket during their online booking. It is obvious in the results that there are still a fraction of respondents rely on the traditional travel agencies both to look for travel information and to book travel services. The results indicate that travel service providers still need to depend on travel agencies in order to keep competitive.

As expected, the results reveal that online travel service delivery has been a growing trend, but travel agency still keeps the main travel service delivery channel in travel industry with the increase of adoption of online booking service in travel industry, since travel agency is still the most preferred channel for customers to obtain travel information, and nearly half of the respondents still rely on travel agency for their future trip.

As insight into the disintermediation hypothesis, as above discussed, the adoption of online travel service delivery has attracted wide customers, and travel agency is facing the disintermediation threat. But the results also indicate that currently travel agency is an even more important channel than the Internet for customers to book travel service, and about 24.3% of online bookers would like to turn back to travel agencies in travel service booking. The results imply that though disintermediation exists in travel industry, but travel agency still has strong market share in travel industry. Disintermediation or not depends on travel agencies' competitive capability in the travel market.

In summary, the results support the following conclusions. First, online travel service delivery has grown as a popular direct distribution channel in travel industry. Second, customers has intentions to book travel service online, while still more of them prefer to the traditional travel agency. There are quite contradictory arguments on the disintermediation hypothesis in the travel industry. It implies that though the phenomenon of disintermediation exists in travel industry, intermediaries are still important for travel service providers to keep competitive. Third, online services provided by travel service providers still need to be improved since the number of online bookers is declined.

This study has offered some valuable insight into studies on the online travel service delivery. A number of limitations of the study need to be acknowledged when we interpret the results. First, the empirical study was conducted just in one country, China. The results are not applicable for most other countries. Second, only airlines were chosen as case in our empirical study. More cases in different travel service organizations will better support the assumptions in the study. In the future further empirical studies on how to evaluate online travel service quality and to meet customer's needs need to be conducted to examine the dimensions of online travel service quality.

Reference

1. M. Porter, Strategy and Competitive Advantage, *Journal of Business Strategy* 79(3), 63-78 (2001).
2. A. Parasuraman, and G.M. Zinkhan, Marketing to and Serving Customers through the Internet: An Overview and Research Agenda, *Journal of the Academy of Marketing Science* 30(4), 286-295 (2002).
3. H.H. Bauer, M. Hammerschmidt, and T. Falk, Measuring the Quality of E-banking Portals, *International Journal of Bank Marketing* 23(2), 153-175 (2005).
4. D. Buhalis, Tourism and Information Technologies: Past, Present and Future, *Tourism Recreation Research* 25(1), 41-58 (2000).
5. R. Law, Internet in Travel and Tourism-Part I, *Journal of Travel & Tourism Marketing* 9(4), 83-87 (2000).
6. R. Law, K. Leung, and J. Wong, The Impact of the Internet on Travel Agencies, *International Journal of Contemporary Hospitality Management* 16(2), 100-107 (2004).
7. D. Buhalis, and M. C. Licata, The future of eTourism Intermediaries. *Tourism Management* 23 (2002), 207-220 (2002).
8. A. Parasuraman, V. Zeithaml, and A. Malotra, E-S-QUAL: A Multiple-item Scale for Measuring Customer Perceptions of Service Quality, *Journal of Service Research* 17(3), 213-233 (2005).
9. C.H. Malone, J. Yates, and R.I. Benjamin, Electronic Market and Electronic Hierarchies, *Communications of the ACM* 30(6), 484-497 (1987).
10. F. Jallat, and M. Capek, Disintermediation in Question: New Economy, New Networks, and New Middleman, *Business Horizons* 2001(March-April), 55-60 (1997).
11. M.E. Nissen, Beyond Electronic Disintermediation through Multi-agent Systems, *Logistics Information Management* 14(4), 256-275 (2001).

12. L. Harris, and K. Duckworth, The Future of the Independence Travel Agent: The Need for Strategic Choice, *Strategic Change* 2005(June-July), 209-218 (2005).
13. P.B. Evans, and T.S. Würster, Strategy and the New Economics of Information, *Harvard Business Reviews* 1997(September-October), 71-82 (1997).
14. Y. Bakos, Reducing Buyer Search Costs: Implications for Electronic Marketplaces, *Management Science* 43(12), 1676-1692 (1997).
15. Y. Bakos, The Emerging Role of Electronic Marketplace on the Internet, *Communications of the ACM* 41(8), 35-42 (1998).
16. J.P. Bailey, and Y. Bakos, An Exploratory Study of the Role of Electronic Intermediaries, *International Journal of Electronic Commerce* 1(3), 7-20 (1997).
17. I. Lewis, and A. Talalayevsky, Travel Agents: Threatened Intermediaries? *Transportation Journal* 1997(Spring), 26-30 (1997).
18. A.C. Tse, Disintermediation of Travel Agents in the Hotel Industry, *Hospitality Management* 22 (2003), 453-460 (2003).
19. R. Christian, Developing An Online Access Strategy: Issues Facing Small-to medium-sized Tourism and Hospitality Enterprises, *Journal of Vacation Marketing* 7(2), 170-178 (2001).

20 A. Poon, The Future of Tour Agents, *Travel & Tourism Analyst* 2001(3), 57-80 (2001).

21. J. Pötzl, Issues in Direct Channel Distribution: A Comparison of Selling via the Internet in the Airline Business and the Fast-moving Consumer Goods Industry, *Electronic Market* 10(3), 153-157 (2000).

22. J.E. Mills, and J. Law, *Handbook of Consumer Behavior, Tourism and the Internet* (The Haworth Hospitality Press, Birmingham, New York, 2004).

23. E. K. Clemons, I.-H. Hann, and L.M. Hitt, Price Dispersion and Differentiation in Online Travel: An Empirical Investigation, *Management Science* 48(4), 534–549 (2002).

24. A. Palmer, and P. McCole, The Virtual Re-intermediation of Travel Service: A Conceptual Framework and Empirical Investigation, *Journal of Vacation Marketing* 11(1), 33-47 (1999).

25. Shengliang Deng, R. Lawson, and L. Moutinho, Travel Agents' Attitudes toward Automation and the Delivery of Service, *Asia Pacific Journal of Marketing and Logistics* 2000(4), 60-72 (2000).

26. N.J., Morgan, A. Pritchard, and S. Abbott, Consumers, Travel and Technology: A Bright Future for the Web or Television Shopping? *Journal of Vacation Marketing* 7(2), 110–124 (2001).

27. Kin-nam Lau, Kam-hon Lee, and Ying Ho. Web-site Marketing for the Travel-and-tourism Industry, *Cornell Hotel and Restaurant Administration Quarterly* 42(4), 55-62 (2001).

28. A. Gupta, Bo-chiuan Su, and Zhiping Walter, An Empirical Study of Consumer Switching from Traditional to Electronic Channels: A Purchase-decision Process Perspective, *International Journal of Electronic Commerce* 8(3), 131-162 (2004).

29. A. Athiyaman, Internet Users' Intention to Purchase Air Travel Online: An Empirical Investigation, *Marketing, Intelligence & Planning* 20(4), 234-242 (2002).

30. A.M. Chircu, R.J. Kauffman, and D. Deskey, Maximizing the Value of Internet-based Corporate Travel Reservation System, *Communications of the ACM* 44(11), 57-63 (2001).

31. China Internet Network Information Centre (CNNIC), The 19th Statistical Report on Internet Development in China (2007), http://www.cnnic.net.cn/uploadfiles/doc/2007/1/23/113530.doc

Research on the Impetus Mechanism of Institutional Repositories

Jun Deng, Qiang Bi
School of Management Jilin University, Changchun, China ,
dengjun9722@163.com, biqiang12345@163.com

Abstract: The paper gives an illustration on the concept, features, functioning and other basic problems of institutional repositories and establishes the concept model of institutional repositories. An analysis of the six major momentum factors determining the institutional repositories development and the interaction of the impetus factors of institutional repositories development are also touched upon.

Preamble

The currently unprecedented progress of modern technology in fields of information and internet has made Institutional Repositories (referred to as IR hereafter) a prime field to carry out open access theoretical and practical research. The ultimate target of IRs is the optimized share of information and knowledge through information and internet technologies and the satisfaction of users' demands for information and knowledge in a bid to promote the innovation and communication of knowledge. However, the current frustrating situation is marked by a lack of exploration and momentum for sustainable development in related fields and a deficiency in research of IRs impetus mechanism. Thus, IRs research facilitates the exploration of inter-relations among related systems in terms of IRs development and provides practical value for IRs progress. Consequently, the analysis of IRs development mechanism justifiably ensures the sustainable development of IRs.

Please use the following format when citing this chapter:

Deng, J., Bi, Q., 2007, in IFIP International Federation for Information Processing, Volume 252, Integration and Innovation Orient to E-Society Volume 2, eds. Wang, W., (Boston: Springer), pp. 123-131.

1   Introduction to IRs and impetus mechanism

1.1   Synopsis on an Institutional Repository

The cognizance of an IR concept is determined by scholars' understanding of the connotation of as well as their perspective on the field. An IR is more likely to be encyclopedic in subject coverage, representing the full range of academic fields of study, especially an IR at universities. It is undeniable that an IR is an integration of institutional intellectual products which acquires knowledge and promotes communication through the collection, storage and management of intellectual results. Thus it is justifiable to say that an IR is a system aiming at collecting, storing, administrating and offering knowledge dissemination and knowledge service. In practice, an IR is a kind of notion as well as a system. When applied as notion, it is a challenge towards traditional academic communicative system which provides a true scientific research model based upon cyber environment and re-orients the roles of authors, librarians and publishers in the process of academic communication through separating the circles in academic publishing including collection, processing and publishing. As a kind of system, an IR provides a convenient platform for authors to publish their research fruits efficiently and enables users to have access to academic resources efficaciously in a bid to enhance scientific productivity.

Consequently, an IR concept model is divided into three levels, namely, users, database storage and management and service, which is illustrated in Figure 1.

Users: It serves as the media between content-forwarder and an IR, which submits digital research results of authors or the third party.

Database storage and management: the core of an IR, which provides data storage, metadata management, data management and dissemination of data.

Service: It provides a unified interface for users, which is responsible for terminal users' interaction. Its services mainly compose data search, data browsing and data downloading.

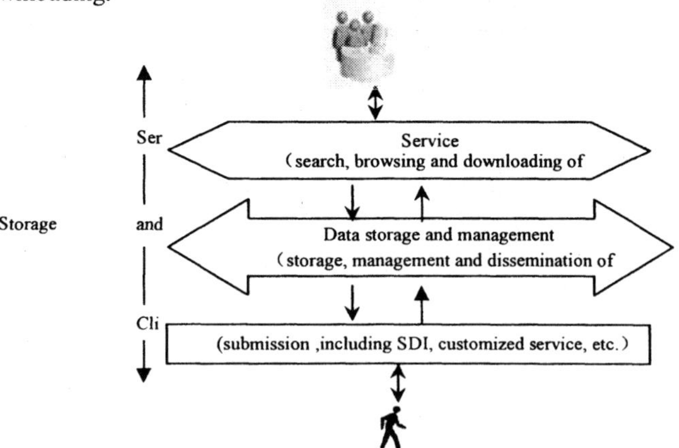

Fig. 1 the Concept model of an IR

General speaking, there are four features in an institutional repository: institutionally defined, focused on scholarly content, cumulation and perpetuation and interoperability. Institutional repositories can create positive outcomes for all interested groups: Authors can gain visibility and enlarged research impact; users can find research more easily; institutions can raise their research profile; and the funders can receive wider research dissemination.

1.2   Impetus Mechanism illustration

Impetus is the factor that precipitates the progress of all existing subjects. Though originally abstract as it is the innate logic which is concealed behind all phenomena of existing things, it is practical and tangible in terms of motion, development and change. Thus impetus mechanism is the impetus which propels the progress, alteration and interaction of all of institutional repositories.

2   Impetus Mechanism of Institutional Repositories

The formation and development of IRs is not immediate but a long process consisting of many complicated factors including academic communication change as well as digital information resources. The impetus comes from digital information explosion's demand for the preservation of digital resources, the impulse of open access movement development, the magnetic power of the share of scientific information and knowledge, the buttress from digital information technology and standard, the support from prime institutions and theoretical as well as practical guidance from related fields(as illustrated in figure 2).

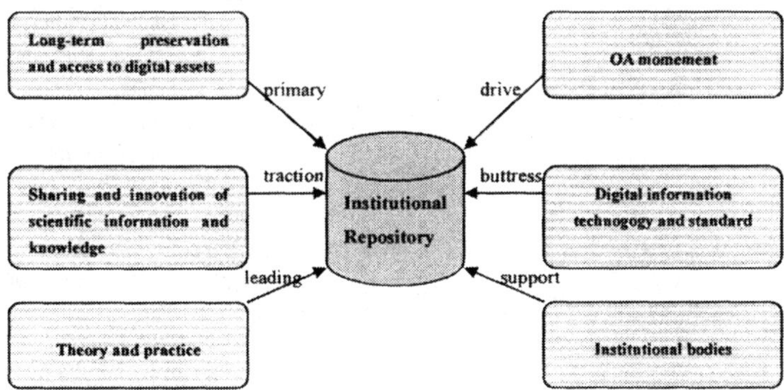

Fig. 2. Impetus Structure of development of IRs

2.1 The Primary Energy of IRs Lies in the Long-Term Preservation and the Storage as Well as the Access to Digital Assets

The primary energy of an IR lies in the long-term preservation and the storage as well as the extraction of digital assets. Since the 20th century, the development of computer technology and internet techniques is gradually modifying scholars' communicative approaches, which are not confined by traditional paper-based communicative channels. An increasing number of scholars have adopted novel communicative methods, which spawns the explosion of digital information resources. The digital information resources are distributed randomly and disorderly with the progress of digital technology and the explosive increase of digital database, hence the organization, preservation and application of digital academic assets have become the prime challenges confronted by scholars. The majority of research results are distributed online through personal cyberspace, websites and other channels, which greatly threatens the preservation and development of digital academic resources and might be inaccessible at any moment. The current situation also suffers a lack of cohesion. Confronted with the chaotic condition of digital information resources, most institutions and scholars yearn to establish an ideal storage database to realize the long-term preservation of valuable digital academic resources, consequently, an IR becomes the prime interface for the preservation and extraction of digital information.

2.2 Open Access Movement is the Prime Impetus for the Development of IRs

Open access serves as the prime and immediate impetus for the development and formation of IRs. Traditional publishing models greatly hinder academic development and communication with the progress of economy and technology. The price rise of serials has greatly exceeded the affordability of libraries which can only cut their limited budgets. To break price barrack hindering academic communications, open access movement has been initiated in international academic fields, publishing fields and media circles in a bid to promote the free circulation of scientific information. Two channels are available in the process of open access. one being OA, which is also called "gold" road, another being Author Self-archiving, which is also known as "Green" Road. There are two kinds of "green" OA repository: one is Subject-repository，where authors deposit in a (usually) central repository used by the community and maintained by an appropriate institution and where relevant material on a subject area is collected together; the other is an institutional repository，where the authors deposit in a repository maintained by their institution thus collecting together in one place the research output of that institution. Though open access approaches are available for some publishers and electronic journals are adopted already, it is not easy work for the creation and realization of OA and OA journals. Current figures show that only about 2,630 [1] journals are open access. Presently, the number of OA journals account for a small proportion of issued journals, as a contrast, IRs have become the main channel during the innovation of traditional academic communication system and the main solution to "scholarly communication crisis". A great deal of institutions and scholars have turned their eyes to the construction and development of IRs, consequently, IRs are accelerating in a startling speed with the progress of open access.

2.3   The Sharing and Innovation of Scientific Information and Knowledge is the Impetus of IRs Development

Communication is the key to academic research and innovation, which targets at the exploration and application of knowledge and information as well as the rejuvenation of knowledge.

In a broad sense, as the most active innovation resource in the information era, scientific information has become a vital approach in breaking through academic barriers and promoting academic integration. Scientific development demands the share of information resources, the optimization of scientific resources and the acceleration of knowledge innovation. In a narrow sense, scholars yearn to expand their influence and attract more readers, to communicate with their counterparts and to share the research results with other researchers. They also want to expand their research horizon, to keep a close eye on academic development and to perfect their research and speed up innovation. In addition, many researchers and teachers are using more informal methods for sharing such as informal networks, wikis, peer-to-peer mechanisms; and providing access through owner created and managed websites. Propelled by the demand, an IR makes it emergence and consequently becomes a key factor in accelerating the pace of scientific information sharing, establishing a new order and speeding up innovations in this field.

2.4   Digital Informational Techniques and Standards are the Pillar Force in Propelling the Development of IRs

The support of information techniques and standards determines the path of the development of IRs as IRs emerge and develop with the development of internet technology and the progress of digital information technology and cyber environment. There is no room for its development without the support of digital information techniques. The development and perfection of related technologies is also the basis for the progress of IRs as the latter becomes a part of digital information resource management in a bid to meet scholars' demand for academic information communication and resource share. A lack of related standards will greatly impair the efficiency of IRs operation. As a consequence, the development of digital information technology and the establishment of related standards mark a profound reform in digital information field and serves as a vital determinant in IRs development. Digital information technologies carry two functions, namely, the development of digital asset management techniques, metadata description and standardization techniques. For example,

• The Open Archival Information System (OAIS) model developed by an international group of information technology organizations spearheaded by NASA's Consultative Committee for Space Data Systems, which provides a "conceptual framework for an archival system dedicated to preserving and maintaining access to digital information over the long run" [2], and offers "a comprehensive logical model describing all the functions required in a digital repository" [3].

• Open Archives Metadata Harvesting Protocol (OAI-PMH)[4]that was developed by the Open Archives Initiative from the library and scientific community, which defines a mechanism for harvesting XML-formatted metadata from repositories and makes the basic interoperability standard.

• A Metadata Encoding and Transmission Standard (METS) [5] developed under the sponsorship of the Digital Library Federation, which provides a schema for encoding descriptive, administrative, and structured metadata in a digital repository or library.

Another function is the development and application of open source software systems. The first step for an IR development is the design of applied software systems. The matured open source software systems that offer technical infrastructure options for implementing all or part of an institutional repository include Archimede[6], CDSware[7], DSpace[8], Eprints[9], Fedora[10], i-Tor [11], Greenstone[12] etc..

The Eprints software has the largest—and most broadly distributed—installed base of any of the repository software systems involved here, and currently over 222 [13] known archives are running on the software. The DSpace software has also generated a great deal of excitement and encouraged wave of institutions around the world to implement institutional repositories, which formed a DSpace Federation and currently over 218[14] known archives are running on the software.

These techniques make IRs resource share possible, realize the interoperability between IRs, and integrate all chaotically-distributed resources in a variety of IRs into the unified system of global information digital operation system. The development and application of open software systems also lowers the cost of the establishment of an IR for an institution. The open source software systems are regarded as the most cost-effective and immediate route to set up and advance the development of institutional repository. The standardization and techniques for digital information and the perfection of related criteria determine IRs development, the construction of digital information resources.

2.5   Institutional Bodies are the Determinant of IRs

The development and realization of IRs are determined by institutional body as they are inter-dependent. Its functions are embodied by the implementation of policies and financial investment. Take self-archiving mandate for example, self-archiving determines the content of an IR as an IR will be vacant without resources. To enrich IRs content resource, many institutions, governments and research organizations have established self-archiving mandate policies. According to ROARMAP[15], Statistics reveals that: three universities adopted departmental-mandate policy, ten institutions adopted institutional-mandate policy , eleven institutions adopted funder-mandate policy, six institutions adopted proposed funder-mandate policy. Besides, University of Southampton Department of Electronics and Computer Science successfully lobbied the UK Parliamentary Select Committee in 2004 to mandate self-archiving; This led directly to the RCUK self-archiving mandate proposal. The self-archiving mandate greatly promotes the development of IRs. Meanwhile, some governments applauding IRs development also invest great amounts of money into IRs programs and ensure their development legally. For example, in the Netherlands, the Dutch government has given 2 million Euros to set-up the infrastructure for IRs at several of the Universities, the Dutch National Library, and the Dutch Academy of Arts and Sciences (Surf, 2003),which named he Digital Academic Repositories(DARE). Also the bipartisan Federal Research Public Access Act, introduced on May 2, 2006 by Senators John Cornyn (R-TX) and Joe Lieberman (D-CT), would require that 11 U.S. government agencies with annual extramural research expenditures over $100 million make manuscripts of journal articles stemming from research funded by that agency publicly available via suitable digital repositories [16].

2.6   Theoretical Research and Practical Development are the Impetus of the Development of IRs

An IR development falls into two categories, namely, theoretical progress and practical progress, which are interactive and bilaterally-influential.

The Association of Research Libraries, Scholarly Publishing and Academic Resources Coalition and the Coalition for Networked Information established SPARC IR Workshop and sponsored a series of academic seminar on institutional repositories, such as the Workshop on Institutional Repositories intended to help academic and research library and IT directors and their senior staffs begin planning for the implementation of repositories in 2002, the conference on the strategies critical to implementing and managing the successful long-term growth of your institutional repository in December, 2004 and on building a successful institutional repository in April, 2005,etc.. Some interested scholars such as Raym Crow [17], Stevan Harnad[18], David Prosser[19], Clifford Lynch[20] and William Nixon discusses and researches the development tendencies of challenges and problems in a variety of fields including technology, theory, law and the like, which greatly speeds up the discussion and research of IRs development and propels the integration of practice with theory. In the UK, the Joint Information Systems Committee (JISC) is funding the development of institutional repositories for several of their leading research institutions [21]. In Canada, Twelve Canadian research libraries have begun a pilot project to implement institutional repositories, which is being coordinated by the Canadian Association of Research Libraries.

Presently, IRs are development in an unprecedented speed and have a trend of globalization. According to statistics, 862 [22] IRs have been established on a global scale, which is the vital foundation for IRs development; the academic study of IRs research deepens the theoretical research of IRs and propels the progress of IRs practice.

3   The Interaction of IRs Development Impetus Factors

IRs originate from different mechanisms and the previously-mentioned six forces are interactive and form a new impetus in determining the development of IRs. From a information technology angle, digital prosperity is achieved in scientific research. With the support of institutional bodies, IRs are to witness a quick development, IRs theories are to witness a penetration and IRs practical fields are to witness an expansion. The support boosts the development and prosperity of the preservation of digital assets and the management skills. Thus IRs development is realized and coordination achieved.

Conclusion and Prospects

Comprehensively-speaking, demand and impetus are the basic power for IRs development, digital information techniques and related standards are the vital supports for IRs development. IRs progress is also determined by institutional bodies, OA movement and the integration of practice and theory.

What deserves special mention is that the development of IRs varies with their determinant factors. Presently, IRs are in their primary process of development and deeper research together with the establishment of related models is compulsory to enhance their popularity in society , to improve the awareness of IRs, to promote the development of IRs and to realize the communication and innovation of scientific communication.

Acknowledgments

The paper is one of the research results of the key research project funded by Ministry of Education, P.R.of China（NO.05JZD00024）

Reference

1. (April 10, 2007); http://www.doaj.org.

2. Brian Lavoie, "Meeting the Challenges of Digital Preservation: The OAIS Reference Model." 2000. OCLC Newsletter 243 (January/February): 26-30. (April 18, 2007); http://digitalarchive.oclc.org/da/ViewObject.jsp?objid=0000001747.

3. Preserving our digital heritage. RLG News 2003, 56 (Spring): 1-3. (April 18, 2007); http://www.rlg.org/en/pdfs/rlgnews/news56.pdf.

4. Open Archives Initiative. (April 18, 2007) http://www.openarchives.org/.

5. METS, (April 18, 2007); http://www.loc.gov/standards/mets/.

6. (April 18, 2007); http://archimede.bibl.ulaval.ca/.

7. (April 18, 2007); http://cdsware.cern.ch.

8. (April 18, 2007); http://www.dspace.org/.

9. (April 18, 2007); http://software.eprints.org/.

10. (April 18, 2007); http://www.fedora.info/.

11. (April 18, 2007); http://www.i-tor.org/en/.

12. (April 18, 2007); http://www.greenstone.org.

13. (April 18, 2007); http://www.eprints.org/.

14. (April 18, 2007); http://wiki.dspace.org/index.php//DspaceInstances.

15. (April 18, 2007); http://www.eprints.org/openaccess/policysignup/.

16. (April 18, 2007); http://www.arl.org/sparc/advocacy/frpaa/.

17. SPARC Senior Consultant.

18. Department of Electronics and Computer Science at the University of Southampton.

19. SPARC Europe Director.

20. Director of the Coalition for Networked Information.

21. University of Nottingham, University of Edinburgh, University of Glasgow, Universities of Leeds, Sheffield and York, University of Oxford, British Library, and Arts and Humanities Data Service.

22. (April 18, 2007);http://roar.eprints.org/index.php.

Study on Influencing Factor Analysis and Application of Consumer Mobile Commerce Acceptance

Gaoguang Li [1] and Tingjie Lv [2]

1 School of Economics and Management, Beijing University of Posts and Telecommunications, Beijing 100876, P.R. China,ligaoguang@gmail.com

2 School of Economics and Management, Beijing University of Posts and Telecommunications, Beijing 100876, P.R. China,lutingjie@263.net

Abstract. Mobile commerce (MC) refers to e-commerce activities carried out using a mobile device such as a phone or PDA. With new technology, MC will be rapidly growing in the near future. At the present time, what factors making consumer accept MC and what MC applications are acceptable by consumers are two of hot issues both for MC providers and f or MC researchers. This study presents a proposed MC acceptance model that integrates perceived playfulness, perceived risk and cost into the TAM to study which factors affect consumer MC acceptance. The proposed model includes five variables, namely perceived risk, cost, perceived usefulness, perceived playfulness, perceived ease of use, perceived playfulness. Then, using analytic hierarchy process (AHP) to calculate weight of criteria involved in proposed model. Finally, the study utilizes fuzzy comprehensive evaluation method to evaluate MC applications accepted possibility, and then a MC application is empirically tested using data collected from a survey of MC consumers.

1   Introduction

Early studies on mobile commerce (MC) suggest that there is a general consumer interest toward MC and service applications. Purchases on web sites, electronic receipts and tickets, mobile content, routine bank services, peer-to-peer payments, and vending are among the potential applications [1]. However, the adoption of MC and services has been slower than expected. Facing on situation of insufficient user acceptance, Different persons have given different explanation from diverse angles. For promoting healthy development of MC, we believe that it is extremely important to understand consumer MC perceptions and acceptance. We believe that there are

Please use the following format when citing this chapter:

Li, G., Lv, T., 2007, in IFIP International Federation for Information Processing, Volume 252, Integration and Innovation Orient to E-Society Volume 2, eds. Wang, W., (Boston: Springer), pp. 132-141.

some important issues (i.e., cost, risk, usefulness, ease of use, playfulness) that can explain why some mobile applications have been successful and why some others have not performed as expected.

In this study we aim to analyze which factors will affect and how to affect consumer adoption to MC and analyze accepted possibility of certain MC application. The theoretical background of the study is based on the technology acceptance model (TAM) and diffusion of innovations theory, which have been suggested by prior studies as applicable frame of reference for MC context. Cited empirical data in the study was obtained from survey to some specialists in the relative field.

The paper is organized as follows. In the next section, we discuss the ingredients of affecting consumer adoption to MC in virtue of TAM and production of other research fields, we then construct a research model for MC acceptance and build an index system for evaluating. In the third section we apply the analytic hierarchy process (AHP) to evaluation of weight of factors in upper model. In succession, choosing a piece of MC applications, we use fuzzy evaluating method to analyze the accepted possibility by consumers. The final chapter discusses our results and suggests future research.

2   Research model

2.1   Perceived usefulness and perceived ease of use

The TAM is an information systems theory that models how users come to accept and use a technology. The TAM was first introduced by Davis et al. in 1986 [2].TAM is a well respected model of IT adoption and use. The model provides a traditional view point about technology acceptance from the users' perspective. The model provides a traditional view point about technology acceptance from the users' perspective.

The core concept of TAM is that perceptions of usefulness, ease of use and other external variables will influence an individual's intention to use IT, which will ultimately influence actual usage behavior [2]. Perceived usefulness and perceived ease of use are the two particular beliefs. According to the model, system usage is determined by the users' attitude towards using the system while attitude towards using is jointly determined by usefulness and ease of use [2]. Perceived usefulness is defined as ''the degree to which a person believes that using a particular system would enhance performance''.

Perceived ease of use is defined as ''the degree to which a person believes that using a particular system would be free of physical and mental efforts'' [2]. Davis also suggested that perceived ease of use may actually be a prime causal antecedent of perceived usefulness. TAM also postulates that perceived ease of use is an important determinant of attitude toward using a system.

2.2   Cost and perceived risk

Much research also indicated that TAM needed integration with additional variables in order to improve its prediction of system use [3]. Chen and Hitt et al pointed out consumers must deal with non-negligible costs in switching between different brands of products or relative services in various markets. Transitioning from wired EC to MC implies some additional expenses. Equipment costs, access cost, and transaction fees are three important components that make MC use more expensive than wired EC. In addition, frustrating experiences, such as slow connections, poor quality, out-of-date content, missing links, and errors have infuriated online users. Unfortunately, consumers must pay for all these frustrations [4]. Some researchers suggested that MC providers should find solutions that reduce the costs and entice present and new customers to access portals anytime, from anywhere.

According to cost-efficiency model, cost is important factors in consumer decision-making of purchase and use. Therefore, the perceived cost is an important factor affecting. It has a negative direct effect on behavioral intention to use. With the increasingly high penetration rate of Internet applications, people are anxious about the diverse types of risks presented when engaging in online activities or transactions. When customers are uncertain about product quality, brands and online services they may worry about an unjustifiable delay in product delivery, providing payment without receiving the product and other illegal activities and fraud . Perceived risk refers to certain types of financial, product performance, social, psychological, physical, or time risks when consumers make transactions online

Credit ratings, bank balances and financial data could be changed without the owner knowing during online transactions. The reliability of online transactions is still far from perfect. Cognitive and affective factors are important variables that prevent people from trusting online services. Pavlou defines this as "the user's subjective expectation of suffering a loss in pursuit of a desired outcome" [5]. Other research also indicated that perceived risk is an important determinant of consumers' attitude toward online transactions. Since intention to use a website for transactions involves a certain degree of uncertainty, perceived risk is incorporated as a direct antecedent of behavioral intention to use. Hence, Perceived risk has a negative direct effect on behavioral intention to use [4].

2.3   Perceived playfulness

For nailing down consumer's intrinsic motivation to computers acceptance, Davis et al introduce into the conception of perceived playfulness. Perceived playfulness is defined as feeling playful and dispensing with thinking over evocable aftereffect possibly. In theory, perceived playfulness affects directly use intention. In American, there were two research carried out to study affection of playfulness. One was the study of 200 American MBA students using word-processing procedure, the other was the research on 40 American MBA students using graphical procedure. The results were showed as follows: there are stronger relationship between usefulness and use intention, at the same time, perceived playfulness and use intention has weaker relationship, perceived ease of use affect actual use through perceived usefulness and perceived playfulness.

Early empirical research on use of Internet shows that perceived playfulness is the main driving force of consumer using Internet. For example, Atkinson and Kydd (1997) validate the relation between use of Internet, perceived usefulness and perceived pleasure through survey on 84 MBA students and 78 masters major in business administration. They find that perceived playfulness has an obvious effect on use of Internet but perceived usefulness is not very obvious when consumer uses Internet for entertainment. They find that there are stronger relationship between perceived usefulness and actual use but weaker relationship between perceived playfulness and actual use when consumer uses Internet for study [6].

Teo et al (1999) research how three factors (i.e., perceived ease of use, perceived usefulness, perceived playfulness) affect consumer use of Internet by means of online questionnaire. Analyzing 1370 questionnaires obtained, they find that Internet users are largely impact by perceived usefulness and perceived playfulness. However, Kydd and Atkinson draw an opposite conclusion, they find that perceived usefulness has a weaker effect on frequent user and perceived has also a weaker effect on online frequency. According to questionnaires of 152 college students in South Korea, Moon and Kim find perceived usefulness and playfulness have an obvious effect on consumer use of Internet. Hence, we believe perceived playfulness has a positive effect on behavioral intention to use.

2.4   Proposed research model

The research model for our study is depicted in figure 1. In the model, based on these arguments, our study integrates TAM and three additional variables (i.e., cost, perceived risk, and perceived playfulness) to model user acceptance in the B2C MC context. The constructs of perceived ease of use, perceived usefulness, behavioral intention to use, and actual use are adopted from TAM. Three other external variables are also integrated into the model.

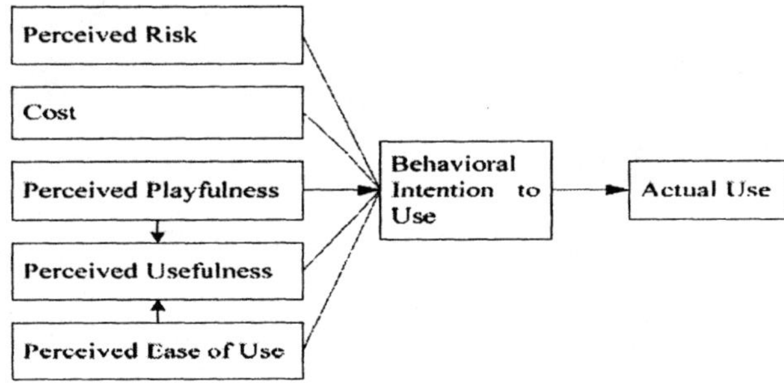

Fig. 1. Proposed MC acceptance model

2.5 Construct criteria system of MC application acceptance

Many variables involved in social, scientific, psychological research can't be measured directly, this variable is named as latent variable, so we measure indirectly latent variable by observable indicators. In the study, there are seven latent variables, namely perceived usefulness, perceived ease of use, behavior intention to use, actual use, perceived playfulness, perceived risk and cost. Observable indicators refer to previous research and actual situation. Previous research was reviewed to ensure that a comprehensive list of measures were included. Those for perceived usefulness, perceived ease of use, behavioral intention to use and actual use were adapted in our model from previous studies on TAM (e.g., [7]). The construct for perceived risk was adapted from the studies of Pavlou and Eastin. The scales for playfulness were based on M. Igbaria et al. and Atkinson et al. The measures for cost were captured using three items derived from Constantinides, Rupp and Smith, and real world experience. For perceived ease of use has slim effect, we omit it. After a series of modifying and adjusting, the evaluating criteria system is depicted in figure 2.

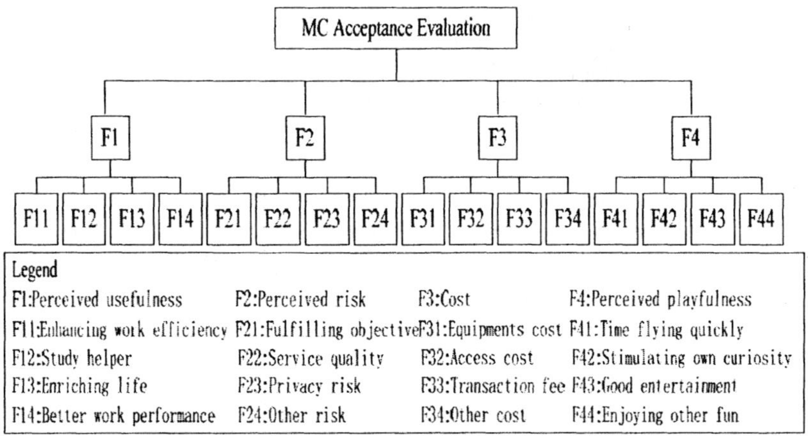

Fig. 2. Criteria system of mc application acceptance & AHP hierarchical diagram

3 Evaluating weight of criteria through AHP

AHP is a multi-criteria decision method that utilizes structured pair-wise comparisons among systems of similar alternative strategies to produce a scale of preference. It has been found to be an effective approach that can settle complex decision. And it has been used by numerous researchers in various fields to handle both tangible and intangible factors and sub-factors. As the AHP approach is a subjective methodology, information and the priority weighs of elements may be obtained from a decision-maker using direct questioning or by a questionnaire method. The AHP procedure is usually summarized as four steps, now we will evaluate weight of factor step by step and prepare for using fuzzy comprehensive evaluation to evaluate possibility of certain MC application acceptance.

3.1   Establish hierarchy structure (Step 1)

In this step, we build a decision hierarchy by breaking a general problem into individual criteria. Figure.2 in section 2 is the AHP hierarchical diagram. The top of the hierarchy is the overall objective, the decision alternatives are at the bottom. The middle nodes are the relevant attributes (criteria) of the decision problem.

3.2   Construct judgment matrix (Step 2)

Next, we gather rational data for the decision criteria and alternatives, using the AHP relational scale suggested by T. L. Saaty. We invite five specialists to carry out pair-wise comparison of elements at each level in the hierarchy. From now on, we take example for perceived usefulness, and other results can obtain in terms of same method. Table 1 show the original pair-wise weighs of the AHP matrices.

Table 1

C	u_1	u_2	u_3	u_4
u_1	1	1/2	2	3
u_2	2	1	2	2
u_3	1/2	1/2	1	2
u_4	1/3	1/2	1/2	1

3.3   Obtain weights of criteria

The relative weights of the criterion of each level with respect to an element in the adjacent upper level are computed as the components of the normalized eigenvector associated with the largest eigenvalue of their comparison matrix. The composite weights of the decision alternative are then determined by aggregating the weights through the hierarchy. Now we will make calculation to judgment matrix and obtain weights of various evaluating criterion.

Firstly, using the following formula:

$$W_i = \frac{1}{n}\sum_{j=1}^{n}\frac{c_{ij}}{\sum_{k=1}^{n}c_{kj}} \quad i=1,2,\cdots,n$$

According to data in Table 1, we can calculate weight vector. $W = (0.299 \; 0.384 \; 0.191 \; 0.126)$

3.4   Consistency test

Constructing judgment matrix should keep thought consistency, only when matrix is consistent totally, there exists $\lambda_{max} = n$ in judgment matrix, however, there exists $\lambda_{max} > n$. Hence, the difference between λ_{max} and n is used to test consistency using CI. The relation between CI and λ_{max} is described as follows:

$$CI = \frac{\lambda_{max} - n}{n - 1}$$

λ_{max} is matrix maximal latent root, and n represents matrix rank, the smaller CI, the better consistency. At the same time, CI is necessary to compare with random consistency index (RI), we can obtain the test value, namely CR, the formula and condition are as follows:

$$CR = \frac{CI}{RI} \qquad CR < 0.1$$

And then we verify consistency of judgment matrix by upper method.

$$CW = \begin{pmatrix} 1 & \frac{1}{2} & 2 & 3 \\ 2 & 1 & 2 & 2 \\ \frac{1}{2} & \frac{1}{2} & 1 & 2 \\ \frac{1}{3} & \frac{1}{2} & \frac{1}{2} & 1 \end{pmatrix} \begin{pmatrix} 0.299 \\ 0.384 \\ 0.191 \\ 0.126 \end{pmatrix} = \begin{pmatrix} 1.330 \\ 1.616 \\ 0.785 \\ 0.513 \end{pmatrix}$$

$$\lambda_{max} = \sum_{i=1}^{n} \frac{(CW)_i}{nW_i} = 4.209 \quad CI = \frac{\lambda_{max} - n}{n - 1} = 0.0697 \quad CR = \frac{CI}{RI} = 0.0774 < 0.10$$

Therefore, compositor result of various criterion weight vectors is satisfied in consistency. In the same way, weights of other criteria (i.e., cost, perceived playfulness, perceived risk) can be calculated and depicted in table 2.

Table 2. Criteria weight and evaluation

Criteria (level 1)	weight	Criteria (level 2)	Weight	A	B	C	D	E
Perceived Usefulness	0.272	F11	0.299	4	0	4	11	1
		F12	0.384	1	1	3	6	9
		F13	0.191	0	0	8	12	0
		F14	0.126	0	3	8	9	0
Perceived Risk	0.319	F21	0.281	0	4	6	8	2
		F22	0.277	2	0	4	6	8
		F23	0.231	2	2	4	4	8
		F24	0.211	0	4	8	8	0
Cost	0.239	F31	0.271	0	0	2	4	14
		F32	0.256	8	2	2	6	2
		F33	0.241	4	2	2	2	10
		F34	0.233	4	0	0	8	8
Perceived Playfulness	0.160	F41	0.028	2	4	4	8	2
		F42	0.258	4	8	4	4	0
		F43	0.238	0	16	0	4	0
		F44	0.218	0	14	4	2	0

4   Analysis of MC applications accepted possibility using fuzzy comprehensive evaluation method

4.1   Fuzzy comprehensive evaluation model

The comprehensive fuzzy evaluation model proposed is based on fuzzy set theory as developed by Zadeh and the analytic hierarchical process developed by Saaty. Zadeh define fuzzy logic underlying models of reasoning which are approximate rather exact. Saaty advocated the use of deductive systems approach in the analysis of complex decision problem. The steps in CFEM are described as follows.

1. Define model input, the set of judgment factors $u_i(i=1,2,...,m)$, for the comprehensive fuzzy evaluation model. $U = \{u_1, u_2, u_3, ..., u_m\}$, U is set of judgment factors.

2. Set the linguistic variable, $V = \{y_1, y_2, y_3, ..., y_n\}$ (comment factor)

Linguistic value $v_i(i=1,2,...,n)$ is the result of evaluation, namely $V = (\text{Very Poor, Poor, Average, Good, Very Good})$. Then give the value by five level measurements, $C = (1 \quad 2 \quad 3 \quad 4 \quad 5)$

3. Define the weightings of the judgment factors, $u_i(i=1,2,...,m)$, W is corresponded fuzzy weightings vector, $W = (w_1, w_2, ..., w_m)$, based on questionnaire results.

4. Constructs the membership function r (v). Membership function is at the core of fuzzy models. The membership function is considered to be the strongest and weakest point of fuzzy set theory. Member functions are the most commonly used.

5. Computer the degree of membership (r_{ij}) and the fuzzy matrix R_i, R_i is

$$R_i = (r_{i1}, r_{i2}, r_{i3}, ..., r_{im})$$

The fuzzy matrix is

$$R = \begin{pmatrix} r_{11} & r_{12} & r_{13} & \cdots & r_{1m} \\ r_{21} & r_{22} & r_{23} & \cdots & r_{2n} \\ \cdots & \cdots & \cdots & \cdots & \cdots \\ r_{m1} & r_{m2} & r_{m3} & \cdots & r_{mn} \end{pmatrix}$$

6. Define the fuzzy judgment $B = W \cdot R$. So as to assess the effects. B is the fuzzy evaluation model, $b_j(j = 1, 2, ..., n)$ is fuzzy evaluation index.

Comprehensive fuzzy evaluation model is $U = \{u_1, u_2, u_3, ...u_m\}$

4.2   Empirical study

4.2.1 Classification of MC Applications

There is potentially an unlimited number of MC applications (Varshney, 2001; Varshney & Vetter, 2002), which leads to a demand for classification, since currently, it is almost impossible to cover the whole range of potential MC products and services (Lehner &Watson, 2001). Yuan and Zhang (2003) argue that value propositions in MC which define the relationship between seller offerings and buyer purchases by identifying how the seller achieves the buyer's needs (Clarke, 2001) originate from mobility and location awareness and are contrary to Internet-based e-commerce. Therefore, they group various MC applications based on these value propositions into six categories, namely ubiquitous communication, Emergency and time critical information services, location-sensitive service, pocket e-wallet, portable entertainment, improving productivity of mobile workforce. In this study, we adopt this classification and take example for ubiquitous communication.

4.2.2 Construct evaluating criteria system

The criteria system is depicted as figure 2. in second section.

4.2.3 Evaluate weight of criteria

The process of evaluating weight of criteria can see from third section, and result is showed in table 2.

4.2.4 Establish judgment matrix

We investigate 20 consumers by questionnaire and let them objective score according to their own perception. The result is showed in table 2.The number of perception in table (i.e., very poor, poor, average, good, very good) represent how many consumers choose the answer.

$$r_{ij} = \frac{c_{ij}}{\sum_{i=1}^{5} c_i} \quad (i = 1, 2, 3, 4,)$$

$\sum_{i=1}^{5} c_i = 20$ is the total number of investigated consumers. According to the formula, we can obtain criteria judgment matrix:

$$R_1 = \begin{pmatrix} 0.2 & 0 & 0.2 & 0.55 & 0.05 \\ 0.05 & 0.05 & 0.15 & 0.3 & 0.45 \\ 0 & 0 & 0.4 & 0.6 & 0 \\ 0 & 0.15 & 0.4 & 0.45 & 0 \end{pmatrix}$$

4.2.5 Fuzzy comprehensive evaluation aiming at objective

$$B_1 = W_1 \cdot R_1 = (0.079 \quad 0.0381 \quad 0.2442 \quad 0.45095 \quad 0.18775)$$
In the same way,
$$B_2 = (0.05078 \quad 0.12149 \quad 0.26474 \quad 0.32727 \quad 0.23125)$$
$$B_3 = (0.19694 \quad 0.04962 \quad 0.07672 \quad 0.24808 \quad 0.42864)$$
$$B_4 = (0.08025 \quad 0.52321 \quad 0.15242 \quad 0.23649 \quad 0.02863)$$
And then, $B = W \cdot R = (0.09761 \quad 0.14459 \quad 0.19534 \quad 0.32416 \quad 0.23195)$

4.2.6 Calculate accepted possibility

$$AD = B \cdot C^T = 3.4292$$
$$ADP = 3.4292 / 5 \cdot 100\% = 68.58\%$$

Therefore, as a whole, accepted possibility of this MC applications (i.e., ubiquitous communication is 68.58%.

5 Conclusions and future work

This research has contributed to the MC field by exploring which factors affect consumer acceptance and MC application acceptance possibility by empirical study.

Some suggestions for future study are outlined here: first, TAM needs to be given additional variables to provide an even stronger model. Although some new factors are already introduced into TAM, for example research by Venkatesh and Davis indicated that both social influence processes and cognitive instrumental processes significantly influenced user, more reasonable variables is necessary to adopt to study consumer mc applications acceptance. Second, other research methodologies can be applied to study mc acceptance in order to do further research with a large population besides TAM. Third, empirical study should be further developed, including questionnaire design, choosing research object, scope of research etc. in this way, we can draw precise conclusion to guide mc healthy development.

References

1. B. Anckar and D. Dincau, "Value Creation in Mobile Commerce: Findings from a Consumer Survey", *Journal of Information Technology Theory and Application.* 4(1), 43-64(2002).

2. F. D. Davis, "Perceived Usefulness, Perceived Ease of Use, and User Acceptance of Information Technology", *MIS Quarterly.* 13(3), 319-340(1989).

3. B. Szajna, "Empirical Evaluation of the Revised Technology Acceptance Model", *Management Science.* 42(1), 85-92(1996).

4. J. H. Wu and S. C. Wang, "What Drives Mobile Commerce? An Empirical Evaluation of the Revised Technology Acceptance Model", *Information Management.* 42, 719-729(2005).

5. P.A. Pavlou, "What Drives Electronic Commerce? A Theory of Planned Behavior Perspective"(2001); http://www-scf.usc.edu/pavlou/14794.pdf.

6. M. A. Atkinson and C. Kydd, "Individual Characteristics Associated with World Wide Web Use: An Empirical Study of Playfulness and Motivation", *Data Base for Advances in Information Systems.* 28(2), 53-62(1997).

7. T. Fenech, "Using Perceived Ease of Use and Perceived Usefulness to Predict Acceptance of the World Wide Web", *Computer Network and ISDN Systems.*30, 629–630(1998).

The role of post-adoption phase trust in B2C e-service loyalty: towards a more comprehensive picture

Matti Mäntymäki

Turku Centre for Computer Science (TUCS)
Turku School of Economics, Information Systems Science
Joukahaisenkatu 3-5 B, 6th floor
20520 Turku
Finland
matti.mantymaki@tse.fi

Abstract. Despite the extensive interest in trust within information systems (IS) and e-commerce disciplines, only few studies examine trust in the post-adoption phase of the customer relationship. Not only gaining new customers by increasing adoption, but also keeping the existing ones loyal, is largely considered important for e-business success. This paper scrutinizes the role of trust in customer loyalty, focusing on B2C e-services by conducting a three-sectional literature review stemming from IS, e-commerce and marketing. The key findings of this study are: 1. Literature discussing the role of trust after the adoption phase is relatively scarce and fragmented 2. In the empirical testing trust is mostly viewed as a monolith 3. Quantitative research methods dominate the field 4. Since trust may play a role during the whole relationship, also dynamic ways to scrutinize trust would be appropriate. Implications of these findings are discussed and ideas for further research suggested.

1   Introduction

Trust has been viewed as one important factor affecting e-commerce adoption within the information systems (IS) and e-commerce disciplines [1, 2, 3]. The nature of trust has been widely discussed and its importance acknowledged also in e.g. e-commerce and marketing research streams [4]. Traditionally IS has been interested in adoption

---

Please use the following format when citing this chapter:

Mäntymäki, M., 2007, in IFIP International Federation for Information Processing, Volume 252, Integration and Innovation Orient to E-Society Volume 2, eds. Wang, W., (Boston: Springer), pp. 142-152.

of technologies, such as Internet or e-commerce. However, from a customer relationship perspective the adoption represents only the first steps. The role of trust in post-adoption phase business-to-consumer (B2C) relationships has not been extensively discussed within the IS and e-commerce disciplines. Therefore, one can ask to what extent adoption alone is enough to explain customer relationships in the e-environment? One can also ponder whether consumers automatically continue usage after the adoption of the service and whether the same factors influencing adoption behavior play a role in the post-adoption phase? [5]

The importance of customer loyalty has been widely acknowledged and discussed in the marketing literature (see e.g. [6-9]). Customer loyalty is viewed as one of the most important factors for e-business' success [see. e.g. 10, 11].

In this study, the customer means an individual consumer, not a corporate customer. With respect to loyalty, the term customer loyalty instead of consumer loyalty or service loyalty is used. Examples of the usage of the term customer loyalty in similar contexts can be found from the e-commerce body of research (cf. e.g. [26, 28, 39]).

In this study, B2C e-services are viewed in a rather wide sense as services that are delivered by commercial organizations to consumers via the Internet. Hence, services that are delivered using other electronic channels than the Internet are excluded from this study.

An increasing share of services is delivered using virtual channels. Hence, the service encounters are moving away from face-to-face interaction towards virtual encounters. Since service encounters are important for the relationship, organizations need to consider how to maintain and develop their customer relationships without the face-to-face component. As a result, understanding the post-adoption behavior requires further scrutiny. The contribution of the paper is three-fold; firstly, it investigates the role of trust in post-adoption phase of B2C relationships in the online environment. Secondly, the paper scrutinizes the academic discussion around trust to identify topical areas of research and provides some longitudinal perspective on the development of the research. Thirdly, it attempts to identify possible paths for further research around trust and e-commerce.

2   Research Approach

The main focus of this paper is to discuss the role of trust in customer relationships of business-to-consumer (B2C) e-services, particularly in customer loyalty. As pointed out by Pavlou and Fygenson [12], consumer behavior has understandably largely ignored IT issues, since they have not been relevant in traditional physical business environment. Thus, this paper is positioned to contribute in narrowing the gap between IS and consumer behavior research as regards the role of trust.

A three-sectional literature review was conducted for this study. Figure 1 illustrates the areas and focus of the review. The first section focused on literature on trust in the Internet environment. To ascertain that the quality of the reviewed literature is sufficient, the top ten IS journals based on the Association for Information Systems Journal Rankings were included to the review. Because the idea is to investigate trust in online environment, articles published prior 1995 were excluded since the commercial usage of the Internet was rather limited before 1995.

The second part of the review concentrated on e-commerce and e-services literature to find and investigate the studies discussing the role of trust in post-adoption behavior, particularly in customer loyalty. The third section of the literature review focused on studies around trust and loyalty in consumer behavior literature within the marketing discipline.

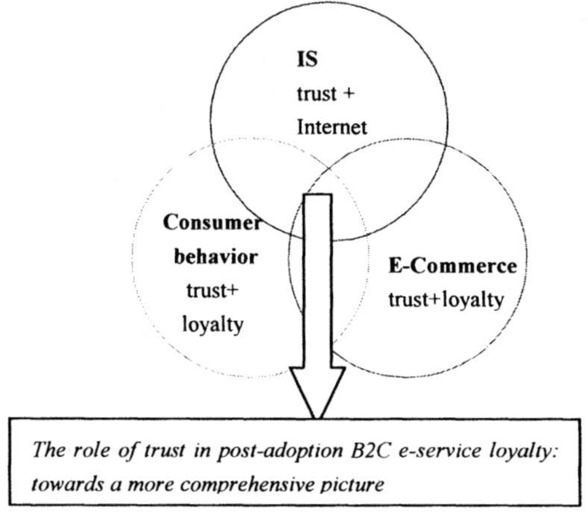

Figure 1. The structure of the study

3 Background

Trust has been in the interest of several disciplines. Trust has a central role in human interactions and hence in the society and economic exchange. The construct of trust can be approached from several directions using various theoretical frameworks. (cf. e.g. [1, 2, 3].)

In the IS literature trust has been discussed in relation to e.g. e-commerce adoption [13], electronic marketplaces [14] and virtual teams [15]. In their studies, McKnight and Chervany [16] and McKnight et al. [2] have strived for bringing the dispositional, institutional and interpersonal aspects of trust into a single framework.

The e-commerce literature has generally focused more on the institutional [17, 18] than dispositional aspect of trust, yet the importance of dispositional trust in e-commerce is also acknowledged [13]. From a managerial perspective, influencing dispositional trust may be challenging since it stems from values and personality whereas institutional trust is built on structures such as laws, regulations, standards etc. that reduce the perceived risk. As a result, creating trust-building mechanisms to nurture trust is often faster and technically easier than trying to influence the psychological dimension of trust.

Most of the online trust-building techniques are based on institution-based trust. Intuitively, institution-based trust seems effective also with B2C e-services. Structural assurances such as escrow services [17], privacy statements [19, 20] and feedback mechanisms [21, 14] are examples of commonly used trust-building techniques in e-commerce. In the case of e-services, the delivery of the service is automated. This reduces the risk of human errors and 'bad' service from the supplier side. On the other hand, the role of the customer in the e-service delivery is amplified. Therefore, achieving a high level of situational normality requires a technical environment where the customer is able to deliver the service without errors.

The view of trust in the literature has also somewhat evolved within the scrutinized period. In the early days, the focus was perhaps more on the security aspects to reduce the risk of fraud or misuse of personal data. The fundamental issue has shifted from convincing people that conducting transactions in the Internet is generally safe, towards lubricating the exchange and minimizing potential causes of inconvenience.

A topical trend is the critical evaluation of trust-building mechanisms [21, 22]. Issues related to feedback rating manipulations in electronic marketplaces and lack of customer attention and awareness of 3rd party assurance seals and privacy policy statements [23, 20] may indicate that trust aspects will remain in the agenda. Increasing customer awareness of the reliability issues of feedback ratings in electronic marketplaces may underscore the significance of appropriate and transparent trust-building measures in the future.

Another topical issue is related to the cultural issues of trust in e-commerce. Traditionally, a vast majority of studies on trust in e-commerce have used populations of US students in the empirical research. Some recent studies have investigated the cultural differences concluding that cultural aspects are an issue that influences trust in e-commerce. [24, 25.]

5   Trust and B2C e-service relationships

IS and e-commerce have discussed trust rather extensively but trust after the adoption phase has this far drawn less attention in these disciplines. Yet, signs of increasing interest towards post-adoption behaviors, e.g. customer loyalty have occurred in the recent IS and e-commerce literature [26, 27]. Table 1 illustrates the articles discussing trust and loyalty in the online B2C context. The articles are found from databases EBSCOhost, Emerald, Elsevier, ProQuest/ABI Inform using search terms 'trust' AND 'loyalty'. Additional search terms, 'web', 'customer/consumer loyalty' and 'e-loyalty' were used to ensure that the most of relevant content is included in the search. From this group, articles focusing on online context and having trust as a variable or otherwise explicitly discussing trust were included. As can be seen from table 1, e-commerce/IS literature scrutinizing trust in B2C e-services is sparse. Traditionally, customer loyalty has been discussed within consumer behavior in marketing and service loyalty within services marketing.

Table 1. Articles on trust and customer loyalty

Article	Area	Theoretical framework & Methods	View of trust	Key Ideas
Luarn & Lin (2003) [28]	E-Service	Quantitative Trust-commitment theory (Morgan & Hunt 1994) Proposed loyalty model	Set of specific beliefs (integrity, benevolence, competence and predictability) Monolith	Commitment as a powerful mediator between trust, satisfaction, perceived value and loyalty Correlation between trust and commitment weaker that satisfaction or perceived value Conceptualization of "traditional" customer loyalty in e-service context
Li et al. (2006a) [5]	E-commerce / web site	Investment model for interpersonal relationships & commitment-trust theory Quantitative	Monolith, however the authors discuss that trust is not undimensional Trust and commitment the predictors for stickiness intention	Commitment is a stronger predictor for stickiness than trust. The impact of trust also mediated by commitment
Flavián & Guinalíu (2006) [29]	E-commerce	Quantitative Proposes a model that relates trust, privacy and security with loyalty to a web site	Monolith	Direct correlation between trust and loyalty, not only intention to buy but also preference, cost and frequency of visits. Perceived security as an important antecedent of trust
Harris & Goode (2004) [30]	E-commerce & E-service (Books.com & Flights.com)	Applying Oliver's (1997) sequential loyalty chain in an online context	Monolith	Trust as a central driver of loyalty, direct correlation notified Oliver's loyalty model is reliable and valid in the online context. nature of online exchange rather relational than transactional

Thatcher & George (2004) [31]	E-commerce	TRA Quantitative	Trust in the Internet Monolith Trust in the Internet not correlated to loyalty, once consumers gain a sufficient level of experience to form a committed relationship to a vendor --> threshold level?	Existing marketing models relevant are for Web shopper behavior. Social involvement magnifies the relation between commitment and loyalty to a vendor.
Flavián et al. (2006) [32]	Website loyalty	Quantitative Explore the influence of perceived website usability on trust and satisfaction and the incidence of these 3 variables on loyalty	Trust as set of beliefs Monolith	The effect of usability on loyalty seems to be conditioned by trust and satisfaction
Li et al. (2006b) [33]	E-Commerce site	The investment model Organizational commitment theory Commitment-trust theory Quantitative	Monolith (focus on commitment)	Trust has a direct impact on behavioral intention (return to the site) and indirect via affective commitment Trust between web site and customer increases likelihood for use intentions.
Gummerus et al. (2004) [34]	Services Marketing Online health-care service	SERVQUAL Satisfaction-loyalty link Quantitative	Monolith Trust as a mediator between service quality dimensions and customer satisfaction	Service quality-trust-satisfaction-loyalty chain Trust as an important mediator of customer loyalty
Cyr et al. (2007) [35]	E-Service	TAM (applied) Quantitative	Monolith, yet the multidimensional nature of trust is discussed	Trust mediates between perceived social presence and e-loyalty
Anderson & Srinivasan (2003) [10]	E-commerce	Loyalty & Satisfaction Quantitative	Monolith	Trust mediates between E-satisfaction and e-loyalty
Ribbink et al. (2004) [36]	Services Marketing	Loyalty literature Quantitative	Trust viewed only as trust to an e-tailer, yet other	E-trust has a moderate direct impact on e-loyalty,

			aspects i.e. dispositional, system-based and interpersonal are discussed.	but weaker than e-satisfaction has. E-trust also mediates between e-satisfaction and e-loyalty
Pitta et al. (2006) [37]	Marketing	Conceptual paper Marketing literature	Multi-dimensional	Trust needs to be nurtured throughout the whole customer relationship to keep customer loyal
Ha (2004) [38]	Marketing	Quantitative web survey Marketing literature	Brand trust Monolith	Brand trust an important factor for relationship length Community keystone for brand trust Brand trust affects commitment
Gefen et al. (2003) [13]	Online shopping	TAM Quantitative	Multi-dimensional	Trust in repeat purchasing
Floh & Treiblmaier (2006) [39]	Internet Banking	Multigroup analysis Quantitative	Monolith	Trust mediates the impact of service quality and web site quality on loyalty.

6   Discussion

6.1   Implications for research

Literature discussing trust after the e-service adoption and its influence on customer loyalty is scarce and fragmented across marketing and e-commerce. In the studies investigating the role of trust with other relationship constructs such as satisfaction, perceived value or commitment, trust is largely viewed as a monolith. This approach leaves the multi-dimensional, complex nature of trust reported in numerous studies largely, ignored in the empirical testing.

Quantitative research methods are dominant within the area of trust and customer loyalty, yet the recent literature also contains a qualitative example [40]. Quantitative methods enable measuring correlations between the key constructs. In the light of previous studies, trust seems to correlate with numerous relationship components. In addition, quantitative methods are only able to provide a static picture leaving the dynamics of trust, also acknowledged by scholars, without further scrutiny.

Due to varying setting of hypotheses in different studies it is problematic to interpret how trust in positioned among the other related constructs such as perceived value, service quality, satisfaction and loyalty. This either underscores the complex, multi-faceted nature of trust, or reflects that capturing 'the true nature' of trust can be challenging.

For this paper the literature review discussing trust and customer loyalty was not conducted systematically but using search terms. This can be viewed as a limitation for the study since it is possible only with a systematic review to ensure that the relevant articles are included. However, if the literature discussing the topic is fragmented across several disciplines and journals, as it is in this case, conducting a systematic, holistic literature review can be somewhat challenging.

6.2 Implications for business

Trust appears to be a central component of customer relationship during the whole customer lifecycle, not only a factor affecting the adoption. However, the relationship between trust and other relationship components may require further clarification. A 'trust threshold' that businesses need to exceed to convince customers may not be static, but shifts over time. As a result, trust management is an ongoing process.

6.3 Future research

Widening the view of trust from monolith to multi-dimensional would draw a more comprehensive picture of trust in the post-adoption phase. Extending the array of methodological choices from strictly quantitative analysis to other methods, such as case study approach or ethnographical research, could potentially enrich the picture of trust in the post-adoption phase. It could also include a longitudinal perspective to better grasp the dynamic nature of trust.

7 Conclusions

This paper has scrutinized the role of trust in post-adoption phase of B2C e-services. Based on the findings of this study, trust seems to be an important, yet multi-faceted factor after adoption, since it correlates with several relationship elements such as commitment and loyalty. Therefore, the development and increasing adoption of e-commerce and e-services have not reduced the importance of trust in understanding online consumer behavior. In this light, further research on post-adoption trust seems appropriate.

Acknowledgements

The author gratefully acknowledges the financial support received from Jenny and Antti Wihuri Foundation, Foundation for Economic Education and Turun Kauppaopetussäätiö (Foundation for Economic Education in Turku).

References

1. M.O.K Lee and E Turban, A Trust Model for Consumer Internet Shopping, *International Journal of Electronic Commerce* 6(1), 75-91 (2001).

2. H.D McKnight, V. Choudhury, and C. Kacmar, Developing and Validating Trust Measures for e-Commerce: *An Integrative Typology Informations Systems Research* 13(3), 334-359 (2002).

3. S. Grabner-Kräuter and E.A. Kaluscha, Empirical research in on-line trust: a review and critical assessment, International *Journal of Human-Computer Studies* 58(6), 783-812 (2003).

4. A.E. Schlosser, T.B. White, and S.M. Lloyd, Converting Web Site Visitors into Buyers: How Web Site Investment Increases Consumer Trusting Beliefs and Online Purchase Intentions, *Journal of Marketing* 70(April 2006), 133-148 (2006).

5. D. Li, G.J. Browne, and P.Y.K Chau, An Empirical Investigation of Web Site Use Using a Commitment-Based Model", Decision Sciences 37(3), 427-443 (2006).

6. R.L. Oliver, Satisfaction: a behavioral perspective on the consumer (McGraw-Hill, New York, 1997).

7. R.L.Oliver, Whence Consumer Loyalty?, *Journal of Marketing*, 63(October 1999 Special Issue), 33-44 (1999).

8. M.T. Copeland, "Relation of consumers' buying habits to marketing methods", *Harvard Business Review* 1(3), 282-289 (1923).

9. J. Jacoby and R.W. Chestnut, Brand Loyalty Measurement and Management (John Wiley & Sons, New York, 1978).

10. R.E. Anderson and S.S. Srinivasan, *E-satisfaction and e-loyalty: a contingency framework, Psychology and Marketing* 20(2), 123-138 (2003).

11. F.F. Reicheld and P. Schefter, E-loyalty – Your Secret Weapon on the Web, *Harvard Business Review* 78(7-8), 105-113 (2000).

12. P.A. Pavlou and M. Fygenson, Understanding and Predicting Electronic Commerce Adoption: An Extension of the Theory of Planned Behaviour, *MIS Quarterly* 30(1), 115-143 (2006).

13. D. Gefen, E. Karahanna, and D.W. Straub, Trust and TAM in Online Shopping, An Integrated Model, *MIS Quarterly* 27(1), 51-90 (2003).

14. S. Ba and P.A. Pavlou, Evidence of the Effect of Trust Building Technology in Electronic Markets: Price Premiums and Buyer Behavior, *MIS Quarterly* 26(3), 243-268 (2002).

15. S.L. Järvenpää, T.R. Shaw, and S.D. Staples, Toward Contextualized Theories of Trust: The Role of Trust is Global Virtual Teams, *Information Systems Research* 15(3), 250-267 (2004).

16. D.H. McKnight and N.L. Chervany, What Trust Means in E-Commerce Customer Relationships: *An Interdisciplinary Conceptual Typology, International Journal of Electronic Commerce* 6(2) 35-59 (2002).

17 X. Hu, Z. Lin, A.B. Whinston, and H. Zhang, Hope or Hype: On the Viability of Escrow Services as Trusted Third Parties in Online Auction Environments, *Information Systems Research* 15(3), 236-249 (2004).

18. P. Ratnasingam, D. Gefen and P. A. Pavlou, The Role of Facilitating Conditions and Institutional Trust in Electronic Marketplaces, Journal of Electronic Commerce in Organizations 3(3), 69-82 (2005).

19. I. Pollach, Privacy Statements as a Means of Uncertainty Reduction in WWW Auctions, Journal of Organizational and End User Computing 18(1), 23-49 (2006).

20. D.B. Meinert, D.K. Peterson, J.R. Criswell, and M.D. Crossland, Privacy Policy Statements and Consumer Willingness to Provide Personal Information, *Journal of Electronic Commerce in Organizations* 4(1), 1-17 (2006).

21. A. Josang, R. Ismail, and C. Boyd, A survey of trust and reputation systems for online service provision, *Decision Support Systems* 43(2), 618-644 (2007).

22. J. Brown and J. Morgan, Reputation in Online Auctions: The Market For Trust, California Management Review 49(1), 61-81 (2006).

23. K.M. Kimery and M. McCord, Signals of Trustworthiness in E-Commerce: Consumer Understanding of Third-Party Assurance Seals, *Journal of Electronic Commerce in Organizations* 4(4) 52-74 (2006).

24. D. Gefen and T. Heart, On the Need to Include National Culture as a Central Issue in E-Commerce Trust Beliefs, *Journal of Global Information Technology Management* 14(4), 1-30 (2006).

25. T.S.H Teo, and J. Liu, Consumer trust in e-commerce in the United States, Singapore and China, Omega - *The International Journal of Management Science* 35(1), 22-38 (2007).

26. S. Otim and V. Grover, An empirical study on Web-based services and customer loyalty, European *Journal of Information Systems* 15(6), 527-541 (2006).

27. F. Wang and M. Head, How can the Web help build customer relationships? An empirical study on e-tailing, *Information & Management* 44(2), 115-129 (2007).

28. P. Luarn and H-H. Lin, A Customer Loyalty Model for E-Service Context, *Journal of Electronic Commerce Research* 4(4), 156-167 (2003).

29. C. Flavián and M. Guinalíu, *Consumer trust, perceived security and privacy policy Three basic elements of loyalty to a web site, Industrial Management & Data Systems* 106(5) 601-620 (2006)

30. L.C. Harris and M.H. Goode, The four levels of loyalty and the pivotal role of trust: a study of online service dynamics, Journal of Retailing 15(6), 139-158 (2004).

31. J.B. Thatcher and J.F. George, Commitment, Trust and Social Involvement: An Exploratory Study of Antecedents to Web Shopper Loyalty, *Journal of Organizational Computing and Electronic Commerce* 14(4), 243-268 (2004)

32. C. Flavián, M. Guinalíu, and Raquel Gurrea, The role played by perceived usability, satisfaction and trust on website loyalty, *Information and Management* 4(1), 1-14 (2006).

33. D. Li, G.J. Browne, and J.C. Wetherbe, Why Do Internet Users Stick with a Specific Web Site? A Relationship Perspective, *International Journal of Electronic Commerce* 10(4), 105-141 (2006).

34. J. Gummerus, V. Liljander, M. Pura, M. and A. van Riel, Customer loyalty to content-based web sites: the case of an online health-care service, *Journal of Services Marketing* 18(3) 175-186 (2004).

35. D. Cyr, K. Hassanein, M. Head, and A. Ivanov, *The role of social presence in establishing loyalty in e-Service environments, Interacting with Computers* 19(1)43-56 (2007).

36. D. Ribbink, A.C.R. van Riel, V. Liljander, and S. Streukens, Comfort your online customer: quality trust and loyalty on the internet, Managing Service Quality 14(6), 446-456 (2004)

37. D.A. Pitta and D. Fowler, Internet community forums: an untapped resource for consumer marketers, *Journal of Consumer Marketing* 22(5), 265-274 (2005).

38. H-Y. Ha, Factors Affecting Online Relationships and Impacts, *The Marketing Review* 4(2), 189-209 (2004).

39. A. Floh. and H. Treiblmaier, What Keeps the E-Banking Customer Loyal? A Multigroup Analysis of the Moderating Role of Consumer Characteristics on E-Loyalty in th Financial Service Industry, *Journal of Electronic Commerce Research* 7(2), 97-110 (2006).

40. K. Pennanen, T. Tiainen, and H.T. Luomala, A qualitative exploration of a consumer's value based trust: A framework development, *Qualitative Market Research: An International Journal* 10(1), 28-57 (2007).

Open Access: How Is Scholarly Information Service System Going?

Nanqiang Xia[1] and Yaokun Zhang[1]
1 Huazhong Normal University, Imformation Management Department
Luyu Road 152, 430079 Wuhan, China
{xnq1955,yaokunzhang}@yahoo.com.cn

Abstract. Open access movement has resulted in a change of the entire scholarly communication environment. Scholarly information service system (SISS) had a significant change which is represented in the emergency of various open access publishing mode and diversification of integrated value-added service providers. This paper analyzed this change, and discussed how academic library should react to the change; also some possible impacts on scientific communication were discussed.

1 Introduction

Nowadays, few scientists take part in the publishing processes of scientific literature which is closely associated with scientific research activities and leave it up to the Third Party, thus gradually form the scholarly information service system (SISS) which is independent of scientific research. SISS is an independent intermediate system which implements the scientific communication process between scientific information creators and users. It usually consists of publishers, issuers, indexing and abstracting service providers, online retrieval service providers and libraries especially academic libraries.

It's a routine that scientists publish their latest research achievements in academic journals since academic journals can both confirm the patent rights of discovery and ensure the timeliness of scientific communication. But since 1990's, international commercial academic journal publishing market has been controlled by several big publishers due to the increasingly fierce mergers and acquisitions. The price raising of academic journals due to the monopoly of academic journals publishing markets leads to a struggling library budgets during 1990s as we told it in terms of "serials

Please use the following format when citing this chapter:

Xia, N., Zhang, Y., 2007, in IFIP International Federation for Information Processing, Volume 252, Integration and Innovation Orient to E-Society Volume 2, eds. Wang, W., (Boston: Springer), pp. 153-159.

crisis" which means "scholarly communication crisis." According to ARL's latest data statistics, compared with the year 1986, serial expenditures in ARL libraries in 2005 had increased by 302%, serial unit cost had increased by 167%, but the serials purchased only increased by 42%[1]. To solve serials crisis goals, academia initiated the open access movement.

The Budapest Open Access Initiative (BOAI) defined open access as: "By 'open access' to this literature, it means its free availability on the public internet, permitting any users to read, download, copy, distribute, print, search, or link to the full texts of these articles, crawl them for indexing, pass them as data to software, or use them for any other lawful purpose, without financial, legal, or technical barriers other than those inseparable from gaining access to the internet itself. The only constraint on reproduction and distribution, and the only role for copyright in this domain, should be to give authors control over the integrity of their work and the right to be properly acknowledged and cited."[2] For academia, Open access is both an already existing informal scientific communication mode (i.e. e-print archive) and a completely new scholarly publishing mode as we call it open access publishing. Further more, we believe that open access represents a circumstance under which the SISS will change a lot or be totally reformed.

2   The architecture of open access SISS

Under the open access circumstance, the SISS has changed a lot which is mostly expressed in the establishment of open access SISS while the traditional SISS still is working and may not varnish in a very long period. The traditional SISS and the open access will be worked together to ensure the effective running of scientific communication. The architecture of open access SISS was shown in figure 1.

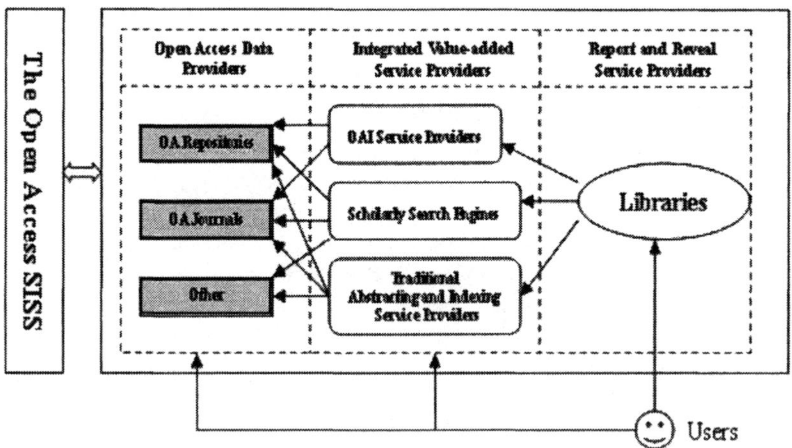

Fig. 1. The architecture of open access SISS

The procedure of the open access SISS is:

· Open access data providers provide resources entity and its related metadata to public through particular ways (i.e. OAI-PMH);

· Data retrieval service providers harvest resources metadata provided by open access data providers and provide integrated data retrieval while also create the linkage to resources entity;

· Data indexing service providers analyze the citing issues and importance of resources through certain mechanism;

· Libraries report and reveal open access resources through resource navigation system, and provide user education, knowledge services etc.

3   The changing points of open access SISS

Compared with traditional SISS, open access SISS has lots of changing points which especially existed in the two aspects below.

3.1   Emergency of various open access data provides

In traditional SISS, scholarly journals mostly adopted peer review system as the only resources while other forms of resources which are also very important to scientific research like preprint were excluded. This problem can be solved in open access SISS properly but may be not so perfect. There are lots of open access data providers in open access SISS, but generally speaking, the two kinds below are the most important.

3.1.1 Open Access (OA) Repository

Sometimes OA repository can be told in terms of e-print archive. BOAI defined e-print archive as "a collection of digital documents."[3] OA repository can be regarded as a collection of digital resources. OA repository depends on self-archiving, that is to say, authors can submit their digital works into the OA repositories. OA repository can be organized by discipline (e.g. arXiv for physics) or institution (e.g. Escholarship Repository for the University of California). It may content research paper (preprint, postprint), technical report, theses and dissertations, course materials, learning objects, data files, audio and video files, institutional records, or any other kind of digital file.

Early OA repository (mostly disciplinary) was introduced as an informal scientific communication mode, not for open access purpose. It's a definite innovation to incorporate OA repository into open access SISS since it can not only improve the pace of communication, but also facilitate the open access movement.

With the fast growing of open access, OA repositories has adopted a uniform protocol called open access initiative protocol for metadata harvesting (OAI-PMH) to accelerate the distribution and access of scholarly resources.

3.1.2 OA Journals

Though OA repository is regarded as a very effective way to achieve open access, there are lots of critiques about it especially in some subjects which are sensitive to experiment data like biology and chemistry. Open access journal, as a substitute for subscription-based journal, has both open access feature and peer review process and, is becoming popular in scholarly publishing arena.

OA journal can be divided into three types according to Sally Morris [4]:

· Partial open access journals

Some publishers routinely make parts of the articles freely available on web as an effective way to attract more readers to their journals. Still this can be seen as a measure of helping non-OA journals to migrate to fully open access journals.

· Delayed open access journals

Some publishers make their previous issues free available on web after a certain period. This mode was adopted by some not-for-profit publishers. For example, Oxford University Press (OUP) had announced a partnership with Oxford University Library Services (OULS) in support of the national SHERPA project in November 2003, allowing worldwide users to freely access the many of the academic articles published by OUP since 2002 [5].

· Fully open access journals

Fully open access journals mean that journals will be freely available on web to everyone once published. According to Directory of Open Access Journals (DOAJ), there are currently 2656 fully open access journals in the directory [6] while this amount is certainly smaller than the accurate one.

3.1.3 Other

Besides OA repositories and journals, there are other types which can also provide open access. For example, personal website especially some world famous scholars' websites, usually contain a lot of valuable resources. Another example is institutional website like ARL's website we cited before.

3.2   Diversification of integrated value-added service providers

Integrated value-added service providers are the essential part of SISS. Without which, scientific communication can not run normally. Since open access is a new environment, it urgently needs the integrated value-added service providers which match it. There are three typical types of integrated value-added service providers in open access SISS.

3.2.1 Providers based on OAI

Providers based on OAI can also be called OAI service providers. An OAI service provider can harvest metadata from many compliant and provide an integrated interface for users to having "one-step" searching. For example, Directory of Open Access, an open access journals directory edited by Sweden Lund university library, besides providing journals browsing, also provides integrated journal articles searching. Another example is Citebase which is a semi-autonomous citation index for the free, online research literature. It can harvest the metadata from OAI-PMH compliant archives, parse and link their references. Citation analysis can also be carried out.

3.2.2 Scholarly search engine

Search engine is not yet a strange thing to scholars since it had been used by many of them to search academic information especially open access resources. But ordinary search engines have quite a lot of information which has no relationship with scientific research thus can hardly fulfill the demands of scholars. Scholarly search engine has filtered non-academic information, and becomes a very important service provider in open access SISS. Scholarly search engine can search and index open access resources efficiently for the relatively mature technology and the wide collaboration with OAI compliant. There are many typical scholarly search engines like Scirus, Citeseer, etc.

3.2.3 Traditional abstracting and indexing service providers

As we all know, traditional abstracting and indexing service providers provide detailed information about research articles (i.e. title, author(s), abstract, keywords, journal, issue), but generally speaking they do not deal with article full-text. In open access environment, due to the free access to full-text, detailed information about article is much more important than article itself. Thus, traditional abstracting and indexing service providers can take the already existed advantage and participate in open access movement with an active gesture while it's also very important for the development of them.

At the present time, some famous traditional abstracting and indexing service providers such as Medline, CA, SCI have been indexing the open access journals. And in 2005, Thomson Scientific released Web Citation Index (WCI) which can be used to retrieve and access open access resources on web. It attempts to connect preprints, institutional repositories, open access journals and other resources together and becomes a consisting part of Web Of Knowledge platform.

4   How are libraries reacting?

In open access environment, users' dependence on libraries' subscription will gradually decrease. This would lead a relatively decline of position of libraries in open access SISS. Libraries should extend its service contents and improve its service modes to seize the opportunity in open access movement.

Libraries have done a lot of work as information "guider" in recent years. A very exciting practice is subject information gateway. Since open access is still a strange word to most people. Libraries should introduce open access ideas and reveal open access resources in effective ways such as put introduction on website of libraries, open lectures on open access etc. According to a investigation about the websites of libraries of Chinese "211" universities conducted by the author, nearly 60% have practices in this form.

Libraries had aware of the importance of to be a part of open access data providers. At the present time, lots of libraries have taken part in the construction of open access repositories mostly institutional repositories. In China mainland, Xiamen university library has established scholarly repository using DSpace software. But large scale practices have not began.

5   Challenge to scientific communication of open access SISS

The establishment of open access SISS give a chance to break out "journals crisis", scientific communication can be improved greatly. In a word, open access SISS combines the advantages of formal communication and its informal counterpart.

But like one coin which has both of two sides, scientific communication also confronts with challenges in open access environment. One of most important challenges is that the base of communication would change.

In traditional environment, the core of scientific communication system is the "peer review system", that is to ensure the quality of academic articles by gatekeeper. The base of scientific communication is peer review, in other words, authority of articles. In open access environment, the base of scientific communication has been derived into whether the resource can be accessed. If one article can be accessed (or indexed), even in a short period, it can be cited. Otherwise, it can't. As we all know, not all the open access resources are high qualified, some of them may be totally wrong. Whether dismissing of peer review process can lead to follow the same errors or not is still a problem which is worth to deep research.

Moreover, the long-term access of some open access resources should be doubted. Both the personal websites and institutional websites are highly unstable while not all the OA repositories provide permanent preservation. The extensive use of these resources may lead to "non-verification" of academic research.

References

1. ARL Statistics 2004-05,
http://www.arl.org/stats/annualsurveys/arlstats/stats0405.shtml.[2007-04-02].

2. Budapest Open Access Initiative: Frequently Asked Questions.
 http://www.earlham.edu/~peters/fos/boaifaq.htm. [2007-04-02].

3. Self-Archiving FAQ, http://www.eprints.org/openaccess/self-faq/. [2007-04-02].

4. M. Sally, "Open Access: How Are Publishers Reacting?", *Serial Review*, 30(4), 304-307 (2004).

5. PRESS RELEASE: OUP Supports Oxford University Library Services "Open Archives" Initiative ,http://www.sherpa.ac.uk/news/oupoulspr.htm. [2007-04-02].

6. Directory of Open access Journals ,http://www.doaj.org/.[2007-04-02].

Analysis and Modelling of Willingness to Receive Reward for Relay in Ad Hoc Networks

Naoyuki Karasawa[1,2], Kyoko Yamori[3,2], Kenji Donkai[2],
and Yoshiaki Tanaka[2,4]

1   Department of Information Engineering, Niigata University
2-8050 Ikarashi, Nishi-ku, Niigata, 950-2181 Japan
karasawa@ie.niigata-u.ac.jp
2   Global Information and Telecommunication Institute
Waseda University
1-3-10 Nishi-Waseda, Shinjuku-ku, Tokyo, 169-0051 Japan
3   Department of Business Administration, Asahi University
1851 Hozumi, Mizuho-shi, Gifu, 501-0296, Japan
4   Research Institute for Science and Engineering, Waseda University
17 Kikuicho, Shinjuku-ku, Tokyo, 162-0044 Japan
kyamori@alice.asahi-u.ac.jp, ken-don@toki.waseda.jp, ytanaka@waseda.jp

Abstract. In ad hoc networks, relay nodes use their limited resources such as battery capacity, CPU, buffer, etc. to support other nodes' communications. This discourages users from joining an ad hoc network and becoming a relay node. Receiving a reward for supporting relay may encourage users to join such networks. This research focuses on the factors of residual battery power, and time during which AC power supply is not available. In this paper, the willingness to receive reward for relay in ad hoc networks is investigated by questionnaire survey. The relation between such factors and the willingness to receive rewards for relay is analysed quantitatively and models of willingness to receive reward for relay are estimated.

1   Introduction

An ad hoc network consists of self-organizing nodes using multi-hop relay. In ad hoc networks, a source node communicates with a destination node via a multi-hop path using other nodes as relay nodes when the source and the destination nodes are out of communication range of each other. While relaying, relay nodes use their limited resources such as battery capacity, CPU, buffer, etc. to support other nodes'

Please use the following format when citing this chapter:

Karasawa, N., Yamori, K., Donkai, K., Tanaka, Y., 2007, in IFIP International Federation for Information Processing, Volume 252, Integration and Innovation Orient to E-Society Volume 2, eds. Wang, W., (Boston: Springer), pp. 160-167.

communications.   This discourages users from joining ad hoc networks and becoming a relay node.

Charging / rewarding methods [1], [2] have been proposed as methods for overcoming problems that occur with relay. In ad hoc networks that use charging / rewarding methods, all nodes have some initial currency. Source nodes can communicate with destination nodes via a path consisting of relay nodes only if the source node can pay at least one unit of currency to each relay node. Nakano et al. [3] showed that charging / rewarding methods reduce unfairness in ad hoc networks and decrease the variance among the nodes induced by frequency of relay. Therefore, rewarding relay nodes can offset disadvantages for relay such as consumption of battery power and processing loads, etc.

In this paper, we investigate the willingness to receive reward for relay using a questionnaire survey in an ad hoc network where relay nodes receive rewards for relay. We focus on residual battery power and the time during which AC power supply is not available. The relation between such factors and the willingness to receive reward for relay is analysed quantitatively. We also discuss how such factors influence willingness to receive reward for relay. Finally, some models of willingness to receive reward for relay are estimated.

2   Questionnaire Survey on the Willingness to Receive Reward for Relay

An overview of the questionnaire survey used to investigate the willingness to receive reward (WTR) for relay in ad hoc networks is described. In this paper, WTR for relay is defined as a reward that is capable of motivating users to relay other nodes' communications. Suppose that ad hoc networks use charging / rewarding methods, which is illustrated in Fig.1. In such ad hoc networks, the relay node receives a reward for relay in proportion to the amount of communication when it relays other nodes' communications.

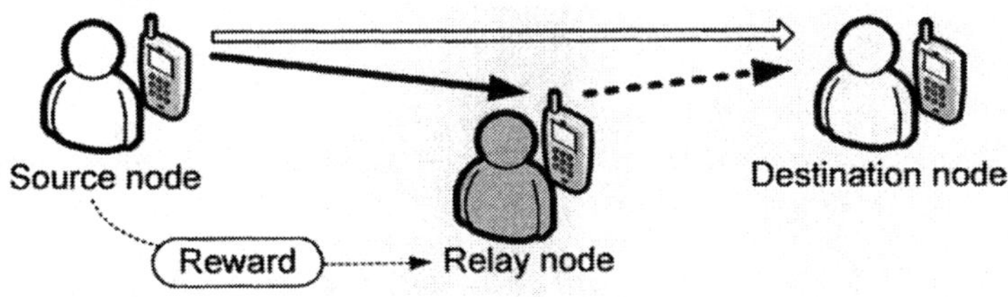

Fig. 1. Ad hoc network using charging / rewarding method.

WTR for relay seems to be affected by several factors. This paper focuses on a type of mobile terminal, the residual battery power during relay, and the time during which AC power supply is not available. In particular, it is expected that WTR for relay depends on residual battery power and the time during which AC power supply is not available. The questionnaire survey is designed to test the following hypothesis.

Hypothesis: There are positive correlations between battery power consumption and WTR for relay and between AC power unavailability duration and WTR for relay.

Here, battery power consumption means the total amount of battery power consumed by several functions of a mobile terminal. AC power unavailability duration means the time during which AC power supply is not available. To test the hypothesis, it is necessary to quantify the relations between various factors and WTR for relay.

Suppose that each node in an ad hoc network uses a mobile terminal. For example, a cellular phone with a wireless LAN device or a laptop PC with a wireless LAN is considered as mobile terminal. In this questionnaire survey, power consumption for relay is not considered, as it is negligible in comparison with the power consumption by LCD display, CPU, and so on. The node is able to use a mobile terminal for 6 hours when the battery power is at 1, i.e. fully charged. The questionnaire assumes various battery conditions. Namely, the battery power consumption is 0, 0.5, 0.75, and 0.92, and the AC power unavailability duration is 3, 6, and 12 hours. The response format of the questionnaire requires the respondent to input an arbitrary value as their WTR for relay with a duration of one minute.

3   Analysis of Questionnaire Results

There are 194 effective responses to the questionnaire (male 131, female 63). The WTR of each sample is normalized so that the maximum value is 1. Only if all WTR values are 0, the normalized WTR values are set to 0. The normalized WTR is summed for each condition and their mean values are taken to be the mean opinion scores (MOS). The MOS thus obtained is used to estimate a WTR curve using regression analysis. Linear, logarithmic, exponential, and power approximations are used for approximation. We determine whether each of the four functions is applicable from their contribution coefficients.

The WTR curve for the relation between WTR and battery power consumption is best approximated as shown in (1),

$$U = \alpha_r \exp(\beta_r r),\qquad(1)$$

where battery power consumption is represented as r and WTR as U. The values of parameters α_r and β_r and the contribution coefficient R^2 are shown in Table 1.

Table 1. Parameters α_r and β_r in (1).

AC ower unavailability duration [hours]	α_r	β_r	R^2
3	0.287	0.715	0.889
6	0.344	0.748	0.925
12	0.462	0.725	0.912

For the relation between WTR and the AC power unavailability duration, the WTR curves estimated by linear approximation are as shown in (2),

$$U = \alpha_t t + \beta_t , \qquad (2)$$

where the AC power unavailability duration is represented by t and the WTR by U. Parameters α_t and β_t and contribution coefficients R^2 are shown in Table 2.

Table 2. Parameters α_t and β_t in (2).

Battery power consumption	α_t	β_t	R^2
0	0.0205	0.241	0.999
0.5	0.0254	0.297	0.998
0.75	0.0330	0.367	0.997
0.92	0.0411	0.498	1.00

Consequently, the WTR curves of the battery power consumption and the WTR curves of the AC power unavailability durations are significant because the contribution coefficients of the estimated regression formulae are sufficiently large. Figs. 2 and 3 show the WTR curves of the battery power consumption and the WTR curves of the AC power unavailability duration, respectively.

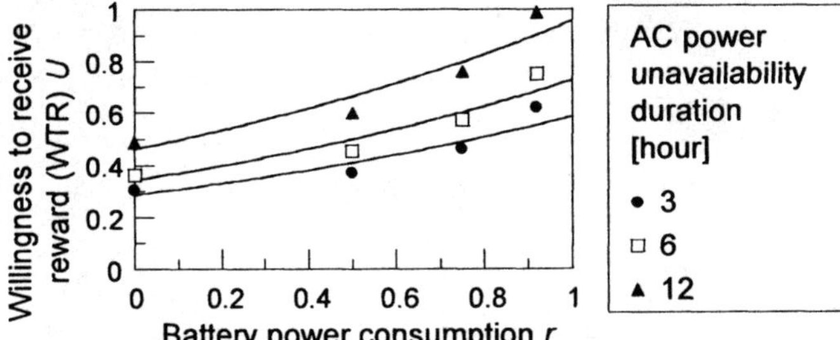

Fig.2. WTR U and battery power consumption r.

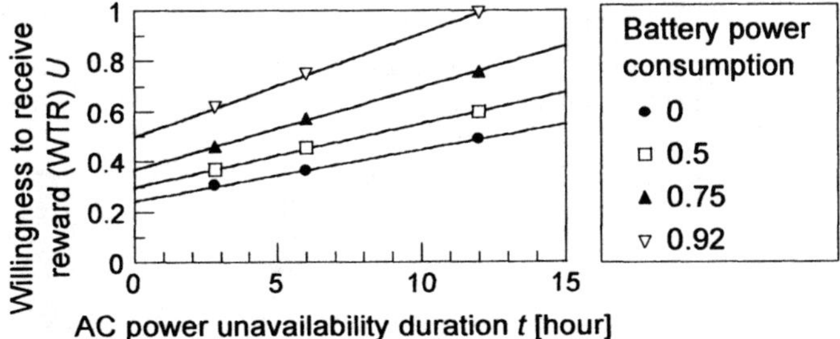

Fig. 3. WTR U and AC power unavailability duration t.

To establish a method of estimating WTR for any battery condition in all cases, we analyse and discuss the relation of factors in the WTR for relay. In this paper, it is assumed that the WTR for relay depends on the battery conditions of the mobile terminal. Battery power consumption and AC power unavailability duration are considered as battery conditions. Therefore, the WTR curve is defined by,

$$U = f(U_r, U_t).\tag{3}$$

Here, U_r is a variable dependent on battery power consumption and U_t is a variable dependent on AC power unavailability duration.

There are two assumptions in (3). It is assumed that U_r and U_t are factors that influence U independently and that U_r and U_t are correlated factors that influence U. In this paper, using these assumptions, we devise WTR curves that fit each model.

5   Estimating the WTR Curve: Independent Factors

In this section, it is assumed that U_r and U_t are independent of each other. Then, the relation between U_r and U_t is given in the form of their sum and we obtain (4).

$$U = a_0 + a_1 U_r + a_2 U_t,\tag{4}$$

where a_0, a_1, and a_2 are parameters. U_r can be approximated by $k_r \alpha_r \exp(\beta_r r)$ where k_r is constant because the relation between WTR and battery power consumption can be approximated by exponential curves from (1). U_t can be approximated by $k_t(\alpha_t t + \beta_t)$ where k_t is constant because the relation between WTR and the AC power unavailability duration can be approximated by linear equations from (2). So, (4) is denoted by (5).

$$U = a'_0 + a'_1 \exp(\beta_r r) + a'_2 t,\tag{5}$$

where a'_0, a'_1 and a'_2 are parameters. Consider $\exp(\beta_r r)$ in (5). In general, it is known that $\exp(x)$ is represented by

$$\exp(x) = \sum_{n=0}^{\infty} \frac{1}{n!} x^n.\tag{6}$$

In this paper, (7) is assumed because the numerical results of $\exp(\beta_r r)$ are sufficiently close to the numerical results of (6) when $x = \beta_r r$ and $n = 2$.

$$\exp(\beta_r r) \approx 1 + \frac{1}{1!}(\beta_r r) + \frac{1}{2!}(\beta_r r)^2 = 1 + \beta_r r + \frac{\beta_r^2}{2} r^2.\tag{7}$$

Using (7) in (5), (8) is obtained.

$$U = a''_0 + a''_1 r + a''_2 r^2 + a''_3 t,\tag{8}$$

where a''_0, a''_1, a''_2, and a''_3 are parameters.

To estimate the WTR curve with the best fit, the WTR curve estimated by (5) and the WTR curve estimated by (8) are compared. First, to devise WTR curve with (5), multiple regression analysis is used. In this multiple regression analysis, $\exp(\beta_r r)$

and t are denoted by predictor variables, and U is denoted by criterion variable. As a result, WTR curve is shown as follows:

$$U = -0.260 + 0.400\exp(\beta_r r) + 0.0299t, \qquad (9)$$

where β_r are determined by t. The contribution coefficient of (9) is 0.918.

Consider β_r in (9). As mentioned in Table 1, β_r is obtained by constrained time t. Thus the curve fitting β_r using various approximation methods are studied. However, we cannot select curves with a good fit because their contribution coefficients are not sufficiently large. Table 1 shows that β_r is irregularly distributed within a narrow range. So, it is assumed that β_r is determined by the mean values. From Table 1, the mean value of β_r is 0.730. We substitute this value into (9).

$$U = -0.260 + 0.400\exp(0.730r) + 0.0299t. \qquad (10)$$

The contribution coefficient of (10) is 0.917.

Then, let us devise WTR curve by (8). For (8), multiple regression analysis is used. In this multiple regression analysis, r, r^2, and t are denoted by the predictor variables, and U is denoted by the criterion variable. The WTR obtained by multiple regression analysis curve is shown by (11).

$$U = 0.177 - 0.177r + 0.651r^2 + 0.0300t. \qquad (11)$$

The contribution coefficient of (11) is 0.970.

Deliberate the WTR curve estimated by (5) and the WTR curve estimated by (8). The contribution coefficient of each WTR curve is sufficiently large. Hence, each WTR curve is significant. In the derivation from (5), β_r is approximated by mean values as an approximate equation. However, there is a model by which the contribution coefficient of an approximate equation of β_r is not sufficiently large. It is considered that the contribution coefficient affects the predictive accuracy of the WTR curve in this model. By contrast, (8) is estimated by approximation using (6). Using (6), it is possible to show (8) basically in the form of a polynomial equation even if degree of a polynomial equation increases.

6   Estimating the WTR Curve: Correlated Factors

In this section, it is assumed that U_r and U_t are correlated. Under this assumption, the relational expression between U_r and U_t is given in the form of the product and (12) is obtained.

$$U = b_0 U_r U_t, \qquad (12)$$

where b_0 is parameter. As in the previous section, substituting $k_r \alpha_r \exp(\beta_r r)$ and $k_t(\alpha_t t + \beta_t)$ into U_r and U_t, (12) is described in (13).

$$U = b_0 \{a_r \exp(\beta_r r)\}(\alpha_t t + \beta_t). \qquad (13)$$

Then, taking a logarithm of both sides of (13), (13) is denoted as follows:

$$\log(U) = b'_0 + b'_1 r + b'_2 \log\{1 + (\alpha_t/\beta_t)t\}, \tag{14}$$

where b'_0, b'_1 and b'_2 are parameters. Consider $\log\{1 + (\alpha_t/\beta_t)t\}$. In general, it is known that x is greater than $\log(1 + x)$ when x is greater than 0. For simplicity, (15) is assumed by using this relation.

$$\log\{1 + (\alpha_t/\beta_t)t\} \approx (\alpha_t/\beta_t)t . \tag{15}$$

Using (15) in (14), (16) is obtained as follows:

$$\log(U) = b''_0 + b''_1 r + b''_2 t , \tag{16}$$

where b''_0, b''_1 and b''_2 are parameters.

To estimate WTR curve that have good fit, WTR curve estimated by (14) and WTR curve estimated by (16) are compared. First, in order to devise WTR curve by (14), multiple regression analysis is used. In this multiple regression analysis, r and $\log\{t + (\beta_t/\alpha_t)\}$ are denoted by the predictor variables, and $\log(U)$ is denoted by the criterion variable. The WTR curve resulting from the multiple regression analysis is shown as follows (See Appendix):

$$U = 0.0182\exp(0.732r)(t + 11.7). \tag{17}$$

The contribution coefficient of (17) is 0.937.

Let us devise WTR curves using (16) and multiple regression analysis in which r and t are denoted by the predictor variables, and $\log(U)$ is denoted by the criterion variable. The resulting WTR curve is shown as follows:

$$U = 0.247\exp(0.729r)\exp(0.0527t). \tag{18}$$

The contribution coefficient of (18) is 0.934.

Deliberate the WTR curve estimated by (14) and the WTR curve estimated by (16). The contribution coefficient of each WTR curve is sufficiently large. Hence, each WTR curve is significant. In particular, it is considered that (18) is simple because there are fewer variables in the WTR curve estimated by (16) than in the WTR curve estimated by (14). For each parameter of (12), the coefficient that affects the whole type is equivalent to b_0 of (12). Then, b_0 of (12) means users' underlying parameters for WTR for relay.

7   Conclusion

In this paper, we focused on the residual battery power and the time during which AC power supply is not available as factors in WTR for relay in ad hoc networks as investigated by questionnaire survey. Based on the results of the questionnaire survey, the relation between battery-related factors and WTR for relay is analysed quantitatively. Two models are considered in this paper: one in which the factors are independent and the other in which the factors are correlated. The best-fit curves of the WTR by relay are estimated in both models. The contribution coefficients of the WTR curves estimated by using both assumptions are sufficiently large.

Consequently, both assumptions produce models with good fits for the WTR for relay.

In future work we intend to analyse WTR for relay along with other factors.

References

1. Buttyan, L., Hubaux, J.: Stimulating cooperation in self-organizing mobile ad hoc networks: ACM/Kluwer Mobile Networks and Applications (MONET) (2003) 579-592.
2. Salem, N.B., Buttyan, L., Hubaux, J.P., Jakobsson, M.: A charging and rewarding scheme for packet forwarding in multi-hop cellular networks: 4th ACM Symposium on Mobile Ad Hoc Networking and Computing (MobiHoc 2003) (2003) 13-24.
3. Nakano, K., Panta, R., Sengoku, M., Shinoda, S.: On performance of a charging/rewarding scheme in mobile ad-hoc networks: 2005 IEEE International Symposium on Circuits and Systems (ISCAS 2005), vol.3. (2005) 2962-2966.

Appendix: Derivation of (17)

The derivation of (17) is described. From (14),

$$\log(U) = b_0''' + b_1'''r + b_2'''\log(t + \beta_t/\alpha_t), \qquad (A1)$$

where b'''_0, b'''_1 and b'''_2 are parameters. Then, multiple regression analysis is used. In this multiple regression analysis, r and $\log(t + \beta_t/\alpha_t)$ are denoted by the predictor variables, and $\log(U)$ is denoted by the criterion variable. The WTR curve resulting from the multiple regression analysis is shown as follows:

$$\log(U) = -4.00 + 0.732r + 1.02\log(t + \beta_t/\alpha_t), \qquad (A2)$$

where α_t and β_t are determined by r. The contribution coefficient of (A2) is 0.957.

From Table 2, α_t and β_t are obtained by r and regression analysis is used to estimate α_t and β_t. As a result, α_t and β_t are approximated by exponential approximation. Then, the estimated results are shown in (A3) and (A4).

$$\alpha_t = 0.0195\exp(0.731r), \qquad (A3)$$

$$\beta_t = 0.228\exp(0.729r). \qquad (A4)$$

The contribution coefficients of (A3) and (A4) are 0.933 and 0.894, respectively. Calculating β_t/α_t using (A3) and (A4), β_t/α_t is 11.7exp(-0.002r). From this result, we obtain (A5).

$$\log(U) = -4.00 + 0.732r + 1.02\log\{t + 11.7\exp(-0.002r)\}. \qquad (A5)$$

Consider $1.02\{t + 11.7\exp(-0.002r)\}$ in (A5). In this paper, to simplify a WTR curve, (A5) is approximated by (A6). Therefore, (17) is obtained from (A6).

$$\log(U) = -4.00 + 0.732r + \log(t + 11.7). \qquad (A6)$$

A Keyword Extraction Based Model for Web Advertisement

Ning Zhou[1], Jiaxin Wu[1,2], Shaolong Zhang[2]

[1] Research Center of Information Resources, Wuhan University, Wuhan, 430072, China

[2] School of Information Management, Wuhan University, Wuhan, 430072, China

logofish@126.com

Abstract. In this paper, a keyword extraction based model is proposed to deal with web advertisement. In our model, we take web advertisement as an information retrieval problem. Web page and advertisement are firstly represented with a simple data structure which will be the source file for keyword extraction based on χ^2-measure for single document. Later we get two vectors to make a retrieval process with a specific similarity function. This model is suitable for common cases of web advertisement. It supports the web page selection in view of advertisement as well as the advertisement selection for specific web page.

1 Introduction

With the rapid growth of internet, web becomes a significant medium of our daily life. More and more people are accustomed to read news, publish their blogs, search information on internet. Internet is turning to be a virtual society where global user exchange and share information as well as service.

Where there is a medium, where there will be advertisement. So web is growing to be a vital place to post advertisements for each company which could be traditional company as well as innovative company. It will be meaningful to construct the model for the post of advisement on web pages. This model must make： 1) An advertisement is post on a web page which latent customer of advisement product will browse. 2) A web page should better include most relevant advertisement to maximize the probability for the user to click. 3) There should be a quantity to show which site or page is the best one to post ads.

There are some obvious problems on web advertisement: 1) the advertisement is not related with the content of web pages, and user has no interest to click.2) Too

Please use the following format when citing this chapter:

Zhou, N., Wu, J., Zhang, S., 2007, in IFIP International Federation for Information Processing, Volume 252, Integration and Innovation Orient to E-Society Volume 2, eds. Wang, W., (Boston: Springer), pp. 168-175.

much unrelated ads make the browsing process to be disappointing. 3) Ads are posted on a large quantity of pages but bring few clicks. 4) Company can't evaluate which site or page is the most beneficial one to post ads until the end of advertisement period.

Many papers pay attention to the web advertisement, but most of them do that in a qualitative way. They give some principles in how to choose and organize the posting strategy, but seldom bring quantitative method to evaluate the ads posting. This paper pays more attention to the data structure of web page and advertisement. Later, based on the data structure, we give a quantitative evaluation of similarity between web page and advertisement which will make it easier to choose the ads for web page and in return, to select web pages for ads.

This paper is organized in 4 sections. Section 2 discusses several recent approaches in web advertisement. Section 3 describes our model in detail. Section 4 gives our experiment result and the work to enhance our model in future.

2 Related Work

Online advertising continues to be a significant source of income for many Internet-based organizations. Banner advertisement is important advertising style for famous websites. Ali[4] extends the problem of scheduling banner advertisement to a more realistic setting, where the customer is allowed to specify a set of acceptable display frequency, the Lagrangian decomposition-based solution was presented to provide good schedules in a reasonable period of time.

Thawani[5] proposed a system for the selection and presentation of advertisements based on detected program events and profiles contained in the home information system. In this system, a comprehensive event prediction and event analysis is performed based on which relevant ads are either selected for transport stream insertion or for caching purposes.

Vincent[3] describes a new advertising agent based on user information. In this agent, the user's interests are discovered by the Order Pattern Mining algorithm and represented in user's profiles with the Gaussian curve transformation. User's profile is used to implement an effective and efficient advertisement mechanism.

Because user's profile is hard to collect, especially user doesn't want to or can't express themselves clearly about their interests to large quantity of products and advertisements, so we put the profile aside. Also the keywords advertisements still a very tidy and meaningful style which is used as the main advertisement style of many search engines, such as Google, Baidu, Yahoo. So we take the advertising as the problem of information retrieval problem of the match between advertisement and web page, and in the end, we could get the similarity as well as a ranked list which is very suitable to the selection of advertisement.

3 Keyword Extraction Based Model

3.1 Data Structure of web Page and Advertisement

In this model, only two kinds of sources are considered, web page and advertisement. We form web page as 5 fields: classID, url, title, meta keywords, text.

classID stands for the category id of given web page in a predefined class catalog which must be carefully designed to cover most of pages; URL is the url of web page such as http://sports.sina.com.cn/; Title is the text in the title field of html source code; Meta keywords is the meta data field in head field of html source code; text is the main text which contains the main content of web page. A html web page should be parsed to get these four field. Then this five construct like the table-1 below.

Table 1. Web page data structure.

classID	sports
url	http://sports.sina.com.cn/cba/2006-12-24/21172659112.shtml
title	I like music and pop star.
Meta keywords	Sports, Basketball, Sina, YiJianlian, CBA
text	Yi Jian Lian gets 23 points; he is a talent basketball player.

Advertisement is divided into 5 fields too: classID, title, keywords, URL, description. Where classID has the same meaning with web page's classID; Title is the title of advertisement; Keywords is related to the company or product; URL stands for the web site of company or the activity site of marketing; description gives a detail description to the product, company or related matter. An advertisement example is in the table-2 below.

Table 2. Advertisement data structure.

classID	literature
url	www.firstbook.org
title	Queen of the Scene
keywords	book, firstbook, literature
description	Grammy-winner Queen Latifah writes, a book for kids.

The structure of web page and advertisement are simple enough to abstract both of them. After getting the structured data source, next process will be the word segmentation and keyword extraction.

3.2 Word Segmentation and Keyword Extraction

In web page structure, text field holds the main meaning. According to vector space model[4], each web page can be seen as a document, text must be segmented as many weighted keywords which all together hold the semantics of a document. Chinese is a kind of language in which there is no separator character (in English, space is separator) to separate the keywords in a sentence. So it is more complex to segment text of Chinese into keywords. We use Hailiang Technology's word segmentation software to implement Chinese word segmentation.

After segmentation of text, we will get a bundle of keywords, and each keyword is called a term in a document. Then we must make each term weighted to assure some term which approximate the semantics of document have larger weight, and vice versa. In traditional way, the weight of given term is calculated in equation-1, called tf-idf scheme[6] after all the documents are processed.

$$w_{i,j} = tf * idf = \frac{freq_{i,j}}{Max_l\, freq_{l,j}} * \log\left(\frac{N}{n_i}\right) \tag{1}$$

Where tf stands for term frequency; $freq_{i,j}$ is the raw frequency of term k_i in the document d_j; maxl $freq_{l,j}$ is the maximum value of the term frequency over all terms which are mentioned in the text of the document d_j. N is the total numbers of documents, n_i is the numbers of document which contains $term_i$.

But when we take web page as the document, the total number of web pages is unstable. At the same time, the text of a web page with a definite URL is also variable, so, td-idf scheme is not suitable here. We apply a single document keyword extraction method presented by [1], which could get weighted keywords based on single document using word co-occurrence statistical information. Because this method is English oriented, we tune it to fit Chinese by using Chinese word-segmentation tool mentioned above.

1. Word segmentation

In the text of web pages, not all the words are meaningful although they maybe appear frequently such as pronoun, conjunction and some frequently used verb. They are treated as stop words which is stored in a stop words list. Noun and verb is the units to segment in a sentence. After all the noun and verb are extracted, the construction of word co-occurrence matrix will be done.

2. Word co-occurrence matrix

In order to construct word co-occurrence matrix, the top N terms with high frequency are extracted by ranking of term frequency in descent order. Then we define the meaning of co-occurrence as: if $term_i$ and $term_j$ appear in a same unit which is predefined, then they co-occur once, and $freq_{i,j}$ should be added one. Here we make the unit as a sentence which is separated by Chinese punctuation such as '。','！','？'.

Our purpose to construct word co-occurrence matrix is to find the most representative terms for a web page. It is time consuming to calculate all possible term pairs. So we just compute the co-occurrence frequency between each terms and top N high frequency terms. It is obvious that the matrix is symmetrical, so $freq_{i,j}$ is equal to $freq_{j,i}$.

3. Calculation of χ'^2 value

Based on co-occurrence matrix, the χ'^2 value is calculated for each term. The higher of the χ'^2 value, the more important of the term to represent the semantics of document. χ'^2 value can be calculated in equation-2.

$$\chi^2(\omega) = \sum_{g \in G} \frac{\left(freq(\omega, g) - n_w p_g\right)^2}{n_w p_g} \tag{2}$$

$$\chi'^{2}(\omega) = \chi^{2}(\omega) - \max_{g \in G} \left\{ \frac{\left(freq(\omega, g) - n_w p_g \right)^2}{n_w p_g} \right\}$$

G as the set of top N frequent terms; g is a member of G; ω as the current term; p_g as (the sum of the total number of terms in sentences where g appears) divided by (the total number of terms in the document); n_w as the total number of terms in sentences where w appears. freq (ω, g) as the co-occurrence frequency between term pair ω and g. We take $\chi'^{2}(\omega)$ as the measure of term ω. The higher value of $\chi'^{2}(\omega)$, the bigger weight of ω should be assigned.

4. Normalization of $\chi'2(\omega)$

$\chi'^{2}(\omega)$ value's range is not between 0 and 1. It should be normalized to [0, 1] in equation-3. Then the weight will be assigned to each term as term-weight.

$$weight_i = \frac{\chi'^{2}(i)}{\max_l \chi'^{2}(l)} \quad (3)$$

Table-3 is an example of keyword extraction results from a web page, which is about the car. After calculating and Normalizing $\chi'^{2}(\omega)$ value, top 6 terms which have higher $\chi'^{2}(\omega)$ value are listed. It shows that a term which have high frequency doesn't necessarily have high $\chi'^{2}(\omega)$ value.

Table 3. Top 6 keywords after keyword extraction.

term	frequency	$\chi'^{2}(\omega)$	normalized $\chi'^{2}(\omega)$
automobile	17	519.22	1
company	11	347.54	0.67
market	8	305.52	0.59
trade	12	222.56	0.43
car	9	206.75	0.40
brand	4	174.92	0.34

5. Similarity

After the extraction of weight for each term in web page, we could extract the weight of terms in the description field of advertisement in the same way.

Both webpage and advertisement can be transformed to vector space model.

1) Keywords vector (KV)

Web page's meta keywords field can be represented as meta keywords vector, by inserting the keywords of title and keywords of high importance in the text field of page into meta keywords vector we will get the keywords vector (KV). Each keyword in KV is assigned in the way below:

Calculate the frequency of $term_i$ in meta keywords and title, then get the maximum frequency to normalize the weight in equation-4.

$$weight_i = \frac{freq_i}{\max_l freq_l} \quad (4)$$

Extracting 10 terms with high weight from text field after the normalization of $\chi'^{2}(\omega)$, then insert it into KV. If existing terms in KV contains the same one of 10 terms, then calculate the weight of the same term in equation-5 below.

$$weight_i = \max(weight_{vi}, weight_{ti}) \quad (5)$$

Where $weight_{vi}$ is the weight of $term_i$ in current KV, $weight_{ti}$ is the normalized weight $\chi'^2(\omega)$ of $term_i$ in text field.

Advertisement' KV can be made by combine the keywords fields, title field and top 5 terms of high normalized $\chi'^2(\omega)$ weight into KV, the calculation formulary of the weight to each term in vector is the same with web page's KV.

2) Content vector (CV)

As described above, we could evaluate the weight for terms in text field of web page as well as description field of advertisement. All of these weighted terms can be transformed to a content vector (CV) which represents the content of text field and description field. Because we extracted the top N terms from text field in to KV, they must be excluded from the CV. Certainly, the highest term-weight will not be 1 anymore, so the normalized $\chi'^2(\omega)$ weight should be calculated again in equation (6) below.

$$weight_i = \frac{weight_i}{\max_I weight_I} \quad (6)$$

$weight_i$ is the normalized χ'^2 value just mentioned above.

With KV and CV, we could define the similarity function between web page and advertisement as equation-7 below:

$$Sim(p_i, a_j) = \alpha * SimV(k_i, k_j)) + \beta * SimV(c_i, c_j) + \gamma * SimV(k_i, c_j) + \delta * SimV(c_i, k_j)$$
$$\alpha + \beta + \gamma + \delta = 1 \quad (7)$$
$$SimV(\vec{v}_i, \vec{v}_j) = \frac{\vec{v}_i \bullet \vec{v}_j}{|\vec{v}_i| \times |\vec{v}_j|}$$

Where p_i is web page i ; a_j is advertisement j; k_i is p_i's KV; c_i is p_i's CV; k_j is a_j's KV; c_j is a_j's CV. α, β, γ, δ is tuning constant, KV contains terms which represent the page or advertisement better than CV, so α, β, γ, δ should reflect the importance of different similarity function and the sum of α, β, γ and δ is 1. We define α=0.45, β=0.15, γ=0.2, δ=0.2; SimV( ) is the cosin function[2] of vector space model.

With the similarity function Sim( ), we could rank the advertisements for each web page to select the top n ads to post. In return, we could also rank the web pages for each advertisement to select the top n web pages to be post.

4   Evaluation and Future Work

To demonstrate our model, we designed the experiment in several steps.

1)   We get 300 web pages from three famous Chinese website: Sohu, Sina, 163. We get 300 advertisements from Google's result lists which are supported by Google AdWords[7].

2)   Every web page and advertisement is constructed in a XML format as source file.

3)   Implement the word segmentation and construct CV index and KV index for each web page and advertisement.

4)   We select 20 web page randomly form 300 source web pages, retrieve with their KV and CV, then find the most similar advertisements according to Sim() function by predefining a threshold θ. then calculate the Precision and Recall. And in

return, we select 20 advertisements randomly from 300 source advertisements. We make the same retrieval process to get the Precision and Recall. Here, Precision is the number of relevant items in retrieval result list divide by the result list's size. Recall is the number of relevant items in retrieval result list divided by all relevant items in source database. The experiment result is shown in Fig. 1 and Fig. 2.

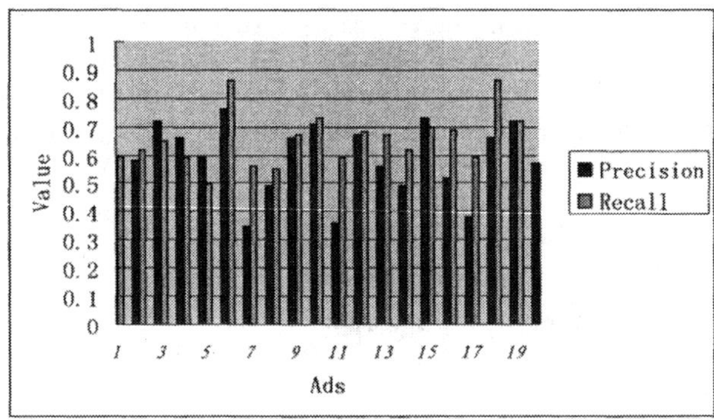

Fig. 1. Precision and Recall of 20 advertisements as the query to retrieve web pages.

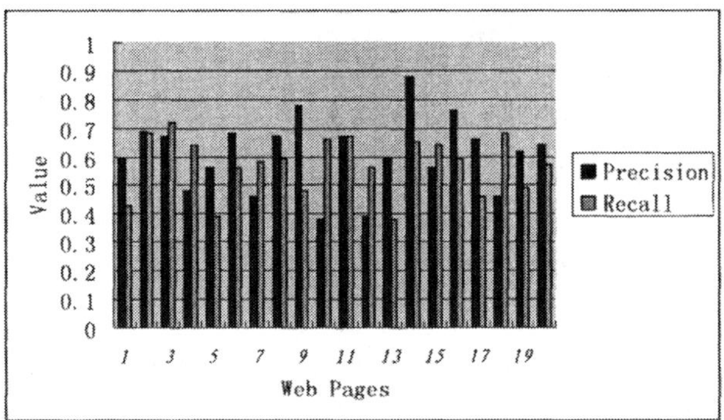

Fig. 2. Precision and Recall of 20 web pages as the query to retrieve advertisements.

In our experiment, the first 5 advertisements and web pages is very relevant, which is suitable to the web advertisement case because there is a limitation for the number of advertisements in one web page.

Our model pays more attention to match the semantics of web page and advertisement by calculating the weight of term in text or description field. But whether customer would like click or how many customers will click greatly rely on the interest of customer and the popularity of that web page. It is reasonable to assume that if page and advertisement have same semantics, customer who is interested in page has great probability to click the advertisement. In the other hand, the frequency of web page browsed and the percentage of target customers who have interest on advertisement is another very important factor. In our future work we will pays more attention on browsed frequency and target customers distribution to further the study of web advertisement.

Acknowledgement

This research is supported by the AOE Important Project of Philosophy and Social Science. The project number is 05JZD00024. It is also supported by NSFC under Grant 70473068.

References

1. Matsuo Y, Ishizuka M. "Keyword extraction from a single document using word co-occurrence statistical information". *Int'l Journal on Artificial Intelligence Tools,* 2004, 13 (1):157~169

2. Ricardo Baeza-Yates, *et al. mordern information retrieval.* 1999, ACM press .

3. Ng V, Kwan-Ho Mok. An intelligent agent for Web advertisements. Cooperative Database Systems for Advanced Applications, 23-24 April 2001 Pages:102~109

4. Amiri A, Menon S. Scheduling web banner advertisements with multiple display frequencies Systems, Man and Cybernetics, Part A, IEEE Transactions on Volume 36, Issue 2, March 2006 Pages:245~251

5. Thawani A, Gopalan S. "Event driven semantics based ad selection". *Multimedia and Expo,* 2004. ICME '04,27-30 June 2004 Pages:1875~1878

6. Salton, G., Buckley, C., "Term weighting approaches in automatic text retrieval." *Information Processing and Management,* 1988.24(5):513-523.

7. Google AdWards, http://www.google.com/intl/zh-CN/ads/. access date: December 21, 2006

Study on Personalized Recommendation
Model of Internet Advertisement

Ning Zhou, Yongyue Chen and Huiping Zhang
Center for Studies of Information Resources, Wuhan University, Wuhan
430072
chenyongyue@hotmail.com

Abstract. With the rapid development of E-Commerce, the audiences put forward higher requirements on personalized Internet advertisement than before. The main function of Personalized Advertising System is to provide the most suitable advertisements for anonymous users on Web sites. The paper offers a personalized Internet advertisement recommendation model. By mining the audiences' historical and current behavior, and the advertisers' and publisher's web site content, etc, the system can recommend appropriate advertisements to corresponding audiences.

1 Introduction

According to the report on the competition and development of Chinese Internet Advertising in 2005 and IAB Internet Advertising Revenue Report of America in 2005(Figure1) [1],[2], Internet Advertising Industry is rapidly growing up, as brings new chances and new challenges for the advertisers and publishers. Web advertising has many forms, such as banners (graphical elements on a web page), their "mutations" displayed in a new layer or new window of the browser [4].

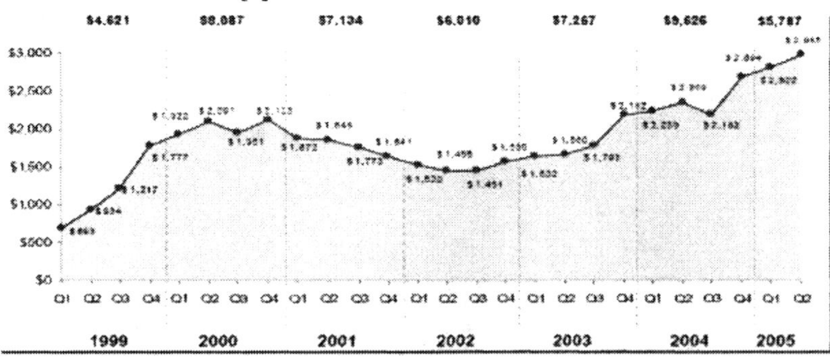

Fig.1. Quarterly Revenue Growth Comparisons in America – 1999-2005 YTD

Internet advertisings can bring profits for websites, but they also cause lots of problems. Online users all passively received Internet advertisements nowadays and even some popping advertisements can't be avoided, which annoys a lot of Internet users and make them try to filter or block them with some software embedded in the browser. In order to solve these problems, we should construct a system to assign suitable advertisements to suitable online users so as to improve the advertising personalization.

The paper offers a personalized recommendation model which can recommend suitable advertisements to the online users according to different interests and tastes. The model is mainly based on an individual's behavior rather than on users' geographical location or other demographic features (e.g. gender, age) [6].

2   Personalized Advertisement Recommendation Model

At present there are various personalized advertisement recommendation models [3],[5],[7],[10],[12]. Furthermore, they are gradually applied nowadays. In the paper, when constructing the model, the model we bring forward mainly account for five personalized factors: current behavior of users, historical behaviors of users, registered information, content of publisher's Web page and advertiser's Web sites, advertising features (Figure 2).

According to Figure2, we can know the basic principle of personalized Internet advertisement model:

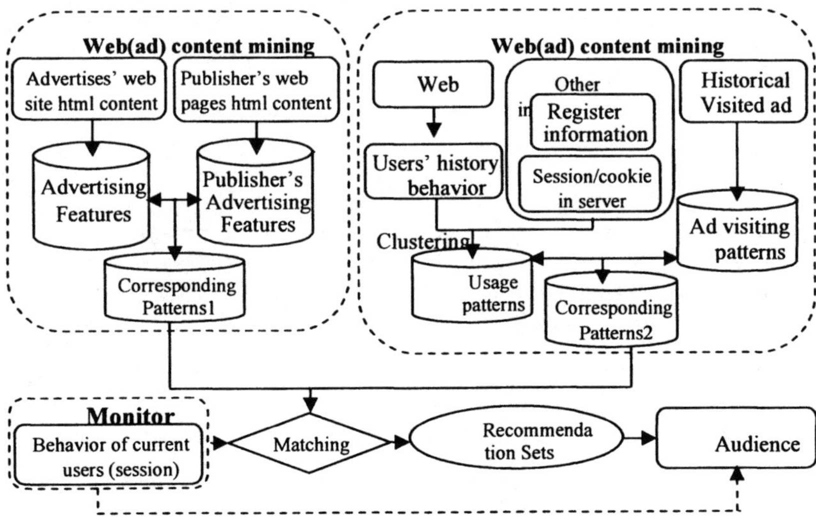

Fig.2. Personalized Internet Advertisement Recommendation Model

The features of Content of publisher's Web page and advertiser's Web sites are extracted to obtain the different categories' features [14], and cluster those advertisements according to the analogous features to form different thematic groups of terms.

• Define the counterparty content to a sort of customers to form the mapping between the advertising content and the type of customers.

- Analyze current behavior, registered information and history behavior of the audiences according to the information of session and Web Log file to learn the personalized features (e.g. requirement, interesting, career, taste, etc.) of different customers, and then judge the type of them.
- Match the clusters of advertisement with the type of audiences and recommend the corresponding advertisement to the different audiences in order to achieve the aim of personalized service.
- When the server is idle or off-line, according the information of session and Web Log file, extract the features of the audiences and then classify them to form different clusters to obtain the personalized patterns.

Behaviors of the current user are derived from the current session. A session is the set of pages watched by the user during one visit to the publisher's web site [6]. The data of the current behaviors include the content of clicked web page, the data of banners, controls, hyperlink, images clicked by the audiences when the audiences visit the website. Those data are monitored by the monitor to judge the type of audiences online. Simultaneously they are stored in the server as the data of historical behaviors.

The data of historical behaviors are derived from the past audience sessions and web log file stored in the database, clustered to obtain typical, aggregated user information offline. One clustering corresponds to one usage pattern of the publisher's web site. Each user session is linked up to the set of advertisements visited by the user during this session. Thus, one usage pattern corresponds to exactly one ad visiting pattern.

Registered information is the information by which server verifies the user's identity when user login the website. Simultaneously, we can learn the user's name, identity and some basic information about the user, such as the salary, profession, interest. Thus, the information can be used to judge the type of audiences as one of reference data.

The site content of the publisher's web pages is automatically processed by Content mining module. Content thematic groups are received using the clustering advertisements extracted from the HTML content of web pages by advertisement features. By text (HTML) content analysis of the advertisement target web site, the model automatically downloads advertiser's web pages and processes only the terms, which occur in the publisher's web pages. As a result we obtain advertising conceptual pattern corresponding to the appropriate publisher's conceptual pattern.

3   Usage Mining

Personalized Internet Advertisement Recommendation Model is mainly based on the technology of data mining. In the model, data mining includes two parts: usage Mining and advertising content mining. Usage mining mostly analyzes the historical behaviors (session, Web Log file, registered information) and the current behaviors of the user so as to obtain the user personalized feature.

3.1   The analysis of the source of data

The data, which are required in usage patterns mining, come from three parts: Web Log file, the session of the current user, the other information (cookies, register information etc.) in the server.

Table 1. The format of Web Log file

Domain	Description
Date	Date, time, time zone for the requested page
IP(client IP)	IP or DNS entrance of the remote host
User name	User name for the telnet
Bytes	Transferring bytes (sending and receiving)
Server	Server, IP address, port
Request	URL query
Status	Return http status sign
Service name	Service name the users require
Consuming time	The time for completing browse
Protocol version	Protocol version for transmission
Cookie	Cookie sign number
Reference	Up page of the current page

Once the web site is visited, a corresponding record is added to the log database in the web server (Table 1) [13]. Web analysis tools create historical behavior pattern by analyzing and processing the Web Log file. We can obtain the current behavior of users by the record of session (When recommending advertisement, the model can compare the current behavior with the historical behavior patterns and learn the audiences' information they need).

Web server can also store the other information such as cookie and querying and retrieval information which the user submits. Cookie is created by the server and records the status information and URL of the user. The data of querying and retrieval information is the record created in the server when the users retrieve the information what they want. Furthermore the register information of the users is stored in the database of the user or the data warehouse. The contents include the audiences' name, age, career and interesting and tasty etc.

3.2   The method of data mining

Data mining mainly consists of three parts: data preprocessing, data mining, user review.

(1) Data preprocessing module (Figure3) preprocesses the data in the Web Log file and the web database/data warehouse. Correlative data are extracted from the Web Server DB and are analyzed their difference to eliminate the variance. Confirm browsing page, users, session of users and the user sequence for visiting website etc. and process the original log files users visit website into transaction DB which will be used during data mining.

• Confirm browsing page. Browsing page requested by the user includes several frames, images and script. Since server records lots of file streams, when confirming to extract the browsing pages, the module generally combines topological structure of sites to filters images (.Gif, .jpeg, .jpg) [11].

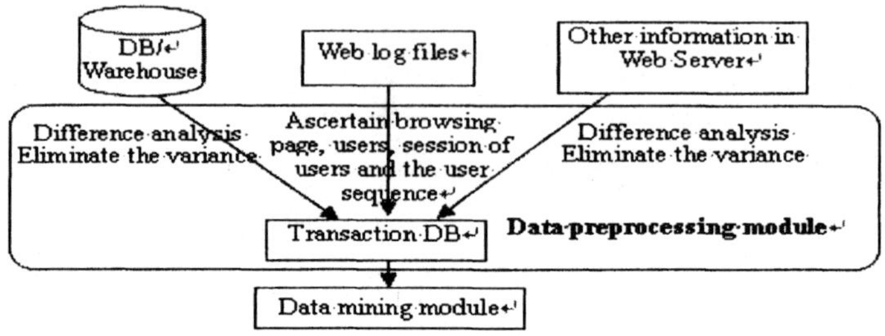

Fig .3. Data preprocessing module

• Confirm the user. The user is the individual visiting servers. In practice, it is difficult to uniquely confirm a user. Users m
• aybe visit server by several agents or computers. Sometimes, the module maybe confirm a user by sever log file, agent and reference page log together.
• Confirm user visiting sequence. In general, server log is arrayed according to IP (assistant key) and visiting time (main key). Thus, finding out all IP sequence according to the visiting time, we can structure user visiting sequence.
• Confirm session of users. During visit at a time, it is most simple to confirm all pages visited by the user according to the length of visiting time.
• Perfect the visiting path. In view of the cache in the client, the users often use the backward function when browsing pages. So we should supply paths to the omitted pages by deducing fore-and-aft pages visited by the user. In addition, when CGI is executed, since the transferred parameters are different, the last output result is different. It is necessary to confirm the displaying page by those parameters.
(2)The structure of data mining module (Figure 4)

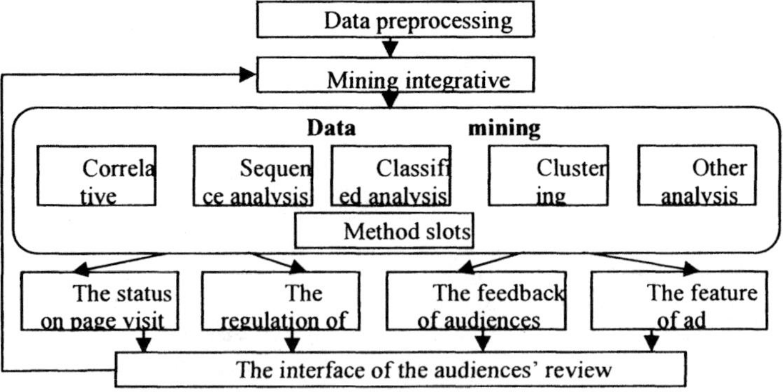

Fig .4. Data Mining module

Mining integrative processor is a mining driver engine. According to different mining requirement, it can use corresponding aggregate rules, choose the most effective sequences of mining algorithms from web data to achieve mining mission, in addition it can add new rules constantly in accordance with feedback information [9]. Web data mining algorithm base is a synthetic algorithm base of data mining analytical method. It can organize kinds of mining method by plugs in, which is convenient, expansible and easily selective. And it can realize the algorithm choice through parameters.

In the analysis of the users' behavior, mainly applications on the common techniques of data mining are as follows. We can learn the users' habit and interesting by correlative analysis and decide the ad recommendation policy. Sequence analysis can forecast the probability of the advertisement which the users require by discoverable behavior in some time point. Clustering analysis can divide users into many clusters in term of their behaviors or feature patterns so as to execute the relevant ad recommendation policy.

(3) The audiences' review is to explain and review the pattern discovered in data mining, and then choose the useful advertisements. It can solve the latent confliction between the mining result and the former knowledge, and evaluate the pattern mined by the Statistic method to decide whether the result should return to data mining module and repeat the former operation so as to get the best and only pattern. After the information extracted by data mining module is processed, it can explain the current and historical phenomena and forecast the things in future so that the decision-maker can make policy by referring to the information extracted from the bygone things.

4   Content Mining

The content is processed in a similar manner. Content features, in the form of terms, are extracted from HTML source of publisher's pages. Next, selected terms are clustered to achieve thematic groups. Since we cluster terms, individual publisher's pages may belong to many clusters. Besides, we take the content of the whole web sites linked by particular banners. Each advertiser's web site is treated like one page from publisher's portal. Advertiser's web sites that contain terms from a thematic group are allocated to this group. In this way we establish a one-to-one relationship between the content of publisher's site and advertisements.

Having content and usage clusters, we can dynamically assign each single user to the most relevant patterns based on their current behavior. This assignment is performed online when user posts a HTTP request. In consequence, the user is suggested advertisements with the content most relevant to the content of pages viewed by them recently. Additionally, advertisements most likely to be clicked by the user have the greater chance to be exposed. It comes from the historical behavior of other users that are similar to the current one: they simply used to click certain banners. Note that the user is assigned to one usage pattern but this pattern corresponds to one clicking pattern.

5   Conclusions and Future Works

The model of personalized advertising recommendation integrates information coming from different sources: web usage mining, web content mining, advertising policy etc. It combines the user session with web log file and improves the veracity to advertisement which the users require. Thus, the same user on the same page may each time be recommended different advertisements in which the audience has an interest so that it can greatly increase the click rate of the advertisement. In all processes in the method (Figure. 2) are performed automatically by the system, which decreases management costs. Consequently, the model not only satisfies the users but advertisers.

Future work will focus on the optimization of online processes and the development of an advertisement scheduling system, which is an important issue when dealing with many advertisers. Furthermore, we should visualize the advertising patterns extracted from the advertisers' web sites and the publisher's site so that the audience can intuitively choose advertisements what they want. In e-commerce, the method can be extended to purchases history and product ratings gathered by the system.

Acknowledgement

This research was supported by t National Natural Science Foundation of China under Grant No. 70473068. Thanks them for their supports during the writing process of my paper.

References

1. *IAB Internet Advertising Revenue Report 2005.* http://www.iab.net/resources/ad_revenue.asp.

2. *The Report about the competition and development of Chinese Internet Advertising in 2005.* http://www.pday.com.cn/research/2006/6201_webads.htm.

3. P. Kazienko, "Multi -Agent System for Web Advertising", *Lecture Notes in Artificial Intelligence* ,507-513 (2005).

4. *Online Advertising.* DoubleClick Inc. (2004).

5. P. Kazienko and M. Kiewra, "Link Recommendation Method Based on Web Content and Usage Mining",http://www.zsi.pwr.wroc.pl/~kazienko/pub/IIS03/pkmk.pdf.

6. P.Kazienko and M. Kiewra, *ROSA-Multi-agent System for Web Services Personalization,* E. Menasalvas et al. (Eds.): AWIC(2003).

7. G Bilchev and D Marston, "Personalized advertising — exploiting the distributed user profile",*BT Technology Journal* (2003)

8.A. Milani, "Minimal Knowledge Anonymous User Profiling for Personalized Services",*IEA/AIE 2005, LNAI 3533,* 709 – 711(2005).

9. W.Y. LIN, "Efficient Adaptive-Support Association Rule Mining for Recommender Systems", *Data Mining and Knowledge Discovery,* 83–105(2002).

10. P. Kazienko, "Multi-agent Web Recommendation Method Based on Indirect Association Rules", *8th International Conference on Knowledge-Based Intelligent Information & Engineering Systems, KES'2004, LNAI 3214, Springer Verla,g* 1157-1164(2004).

11. D. Johansen and R.V. Renesse, "WAIF:Web of Asynchronous Information Filters",*Future Directions in DC 2002, LNCS, 2584* 81–86(2003).

12. J. Chen and J. Huang, "Design and Implementation of Internet Advertising Analysis System Based on OLAP",*Application Research of Computers* (2004).

13. M.J. XIA and J. Zhang, "Web Mining Application: Customized Internet Advertising", *Journal of Zhong Yuan institute of Technology* (2003).

14. X.L. Fan, "Research and Achievement on Personalized E -commerce Site", *Computer Application* (2002).

An Analysis on Modes of Scientific and TechnologicaInformation Integration Services in the E- environment

Ping Wang, Weidong Zhang, Ye Yuan, Xueyan Song
School of Management, Jilin University, Chang chun, China
wdzhang@jlu.edu.cn

Abstract. During the combination of knowledge and capital, science and technology intermediaries are demanded to provide information integration services. Science and technology intermediaries play an important role in quickening the commercialization of research findings, developing new and high technology industry, and promoting regional scientific and technological innovations. With the influences of the computer age on science and technology information services as the starting point, the thesis makes a large-scale survey of websites of state and provincial comprehensive science and technology intermediaries, and based on this, the overall framework of scientific and technological information integration services under the E-environment is established, and furthermore, the functions and structures of different subsystems are systemically analyzed in the modes of scientific and technological information integration services.

1 Introduction

The arrival of the era of network poses a great convenience for the information services of science and technology intermediaries. As online scientific and technological information services break down the time and space limitations, any innovation subject can access information quickly. The network dissemination of scientific and technological information makes it more transparent, and thus quickens the fusion of knowledge with capital. Integration services of scientific and technological information in the network environment have become a reality. Integrated services effectively integrate all elements of information resources organically into an overall dynamic process, which is displayed to its users through the network, and enable users to quickly access services based on the theme of 'one-

Please use the following format when citing this chapter:

Wang, P., Zhang, W., Yuan, Y., Song, X., 2007, in IFIP International Federation for Information Processing, Volume 252, Integration and Innovation Orient to E-Society Volume 2, eds. Wang, W., (Boston: Springer), pp. 184-192.

stop', which is very convenient for users to make personalized options and professional use.

2   Statistical analysis of websites of science and technology intermediaries

2003 is the year of 'construction of science and technology intermediaries' prescribed by the Ministry of Science and Technology of China. [1] Science and technology intermediary websites have developed rapidly. Science and technology intermediary, as an aggregate concept, can be roughly divided into the following 12 categories: Productivity promotion center, Science and technology entrepreneurial service centers, Scientific and technological information agencies, Science and technology assessment and advisory bodies, Technology transactions, Venture investment and financing services, Agricultural extension services, Tech services sector, Professional agent, Trade or professional associations, Science and technology talents service providers and Management consulting agencies. [2]Due to its numerousness and diversity, it is very difficult to carry out disaggregated statistical analysis on these websites, and therefore, since the beginning of 2007, the authors of this thesis have only selected science and technology information agencies and make a sample analysis, by means of visiting websites. The samples include the national and provincial scientific and technical information network platforms, in which 75 national science and technology information websites are surveyed, and 136 provincial ones are involved. The provincial science and technology information network platforms cover all the mainland provinces, autonomous regions and municipalities, and the average number of samples of each province is 3 to 5.

2.1   Analysis of Problems

In general, the overall quality of Chinese scientific and technological information website construction is of sorts, which is embodied in the following aspects:
①Lack of standardization resulted from the too large number of websites.
②Loss of characteristics resulted from diverse columns.
③ Redundant construction.
④Unsound mechanism of scientific and technological information dissemination.
⑤ Stereotyped service means.
⑥Low degree of specialization, personalization, and intellectualization of services.

2.2   Solutions

Based on the above analysis of problems, the authors of this thesis think that it is very necessary to construct a scientific and technological information service mode which highly integrates resources, technologies and services. Modes of scientific and technological information integration services in e-environment are expected to reach the following goals.

2.2.1 Integration of resources --- optimization of information dissemination.

The problem of resources allocation facing scientific and technological information websites should be solved from both macro and micro perspectives. As a whole, governments should concentrate manpower and material and financial resources to build comprehensive scientific and technological information portals, integrate public scientific and technological information databases, commercial scientific and technological information databases, databases of patents, databases of research findings and so on, and invest more in information organization technology and intelligent retrieval technology. Meanwhile, scientific and technological information websites of other regions and in other industries can focus on construction of distinctive information databases, which can share information interactively with platform of scientific and technological information portals. On the basis of such macro-view of platform, scientific and technological information services tend to be improved and optimized. At the micro level, scientific and technological information websites should unite columns and stress features by collecting information from enterprises, research institutes, universities and governments, then organizing them carefully and publishing them timely.

2.2.2 Integration of technologies --- intellectualization of information services.

The main trend of information services is rising of online services. Modern technologies like intelligent retrieval, personalized push and semantic web have been extensively used applied in information service field. When integration of information technologies is done, experts' intelligence factors should be taken into consideration. Online reference and consultation services, which combine information technologies with expert intelligence, will meet users' high-level demands effectively.

2.2.3 Integration of services --- 'one-stop' trip.

With abundant information resources, modernized information technologies, and diverse means of services, users' demands for information can be met sufficiently. With integration of a variety of service functions like navigation, intelligent retrieval, online reference and consultation, personalized services and link services, users can get access to information they need on one website timely and accurately.

3   Modes of scientific and technological information integration services in the e-environment

Scientific and technological information integration services are mainly reflected in two aspects: First, the integration of scientific and technological information resources is the foundation of providing effective services. Science and technology intermediaries need to integrate regional, trade or even global resources, including information of scientific research findings, patents, enterprise technology needs, talents and scientific and technological literature resources, to provide users with specialized services. Second, the integration of information services is not only integrated information resources services. The focus is no longer the provided information resources themselves, but has been shifted to specific problems the enterprise seeks to solve. Through information integration services, users are allowed to enjoy 'one-stop' information supply, to reach an overall solution, and eventually a blend of knowledge and capital will be realized, which will be transformed into economic benefits in reality. [3] The modes of scientific and technological information integration services need to be constructed on such basis.

3.1 Overall framework of modes of science and technology information integration services

The overall framework of modes of science and technology information integration services is designed on the basis of two layers: information layer and service layer (see figure 1). Based on database of science and technology information, database of users and enterprises information, and database of policies and regulations, information layer mainly deals with several issues such as organization, dissemination, and retrieval of information resources, and integration of users information; on the service layer, services which are mainly aimed at specific users are integrated, including online reference and consultation services, personalized services, professional training services, agency services, etc.

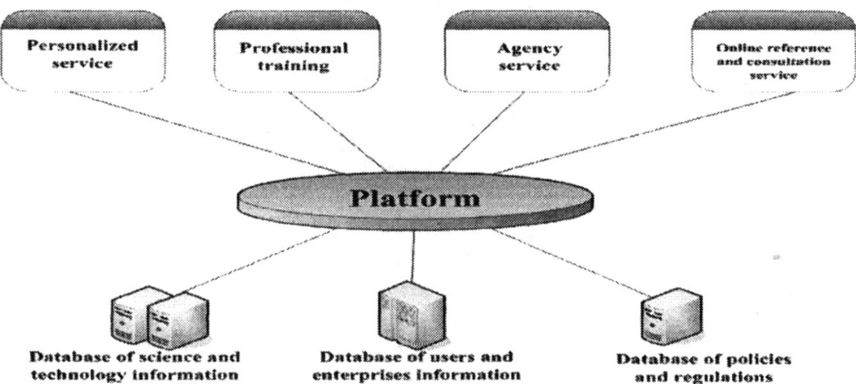

Figure 1. overall framework of science and technology information integration services

3.2 Function modules of modes of science and technology information integration services

3.2.1 Module of science and technology information dissemination

Science and technology information dissemination system is an important indicator which is used to examine integration services of science and technology intermediaries from the perspective of resources supply, and is also the foundation of science and technology information services. As to the demands of specific users, science and technology intermediaries collect, organize, and integrate information, and disseminate it on internet platform, so that the demand of different innovation subjects is met. Science and technology information resources dissemination system is designed mainly on the following four layers (see figure 2): Enterprise Information Dissemination Platform, Science and Technology Information Dissemination Platform, Professional and Technical Data Release Platform, and Policies and Regulations Dissemination Platform.

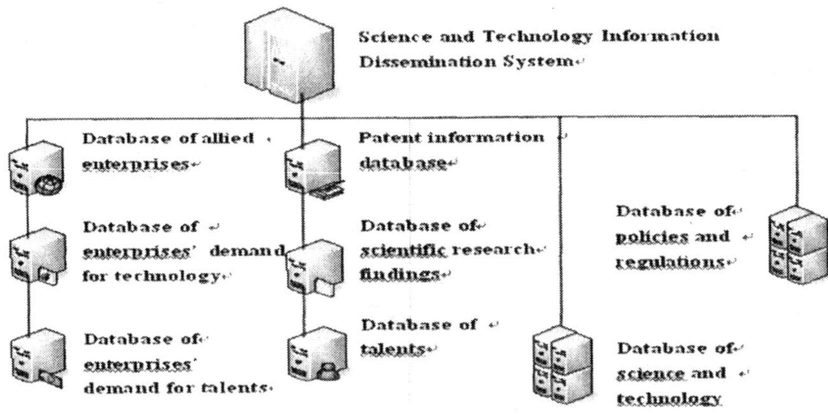

Figure 2. structure of modules of science and technology information resources dissemination

3.2.2 Module of Cross-database Integrated Retrieval

Cross-database integrated retrieval, based on various databases set up in science and technology information resources dissemination system, integrates many databases of scientific and technological information effectively, as a result of which, users can accomplish retrieval of all the databases available under only one interface. Users do not need to log in and retrieve different databases one after another, and furthermore, with simple and swift the process of retrieval, and unified research interface format, the burdens on users are reduced. The integration of cross-database retrieval is also embodied by the realization of functions like links between cross-database citations, links between knowledge elements, knowledge hubs, intellectual research, etc. Hence, the use efficiency is improved. [4]

Retrieval interface is supposed to design navigation systems for users. Navigation database is set up through collection, analysis, selection, organization, and description of various scientific and technological information resources, which enables a user to be aware of his or her location, and accurately select database to get access to information, and in this way, the user is unlikely to get lost (see figure 3).

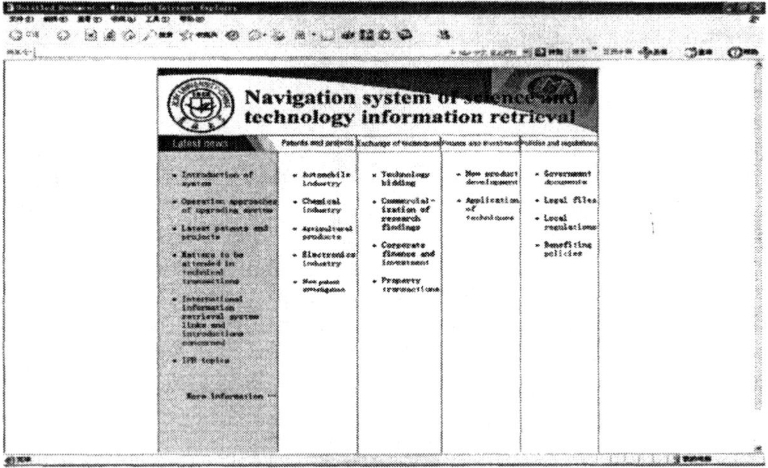

Figure 3 navigation function of science and technology information integration

3.2.3 Module of Online Reference and Consultation Services

Online reference and consultation services system of scientific and technological information is digital form which has the traditional expert advisory services as foundation. It combines traditional forms of reference, and uses the e-commerce online customer service experiences for reference. It meets users' different demands for information recurring to reference desk, telephone, FAQ databases, e-mail, web forms, bulletin boards or discussion groups, online chat, a common browser, internet-advisory services, network meetings of advisory services, expert advisory services, and cooperation in the digital reference services. [5] (see figure 4)

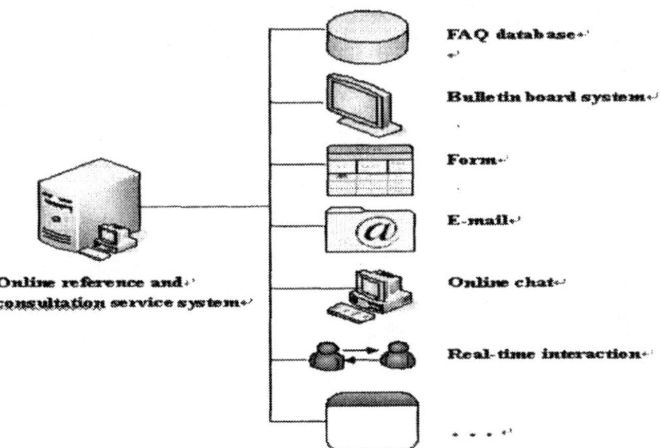

Figure 4. framework of online reference and consultation service system

3.2.4 Module of Personalized Services

Personalized services system is based on specific demands of specific users. Personalized services system of scientific and technological information is mainly targeted at technology-based small and medium-sized enterprises which have a big demand for technology. Customization and push of information are considered the core of personalized service system. [6] Customization is one of the effective ways of understanding users' demand, through which, personalized information about users can be obtained, and users' demand can be comprehended, and more accurate services will be offered to users. The so-called push technology refers to a kind of information sending technology, which is achieved by tracking users' network activities, extracting, tracing and analyzing users' personal interests and hobbies, forming a user model, and then referring to users' customization. Push services also regularly or irregularly take the initiative to 'push' users special information they are interested in. Construction of user model is a critical component of personalized information service system. User model is mainly realized through push server which sets up model of user information by guiding users and extracting and analyzing users' interests. (see figure 5)

① Visitors to information integration platform of a science and technology intermediary have to land user interface, and fill in the corresponding registration information (new visitors). User interface offers options reflecting user's basic features, such as age, occupation, education and personal profiles, and such options serve as the basic elements of database of users.

② With the entry of user basic information into database of users, user model is set up. Analyses are made on basic elements of users and tracks in which users get access to archives resources, then the most basic characteristics of user demand are extracted, and therefore, foundation of realizing personalized services has been laid.

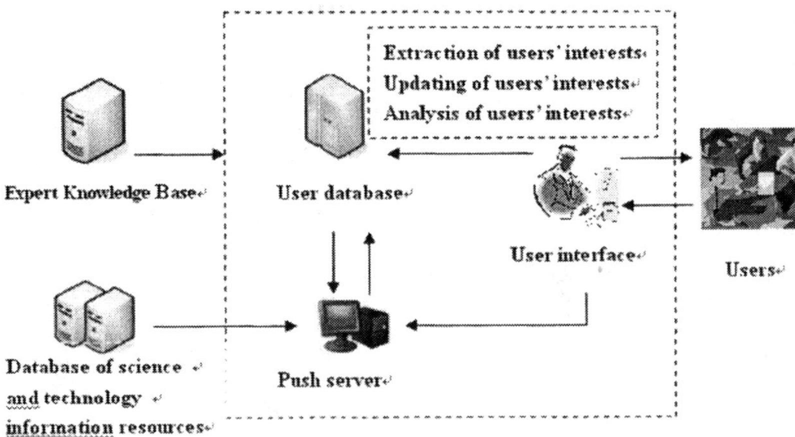

Figure 5. flow of personalized services of science and technology information

③A user submits demand to intellectual retrieval system, the demand enter into push server which makes the initial matching search according to the user's retrieval order, but the information obtained at this moment cannot be provided to the user. Simultaneously, push server enters into database of users to research for the user's historical documents, and then put the user's descriptive information in user model to analyze and filter the user's interests.

④ Comparison is made between user interests and the information obtained initially and than some content is extracted, so the ultimate retrieval content is fixed and is pushed to users. Meanwhile, the user's application of this time will be stored in database of users. Push server will periodically identify the latest information which a user is interested in, and push technological information catalogues irregularly through e-mail, nurturing the stable user groups. When providing users with information services, expert intellectual knowledge database also plays a key role.[7]

3.2.5 Other Services

① Convergence of information about the latest developments of science and technology. Science and technology information integration service system possesses a special retrieval system which, with the help of human work, collects and converges the latest technological developments, news and policies, after that, releases them on the websites of science and technology intermediaries quickly and timely.[8]

② Professional training services. Professional training services may take the form of training class or online training, and training content includes professional business administration, use of database, or examination of scientific and technological information.

③ Agency services. Science and technology information integration service system submits online forms. Users can entrust science and technology intermediaries with such operations as investigating new scientific developments and downloading scientific and technological information by filling in an online agency standing order.

4   Conclusions and Outlook

Since China's science and technology intermediary service system is still in a stage of development, and the overall level of information integration services is not high enough, modes of science and technology information integration services constructed in the thesis are just a framework which is feasible in theory. Many problems remain to be solved in practice.

(1)Of government support. Governments should offer greater support in terms of policies, funds, and technology, and construct a perfect and efficient information service platform in collaboration with enterprises, universities, research institutes and science and technology intermediaries.

(2) Of intellectual property rights. authorization of database constructors has to be obtained when integration of different databases is conducted, and besides, rational utilization is preferred and malicious download and abuse should be avoided.

(3) Of economy. investment income and interest is a problem which future science and technology intermediaries, enterprises, research institutes, universities and governments will have to face.

(4) Of technology. It remains to be further studied how to integrate different types of information into one system.

References

1. People's Republic of China Ministry of Science and Technology, 2003: *Year of 'Construction of Science and Technology Intermediaries'*
(Apr.21,2007)http://www.most.gov.cn/kjjr/jyjl/200303/t20030321_9568.htm.

2.*Questionnaire of Science and Technology Intermediaries,*
(Feb.25,2007)http://www.lninfo.gov.cn/.

3 Qiang.B, H.Y. Shi, *Research on Modes of Information Integration Services [J]*, Library and Information Service, 2004(9).P30-33.

4.web of CNKI,(Apr.25,2007);http://www.cnki.net/index.htm.

5.*IFLA Digital Reference Guide* .(Apr.25,2007).
http://zsdh.library.sh.cn/vrdguide.htm.

6.Y.L. Hao.*Push Technology--The Realzation of Personalized Information Service on Network.* Journal of Information 2002（10）.P55.

7 W.D. .Zhang, P. Wang, *Study on Personalized Service Modes Driven by Archive User,* Archives Science Bulletin.2007（2）P85.

8. Y. et.al. *Construction Ideas of Patent Information Integration Platform*, Information Science: Theory and Application.2007（1）P91.

QoE: Quality of Experience: **A Conceptual Essay**

Regis Cabral
Digital Media Laboratory
Applied Physics and Electronics
Umeå University
SE-901 87 Umeå universitet Sweden
regis.cabral@tfe.umu.se,
http://www.medialab.tfe.umu.se/

Abstract. The ICT industry and services are on the verge of substituting quality of service and utility functions with quality of experience, QoE. While intuitive, QoE, has eluded the research community. QoE takes into account what the user is experiencing with new products and services. Once this information is collected, it becomes an input in the development of the new product or new service. But how does one measure directly quality of experience? In this conceptual paper, I discuss from an ICT perspective, the utility function and quality of service, QoS. I also present how active interested the industry is in QoE. I concluded with some key points that may serve as a guideline in the process of constructing the QoE function.

1   Introduction

In recent years, the ICT industry and related services have highlighted that concepts such as quality of service and even utility functions, while useful, have failed in contributing to product and service development from the perspective of the consumer. One can say that quality of service has even failed in capturing the needs of the consumer. The concept of quality of experience, QoE, is emerging as an alternative. The concept seems to be easy to understand intuitively. Nevertheless, QoE has eluded the research community. One takes into account what the user is experiencing with new products and services. Once this information is collected, it becomes an input in the development of the new product or new service. Other fields, beyond ICT, like the health sector or the food sector, have a long history of using qualitative approaches to deal with similar issues. But quality of experience, while

---

Please use the following format when citing this chapter:

Cabral, R., 2007, in IFIP International Federation for Information Processing, Volume 252, Integration and Innovation Orient to E-Society Volume 2, eds. Wang, W., (Boston: Springer), pp. 193-199.

similar to consumer satisfaction, it is not the same. Consumer satisfaction has been used has a proxy for QoE and surveys and questionnaires have been common approaches. But how does one measure directly quality of experience? In this conceptual discussion, I present some (but not all) concepts that are relevant to the ICT sectors, such as utility function and quality of service. Then I attempt a definition of QoE and enter suggestions about how to measure it directly.

2   Relevant concepts[1,2,3,4,5]

2.1 The utility function

It may come as a surprise to many that the concept of utility has not been defined 100% unequivocally. Nevertheless, the utility functions is assumed to be properly and well defined. Engineers use it as a standard instrument to compare technologies. But is it well defined? If we open standard works or encyclopedias in economics, it is clear that the concept of utility emerged in history as a way to measure a user satisfaction with products or services. So a society would aim at maximizing its utility. That is, society should strive at making all, (and if not all the greatest number,) of its members happy. An important name in utilitarianism was John Stuart Mill.

The difficulties at measuring something as "irrational" as happiness, forced economists to reconsider utility as a behavioral measure. So a behavior became rational when it maximizes utility – what ever that might be. Utility became a curve representing how a society or an individual consumed, or accepted, goods and services, to a certain satisfaction level. How to best achieve an efficient use of these goods and services so as to maximize this utility function became a social and individual objective in economics.

It is very relevant for a discussion of quality of experience to consider that there are two types of utility, cardinal and ordinal. The former relates to magnitudes while the later to ranking. In both cases one is referring to a society or a consumer's preferences. It is clear that ordinal utility represents a behavioral choice but does not tells us what the user is experiencing and neither which product is better or worst. Cardinal utility functions have, for all practical purposes, disappeared from neoclassical economics. What has happened is that consumer purchase preferences have became, in practice, proxies for utility functions. It is assumed that what consumers choose has been chosen rationally to maximize their utility. Mathematical formulations have followed from this. Or alternatively, mathematical formulations have been interpreted this way. Utility functions are (quite often linear and well-behaved) ranking of user's possible choices from a consumer set. It is assumed that what the consumer chooses is what the consumer prefers, no matter what the consumer experiences. In the expected utility models, consumers and society are expected to avoid risk in their choices. The key names were von Neumann and Morgenstern.

Difficulties with utility, particularly when monetary and price issues emerged, required economists to consider marginal utility. Utility reduces to that which is used at the margin. But different consumers will attribute different marginal utilities to the same product or the same service. Theories of marginal utility may confront difficulties not only because of this but also because of the attempts to associate this marginal change to quantifiable entities or measures. Quantification may be possible if the marginal utility changes can be associated to changes from one economic state to another. But again this does not tells us much about the quality of the experience the consumer may be having. And this is so, even in microeconomics where consumers have to maximize their utility with their choice of money allocation, given several goods, services and savings to choose from. It is straightforward to show that in most cases the problem has several solutions. In addition, consumers may have a behavior described as satisficing, which means just choosing what is good enough even if it is not the best – the bounded rationality behavior. Utility is also a function of knowledge, information, energy, time and other factors. This means that the utility function may be describing a choice but not the maximization of the quality of experience of the consumer.

2.2 Quality of Service - QoS

While ICT engineers use utility functions to develop their products and services., there emerged a need to offer to consumers the best possible service, given resources, infrastructures and technology. QoS is used widely in the ICT sector with this purpose. In contrast to the utility function, quality of service is very clearly defined, including in several international standards. For instance in telephony, QoS is "a set of quality requirements on the collective behavior of one or more objects", according to ITU standard X902 [2]. Given a network that combines several technologies, including IP-routed networks, QoS will give us a measure of the network's capability to provide the best possible service given a selected network traffic. The QoS function must take into account factors such as bandwidth, latency and loss characteristics. The QoS function also allows for service providers to measure the extent to which providing one flow of information through the network does not impair other flows. Without a measure of QoS it is not possible to provide such services as WAN and IOS.

There is another important contrast to the utility functions. QoS are actually control mechanisms. Users, application softwares and data flows have priorities in the networks and it is QoS that determines who goes first, given the actual limited physical qualities of the network. With QoS a traffic control that guarantees traffic without quality impair is possible. With this in mind it is clear that QoS is not the same as high performance. We can not measure QoS directly with low latency or low bit error probability for instance, although these can be used as proxies or indicators of QoS.

QoS can be affected by many factors, for instance networks delays, out of order deliveries, dropped packets and errors in general. Providers make an extreme effort at not loosing packages from origin to destination.

Some current network services would be impossible without QoS, for instance streaming multimedia, IPTV, and asynchronous transfer mode (ATM) with one of its key applications VOIP. QoS statistics show that networks that provide QoS can be as much as for times more reliable than a network without QoS.

It is also clear that if there is substantial capacity in the bandwidth than one can operate without QoS. It is here that one can see the difference between QoS and quality of experience, QoE. The user or consumer may have a good quality of experience even when QoS is not in place. ICT providers can not evaluate QoE from QoE and vice-versa. But, they actually need to know QoE to determine their customer relations.

3. Quality of Experience – QoE - What is it?

Quality of experience can not be considered a "new" concept. In several business sectors, there has been serious attempts to take into account the customer's perspective. Product developers, particular in the consumer goods sectors, have constantly asked themselves about what needs to change in a product in order to meet the needs of the consumer. But QoE is also a reaction to mass production society. But it has been very difficult to measure it objectively. The use of questionnaires and interviews has proved problematic, particularly for the fast growing and fast changing ICT sector. Here I will not considere the parallel and similar issue that has been under consideration in the medical sector. Since health is directly related to the patient quality of experience with the medical service, medical providers have been looking into this issue also.

In the ICT sector is has long been considered that QoE is subjective. It is our contention that it is possible to quantify or at least measure QoE. That is, it is possible to take the user into account in the services provided, even if dependent on the user's previous experiences. QoS, particularly when measured by the Mean Opinion Score (MOS) has been used as a proxy for QoE, but it is limited because it requires a highly controlled environment.

Since the great contributions of Harrison White [7], networks have been well established as a research tool. In the case of innovation this has been facilitated by the acceptance and implementation of national and regional systems of innovation. Such understanding of the dynamics of networks gives us a point of departure to consider the very important issue of quality of experience. QoE is of fundamental interest for video mobile service, as has been highlighted by Nokia and Ericsson literature. QoE is expected to replace both utility functions and quality of service. Quality of experience, in contrast to quality of service, QoE, takes into account how a user, particularly in the video mobile networks, assesses and evaluates a service/product innovation in relation to existing services/products. Basically, QoE will measure if an innovation will reduce or increase the transaction costs (and not only monetary costs) from the perspective of the user's experience. QoE is an emerging but very difficult concept and has baffled large corporations like Nokia and Ericsson. The literature is so far internal or limited, with exception of the health sector, from which ideas can be imported. QoE is of fundamental importance for the positioning of Finland and Nokia in the European and in the global market [8]. So far, has neither Ericsson nor Nokia been able to successful address the issue of how to measure QoE. There are indications that Samsung may be on the right track, although mobile video providers may enter higher demands on technology producers. This has recently been highlighted by the work of M.A Sasse, UCL [9], as well as by the seminars promoted by the German telecom interests. In Sweden, the dissertation of Jiong Sun on Streaming Video has also reinforced the need to advance on this front [10]. An important alternative is to develop intelligent video displays [11].

Over all, QoE will become more important than quality of service and for management, and management theory/economics, and probably more important as the utility function. Moreover a functional QoE may give an extra innovative edge to companies in Sweden's and Finland's science parks and incubators [12, 13, 14]

Certainly a number of companies are capitalizing on the possibilities of measuring QoE. This includes for instance LCC International, which has announcement for "wireless turn-key services, ... and end-user 'Quality of Experience' solution". LCC suggests that it is measuring the "actual consumer experience". LCC is highlighting that it is tracking, among other things, consumers' download options and thus identifying preferences. Their preliminary results indicate that fewer than 20% of customers are satisfied with their experience with mobile content services [15]. Another company is Nominum but their product description indicates a high quality in QoS. This would improve reduce problems for customers QoE [16].

4. Can we measure QoE?

The industrial interest in QoE and its measuring is demonstrated by the large number of entries in Google – over 250000 relevant entries by 15 May 2007. The academic work in the economics and theory of QoE has been restricted to the economics of experience. But a search for a metric is most relevant [17]. So the belief is that QoE can be measure and that it can be done quantitatively. Efforts such as the Quality of Experience Initative, led by Zandan and supported by LCC, Freever, mBlox, Motricity, Musiwave, and Vodafone reinforces the perception here presented about the importance of QoE [18]. Ericsson is also moving in this direction, as indicated in its "User Service Performance white Paper of February 2007 [19].

What is it that we know so far?
1. QoE is not the same as QoS
2. The two may occur at the same time, but one does not necessarily leads to the other
3. QoS is not sufficient for the development of products and services that take into account the customer's experience
4. Utility function is not sufficient for the development of products and services that take into account the customer's experience
5. QoS is not the same as the utility function
6. QoE is not the same as the utility function
7. But it is very likely that there is a relationship between utility and QoE

8. QoE is a function of behavioral variables that may be possible to measure quantitatively.
9. Some of these measures may be physiometrical and psychometrical.
10. In case of mobile telephony this may be possible directly through the mobile phone in participating populations
11. Utility is one of the variables of the QoE function

References

1. M. Blaug, *The Methodology of Economics or How Economists Explain* (Cambridge Univ. Press, Cambridge, 2nd ed, 1992).

2. T. Eggertsson, *Economic Behavior and Institutions* (Cambridge University Press, Cambridge, 1999).

3. F. Fisher, *The Identification Problem in Econometrics* (McGraw-Hill, New York, 1966).

4 .U. Mäki, *Fact and Fiction in Economics: Models, Realism and Social Construction* (Cambridge University Press, Cambridge, 2002).

5 .S. S. Stevens, Measurements, Psychophysics and Utility, edited by C. W. Churchman and R. Philburn, Measurement: *Definitions and Theories* (New York: John Wiley, New York, 1959), pp. 18-63.

6. ITU (February 2003); www.itu.int/itudoc/itu-t/com17/activity/cat004_ww9.doc.

7. J. Moody, review of Harrison White's Markets from Networks: *Socioeconomic, Models of Production Social Forces*, 81 (2), 663-664 (2002).

8 .NOKIA, (October 2004), Quality of Experience (QoE) of Mobile Services: Can It Be Measured and Improved? http://whitepapers.silicon.com/0,39024759,60104519p-9000457q,00.htm

9 . *Angela Sasse* (May 2007); http://www.cs.ucl.ac.uk/staff/a.sasse/angelasasse.html.

10 .J. Sun, Football on Mobile Phones. Algorithms, Architectures and quality of Experience in Streaming Video (PhD Dissertation, *Department of Applied Physics and Electronics*, Umeå University, 2006).

11 . C. Kim, J. Ko, I. Ahn, M. Usman, J.H. Kwon, J. Park, Y. H. Joo, and Y. J. Oh, Intelligent Video Display to Raise Quality of Experience on Mobile Devices, Applications of Digital Image Processing XXIX. *Proceedings of the SPIE* 6312, pp. 63120N (2006).

12. A.-V. Anttiroiko, Editorial: Global Competition of High-Tech Centres, *International Journal of Technology Management* 28 (3/4/576), pp. 289-323 (2004).

13. R. Cabral, The Cabral-Dahab Science Park Management Paradigm: *An Introduction, International Journal of Technology Management,* 16, pp. 721-725 (1998).

14. R. Cabral, The Cabral-Dahab Science Park Management Paradigm applied to the case of Kista, Sweden, *International Journal of Technology Management* 28 (3-6), pp. 419-443 (2004).

15. LCC (February 13, 2007) LCC Solution Measures 'Quality of Experience'; http://www.mobilemarketingmagazine.co.uk/2007/02/lcc_solution_me.html.

16 .Daily News (2007), Nominum Enhances Products For Wireless Quality Of Experience, *Daily News*;
http://newsblaze.com/story/20070206160437youn.np/topstory.html.

17 .EMA (March 22, 2006), Adopting the ultimate service metric: A checklist for an effective Quality of Experience solution, *Enterprise Management Associates (EMA)*, http://www.compuware.com/default.asp.

18. MEF, London (May 2007); http://www.m-e-f.org/index.php?id=43.

Ericsson, (February 2007) Ericsson User Service Performance, February 2007, White paper 284 23-3106 UEN Rev A;
http://www.ericsson.com/technology/whitepapers/3106_user_service_performance_A.pdf.

Inter-organization Cooperation for Care of the Elderly

Ricardo Costa1, Paulo Novais2, José Machado2 , Carlos Alberto3 and José Neves2

1   College of Management and Technology - Polytechnic of Porto, Felgueiras, Portugal rfc@estgf.ipp.pt
2   DI-CCTC, Universidade do Minho, Braga, Portugal {pjon,jmac,jneves}@di.uminho.pt
3 Hospital Geral de Santo António, EPE, Porto, Portugal calberto.admn@hgsa.min-saude.pt

Abstract .With the growing numbers of the elderly population, the society is face to face with a set of new problems, namely the lack of resources to assist their living in a noble mode. Nevertheless, with the use of new computational technologies and novel methodologies for problem solving, some solutions to these problems are emerging (e.g., remote sensing/assistance/supervision). Therefore, it is our goal to show that under such scenarios, it is possible to bring into play different interconnected virtual organizations, through which will be provided to the population, in general, and the elderly, in particular, a number of services (e.g., healthcare, entertainment, learning), without delocalization or messing up with their routine.

1   Introduction

Once the human population is progressively ageing, it matters that the elderly in need of special attention, is growing. Old age brings new problems (e.g. entertainment, health, lowliness), aggravated with the lack of specialized human resources to assist their necessities. Besides that fact, one may point out, for example, that pressure exists in government and society (e.g. budgetary restraints, cost of medical technologies and cost of internment) that will force readjustments of actual entertainment and/or health care practice, which may also affect other co-related public systems [1, 2].

This work looks at the role that inter-organization cooperation and learning plays within the innovative processes of a smart home for care of the elderly, and, suggests a framework that allows a set of organizations to strategically model a collaborative

Please use the following format when citing this chapter:

Costal, R., Novais, P., Machado, J., Alberto, C., Neves, J., 2007, in IFIP International Federation for Information Processing, Volume 252, Integration and Innovation Orient to E-Society Volume 2, eds. Wang, W., (Boston: Springer), pp. 200-208.

environment that is conducive to innovation. The major idea is to enhance elderly quality of life, allowing them an "active ageing", thus being able to participate in social, economic, cultural, spiritual, civic and family affairs, physically and labor, remaining active contributors to their families and communities [1]. The path to pursue, in order to achieve the presented idea, relies on a mix of different sensibilities from Artificial Intelligence, such as Decision Trees and Automated Learning, coupled whit different computational paradigms and methodologies for problem solving, such as Agent Based Systems and Group Decision Support Systems [3], thus being able to achieve a high level of "intelligence" in what may be denominated as "Smart Healthcare Homes" [4].

1.1   Inter-organization Cooperation

In Inter-Organization Cooperation there are factors that tend to be surrounded in the local milieu, which according to Dosi [5], can be seen as the social embedded processes that allow organizations to obtain outside complementary knowledge and be innovative in the course of interaction among different actors, i.e., the local or regional milieu needs to include not only the substances related to the service structure or economics terms, but also social, cultural and institutional ones [6]. Thus, in the interaction of the different actors, the cooperation elements can be found in a kind of common language, social relationship, norms, values and institutions, which in our work will be set in terms of an extension to the logic programming language, being their knowledge bases built as logical theories that found their foundations on this extension [7]. Conclusions are supported by deductive proofs, or by arguments that include conjectures and motivate new topics of inquiry, i.e., if deduction is fruitless the agent inference engine resorts to abduction, filling in missing pieces of logical arguments with plausible conjectures to obtain answers that are only partly supported by the facts available (to the inference engine).

2   Business Integration for Healthcare

Our objective is to present an intelligent multi-agent system that will be able to monitor, interact and serve its costumers, being those elderly people and/or their relatives. This system will be interconnected, not only to healthcare institutions, but also with leisure centers, training facilities, shops and relatives, just to name a few. The VirtualECare Architecture is a distributed one with different components interconnected through a network (e.g. LAN, MAN, WAN), each one with a different role (**Fig**).

This solution helps healthcare providers to integrate, analyze, and manage complex and disparate clinical, research and administrative knowledge. It provides tools and methodologies for creating an information-on-demand environment that can improve quality-of-living, safety, and patient care.

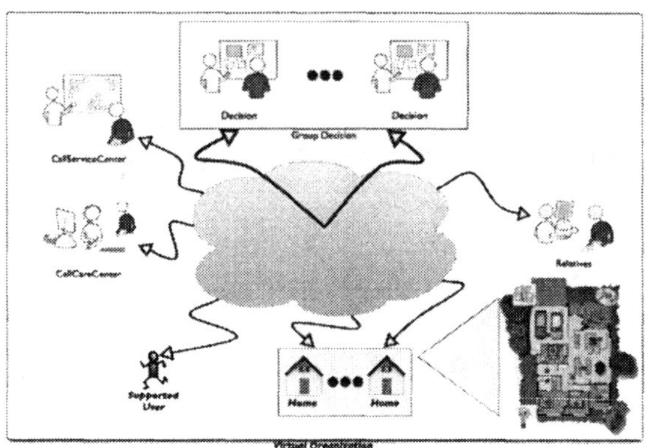

Fig 1. The System's Architecture, VirtualECare

3   Decision Making

To model the call centers it is necessary to establish the steps for the creation of a virtual community of agents, i.e. a Multi Agent System (MAS). The importance of maintaining a community of agents is directly related to the need of obtaining information, among others, about their credibility, reputation, as well as their past behaviors, i.e.:

Agent(Id)::area_of_expertise ∧ organizational_factors ∧ interest_topics ∧
disponibility ∧ credibility ∧ reputation ∧ availability.

where *Id, area_of_expertise, organizational_factors, interest_topics, disponibility, credibility, reputation* and *availability* denote, respectively, the identification of the agent, the set of areas where the agent is an expert, the information about the institution where the agent is enrolled (e.g. employee numbers), the interest topics for the agent, the disponibility, credibility, reputation of the agent and its availability at a given moment. The community of agents is given as a set of N agents, {AgP$_1$, AgP$_2$, ... AgP$_N$}, denoted by AgP. The availability of each agent can be classified according to three states: **uncommitted, committed**, or **in action**. An uncommitted agent stands for someone that may or may not join the MAS. A committed agent has agreed to be part of the MAS, but the inclusion process has not yet started. At last, an agent in action is someone involved in a task that already began.

3.1 Incomplete Information

The agent's KB has two different types of knowledge: the positive knowledge (that is known to be *true*), and the negative one (that is known to be *false*). All the rest is *unknown* [7]. Indeed, the view of logic programming accepted in this paper is strictly declarative. The adequacy of a body representation of knowledge in a logic programming language means adequacy with respect to the declarative semantics of that language. Given a First Order Language (FOL), an Extended Logic Program (ELP) is a set of rules and invariants of the form:

$$H \leftarrow B_1 \wedge ... \wedge B_n \wedge \neg C_1 \wedge ... \wedge \neg C_m \, (m > 0, n > 0)$$

where H, B_1, ..., B_n, C_1, ..., C_m are objective literals, and, in integrity rules, H is $\perp$ (contradiction). An objective literal is either an atom A or its explicit negation $\neg A$, where $\neg\neg A = A$. $\neg L$ is called a default or negative literal. Literals are either objective or default ones. The default complement of objective literal L is $\neg L$, and of default literal $\neg L$ is L. A rule stands for all its ground instances wrt (with respect to) FOL. A set of literals S is non-contradictory iff there is no $L \in S$ such that $\neg L \in S$. For every pair of objective literals {L, $\neg L$} in FOL we implicitly assume the integrity rule $\perp \leftarrow L, \neg L$. The main idea here is to compute all consequences of the program, even those leading to contradiction, as well as those arising from contradiction. Suppose that in the KB of the AgR the information related to the areas of expertise of the AgP_i identified as Peter, is represented in Program 1 [7].

```
area_of_expertise('Peter', pediatrics).
¬area_of_expertise('Peter', oncologist).
```

Program 1. It contains information related to the expertise areas of a specific agent.

If the KB is questioned if the area of expertise of Peter is Pharmacy the answer should be unknown, because there is no information related to that. On other hand, situations of incomplete information may involve different kinds of nulls. The ELP language will be used for the purpose of knowledge representation. One of the null types to be considered stands for an unknown value, a countable one (i.e. it is able to form a one-to-one correspondence with the positive integers). As an example, let us suppose that one of the agents that belong to the agent community AgP, at the registration phase, does not specify its interest topics; it just informs that it has interest topics. This means that the interest topics of the agent are unknown (Program 2).

```
¬skill(A,B) ← not skill(A,B) ∧ not exceptiontskill(A,B).
exceptionskill(A,B) ← skill(A, something).
skill('John', something).
```

Program 2. Information related to the agent interest topics.

Another type of null value denotes information of an enumerated set. Following the previous example, suppose that an agent does not give information related to its availability, but its state of affairs is one of the three: **uncommitted, committed** or **in_action** (Program 3).

$\neg$availability(A,B) $\leftarrow$ not availability(A,B) $\land$ not exceptionavailability(A,B).
exceptionavailability('John',committed).
exceptionavailability('John',uncommitted).
exceptionavailability('John',in_action).
$\neg$((exceptionavailability('John',A) $\lor$ exceptionavailability('John',B)) $\land \neg$
(exceptionavailability('John',A) $\land$ exceptionavailability('John',B)).

/* This invariant denotes that the agent states of committed, uncommitted and in_action are disjointed */

Program 3. Information related to the agent's availability.

3.2   Quality of Information of the Agent`s Profile

The quality of information about an asset K (given in terms of the quality of information that emerges from the extension of predicate K) is given by $Q_K = 1/Card$, where $Card$ denotes the cardinality of the exception set for predicate K, being K disjunctive.   One   the   other   hand,   if K contradicts   disjunction,

$$\binom{Card}{1} + \binom{Card}{2} + ... + \binom{Card}{Card}$$ will stand for the cardinality of the combined set

of terms that make the extension of predicate K (with respect to a particular asset $K)$

(where $\binom{Card}{p} = \dfrac{Card!}{p!(Card - p)!}$ gives the number of combinations of $Card$

elements,   taken p to p, where $o \leq p \leq Card$). Q_K is, in this case, given in the form:

$$Q_k = \frac{1}{\binom{Card}{1} + \binom{Card}{2} + ... + \binom{Card}{Card}}$$

The quality of the information that the system detains about agent AgPj, may now be defined as follows [Marreiros, 2006]:

$$Q^{AgP_i}(Profile_{AgP_j}) = \frac{\sum_{k=1}^{N} Q_k^{AgP_j} * W_k^{AgP_i}}{\sum_{k=1}^{N} W_k^{AgP_i}}$$

where N stands for the number of assets of the profile, $Q_k^{AgP_j}$ is the quality measure of K and $W_k^{AgP_i}$ denotes the contribution of K to the agent's profile. It is now possible, based on a set of (evolving) Decision Trees (DTs), to follow, day in, day out, the elderly. However, DTs are not simple representations of a decision making process, they may also apply to categorization problems, i.e., for example, instead of saying that one wish to represent a DT to plan what to do, on a weekend,

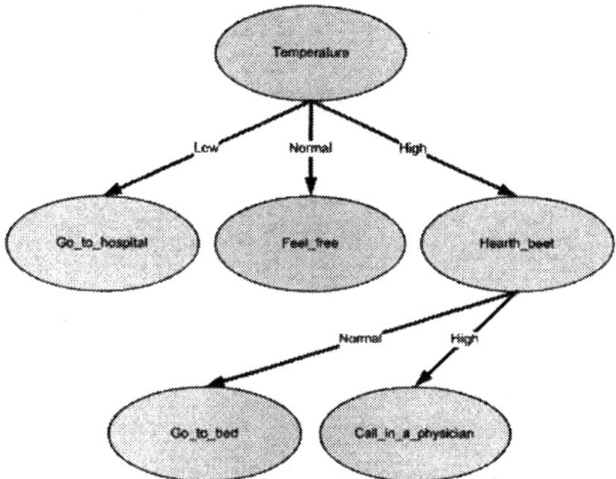

we could ask what kind of weekend is to be expected. This could easily be phrased as a question of learning a DT to decide in which category a weekend fits in (e.g., *if* it rains and it is windy *then* it is a weekend not to be remembered).

Fig 2. Decision Tree to watch the Elderly State of Health

One may now look to the process of DTs construction (e.g., to decide what to do at the weekend). One may use some background information as axioms and deduce what to do (e.g. one can know that the family is in town and that they like going to the cinema). Then, using, for example, Modus Ponens, we may decide to go to the cinema. Another way to stand around, it is by generalizing from previous experiences (e.g. let us consider all the times we had a really good weekend). If this is the case, one is using an inductive, rather than deductive method to construct the DTs (in this case one is using, for example, Modus Mistakens). Therefore, one may have Figure 2 and Figure 3.

On the other hand, there is a link between decision tree representations and logical representations, which can be exploited to make it easier to understand (to read) learned DTs. If we think better about it, every DT is actually a disjunction of implications (i.e., if ... then statements), and the implications are Horn clauses, i.e. a conjunction of terms implying a single term (Program 4).

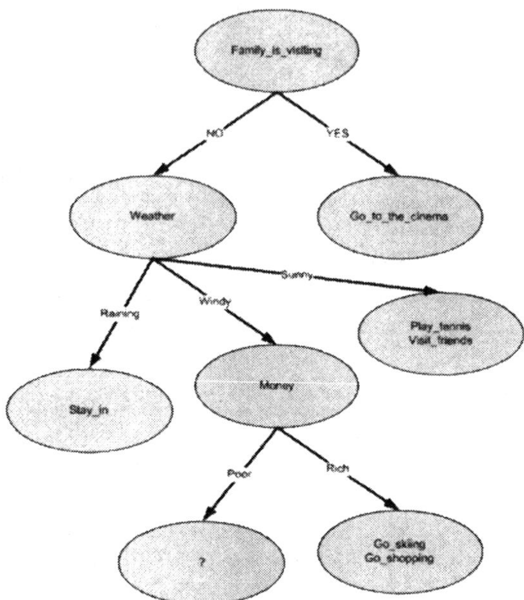

Fig 3 . Decision Tree to gaze at the Elderly Weekend Planning

if family_is_visiting then go-to-the-cinema ∨
if ¬family_is_visiting ∧ weather_is_sunny then play_tenis ∧ visit_friends ∨
…

Program 4 - Reading from the root node to each leaf node.

The DTs depicted in Figures 2 and 3 may now be given in terms of logic programs or theories. For Figure 3 one may have (Program 5):

if family_is_visiting then go-to-the-cinema.
if ¬family_is_visiting ∧ weather_is(weather, sunny) then play_tenis.
if ¬family_is_visiting ∧ weather_is(weather, sunny) then visit_friends.
…
if ¬family_is_visiting ∧ weather_is(weather, windy) ∧ money_is(money, rich) then go_shopping.
if ¬family_is_visiting ∧ weather_is(weather, windy) ∧ money_is(money, rich) then go_skiing.
¬((go_shopping ∨ go_skiing) ∧ ¬(go_shopping ∧ go_skiing)).
/* This invariant denotes that the options of going to shop or going to skiing are disjointed */
…
family_is_visiting.
¬ family_is_visiting.

¬((family_is_visiting ∨ (¬ family_is_visiting)) ∧ ¬(family_is_visiting ∧ (¬ family_is_visiting)).
/* This invariant denotes that the occurrences family_is_visiting and
¬ family_is_visiting are disjointed */

¬ weather_is(weather ,X) ←
        not weather_is(weather ,X) ∧ not exceptionweather_is(weather ,X).
weather_is(weather ,sunny).
weather_is(weather ,windy).
weather_is(weather ,raining).

¬ mone_is(money ,X) ←
        not money_is(money ,X) ∧ not exceptionmoney_is(money ,X).
money_is(money ,rich).
money_is(money ,poor).

Program 5 - Decision Tree Meta-Logic Program to gaze at the Elderly Weekend
Planning.

The call centers (i.e. the ServiceCallCenter and the CareCallCenter) may now
receive from the premises under monitoring the elderly plans for the weekend,
knowing also how good or bad they are, being therefore in a position to make the
right judgments (Figure 4).

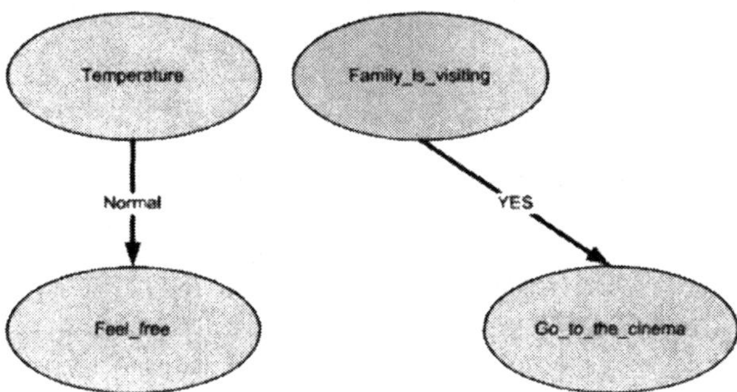

Fig 4 . Messages sent to the call centers

An advice is got in return (e.g., you may go with your family to the cinema). This
advice is given not only in terms of the factual information gathered by the sensors,
in terms of the DT or corresponding logical formulae depicted in Figure 2, but also
attending to an evaluation of the quality of information of such formulae [8].

4 Conclusion

Based on a set of evolving DTs, it is possible not only to monitor the day in, day out of the elderly, but provide some useful advice. In future work, and attending to such scenarios, we may use collaborative networks as a support for different, but interconnected virtual organizations, that could provide to all the population in general, and the elderly, in particular way, a certain amount of remote services (e.g. healthcare, entertainment, learning), without delocalizing or messing up with their routine, in a more effective and intelligent way.

References

1. Giráldez, M., Casal, C.: The Role of Ambient Intelligent in the Social Integration of the Elderly. *IOS Press* (2005)

2. Camarinha-Matos, L.M., Afsarmanesh, H.: Virtual Communities and Elderly Support. Advances in Automation, Multimedia and Video Systems, and Modern Computer Science. WSES (2001) 279-284

3. Marreiros, G., Novais, P., Machado, J., Ramos, C., Neves, J.: An Agent-based Approach to Group Decision Simulation using Argumentation. International MultiConference on Computer Science and Information Tecnology, Workshop Agent-Based Computing III (ABC 2006), Wisla, Poland (2006) 225-232

4. Augusto, J.C., McCullah, P., McClelland, V., Walden, J.-A.: Enhanced Healthcare Provision Through Assisted Decision-Making in a Smart Home Environment. 2nd Workshop on Artificial Inteligence Techniques for Ambient Inteligence (2007)

5. Dosi, G.: "Sources, procedures and microeconomics effects of innovation". *Economic Literature* 26 (1998) 1120-1171

6. Malmberg, A.: "Industrial Geography: agglomeration and local milieu". Progress in Human Geography, Vol. 20 (1996) 392-403

7. Neves, J.: "A Logic Interpreter to Handle Time and Negation in Logic Data Bases". In: ACM (ed.): *The Fifth Generation Challenge* (1984) 50-54

8. Marreiros, G., Santos, R., Ramos, C., Neves, J., Novais, P., Machado, J., Bulas-Cruz, J.: Ambient Intelligence in Emotion Based Ubiquitous Decision Making. Proceedings of the International Joint Conference on Artificial Intelligence (IJCAI 2007) - 2nd Workshop on Artificial Intelligence Techniques for Ambient Intelligence (AITAmI'07) (2007)

An Investigation and Analysis of e-Services in Major Subject Based Information Gateways in the World

Ruhua Huang1   Chang Liu2
*1 Ruhua Huang, Center for Studies of Information Resources
, Wuhan University, Wuhan, P.R.China, 430072
ruhua2003new@yahoo.com.cn
2 Chang Liu, School of Information Management, Wuhan
University, Wuhan, P.R.China, 430072
liuchang_cl@hotmail.com*

Abstract. Subject based information gateways (SBIGs) aim at providing professional quality-assured information resources and multifold e-services. However, since the information resources construction of SBIGs has gained lots of acclamations, much attention should be paid on e-services to attract users. Only through expedient services provided by SBIGs, can users be faithful supporters. But e-services of them have infrequently been discussed, so we looks into e-Services of ten major SBIGs in the world, with focus on their browse, search and value-added information services. The e-service in SBIGs are uneven, most of them lack in efficient services. Based on the investigation and analyses, the paper concludes with some suggestions using theories of user-centered and service-centered for improving e-services in SBIGs. The methodologies of investigation, analysis, comparison, case study and statistics are used to do this research.

1   Introduction

The growth of Web information continues to challenge users seeking relevant and high-quality resources on the Internet. Major search engines, such as Google and Yahoo, respond to this challenge by increasing the size of their databases and offering more powerful searching and ranking features. But they often lack the structured browsing and controlled vocabulary support. Thus, Subject Based Information Gateways (SBIGs) emerged as a response to weakness of Internet search engines. "Subject gateways are online services and sites that provide searchable and browsable catalogues of Internet based resources. Subject gateways will typically focus on a related set of academic subject areas. [1]"

Nowadays, a number of SBIGs have been developed to help users find high quality resources on the Internet. They tend to be used widely in the research, educational or cultural domains. As a result, SBIGs play a crucial role in the

---

Please use the following format when citing this chapter:

Huang, R., Liu, C., 2007, in IFIP International Federation for Information Processing, Volume 252, Integration and Innovation Orient to E-Society Volume 2, eds. Wang, W., (Boston: Springer), pp. 209-217.

education and research innovation, and have been conceived and carried forward as an integral part of national cyberinfrastructure in some countries.

SBIGs employ subject specialists and information professional to identify, evaluate, catalogue and organize Internet resources for inclusion in browsable and searchable Web-based gateway services to support user with quality-controlled resources and e-Services.

At present, the e-services of SBIGs are infrequently investigated especially for the comparison of them. This paper is an attempt to provide a detailed survey on e-Services of SBIGs and to offer some suggestions on improving them. The ten major SBIGs studied in this paper are from different countries of the world. BUBL Information Service (BUBL), intute and Biz/ed are from U.K., INFOMINE, Librarians' Index to the Internet (LII) and Gate way to 21st Century Skills (Gateway) from U.S.A., WWW Virtual Library (VL) from Switzerland, EdNA Online: Education Network Australia (EdNA Online) from Australia, MathGuid from Germany, and Chinese National Science Digital Library (CSDL) from P. R. China.

2   Browse Services in SBIGs

Provide browsing of quality manually catalogued resources are essential services for SBIGs. In this part, we investigate browse services provided in the ten SBIGs.

Table 1. Browse Modes in Major SBIGs (arranged alphabetically by the SBIGs' name)

Gateway	Country	Browse Mode
Biz/ed	U.K.	By subject, status or sections
BUBL	U.K.	By DDC, alphabetical order, subject menus, countries and resource type
CSDL	P. R. China	By subject
EdNA Online	Australia	By website area and all education topics
Gateway	U.S.A.	By subject, type, level, keywords, mediator, beneficiary and price code
INFOMINE	U.S.A.	By subjects, keywords, authors, titles and resource types
intute	U.K.	By subject headings
LII	U.S.A.	By subject
MathGuide	Germany	By subject, source type and journal list
VL	Switzerland	By subject

Table 1 shows all the ten described SBIGs provide browsing services, nine of them support browse by subject, typically based on classification schemes. Some even add other browsing mode according to their characteristics. Gateway provides seven browse choices and it is the best integrated one among the ten.

3   Search Services in SBIGs

Searching presents modes of SBIGs' information retrieval system. To carry out a search combining different search fields help focusing search on specific kind of information. Meanwhile, a search query by using search operators can make search results more relevant and precise. The focus of this part was on the investigation of search services in the ten SBIGs. It consists of three main parts: search modes, search fields and search operators.

3.1   Survey on Search Modes in Major SBIGs

Table 2. Search Modes in Major SBIGs

Gateway	Search Mode		
	Simple	Advanced	Others
Biz/ed	√	√	
BUBL	√	√	Combined search
CSDL	√	√	
EdNA Online	√	√	Distribute search, sector search, Browse category search
Gateway	Faceted search		
INFOMINE	√	√	
intute	√	√	
LII	√	√	Facet navigation
MathGuide	√	√	
VL	√	√	

It can be seen from table 2 that the studied SBIGs use different modes to provide search services, including simple search, advanced search, combined search, distribute search, sector search and faceted search. Generally speaking, the most common search method is the simple search and advanced search mode options. Simple search in these SBIGs only supports search in some limited fields, while advanced search combines a wide variety of search fields and several displayed choices. The advanced search in every SBIG has its special functions, taking CSDL as an example, it provides the function of conserve searching data and offers them to user when they log in next time.

Some characteristics with regard to searching should be pointed out. Several of them add combined search, distribute search, sector search as a supplementary. Faceted search is also used in such well-developed SBIGs like LII, Gate way to 21st Century Skills and EdNA Online. Faceted search, which combines the processes of searching for specific words and phrases with browsing resources based on subject facets, is an excellent way and also a trend in searching area.

3.2   Survey on Search Fields in Major SBIGs

Table 3. Search Fields in Major SBIGs

Gateway	Search Fields
Biz/ed	keywords
BUBL	title, subject terms, author, description, resource type

CSDL	title, classification, subsidiary title, editor, author, publisher, URL, publish year, type of institution and resources, language, record type
EdNA Online	title, subject, audience, creator, date, description, EdNA category, identifier, location, publisher, search area, search site, thesaurus selecting, repository selecting
Gateway	title, keywords, full text, description
INFOMINE	title, subject, author, keyword, description, full text ,subject categories, record origin(expert created or robot), resource access, resource types
intute	title, description, keywords, subject groups, resource type
LII	title, URL, description
MathGuide	title, keywords, names, MSC, codes, language, country, source type, dates, last update, text,
VL	title, subject, author, keyword, description, words forms(all or exact), use synonyms (yes/no), document types, URL matches

Table 3 shows that the search fields which are frequently used in SBIGs are: title, subject, author, keyword, description and document types. The number of search fields in each SBIG is very variable, from 5 of LII to 14 of EdNA Online. Each of them designs a variety of useful fields. VL uses match, search for, words forms and synonyms fields to help users express search terms precisely and conveniently, so does Biz/ed. INFOMINE set record origin fields to identify the manually quality-controlled resources or robot-generated databases, as well as set resource access fields to separate the free access resources from the paid ones. EdNA Online allows search result to be restricted from all sites or Australian sites via search site field, from all types of EdNA resources or any sector of them via search area field, from the internal EdNA resources or some well-recognized repository outside via the repository selecting fields. Comparatively speaking, the SBIGs which used faceted search like LII and Gate way to 21st Century Skills have few fields but higher search efficiency and convenience than others.

3.3   Survey on Search operators in Major SBIGs

Table 4 shows a statistic as follows. In SBIGs described above, 100% of them support Boolean logic, 70% support truncation, half provide phrase operator. However, several SBIGs use other search operators like parentheses, fuzzy, proximity and spell-check. For example, INFOMINE and VL support parentheses, but LII provide the greatest number of search operators. Additionally, some of them integrated search operators into the interface as a search box, which means that SBIGs become more and more intellectual and humane.

Table 4. Search Operators in Major SBIGs

Gateway	Search Operators			
	Boolean Logic	Truncation	Phrase	Others
Biz/ed	AND,OR			
BUBL	AND,OR,NOT	*, ?		
CSDL	AND, NOT(-)		" "	
EdNA Online	AND,OR,NOT			

Gateway	AND,OR,NOT	*	" "	Spell-check
INFOMINE	AND,OR,NOT	*	" ", ||	Proximity(Near"n ")
intute	AND,OR,NOT	*	" "	
LII	AND(+),OR,NOT(-)	*	" "	Spell-check, stemming
MathGuide	AND,OR,NOT	?		
VL	AND(&),OR(|),NOT(~)	*		Fuzzy
Total	100%	70%	50%	40%

4 Survey on Value-added Information Services Provided by SBIGs

Table 5. Value-added Information Services in Major SBIGs

Gateway	Information Services					
	Virtual reference service	Newsletter	Archi-ves offer	Information push	Persona-lization service	Others
Biz/ed		√	√			
BUBL	√		√			
CSDL	√	√		√	√	Subject's forum
EdNA Online	√	√	√	√	√	Group space
Gateway	√	√			√	
INFOMINE	√			√		
intute	√	√			√	Job search
LII		√		√		
MathGuide	√					
VL		√	√			
Total	70%	70%	40%	40%	40%	30%

Table 5 shows that the value-added information services provided by the ten SBIGs focus on several types listed above. Virtual reference services(VRS)and newsletter are the most frequently provided services in SBIGs, the follow ones offered is information push, archives offer and personalization services.

The first kind of virtual reference service mode is to reveal general reference resources. For instance, BUBL exploits a directory of UK organizations and institutions. MathGuide collects journal information about math. INFOMINE even integrate Google, Altavista, All the Web, Hotbot, Teoma and Wisenut to be a meta search engine and recommend Internet search engines &finding tools to users. Only Gateway provides "ask and answer questions" service. Newsletter service often selects news in the related subject areas, users can subscribe by email or RSS or just read online to get this service from some SBIGs like LII.

Information push is more and more prevail, both users and the websites can get benefit from it. In SBIGs, the email notification service will keep users informed of the latest information resources they customized. Establishing archives is a method to preserve precious resources. BUBL provide "E-LIS", an open archive for Library and Information Science. VL also set out the archives of papers, presentations, audio materials and history about it. The most noteworthy example is that the personalized service of intute is classified to certain groups of users particularly and pertinently.

Virtual training should be a very useful service to improve users' information literacy, but only intute supports it. Other special kinds of information services are job search by intute, subject's forum by CSDL, group space by EdNA Online.

5   Suggestions for Improving e-Services in SBIGs

Although the studied SBIGs are appreciated by their user communities, they face challenges from automated search engines. Powerful search engines including Google have used advanced techniques to improve the quality of search results. In order to advance and perfect the quality of e-Services of SBIGs, some areas for future developments are given below.

5.1   Reforming Browsing and Searching Interfaces

While the SBIGs have developed many kinds of searching and browsing ways, some future work might include further enhancements of the searching and browsing interfaces. Surveying the SBIGs, we find that the concision, practicability and amicability have great influence on users' willing of using SBIG. Analysis of Renardus usage logs also suggests that "systematic browsing of large information systems with the help of classification hierarchies seems to be widely accepted by users, especially when there is graphical support" [2].

LII doesn't provide so many search modes as other SBIGs, but it is the most wieldiest one. In LII, users do not have to spend time on scanning the dazzling interfaces and deciding which one they should log in or log out. The whole interface of the gateway is quite clear with an obvious navigation system, which allows user switching between searching and browsing. It is also a secret of LII's success, despite of the specialization.

5.2   Progressing Integration of Resources and Services

Integration should mean enhancing and maximizing the value of existing infrastructure services and combining their service delivery with new mechanisms which exploit new technologies [3]. Integrated access to digital resources depend on the uniform descriptions of information resources. Nowadays, the development of metadata and new technical architectures make it possible. The integration of information resources aims at better e-services. Service-centered must be the principle in the progress of SBIGs.

Except such basic services as browse and search options, SBIGs should provide additional, valued-added services, such as producing thesauri, delivering training, setting up personalized alerts for new online resources and giving advice on users' searching, and integrate all these services so that end users can get one-site services. Intute is a typical illustration. In July 2006, it re-launched as a single service through integrating eight good U.K. SBIGs (Altis, Artifact, BIOME, EEVL, GEsource, Humbul, PSIgate and SOSIG) to centralize the forces and actualize the supplement among them. Intute provides united services and has more achievements in the world than before.

In order to enhance information services in SBIGs, the UK's Joint Information Systems Committee (JISC) funded a two-year project ending August 2003——The Subject Portals Project. The portal services include a single sign-on access management system; a cross-searching tool; a user profiling system; and other "additional services" [4]. This system is a successful model, which has integrated basic and value-added services.

5.3   Strengthening Investigation and Feedback of User's Requirement

User-centered has been always the ideal of all services including e-services in SBIGs. A SBIG must assess accurately the needs of the prime target audience and meet the needs of its user community. At present, there are three kinds of communication between providers and users in SBIGs: virtual reference, information push and users' feedback. Although SBIGs have diversified traits, the ultimate purpose is to improve their services. The communications help both users and providers.

It is a piece of good news that most SBIGs discussed above emphasize information push services. Nevertheless, the implement of VRS is not so optimistic. Real-time reference service is not provided by these SBIGs, what they offer are just related reference resources. Theories and practices of multiple models of virtual reference service should be applied to further development of SBIGs. The users' feedback is helpful for providers to improve services. The current users' feedback system is not consummate enough for users to estimate effectively. Enhancing and perfecting the construction of the SBIGs' communication system is still a handicap for the developers to conquer.

Besides direct communication between users and providers, some deep investigation and analysis should be done among users. In 2001, an evaluation study was done with attempts to evaluate ADAM in terms of real searching behavior obtained by users' feedback and provides some detailed information on who these digital users are, how often they use the service, etc [5].

5.4   Paying Attention to Promotion of e-Service

In order to become a popular service and gain acceptance as a valid information retrieval tool amongst its target audience, a SBIG should use a number of methods and a variety of media to promote itself and its services like other successful commerce case. News about a particularly important milestone of SBIG, or a new service or interface released should be posted to the target audience in a number of newsgroups and e-mail discussion groups by information push services, it is the basic way which the SBIGs usually do. Some other methods are still needed, for example, publishing advertisements on various media like TV, radio, high-click rate websites, even distributing small gifts with some information of SBIGs on including calendars, pens, cups and unusually-designed leaflets.

Some SBIGs has done very well in this way. Ongoing promotion, by a variety of methods, has been recognized as a means of raising awareness of the development of the Edinburgh Engineering Virtual (EEVL) amongst its target audience. As a result, usage of EEVL has rapidly increased in recent months, with current figures indicating a daily average of over 9,000 page views [6].

6   Conclusion

Despite the variety of search engines in use and the proliferation of search tools, there is still a need for human intervention to guide the search process by adding a subject gateway [7]. SBIGs should save users' time, connect them to quality-controlled resources and services to support their learning, teaching and research. The key issues which need to be addressed for the future development of information services in SBIGs are: continued quality of services, reinforced the value of existing service provision methods, sustainability of services and service integration [8].

In order to provide a better and more sustainable subject orientated service to a wider audience, more efforts should be put on the specialization, efficiency and accuracy of e-Services in SBIGs. Increased collaboration between SBIGs would be a good solution, for example, exchange records, cross-browsing, cross-searching, mirroring remote service, cooperative digital reference services, shared development of technological solutions and online tutorials, etc. This includes cooperation between SBIGs in a subject area and cooperation between SBIGs in different countries as well as international collaboration.

Acknowledgment

This research was supported by the National Planning Office of Philosophy and Social Science, P.R. China (Project No. 06&ZD031).

References

1.   What   is   a   subject   gateway?   (May   16,   2007); http://www.desire.org/html/Subjectgate ways/subjectgateways.html.

2. M. Day, T. Koch, H. Neuroth, Searching and browsing multiple subject gateways in the Renardus Service, Proceedings of the RC33 Sixth International Conference on Social Science Methodology. Amsterdam, Stuttgart(2004).

3. Debbie Campbell, "Australian subject gateway: political and strategic issues", *Online Information Review*. Vol. 24, 73-77 (2000).

4. Ruth Martin, "The subject portals project: Enhancing the delivery of subject-based information to the UK further and higher education community", *The Serials Librarian*. Vol. 45, 39-48 (2004).

5. Maria Monopoli, David Nicholas, A User Evaluation of Subject Based Information Gateways: Case Study ADAM, Aslib Proceedings. 53(1), 39-52 (2001).

6. Roddy MacLeod, "Promoting a subject gateway: a case study from EEVL" (Edinburgh Engineering Virtual Library), *Online Information Review*. Vol. 24, 63(2000).

7. Krishnamurthy, M,"Designing a gateway interface: conceptual framework for library and information science", *Information Studies*. Vol.11, 195-204(2005).

8. Nejdl Wolfgang, Innovative information and knowledge infrastructures - How do I find what I need?, Advances in information systems. Proceedings lecture notes in computer science. 4243, 34-37(2006).

Design of Web-based Management Information System for Academic Degree & Graduate Education

Rui Duan[1], Mingsheng Zhang[2]

[1]Northwestern Polytechnical University, Xi'an, Shanxi, 710072,
duanrui@mail.ccnu.edu.cn

[2]Huazhong Normal University, Wuhan, Hubei, 430079,
mszhang@mail.ccnu.edu.cn

Abstract: For every organization, the management information system is not only a computer-based human-machine system that can support and help the administrative supervisor but also an open technology system for society. It should supply the interaction function that face the organization and environment, besides gather, transmit and save the information. The authors starts with the intension of contingency theory and design a web-based management information system for academic degree & graduate education which is based on analyzing of work flow of domestic academic degree and graduate education system. What's more, the application of the system is briefly introduced in this paper.

1   Introduction

In college and university, the all functions and whole process of management are an open system of general management. It includes the academic record management, cultivating scheme management, course management, grade management, degree management and directing the students to take up an occupation, etc. Every function department involved in the system has respective special information requirements and there are diversified information connections among them. "The web-based management information system for academic degree & graduate education" is based on the contingency theory and tries to more efficiently manage the academic degree & graduate education from the interrelation and dynamic activity in system.

Please use the following format when citing this chapter:

Duan, R., Zhang, M., 2007, in IFIP International Federation for Information Processing, Volume 252, Integration and Innovation Orient to E-Society Volume 2, eds. Wang, W., (Boston: Springer), pp. 218-226.

1.1 Known Results

The basic assume of contingency theory is organization, environment and every subsystem should achieve consistency. The contingency viewpoint is a systemic concordant thought and can solve problems. These thought let manager starts with whole and carry on management with the aim of realize the whole target. Its significance is focusing on that change of management is consistent with the change of people, time, place and environment. It focuses that using different strategy in change environment.

Management Information System, namely MIS, is a human-machine system that uses systemic thinking and has the modern communication techniques as the basic information disposal means and transfer tools. It can supply the information service to managers. MIS is a unified system or integrated system, that is to say MIS carries on the management staring with the whole status, entirely considers every factor and ensures the share datum in each function department, in order to decrease the data redundancy and ensure data compatibility and consistency.

One the one hand, the application of web-based management information system decreases the middle-level management layers and makes the structure of organization more flat; on the other hand, it strengthens the communication channel of inter-organization. At the same time, it makes the application system quicker and reduces the cost.

The web-based management information system for academic degree & graduate education utilizes the B/W/D structure. The work principle of traditional C/S structure is user puts forward data requirement to client computer by application, client computer puts in the requirement to server by network, server' database management system execute the data processing mission, and then the datum that user needed are transmitted to client computer, finally, client computer completes the processing of the needed datum. However, in B/W/D structure it is just need to install a Browser on client computer, middle-layer of system utilizes web server. The web server acts as not only an agent of client but also a client of database. At the same time, it takes charge of monitoring and answering the requirements of web client browser.

Because the various countries' graduate student management systems and management ways are different, the various countries' degree and graduate student education administration aspects also present the big differences. The domestic units raising graduate student usually make the degree and the graduate student education management information system in terms of their own raise pattern and the management characteristic. Viewing the graduate student education management information system the present various universities using, the following characteristic present:

(1) The degree and the graduate student education management information system lack the unified plan, each part of coordination is insufficient, data sharing between system and the integration is bad.

(2) The system service content is unitary. It mainly limits at the teaching administration, the academic record management, etc. However, there is almost not the information management system of directly unify the management of academic degree & graduate education.

(3) The main bodies of the service object are superintendent or in-school graduate student. Few are management information system that serves teacher and provides the many service function for the society, particularly few based on the web.

(4) The base data preparation insufficiency, the massive data dissociation outside the system. Both of them create the non-convenient use of the system.

Generally speaking, at present the degree and the graduate student education management information system and the degree and the graduate student education development have many inadaptable places.

The web-based management information system for academic degree & graduate education can more efficiently adapt to the changing conditions and make inter-department more harmony and unification. What's more, it can realize remote information resource of graduate education management's sharing and management. It is the diligently informationization work direction of various degrees and graduate student education administration department, at present and the next section of times, to realize the information resource's sharing and management.

1.2   Our Goals

Unifying our actual work and work requirement, we have conducted the thorough research on the degree and graduate student education management information system, which based on the web. Through the service flow analysis of the degree and the graduate student, and carrying on the system demand analysis, we designed the scientific, standard, integrated highly, function-entirely, based-on-web degree and the graduate student education management information system. And this system has following characteristic:

First and most important, highly integrated, unified constructed data platform, is advantageous for the management and facilitates the application. It may cover each aspect of the Chinese degree and the graduate student education administration and serve.

Next, it takes each service flow and the main function design subsystem of the degree and the graduate student education as the central design subsystem, rather than the degree and the graduate student education administration department. For efficiency, it makes the organization's structure more flat.

Once more, the service object and the user of the traditional management information system mainly are the administrative personnel in the graduate student education. This design will implement the humanist thought. The service object expands and the graduate student, teacher will be the main body members who participate to use this system. It will also provide the service function for the society.

At present, we have realized such subsystem functions of this system: graduate student school register management, the raise plan and the curriculum manage, the raise project management, the result management, the degree management, the user jurisdiction management, etc.

2   Research and design

2.1 system analysis

In order to design Web Information System for Academic Degree and Graduate Education, I use degree and graduate education of the HuaZhong normal university as the research subject.

2.1.1 The Primary Service Analysis

The main target of the degree and graduate student education management information system mainly is the discipline, the scholar, the students.

The discipline mainly was refers to have already to obtain the doctor degree and the master's degree authorization discipline specialty in the school. Under various disciplines has the basic situation to introduce, the troop constructs, the scientific research situation, the achievement and the prize situation, the key discipline, the key laboratory and so on.

The scholars mainly refer to the teacher to instruct the graduate student, including the graduate student instructor and the doctor instructor.

The students mainly refer to the graduate student in the school. It is to achieve the enrollment, training, degree management, student management, and employment of information management, in addition, also provide some of the information published on the Internet to collect and search functions, including enrollment plans of exam results in-school performance, degree and distribution of information.

2.1.2 The System Goals

Based on the above analysis, in order to meet school building and development needs, the system should meet the following development goals.

- System performance goals:

Usability: the management information system development should be the system's utility primary position, graduate education management information system design; the school should meet the graduate education management. The mechanism to operate should be in the first place.

Sophistication: Based on the pledge to meet the needs of the existing business, a certain system to maintain the advanced nature to make the system as growth in its life cycle. We must also consider the convenience of the system maintenance.

Integrity: the adoption of the system design and construction, so that the whole school graduate education information data reunification give full play to the entire system's overall efficiency.

Security: On the one hand we must guarantee the uniformity of the data and sharing, on the other hand we must guarantee the security of the data. Prevented the system suffers the attack and prevented the data is compiled to change and so on.

- The System Function Goal

We establish one information platform to be able to cover the entire degree and graduate student education administration service work, to satisfy the different management level to each kind of information demand.

Operation to achieve the following major functions: Data input, including mass introduction; Data Processing, including scheduling, and statistics; Data output, including data is derived, data backup, statements and print form; Data inquiries to various conditions, and other forms of inquiry.

2.1.3 System E-R figure

This system refers to subject, scholar, graduate student, department, course, program, production, award, punish, and so on. The mostly substantiality in this system see Figure 1.

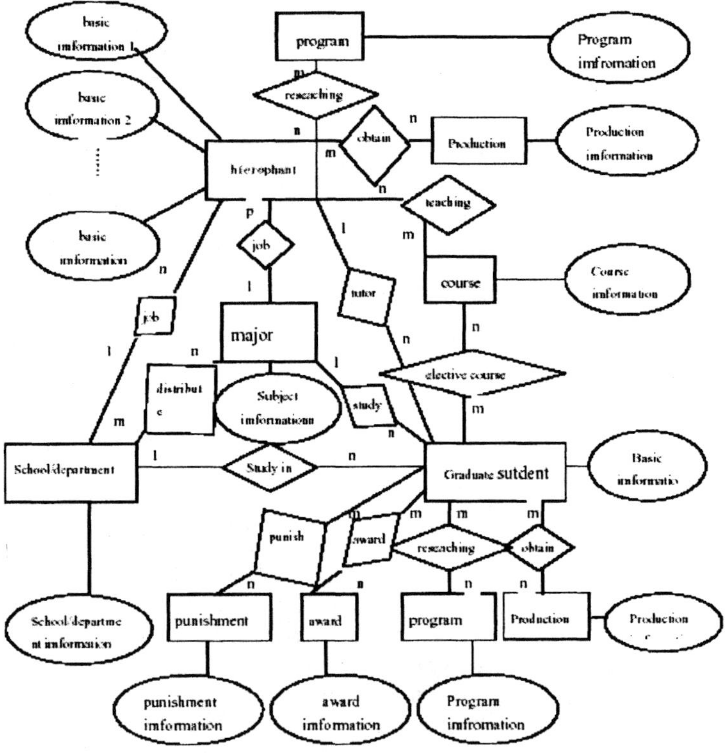

Figure 1 ADGEMIS mostly substantiality E-R figure

2.2 system design

2.2.1 Collectivity system design

Information System refers to many parts and data. Its target is realization of a comparatively stable concerted management environment. When design it, at first should master the whole structure, seize the keystone, carve up the hierarchy, and then fractionize one by one. According to the each part of the Academic Degree and Graduate Education，carve up the whole system to 10 system: Subject management, hierophant management, School register management subsystem, training plan and course management subsystem, training plan management subsystem, score management subsystem, degree management subsystem, obtain employment management subsystem, basic information maintenance subsystem, user power management subsystem.

2.2.2 System structure

Design of Web Information System for Academic Degree and Graduate Education are shown in figure 2.

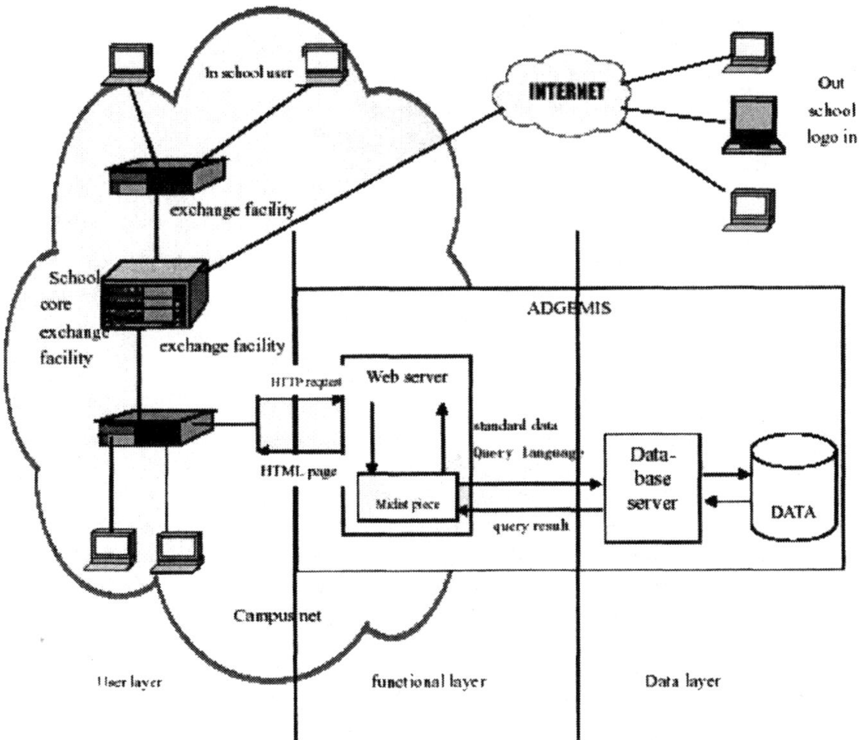

Figure2 system structure figure

In the database storage and handling of centralized storage and processing of information is centralized service model, academic degree and graduate education management information system (ADGEMIS) can be set up in graduate school (department), can be set up in schools center room. In the operating mode of using B/W/D framework internal and external users can through the web browser trip and academic degree and graduate education management information system (ADGEMIS).

The system is divided into user layer (also known as denote layer), the functional layer (also known as logic layer), the data layer, internal and external users through the use of the Internet web browser visits (including data maintenance and inquiry, etc.) for academic degree and graduate education Management Information System (ADGEMIS), HTTP request through the middleware layer functions (data transmission, analysis, processing, collating, sorting, printing and other functions) to the calling data server data requests, The database server will query result back to the function layer, the functional layer through the web browser will be back to the user.

3 Realizations

The academic degree and graduate education management information system has been realized and tested in the management of more than two thousand of grade 2006 graduate students in HuaZhong Normal University. The test and application includes the functions of recruiting graduates, academic record management, cultivating scheme management, constituting of individual cultivating plan, choosing course online, grade management and degree awarding management, etc. The fact proves that the system improved the work efficiency and service quality; the work period has averagely reduced 75%. At the same time, it has been all-round tested the system's security, toughness, compatibility and integrality of database and redundancy, etc. At present, the system is running all right.

4. Conclusions and Forecast

Our web-based information management system has almost realized the functions of the subsystems of academic record management, cultivating scheme management, constituting of individual cultivating plan, choosing course online, grade management, degree awarding management, user power management, etc.

Khazanchi (2005) put forward a point of view that traditional match of "mission-technique" is not equal to the improvement of mission performance. From the viewpoint of contingency theory to define math, it should use the match of "organization-technique" to answer the question of "when and in what condition does utilize the information technology to improve origination performance?" He put forward the conception of IT appropriateness. So we combine the experiences of study and development of information management system and consider that the following aspects should to note in the development of web-based information management system.

(1) Research, design, development and management of information systems, must be "people-oriented" concept as a system design starting point and end-result; the system should obtain the support of collaborator.

(2) Research, design, development and management of information systems should give attention to both inter and outer origination's management and technique environment. At the same time, it should pay attention to the actual benefit after putting in practice of the system and the status of improvement of organization productivity, in order to perfect and adjust ceaselessly.

(3) Security strategies. Once the information system and network connectivity, it must consider the network and information systems security. Network and information systems security include physical security and logical security. Physical security is the use of network hardware, maintenance and management; logical security, mainly from the perspective of software made to the main data confidentiality, integrity and availability, and so on. The same time, must use the form of rules and regulations to manage information systems.

Computer technology, information technology and network technology to the rapid development both graduate and post-graduate education management with a daunting challenge, but also to improve our management to provide a good tool and means will further promote graduate education management information process.

Academic degree and graduate education is the vigorous development of colleges and universities to improve their level of the important links for building a "comprehensive research university" is a vital element.

Academic degree and graduate education management information system as a digital campus, part of the information, College to improve the management level, efficiency, service quality, proceed to raise academic standards and the quality of graduates will have far-reaching significance.

References

1. W.M. Chen, H. Qi, Academic Degree and Graduate Education information management in information times. *Academic Degree and Graduate Education*, 2003(2)

2. X.J. Zhou, The Time transformation of the Academic Degree and Graduate Education. *Educational Research and Experiment*, 2005(1)

3. S.Q, Wang, etc. Study on the development of Management Information System for Graduate Education. *Scientific & Technical Information of GANSU*, 2003(4)

4. X.C. Lu, Design and Implementation of Academic Degree Theses Management System Based on Web. *Computer Knowledge and Technology*, 2005(2)

5. W.P. Song, etc. Authorization of User Privilege on the Basis of Web Information System. *Computer Engineering and Application*, 2004(35)

6. The 1999 National Survey of Information Technology in US Higher Education: The Continuing Challenge of *Instructional Integration and User Support.October,1999.*The Compus Computing Project

7. Bieg, Claudial Diehl, Stephan .Educational and technical design of a Web-based interactive tutorial on programming in Java. Science of Computer Programming .2004, 53(1):25-36

8. D. Khazanchi, Information Technology (IT) Appropriateness :The Contingency Theory of "FIT" and IT Implementation in Small and Medium Enterprises.*The Journal of Computer Information Systems* ,2005, 45(3) :88-95

9. Bechtel Government Projects Estimating Standards Team., Bechtel's Proposed Approach to Baseline Ownership, Contingency, *Rate and Escalation Applications on DOEProjects*. March 24, 2000.

10. Bowman, C. Collier, Nardine, A contingency approach to resource-creation processes. *International Journal of Management Reviews;* Dec2006, Vol. 8 Issue 4, p191-211, 21p

11. *Organization and management: A Systems and Contingency Approach.* 1985 by McGraw-Hill, Inc.

A Process Model of Partnership Evolution Around New IT Initiatives

Timo Kestilä[1], Lauri Salmivalli[2], Hannu Salmela[1], Annukka Vahtera[1]
1 Turku School of Economics, Information Systems Science
2 Turku School of Economics, Pori Unit, Welfare Economics

Abstract. Prior research on inter-organizational information systems has focused primarily on dyadic network relationships, where agreements about information exchange are made between two organizations. The focus of this research is on the processes through which IT decisions are made within larger inter-organizational networks with several network parties. The research draws from network theories in organization science to identify three alternative mechanisms for making network level commitments: contracts, rules and values. In addition, theoretical concepts are searched from dynamic network models, which identify different cycles and stages in network evolution. The empirical research was conducted in two networks. The first one comprises of four municipalities which began collaboration in the deployment of IT in early childhood education (ECE). The second network involves a case where several organizations, both private and public, initiated a joint effort to implement a national level electronic prescription system (EPS). The frameworks and concepts drawn from organizational theories are used to explain success of the first case and the failure of the latter case. The paper contributes to prior IOS research by providing a new theory-based framework for the analysis of early stages of building organizational networks around innovative IT initiatives.

1   Introduction

Despite the critical role of computers in inter-organizational arrangements, coordination of IT decisions within these networks is a fairly unexplored area, both in research and in practice. The processes through which the orchestration of IT in networks takes place are largely hidden. However, many initiatives to coordinate IT decisions fail within networks. These failures are not necessarily very visible and thus get very little attention.

Please use the following format when citing this chapter:

Kestilä, T., Salmivalli, L., Salmela, H., Vahtera, A., 2007, in IFIP International Federation for Information Processing, Volume 252, Integration and Innovation Orient to E-Society Volume 2, eds. Wang, W., (Boston: Springer), pp. 227-236.

This research investigates the processes through which networks can reach agreements on the use of IT. The research problem is formulated as follows: *How to build and maintain inter-organizational cooperative network for IT collaboration?* The practical objective is to provide methods for managers starting up inter-organizational network to foster a specific IT related collaborative idea. It is suggested, however, that the networks differ in terms of dominant coordination mechanisms. Hence, the group should employ methods that fit with the general coordination style of the network.

We acknowledge the dynamic nature of networks: the explanations for outcomes are process theories, rather than variance theories [1]. Preconditions and situational variables are not, as such, sufficient to explain outcomes. The outcomes result from the interplay between initial conditions, contextual changes, and process events and Ring and Van de Ven (1994) argue that there are less empirical knowledge about how Inter-Organizational Relationships (IORs) emerge, grow, and dissolve over time than there are about success factors and failures of IORs [2]. Therefore, it is relevant to ask, how the inter-organizational relationships are being developed. Field work in this article has done in two networks. One was a relative failure and the second one was success. Both ICT networks were in early stages and research was conducted with action research approach.

2   A process model of partnership evolution

Within Information Systems Science, the research draws from the research tradition around Inter-Organizational Systems (IOS). Research on strategic IS management, and more recently that of IT governance, will also be used as a theoretical background. While most of the studies in this area address IS management and governance mainly as taking place within a single firm, some researchers have already identified the need to incorporate network level considerations. For instance, Finnegan et al. argue that there is growing need for inter-organizational IS planning [3]. This argument is further developed by Salmela and Spil [4].

Perhaps the most fundamental difference between a network and an organization is the lack of a single authority to ensure coordination of actions. Absence of a single authority has led networks to employ a wide array of mechanisms to be used for building and maintaining commitment to joint efforts. These mechanisms have intrigued researchers in many fields, such as economics [5], strategic management [6], organization science [7], marketing [8], sociology [9], information systems [10] [11] and strategic information systems planning [12].

An inter-organizational relationship (IOR) can be defined as *"a social action system on the premise that it exhibits the basic elements of any organized form of collective behavior"* [13]. These IORs include strategic alliances, partnerships, coalitions, joint ventures, franchises, research consortia and various forms of network organizations [2].

The effects of the contingencies on inter-organizational cooperation vary between different types of IORs. Four basic types can be identified ([14]): *Hierarchical, Solar, Centreless* and *Swingle*. According to Wilson (1995) a process model for the development of inter-organizational relationship includes the following steps: partner selection, purpose definition, relationship boundaries setting, relationship value creation and relationship maintenance[15]. Ring and Van de Ven (1994) claim that the development and evolution of a cooperative inter-organizational relationship consists of a repetitive sequence of negotiation, commitment and execution phases [2].

The framework is presented in Figure1where each phase is assessed in terms of efficiency and equity. Even though the temporal occurrence of these phases may be almost simultaneous in simple transactions, the duration of each stage varies according to the uncertainty of issues involved, the reliance on trust among the parties to a cooperative IOR and the role relationships of the parties.

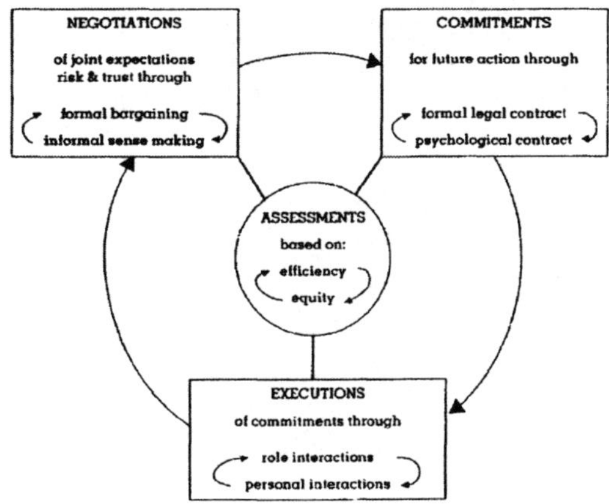

Figure 1: Process Framework of the development of cooperative Inter-organizational relationships [2]

Below, a more detailed description of different stages is given:

• **Negotiations stage**: In this stage the parties develop joint expectations about their motivations, possible investments and perceived uncertainties of a business deal they are exploring to undertake jointly. The focus in this stage is on the formal bargaining processes. These processes are often necessary in order to provide participants opportunities to assess uncertainty associated with the deal, the nature of each other's role, the other's trustworthiness, their rights and duties, and possible efficiency and equity of the transaction as it relates to all parties.

• **Commitments stage**: Participants reach an agreement on the obligations and rules for future action in the relationship. The terms and governance structure of the relationship are established in this stage. These agreements are either aggregated in a formal legal contract or informally understood psychological contract.

• **Executions stage**: In this stage, the commitments and rules of action are carried out. Initially, parties' formally designated role behavior reduces the uncertainty and makes interactions among parties also more predictable. After a while, parties may become more familiar with each other and they may increasingly begin to rely on interpersonal relationships.

In many cases, a cooperative IOR may need to remain in effect for a long time. Misunderstandings, conflicts and changing expectations are inevitable and they might cause renegotiations. In the final cycle of the process, the parties may conclude that the relationship should be terminated. This typically occurs when the parties have lived up their promises and the deal is completed. Ring and Van de Ven (1994) assume that participative organization have motivations to the network [2]. In this paper we assume that in pre-stage and early stage the motivation exist but it is unconscious and weak and is therefore needed to be strengthened.

Transaction economy has traditionally seen two possible ways for managing exchange: *hierarchy* and *market*. *Market exchanges* are transactions between separate entities whereas *hierarchical relationships* are coordinated through unitary organizational structures [16]. Ouchi has expanded Williamson's model by adding *clan* as one form of exchange and has renamed hierarchy to *bureaucracy*. [17]

According to Rodríguez et al. (2007) all three kind of governance mechanism play different but essential role in stimulating effective inter-organizational collaboration [18]. In Figure2 we describe these mechanisms and key motivations behind it. The mechanisms are present constantly and have to be considered in every phase of IOR process.

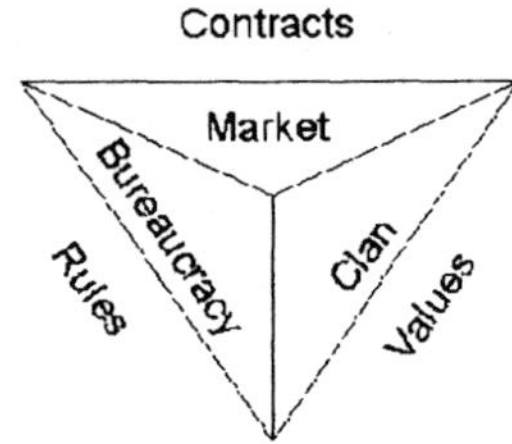

Figure 2: Coordination mechanism and key motivators [17]

In this paper we combine Ring and Van de Ven (1994) process framework in Figure and Ouchi's coordination mechanisms in Figure [2, 17]. Market, bureaucracy and clan mechanism are constantly present in properly operating inter-organizational union. Market and bureaucracy are needed for manage participants opportunism and clan for creating value and fairness [19]. In Figure 3 is presented the framework for analyzing IOR in different stages. This framework will be used to analyze our two cases.

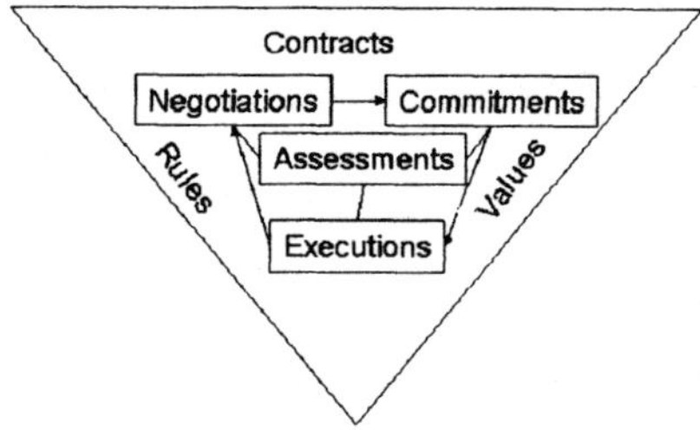

Figure 3 Framework for creating IOR

4   Cases

In this chapter we introduce two eGovernment projects in Finland where the authors have been participating as *action researchers*.

Rapoport [20, 499] has defined action research as: *"Action research aims to contribute both to the practical concerns of people in an immediate problematic situation and to the goals of social science by joint collaboration within a mutually acceptable ethical framework."* This twofold view of the objectives of action research - to solve a problem for a client and to advance science - is, perhaps, the most fundamental feature of action research [21, 22]. Because action research is a qualitative research method with a small sample size, it is vulnerable to positivist critics [23]. Because it attempts to contribute to practical concerns, it is sometimes confused with applied research or consulting [24]. However, action research can follow rigorous guidelines. One of the principal guidelines for conducting action research is that researchers should make their reasoning explicit and organize it in such a way that it is testable [25]

Data was collected from documents, interviews and participatory observation (including researcher diary and group discussions). The first case can be considered as successful IOR venture and the second one as relatively failed IOR.

The first case describes four municipality's common ICT governance project. Participants were daycare professional and their management. The second reports findings from fifteen semi-structured interviews made to main actors in the Finnish Electronic Prescription System (EPS) pilot. Interviewees were on the management level in their organizations.

Case 1: ICT in the Finnish Early Childhood Education

This case demonstrates the creation of ICT utilization oriented network in the context of early childhood education (ECE). In Finland, every child has a statutory subjective right to receive public day-care and the municipalities are responsible to organize a placement according to demand.

The creation of ICT utilization oriented network began in 2004. In the first phase in 2004–2005 the initiative business idea was developed and the possible actors to the network were outlined. In the fall of 2005 the foundation of the network was established. In the early 2006 the participative organizations made an agreement about a common development project and filled in a funding application for one year long developing project to the Finnish Ministry of Social Affairs and Health. The positive decision was received in May 2006 which led to an establishment of a steering group with representatives from four municipalities and two universities in South-West Finland.

The initial developing work started in fall 2006 with orientation lecture. A total of 50 ECE professionals with different professional backgrounds varying from the Director of ECE to daycare teachers and administrative officers participated in the developing process. Altogether over 150 people were involved in the network to a certain degree during the years 2004–2007. The negotiations and planning for the follow-up development project began in the beginning of 2007. Three municipalities decided to continue cooperation, and new funding application for two year's follow-up development project was filled. In spring 2007 the follow-up project was admitted a funding decision.

Case 2: Implementation of Electronic Prescription System

The second case reports findings from the Finnish Electronic Prescription System (EPS) pilot. In 2000 the Ministry of Social Affairs and Health set a project to suggest a national concept for ePrescribing. The construction of the system took 2 years, and the first clinical pilot started in 2004. By the end of 2004 two out of the four piloting health care units had implemented the EPS integrated into Electronic Patient Record (EPR), pilot pharmacies still used a stand-alone system, which was not integrated into pharmacy systems and created extra work at the pharmacies. In June 2005, the third integrated EPS and the first integrated pharmacy system were implemented. The amount of produced e-prescriptions remained very small during the pilot and at the end of 2005 only approximately 800 electronic prescriptions had been dispensed (there are approximately 40 million dispensed prescriptions in Finland annually). In June 2006 the EPS pilot was ended, because it had "reached the objectives set to it".

5 Discussion

We divided the both cases in three different stages based on our framework.

Negotiations stage

In the *ECE case* the participation of one particular ECE researcher in was important to the project's success. She had worked as researcher in many ECE development projects and was therefore familiar for most of the ECE managers. The presence of the ECE researcher invoked confidence among the ECE participants and further interpreted IS researchers' ICT based concepts and terms to the ECE professionals.

During the development process one seminar for ECE software vendors was organized. The firms were not interested in participating networks. Behind the refusals were many reasons: cooperation with competitor is always difficult and the advantage from participation was difficult to see. We argue that the main reason in the terms of our coordination mechanism framework was incompatible values between competitors and especially between the ECE people.

In the *EPS case* the preliminary work was thoroughly prepared. The Ministry of Social Affairs and Health set already in 2000 a preliminary disquisition project in order to suggest a national model for electronic prescription in order to harmonize the development. The work was done in line with the Finnish National eHealth Strategy, in collaboration with experts in different fields. In 2001 published expert report described alternative architectures for a national EPS, their strengths and weaknesses. The Ministry selected in 2002 four health care organizations and Pharmacy Association and University Pharmacy selected a couple of nearby pharmacies in four different regions for clinical tests of the pilot system. Yet it can be argued whether the negotiations stage really achieved to develop joint expectations about the motivations of the project. The interviewees claimed that the objectives of the pilot were expressed vaguely in the first place.

Commitments stage

In the first, *ECE case*, the researchers presented preliminary proposal to the managers and asked what their personal level commitment to participation were and what was their organizations' interest. The discussions with the managers increased organizations' interested in participating to the network. The development project needed funding. In Finland state supports municipalities in their development projects. The funding application form has to include things like project plan, governance model, budget etc. The application form serves as a legal agreement between the participating municipalities, too. According to our framework was the application market-based agreement, which created some administrative and bureaucratic structure and had symbolic value, too. In the application phase the role of the contract is essential. The contract created some rules, too. The inter-organizational contract in turns enforced commitment of the members from participating organizations [2]. After the positive funding decision was received, the actual inter-organizational cooperation started fast. A steering group with chairman was established, and development work plan was specified. The agreements about fiscal matters between participating organizations were signed. The members of the steering group had worked with the initial application together and had therefore created a common value space for this project.

In Finland health care is strictly regulated by legislation. The *EPS* pilot suffered from incompleteness of legislation which in turn hindered the pilot. An experimental decree on electronic prescribing was issued in 2003. It laid down provisions on preparing, signing, technical content, altering and delivery of electronic prescriptions. There were also provisions on informing patients and obtaining their consent, defining the rights of access to database and maintaining information in the national database. Yet the situation would have been eased if actors had have contracts among each other defining the rights and responsibilities in the pilot.

The interviewees claimed that they were committed to EPS implementation project, and generally respondents didn't see that there were any major conflicts of interest. Yet, some respondents argued that a certain trusteeship organization was having its own agenda, and is hindering the work of steering group. Participating organizations did not receive any financial incentives for participation, but instead they were expected to allocate resources for the pilot. Hence, members participated the project among their other tasks.

Executions stage

In the end of 2007 the negotiations for a new *ECE* development project began. Members in the steering group and workgroups were asked how and which of the development proposals should be implemented. According to the answers, the foundation for further development project was formulated. Three municipalities showed their interest to continue IOR cooperation. Funding application was delivered to Ministry of Health and Social Affair. After positive decision a two year long development project started.

The *EPS pilot* was a peculiar combination of different governance methods. The construction of the system took 2 years, and the first clinical pilot started in 2004. By the end of 2005 two out of the four piloting health care units had implemented EPS integrated into an electronic patient record (EPR), and in one area an integrated pharmacy system was implemented to dispense electronic prescriptions. The amount of electronic prescriptions remained very small until the end of the pilot. As one of the biggest reasons for this was that the pilot was foremost seen as a technical pilot. This was reflected among other things as low usage in the actual use.

The actual management was conducted through national steering group which had little normative rules to affect the pilot, some of the interviewees referred to it as a debating club. The steering group coordinated the locally organized pilots with a small budget. Additionally, the pilot was coordinated at first hand by a part-time project manager designated by the Ministry of Health. The project manager had little means to influence the network, as the contractual jurisprudence was lacking, the project lost its final coordination mechanism. Furthermore, in the spring 2005 the organization of the national e-prescription pilot was changed thoroughly; the part time project manager of the pilot was changed to a major consultancy company, which re-organized the administration of pilot entirely.

There was a broad conception among interviewees that the execution of the pilot was a failure. Time scale of the project was drawn out constantly, the pilot was under-resourced both in terms of money and personnel, and responsibilities were not clear. Several interviewees reported that steering group was too large, and decision-making was difficult. Decision-making was aggravated furthers because there was no prepared drafts on basis of decision making. As the objectives and benefits to be attained were expressed loosely there was no clear common objective for all the organizations to pursue. In order to overcome the obscurity of the pilot, it would have needed hierarchy. Organization of health care in general is still very hierarchical and some of the actors were expecting firmer steering for the pilot.

6 Summary

This paper introduced briefly a process model of partnership evolution in new IT initiatives. The model is still in its infancy and needs still further research. However, some preliminary thoughts can be presented based on these two cases. The cases shared some similarities and some differences in e.g. the magnitude and organization of the projects. Both cases shared similar network-like organization, but the outcomes of the projects varied significantly. First case was a success and second one a relative failure.

Based on this study It seems evident, that clan based mechanism is important for successful network. Market and hierarchy are essential, but in they are not adequate in initial stage of network. The role of contract is to create trust and symbolic value for network. The presented framework in **Figure** explained outcome in two cases. Despite that the reliability and validity of the framework need still more study. It still indicates that IOR has three coordination mechanisms with three dimensions that should be taken into consideration.

References

1.   Markus, M. and D. Robey, *Information Technology and Organizational Change: Causal Structure in Theory and Research. Management Science,* 1988. **34**(5): p. 583-598.

2.   Ring, P.S. and A.H. Van de Ven, *Developmental Processes of Cooperative Interorganizational Relationship.* Academy of Management, 1994. **19**(1): p. 90-118.

3.   Finnegan, P., R.D. Galliers, and P. Powell. *Guidelines for Effective Information Systems Planning in Inter-organisational Environments. in Proceedings of the Seventh European Conference on Information Systems.* 1999. Copenhagen: Copenhagen Business School.

4.   Salmela, H. and T. Spil. *Strategic Information Systems Planning in Inter-Organizational Networks: Adapting SISP Approaches to Network Context. in 2nd European Conference on IS Management, Leadership and Governance.* 2006. Paris.

5.   Williamson, O.E., *The Economic Institutions of Capitalism. Firms, Markets, Relational Constructing.* 1985: The Free Press.

6.   Thorelli, H.B., *Networks: Between Markets and Hierarchies. Strategic* Management Journal, 1986. **7**(1): p. 37-52.

7.   Ouchi, W.G., *A Conceptual Framework for the Design of Organizational Control Mechanism.* Management Science, 1979. **25**(9): p. 833- 847.

8.   Wilkinson, I., *A History of Network and Channels Thinking in Marketing in the 20th Century.* Australasian Marketing Journal, 2001. **9**(2): p. 23-52.

9.   Leblebic, H., et al., *Institutional Change and the Transformation of Interorganizational Fields: An Organizational History of the U.S. Radio Broadcasting Industry.* Administrative Science Quarterly, 1991. **36**(3): p. 333-363.

10.   Malone, T.W., J. Yates, and R.I. Benjamin, *Electronic Markets and Electronic Hierarchies: Effects of Information Technology on Market Structure and Corporate Strategies.* Communications of the ACM, 1987. **30**(6): p. 484-497.

11.   Choudhury, V., *Strategic choices in the development of interorganizational information systems.* Information Systems Research, 1997. **8**(1): p. 1-24.

12.   Johnston, H.R. and M.R. Vitale, *Creating competitive advantage with interorganizational information systems.* MIS Quarterly, 1998. **12**(2): p. 153-165.
13.   Van de Ven, A.H., *On the Nature, Formation, and Maintenance of Relations Among Organizations. Academy of Management Review,* 1976. **1**(4): p. 24-36.
14.   Williams, T., *Interorganisational Information Systems: issues affecting interorganizational cooperation.* ELSEVIER, Journal of Strategic Information Systems, 1997. **6**(3): p. 231-250.
15.   Wilson, D.T., *An Integrated Model of Buyer-Seller Relationships.* Journal of the Academy of Marketing Science, 1995. **23**(4): p. 335-345.
16.   Williamson, O.E., *Markets and Hierarchies: Analysis and Antitrust Implications.* 1975, New York: Free Press.
17.   Ouchi, W.G., *Markets, Bureaucracies, and Clans.* Administrative Science Quarterly, 1980. **25**(1).
18.   Rodríguez, C., et al., *Governance, Power, and Mandated Collaboration in an Interorganizational Network.* Administration & Society, 2007. **39**(2): p. 150-193.
19.   Jarillo, J.C., *On Strategic Networks. Strategic Management Journal,* 1988. **9**(1): p. 31-41.
20.   Rapoport, R.N., *Three Dilemmas of Action Research. Human Relations,* 1970. **23**: p. 499-513.
21.   Baskerville, R.L. and T. Wood-Harper, *Diversity in information systems action research methods. European Journal of Information Systems,* 1998. **7**(2): p. 90-107.
22.   Susman, G.I. and R.D. Evered, *An Assesment of the Scientific Merits of Action Research. Administrative Science Quarterly,* 1978. **23**(4): p. 582-603.
23.   Checkland, P., *From Framework through Experience to Learning: The Essential Nature of Action Research. Discussant's comments,* in *Information Systems Research: Contemporary Approaches & Emergent Traditions,* H.-E. Nissen, H.K. Klein, and R. Hirscheim, Editors. 1991, Elsevier: Amsterdam.
24.   Jönssön, S., *Action Research, in Information Systems Research: Contemporary Approaches & Emergent Traditions,* H.-E. Nissen, H.K. Klein, and R. Hirscheim, Editors. 1991, Elsevier: Amsterdam.
25.   Argyris, C., *Reasoning, Learning and Action: Individual and Organiational.* 1982, San Francisco: Jossey-Bass Publishers.

Design of a Web2.0-based Knowledge Management Platform

Weijun Wang, Rui Xiong, Jing Sun
*Department of Information Management, HuaZhong Normal University,
Wuhan 430079, China*
wangwj@mail.ccnu.edu.cn, rayze1228@126.com, daneyrong@163.com

Abstract: Knowledge Management Platform plays an important role in helping spread knowledge of individuals or groups across organizations. Many current knowledge management platforms met with deficiencies of poor tacit knowledge exploitation, slow knowledge update, limited knowledge sharing and weak user participation. This paper attempts to find solutions to those problems by integrating Web2.0 with knowledge management, and design a Web2.0-based Knowledge Management Platform. A Web2.0-based knowledge management model is put forth, and the framework and technology architecture of our platform has also been researched.

1   Introduction

Knowledge and the capability to create and utilize knowledge has become the most important source of a company's sustainable competitive advantage. The major obstacle to classical knowledge management approach is that knowledge workers hesitate to release their tacit knowledge and give up sharing autonomy [1]. Researches about constructing Knowledge Management Platform or System generally emphasized much on the "technologies" employed by organizations to better retain and utilize organizational knowledge [2, 3], while less attention was paid to user participation which also plays a key role in supporting knowledge sharing within and between organizations. Actually, knowledge is inextricably bound up with human cognition and social factors [4], reusing, diffusing and maintaining knowledge should be a participatory activity of all the involved people [5].

Web2.0 is characterized by being user-centered, harnessing collective intelligence and social network formation. We believe Web2.0 is a return of human and social factors, but these undoubted significant factors are nearly at risk of being

Please use the following format when citing this chapter:

Wang, W., Xiong, R., Sun, J., 2007, in IFIP International Federation for Information Processing, Volume 252, Integration and Innovation Orient to E-Society Volume 2, eds. Wang, W., (Boston: Springer), pp. 237-245.

neglected by the building of KM Platform. Thus, there arises a demand on the integration of recent knowledge management (KM) with ideas of Web2.0.

The objective of this paper is to analyze how to integrate the ideas, methods and technologies of Web2.0 with the building of KM Platform, and propose a framework and technology architecture for designing a Web2.0-based KM Platform capable of promoting knowledge communication, sharing and tacit knowledge exploitation.

2 Knowledge Management Model Based on Web2.0

2.1 Web2.0 Applications in KM

Blog, Wiki, Social Bookmark, SNS, RSS, Instant Messenger and Forums are all typical applications of Web2.0. As shown in Figure 1, we based on Nonaka's SECI model [6, 7], explain how Web2.0 can influence on the conversion between tacit and explicit knowledge, especially its efficacy on the promotion of making tacit knowledge explicit.

Tacit to Tacit (Socialization)	Tacit to Explicit (Externalization)
Eg: IM(Instant Messenger), Forums	Eg: Blog, Wiki, SN(Social Network)
Explicit to Tacit (Internalization)	Explicit to Explicit (Combination)
Eg: Learning from others' Blog, Wikis…	Eg: Social Bookmark, Folksonomy

Fig. 1 Web2.0-based Conversion of Knowledge between Tacit and Explicit Forms

• Socialization: Socialization is the process of converting new tacit knowledge through shared experiences. Traditionally, it is achieved by apprenticeship and informal meetings, which has specified restrictions with certain time and people. While in Web2.0, this process can be realized by discussing through IM or Forums, in which experiences are described and shared without limits.

• Externalization: Tacit knowledge is difficult to be articulated into explicit knowledge. But Web2.0 can provide a brand new approach for the conversion. For example, blog provides every user with a personal space to freely publish their ideas, experiences, reflections etc., and viewers can make comments and evaluations; Wiki provides a collaborative workspace to generate, accumulate, and perfect knowledge. Through the way of self-expression like telling a story on Blogs and collaboration work on Wikis, some proportion of a person's tacit knowledge may be captured in explicit form. Meanwhile, enhanced trust can be forged in Social Network, which will benignly promote this process.

• Internalization: In order to better understand, internalize and act on information, individuals should embody explicit knowledge into tacit knowledge. By reading others' Blogs or Wikis about their jobs and the organization, and reflecting upon them, people can internalize the explicit knowledge written in them to enrich their tacit knowledge base. We believe "learning by reading" can help viewers re-experience what others previously learned, and get the opportunity to create new knowledge by combining their existing tacit knowledge with the knowledge of others, and finally put them into practice.

• Combination: The information self-organization mechanism in Web2.0 can help combine existing explicit knowledge into a more complex and systematic set. Social Bookmark is an online activity that allows users to save and categorize a personal collection of bookmarks and share them with others [8], and Folksonomy is a collaboratively generated, open-ended labeling system that enables users to categorize content by tags.

Other Web2.0 applications are also useful in knowledge conversion and utilization. Take RSS (Really Simple Syndication) for example, it enables recipients to decide which RSS feeds they want delivered, so as to keep received messages on target [10].

2.2 Web2.0-based Knowledge Management Model

As shown in figure 2, under the participation architecture of Web2.0, individual user can write blogs, edit wikis, establish Social Bookmarks, join Forums etc. In the interaction process, individuals will be connected through various social familiarities ranging from common interests to collaboration group to form a SN (Social Network) like project teams or other collaboration groups. These individuals and SNs will ultimately build up a tremendous virtual knowledge community.

In the knowledge community, every user is considered as an important knowledge body, contextual factors including generalized trust, pro-sharing norms will motivate more people participate in the creation, sharing and communication of knowledge. Moreover, people keep learning from each other during the interaction processes, the utilization and innovation of knowledge can also be achieved in assembly. In all, the interactive potential of Web2.0 applications is huge to develop.

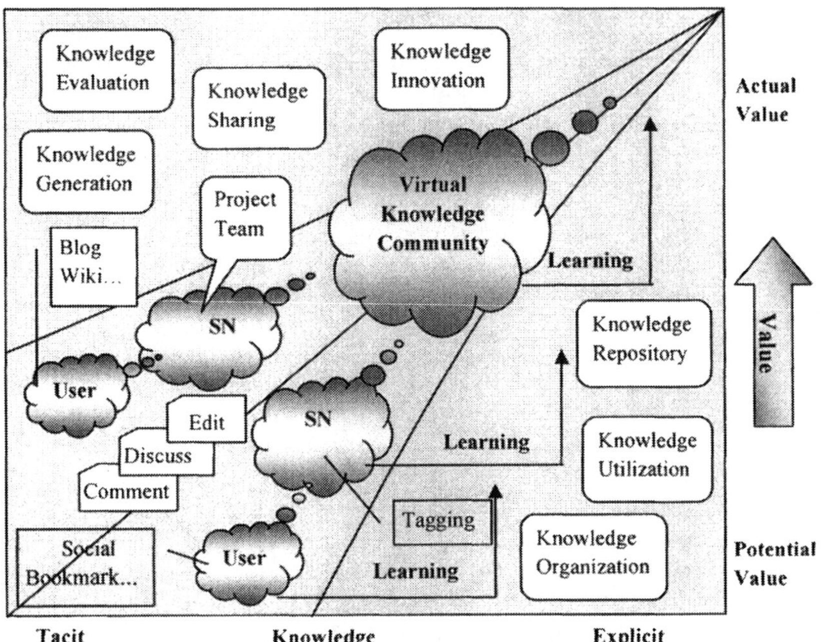

Fig. 2 Web2.0-based Knowledge Management Model

3 Design of Platform

3.1 Deficiencies of traditional KM Platform

Deficiencies of traditional KM Platform can be concluded as follows:

(1) Lack in effective ways to develop and utilize tacit knowledge hidden in the minds of users;

(2) It is difficult to integrate those highly decentralized knowledge embodied by ordinary staff, customers or partners. The knowledge creation, update and maintenance work of system only relies on a small number of experts, executives and technicians.

(3) Only pay attention to formal, final intellectual achievements, but neglects the learning and innovation process;

(4) Lack of interactivity and flexibility, users passively participate, and their personalized knowledge needs are difficult to be met.

3.2 Platform Framework

In this paper, we are not going to establish a complete set of KM Platform, but to focus on how to integrate Web2.0 with KM Platform in order to take full advantage of Web2.0, and make up deficiencies of traditional KM Platform. Based on theoretical background discussed above, the framework for a Web2.0-based Knowledge Management Platform is depicted in Figure 3.

(1) Users: The system users cover a wide range, including internal employees of different management layer, specialized knowledge management personnel and external customers, suppliers, dealers, etc. Among them, members of the enterprise are the main knowledge contributors, but customers, business partners can also provide many valuable and worth digging information.

(2) Knowledge Portal: Knowledge Portal is the entrance to the platform. On Knowledge Portal, information and knowledge are centralized expressed in an easily understandable way. Internal and external users get access to the portal separately via Internet and Intranet. They can make RSS/Keywords subscription to customize their Personalized Knowledge Page (PKP) so as to meet their individual demands.

(3) Knowledge Application : It is composed of four parts - content module, interactive module, Knowledge Assessment Module and search engine:

• Content Module: The content modules integrate Web2.0 applications such as Blog, Wiki, Social Bookmark, Forum, IM and other information resources from both inside and outside of enterprises into the platform.

• Interactive Module: It refers to collaboration & communication functionalities on the platform. We can complete project cooperation with Wiki, real-time communication with IM, views exchange with Blog, group discussion with Forums.

• Knowledge Assessment Module: The platform lets people identify, rate, and rank the information that's important to them, and a Knowledge Assessment Module is used to record the knowledge contribution of every user. If a person gets the highest rank, he or she will receive an organization reward as well as the intrinsic knowledge self-efficacy and enjoyment in helping others. This can motivate other knowledge workers to contribute more.

• Search Engine Module: The rich information resources on Web2.0-based KM Platform are mostly in text format, a full-text search engine is required to help users find the information they need.

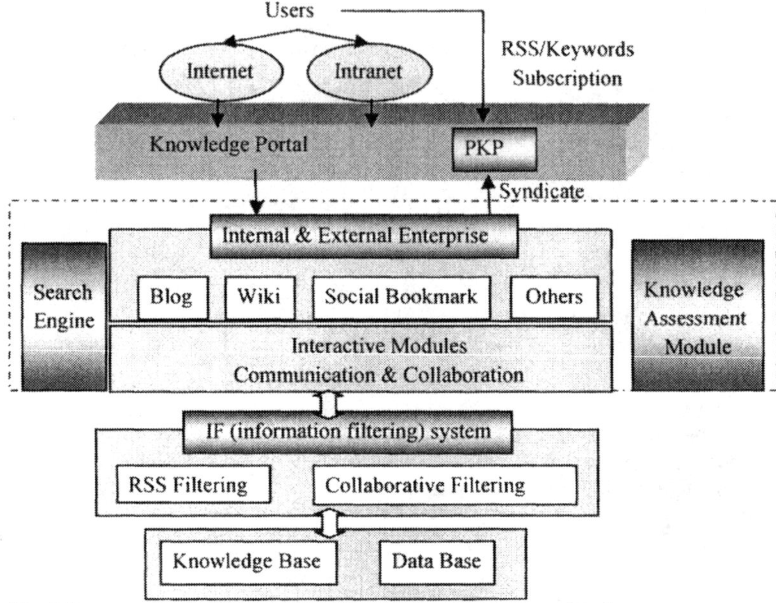

Fig. 3 Framework of a Web2.0-based Knowledge Management Platform

(4) Information Filtering(IF): The goal of our Information Filtering is to screen out irrelevant data from incoming streams of data items in accord with a user's profile. As shown from Foltz and Dumais' study [12], filtering did improve if more than one technique is integrated. Thus, we want to apply two filtering techniques according to features of Web2.0:

• RSS Filtering: RSS can simulate real time information delivery using automated client pull technology. Since RSS is XML-based format, while most current Web information still uses HTML instead of XML, a information mediator is needed to download RSS feeds available on the network and also translate certain HTML sources into RSS format. Then, those RSS document can be classified into database for browsing and retrieval, and users can make RSS/Keywords subscription, receive information directly.

• Collaborative Filtering: Collaborative filtering automates human recommendations on the basis of its being relevant to other users having similar tastes (habits) [13]. It can predict users' potential information needs from a more comprehensive "user model". The platform compares the URLs that users have visited, their bookmark folders, or tags they have established, to identify similar users, and recommend relevant information to certain users.

(5) Knowledge Storage: Knowledge Storage is the "memory" of enterprise's data, information and knowledge. It mainly consists of database and knowledge base.

4 System Technology Architecture

In order to implement the system framework proposed above, and achieve the objective of providing the right knowledge or information to the right person at the right time, we establish technology architecture composed of five parts, as is shown in Figure 4.

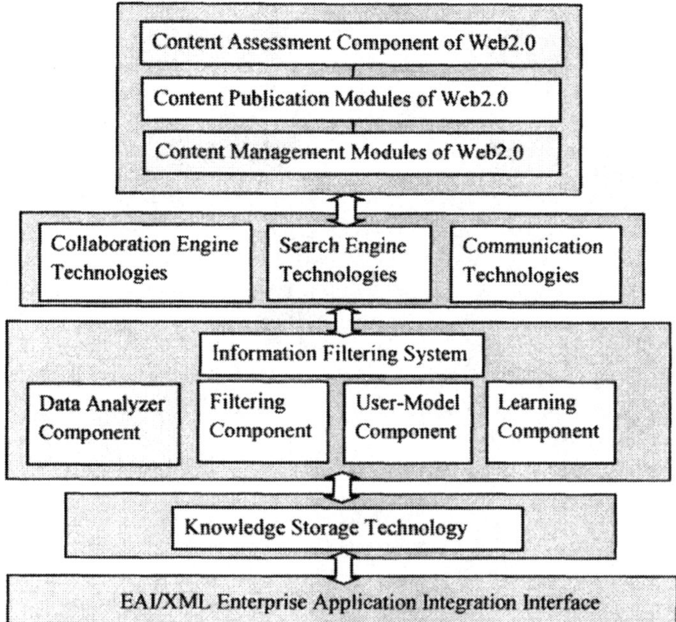

Fig. 4 Technology Architecture of a Web2.0-based KM Platform

(1) Content: The Content Assessment Component support functionalities of quantity counting and quality evaluation of staff's knowledge contribution; the Content Publication and Management Modules of Web2.0 are supported by typical technologies and application standards of Web2.0 like Ajax, Mash-up, REST, Tagging, these new Web2.0 capabilities bring about enhanced interactivity and responsiveness, in-line editing, intuitive drag-and-drop, and intelligent page refresh[14];

(2) Applications Support: The Collaboration and Communication Engines are web2.0-based application that enables project teams to eliminate face-to-face work, enhance user feedback functionalities, and streamline the process for creating, storing, editing, approving, sharing and comunicating of Web2.0 contents.

(3) IF System: The generic model of RSS filtering and collaborative filtering system include four basic components: a data-analyzer component, a filtering component, a user-model component and a learning component [15]. It is designed to integrate and classify a lot of dynamic information, improve users' efficiency to access information resources they need [16].

(4) Storage Technologies & Integration Interface: Knowledge Storage technologies support the access, retrival of data, information and knowledge; to avoid the emergence of "isolated islands of information", we can use the EAI/XML-based data standards to link heterogeneous systems, applications and data sources of the enterprise, so that seamlessly sharing and exchange of data among the whole enterprise's ERP, CRM, SCM and database systems can be achieved[17].

5 Conclusions

In this paper, we use Nonaka's model to explain how Web2.0 promote the conversion between knowledge in explicit and tacit forms, and put forth a Web2.0-based Knowledge Management Model. Based on the objectives of fully taking advantage of Web2.0 to make up deficiencies of traditional KM Platform, we design a Web2.0-based KM Platform; propose its framework and supportive technology architecture. The core advantage of our platform is its powerful user interaction, which drives the creation, organization, communication and sharing of knowledge in enterprise.

However, the platform still needs constant improvement. From our perspectives, current Web2.0 pages still lack of semantic description, which cause problems with information reuse and structured access [18]. To further reveal the semantic links between contents will be our major research goals in the future.

Acknowledgments

This research was supported by the National Social Science Foundation of China under Grant 06BTQ019.

References

1. H.L. Yang, H.C. Ho, "Emergent standard of knowledge management: Hybrid peer-to-peer knowledge management", *Computer Standards & Interfaces* 29,413–422 (2007).

2. M. Alavi and D.E. Leidner, "Review: Knowledge management and knowledge management systems: Conceptual foundations and research issues", *MIS Quarterly* 25(1), 107-136 (2001).

3. S.M. Richardson, J.F. Courtney, and J.D. Haynes, "Theoretical principles for knowledge management system design: Application to pediatric bipolar disorder", *Decision Support Systems* 42(3), 1321–1337(2006).

4. J.C. Thomas, W.A. Kellogg, and T. Erickson, "The knowledge management puzzle: Human and social factors in knowledge management".
http://www.research.ibm.com/journal/sj/404/thomas.html

5. J. Euzenat, "Corporate memory through cooperative creation of knowledge bases and hyper-documents". http://www.inrialpes.fr/sherpa/papers/euzenat96b/euzenat96b.html.

6. I. Nonaka, "The Knowledge Creating Company," *Harvard Business Review* 69, 96–104 (1991).

7. I. Nonaka and H. Takeuchi, *The Knowledge Creating Company*, Oxford University Press, Oxford, UK (1995).

8. N. Wang, "Tacit Knowledge Management Strategy of Virtual Enterprise under the Web2.0 environment", *Information Studies: Theory & Application*, 30(2) (2007)

9. Definition of Social Bookmarking, http://en.wikipedia.org/wiki/Social_bookmarking.

10. G. Gruman, "Really Simple Syndication (RSS): as a Knowledge Management Tool".http://www.cio.com/article/24442/Really_Simple_Syndication_RSS_as_a_Knowledge_Management_Tool.

11. A. Kankanhalli, B. C.Y. Tan, "Contributing Knowledge to Electronic Knowledge Repositories: An Empirical Investigation".
http://www.iscs.nus.edu.sg/~atreyi/papers/EKRcontrib.pdf.

12. P. W. Foltz and S. T. Dumais , "Personalized information delivery: An analysis of information filtering methods". *Communications of the ACM* 35(12), 51-60 (1992).

13. P. Maes and R. Kozierok , "Learning interface agents". *Proceedings of AAAI*, 459-465 (1993).

14. WebSphere Portal's Web 2.0 Makeover, http://www-03.ibm.com/developerworks/blogs/page/Turbo?tag=web2.0

15. U. Hanani, B. Shapira and P. Shoval, "Information Filtering: Overview of Issues, Research and Systems". *User Modeling and User-Adapted Interaction* 11, 203-259 (2001)

16. D. Oard, "Information Filtering", http://www.glue.umd.edu/-oard.

17. B. Ma, "The Building of a Portal-based Enterprise Knowledge Management System", *China Management Informationlization*, 11, 13-16 (2006).

18. H. L. Kim, "Toward the semantic web2.0", http://www.blogweb.co.kr/wp-content/uploads/2006/11/haklae_SKK_SW2.0_20061027.pdf.

An Access Control Model of Workflow System Integrating RBAC and TBAC

Xiangning Zhou [1] and Zhaolong Wang [2]
1 School of Information and Electronic Engineering
ShanDong Institute of Business and Technology, Yantai 264005, China
E-mail: dulier@tom.com
2 Network Center YanTai University, Yantai 264005, China

Abstract. Basing on the integration of two models, RBAC and TBAC, an access control model called Role-Task Based Access Control (R&TBAC) is given, which takes two parts as combining sites, one is the role and trustee, the other is the role permission assignment and trustee permissions. A set of fundamental conceptions, a series of authorization processes, a formalized description and some modeling tools about this model are given. This model has both intuitionistic and dynamic characteristics. It also has some other advantages, such as economical for memory space, convenient to maintain and control etc.

1   Introduction

Adding some dynamic characteristics for RBAC96 model [1], such as task state [2], recycle time [3], or using TBAC model [4-6] directly can achieve the access control in the workflow system. But in some systems including the workflow technology, some abstracting ways of RBAC are needed to divide and describe some activities connected with access control in the system. At the same time, some descriptive ways of TBAC are also needed to describe the dynamic characteristics in the system.

In order to meet the above needs, a new model called R&TBAC is given, which based on roles and tasks. The descriptive capability and security of the model has also been analysed.

2   The necessity of using RBAC and TBAC integrated

First of all, the station is corresponding to the role in the RBAC. So using the PA matrix in the RBAC to control access is benefited to understand. But in the workflow system, taking tasks into the PA matrix directly will lead the rows of the matrix increasing sharply. In the mean time, the dynamic permission about authorize/revoke is needed in the RBAC model.

Secondly, the schedule and constraints in the workflow can be well described by the concept "depending" in the TBAC model. For that matter, TBAC is better than RBAC. But during the application of the TBAC model, for the trustee who wants to execute some public processing flow is crowded, the more popular the public process is, the more resource kinds the processing flow needs to access. So if every trustee has the permission of each kind of the resource, the number of records in the permission of the public processing flow will increase sharply. Of course, dividing the public processing flow into some different processing flows can solve this problem, but it needs a great deal of reduplicate codes, which induce the descend of maintainability.

So basing on the experience in real OA system development, a new access control model R&TBAC is proposed, which integrates the RBAC and TBAC and adopts static and dynamic permission altogether.

3   R&TBAC access control model

3.1   Basic definitions

Some definitions about the R&TBAC are as follows:

Definition 1 The basic definitions set in the R&TBAC ={User (U), Role(R), Authorization step (As), Permission (P)}.

Hereinto:

(1)   User (U) is the user set, which includes all the users in the system.

(2)   Role (R) is the roles set, which includes all the roles abstracted from departments and duties.

(3)   Authorization step (As) is authorization step, which means one process in a workflow. It is the minimum process unit that can be controlled in the access control.

(4)   Permission (P) includes all the access permissions that can be authorized to users. Resource (res) and operation (op) to this resource can be called access permission.

The definitions derived from the basic definitions are as follows:

Definition 2 The derived definitions set in the R&TBAC ={Trustee (T), Authorization unit (Au), unit Permission (uP), trustee Permission (tP), Session (S)}.

Hereinto:

(1)   Trustee (T) includes all roles that have been authorized the authorization step.

(2)   Authorization unit (Au) is an authorization step organization, which may include one or many authorization steps logically connected. Au is corresponding to the real tasks. Normally Au has two kinds, one is general Au and the other is atomic Au. In the former, authorization steps will be executed orderly, while in the latter, every As connects with each other closely, which results in the whole failure if one fails.

(3) unit Permission (uP) is a subset of Permission, which includes all access permissions that can be authorized to trustee by As or Au.

(4) trustee Permission (tP) includes all access permissions that have been authorized to trustee by As or Au. tP is a subset belong to uP.

(5) Session (S) includes all sessions. By session, users can be or not be a role.

Based on **definition 1** and **definition 2**, there are some relations and constraints among the definitions.

Definition 3 The relations and constraints set among the definitions in the R&TBAC ={Role Hierarchy (RH), Dependency (D), User Role Assignment (URA), Role Permission Assignment (RPA), Constraint}.

Hereinto:

(1) Role Hierarchy (RH) is partial order relation in the Role(R). It is called role hierarchy relation.

(2) Dependency (D) is the relations between As or Au. It includes sequence dependency, failure dependency, divided permission dependency and agency dependency.

(3) User Role Assignment (URA) assigns relations for users and roles. The relations mean a many to many mapping, from user (U) to role (R), which show the user is assigned to be a role.

(4) Role Permission Assignment (RPA) assigns relations for roles and permissions. The relations mean a many to many mapping, from permission (P) to role (R), which show the role is assigned permission.

(5) Constraint means all criteria on the mapping.

3.2   Authorization processing in R&TBAC model

The authorization can be expressed by five-parameter set (S, O, op, L, As). S means the main body, corresponding to the role in the model. O means object, corresponding to the resource in the model. Op is operation. L is the abbreviation of lifecycle. As is authorization step. The above five-parameter set means the subject (S) has the access permission to operate op on object (O) during the lifecycle (L) activated by As. The detailed processing is as follows:

1. Initialization

Initialize all roles (R) and RH. URA and RPA should be assigned. Initialize all As and Au. The relations between As and As, Au and Au should be assigned. T and uP should be assigned to every As.

2. The dynamic authorization should be finished in the workflow.

A. Using the following way, the trustee's tP can be gotten.

(1) According to URA and T, the role (r) connected to As is confirmed.

(2) According to r and RPA, all r' authorizations can be confirmed. It is called rPA.

(3) The joinset of rPA and uP is the tP.

B. Using the following way, authorize, revoke and period of validity can be gotten.

(1) Before the As is activated, five-parameter set is void and all permissions in tP can not be used.

(2) As soon as the As is activated, the lifecycle (L) of every five-parameter set begin to count down. At the same time, trustee (t) owns his permissions in the tP.

(3)   In the life cycle, five-parameter set is available.

(4)   When the As stops, five-parameter set is invalid. And all permissions in the tP are revoked.

(5)   When As is not activated again, all five-parameter sets that describe tP are all invalid. And all permissions in the As are revoked.

3.3   The formalized description of R&TBAC

The brief model of R&TBAC is shown as **fig.1**. The figure only shows the referred and modified parts. The other parts of model RBAC and model TBAC can be found in references [1,5,6]). The formalized description is as follows:

(1)   URA $\subseteq$ U$\times$R;

(2)   RPA $\subseteq$ R$\times$P;

(3)   RH $\subseteq$ R$\times$R;

(4)   Wf is made of a series of Au, the relations between the Au is Au $\times$ Au $\subseteq$ 2^D D={sequence dependency, failure dependency, divided permission dependency, agency dependency};

(5)   The mapping between Au and T is 1:n; H(Au) $\rightarrow r, H$ is a function selecting a role (r) from T, hereinto: $r \in$ T, T=$\{r_1, r_2, ..., r_n\}$.

(6)   The relationship between Au and uP is 1:1. The formula I (Au) $\rightarrow$ uP means I is a function used to initialize uP as soon as Au is initialized.

(7)   The relationship between Au and tP is 1:n. The formula F (Au, RPA, r) $\rightarrow$ tP, r $\in$ T, F is a function used to initialize tP. It can get a sub set tP from uP according to RPA and r, hereinto, tP=$\{p_1, p_2... p_n\}$.

(8) G (Au, P_1) $\rightarrow$ P_2, $P_1 \subseteq$ tP, P_2 = tP $-$ P_1, G is a function used to revoke the authorization.

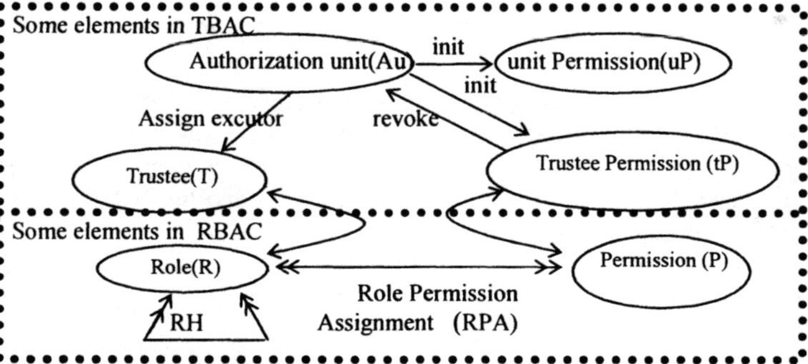

Fig.1. The brief model of R&TBAC

3.4 The descriptive tools of R&TBAC

In the R&TBAC model, the signs in TBAC model are continued to use. The set operators shown in Tab.1 and the authorization matrix shown in Tab.2 are the descriptive tools of R&TBAC.

Table 1. The set operators used in R&TBAC

Sign	Examples	Description
=	Set1={ role1,role2,…}	The set1 includes role1, role2…
	Set1=Set2 ∩ Set3	The Set1 is endued with the joinset of Set2 and Set3.
∈	User1 ∈{role1,role2,…}	User1 can acts as role1 or role2 …
∪ ∩ ⊃ ⊂ ⊇ ⊆		Same meaning to set operations.

Table 2. The authorization matrix used in R&TBAC

Role	Resource	Operation (op)	Lifecycle (L)	Authorization step (As)

The authorization matrix can select one or many columns according to the situation. The wildcard character can be used in the selected columns, such as, in the RPA, only three columns are selected, role, resource, operation, shown in Tab.3

Table 3. The authorization matrix example used by RPA

Role	Resource	Operation (op)	Description
*	A	R	All roles can execute the operation (R) to A.
Role1	B	W	The role1 can execute the operation (W) to B.
Role2	C	*	The role2 can execute all operation to C.

4   The descriptive capability and security analyze of R&TBAC model

R&TBAC model has strong descriptive capability. It inherits the intuitionistic characteristic of RBAC model and the dynamic characteristic of TBAC model. The concept R and uP are encapsulated by As and Au, which makes the concept As and Au accords with the true working better. The united static authorization matrix (RPA) has global restriction and control, while the dynamic authorization matrix uP can change and control according to the needs flexibly. The two matrix have complementary advantages. In practical development, it can save the memory and improve the work efficiency and maintainability.

R&TBAC model fits two famous principles about security. One is the least privilege principle. The combined usage of trustee (T), lifecycle (L), unit permission (uP) and role permission assignment (RPA) makes every trustee (t) only get its sufficient and necessary permission in every As. The other principle is separation of duty. R&TBAC model adopts divided permission dependency and the constraints among roles to control the responsibilities among users and operations, which makes it easy and efficient.

5   Conclusion

Every element in the RBAC and TBAC model has been abstracted and defined in R&TBAC. And the needed relationships in the workflow have been combined in R&TBAC model, which can express the workflow's control mechanism clearly. The R&TBAC model has been used in the OA project of Yantai University. It has been validated that the model has excellent descriptive capability, high security and easy to implement.

References

1. R.S. Sandhu, E.J. Coyne and H.L. Feinstein, et al. Role Based Access Control Models. *IEEE Computer*, 29(2), 38-47(1996),

2. S. Kandala and R. Sandhu,*Secure Role-based workflow Models.* Proc of the 15th IFIP WG 11.3 Working Comference on Database Security. Niagara, Ontario, Canda, Kluwer Academic Publishers(2002).

3. X.M. Wang, Z.T. Zhao and K.G. Hao, "A Weighted Role and Periodic Time Access Control Model of WorkFlow System". *Journal of Software,* 14(11), 1841-1848 (2003).

4. R.K. Thomas and R.S. Sandhu, *Towards a task-based paradigm for flexible and adaptable access control in distributed applications.* Proc of the 1992-1993 CM SIGSAC New security Paradigms Workshops. Little Compton,Rhode Island, US:ACM Press (1993).

5. R.K. Thomas and R.S. Sandhu, *Conceptual Foundations for a Model of Task-based Authorizations,*Proc of the 7th IEEE Computer Security Foundations Workshop. Franconia NH:IEEE Com , 66-79(1994).

6. J.B. Deng and F. Hong, "Task-Based Access Control Model", Journal of Software, 14(01), 0076-0082(2003).

Study on Technological Innovation Risk of China's e-Services

Xiaobin Lu

School of Information Resource Management, Renmin University of China,
Beijing 100872

Abstract. Technological innovation risks of China's e-Services include such factors as policy, economy, technology, market and resources. Based on analyzing the above factors, the Article has designed the assessment system for technological innovation risk of China's e-Services, discussed on the assessment method of analytical matrix and proposed the particular measures for preventing China's e-Services technological innovation risk.

Technological innovation of e-Services is the core power for e-Business. The development and the success in technological innovation of e-Services will bring huge interests for e-Business, but due to the systematic and complicated features of technological innovation for e-Services, it is also a high-risk activity [1].

The research group of the program for the National Natural Science Foundation of China (70573119), "Demonstrative Study on Technological Innovation of China's Information Service" and New Century Excellent Talents in University (NCET-04-0049), "Theoretical Study and Case Analysis on Technological Innovation of China's e-Services" had investigated 30 e-Business websites in China (e.g.,Alibaba.com, ebay.com, ChinaCCM.com, Made-in-China.com, joyo.com , etc.) during 2005-2006. The content of questionnaire comprises 4 respects (Table 1).

Table 1. .Content of Questionnaire

Types of investigation	Objects of investigation	Amount of questionnaire	Explanation of questionnaire
Technological innovation risks	30 e-Business websites in China	28 (available), 2 (no available)	Main person in charge of e-Business websites

The conclusions have been obtained on the basis of analysis of the content of questionnaire: 65% of e-Services technological innovation projects have made technological achievements, but only 9% of e-Services technological innovation projects have been marketed. Because of the high risk and the risk's uncertainty, complicity and objectiveness, when the enterprises undertaking e-Business carry out technological innovation of e-Services, failure has always been in companion. Consequently, many of the enterprises, especially small and medium enterprises fear excessively the risk that they shrink back at the sight of e-Services technological innovation and dare not to undertake e-Services technological innovation and thus lose the fine opportunity for development.

The excessively high risk of e-Services technological innovation will not naturally determine the fate of the results of e-Services technological innovation, while they will depend on the effective management over the innovation process [2]. If we carry out the total analysis and investigation over all the segmental risk factors affecting the success and failure of e-Services technological innovation, have a full understanding of innovation risks and formulate better prevention measures for these possible risks, technological innovation risks of e-Services will be minimized.

1   Factor Analysis on Technological Innovations Risks of China's e-Services

1.1   Policy risk factor

China's economic development target in different periods and changes of social demand will all influence the orientation of e-Services technological innovation. Changes in the government's overall economic development planning, regional development planning and development planning for information industry and e-Business will all cause risks to China's e-Services technological innovation. Projects in compliance with the government's development target, development planning and policy for information industry and e-business will be supported and sponsored by the government and enterprises; otherwise, they may be restructured by the government for development and may encounter the policy risk. The change of the government's macro development target influences the change of social demand. It will be easy for those projects of e-Services technological innovation in compliance with the development demand of e-business to obtain social support and reduce the risks in commercialization of innovation [3].

1.2   Economic risk factor

Development of China's economic circumstance has a major influence over the success or failure of e-Services technological innovation, as is mainly reflected in the people's online shopping capacity and market demand. With the economy flourishing, the people's online shopping capacity is strong and market demand is vigorous, as will promote the activities for e-Services technological innovation and reduce the risk in marketing the technological innovation of e-Services; otherwise, it will not be beneficial to undertake the activities for technological innovation of e-Services and increase the marketing risk. The development of China's economic circumstance will directly influence the financing for the technological innovation of e-Services.

1.3 Technical risk factor

Technical factor is the objective reason for technological innovation risk of e-Services for the uncertainty of technological research and difficulty of innovation technology will directly determine the technological innovation risk of e-Services. As for some copy and transform innovation projects with breakthrough in key technology and mature supporting technologies, the technical risk of innovation will be reduced to a great extent, while for those projects of the essential innovation with comparatively high technical standard that will bring enterprises high returns once a breakthrough is made in the key technology, the innovation risk will be comparatively high.

1.4 Market risk factor

Technological innovation of e-Services is a process of integrating the market opportunity with the technical opportunity. The marketing and commercial benefit is the final standard for testing if the innovation is successful or not. Therefore, market factor is the key factor influencing technological innovation risk of e-Services in China, including mainly: ① improvement of market regulations: with incomplete regulations, different types of tort will appear and innovators will not be able to enjoy the expected innovation returns. ② Status of market demand: the consumers' preferential and its duration, scale of market demand and opportunity for a high tide of market demand will all influence the marketing of innovation products [4].

2 Design of Assessment System for Technological Innovation Risks of China's e-Services

According to the above analyses on the risk factors, we will design the comprehensive indicators system for technological innovation risks of China's e-Services in the five respects of environmental factor, market factor, technical factor, financial factor and management factor.

2.1 Environmental factor

a. Policy and law environment: the indicator is used to display the uncertainty of policy and law environment. China's policy and law environment has to a great extent determined the speed, direction and scale and even success or failure of technological innovation for e-Services. b. Macro economic situation: it is an indicator used to describe the influence of China's overall economic status on the technological innovation for e-Services. Generally, with the economy flourishing, the technological innovation risk is low, while with the economy depressing, the risk is high.

2.2   Market factor

c. Market acceptance capacity. Technological innovation products of e-Services are brand-new products. With the products introduced, it is not so easy for consumers to timely understand about their performance that they will keep an attitude of wait and see or make a wrong assess. Therefore, it is difficult to estimate accurately if the market can accept and how big the market capacity is. d. Extent of not being influenced by the competitors. In all the stages of executing technological innovation projects of China's e-Services, there will be always competitors or potential competitors and thus it is definite that they will be influenced by the competitors, while the extent of influence depends on the number, strength and competing measures of competitors. e. Promotion capacity. Objectively speaking, if market potential is excessively strong or the barrier for marketing is comparatively sold, it will cause difficulties for promoting the technological innovation products of China's e-Services. Subjectively speaking, the indefinite market orientation for technological innovation products of e-Services is the main reason for unfavorable market promotion.

2.3   Technical factor

f. Technical force. This comprehensive indicator is reflected in: firstly, e-Business companies' strength of scientific research force and technical accumulation; secondly, technical equipment, process and experimental conditions of enterprises undertaking e-Business. g. Technical leadership: i.e., the extent of the technology of the innovation activity leads the current average standard. h. Technical difficulty. In the stage of production, the more difficult the technology, the higher technical risk and production risk will be brought to the enterprises undertaking e-Business. With the new products marketed, the higher the technical difficulty, the stronger the access barrier is for the competitors and the market risk is low. i. Technical prospect. At birth, the technological innovation products of China's e-Services are normally incomplete and even rough. The innovators are not sure if they can soon improve the products under the current technical conditions. Additionally, it is uncertain if the new products can bring the anticipated effect and will be eliminated or restricted for selling due to the technical defects. The uncertain factor of all these technical prospects will possibly cause a risk for the technological innovation of China's e-Services.

2.4 Financial factor

j. Financial strength of enterprises undertaking e-Business. The financial strength of enterprises undertaking e-Business is an important aspect reflecting their projection capacity for innovation and capacity of bearing risks. k. Financing capacity of enterprises undertaking e-Business. In carrying out the technological innovation activities of e-Services, enterprises undertaking e-Business not only need to have strong financial capacity, but also strong financing capacity to handle all different possible emergencies and other emergent financial demands. l. Status of financial operation. The financial operation status of the enterprise undertaking e-Business enterprises can show risk potential of the project.

2.5 Management factor

m. Comprehensive qualification of the project in-charge. Here, the project in-charge is extensively defined: it can mean an in-charge of a project as well as the steering group of the project. The comprehensive qualification of the project in-charge covers his work experiences, knowledge standard, organization and management capacity, occupational morality and sense of innovation and risk. n. Performance of organizational structure: i.e., the effect and function on the technological innovation project of e-Service by the setup and operation of the organizational structure [5].

3   Assessment Method of Analytical Matrix for Technological Innovation Risk of China's e-Services

3.1 Analytical matrix

Analytical matrix is shown in Table 2, whereas Aij indicates a stage in the e-Services technological innovation, having a risk factor with a certain feature.

Table 2. Analytical Matrix for Technological Innovation Risk of e-Services

Stages of innovation	Technica l risk	Market risk	Financing risk	Production risk	Manageme nt risk	Policy risk
Innovation assumption	A_{11}	A_{12}	A_{13}	A_{14}	A_{15}	A_{16}
Survey and evaluation	A_{21}	A_{22}	A_{23}	A_{24}	A_{25}	A_{26}
R & D	A_{31}	A_{32}	A_{33}	A_{34}	A_{35}	A_{36}
Pilot experiment	A_{41}	A_{42}	A_{43}	A_{44}	A_{45}	A_{46}

Batch production	A_{51}	A_{52}	A_{53}	A_{54}	A_{55}	A_{56}
Market sales	A_{61}	A_{62}	A_{63}	A_{64}	A_{65}	A_{66}

3.2   Risk dimension of analytical matrix

(1) Technical risk: means the possibility of innovation failure due to the uncertainty of technical factor and its change in the technological innovation of e-Services.

(2) Market risk: means the possibility for technological innovation failure of e-Business due to uncertainty of relevant market factor and its change.

(3) Financing risk: means the possibility for innovation failure due to uncertainty of factor and its change influencing the fund raising, use and repayment for the technological innovation of e-Services.

(4) Production risk: means the possibility for innovation failure due to uncertainty of factor and its change in the production system in the technological innovation process of e-Services.

(5) Management risk: means the possibility for innovation failure due to the management error in the technological innovation process of e-Services.

(6) Policy risk: means the possibility for innovation failure due to the unfavorable influence of the central or local government's law, regulations, principle and policy and their change on the technological innovation project of e-Services.

For a technological innovation project of e-Services, according to the analytical matrix of risks, we can analyze systematically the possible risks and study the probability of occurrence and the possible loss extent so as to decide on the risks and carry out the effective risk management accordingly. Therefore, analytical matrix for technological innovation risk of e-Services has the following significances: ① it is beneficial to make clear risk factors for technological innovation of e-Services and their co-relation; ② since in practice the technological innovation activities of e-Services are carried out at levels and in stages, innovation risk matrix can cooperate better in the risk management; ③ innovation risk matrix can provide risk analysis, estimation, control and investigation before, during and after the technological innovation activities of e-Services technological innovation, from which to find the rules so as to benefit the enterprises undertaking e-Business avoid the risks in innovation activities.

4   Preventive Measures for Technological Innovation Risks of China's e-Services

4.1   Strengthen the governmental support and guidance to technological innovation of China's e-Services

(1) Establish the information supporting system

In the current commercial environment with rapid changes, for e-Business, it is critical to grasp such latest information as the governmental research achievements with potential and the production and operation of competitors. In China, many of the enterprises undertaking e-Business have inadequate sense of innovation for their technical progress, development of production technology development production and management skills for operation. Especially, it is extremely difficult for some small and medium enterprises to obtain high-quality and accurate information due to their isolated operation and lack of opportunities to exchange and learn with their colleagues. Therefore, it is necessary to strengthen the government's technical information service. For instance, through FEDWORLD network server, American National Technical Information Service provides customers with dial-network or INTERNET network information service and through the "chain" e-Supermarket provides the public with the wider and timely governmental information resources. These experiences are worth of reference [6].

(2) Regulate the intermediate service system for transform of innovation achievements

In order to raise the overall benefit of technological innovation for China's e-Services, it is necessary to further cultivate and regulate the technical exchange market, energetically develop the productivity promotion center, business service center, technical broker and technical consulting companies and other intermediary organizations so that they can play an important role in the fields of achievement promotion, information provision and personnel training and build a bridge for the technological and economic integration. Additionally, it is also necessary to improve the auxiliary legal service organizations such as the technical contract arbitration committee, intellectual property firms, court for intellectual properties and promote the effective operation of technical market.

(3) Formulate effective technological policy

To cultivate the national technological innovation system for e-Services, it is not only to give a play to the market mechanism, but also more importantly to have the powerful policy guidance. America adopts a highly-developed free market economy system, but also the powerful governmental interference. Therefore, to formulate the national e-Business policy, China should also be deeply aware of the international competition environment China is faceting and the problems encountered in China's e-Business development, stress truly the features and comparative advantages of China, improve the relevant auxiliary policy and regulations and gradually generate the policy system with the technical progress of e-Services as the subject.

(4) Establish and regulate the venture investment mechanism

Development of venture investment industry is beneficial to guide the social idling capital fro investment in the technological innovation of e-Services, accelerate the industrialization of the achievements in technological innovation and reduce the loss due to the settlement and idling of scientific research achievements. For China's venture investment industry to really improve and develop and play a leading role in the technological innovation of e-Services, it is necessary to speed up the establishment of market economy system, i.e., to develop and improve the securities market, property exchange market, technology exchange market, establish the "secondary stock market" and accelerate the establishment of modern corporate system so as to create a fine market environment for the venture investment enterprises.

4.2   Improve the risk management for the technological innovation of China's e-Services

(1) Intensify the market survey and market forecast before the technological innovation of e-Services

Firstly, it is necessary to analyze the external operation environment, stress on understanding the law and regulations, trade policy, industrial policy, technical policy, and culture, nationality, religion and public psychology related to the technological innovation of e-Services so as to ensure the innovation products will not be constrained by the national law, regulations and policy and comply better with the requirement of social environment. Secondly, the success in technological innovation of e-Services does not necessarily mean an economic success. Time is the opportunity cost for a new and high technology to be transformed into innovative products with economic advantages, while the excessively early or late marketing of innovative products will both lead to a failure. Enterprises undertaking e-Business should carry out deliberate market study, timely discover new market and identify the declining of the current market and undertake the technical forecast and economic forecast.

(2) Stress on self competitive advantage and cautiously select the direction for the technological innovation of e-Services

For enterprises undertaking e-Business, if the elimination ratio is not so high in the initial stage of technological innovation for e-Services, it is possible move some development projects with impossible technical success or market success to the later stage of innovation, as will settle and collect the risks and eventually lead to increase or further expansion of risks and even cause the operation crisis of enterprises. Therefore, the enterprises undertaking e-Business must undertake corresponding countermeasures and formulate, in combination with their features and market status, different feasible optional solutions and carry out multi-stage assessment, set the control point of risks in the initial stage of innovation as far as possible and relief the possible risks as early as possible.

(3) Implement the progress control and risk monitoring for technological innovation of e-Services

It is necessary to establish the effective regulation and control mechanism, while the management should change along with the change of innovation activities. It is to raise the flexibility of organization as well as to strengthen the rigidity of organization, for an integration of the flexible and variable, planned and intentional supervision, control and management. It is necessary to constantly raise the technical qualification of engineering technical personnel and production workers and enhance the market sense of marketing personnel. Since there may be risks of different features in the entire process of technological innovation for e-Services technological innovation, such as technical risk, market risk, management, decision and other risks, in considering the assessment for the innovation project, it is not only necessary to carry out the pre-event study, but also the interim and post-event studies and to assess all the stages: i.e., the one single assessment is changed for a multi-stage assessment and the single decision making to the multi-stage decision making.

4.3   Stress on the application of prevention technology for technological innovation risk of China's e-Services

(1) Risk transfer

Risk transfer for technological innovation of e-Services means that part or all of the innovation risks are transferred from one undertaking entity to another undertaking entity, in two modes: ① financial transfer: the undertaking entities of innovation activities remains, but the undertaking entities of risk loss have increased. Through participating in the project insurance and absorbing external investment, the enterprises undertaking e-Business carry out such transfer. ② Objective transfer: it is to transfer part or all of the innovation activities from one undertaking entity to another undertaking entity, in such modes as technical transfer, consigned development, joint technological innovation, etc. Since the risk transfer of innovation is normally accompanied with the benefit transfer or payment of certain risk cost, it is necessary for the enterprises undertaking e-Business to weigh carefully if to transfer risks and which mode to be taken for risk transfer. Normally, when the technical risk and business risk is not greater than the financial risk, the financial transfer can be adopted. When the technical risk or business risk is greater, the objective transfer can be adopted.

(2) Risk distribution

Risk distribution for technological innovation of e-Services technological innovation means to reduce the overall risk by selecting the composition of proper technological innovation projects and carrying out the composed development of innovation. Theoretically speaking, when the mutual independence between different projects in the innovation project composition is stronger or of negative association, it will be more beneficial to reduce the overall risk of the project composition. However, due to the available conditions of Chinese enterprises undertaking e-Business, such as fields with technical advantages and market share, it is difficult for them to be independent and non-associated in selecting the project composition. Besides, the excessive independence between projects will increase the innovation cost and enhance the innovation difficulty due to the non-effective sharing of technical resources, human resources and production resources. Therefore, it is necessary to maintain a certain association between projects if to distribute technological innovation risks by means of project composition.

(3) Risk control

Risk control for technological innovation of e-Services means to carry out pre-control over the innovation risks and reduce the possibility of risks and loss of the existing risks under the circumstance of having thorough identification and analysis on the risk factors of innovation. Risk factors for technological innovation of China's e-Services include controllable risk factor and uncontrollable risks factor. Some factors for decision-making risk, technical risk and production risk are in the category of controllable factors, which can be prevented and controlled by means of planning, organization and coordination. As for the uncontrollable factors of risks due to macro policy environment and market demand, such risk prevention modes as risk transfer and distribution. Chinese enterprises undertaking e-Business can also establish the risk alarming system for innovation to carry out the assessment and forecast of risks, deliver timely different-extent alarming as per nature and extent of risks and carry out the pre-control over the technological innovation risk of e-Services.

References

1. WmChi and Zq Lin. Technical Composition of and Key Problems for Current e-Business. Guangdong Education, 2006 (4), pp. 57-59

2. Mx Huang and Xl Li. Study on Quality of e-Service. Information Journal, 2005(8), pp.20-22

3. Hx Xie. Demonstrative Study on Technological Innovation Risks of Search-engine Enterprises. Library information Service, 2007(2), pp. 18-22

4. Hg Qin and JCui. Type, Reason and Countermeasures of Enterprises' Technological Innovation Risk. Business Study, 2002(242), pp. 23-25

5. Xiaobin Lu. Study on Technological Innovation Models for Chinese Consulting Enterprises. Library information Service, 2007(2), pp. 10-14

6. Julie Gable. Innovations in Information Management Technologies. Information Management Journal. Lemexa: Jan/Feb 2004. Vol. 38, pp. 156-159

Research of Default Rules Mining Model
Based on Reduced Lattice

Xinyuan Lu [1], Huili Zhang [2], and Jinlong Zhang [3]
[1] Department of Information Management, Huazhong Normal University,
Wuhan, 430079,China, luxy@mail.ccnu.edu.cn
[2] College of Humanities, Xi'an University of Archtecture and Technology,
Xi'an, 710055,China,xy-hx@163.com
[3] College of Management, Huazhong University of Science & Technology,
Wuhan 430074, China, jlzhang@mail.hust.edu.cn

Abstract. In order to solve the decision question with incomplete information and uncertainty of risk factors during the risk decision, the concept of reduced lattice is introduced into project risk management in this paper, then the default rule mining model based on the combination of rough set and reduced lattice is constructed, and created a series of subsystems from the known decision system at different reduced levels, then form a reduced lattice, and then deduce its own rule set at each reduced lattice. At last, an example is introduced to demonstrate the method and model above detailed.

1   Introduction

During the reasoning of rough set, It always supposes that a attribute of each object has only one value matched it, so the equivalent relationship of the value region can be make certain uniquely, which means it is very convenient to dispose the data. But in many occasion, the information are incomplete or lacked, and the descriptions of the objects are not reasonable, so the decision of incomplete information in the complicated system is inevitable. Assume that a decision support system is expressed by $S = (U, C \cup D, V, f)$ using the theory of rough set. Given a class $E_i \in U / Ind(C)$, and if all the objects in E_i are reflex to the same decision class $X_i \in U / Ind(D)$, then all the rules are certain, which means its reliability is 100%. But in facts, the objects can not reflex to the same decision class completely because of the missing information, and it means the rules are not 100% reliable, which is result in the coming into being of default rules.

Please use the following format when citing this chapter:

Lu, X., Zhang, H., Zhang, J., 2007, in IFIP International Federation for Information Processing, Volume 252, Integration and Innovation Orient to E-Society Volume 2, eds. Wang, W., (Boston: Springer), pp. 262-270.

Some scholars have make correlative research in this fields, such as: Skowron.A put forwarded the method of Boundary Region Thinning (BRT) to mine the default rules[1], Mollestad presented the method of selecting the default rules from incomplete information using theory of lattice and searching tree[2].Wang Yaying concluded the method of reduced lattice, and classify the knowledge into several kinds, then mined the default rules in different kind[3,4,5].Under this background mentioned above, this paper construct the default model mining model based on rough set and reduced lattice. The main process of this method are: given the reliability value μ of the rules, and construct the lattice according to different reduced levels using the rough set theory, then find out all the rule which matched the value of μ for each node in different layer. Finally, using those rules to make decision and reasoning, and find the result according to top-priority of each rule.

2   Construction of reduced lattice

The concept of lattice was presented by Wille.R in 1982, which is a two-dimensional hiberarchy, and it is also a useful mathematics tool to analyze the data. The lattice includes two meanings: inherent and extension characters of objects. In essential, the lattice describes the relationship between the object and it attributes, and it also indicates the relationship between generalities and particularity. The lattice is only influenced by the data itself, but not influenced by the order of the data or the attributes [6,7].

Suppose N expresses the number of decision attributes in a *DSS*, the initial lattice can be constructed through the method of projection. The top layer has only one node, all the node in the same layer has the same attributes (equal to the number of layer), with the decrease of layer, the number of node is decreased, so there is no node in the layer *0*. Obviously, the number of node in the layer k is C_N^k, which are deleted a attribute from the layer $k+1$, and the relationship between the neighbor nodes are successive. But in the initial lattice, each node is the subsystem of the initial system, the rules of each node is repeated because of the attributes are redundancy, which means that the computing process is very perplexing, so it is necessary to simplify the initial lattice.

Define1: Use the concept of reduced in Rough set, suppose there is a lattice of the node, if the attributes set of the node is positive to the set of decision attribute, then we can define the node as reduced node, otherwise, the node is un-reduced. If all the nodes in the lattice are reduced, then the lattice is defined as *Reduced Lattice.*

Define2: In a reduced lattice, if a node in layer k is un-reduced, then its reduced form can be found out (the reduced maybe more than one form). Generally, assume the number of attributes is $m(m \leq k)$ in a reduced form, if node in the layer from $m+1$ to k whose attribute set includes this reduced, then the node can be deleted, which means the node is superfluous, and this does not influence the obtaining of default rules.

The main course of construction of reduced lattice include: Firstly, the attribute sets can be ascertained from the initial data, then choose the value range of the attribute sets, and disposal those data preliminarily such as discrete, so the *DSS* of

$S = (U, C \cup D, V, f)$ can be gained. Secondly, construct the initial lattice according to the number of attributes, then the reduced lattice can also be calculated from the initial lattice. The main steps are as follows:

Step1：Initialize the nodes in each layer, $node[i] = C_N^i \ (i = 0, 1, 2 ... N)$, and all the nodes are signed with "*un-reduced*", *i=N*, which means the layers of the information system;

Step2：Set $j = node[i]$, which means the number of the nodes in each layer;

Step3：For the un-reduced node j in layer i, find out every reduce form of the node;

Step4：If the reduce form is itself, then change the sign symbol is changed with "*reduced*", and set $node[i]=node[i]$-1, then switch to Step6;

Step5：Change all the sign symbol of each *reduced* node, and delete the superfluous *un-reduced* node according to character of reduce lattice, then calculate the new numbers of the *un-reduced* node which denoted with $node[k]$, where k means the layer having been modified;

Step6：Set $j = node[i]$, if $j \neq 0$, switch to Step3;

Step7：Set $i = i\text{-}1$, if $i =1$then stop the algorithm, otherwise, switch to Step2.

3、 The searching and optimizing of default rules

In the initial lattice, use $N_i^{(q)}$ denote the node of "i" in layer q, and the decision support system is $S = (U, C_i^{(q)} \cup D)$, all the rules in this layer corresponding are listed:

$$U \ / \ Ind(D) = \{Y_1, Y_2, ... Y_m\}$$

$$U \ / \ Ind(C_i^{(q)}) = \{X_1, X_2, ... X_t\}$$

If $(X_k \cap Y_j) \neq 0$ (k=1,2,$\cdots$,t；j=1,2,$\cdots$,m), then a default rule can be created: $Des(X_k) \rightarrow Des(Y_j)$,its reliability is expressed with $R(X_i, Y_j)$:

$$R(X_i, Y_j) = \frac{Card(X_i \cap Y_j)}{Card(X_i)} \tag{1}$$

Its support is expressed with $S(X_i, Y_j)$:

$$S(X_i, Y_j) = \frac{Card(X_i \cap Y_j)}{Card(U)} \tag{2}$$

Suppose R_{tr} denotes the given criterion reliability, If $R(X_i, Y_j) = R_{tr}$,then the rule corresponding can be put into the rules set. If some $R(X_i, Y_j) < R_{tr}$, then all the rules' reliability of the successive node are also less than μ_{tr} , which means if some $R(X_i, Y_j) < R_{tr}$,then all the process of calculating can be overleaped, and we can only conserve the rules which accord with $R(X_i, Y_j) > R_{tr}$. So the reduce lattice and rules can be simplify continuatively.

To each node in the reduce lattice, the rule can be found out correspondingly. If the rules set is empty, then the node can be deleted, and if there more than one node accord with the R_{tr}, then construct the new rules set which are suited the criterion. If the rules set is no-empty, then choose the top-priority rule as the output rule.

The top-priority of appraisement criterion in every default rules are as follows:

1) The rules in top-layer have the top-priority, which means the connotative information can be used totally.

2) If the rules in the same layer, then assuring rules are top-priority, which means that the $R = 1$ has the top-priority;

3) If some rules are in the same layer, and each rule have the character of $R = 1$, then the more "support" has the more top- priority;

4) If some rules are in the same layer, and all the $R < 1$, then the number of appraisement function is bigger means the rules has the more top-priority. The appraisement function is defined as follows:

Assume all the rules have some conclusion of $(d_1, d_2, \dots, d_r)$, and the rule of d_i is $(r_1, r_2, \dots, r_r)$,then the appraisement function of d_i is below:

$$v(d_i) = \frac{\sum_{j=1}^{m} S_j}{\sum_{j=1}^{m} (S_j / R_j)} \qquad (3)$$

Where, S_j、 R_j express the *Support* and the *Reliability* of the rule r_j respectively.

4、 Example

Suppose there is a IT project ,ant its decision system is $S = (U, C \cup D, V, f)$, and the sample number of each object is expressed with K, the believe threshold of each rule is denoted by $R_{tr} = 0.75$,which are showed in Tab.1.

The main algorithms and steps are as follows:

Step1: Construction the initial lattice, and set $N=4$, which means there are 4 condition attributes. The number of node in each layer is: $node[i] = C_4^i = \{1, 4, 6, 4, 1\}$ $(i = 0, 1, 2, 3, 4)$, which are showed in Fig.1.

Step2: In the initial lattice, each node is signed with no-reduction symbol. Set $i = 4$, and simplify the nodes in $i=4$ layer. There is $j=node[4]=1$ node which is no-reduced in this layer, this node is $\{abcd\}$. The two reduced sets $\{b,c,d\}$ and $\{a,b\}$ can be calculated, so the node "bcd" and "ab" in the initial lattice can be signed with reduced symbol. As a result , $node[3]=3$, $node[2]=5$. So we can deleted the node "$abcd$" which included the reduced of $\{b,c,d\}$ in $i=4$ layer, the $node[4]=0$. By the same way, the node of "abc、 abd" can also be deleted which included the reduced

$\{a,b\}$ in $i=3$ layer, so the $node[3]=1$.Because of $j=node[4]=0$, $i=i-1=3$, so it switch to $i=3$ layer.

Step3: set $i = 3$, all the nodes can be reduced in this layer. Because there is only $j=node[3]=1$ no-reduced node "acd", and its reduced is $\{a,d\}$, so the node of "ad" can be signed with the symbol of reduced. Then $node[2]=4$, and the node "acd" which included $\{a,d\}$ can be deleted, so the $j=node[3]=0$, $i=i-1=2$, and it switch to $i=2$ layer.

Step4: set $i = 2$, the node in this layer can be reduced: there are $j=node[2]=4$ no-reduced nodes, because each node's reduced is itself, so each node can be signed with the symbol of reduced. Then $node[2]=0$, $i=i-1=1$, so all the nodes are reduced and finish all the process. As showed in Fig.2:

Tab.1   Decision table of information

U	Sample	Condition attributes				Decision attributes
	K	a	b	c	d	D
x_1	15	1	1	2	2	1
x_2	10	2	1	2	3	1
x_3	10	2	2	1	2	1
x_4	60	1	2	1	3	2
x_5	10	1	3	2	3	2
x_6	30	2	3	1	2	3
x_7	25	3	2	1	2	3
x_8	40	3	2	3	1	3

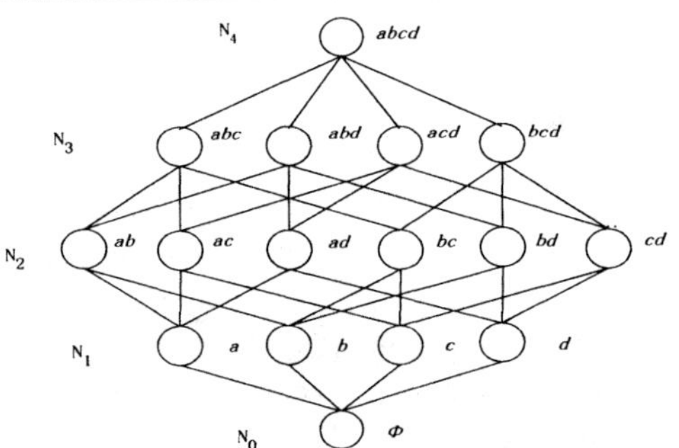

Fig.1 Initial lattice

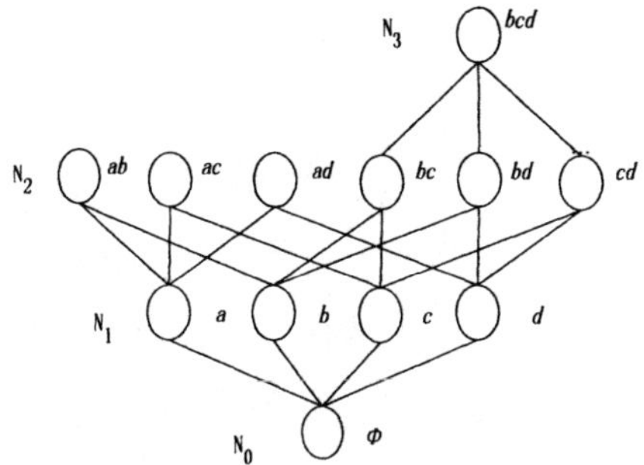

Fig.2 Reduced lattice

To each node of the reduced lattice in Fig.2, find out all the rules for each node, and put those rules into a set, the reliability and support can also be calculated according to formula （1） and （2）. For example, the rule and its reliability and support of the node "*bcd*" are as following:

$$b_1c_2d_2 \rightarrow D_1, \quad R=15/15=1.000, \quad S=15/200=0.075;$$
$$b_1c_2d_3 \rightarrow D_1, \quad R=10/10=1.000, \quad S=10/200=0.050;$$
$$b_2c_1d_2 \rightarrow D_1, \quad R=10/(10+25)=0.286, \quad S=10/200=0.050;$$
$$b_2c_1d_3 \rightarrow D_2, \quad R=60/60=1.000, \quad S=60/200=0.300;$$
$$b_3c_2d_3 \rightarrow D_2, \quad R=10/10=1.000, \quad S=10/200=0.050;$$
$$b_3c_1d_2 \rightarrow D_3, \quad R=30/30=1.000, \quad S=30/200=0.150;$$
$$b_2c_1d_2 \rightarrow D_3, \quad R=25/(10+25)=0.714, \quad S=25/200=0.125;$$
$$b_2c_3d_1 \rightarrow D_3, \quad R=40/40=1.000, \quad S=40/200=0.200;$$

In the same way, all the rules, its reliability and its support of each node can be calculated with the method mentioned above, which are showed in Tab.2:

Tab.2 The rules set of reduced nodes

Node	Rule	Reliability (R)	Support (S)	Node	Rule	Reliability (R)	Support (S)
a	$a_1 \rightarrow D_1$	0.176	0.075	ad	$a_1d_2 \rightarrow D_1$	1.000	0.075
	$a_1 \rightarrow D_2$	0.824	0.350		$a_1d_3 \rightarrow D_2$	1.000	0.350
	$a_2 \rightarrow D_1$	0.400	0.100		$a_2d_3 \rightarrow D_1$	1.000	0.050
	$a_2 \rightarrow D_3$	0.600	0.150		$a_2d_2 \rightarrow D_1$	0.250	0.050
	$a_3 \rightarrow D_3$	1.000	0.325		$a_2d_2 \rightarrow D_3$	0.750	0.150
b	$b_1 \rightarrow D_1$	1.000	0.125		$a_3d_2 \rightarrow D_3$	1.000	0.125
	$b_2 \rightarrow D_1$	0.074	0.300		$a_3d_1 \rightarrow D_1$	1.000	0.200
	$b_2 \rightarrow D_2$	0.444	0.050		$b_1c_2 \rightarrow D_1$	1.000	0.125
	$b_2 \rightarrow D_3$	0.482	0.325		$b_2c_1 \rightarrow D_1$	0.105	0.050
	$b_3 \rightarrow D_2$	0.250	0.050		$b_2c_1 \rightarrow D_2$	0.632	0.300
	$b_3 \rightarrow D_3$	0.750	0.150	bc	$b_2c_1 \rightarrow D_3$	0.263	0.125
c	$c_1 \rightarrow D_1$	0.080	0.050		$b_2c_3 \rightarrow D_3$	1.000	0.200
	$c_1 \rightarrow D_2$	0.480	0.300		$b_3c_1 \rightarrow D_3$	1.000	0.150
	$c_1 \rightarrow D_3$	0.440	0.275		$b_3c_2 \rightarrow D_2$	1.000	0.050

Node	Rule	R	S	Node	Rule	R	S
	$c_2 \rightarrow D_1$	0.714	0.125	bd	$b_1d_2 \rightarrow D_1$	1.000	0.075
	$c_2 \rightarrow D_2$	0.286	0.050		$b_1d_3 \rightarrow D_1$	1.000	0.050
	$c_3 \rightarrow D_1$	1.000	0.200		$b_2d_1 \rightarrow D_3$	1.000	0.200
d	$d_2 \rightarrow D_1$	0.312	0.125		$b_2d_2 \rightarrow D_1$	0.286	0.050
	$d_2 \rightarrow D_3$	0.688	0.275		$b_2d_2 \rightarrow D_3$	0.714	0.125
	$d_3 \rightarrow D_2$	0.750	0.350		$b_2d_3 \rightarrow D_2$	1.000	0.300
	$d_3 \rightarrow D_1$	0.250	0.050		$b_3d_2 \rightarrow D_3$	1.000	0.150
	$d_1 \rightarrow D_3$	1.000	0.200		$b_3d_3 \rightarrow D_2$	1.000	0.050
ab	$a_1b_1 \rightarrow D_1$	1.000	0.075	cd	$c_2d_2 \rightarrow D_1$	1.000	0.075
	$a_1b_2 \rightarrow D_2$	1.000	0.300		$c_1d_3 \rightarrow D_3$	1.000	0.300
	$a_1b_3 \rightarrow D_2$	1.000	0.050		$c_2d_3 \rightarrow D_2$	0.500	0.050
	$a_2b_1 \rightarrow D_1$	1.000	0.050		$c_2d_3 \rightarrow D_1$	0.500	0.050
	$a_2b_2 \rightarrow D_1$	1.000	0.050		$c_1d_2 \rightarrow D_1$	0.154	0.050
	$a_2b_3 \rightarrow D_3$	1.000	0.150		$c_1d_2 \rightarrow D_3$	0.846	0.275
	$a_3b_2 \rightarrow D_3$	1.000	0.325		$c_3d_1 \rightarrow D_3$	1.000	0.200
ac	$a_1c_2 \rightarrow D_1$	0.600	0.075	bcd	$b_1c_2d_2 \rightarrow D_1$	1.000	0.075
	$a_1c_2 \rightarrow D_2$	0.400	0.050		$b_2c_1d_3 \rightarrow D_2$	1.000	0.300
	$a_1c_1 \rightarrow D_2$	1.000	0.300		$b_3c_2d_3 \rightarrow D_2$	1.000	0.050
	$a_2c_1 \rightarrow D_1$	0.250	0.050		$b_1c_2d_3 \rightarrow D_1$	1.000	0.050
	$a_2c_1 \rightarrow D_3$	0.750	0.150		$b_2c_1d_2 \rightarrow D_1$	0.286	0.050
	$a_2c_2 \rightarrow D_1$	1.000	0.050		$b_3c_1d_2 \rightarrow D_3$	1.000	0.150
	$a_3c_1 \rightarrow D_2$	1.000	0.125		$b_2c_1d_2 \rightarrow D_3$	0.714	0.125
	$a_3c_3 \rightarrow D_3$	1.000	0.200		$b_2c_3d_1 \rightarrow D_3$	1.000	0.200

All the rules can be extracted from Tab.2, which accord with $R_{tr} \geq 0.75$, and the rules set can be showed in Tab.3:

Tab.3 The rules set of reduced nodes（ $R_{tr} \geq 0.75$ ）

Node	Rule	Reliability (R)	Support (S)	Node	Rule	Reliability (R)	Support (S)
a	$a_1 \rightarrow D_2$	0.824	0.350		$a_1d_2 \rightarrow D_1$	1.000	0.075
	$a_3 \rightarrow D_3$	1.000	0.325		$a_1d_3 \rightarrow D_2$	1.000	0.350
b	$b_1 \rightarrow D_1$	1.000	0.125	ad	$a_2d_3 \rightarrow D_1$	1.000	0.050
	$b_3 \rightarrow D_3$	0.750	0.150		$a_2d_2 \rightarrow D_3$	0.750	0.150
c	$c_3 \rightarrow D_1$	1.000	0.200		$a_3d_2 \rightarrow D_3$	1.000	0.125
d	$d_3 \rightarrow D_2$	0.750	0.350		$a_3d_1 \rightarrow D_1$	1.000	0.200
ab	$a_1b_1 \rightarrow D_1$	1.000	0.075	bd	$b_1d_2 \rightarrow D_1$	1.000	0.075
	$a_1b_2 \rightarrow D_2$	1.000	0.300		$b_1d_3 \rightarrow D_1$	1.000	0.050
	$a_1b_3 \rightarrow D_2$	1.000	0.050		$b_2d_1 \rightarrow D_3$	1.000	0.200
	$a_2b_1 \rightarrow D_1$	1.000	0.050		$b_2d_3 \rightarrow D_2$	1.000	0.300
	$a_2b_2 \rightarrow D_1$	1.000	0.050		$b_3d_2 \rightarrow D_3$	1.000	0.150

	$a_2b_3 \rightarrow D_3$	1.000	0.150		$b_3d_3 \rightarrow D_2$	1.000	0.050
	$a_3b_2 \rightarrow D_3$	1.000	0.325		$c_2d_2 \rightarrow D_1$	1.000	0.075
	$a_1c_1 \rightarrow D_2$	1.000	0.300	cd	$c_1d_3 \rightarrow D_3$	1.000	0.300
	$a_2c_1 \rightarrow D_3$	0. 750	0.150		$c_1d_2 \rightarrow D_3$	0.846	0.275
ac	$a_2c_2 \rightarrow D_1$	1.000	0.050		$c_3d_1 \rightarrow D_3$	1.000	0.200
	$a_3c_1 \rightarrow D_2$	1.000	0.125		$b_1c_2d_2 \rightarrow D_1$	1.000	0.075
	$a_3c_3 \rightarrow D_3$	1.000	0.200		$b_2c_1d_3 \rightarrow D_2$	1.000	0.300
	$b_1c_2 \rightarrow D_1$	1.000	0.125	bcd	$b_3c_2d_3 \rightarrow D_2$	1.000	0.050
bc	$b_2c_3 \rightarrow D_3$	1.000	0.200		$b_1c_2d_3 \rightarrow D_1$	1.000	0.050
	$b_3c_1 \rightarrow D_3$	1.000	0.150		$b_3c_1d_2 \rightarrow D_3$	1.000	0.150
	$b_3c_2 \rightarrow D_2$	1.000	0.050		$b_2c_3d_1 \rightarrow D_3$	1.000	0.200

It can be concluded from the Tab.3 above, the default rules mining model of educed lattice can provide the satisfying decision rule according to the different layer. Due to its mechanism resemble humans' thinking, those method is very useful and flexible, it can conveniently arrive at a conclusion as good as possible at the matching rule sets according to the given criterion.

5、 Conclusion

The advantages of the method mentioned above in this paper are as follows: 1) The reliability and support can be given when the data and information are incomplete. 2) The satisfying results can be approved when the data is inconsistent, which means that the system has the character and ability of allowable error. 3) The decision maker can choose the different layer and node freely.4) The default rules are simple and regular, especially unrepeated, which is propitious to make decision according to the new data.

6、 Acknowledgement

This research was supported by the National Natural Science Foundation of China （70571025）, and also supported by the DanGui Project of Huazhong Noraml University（06DG024）.

References

1. Skowron A, Polkowski L, Komorowski J. Learning Tolerance relations by Boolean descriptors, *Automatic Feature Extraction from Data Tables.* In:Tsumoto[C]. Kobayashi,Yokomor,Tanka,and Nakamura.RSFD, 1996:11-17
2. Mollestad T.A Rough set approach to default rules data mining[D]. Norway: the Norwegian Institute of Technology,1996
3. Wang Yaying, Shao Huihe. A Rough Set Model to Mine Default Rule *Journal of Shanghai Jiaotong University.* 2000 ,5:691-694
Hu Keyun; Lu Yuchang; Shi Chunyi. Advances in concept lattice and its application[J].

Journal of Tsinghua University. 2000,9:77-81
4. Marzena Kryszkiewicz. Rough set approach to incomplete information systems[J]. *Information science,* 1998, 112: 39-49
Marzena Kryszkiewicz. Rules in incomplete information systems[J]. *Information science,* 1999, 113: 271-292
5. Zdzislwa Pawlak. Rough sets and intelligent data analysis [J], *Information sciences,* 2002,147:1-12
6. Wu Bing. Web mining model based on rough set theory. *Journal of southeast university*[J]. 2002.3:54-58
7. Wille R. Restructuring Lattice theory: An Approach Based on Hierarchies of Concepts[C].In: Rival I ed. Ordered Set.Dorerecht-Boston:Reidel.1982:445-470
8. Lu Xinyuan.*A sutydy on the risk decision rules mining of IT project* [M], Hubei People Press,2006,
9. MO Xiangqun. Risk management of software project schedule [J]. *Computer and Information Technology,*2002,4:67-70
10. Jian Lirong, Da Qing li,Chen Weida. A method of rule induction based on rough set theory in inconsistent information system [J]. *Chinese Journal of Management Science.* 2003,8: 91-95
11. Pang Sulin, Li Rongzhou, The decision mechanism of credit risk for banks with imperfect information [J]. *Journal of South China University of Technology,* 1999.8
12. Pawlak Z. Rough sets[J].*International Journal of Information and Computer Science,*1982,11:341-356.
13. Wang Guoyin. *The Rough set theory and the knowledge acquirement [M].* Xi'an:Xi'an Jiaotong university press,2001,.5.
14. Holt, Gary D. Classifying construction contractors: a case using cluster analysis (Periodical style). *Building Research & Information,* 1997, 25(11): 374-378
15. Chinyio, E. A., Olomolaiye, P. O., Kometa, S. T. and Harris, F. C., A needs-based methodology for classifying construction clients and selecting contractors (Periodical style). Construction Management & Economics, 1998, 16(1): 91-95
16. Koen Milis, Roger Mercken, The use of the balanced scorecard for the evaluation of Information and Communication Technology projects (Periodical style). International Journal of Project Management, 2004(22): 87-97
17. M. Banerjee, S. Mitra, S.K. Pal, Rough fuzzy MLP: knowledge encoding and classification, IEEE Trans. *Neural Networks 9* (Nov) (1998) 1203 – 1216.
18. XU Zeshui. A method for multi-objective decision making with incomplete information [J]. *Operations research and management science* 2001.6
19. Liao Xiuwu; Tang Huanwen. A new group decision-making approach with incomplete information [J]. *Journal of Dalian University of Technology* 2002.1

WSDRI-based Semantic Web Service Discovery Framework

Xu Sun[1], YanLi Xu[2],MingRong Mao[3] and Ming Dong[4]

1 Renmin University of China, the School of Information, 100872 Peiking,
xu2002261@163.com,

2 Renmin University of China, the School of Information, 100872 Peiking,
xu_yanli@163.com.

3 Nanjing Normal University, Information department, 210042 Nanjing,
mrmao@njnu.edu.cn

4 Renmin University of China, the School of Information, 100872 Peiking,
dongming3699@126.com

Abstract. In the research of Web Service [1, 2], semantic information should be automatically discovered, selected and composed. These automations can make usage of Web Service easily. In this paper we propose a framework to facilitate the discovery of Web Service. In this framework, we use WSDRI (Web Service Discovery Information) to describe the semantic information. This framework which refers to client and Match Server is based on WSDRI. Then we evaluate the framework through the application on the internet to find that the framework is effective. Following this framework, it could be easy to discover the information of Web Service especially the semantic information.

1 Introduction

Now enterprise application begin to shift from single way to collaboration way. An application can be formed by web applications that base on the Browser/Server structure. And more and more applications come into distributed compute supported by many technologies such as CORBA, Java. Because of this environment and such technology, Web Service [1, 2] comes forth. Web service is a coupled component that can be programmed via any program language such as Java, C#. It exposes its interface on the Internet and some clients can request it. And Web Service is a standard including Hypertext Transfer Protocol, XML, SOAP, WSDL (Web Service Description Language) and UDDI[8]. If Web Service follows these technology standards, a client can call the Web Service via UDDI. There are many researches in this field. For example Wolfgang Hoschek proposed the web service discovery

---

Please use the following format when citing this chapter:

Sun, X., Xu, Y., Mao, M., Dong, M., 2007, in IFIP International Federation for Information Processing, Volume 252, Integration and Innovation Orient to E-Society Volume 2, eds. Wang, W., (Boston: Springer), pp. 271-281.

architecture [14]. It specified a small set of orthogonal multi-purpose communication primitives for discovery. And to integrate the information, he used XML data model. And then Ronan Barrett and Claus Pahl addressed service composing with a modeling approach, a non-intrusive decentralized interaction mechanism and a solution for dynamic deployment of the composition. Their novel approach combined a Model Driven Architecture using UML 2.0, for modeling and subsequently generating Web service compositions, with a method for achieving decentralized communication amongst services. They also provided a Web service based facility for enabling the dynamic deployment of compositions [15].

We think Web Service description should contain enough semantic information. This information is associated with some Web Service. When discovering a Web Service, this semantic information should be offered by a client. Via WSDA, at runtime, application can discover and adapt the suitable Web Service [14]. A simple description language SWSDL (Simple Web Service Description Language) is used to describe a Web Service [14] .But in this paper, we do not use another simple language to describe Web Service, and instead, we use a formalized method to figure out what information a client should offer, and how is Web Service discovered. We assume that we can use the present technology such XML to represent the related information about Web Service.

But the service providers should describe the Web Service using a certain language and register the services for some client can find it. At present the OWL [13,10] language should be considered. OWL can be used to explicitly represent the meaning of terms in vocabularies and the relationships between those terms. But we can use OWL-S [10]. OWL-S is ontology for services created by the Darpa Agent Markup Language (DAML) group (Martin et al., 2005). The ontology is broken into three parts: the Service Profile describes the capabilities of the service; Service Model describes how the service works internally; and Service Grounding describes how to access the service [6]. The OWL-S ontology is useful in that it provides a uniform mechanism for describing the semantics of a Web service. We use a tool to make us easy to construct the OWL files. We do not discuss the OWL language. We only offer a framework for discovering Web Service, and the framework is independent on some language, because we describe it using formal language.

In this paper we define some procedures and these procedures use the information of the semantic information to discover Web Service. These procedures run at client and Match Servers. The Semantic Information, which is named in paper as WSDRI (Web Service Discovery Routine Information), transfer between Match Servers. We apply the event-driven model to the framework; And the procedures we define in this paper, are all embedded in this model.

2   What is WSDRI

Semantic Web services are the emerging technology promising to become one of the future key enables of the semantic web. Now in this field, experts are researching many aspects of the semantic web, such as the standards of web service, the infrastructures, the match algorithms, the method to describe the semantic and so on. But Web Services are generally described using XML-based standards, namely

WSDL, UDDI, and SOAP [9,11,12]. In addition to these low-level standards, work is on-going to create standards that allow services to be combined into a workflow, e.g. WS-BPEL (Web Services — business process execution language), and also to define permissible message exchange patterns and contents, e.g. ebXML [14]. However, few of these standards provide a way to describe a Web Service in terms of explicit semantics. For a given service you maybe do:

(1) What kind of service it is (2) What inputs it requires (3) What outputs it provides, what needs to be true for the service to execute

The first of these requirements is partly addressed by UDDI, in that a category and human-readable description can be assigned to a Web Service in a registry to aid discovery [3, 5]. This provides only limited support for automated discovery since a computer will not understand the description or what the category means. The second and third of these requirements are partly addressed by WSDL in that XML tags can be attributed to inputs and outputs. A computer can easily match these, but again has no notion of their meaning or relationship to other pieces of data. Fundamentally, most of the hard work is left to the human user who must interpret the descriptions provided to the best of their abilities [4].

But the above discussion lacks the information to describe more features of Web Service. In this paper, we use Web Service Discovery Routine Information (WSDRI) (Fig.1) to conquer these disadvantages.

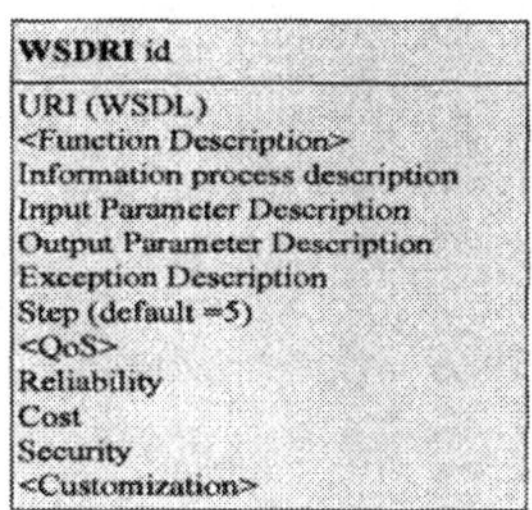

• **Fig.1.** The description of WSDRI

WSDRI id expresses the identification of the request for Web Service.

URL expresses Web Service's WSDL. If a client wants an explicit Web Service, this field should be assigned a value.

Function description expresses the function of Web Service. It includes: Information Process Description, Input Parameter Description, Output Parameter Description and Exception Description.

We think that there should be some criterions about Information Process Description (IPD), output description, input description, and exception description. And these criterions should also contain semantic information to help to match. In function description, we think IPD is very important and there should be an industry standard to specify IPD. It should be defined as Standard Information Procedure of Industry (SIPI) that is defined by industry or Standard Information Procedure of Business (SIPB) that is defined by some company. And a certain SIPI or SIPB can describe an Information Process. Every service provider should had better follow these standards and provide more semantic information.

Step (default = 5) expresses that how many Match Servers the WSDRI should transfer in one direction.

QoS expresses the constraints of a Web Service's quality. It includes reliability cost, security and so on.

Customization expresses that the client can define some extra constraints about Web Service.

About the WSDRI, we can formalize the data structure, as follows:

Need WebSevice:={ function description} ***with*** {non-function description}
{function description}:={
        InformationProcessDescription:={semantic information};
        OutputParam:={semantic information};
        InputParam:={semantic information};
        Exception:={semantic information};
}
Step:={5};
{non-function description}:={
        Cost:={numeric};
        Security:={encrypt standard};
        Time:={n seconds};
        Customization:={non-function description}}

The service provider should offer enough semantic information to register its Web Service and this is out of the scope of this paper, so we assume there is lots of information in internet or managed by the Web Service Discovery Framework.

3   The Web Service Discovery Framework

3.1   General introduction of the framework

On the Internet, there should be several hosts which run match software. These hosts can use WSDRI to match the semantic information. We name these hosts as Match Server. Some client sends WSDRI and the framework can return a set of Web Service to this client (Fig.2). The Match Server is linked as a chain (We will talk the match server chain at **3.2**):

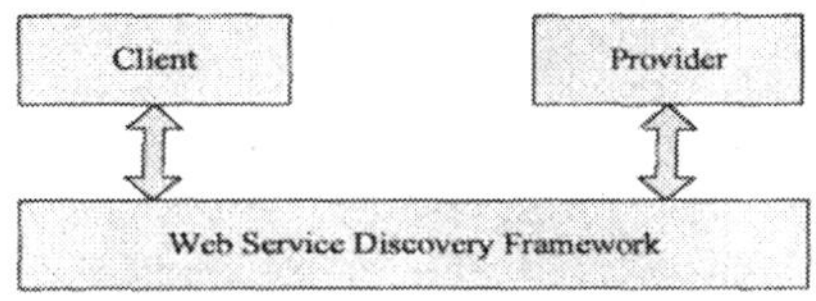

• **Fig.2.** usage of Web Service Discovery Framework

For Match Server to use WSDRI to discover the Web Service, we define such processes as follows:

SendWSSemantic:

(1) InParam: WSDRI (is identified by requestor's URL and the WSDRI id)(2) OutParam: None(3) Called by client

CombineResults:

(1) InParam: ArrayList (two results)(2) OutParam: an array list of Web Service in which there is no the same element.(3) Called by client

MatchSemantic:(1) InParam:WSDRI, WSDLs (a set of Web Service)(2) OutParam: None(3) Call by Match Server

SendNextChainServer:(1)InParam: inWSDRI (a copy of WSDRI), outNextSetofWS (a set of Web Service)(2)OutParam:None(3)Call by Match Server

SendSetofWS:(1) InParam: a set of Web Service; WSDRI (2) OutParam: None(3) Call by Match Server

We use Event System to invoke this function. The event is a Message Object. We use the kind of object to decide which handler is called. So we define such types:

WSSMsg (Web Service Semantic Message) expresses that in client the queue of Web Service Semantic Description is not empty, and then the handler SendWSSemantic is called.

WSCMsg (Web Service Combine Result Message) expresses that in client the two results received and the handler CombineResults is called.

WSMMsg (Web Service Match Semantic Message) expresses that in Match Server the WSDRI is received and the match software will call the handler MatchSemantic .

WSSSMsg (Web Service Send Set Message) expresses that if the WSDRI get the end of Web Service Chain (WSC) or the *Step* field of the WSDRI is reduced to zero, the handler SendSetofWS will be called.

We assume that in client and Match Server there are some queues.

In client there are:

1. Semantic Request Queue stores the WSDRIs. In client every request for a Web Service is associated with a WSDRI.

2. Result Queue expresses that one WSDRI will generate two results and when the two results return, they will be saved in this queue. Every element is divided into two units to save the two results.

In Match Server there are:

1. Match Semantic Queue expresses that WSDRI which was received from a client or another Match Server will be saved in this queue.

2. Final Result Queue expresses that when the *Step* field of the WSDRI is reduced to zero, the set of Web Service in current Match Server will be saved here and waits to be sent to the client.

3.2   Procedure definition

The framework works based on the mentioned procedure at the above sections. So we now define the procedures in this section. First we define the SendWSSemantic () procedure and this procedure is used in client. The client uses this procedure to send the WSDRI to a default Match Server.

```
SendWSSemantic (inWSDRI):={
IF validate (inWSDRI) =TRUE
        THEN SYSTEM . send (inWSDRI)
Else
        {require More Details}

}
```

WSDRI should have some essential elements. So we call function validate () to confirm if inWSDRI (inWSDRI is a copy of WSDRI) is integrity. We think such essential elements are: function description, output description, input description. Finally we use a system call send () function via a default Match Server URL to send WSDRI to Match Server.

Every Match Server receives WSDRI, the function as follows we define should be invoked.

```
MatchSemantic (inWSDRI, inPreSetofWS){
IF inWSDRI. Step<MaxStep
        THEN set inWSDRI.Step  inWSDRI.Step-1
Set tmpSetofWS:={
Select WSDL from ontology Server linking to the Match Server where Semantic
Server SUPER inWSDRI
    }
Set outNextSetofWS :={ UNION (tmpSetofWS, inPreSetofWS)}
IF inWSDRI. Step<0 OR (NextMatchServer is NULL OR PreMatchServer is
NULL)
    THEN SendResultModule (inWSDRI.URL , outNextSetofWS)
    ELSE
        SendNextChainServer (inWSDRI, outNextSetofWS)
}
```

Before discussing the above function, we first introduce the Match Server Chain (Fig.3).

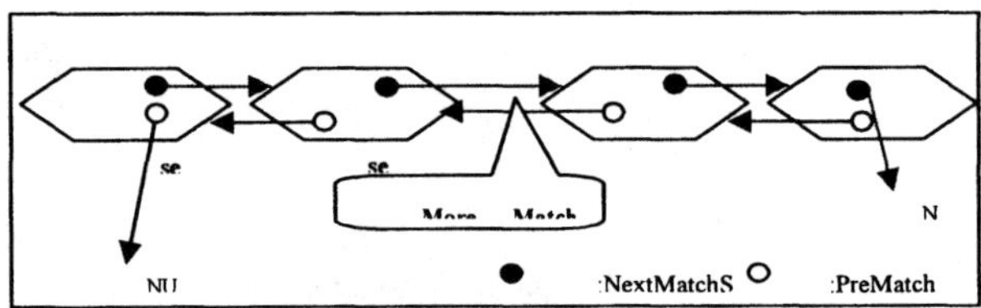

• **Fig.3.** The interior structure of the match server

But in this framework we assume that all Match Server are inter-linking like as a bidirectional link-table(Fig.3) and we use PreMatchServer and NextMatchServer to identify the preceding and next server.

In function MatchSemantic (), the Match Server first check the Step field and determine if the WSDRI should be completely processed; and if the result can be send client by calling the SendResultModule. About modules we will discuss at the next chapter.

In MatchSemantic () procedure, procedure SendNextChainServer () is called. Because the Match Server is a chain, and the *step* is not zero, the procedure will be called. The definition is following as:

SendNextChainServer (inWSDRI, outNextSetofWS) {

IF FROM(inWSDRI)=PreMatchServer

THEN SYSTEM . SendNext(NextMatchServer , inWSDRI , outNextSetofWS)
    ELSE

        IF FROM(inWSDRI)=NextMatchServer

THEN SYSTEM . SendNext(PreMatchServer , inWSDRI , outNextSetofWS)

ELSE {

SYSTEM . SendNext(NextMatchServer , inWSDRI , outNextSetofWS)

        SYSTEM . SendNext(PreMatchServer , inWSDRI , outNextSetofWS)

}

}

SendNextChainServer () should decide which URL the WSDRI should be send to. In Match Server chain , if a WSDRI is received, and its source URL is PreMatchServer, the WSDRI should be send via the NextMatchServer, and otherwise via the PreMatchServer. And if the WSDRI is from a client, the WSDRI will be send via PreMatchServer and NextMatchServer. FROM () is to fetch the source URL.

When in a Match Server Chain some a Match Server receives a WSDRI from a client, the WSDRI will be send to two servers, one is PreMatchServer and the other NextMatchServer. And so the two directions will be generated two result sets and the client will receive them. And the following procedure is necessary. It use UNION operation to merge two returned results. The procedure CombineResult () is called when the WSCMsg message happens.

CombineResult (firstResult, secondResult, outOptionalResult) {

Set outOptionalResult: =UNION (firstResult,secondResult)

}

3.3   Module definition

As we mentioned in the previous sections, we think that the framework is based on the message-driven model. In this section we will discuss the relative aspects about the model.

First, in this section we only use one procedure as follows we define:

SendSetofWS (URL, inSetofWS){

SYSTEM. Send (URL, inSetofWS)

}

The procedure is called when the final result set is formed, and the message WSSSMsg generates in Match Server. But before this the final result should be save in the Final Result Queue. This procedure is simply calling the System function Send ().

We think that there should be some modules that generate event and set some environment variables to offer the executing environment for the event handler. So we define some Modules run at client and Match Server:

1. ClientModule:This module run in client and generate event: WSSMsg (Web Service Semantic Message), MSCMsg (Web Service Combine Message). And it can operate Semantic Request Queue and Result Queue.

2. MSModule:This module runs in Match Server and generate event: WSMMsg (Web Service Match semantic Message). And it can operate Match Semantic Queue. This module calls Send Result Module.

3. SendResultModule:This module runs in Match Server and generates WSSSMsg. And it can operate Final Result Queue.

Then we formalized the three modules as follows:

ClientModule
Begin
 Suspend on PORTxxx until WSDRI ***is listened*** {
 Add WSDRI ***to*** SemanticRequestQueue
 Generate WSSMsg

}

 Suspend on PORTyyy until Set of Web Service ***is listened*** {
 Add Set of Web Service ***to*** Result Queue
 IF two result sets that refer to the same WSDRI return ***Generate*** MSCMsg

}
End
MSModule
Begin
 Suspend on PORTzzz until WSDRI is ***listened*** {
 Add WSDRI ***to*** Match Semantic Queue
 Generate WSMMsg

}
End
SendResultModule
Begin
 Add Set of Web Service ***to*** Final Result Queue
 Generate WSSSMsg
End

And if some event is generated, we use the macro ***BEGIN_ EVENT*** and ***END_ EVENT*** to determine which procedure should be invoked.

In client:
BEGIN_ EVENT
 WSSMsg ***Associated with*** SendWSSenmatic
 WSCMsg ***Associated with*** CombineResult
END_ EVENT
 In Match Server:
BEGIN_EVENT
 WSMMsg ***Associated with*** MatchSemantic
 WSSSMsg ***Associated with*** SendSetofWS
END_EVENT

4   Conclusion and Future work

4.1   Conclusion

This paper has presented the Web Service discovery framework. We use WSDRI to describe the semantic information about a Web Service including the input parameter, output parameter and some of the function and non-function information, conquering the deficiency of the WSDL and the UDDI.

This framework integrates the main features of Web Service. The semantic information of Web Service is published in the framework by the service providers. So the client only provides the semantic information like a natural language but not like the program interface, and the framework can complete the discovery of Web Service. In client eyes, discovery of Web Service is easier via WSDRI.

About our work at the previous mention, we conclude our research and the Web Service discovery framework can describe as following chart (**Fig.4.**):

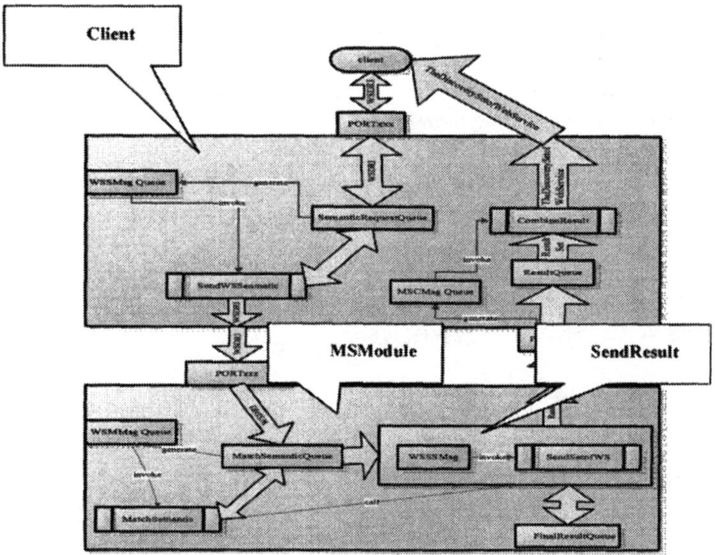

• **Fig.4.** The detail structure of the Web Service Discovery Framework

If a Client has a Web Service requirement and the WSDRI will be generated. At this time event WSSMsg will be generated and WSDRI will be saved in a queue, Semantic Request Queue, and the event handler SendWSSemantic will be called.

When a Match Server receives a WSDRI, the event WSMMsg will be generated and the received WSDRI will be saved in Match Semantic Queue. In the Match Server, because WSMMsg occurred, the corresponding handler MatchSemantic will be called. But if the value of *Step* field of WSDRI is reduced to zero, the current set of Web Service will be the final result set and this set will be sent to the responding client. When the client receives two sets of Web Service that is identified by the same WSDRI id, the event WSCMsg will be generated and the two result sets will be saved in a queue Result Queue. Because the event WSCMsg occurred, the handler CombineResults will be called. Then the client can get a set of Web Service from the framework works in the Internet.

4.2   Future work

Though the framework is effective, there are some shortcomings. In order to complete the framework fully we should do the next in the future.

1. We think that in Web Service how to process the data is very important and that is the most part of the function. We will embark on research the SIPI and SIPB. This can describe the meaning of semantic information fully, as a part of the WSDRI. Now the description of that is insufficient.

2. We will develop a system or prototype to implement the framework and try to find more dimensions about WSDRI. We think the technology of developing this framework is not difficult. This prototype will follow our framework. Many program languages all support the development of module of the framework, such as Java. But considered the efficiency of the framework we will use the C++ language.

3. We will develop some algorithm to evaluate the Web Service that be returned from the Internet and then we will make the auto-selection and the auto-composition coming true. An auto-selection and auto-composition is considered the next most important work in the research of web service. If these come true, the web application will be produced automatically.

References:

1. Max Haustein, Klaus - Peter L#hr. JAC- Declarative Java Concurrency, Concurrency and Computation: Practice and Experience, 2006, pp.519~546.
2. Gerald C. Gannod, John T. E. Timm, Raynette J. Brodie. Facilitating the Specification of Semantic Web Services Using Model-Driven Development. IDEA Group Publishing, Volume 3(3), 2006, pp.61-81.
3. Jyotishman Pathak, Neeraj Koul. A Framework for semantic Web services discovery. ACMWIDM, 2005.
4. M. Altenhofen, E. B¨orger, J. Lemcke. An execution semantics for mediation patterns. In C. Bussler, D. Fensel, U. Keller, and B. Sapkota, editors, Proc. of 2nd WSMO Implementation Workshop WIW'2005.
5. A. Barros, E. B¨orger. A compositional framework for service interaction patterns and communication flows. International Conference on Formal Engineering Methods (ICFEM 2005), volume 3785, 2005, pp.5–35.
6. A. Barros, M. Dumas, P. Oaks. A critical overview of the web series choreography description language (WS-CDL). White paper, 24th of January 2005.
7. D. Skogan, R. Gronmo, I. Solheim, "Web service composition in UML", In: Proceeding of the 8th International IEEE Enterprise Distributed Object Computing Conference (EDOC'04), pp. 47–57, Sep, 2004

8. L. Li, I. Horrocks. A software framework for matchmaking based on semantic web technology. In Proc. of the Twelfth World Wide Web Conference, 2003.
9. Bijan Parsia. Semantic Web Services. Bulletin of the American Society for Information Science and Technology, May, 2003, pp.12-15.
10. Methmet Sayal, Akhil Sahai, Vijay Machiraju, Fabio Casati. Semantic Analysis of E-Business Operations. Journal of Network and Systems Management, May 2003, pp .13-37.
11. Maedche A, Staab S. Services on the Move – Towards P2P-enabled Semantic Web Services. In: Proceedings of 10th International Conference on Informa- tion Technology and Travel & Tourism, ENTER 2003, Helsinki, 2003.
12. C. Goble, D. D. Roure. The Grid: An Application of the Semantic Web. ACM SIGMOD Record Volume 31(4), December ,2002, pp.65-70.
13. P.H. Alesso, C..F. Smith, Developing Semantic Web Services, A K Peters ltd, Wellesey MA, Canada, Date, 2004, pp.165-272.
14. Wolfgang Hoschek . The Web Service Discovery Architecture . CERN IT Division . European Organization for Nuclear Research .
15. Ronan Barrett, Claus Pahl, Lucian M. Patcas, John Murphy. Model Driven Distribution Pattern Design for Dynamic Web Service Compositions ICWE'06, July 2006, pp.11-14.

Virtual Team Governance: Addressing the Governance Mechanisms and Virtual Team Performance

Yihong Zhan[1],Yu Bai[2],Ziheng Liu[3]
1 Graduate Department, Central China Normal University,
zyh@mail.ccnu.edu.cn
2 Information Management Department ，Central China Normal
University, Baiyu926@sohu.com
3 The Department of Information Technology ，Central China
Normal University,Lzh20201@yahoo.com.cn

Abstract. As technology has improved and collaborative software has been developed, virtual teams with geographically dispersed members spread across diverse physical locations have become increasingly prominent. Virtual team is supported by advancing communication technologies, which makes virtual teams able to largely transcend time and space. Virtual teams have changed the corporate landscape, which are more complex and dynamic than traditional teams since the members of virtual teams are spread on diverse geographical locations and their roles in the virtual team are different. Therefore, how to realize good governance of virtual team and arrive at good virtual team performance is becoming critical and challenging. Good virtual team governance is essential for a high-performance virtual team. This paper explores the performance and the governance mechanism of virtual team. It establishes a model to explain the relationship between the performance and the governance mechanisms in virtual teams. This paper is focusing on managing virtual teams. It aims to find the strategies to help business organizations to improve the performance of their virtual teams and arrive at the objectives of good virtual team management.

1 Introduction

The virtual environment and various communication technologies have created a new context for leadership and teamwork. As technology has improved and collaborative software has been developed, virtual teams are becoming a more common type of work unit and play an increasingly role in organizations [1]. Virtual teams with geographically dispersed members spread across diverse physical locations have become increasingly prominent. Virtual team is supported by advancing communication technologies, which make virtual team able to largely transcend time and space and to work together and accomplish projects or goals with the combining of the skills of different members in different locations and organizations with different functions [2].

Virtual teams have changed the corporate landscape, which are more complex and dynamic than traditional teams since the members of virtual teams are spread on diverse geographical locations and their roles in the virtual team are different. Therefore, how to realize good governance of virtual team and arrive at good virtual team performance is becoming critical and challenging. Good virtual team governance is essential for a high-performance virtual team. This paper explores the performance and the governance mechanism of virtual team. It establishes a model to explain the relationship between the performance and the governance mechanisms in virtual teams. This paper is focusing on managing virtual teams. It aims to find the strategies to help business organizations to improve the performance of their virtual teams and arrive at the objectives of good virtual team management.

2 Virtual Team Governance Mechanisms

Virtual teams are heavily dependent on the advanced information and communication technology. The most distinctive features of virtual teams are that they cross boundaries of space and that teams interaction is mediated through communication technology, for example e-mails, videoconferences and so on. The formation of virtual team facilities companies of various kinds of knowledge and expertise collected in the group working process [3]. Virtual team is becoming common in companies. Thus how to realize good virtual team governance and arrive at good virtual team performance have become critical in organizations. Virtual teams can help organizations to harness, integrate and apply knowledge and expertise that are distributed across organizations and in pockets of collaborative networks [4]. Good management of virtual team is an important orientation of business organizations. In virtual team governance the following mechanisms are of importance in improving the performance of virtual teams: control, trust and cooperation.

2.1 Control Mechanism

Control is a helpful mechanism to realize efficient performance of routine partitioned tasks in virtual team work. In virtual team work, there are various kinds of above-mentioned routine tasks, for example, regular videoconference, and regular online report and so on. Control is an important mechanism that may help to ensure confidence in cooperative behavior in virtual team. Control mechanism is generic policies or activities that may generate different levels of control. The level of control has a direct influence on the level of trust within a virtual team [5]. Ensuring control is quite difficulty, since both high-level and low-level control can result in the dysfunction of virtual team and loss of the advantages of virtual team. Control mechanism can limit the performance of innovation capability in virtual teams as well. It should be applied with some other mechanisms in virtual team management.

2.2   Trust Mechanism

Trust is a complex, multifaceted phenomenon, which can function as a highly effective coordinating mechanism in virtual team management. Trust is selected as an important affect-based focus in virtual team management because of its importance to team member perceptions and behaviors towards their team and its importance to individuals working as part of a virtual team. Virtual team is of high dynamics and flexibility, which requires high levels of mutual trust and cooperation in virtual team work and management. It is impossible to monitor and control geographically distributed employees in the virtual team [5]. In virtual team case, trust is a good mechanism to manage people who work in different locations with the help of modern communication technology if companies want to enjoy the benefits of virtual teams. The feature of being virtual requires trust mechanism to make virtual team work. Trust can also help to improve relationships, mutual understanding and knowledge sharing in the virtual team. But ensuring trust is difficult. In virtual team governance, having too much trust can be dysfunctional. In virtual team governance, trust should be combined with control, which can mitigate the weakness of low-trust in control mechanism.

2.3   Cooperation Mechanism

In virtual team all the members are working based on the cooperation with different partners in different locations. The members of virtual team are not only dependent on each other, but also responsible for each other. The members of virtual team are supporting each other and helping each other in their work in the virtual environment. Cooperation mechanism helps virtual team in organizations to enhance the competitive strategies of their businesses by cooperation, which can increase the flexibility, responsiveness and cost efficiency as well as the reduction of operational and transactional costs in working process in organizations. Cooperation is perceived as a strategic drive aimed at improving the internal and external resource utilization and the overall profitability of organizations as well [6].

Cooperation mechanism is always used with the trust mechanism in virtual team management. With the advent of cooperation in virtual teams, direct control is no longer so important. Instead trust serves as an important aligning mechanism for geographically dispersed workers. Without trust, virtual teams could not be effective. Individual members in virtual team can cooperate together only if mutual confidence or trust is present among the members in the virtual team [7]. Just as discussed above, the three different governance mechanisms - control, trust and cooperation mechanisms, should be applied in virtual team management together, not only one mechanism, which can help organizations to take advantages of the three different governance mechanisms and minimize the disadvantages of them, meanwhile to realize the good performance of virtual team.

3 Performance of Virtual Team

There are many potentially important factors that could impact the performance of virtual teamwork in various ways. In this paper we address four aspects of the performance of virtual team. We examine the knowledge management capability, communication capability, shared understanding capability and innovation capability of virtual team to explore the performance of virtual team. Good performance and capability of virtual team is the goal of organizations. Different working capabilities of virtual teams play important roles in the strategic positioning of organizations' performance and the efficiency of virtual team.

3.1 Knowledge Management

Knowledge management is an important aspect to evaluate the performance of virtual team. In virtual team knowledge management consists of knowledge learning and knowledge sharing. As above-mentioned, organizations aim at harnessing, integrating and applying knowledge and expertise that are distributed across organizations through virtual team. In virtual team working, knowledge sharing and knowledge learning is the basic requirement for all members in virtual team, which is important for cooperation in virtual team and for the successful utilization of new knowledge produced in the virtual working process [4]. Knowledge management is the prerequisite to transform the knowledge collected and created in virtual team work into the asset of organization, which can influence the efficiency and performance of virtual team.

3.2 Communication

In virtual team, all the members, who are working together based on modern information technology, are located in different locations. The members never or rarely meet face-to-face in their working process. Thus communication based on modern technologies becomes quite vital for the collaboration in virtual team. The communication methods in virtual team include videoconference, text-based chat and sharing, and face-to-face meeting, though face-to-face meeting rarely happen in virtual team [8]. Communication is the basic working tool in virtual team. Good communication capability can help virtual team to improve their efficiency on ideas, knowledge and skills exchange, improving understanding among members, producing more new knowledge, and making innovation. In a word, communication based on modern information technology is the basic thing what the members in virtual team should do.

3.3   Shared Understanding

Shared understanding in virtual team is more than a common goal that all the members in the virtual team recognize. Shared understanding involves embracing the strategic direction of a team, including an understanding of the knowledge and expertise each member possesses the role of different members in the team, and how they should interact with each other in order to realize the overall goal of the team. Shared understanding in virtual team can help to establish the cooperation relationship in the entire working process and make the virtual team relationship work very well [2]. It can also encourage the members in virtual team to care more about the whole team work, but not their specific contribution. Shared understanding can help virtual team to cooperate very well, which is the prerequisite for good performance of virtual team.

3.4   Innovation

Innovation capability is quite vital for organizations to achieve competitive advantages in the competition with other organizations. Organizations are aiming at make innovation and achieve superiority on technology, product and market through virtual team [6]. Making innovation is the final goal of virtual team. Good innovation capability means good performance of virtual team.

4 The Governance Model of Virtual Team

Based on the above discussion on governance mechanism and performance of virtual team, we establish a governance model of virtual team (See Figure 1). This model illustrated that in virtual team management, the three mechanisms, including trust, cooperation and control mechanism, should be applied together, but their importance in management is different (See Figure 1). Trust is of the highest importance and control is of the less.

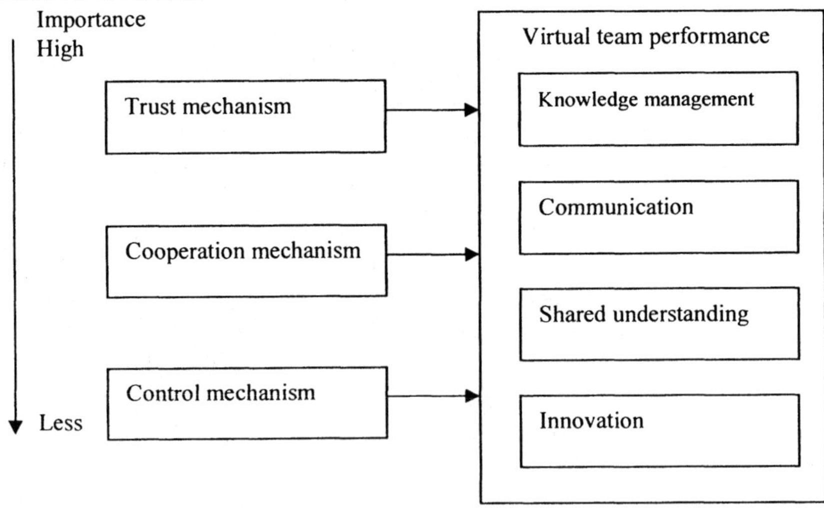

Fig 1. The Governance Model of Virtual Team
Successful application of the three mechanisms in virtual team management can help improve the performance of virtual team, including knowledge management, communication, shared understanding and innovation. For example, trust can encourage the shared understanding among members in virtual team and the knowledge sharing and knowledge learning between each other, which can improve the innovation capability of virtual team. But too much trust might result in business lost as well. In that case control can help to monitor the behavior of members. Over control can limit the innovation capability of virtual team as well. Thus balance the control and trust mechanism is important in virtual team management.

5 Conclusion

In this paper some basic concepts and ideas on governance mechanisms and the performance virtual team are discussed. The relationship between the governance mechanism and virtual team performance is explored as well based on a governance model of virtual team. It is concluded that in virtual team management different governance mechanisms should be applied together in order to realize good performance of virtual team, and proper mechanisms applied in virtual team management based on the characteristics of virtual team can improve the innovation capability of virtual team. This paper offers some guide to both practitioners and researchers how to realize good virtual team governance and the prerequisites for virtual team to conduct good performance and reach their business goals.

References

1. G. Hertel, U. Konradt, and B. Orlikowski," Managing Distance by Interdependence: Goal Setting, Task Interdependence, and Team-based Rewards in Virtual Teams", European *Journal of Work and Organizational Psychology* 13, 1–28 (2004).

2. L.M. Peters, and C.C. Manz, "Identifying Antecedents of Virtual Team Collaboration", *Team Performance Management* 13(3/4), 117-129 (2007).

3. H.P. Andres," The Impact of Communication Medium on Virtual Team Group Process", *Information Resource Management Journal* 19 (2), 1-17 (2006).

4. M. Alavi, and A. Tiwana, "Knowledge Integration in Virtual Teams: the Potential Role of KMS", *Journal of the American Society of Information Science and Technology* 53(12), 1029-1037 (2002).

5. M.J. Gallivan, "Striking a Balance between Trust and Control in a Virtual Organization: A Content Analysis of Open Source Software Case Studies", *Information System Journal 11*, 277-304(2001).

6. H. Matlay, and P. Westhead, Innovation and Collaboration in Virtual Teams of E-entrepreneurs: Case Evidence from the European Tourism Industry, Entrepreneurship and Innovation, 8(1), 29-36 (2007).

7. J.A. Holton, "Building Trust and Collaboration in a Virtual Team", *Team Performance Management: An International Journal* 7 (3/4), 36-47 (2001).

8. L. A. Hambley, T. A. O'Neill, and T. J.B. Kline, Virtual Team Leadership: The Effects of Leadership Style and Communication Medium on Team Interaction Styles and Outcomes, Organizational Behavior and Human Decision Processes 103, 1-20(2007).

Government Information Access: A decisive Factor for E-Government

Yikun Xia 1   Cui Huang2
1 Yikun Xia, Center for Studies of Information Resources,
Wuhan University,Wuhan, P.R.China, 430072
xykwhu@126.com
2 Cui Huang, School of Public Management, Zhejiang University,
Hangzhou, P.R.China, 430072
huangcui@x263.net

Abstract. In recent years we are witnessing enormous development of e-government, which has brought about great changes in our society. This study examines the relationship between the levels of e-government and the quality of government information access, pointing out that e-government principles are based on the assumption that government information should be accessed among all kinds of organizations. In contrast to government webs' rapid growth, the low quality of government information access has been a dilemma which impacts the usability and efficiency of e-government. This paper also analyzes blocking factors about information access in China, draw a conclusion that on-line government information access should be the key factor of e-government which steps should be taken to enhance accessibility to government information.

1   Introduction

Through over ten year's development, E-Government becomes a fundamental part of government's public service reform agenda. In China, by the end of Jun 2006, the population of government websites using the DNS of ".gov.cn" has reached almost 12 thousand. At present, 96% of departments of state council in our country have established government websites and nearly 90% of governments at provincial level, 96% of governments at municipal level and 77% governments at country level have their own government websites. [1] With more and more funds, technology and devices added, the hardware environment of E-Government gets better and better, while the conditions for information access is not simultaneously promoted, the gap between information richer and poorer becomes more largely than ever, so the issue of government information access is put on the agenda.

As the necessity of the times, the appearance and the widespread application of e-government not only changes government information flow and work system, but also plays a decisive role in information access, improving government information sharing and thus building the social information justice. Therefore, the aims of this paper are to (i) provide a brief review about the great changes of government information access brought by e-government, (ii) to investigate the relationship between government information access and e-government, (iii) to determine obstacles of on-line government information access in China, (iv) to propose a model to develop e-government on the base of government information access.

2   Government Information Access: Key Characteristic of E-Government

2.1   Changes of Information Access in E-Government Environment

Although users, information providers, information channels and information environment are all important factors for information access and should be given equal attention, so far as government information access is concerned, owing to the actual unequal positions of information owners and information demanders, the power to control information access is always unilaterally held in government .How to accelerate government information flow and eliminate information monopoly becomes the main problem. Because "electronic information access strategies and programs are a consistent feature of e-government initiatives [2]", e-government provides a realistic way.

"Access" means different information to different users at different time, today, it is controlled by technologies available. Because "this kind of change demands a foundation of valid information exchange between government and the citizen." [3] The development of web technology not only laid substantial technological foundation for e-Government, but also created unprecedented conditions and advantages to improve and promote government information sharing.

>   The expansion of information access users

The development of e-government moves citizens out of line onto the internet successfully, making anyone any organization gain information from the open online information source with lower cost. In South Korea, citizens do not need to visit government offices because 75% of the required documents can be issued online[4]. In the United States, three-quarters of e-government users believe that e-government has made it easier and more convenient for them to stay informed about government services[5].

>   The improvement of information access effect

Information access effect differs in the level of detail, the quantity or type of data exchanged. It is dependent on a common way to integrate diverse information residing in different government departments. So e-government is looked as the second revolution in government information service domain after the information resources management idea, providing prompt one-stop service on line, integrating all kinds of information resource have already promoted public information demand, realizing the breakthrough and the innovation in the method and pattern of government information service.

> The content deepening

The complicated combination of data and kinds of web language and technical factors further enriches the manifestation of government information online. On the one hand, the integrated use of text, image, video and audio improves the expressiveness and influence of government information communication on website, attracting more and more people to visit government website, on the other hand, an e-government framework requires transparency of information which stimulates information flow and transfers massive amounts of unused government information to useful information needed in social life.

> The demonstration of information access benefits

The experience features of information products not only caused different users' effect, but also made it difficult to judge the benefits of e-government directly. The effect of government information access are not only reflected in the great changes brought about after government information was open and communicated , but also in the organic connection of government information process and government affairs process, make information access and information implementation intersect and furthermore promote government administrative reform process.

> The changes in the structure of information access

E-Government broke the previous order of up-down government information access and replaced it with a process of interact information access. Bottom-up or lateral information flow not only constructs intersected network for government information access, but also enables the users to become important participants in the chain of government information producing, hence improve the relationship between users and government department, making e-government stage advanced to the more superior transaction model from the information model gradually

2.2   Government Information Access: Demonstrating Benefits of E-Government

In United States, "Citizens not only visit government Web sites, but also use the information they find. Close to two-thirds of government Web site users say they have sought information on public policy issues via government sites, while Seventy-two percent said their use of government Web sites has improved the way they interact with state government at least a little[6]. "In Britain, the vast majority of government services can be obtained from the government websites. The practice of e-government's in Western countries demonstrates that obtaining necessary documents and information from government websites has gradually played an increasingly important role in the public domain.

In attention extremely limited time, stressing information access truly reflects the core value of e-government:

First, information access has become an important factor of e-government practical effect evaluating, because in essence, the difference of a 'good' government and a 'bad' government is reflected in how to predominate and handle information. And, the distinguish between e-government and e-commerce mainly lies in the social information justice maintenance, emphasize the equal opportunity of information access. The past e-government models whether based on technology-centered or government-centered were only adapted to convenient government itself, which is difficult to be utilized by citizen. However, the outstanding nature of e-government model should provide an open channel for the users to access public information.

Second, government information access is an inevitable choice for the transformation of government information workflow, the innovation of government management and the accomplishment of e-government goal. Information is the key factor to successful innovation, in terms of content, government information is e-government's "blood", to some extent, the successful e-Government is critically dependent on the access effect of its integral information.

Third, the stress of information access is also the maintenance of user's right of information freedom. The current way of government's web site design and information integration is ruled by customer-centric principle. The e-government assessment reports made by Accenture Company have well reflected this trend that e-government should pay more attention on customer feelings, for example, in 2003,the subject was "e-Government Leadership: Engaging the Custom", in 2005, "Leadership in Customer Service: New Expectations, New Experiences", in 2006, "Leadership in Customer Service : Building the Trust"(2006).
"In the future society, the on-line information will become the distinct characteristic of democratic system" [7], Through the improvements of information access, government will provides a new framework of thinking and acting for information management, coordinate the interests of all parties and maximize the effectiveness and value of government information. Meanwhile, as a "checks and balances", public access is an independent way for citizens to know what their government is doing (fig Description of the relationship between information access and e-government).

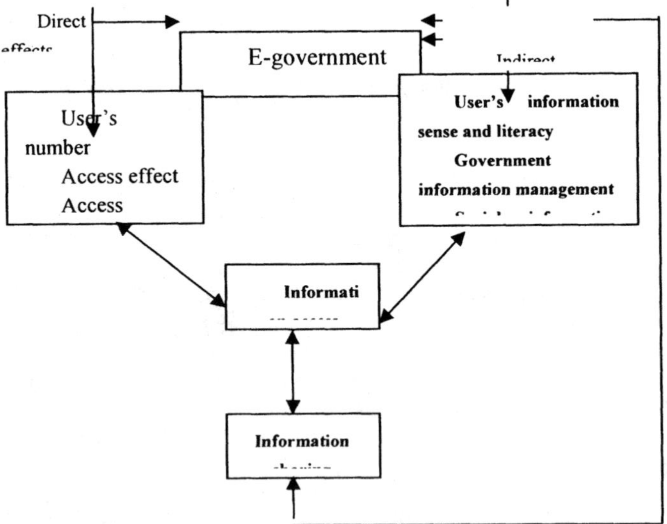

Fig.1. Description of the relationship between information access and e-government

3 The Low Effect of Government Information Access: the Main Restricting Factor on the Success of E-Government

3.1 Connotation of Government Information Access Online

Being the "Out put" of e-government, government website can be a contact platform for G2C(government to citizen). From the perspective of users, whether based on technology or content, government information access is a very broad concept. Putting aside the technical factors, such as the status of interfaces, system interoperability, web site security, only judged from the perspective of information content, the quality of government information access can be examined from characteristics among information scope, content and user's participation:

The scope refers to the width, depth, time span and the format diversity of information and so on.

The content includes authenticity and accuracy, timeliness, relevance, integrity and easier usability (conditions of information organizing, ease of access).

The user's participation focuses on both user's amount and constitution of occupation.

Information access in e-government is assumed to be able to collect,manage, evaluate information used and identify needs. It thus needs relative resource management of human being, computers, users, information training and digital data. Because "this demand for direct access to government information, from both inside and outside government, is influencing the design and management of these information services. [8]".

3.2 The Negative Influence on E-Government Due to the Low Effect of Government Information Access

"As states migrate most of their public information to the web, access is improved for many people. However, states need to take care that this on-line migration does not provide new obstacles to others. [9]" In fact, even in developed countries, ignorance of government information access has greatly impaired government website's usability , thus the popularization of e-government still faces challenge. A survey conducted by the United States showed that nearly half of the population had never used the Internet and 57% of them said that they were not interested in the Internet service[10]. In Britain, only 10% of the citizens had interactive activities with government through Internet[11].

Various surveys show that, although most government departments have built up their own websites, few people noticed whether the government website was designed to facilitate the public. On the one hand, the low effect of government information access has caused a large number of government websites stagnate at a lower stage of simply information release and in turn, the degree of government computerization determines whether the public use online e-government services. Therefore, it is often the case that citizens have difficulty in access public information, thus implying a lack of information transparency. only when government websites that are built on the basis of convenient to information access can really attract participation from the public and establish more democratic governments. The government website construction must be developed centering on information access so that e-government can become an advanced perception and ideal model.

3.3   Analyzing Restriction Factors on Chinese Government Information Access

In practice, the technical dependence of e-government provides the opportunity for technical bureaucrat to control government website operation and information publicity and utilization. the current e-government in our country is lack of effective information access. In 2006, the main web services used by Chinese Internet users is browsing news, search engines and delivery of Email, E-government ranks No. 24, taking up only 5.4%[12]. According to factors analyzing on government information access, the main problems in our country are as follows:

➢   Low total supply quantity .On the one hand, because of the lack of government information openness, a lot of government information is limited in specific government system because of fear losing autonomy; on the other hand, the isolation between government website designers, information management staff and government affairs processing results in discrepancy between internet government information process and government affairs process. In 2005, only 44.5% of all the government websites released over 60% of information, while 21.7% of the websites released less than 20% of information [13].

➢   Broadly scope and depth insufficient. According to various Internet survey results, the main information content provided on Chinese government websites are in turn of government news, government function/business introduction, statistic data/materials search, laws and regulations/policy documents, etc. Although there are lots of categories of content, the depth of information processing can't satisfy users' need, and in particular, the structure of government information supply can't match that of users' information need also, the inefficiency in government information access caused by the differences between demand and supply will then affect social popularization of e-government.

➢   Single manifestation and insufficient interactive usability. Government information on-line is mainly displayed in static forms, with few dynamic forms like image, video and many text databases, and the lack of multimedia information and full text databases severely impairs the vivacity and attraction of government website. Besides, government information updates slow, the most quickly updating information type is government news, while the most slow update type is necessary information needed in social life like business guide.

➢   Imbalance distribution of information. There is an obvious tendency in government information distribution from different government websites, eastern provinces full of information whereas western provinces lack of it. At the same time, the content and quality provided on government website might be different because of different attributes and levels of government institutions. The amount of government information owned and provided by central government and municipal government websites is not at same level.

➢ A bureaucratic access way. On the one hand, many government websites were designed without taking accessibility account and caused disorder in government information classifying. According to statistics, the percentages of websites whose services are categorized by users in municipal and country-level governments are only 8.7% and 3.2% respectively, while the percentages of those categorized basically by government departments are as high as 48.1% and 50.4% respectively[14]; on the other hand, since they are designed primarily for simple information releasing, they also lack efficient support for representing the exchange of complex information and forming interaction between officials and users.

➢ High access cost. cost is an important factor in determining users' information access methods. No matter examined from the popularization of information infrastructure, or users' surfer fee, or time cost, government information access in our country is not inexpensive. And the high cost in turn result in the drop of government information using and inefficiency of e-government.

4 Conclusion

"Information age can be taken as an opportunity of liberation, but only when information providers keep supporting the objective of equally accessing information, technology can open various information sources" [15]. In a certain sense, the success of E-Government depends on the degree of government information access realization. So, it is necessary for us to take steps as follows:

➢ Recognize the importance of information access, taking the availability of information as the starting point during website planning, design and management.

➢ Design and construct E-Government project aimed at the principle of convenient user's information access, clearing up all kinds of barriers to broad government information access and building an effective E-Government pattern finally.

➢ Provide multiple information access channels, to expand the information service target and scope, and to push and integrate all the users into the digital ages as far as possible.

➢ Provide relevant training in order to expand public ability of information access.

Acknowledgments

This research is supported by National Planning Office of Philosophy and Social Science, P.R. China(07BTQ017).

References

1. The 18th report of Chinese internet development status statistics. http://www.cnnic.cn/uploadfiles/doc/2006/7/19/103601.doc

2. Sharon S. Dawes, Theresa A. Pardo, and Anthony M. Cresswell, Designing electronic government information access programs: a holistic approach, *Government Information Quarterly*, 21 (2004), pp.3–23.

3. Hart-Teeter. The New E-Government Equation: Ease, Engagement, Privacy & Protection.
http://coexgov.securesites.net/admin/FormManager/filesuploading/egovpoll2003.pdf   (current 10 July.2007)

4. Young-Jin, Shin. Establishing e-Government through Government Information Sharing. http://egov.epfl.ch/UserFiles/File/Shin_Presentation.pdf. (current 10 July.2007)

5. Hart-Teeter. The New E-Government Equation: Ease, Engagement, Privacy & Protection. http://www.excelgov.org. (current 10 July.2007)

6. Jody Condit Fagan and Bryan Fagan. An accessibility study of state legislative Web sites. *Government Information Quarterly*, 21 (2004), pp.65–85.

7. Douglas Holmes. eGov: eBusiness Strategies for Government. *Nicholas Brealey Publishing*, (2003), pp.212

8. Sharon S. Dawes, Theresa A. Pardo, and Anthony M. Cresswell. Designing electronic government information access programs: a holistic approach. *Government Information Quarterl*, 21 (2004), pp.3–23

9. Jody Condit Fagan and Bryan Fagan. An accessibility study of state legislative Web sites. *Government Information Quarterly*, 21 (2004), pp.65–85.

10. Lenhart, A., Rainie, L, Fox, S., Horrigan, J., and Spooner, T. Who's not online: 57% of those without Internet access say they do not plan to log on. Pew Internet & American Life Project. http://www.pewinternet.org/. (current 10 July.2007)

11. Booz, Allen, Hamilton. International e-economy benchmarking: the world's most effective policies for the e-economy. http://www.itis.gov.se/publikationer/eng/ukreport.pdf(current 10 July.2007)

12. The 19th report of Chinese internet development status statistics. http://www.cnnic.cn/uploadfiles/pdf/2007/1/23/113114.pdf

13. The report of Chinese internet information resource 2005. http://www.cnnic.net.cn/download/2005/20050301.pdf (current 7 July.2007)

14. CCID Consulting Stock Ltd. The report of performance assessing on Chinese government websites2004. http://www.ah.gov.cn/otherimages/baogao.pdf(current 7 July.2007)

15.Jody Condit Fagan and Bryan Fagan. An accessibility study of state legislative Web sites. Government Information Quarterly 21 (2004) 65–85

An Algorithm for Semantic Web Services Composition Based on Output and Input Matching

Ying Li and Baotian Dong
School of Traffic and Transportation, Beijing Jiaotong University, Beijing,
100044, China
ling.ly@sohu.com

Abstract. Existed methods for automatic web services composition based on output and input matching are limited to deal with simple Composition Request (CR) which can only be satisfied by linear composition plan, but complicated CR asks for netty plan because the structure of netty plan can be complicated enough to deal with complicated problem while the structure of linear plan is too simple to do that. In order to overcome the shortcoming of the existed methods, a new algorithm is proposed in this paper which can deal with not only simple CR but also complicated CR. A web services connection matrix is used in the proposed algorithm. This matrix is constructed based on the services which participate in a composition to express all output and input matching relations among services. With this matrix, both simple CR and complicated CR can be processed.

1 Introduction

Automatic Web Services composition becomes one of the most challenges in the research area of web services because composing existed web services to form a new one can add value to those web services. There are two fundamentally different ways to handle automatic services composition[1]: one way is to start with the pre-defined generic composition and perform 1-1 search to replace every generic element of a composition with a real service; the other way is to describe a set of goals and try to achieve them by building the whole process from scratch. In the second way, how to build the whole process depends on the relation between services. There are several types of relation between services, such as interoperation relation [2], effect and precondition relation [3] and output and input matching relation [3, 4, 5]. The last two relations can be judged through properties of service because IOPE (Input,

Please use the following format when citing this chapter:

Li, Y., Dong, B., 2007, in IFIP International Federation for Information Processing, Volume 252, Integration and Innovation Orient to E-Society Volume 2, eds. Wang, W., (Boston: Springer), pp. 297-307.

Output, Precondition and Effect) are properties of semantic web services while the first relation can not. Furthermore, I/O parameters are the basic properties of services while P/E parameters are not; therefore research of automatic services composition focuses on output and input matching relation between services.

A composition plan can be expressed as a direction graph with service(s) as node and relation as edge. Each node (except start node and end node) has only one prior node and only one successive node in a linear plan while each node has at least one prior node and at least one successive node in a netty plan. The existed methods for automatic web services composition which are based on output and input matching try to find out all composition plans for a Composition Request (CR), but just acquires linear plans. These methods will be malfunction when they handle CR which can only be satisfied by netty plan. Linear plan can only express simple services composition while netty plan can express both simple composition and complicated composition, so the existed composition methods which are limited to deal with simple composition can not handle complicated composition. In order to overcome the shortcoming of the existed methods, a new method for automatic services composition based on output and input matching is proposed in this paper. The new method can deal with CR satisfied not only by linear plans but also by netty plans through using a web services connection matrix constructed on the services which participate in the composition. In addition, this method is for the semantic web service which is based on ontology [6] because web service is developing toward semantic web service.

2   Assumptions and Expressions

2.1   Assumptions

- Using ontology to express input/output parameters of web services.
- A web service provides a single functionality.

2.2   Related Expressions

- An entity in ontology can be expressed as a set of attributes, that is $\varepsilon = \{a_1, a_2, ..., a_n\}$, where ε is an entity and a_i $(i = 1, 2,..., n)$ is an attribute.
- I/O parameters of semantic web services based on ontology can be expressed as entities of ontology. A kind of parameters of service is a set of entities, that is $P = \{p_1, p_2,..., p_n\}$, where P can be I/O and p_i is a set because it is an entity. If a service is w, its set of input parameters is $w.I = \{i_1, i_2,..., i_m\}$, and its set of output parameters is $w.O = \{o_1, o_2,..., o_n\}$.
- Symbol "||" is used in this paper to denote the cardinality of a set, e.g. $|X|$ denotes cardinality of set X.

- Give two entities $\varepsilon_1 = \{a_1, a_2,..., a_n\}$ and $\varepsilon_2 = \{b_1, b_2, ..., b_m\}$. (1) If $\forall \ \varepsilon_1.a_i$, $(\exists \ \varepsilon_2.b_j)(\varepsilon_1.a_i = \varepsilon_2.b_j)$, then $\varepsilon_1 \subseteq \varepsilon_2$; if $|\varepsilon_1| = |\varepsilon_2|$, then $\varepsilon_1 = \varepsilon_2$.

- Give two entity sets $\delta_1 = \{p1, p_2, ..., p_m\}$ and $\delta_2 = \{q1, q_2, ..., q_n\}$. (1) if $\forall\ p_i \in \delta_1$, $(\exists\ q_j \in \delta_2)\wedge(p_i \subseteq q_j)$, then $\delta_1 \widetilde{\subseteq} \delta_2$, it means δ_1 is approximately subsumed by δ_2. (2) if $\exists\ p_i \in \delta_1$, $(\exists\ q_j \in \delta_2)\wedge(p_i \subseteq q_j)$, then $\delta_1 \cap \delta_2 \neq \varnothing$.
- Give a entity set $\delta = \{p_1, p_2, ..., p_m\}$ and a entity p, if $(\exists\ p_i \in \delta)(p_i \supseteq p)$, then $p \widetilde{\in} \delta$, it means p approximately belongs to δ.

3 Web Services Connection Matrix (WSCM)

The relation of two services can be expressed by the connection degree between them and the set of matching parameters (I/O) between them. WSCM is used to express all the relations between random two services in a set of services.

Definition 3.1 (WSCM): suppose a set of services is S ($|S|$=N), its WSCM is a N×N matrix with the sequence numbers of its rows/columns being all services from S; its element m_{ij} is a duality tuple <X, Y>, X is the connection degree between w_i and w_j, and Y is the set of matching parameters between w_i and w_j.

Connection degree is calculated by formula (1) while the set of matching parameters is calculated by formula (2).

$$ConDegree(w_1, w_2) = \frac{|\ w_1.O \cap w_2.I\ |}{|\ w_2.I\ |}\quad (1).$$

In formula (1), $\forall\ p_i \in w_2.I$, if $\exists q_j \in w_1.O\ \wedge\ q_j \supseteq p_i$, then $p_i\ \widetilde{\in}\ (\ w_1.O \cap\ w_2.I)$.

$ConPSet(w_1, w_2) = \{p_i\ |\ p_i \in w_2.I \wedge p_i \widetilde{\in} w_1.O, 1 \le i \le |\ w_2.I\ |\}$ (2).

In formula (2), $\forall\ p_i \in w_2.I$, if $\exists\ q_j \in w_1.O\ \wedge\ q_j \supseteq p_i$, then $(p_i \in w_2.I)\wedge(p_i \widetilde{\in} w_1.O)$.

Note: WSCM can express a direction graph with service (expressed by row or column) as node and element (X $\neq$ 0 and Y $\neq$ $\varnothing$ >) as edges. 3 properties of WSCM are described as follows:

Property 1: WSCM is an asymmetry matrix with all diagonal elements being <0, $\varnothing$ >.

Property 2: Suppose service w_j receives outputs from k services as its inputs, then there are k elements m_{x_ij} (i=1, 2,..., k) with $m_{x_ij}.X > 0$ and $m_{x_ij}.Y \neq \varnothing$ in WSCM;

Property 3: Suppose service w_i provides its outputs to k services as their inputs, then there are k elements m_{ix_j} (j=1, 2,..., k) in matrix with $m_{ix_j}.X > 0$ and $m_{ix_j}.Y \neq \varnothing$.

4 Composition Algorithm

4.1 Concepts and Theorems about Web Services Composition

Definition 4.1 (Graph for Web Services Composition, GWSC): give a CR, suppose set of candidate services is Φ_C, the set of user's inputs in CR is U_I while the set of requested outputs is U_O; $G(V, E)$ is a direction graph with service from Φ_C as its node and the output and input matching relation between services as its edge. If G satisfies: (1)The tail node w_t and the head node w_h of each edge satisfy: $w_t.O \cap w_h.I \neq \varnothing$; (2)Is a connected graph; (3) has only one node called w_s with only outward edges and $w_s.I \tilde{\subseteq} U_I$; and has only one node called w_e with only inward edges and $w.I \tilde{\supseteq} U_O$; every service (except w_s and w_e) comes from Φ_C; (4) the inputs of any node except w_s can be satisfied. Then G is a GWSC for CR based on Φ_C.

Note: for simpleness, we do not strictly differentiate between service and node because a node is a service in a GWSC for a CR. Proof about 5 theorems in this paper is omitted for the limited space.

Theorem 1: suppose CR has a GWSC(V, E), the set of user's inputs is U_I and the set of requested outputs is U_O, then $V - \{ w_s, w_e \} = \bigcup\limits_{i=1,2,\ldots,N} S_i$, and (1) $\forall\ w_i \in S_1$, $w_i.I \tilde{\subseteq} U_I$; (2) $\forall\ w_i \in S_i$ $(i=2,\ldots,N)$, $(\exists w_j \in S_{i-1})(w_i.I \cap w_j.O \neq \varnothing)$; (3) c $w_i \in S_N$, $w_i.O \cap U_O \neq \varnothing$, and $(\bigcup\limits_{w_{x_i} \in (S_1 \cup S_2 \cup \ldots \cup S_N)} w_{x_i}.O) \tilde{\supseteq} U_O$. S_1 , S_2 ,…,S_N are called N subset of services for GWSC, and S_i is called the ith subset of services for GWSC.

Definition 4.2 (useless service): suppose a GWSC(V, E) for a CR, and $\exists w_i \in V$, if $w_i.O \cap U_O = \varnothing$ and $(\nexists w_j \in V)(w_i.O \cap w_j.I \neq \varnothing)$, then w_i is a useless service.

Definition 4.3 (prior service and successive service): suppose two services w_1 and w_2, if $\exists\ p_i \in w_2.I \wedge p_i \tilde{\in} w_1.O$, then w_1 is the prior service of w_2 while w_2 is the successive service of w_1.

Note: deleting a service in a GWSC for a CR may cause its prior service to become a useless service and the inputs of its successive service to be unsatisfied. If the inputs of a service can not be satisfied, it can not be executed normally, so the inputs of its successive service can not be satisfied. Therefore deleting services may cause a chain reaction of the inputs of its direction and indirection successive services being unsatisfied.

Definition 4.4 (The Biggest Graph of Web Services Composition, BGWSC): suppose CR has a GWSC based on set of candidate services Φ_C, N subsets of GWSC are S_i $(i=1,2,\ldots,N)$, if $\nexists\ w_i \in (\Phi_C - V)$ and $w_i.I \cap w_j.O \neq \varnothing$ $((w_j \in (S_1 \vee S_2 \vee \cdots \vee S_{N-1}))$, then the GWSC is the BGWSC for CR based on Φ_C.

Definition 4.5 (the Smallest Graph of Web Services Composition, SGWSC): suppose CR has a GWSC (V, E) based on set of candidate services Φ_c, if w_e will be deleted because of the chain reaction of inputs of services being unsatisfied caused by deleting any service (except w_s and w_e) in V, then the GWSC is a SGWSC for CR based on Φ_c.

Note: the deletion of w_e means that the quested outputs can not be acquired.

Definition 4.6 (a call to a service): Suppose service w_i and its prior services is in set $\theta = \{ \ w_j | \ w_j.O \cap \ w_i.I \neq \varnothing \ \}$, if θ has a subset $\theta_c = \{ \ w_j \ | (\bigcup_{w_j \in \theta} w_j.O \supseteq w_i.I) \wedge ((\forall w_\alpha \in \theta)(\bigcup_{w_j \in \theta} w_j.O - w_\alpha.O) \not\supseteq w_i.I) \}$, then θ_c is a call to service w_i.

Definition 4.7 (a list of calls for a set of services): suppose a set of services is w_i $(i=1,2,\ldots,k)$ and the calls to w_i is set $\psi_i = \{ \theta_{ij} | j=1,2,\ldots,m_i \}$, then $\xi = \{< w_i , \ \theta_{ij} >| \theta_{ij} \in \psi_i ; i=1,2,\ldots,k; \ 1 \leqslant j \leqslant m_i \}$ is a list of calls for w_i $(i=1,2,\ldots,k)$.

Note: the number of different lists of calls to a set of services can be calculated by formula (3).

$$\prod_{i=1,2,\ldots,k} |\psi_i| . \qquad (3)$$

Definition 4.8 (share service, valid edge and invalid edge): in a GWSC for a CR, if a service has at least two calls to itself, it is a share service. Each edge between the share service and one of its prior services which belongs to at least one call is a valid edge. If an edge is not a valid one, it is an invalid edge.

Theorem 2: suppose CR has a GWSC based on set of candidate services Φ_c, and then CR will have only one BGWSC and at least one SGWSC based on Φ_c.

Theorem 3: suppose a CR has k SGWSCs based on set of candidate services Φ_c: $G_1, G_2,\ldots, G_k$, and the BGWSC for the CR based on Φ_c is G_{MAX}, then: $\forall G_i$ $(i=1, 2,\ldots, k)$, G_i is a sub-graph of G_{MAX}.

Theorem 4: suppose a CR has a GWSC based on a set of candidate services and this GWSC has at least a share service, then the CR has at least two SGWSCs.

Theorem 5: suppose a CR has a GWSC, and service w in this GWSC has k prior services w_i $(i=1, 2,\ldots, k)$ and $\sum_{i=1,2,\ldots,k} ConDegree(w_i, w) < 1$, then these k prior services can not form a call to w.

4.2 Mechanism of the Composition Algorithm

4.2.1 The method of searching for all SGWSCs from the BGWSC for a CR

The BGWSC for a CR can be acquired according to theorem 1 and this BGWSC is the only one according to theorem 2. All SGWSCs can be acquired from a BGWSC according to theorem 3. Whether a BGWSC contains more than one SGWSC or not can be judged based on theorem 4. The number of SGWSC of a CR can be calculated by formula (3) because a list of calls for the set of share services in the BGWSC decides a SGWSC. All different SGWSCs can be found through searching for all different lists of calls for the set of share services in a BGWSC.

Useless services can be deleted from a BGWSC to decrease the number of services before extracting SGWSCs. When extract a SGWSC, for each share service, take one of its calls from a list of calls, and delete the edges which tail nodes (services) do not belong to that call, then a share service becomes a non share service. Deleting edges may result in useless services. Therefore, useless services checking and deletion should be done after deleting an edge. Some non share services may have invalid edges in a BGWSC, these invalid edges should be deleted after transforming all share services to non share ones. When there are not share services, useless services and invalid edges, there is no a service which can be deleted from this GWSC, and this GWSC is a SGWSC.

Extracting a SGWSC from a BGWSC is done in the WSCM of the BGWSC for a CR by deleting useless services and invalid edges and transforming share services to non share services. The methods of doing so are given as follows:

(1) The method of deleting useless services

In the WSCM of a GWSC, if the connection degree value of every element in a row is 0, the service corresponding to this row is a useless service. Scan the WSCM to find out all such rows and delete them and their counterpart columns. Deleting useless service may result in its prior services becoming invalid ones, so delete useless services repeatedly until there is no more useless service in the WSCM.

(2) The method of deleting invalid edges

Deleting invalid edges is to find out valid edges for a node in fact. Searching for valid edges follows criterion 1: every service in a GWSC should receive outputs from its prior services as few as possible. Following this criterion, the number of nodes in a GWSC can be decreased and the execution efficient of the GWSC can be improved. The method of searching for valid edges following criterion 1 is described as follows:

In the WSCM of a GWSC, for w_j:

A. if $m_{ij}.X=1$, then edge $<w_i, w_j>$ is a valid edge.

B. if $(\bigcup_{1\leq i\leq N} m_{ij}.Y \supseteq w_j.I) \wedge ((\forall m_{\alpha j})(\bigcup_{1\leq i\leq N} m_{ij}.Y - m_{\alpha j}.Y) \not\supseteq w_j.I)$, then edge $< w_i, w_j > (1\leq i\leq N)$ is a valid edge.

(3) The method of transforming a share service to a non share service

Transforming a share service to a non share service is to delete those prior services which do not belong to specified call of the share service. After transforming, useless services checking and deletion should be done because deleting service may result in useless services.

4.2.2 The method of searching for all calls to a share service

A prior service whose connection degree value with the share service is equal 1 can form a call to the share service by itself. According to theorem 5, only the prior service whose connection degree value with the share service is less than 1 needs to join with other services to form a call to the share service. Different combinations of prior services form different calls. Use multitree with weight to find out all different combinations of prior services of a share services. The weight of the multitree is the connection degree.

Put all prior services whose connection degree value with the share service are less than 1 in set θ_w. Construct a multitree with weight for every service in θ_w. Suppose the share service is w_j and a prior service of w_j is w_i, then the multitree constructed for w_i is called $w_j - w_i$ tree. The way to construct such a tree by BFS (Breadth First Search) is described as follows:

(1) The root node of the tree is a null service and w_i is the only child node of the root node.

(2) Scan all leaf nodes from left to right. If a leaf node and all its ancestor node (except the root node) can form a call to w_j, then this node can not have a child any more; otherwise, select from θ_w all services which are neither the ancestor nodes of the leaf node nor the brother nodes on the left side of the leaf node to be child nodes of this leaf node. If neither one service can be selected from θ_w, this leaf node can not have a child any more. Repeat 2 until all leaf nodes can not have any child node.

Get all calls containing w_i from $w_j - w_i$ tree and put them in set C_i, combine C_i $(i=1, 2,...,| \theta_w |)$ and delete repeated calls and get a new set which is the set of calls to w_j). If two calls are the same or one call subsumes another call, they are repeated calls.

4.2.3 The method of finding out all lists of calls for a set of share services

Suppose there are m share services $w_1, w_2,..., w_m$ in a GWSC, and the set of calls to w_i is $\psi_i (i=1, 2,..., m)$. Use multitree which is created by BFS to search for all different lists of calls for these m share services. The multitree has $m+1$ levels and its null root node is in level 0. Each node in level i-1 has $<w_i, \theta_{ij} > (\theta_{ij} \in \psi_i; j=1, 2,...,| \psi_i |)$ as its all child nodes, so nodes in the same level have the same child nodes. Each leaf node and all its ancestor nodes (except the root node) form a list of calls for these share services. Two random lists of calls are not the same because nodes in each level are different.

4.3   Steps of the Algorithm

(1) Sub-algorithm of deleting useless services: DeleteUServ (WSCM, Φ), Φ is the set of services of WSCM.

Step 1: Scan each row in WSCM. If $\forall w_i \in \Phi$ $(i=1, 2,..., | \Phi |)$, $\nexists m_{ij}.X=0$ $(j=1,2,...,| \Phi |)$, return; otherwise delete row w_i and column w_i from WSCM, $\Phi = \Phi -\{ w_i \}$, go to step 1.

(2)Steps of composition algorithm

Give set of candidate services Φ_c , the set of user's inputs U_I and the set of user' requested outputs U_O. CallsToAserv () and ListsOfCalls () are sub-algorithms. The first one is to get all calls to a share service and the second is to get all lists of calls for all share services in a GWSC.

Setp1: if $U_I \supseteq U_O$, go to step 2; otherwise if $\Phi_c \neq \varnothing$, get a service w from Φ_c, if $w.I \widetilde{\subseteq} U_I$, let $\Phi_S = \Phi_S \cup \{w\}$, $\Phi_c = \Phi_c - \{w\}$, $U_I = U_I \cup w.O$. If $(\Phi_c = \varnothing) \wedge (U_I \widetilde{\not\supseteq} U_O)$, return the message of composition failure and terminate the algorithm; otherwise go to step 1.

Step 2: calculate the web services connection matrix for Φ_S and let the matrix to be $WSCM_{\Phi_S}$.

Step 3: DeleteUServ $(WSCM_{\Phi_S}, \Phi_S)$, let $\Phi_{tmp} = \Phi_S$, $\varpi = \varnothing$, N=0, $\chi_{SGWSC} = \varnothing$, $\Omega = \varnothing$.

Step 4: if $\Phi_{tmp} = \varnothing$, go to step 7; otherwise get a service w_j from Φ_{tmp}, and let $\Phi_{tmp} = \Phi_{tmp} - \{w_j\}$. Scan column w_j in $WSCM_{\Phi_S}$, and let $\sigma_j = \{w_i | m_{ij}.X=1\}$, $\sigma'_j = \{w_i | 0 < m_{ij}.X < 1\}$. If $|\sigma'_j| \geqslant 3$ and $\bigcup_{w_i \in \sigma'_j} w_i.O \widetilde{\supseteq} w_j.I$, let $\sigma_{tmp} = \sigma'_j$, if $|\sigma_j| > 0$, $\psi_j = \bigcup_{w_i \in \sigma_j} \{\{w_i\}\}$, go to step 5; otherwise if $(|\sigma_j| > 1) \wedge (\bigcup_{w_i \in \sigma'_j} w_i.O \widetilde{\not\supseteq} w_j.I)$, $\psi_j = \bigcup_{w_i \in \sigma_j} \{\{w_i\}\}$; else if $(|\sigma_j| > 0) \wedge (\bigcup_{w_i \in \sigma_j} w_i.O \widetilde{\supseteq} w_j.I)$, $\psi_j = \bigcup_{w_i \in \sigma_j} \{\{w_i\}\} \cup \{\sigma'_j\}$. Go to step 4.

Step 5: if $\sigma_{tmp} = \varnothing$, if $|\psi_j| > 1$, let $\varpi = \varpi \cup \{<N+1, w_j, \psi_j>\}$, go to step 4; otherwise get a service w_R from σ_{tmp}, and let $\sigma_{tmp} = \sigma_{tmp} - \{w_R\}$, $\psi' = \varnothing$, $\omega_{CH} = \sigma'_j - \{w_R\}$, $V = \varnothing$, $E = \varnothing$, $\psi' = $CallsToAserv$(w_R, \omega_{CH}, \psi', V, E)$.

Step 6: if $\psi' = \varnothing$, go to step 5; otherwise get an element α from ψ', let $\psi' = \psi' - \{\alpha\}$. If $(\exists \beta)(\beta \in \psi_j) \wedge (\beta \supset \alpha)$, let $\psi_j = (\psi_j - \{\beta\}) \cup \{\alpha\}$; Otherwise if $(\not\exists \beta)(\beta \in \psi_j) \wedge (\beta = \alpha)$, let $\psi_j = \psi_j \cup \{\alpha\}$. Go to step 6.

Step 7: if $\varpi = \varnothing$, let $WSCM'_\Phi = WSCM_{\Phi_S}$, $\Phi' = \Phi_S$, go to step 10; otherwise let $v_R = t$ (t is the root node of the tree and it is also an empty node), get a element $<x, w_x, \psi_x>$ from ϖ, let $l=0$, $H=|\varpi|$, $V = \varnothing$, $E = \varnothing$, $\Omega = $ListsOfCalls $(v_R, w_x, \psi_x, \varpi, l, H, V, E)$.

Step 8: if $\Omega = \varnothing$, go to step14; otherwise get an element ξ from Ω, let $\Omega = \Omega - \{\xi\}$.

Step 9: if $\xi = \varnothing$, let $\varphi = \Phi'$, go to step 10; otherwise get an element $<w_j, \theta_j>$ from ξ, let $\xi = \xi - \{<w_j, \theta_j>\}$, $\omega = \{ w_i |(w_i \notin \theta_j) \wedge (w_i.O \cap w_j.I \neq \varnothing), 1 \leqslant i \leqslant |\Phi'|\}$, if $|\omega| > 0$, let $m_{ij} = <0, \varnothing >(w_i \in \omega, 1 \leqslant i \leqslant |\Phi'|)$ in $WSCM'_\Phi$. DeleteUServ ($WSCM'_\Phi, \Phi'$), and go to step 9.

Step 10: if $\varphi = \varnothing$, go to step 13; otherwise get a service w_j from φ, let $\varphi = \varphi - \{ w_j \}$, if $\exists\, m_{\alpha j}.X=1$, let $m_{ij} = <0, \varnothing >((0<i<|\Phi'|) \wedge i \neq \alpha)$; Otherwise let $\eta = \{w_i | 0 < m_{ij}.X < 1\}$. If $|\eta| > 0$, let $\theta = w_j.I$, go to step 11; otherwise go to step 13.

Step 11: if $\theta = \varnothing$, go to step 12; otherwise get a service w_α from η, let $\eta = \eta - \{ w_\alpha \}$, let w_α satisfy $|\theta - m_{\alpha j}.Y | = \underset{i=1,2,\ldots,|\Phi'|}{MAX}\{| w_j.I - m_{ij}.Y |\}$, let $\phi = \phi \cup \{ w_\alpha \}$, $\theta = w_j.I - m_{\alpha j}.Y$, go to step 11.

Step 12: $\omega = \{w_i |(w_i \notin \phi) \wedge (w_i.O \cap w_j.I \neq \varnothing)\}$, let $m_{ij} = <0, \varnothing >(w_i \in \omega \} \wedge m_{ij}.X \neq 0, 1 \leq i \leq |\Phi'|)$. DeleteUServ ($WSCM'_\Phi, \Phi'$), and Go to step 10.

Step 13: $\chi_{SGWSC} = \chi_{SGWSC} \cup \{\Phi'\}$, if $\Omega = \varnothing$, go to step 14; Otherwise let $WSCM'_\Phi = WSCM_\Phi$, $\Phi' = \Phi_S$, go to step 8.

Step 14: Get all SGWSCs from χ_{SGWSC}, and calculate the QoS (Quality of Service) value for each SGWSC according to certain selection policy. Return the SGWSC with the optimized QoS value and terminate the algorithm.

In the algorithm describe above, step 1 acquires BGWSC; step 2 calculates WSCM for BGWSC; step 3 deletes useless service in BGWSC; step 4, 5 and 6 find out all share services from BGWSC and the sets of calls to each share service; step 7 acquires the set of lists of calls for all the share services; step 8 and 9 transform every share service to non share service; step 10, 11 and 12 delete invalid edges; step 13 puts a SGWSC into the set of all SGWSCs; step 14 acquires the SGWSC with the optimized QoS value. If there is not any proper composition which can meet the CR, the algorithm will return the failure information.

5   Related Works

Method in [4] uses heuristics to select the most proper service from the discovered services in each services discovery phase and acquires only one linear composition plan which contains the least services. Therefore, this method is used in the case that all the composition plans are linear for a CR and the CR requires the optimized composition plan which contains the least services.

Method in [7] uses entity matching to select the most similar service in the candidate services and acquires a composition as a tree. This tree is created from leaf nodes to the root node and a composition plan is a path from the root node to a leaf node of the tree. Some composition plans may be omitted during the discovery of services in non leaf nodes. This may cause the optimized plan for a CR to be lost.

Methods in [3, 5] acquire a composition as an expression in which services are linked by sequence or nondeterminism operator while the parallel operator is used to link two inputs. An expression without any nondeterminism operator is a composition plan, so an expression with any nondeterminism operator will be divided into several expressions. Therefore, the composition plan is also linear.

In conclusion, the methods which use output and input matching to find out composition plan for a CR can only get linear composition plan, so they are limited to particular cases that CRs can only be satisfied by linear composition plans. Furthermore, method in [4] is limited to plan which contains the least services, method in [7] is likely to lose some plans. The method in this paper is more general than the existed methods for it can get not only linear but also netty plan so it can be used in general case, moreover this method will not lost any plan.

6   Conclusion and Future Work

It is a very important method for non predefined composition to utilize the output and input matching between services. The existed methods based on such matching can only deal with those CR which can be satisfied by linear composition plan, and it will be malfunction when the CR can only be satisfied by netty composition plan. In order to overcome the limitation of the existed methods, a new method is proposed in this paper which is also based on the output and input matching. The existed methods only focus on services discovery but ignore relation discovery, so they can only acquire linear plans with simple structure. On the contrary, the proposed method in this paper focuses on both services discovery and relations discovery because it searches for all relations among services after services discovery. The proposed method can acquire not only linear composition plans but also the netty plans just because it finds out all relations among the discovered services. In the proposed method, the set of selected services is found first; then a connection matrix for the set is constructed to find out all relations among the selected services; next certain operations are done to the matrix to find out all composition plans for a CR. The optimized plan is acquired by calculating QoS value for each plan and selecting the optimized one.

In future work, we will research on how to improve the efficiency of our method when the services which participate in a composition are on the increase.

References

1.N. Milanovic and M. Malek, "Architectural Support for Automatic Service Composition", *Proceedings of the 2005 IEEE International Conference on Services Computing (SCC'05)*, 2,133-140(2005).

2.B. Medjahed and A.Bouguettaya, "A Multilevel Composability Model for Semantic Web Services", *IEEE Trans. Knowledge and Data Eng,* 17(7),954-968(2005).

3. L. Freddy, L. Alain and N.S. Ecole, "Semantic Web Service Composition through a Matchmaking of Domain", *European Conference on Web Services (ECOWS'06)* ,33-242(2006).

4. S.C. oh, B.W. On , E.J Larson and D. Lee, "Web Services Discovery and Composition as graph search problem", *Proceedings of 2005 IEEE International Conference on e-Technology, e-commence and e-servic* ,784-786(2005).

5. L. Freddy, L. Alain and N.S. Ecole , "Semantic Web Service Composition Based on a Closed World Assumption", *European Conference on Web Services, (ECOWS'06)* 171-180(2006).

6. T.R. Gruber, "A Translation Approach to Portable Ontology Specifications", *Knowledge Acquistion,* 5(2), 199-220(1993).

7. A. Lerina, C. Gerardo and C. Anna, "An algorithm for Web service discovery through their composition", *Proceedings of the IEEE International Conference on Web Services (ICWS'04)* , 332-339(2004).

Ecological Analysis on Evolution of Information Systems

Ying Liu[1], Shu-ren Zhang[2], Mei-qi Fang[1]
1 Information School, Renmin University of China
59# Zhong Guan Cun Street, Hai Dian District, Beijing,100872, China
{ying.liu, fangmq}@ruc.edu.cn,
WWW home page: http: // ecolab.ruc.edu.cn
2 School of Management, Hangzhou Dianzi University,
Hangzhou Zhejiang 310018, China
zhangshuren@gmail.com

Abstract. Information systems nowadays are growing and changing with a high speed. The flourish of system applications and participators imply opportunities and enthusiasm. Knowledge of the systems' evolution will be important to grasp the trend and so find a direction in the new era. To study the complicated and fast changing web environment, the article refers to ecological analysis. Two evolving models, agent emergence model and system integrated model, are studied. The evolving pattern of typical web applications is studied. According to the analysis, some potential opportunities are declared. Then collaborative structure of web components in integrated systems is analyzed based on network perspective. Popularity of web components and cluster structure of integrated systems, as well as their meanings, are discussed.

1 Introduction

Since Internet widely applied around the world, information systems connect and collaborate with each other. Internet links not only the static web pages, but different Information Systems (IS) as well. Recently great changes are taking place in the area of web. From a macroscopic perspective, some basic evolving rules exist in these changes. So there is a challenge for researchers to understand the existing tangled relationship on web and to find out the basic mechanisms. Once we grasp these rules, we can get prepared consciously before the changes take place in reality.

This article studies the evolution of information systems especially in recent fast changing Web2.0 era. [7] The approach of Information System Ecology is proposed. Some useful concepts from biology are referred. Evolution of information systems is

Please use the following format when citing this chapter:

Liu, Y., Zhang, S.-R., Fang, M.-Q., 2007, in IFIP International Federation for Information Processing, Volume 252, Integration and Innovation Orient to E-Society Volume 2, eds. Wang, W., (Boston: Springer), pp. 308-315.

studied by analogy to that of species in ecology. Approach of network analysis is also referred. Two kinds of evolving models are discussed. For each model, supporting evidences in reality and potential applicable fields are presented.

2   Position of Information Systems Ecology

Ecological analysis on information systems includes the study of patterns forming, evolving, and also some interactive behaviors among systems. It is important to notice that this study is different from information ecology or organizational ecology. Comparison among the three fields may make the position of IS Ecology clear. Information ecology focuses on imitation, creation and diffusion of information from organizational perspective, and is mainly on the ecological behavior within an information system or virtual community. [1, 2] Organizational ecology utilizes biological analogy and statistical analysis, trying to understand conditions under which organizations emerge, grow, and die. [3, 4] So the basic unit in these two fields is organization of users. In contrast, basic unit here is information system. User communities now are treated as component of the information system or external environment, although they still play an important role in interactive collaboration and evolution of information systems.

These related research fields is helpful despite of differences. Their relationship can be shown clearly by the following Fig. 1. IS Ecology locates in the intersection of Information System, Organizational Evolution Theory and Ecology. We can draw on ideas from these related fields, especially, from study on organizational ecology, which covers organizational evolution theory and ecology and also already exhibits effectiveness. [5]

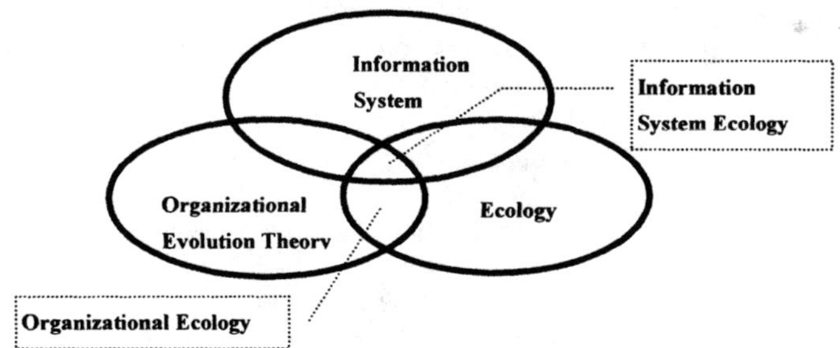

Fig. 1 Relation among three areas and the position of IS Ecology

3   "Cropper Principle" and Agent Emergence Pattern

Web 2.0 is mentioned more and more frequently as the name of a kind of system style. [7-9] Various web applications are flourishing nowadays and "grass root" plays a more important role on the stage of web. In this paragraph, the development of some typical technologies in Web2.0 will be studied. Some concepts and theories from biological fields enlightened our understanding of new phenomena in this area.

In our opinion, emergence of web applications recently can be considered analogical to the Cambrian Explosion to some extend. There are different explanations for the Explosion in biology. Steven M. Stanley of Johns Hopkins University provides a popular ecological theory. [10] He argued "cropping principle" provides a biological control. In one word, the theory explains that the organic diversity comes from "cropper" emergence. It means a "cropper" that feed on some existing species will emerge, along with the growing of species. And this process will continue, as the population of "cropper" grows to some extend, higher level "cropper" comes into being.

We find this theory can be also referred to explain the evolution of information systems. As we all know, web applications exhibit high diversity and extensive collaborating connections. While at the very beginning, the interaction among systems is limited when few of them adopted key technologies such as Ping, Trackback, RSS, Social Tags and etc. [11-13] We define these evolving pattern as "cropper principle" when a new system derives from another system that has developed to certain scale.

3.1   Agent Emergence Pattern of Ping

Take the evolution of Ping as an example, this process can be explained more clearly. (See Fig2) Ping is a kind of technology employed to detect real-time updating of social web sites, say group members' Bolgs here. [14] At the beginning, a few intra-organization Blogs were inspected by a closed, directional Ping monitor. The Blog systems named as Ping source (now it refers to all systems that can send Ping messages) send Ping messages to Ping monitor. The monitor's interface opens to certain sources selectively, and system settings will have to be changed when changing cooperating group. So the cooperation among systems is local, closed and exclusive. (Fig. 2a) As the massive application of Blog systems, some Ping monitors begin to open the interface and allow Blogs add Ping connection by itself to inspect more systems distributed all around the world. So the open Ping monitor comes into force. We call this kind of open monitor as Ping pool. (Fig. 2b) The precondition for Ping pool is existence of large numbers of Ping sources. Weblogs.com is the pioneer of Ping pool. As it can conveniently collect a great deal of changing messages in time, other Ping monitors begin to imitate it. So a lot of Ping pool systems come into being. (Fig. 2c) The cooperation among systems evolves from N:1 to N:M pattern. Along with the similar increase in number of Ping pools, Ping sources that have to send message to multiple Ping pools also increase. It brings inconvenience to both sides, especially to the Ping sources. Those Ping messages sent out to multi-systems waste the bandwidth and reduce efficiency. So some Ping Pools change their strategy. They take charge of transmitting messages to other Ping Pools to attract more Ping sources' direct connections. We call this kind of Ping Pool as Ping Transmit Agent (such as PingOMatic, PinGoat etc.) (Fig 2d) Basic phases in the evolving process can be shown as following Fig. 2.

The emerging agent releases Ping source systems from low efficiency, as they needn't issue messages to many systems simultaneously. The same effect can be completed by only sending messages to a Ping Transmit Agent. The emergence of agent changes system cooperating patterns from N:M to N:1:M. We can summarize this evolution pattern as agent emergence represented by "N:1→N:M →N:1:M".

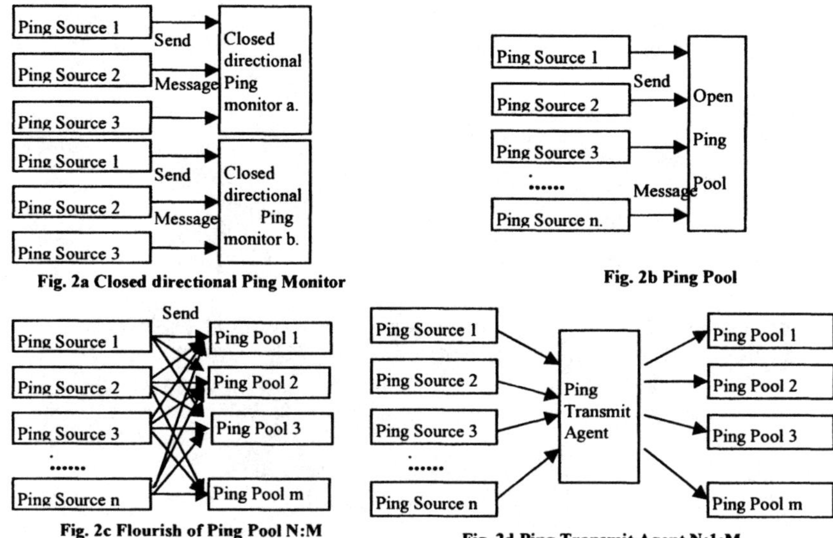

Fig. 2a Closed directional Ping Monitor

Fig. 2b Ping Pool

Fig. 2c Flourish of Ping Pool N:M

Fig. 2d Ping Transmit Agent N:1:M

Fig. 2 Evolution Process of Ping

3.2   Application Proposal

We can get some insight on system development from the evolving pattern study. Potential opportunities may be detected, which will help us get prepared consciously. In other words we can forecast what will probably emerge in web technology development by observing what already happened in related areas.

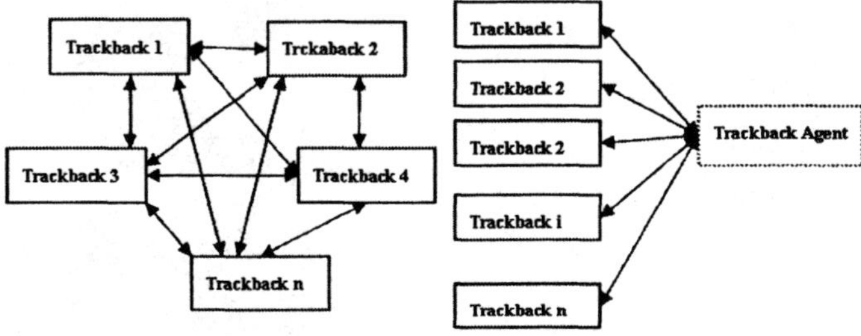

Fig. 3 Niche vanity in Track Back

For example, we focus on the technology of Trackback. Each system supporting Trackback develops interaction with other congeneric systems, which forms bidirectional equal interaction among systems.(See Fig. 3 left) The interaction now is "many to many" pattern. According to "N:1→N:M →N:1:M" agent emergence pattern, Trackback agents will emerge sooner or later.(Fig. 3 right) Features and functions of the new system can be also predicted. It should be the agent systems that take charge of managing the Trackback interactions between two systems. Assisted by these agents requirement from a system is inducted to proper branch interface, and then sent to the objective system through established connection. Trackback agent will be useful in centralized verification, like cooperating anti-spam, reputation assessment and so on.

4   Network Analysis and System Integrated Model

Open fabric is the key to gain adaptability and also the key to survive for information systems nowadays. Special web components are designed to be integrated easily. Some components including Google API, Yahoo API, and etc. are widely applied in many systems. The principle is to integrate functional components in a system in stead of redesigning from nothing. In this way, new integrated systems emerge quickly. We define this phenomenon as system integrated model.

The collaborative relationship of the components can be studied by network analysis approach. Network analysis is a kind of structure analysis. Graph theory provides necessary theoretical technology. [15] It provides us a brand new perspective to understand the environment, and it also introduces a set of new concepts, methods and tools. In this perspective, the key to understand behavior is the holistic structure, the opportunities and restricts from position. To study the collaboration of components, here nodes represent components and a tie occur when there exists a system combined the two components represented by the nodes on both ends. Then we get the collaborative network. So the topology can be visualized, and some quantitative properties like centrality and cluster structure can be calculated and analyzed. Evolving trend of the network also can be studied based on time related data. The analysis may help us making wise decision when choosing components for a new system.

An on line system — Programmable Web —collects mainstream programmable web components and mixed applications. (It can be accessed at http://www.ProgrammableWeb.com/mashup.) We collect the real data from the webpage to build up the network. The sampling was conducted in a series of three times. The analysis employed network analysis tool – UCINET. [16] We'll show our study on centrality, sub-group cluster of the component collaborative network.

4.1   Centrality

From network analysis perspective, centrality is an important quantity indicator to measure the power of a node from its position. There are many kinds of centrality in different level, for example Degree Centrality, Betweenness Centrality, Closeness Centrality, and Harmonic Closeness Centrality.

As our interest is mainly on the evolving pattern of the whole network, we refer to the Harmonic Closeness. We calculate the closeness centrality value in the way

Stephenson and Zelen proposed, as it provides the normalized centrality information for each node in the whole network context. Centrality of a vertex i is the harmonic mean of the measures between i and all other vertices in the network. [17] We list the rank of this value for some popular web components in Table 1. The number in the table cell means the rank value of the harmonic closeness centrality calculated for the component, and "1" means the highest in the network. The first column is the name of the component, and the column 2, 3, 5 correspond to the data collected in three different dates, which is shown in the first row. The column 4 and 6 display the different in rank number in the latest two investigation samples.

Table 1. Harmonic closeness Rank

	Dec 5th	Jan 15th	Difference	Feb 1st	Difference
Amazon	1	2	−1	1	1
Flickr	2	1	1	2	−1
GoogleMap	3	3		3	
Technorati	7	4	3	4	
del.icio.us	4	5	−1	5	
eBay	14	6	8	6	
GoogleAPI	6	7	−1	7	
A9	27	8	19	8	
VirtualEarth	5	9	−4	9	
YahooMaps	23	17	6	10	7
FeedMap	8	15	−7	12	3

From Table 1 we can see the changing position of the components. We highlight the obvious difference. A9, Yahoo Maps, eBay and Technorati are the components growing fast, and FeedMap and VirtualEarth are the two descend greatly in the list. From the changing value of the harmonic closeness of those web components, we can imagine corresponding change in their popularity and influence. The components that are going up in the rank list represent the trend of technology to some extend. It displays the choices of most integrated systems. Based on this observation and analysis, we can select a component more purposefully when there are some options.

4.2 Cluster Structure

Based on the study of web components, we can further analyze integrated information systems. Cluster study of the systems will help us detect the "species". Fig. 4 is a visualization of systems cluster study. Nodes in the figure are integrated systems building on web components discussed above. The UCINET algorithm "Cliques" produces a census of all cliques, which means maximal complete subgraph. Frames mark in Fig. 4 is according to those results. "Species" are defined in this way here. This visualization makes the structure obvious and easy to understand. It is helpful for information systems to find their latent rivals or cooperators. In a more complicated and confusing business environment, this ability is more and more important for practitioners of e-commerce.

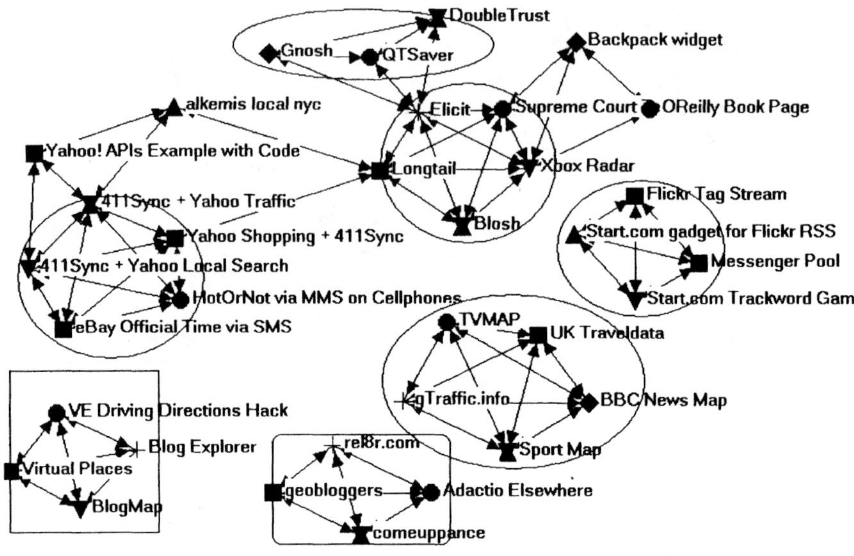

Fig. 4 System ecology and species

5　Conclusions and Further Studies

The fast developing applications of information systems attract our interests. Key technologies related applications and integrated systems are studied. By ecological analysis, we found "cropper principle" works in the evolution of Ping related systems. Based on this analysis, the potential opportunities in Trackback related systems are discussed. Further, according to the trend of open fabric in information systems, our study focuses on integrated systems. Network analysis approach is referred to study the collaboration of web components and also the structure of integrated systems. The popularity of different component at different time is studied through harmonic centrality. And the whole structure of integrated systems is studied by cluster analysis.

The ecological analysis on information systems helps us to grasp the rule of their evolution. To some extend it provides us capability to forecast the changing. The high speed developing and changing of information systems is still on going, the capability can instruct our direction.

Further studies in this area need more of our work. There are lots of useful concepts and theories from ecology can be introduced to information systems analysis. Systemic investigation could be interesting. And the new systems is growing and changing quickly, so we have a growing dataset. We should develop some automatic data-gathering technique to collect useful information from the online resources. Some adaptation of network analysis is also expected to fit for the certain purpose.

References

1. T.H. Davenport, L. Prusak, *Information Ecology: Mastering the Information and Knowledge Environment*, Oxford University Press, New Your, NY, (1997)

2. Y. Malhotra, *Information Ecology and Knowledge Management: Toward Knowledge Ecology for Hyperturbulent Organizational Environments, Encyclopedia of Life Support Systems (EOLSS)*, UNESCO/EOLSS Publishers, Oxford, UK. (2002)

3. M.T. Hannan, J. Freeman, *Organizational Ecology*, Cambridge, MA: Harvard University Press. (1989)

4. G.R. Carroll, M.T. Hannan, *The Demography of Corporations and Industries*, Princeton, NJ: Princeton University Press. (2000)

5. J.A.C. Baum, J.V. Singh, Organizational Niche and the Dynamics of Organizational Founding. *Organization Science*, 5(4):11. pp 483-501 (1994)

6. E.R. Pianka, Competition and niche theory, *Theoretical Ecology*, Second Edition edited by R. M. May, Chapter 8 (Blackwell, 1981) pp. 167-196

7. T. O'Reilly, What Is Web 2.0, Design Patterns and Business Models for the Next Generation of Software (2005, 9),
http://www.oreillynet.com/pub/a/oreilly/tim/news/2005/09/30/what-is-web-20.html

8. T. O'Reilly, Web 2.0 Compact Definition, (2006, 10)
http://radar.oreilly.com/archives/2006/12/web_20_compact.html

9. D. Hinchcliffe, The State of Web 2.0, 2006, 4.
http://web2.wsj2.com/the_state_of_web_20.htm

10. S.M. Stanley, An Ecological Theory for the Sudden Origin of Multicellular Life in the Late Precambrian, PNAS 1973 70: 1486-1489 *Proceedings of the National Academy of Sciences* (1973)

11. "TrackBack Technical Specification",
(http://www.movabletype.org/docs/mttrackback.html)

12. T. Hammond, T. Hannay, and B. Lund, The Role of RSS in Science Publishing, "Syndication and Annotation on the Web", *D-Lib Magazine*, Nature Publishing Group, (2004, 12) (http://www.sythe.org/rss/12hammond.html)

13. A. Mathes. Folksonomies - Cooperative Classification and Communication Through Shared Metadata [EB/OL], http://www.adammathes.com/academic/
computer-mediatedcommunication/folksonomies.html. 2004)

14. M. Jensen, E. Alternatives, A Brief History of Weblogs, *Columbia Journalism Review*, 2003 (5)

15. S. Wasserman, K Faust, D. Iacobucci, *Social Network Analysis: Methods and Applications*. Cambridge, Cambridge University Press (1994)

16. S.P. Borgatti, M.G. Everett, and L.C. Freeman, *Ucinet 6 for Windows*, Harvard: Analytic Technologies. (2002)

17. R.A. Hanneman, and M. Riddle, *Introduction to social network methods*, Riverside, CA: University   of   California,   Riverside   (2005)

Humanized Mandarin E-Learning Based on Pervasive Computing

Yue Ming，Zhenjiang Miao
Institute of Information Science,
Beijing JiaoTong University，Beijing 100044, P.R. China
Email：myname35875235@126.com

Abstract. E-Learning environments designated to facilitate long-distance learning are gaining popularity. Pervasive computing has a great potential for many next-generation IT applications. This paper describes pervasive computing system design and implementation for Mandarin e-learning. We propose a Human-centered Pervasive Computing System Model (HPC) and Layered Architecture Analysis and Design Method (LAAD). Based on the HPC model and LAAD method, a pervasive computing based Mandarin e-learning system is designed and implemented. Its design and implementation issues are discussed in details.

1   Introduction

The impact of technologies has brought in many changes in the field of on-line education. The spectacular development of Internet provides motivation for studying the impact of new technologies on a natural area of education like e-learning. But our investigation indicates that the teaching systems of e-learning are lack of intelligence. Those systems cannot provide learners with personalized services.

As a result, we consider merging the e-learning system with pervasive computing platform. The "any- time, anywhere, and human-centered" feature of pervasive computing makes it a perfect technology for e-learning [1].

With Chinese opening and fast economy development in recent years, the communication between China and the world becomes more and more important in a wide range. So Mandarin, the important communication tool and culture carrier that lets the foreign country know China, attracts more and more governments, educational organizations and corporations. In order to facilitate the foreign learners,

Please use the following format when citing this chapter:

Ming, Y., Miao, Z., 2007, in IFIP International Federation for Information Processing, Volume 252, Integration and Innovation Orient to E-Society Volume 2, eds. Wang, W., (Boston: Springer), pp. 316-323.

we design a pervasive computing Mandarin e-learning system and hope this system can make Mandarin learning conveniently and efficiently. In our work, we synthetically apply Human-centered Pervasive Computing System Model (HPC) and Layered Architecture Analysis and Design Method (LAAD) [2].

In section 2, we introduce the HPC and LAAD and describe the system requirements of a pervasive computing based e-learning system. Section 3 presents speech and tone recognition methods and the process of speech synthesizer for virtual audio teacher. Section 4 describes e-learning and m-learning system, especially the use of m-learning. Section 5 introduces personalized agent as the main advantage of our system. In section 6, we give the structure of IP-to-PSTN gateway and discuss the server. Finally, we describe the whole system design and implementation.

2 System Model and Its Human Core Layer: System Requirements

To consider key pervasive computing components as a whole, we propose the following Human-Centered Pervasive Computing System Model in [1]. This model can be illustrated in Fig.1.

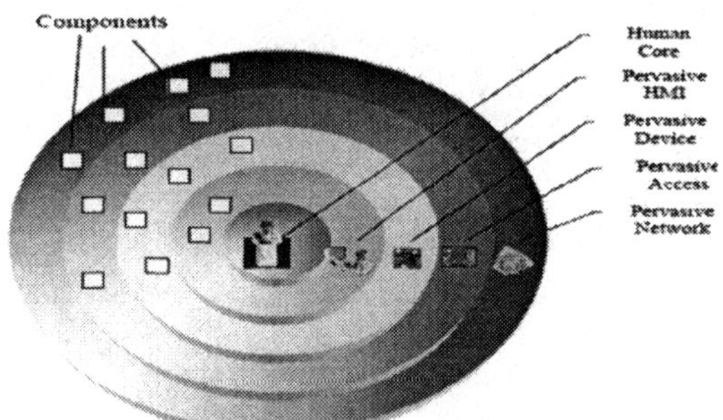

Fig.1 Human-centered Pervasive Computing system model (HPC)

We basically consider a pervasive system as five layers: Human/system requirements are major issues considered in Human core layer based on various different applications; Pervasive HMI layer considers the human and pervasive device natural interaction issues; Pervasive Device layer is for all devices human core user directly or indirectly interacts no matter whether they are visible or invisible; Pervasive Access layer is the bridge to connect the pervasive user device to the network environment; Pervasive Network layer as the system environment is the basis for pervasive computing system, which includes all the networks we can name today and future as long as the network connects to the internet directly or indirectly.

For a real pervasive computing system development, we have to analyze the application's requirements first and then design the system to meet the requirements. To mapping that to the HPC model, the requirement analysis is in the Human Core Layer. We call it Layered Architectural Analysis and Design method (LAAD).

In our system, we consider many issues such as how to recognize and evaluate the utterance of foreign learners as follows:

·For beginner, our system will deliver prepared easy content to students, and ensure that the content reaches them anytime no matter where they are.

·It brings in feedback and ensures students to hear natural pronunciation.

·For outstanding learners with great fluency, the evaluation was executed with a brief quiz offered at the end of the lecture.

·If the learner feels tired, the system can make studying more interesting by numerous means like hearing/seeking someone, arranging a cartoon or game, etc.

The prominent advantages of our system: teach students in accordance with their aptitude (humanizing) and condition with flexible time and space. The system also facilitates communication between the teacher and the students.

3 Pervasive HMI Layer: Speech and Tone Recognition, Speech Synthesizer for Virtual Audio Teacher

The components in this layer are Context Awareness, Computing Paradigms for HMI, Multi-modal interaction, User Interfaces, etc [1, 2].

Fitting to the difference of each learner's timbre, the speech recognition should be speaker-independent Mandarin speech recognition.

Our speech recognition component is firmly based on the principle of statistical pattern recognition [3]. When students' utterance inputs into system, a front-end signal processor with a sequence of acoustic vectors converts the speech waveform and the language model computes its probability. For each phone there is a corresponding statistical model called a hidden Markov model (HMM). The sequences of HMMs needed to represent the postulated utterance are concatenated to form a signal composite model and the probability of that model generating the observed sequence is calculated.

Mandarin is tonal language. The Mandarin four different tones include a lot of important information. So we process the tone recognition separately. The pitch contrail can distinguish four Mandarin tones efficiently, and then an event detection pitch detector based on the dyadic wavelet transform which can detect the catastrophe point of speech signal when people speak [4].

One of the main barriers to on-line distance education is the feeling of alienation and isolation reported by students. Developing a sense of community among students is one of the critical factors in changing from lecturer-centered to student-centered approaches in the mode of teaching and learning. Presently, corpus-based Mandarin TTS component consistently produces the most natural and pleasant synthesized voice. Our system also has the TTS function module used as system virtual teacher.

With a view to natural speech, we built a large Mandarin text-to-speech corpus [5]. It is designed for both statistical prosody modeling, and context dependence of phonemic features. This approach may ensure the concatenated voice to have high intelligibility as well as naturalness of intonation. During the course of learning, the foreign learners are able to hear the "professor" anywhere, anytime and at any place.

4.   Pervasive Device Layer: E-learning and M-learning

This layer is mainly referred to the user interacted devices and related software. The components are Sensors and Actuators, Smart devices, various user devices such as PDA, Embedded System OS, etc [1, 2].

Complete independence of both location and time is often emphasized as the main advantage of e-learning. However, in traditional e-learning the minimum hardware and software requirements are still a Personal Computer (PC) and the HTML language of the Web. Consequently an absolute independence in location is not providing. These independencies are still not fulfilled with notebook, because a real independency in time and location means learning wherever and whenever a person wants to have access to learning material. Mobile learning (m-learning) is the next generation of e-learning and is based on mobile devices and the WML language.

M-learning can be a wide range of educational activities on PDA and mobile phone: Mandarin vocabulary lessons via mobile phone email; 'just-in-time' administration (scheduling, study prompts, and reminders) via mobile phones; language-oriented problem-asked learning modules on PDA; and recorded Mandarin listening materials accessed on mobile phones. They show that the unique combination of features in mobile devices - portability, connectivity, and low cost.

Mobile devices perform the functions of desktop computers, with the advantages of simplicity and improved access. But three limitations prevent mobile devices from replacing desktop PCs: bandwidth, running costs, and text input speed.

4   Pervasive Access Layer: Personalized Agent

The components in this layer are context awareness and reasoning, service management, etc [1, 2]. We use a framework [6] to design and maintain language curricula (Fig.2), which advocates continuously evaluating needs, objectives, tests, materials, and teaching. We focus on evaluation, teaching and materials, including mobile hardware and software.

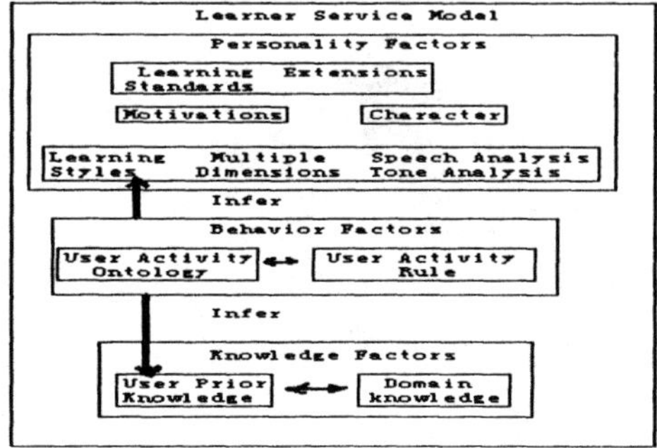

Fig.2 Conceptual design of learner model

It is suitable to design a personalized agent for this layer which is typically composed of the learner service model depicted as Fig.2. The learner model is composed with three sub-categories: Personality Factors, Knowledge Factors and Behavior Factors which are inferable from elements of behavior factors in the Fig.2.

The Personality Factors are composed of four groups of elements. Learning standards elements contain dimensions such as Personal, Preference, and Portfolio, etc. They are coupled with extensions features so that distributed e-learning systems are the summation of mentality requirements, which affected not only the style of interaction, but also the style of behavior in learning (speech and tone).

The Knowledge Factors are composed of learner prior knowledge and domain knowledge. The domain knowledge represents the view of the e-learning systems. The learner prior knowledge represents the concepts associated with learning materials which have been provided by distributed e-learning systems to the learner.

Personality Factors and knowledge Factors are updated as new data for behavior factors are received. Data mining techniques can find the association rules [7].

In our system, the context sensed and used by the agent contains time and spatial contexts, and learner preferences profile. The use of context information (e.g. location, time, and mental states, etc.) has significant potential to simplify the learner's interaction with a complex system. If there is an agent who knows learner's studying level, it can help to find a lesson that satisfies what he needs automatically.

Personalized agent makes e-learning become intelligent, which would provide personalized knowledge service for learners and improve the learning quality greatly.

5   Pervasive Network Layer: IP-to-PSTN gateway and Server

This layer is mainly referred to the network hardware infrastructure and related software modules. The components are Gateways, Servers, Network Resource etc [1].

Today, with the expansion of the Internet, voice services are being provided increasingly with packet-switching networks based on Internet protocol (IP) technologies, i.e., voice-over-IP (VoIP). To realize complete voice calls between endpoints in the Internet and ones in the PSTN, VoIP service providers use IP-to-PSTN gateways, which serve as bridges between the PSTN and IP networks [8].

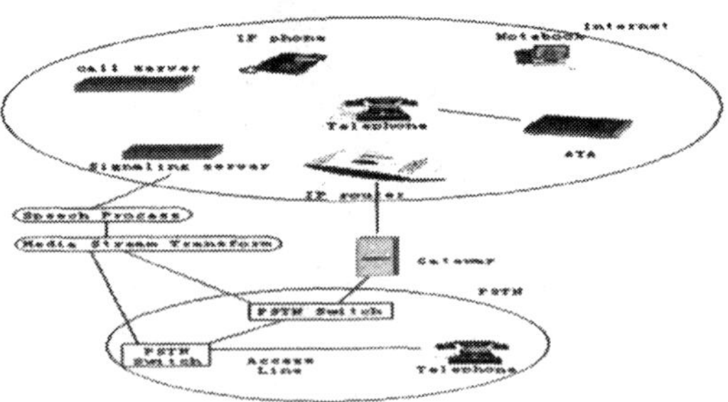

Fig.3 IP-to-PSTN gateway in a VoIP network

In our system, the gateway connects to a LAN port on the user's IP router, and PSTN access line. It produces the bridge of a voice call between Internet endpoint devices, such as a soft phone. Fig.3 illustrates the typical position of the gateway. It also includes a call server and a signaling server. A call server is used in the call establishment phase to set up IP communication between an IP device, such as an IP phone, computer, or analogue telephone adapter (ATA) and an IP-to-PSTN gateway. A signaling server may be involved in call establishment if speech process is used.

The system can afford voice-mail communication between the foreign learners and their teacher. Depend on the voice-mail component, the system can send the learners' information which is collected automatically by system to their teacher.

Another important Network Layer Component is Server. Therefore, we apply Java Applet, which dispenses heavy processing burden of the server to the clients. Unlike standard Web pages, which users simply visit and browse, applet-enhanced pages let the learner manipulate applet components and dynamically interact with information, which is distributed into client-side to lessen server's burden.

When applets incorporate large information domains, they begin to resemble complex desktop applications. In an applet, as in an application, learner might have to move between different screens of information that comprise the applet's domain. Each component would have its own view; to access both learners must be able to navigate between the views. It is different than navigating between Web pages, because all applet code resides in the HTML on a single Web page and the browser's navigation tools navigate "between" pages.

6   System Design and Implementation

Based on the above design discussion, we design our Pervasive Computing Mandarin e-Learning System as in Fig.4. Java is used due to the isomerism of platform, and JSP used to design the web page.

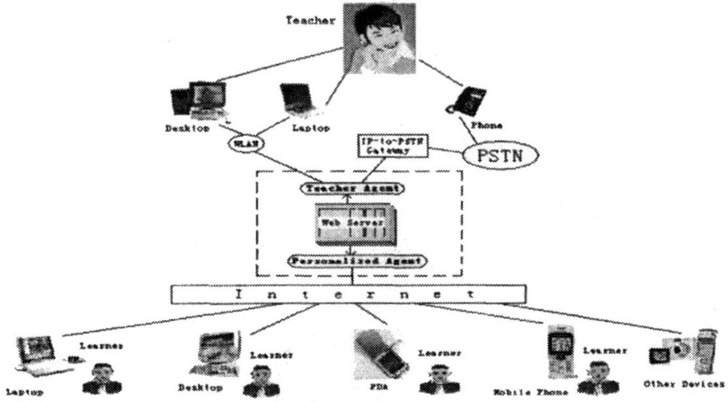

Fig. 4 Pervasive Computing Mandarin e-Learning System

As one focus is humanizing pedagogy, a major part of our work is to evaluate and analyze learner's language learning activities, and adjust the curriculum contents based on his activity situation. The work process is as follows: firstly, he interacts with the teaching server through Internet; and puts forward his personalized learning requests according to his knowledge structure and learning plan. Then, learner service center analyzes the learner's learning history and demands, creates personalized agent which stands for his learning requests and preferences. Finally, the system distributes the personalized learning services to the learner so that the learner obtains the learning resource or personalized learning guide.

After certain personalized course, a group of test is presented for the learner. His answer is analyzed though personality-analyzing agent. The analysis results are saved in his personalized learning database, which is the basis for the next learning.

This section gives system's implementation discussions. The foreign learner can log in our e-Learning system by his ID and password through Internet in the Fig.5.

Fig.5 Pervasive Computing Based Mandarin E-learning System Home Page

An example of Mandarin e-learning lessons is shown in Fig.6. For each Mandarin word, we all provide its mean in English, Real-time pronunciation, learner's pronunciation, Speech Recognition and Tone Recognition.

The overall pronunciation of each utterance is rated on a scale of 1-100. In terms of the related theories of speech analysis discussed above, the e-learning system will process the learner's Mandarin speech and the result in Fig.6.

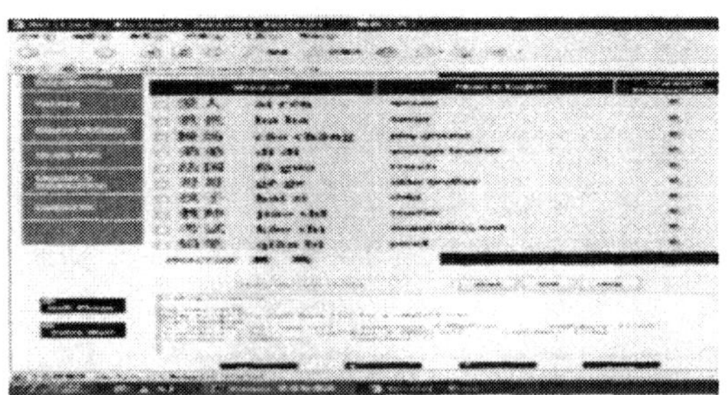

Fig.6 Learner's Pronunciation Exercise Page

7   Conclusions

This paper describes a pervasive computing system design and implementation for Mandarin E-learning. We study its implementation using the LAAD method based on the HPC Model. We analyze the foreign learners' requirements and discuss the implementation in pervasive environment.

Generally the key advantages of our system are: (1) The learner can access our Mandarin e-learning system anytime and anywhere without any restrictions as the system is a pervasive computing based system; (2) It is a humanized learning system which can adjust the learning contents and their presentation formats based on the learner's preferences and his real-time learning states.

This gives us bright hope in the success of our scheme and we are convinced that such a scheme will indeed become practical and scalable for its deployment over Internet for Mandarin e-learning.

Acknowledgments

This work is supported by National 973 Key Research Program 2006CB303105, National 973 Key Research Program 2004CB318110 and University Key Research Fund 2004SZ002.

References

1. Z.J. Miao, B.Z. Yuan, M.S. Yu, "A Pervasive Multimodal Tele-Home Healthcare System", *Journal of Universal Computer Science*, Vol. 12, No. 1 (2006), 99-114

2. W. Su, Z.J. Miao, "A pervasive Computing System Design and Implementation For Mandarin e-Learning", *The First International Symposium on Pervasive Computing and Applications*, Urumchi, China, Aug. 2006, 394-398

3. S. Young, "Large Vocabulary Continuous Speech Recognition: a Review", Cambridge University Engineering Department, 1-23

4. Y. Ming, Z.J. Miao, W. Su, "Tone Analysis for a Pervasive Computing Mandarin e-Learning System", The Second International Symposium on Pervasive Computing and Applications, Birmingham, UK, Jul. 2007

5. Q. Shi, X.J. Ma, W.B. Zhu, W. Zhang, Q.S. Li, "Statistic Prosody Structure Prediction", Speech Technology Group, IBM China Research Lab

6. C. Houser, P. Thornton, and D. Kluge, "Mobile Learning: Cell Phones and PDAs for Education", Computers in Education, 2002. Proceedings International Conference on, Dec. 2002, Vol.2, 1149-1150

7. Q.Y. Gu, T. Sumner, "Support Personalization in Distributed E-learning Through Learner Modeling", Information and Communication Technologies, 2006. ICTTA '06. 2nd, Vol 1, 610-615

8. A. E. Conway, "IP Telephone with a Personal IP-PSTN Gateway: Architecture and PSTN-Line Sharing Application", Verizon Laboratories, 132-136

The Agent of extracting Internet Information with Lead Order

Zan Mo [1], Chuliang Huang[2], and Aijun Liu[3]

1 Associate professor at School of Economic and Management,
Guangdong University of Technology, 510090 Guangzhou, China
Email: mozan@126.com
2 Graduate student at School of Economic and Management,
Guangdong University of Technology, 510090 Guangzhou, China
Email: chuliang750@163.com
3 Graduate student at School of Economic and Management,
Guangdong University of Technology, 510090 Guangzhou, China
Email: laijnking@gmail.com

Abstract. In order to carry out e-commerce better, advanced technologies to access business information are in need urgently. An agent is described to deal with the problems of extracting internet information that caused by the non-standard and skimble-scamble structure of Chinese websites. The agent designed includes three modules which respond to the process of extracting information separately. A method of HTTP tree and a kind of Lead algorithm is proposed to generate a lead order, with which the required web can be retrieved easily. How to transform the extracted information structuralized with natural language is also discussed.

1 Introduction

In the era of e-commerce, only the one who can quickly access and distinguish information can gain business opportunities. Currently, Internet has developed into the world's largest information base and the main channel of global e-commerce, of which the WWW (World Wide Web) develops most rapidly. WWW offers users the information they need in the form of hypertext, including technical material, business information, news, entertainment, and other information of different types and forms. The information constitutes an unusually huge heterogeneous, open distributed database. Searching information which we are interested in such a large ocean of data is very difficult. It needs some smart technology of information extraction then, which is also the urgent bottleneck of the process of carrying out e-commerce.

The agent, developed in recent years, has been proved as the right professional assistant in this field. It can access specific information from the WWW, and arrange the information into the forms we need, such as: collect and collate information, manage

Please use the following format when citing this chapter:

Mo, Z., Huang, C., Liu, A., 2007, in IFIP International Federation for Information Processing, Volume 252, Integration and Innovation Orient to E-Society Volume 2, eds. Wang, W., (Boston: Springer), pp. 324-332.

financial affairs, health consult, tour guide, etc. This paper describes a knowledge-based information extraction agent, which can extract meaningful information from the Internet website on the support of domain knowledge [1-4].

In the section 2 of this paper, we describe some common questions for extracting information from websites, which were caused by the non-standard and skimble-scamble structure of Chinese websites. For dealing with the above questions, we divide the process of extracting meaningful information from internet into three steps in the section 3, and try to design an agent which includes three modules responding to these steps. In the section 4, firstly, we research on the method to generate the Lead based on HTTP Tree in detail, through which users can retrieve the required website easily, then we extract information with the method of DOM from retrieved web page, and finally we discuss how to structure the extracted information.

2   Question Description

Freitag [5] and Kushmerick[6] pointed out separately in their papers that: Information extraction is a complex problem because many of the electronic sources connected in the Web do not provide their information in a standard way. The representational manner of website information, which is semi-structure, is more complex. The inherent heterogeneous and dynamic properties of www make it difficult to access the information we need. These can mainly be depicted as following:

1) The specialty of information source elements. Website documents, in which there exist hyperlinks, are the basic elements that composing information source. For each document, from the perspective of object model, is a kind of tree structure. This is different from RDS (Relationship Data Base) or OODB (Oriented Object Database), for the basic information source elements of RDS and OODB are consisted of records. For this reason, manipulation and query of information source are different from RDS and OODB.

2) The independency and dynamic properties of information source. With the change of time, the content and mode of information source change as well. Generally speaking, the models of RDS and OODB change little when designs are finished; the main work is adding, deleting and maintaining the records. However, the change of the mode of information source of www is more frequent. In addition to the mentioned above, the hyperlink relationship of documents often changes quite a lot.

3) HTML is a tool to format information. Browser can explain HTML clearly and express it exactly. However, browser itself knows nothing about what the information is. That is to say, the machine itself can not understand the content of what HTML displays. However, we can understand the content of information very well with its help.

4) Information is expressed in manner of words or tables, but it is not convenient to be extracted by other programs or structure method.

For the first problem, it needs a suitable way to describe the information source which takes the document as a basic element. No. 1 and No. 2 issues are interrelated. For the dynamic varying information source, it needs to generate an information describing method quickly, which can adapt to the changed structure. This paper uses the HTTP tree to describe the relationship between web pages and the method to retrieve the web page. Even if the relationship between websites has changed, we are still able to use the HTTP tree to generate a new method to find out the websites we need. For the third problem, we can describe the required information from the websites through the document object model. Document object models are mainly used to describe the structure and content of each element inner HTML. The content or structure in each element is not limit. As for the content, it can be any usable data model, such as text, graph, sound and cartoon, etc. While for the structure, elements may be composed by simple structure and complex structure. Simple structure means atom element, while complex structure compound elements. Each compound element consists of many sub-elements, and sub-element may also be atom element or compound element. Thereby, it is feasible to use dot '.' to describe the websites which have hierarchical structures. For the fourth problem, we can structure the text information by using the concept node method with the support of domain knowledge.

3   Design of the Agent Model for Extracting Information

Base on the above analyses, the process of extracting meaningful information from internet can be divided into three steps. Firstly, we retrieve the website we need, then extract the needed information and finally structure it. Through these three steps, information on the fixed website can be packaged as a fine source with the fine structure. So, we design an agent, which includes three independent modules. These modules are responding to these three steps to deal with the information. And they can be modified properly to reuse, even if their application domain has been changed.

Fig.1 has shown the details of the theoretic model of information agent, which can be described as following:

Phase 1. The agent module 1 connects the website sources via protocol such as HTTP (Hypertext Transport Protocol), and gets the web URL, which represents a pointer to a resource on the WWW. Then it retrieves the web page with the support of the HTTP Tree model with Lead Order.

Phase 2. With the method of document object model (DOM), the module 2 extracts information from the resulting website which resides on a temp base, and then resides on the temp base again.

Phase 3. The transform module constructs the resulting information with the natural language, and finally gets the information that we are interested in.

4   Hypertext Digraph and Lead Order

Define 1. Digraph D is defined as a couple (V, U), where V is a nonempty set, and its elements are called **peak**; U is a subset of the order-set $V \times V$, its elements are called **arc**. The two ends associated the arc have a certain order, **arc** (u, v) is different from **arc** (v, u).As for **arc** a= (u, v), we can call that u is the jumping-off point of the arc while v is the end-point.

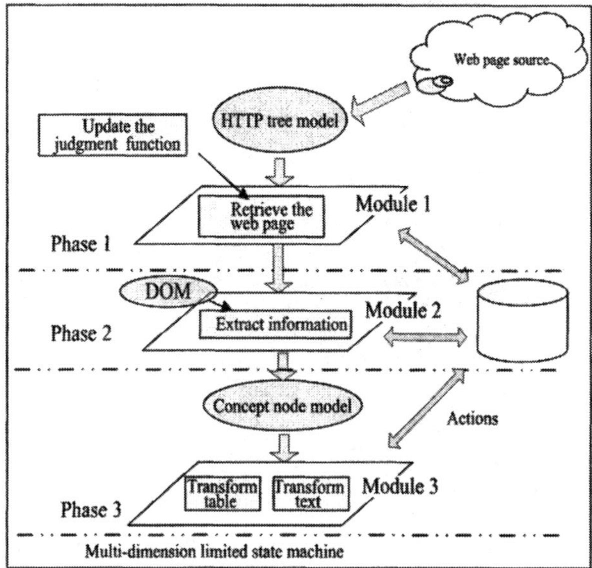

Fig. 1. The theoretic model of information

As shown in the chart A of Fig. 2, document which obeys to HTML syntax is called a *peak*, and the link relationship between two documents is called an *arc*. This link relationship has two forms to show, one is "**Get**" method of HTTP, and the other is "**Post**" method of HTTP.

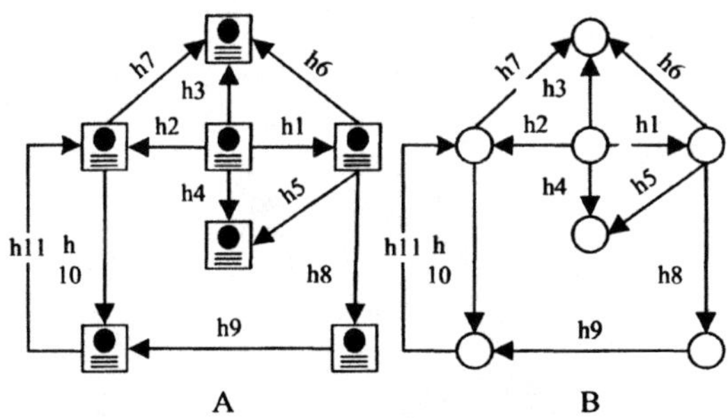

Fig. 2. Te Hypertext Digraph

Define 2. If each arc of Digraph D has been labeled with link method, then the Digraph D is called **Hypertext Digraph**. Generally speaking, the method to link two websites can always be either **Get** or **Post**. For example, if web V_0 and V_1 are linked with the Post method, then we can express this link as ***Post*** (V_0, V_1), otherwise, ***Get*** (V_0, V_1).

If an arrow diagram can be drawn from the start point to the end for each **arc** *(u, v)* in the Hypertext Digraph with *h* labeling the corresponding arc, the Hypertext Digraph D can be expressed by a geometrical figure as chart B of Fig. 2.

Define 3 The number of arcs which begin with the peak v is called **out-degree**, marked as $d_p^+(v)$.In Hypertext digraph, the number in the set which includes all non-local website pages linked by the initial web page with post method is out-degree, marked as $d_p^+(v)$.

Define 4 The number of arcs which end with the peaks *v* is called **in-degree**, marked as $d_p^-(v)$ .In Hypertext digraph, the number in the set which includes all non-local website pages linked by the initial web page with Get method is in-degree, marked as $d_p^-(v)$;

Define 5 In Hypertext digraph, the number of all local website pages linked by the initial knowledge website with Get method is called **sub-degree**, marked as $d_c(v)$.

As Fig.3 shows, web V is the initial knowledge web, it links three non-local websites V_{g1}, V_{g2}, and V_{g3}, with the Get method, and links two non-local websites V_{p1}, V_{p2} with the Post method, and meanwhile, it links three local websites V_{c1}, V_{c2}, V_{c3}, which have relation with the initial knowledge web. So we can say, for the initial web V, $d_p^+(v)$ is 3; $d_p^-(v)$ is 2 and $d_c(v)$ is 3.

In the Digraph, a triple h is used to label each corresponding arc, and regarded as a link method of HTTP. The h can be expressed as following:

{HTTP Method, URL, Parameter}

There are two HTTP Methods: ***Post*** and ***Get***. URL is Uniform Resource Locator pointing to documents. ***Parameter***, standing for h's parameter, is a quadruple :{[$d_p^+(v)$], [$d_p^-(v)$], [$d_c(v)$], [*child.h*]}, whereas, $d_p^+(v)$, $d_p^-(v)$ denotes the aimed web pages' out-degree and in-degree separately , $d_c(v)$ denotes the aimed web pages' sub-degree, and [*child.h*] denotes the HTTP method to link the aimed website and its sub-page.

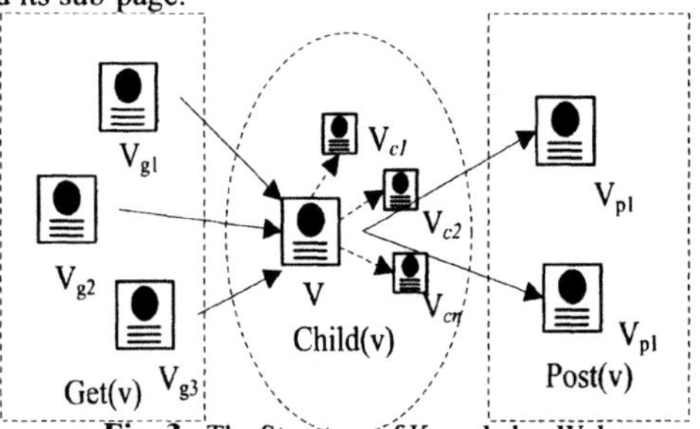

Fig. 3. The Structure of Knowledge Web

Define 6 The limited non-empty sequence $w = v_0 h_1 v_1 ... v_{k-1} h_k v_k$, where the items are alternate with ***peak*** and ***arc***, the start point of h_i is v_{i-1}, and end point is v_i $(i =1, 2, 3... k)$. if there is no same arcs in w, the w can be called a direct chain, where v_0 is the start point, v_{ki} is the end point, and k is its strength, namely, q (v_0, v_k) is a direct chain. The direct chains with non-similar peak are called direct paths, and the direct chains which have superposition of start point and end point are called direct loops. If there is a direct ***path (u, v)*** in Digraph **D**, we can regard that the peak u can reach to v. So, $h_1 h_2 ... h_k$ are called the ***Lead*** of direct ***path (u, v)***.

Suppose **D** *(u, v)* was a Hypertext Digraph, where u and v are two random peaks, then we can get the following natures based on Graph Theory:

Nature 1 *If u* can reach v and vice versa, then **D** was strongly connected or bi-directionally connected.

Nature 2 *If u* can reach v or vice versa, then we say that **D** was weakly connected or single-directionally connected.

Nature 3 If there is a peak w to reach u and v for each couple peak u and v, then **D**

was drafted strongly connected.

If the HTML documents are organized according to strongly directed or weakly directed digraph, then it is much easier to access the HTML documents. So the required web page can easily be found in a website by constructing a series of lead. The **Lead** is h :{ GET, URL, NULL}. If the required website can't be reached directly, according to Nature 3, then we should consider using peak w to reach the required web, thus a Lead should be generated to guide the user to reach the web.

In view of the character of web, Lead order can be generated by using the improved *Kruskal* algorithm [7]. The central thought of the Lead Order algorithm is that: firstly, take the pointed peak V_0 as the initial peak, then choose the point which has the maximal out-degree and associated with V_0 without loop with the Lead order—if there are two or more points having similar maximum of out-degree or in-degree, we can choose the point which has maximal sub-degree, then add it into Lead order. Through several iterations, the algorithm stops until the degree is less than the pointed variable. Finally the Lead

order is generated as this form: $V_0\{Get,\ URL,\{ d_p{}^+(v_0) =5\}\}V_1\{Post,\ URL,\ \{ d_p{}^-(v_1)=3 \}\}V_2\{Post,\ URL,\ \{ d_p{}^-(v_1)=3 ,child1.\{Get,\ URL,\ d_p(v_{2.1})=3 \}\}\}\ldots\ldots V_{k-1}h_kV_k.$

Fig. 4 has described the pseudo code of Lead algorithms.

The lead mentioned above could only find one website that we are interested in. However, in some cases, the interesting webs are a correlated group set. We need not construct all leads for every interesting website, but just construct a common lead order with **wild-card**. By using the common lead order, the HTML documents can be leaded from one to many. According to the data matched with wild-card, the common lead is divided into two kinds: one matches the document object model element, and the other matches all value range of the node parameters.

We can construct a lead h as following:

$h = \{\ Get\ ,\ document.div[0].table[0].tr[0].td[0].ol[0].li[i:*].p[0].a[0].href\ ,\ parameter\}$

Where,* is a *wild-card*, which expresses the sub element 'li' of **document.div[0].table[0].tr[0].td[0].ol[0]** in document. For example: **li[i:1-5]** expresses sub element of the first to fifth li. Specifically, the wild-card * expresses all sub element of **ol[0]**.

Procedure: Lead Order

Lead: = the empty set of Lead order

V_0:= the pointed initial peak

While $d_p(v_i) <= \varphi$ $(\varphi >= 0)$ //****φ denotes the

threshold variable, and is a

integer***//

BEGIN

V_i: = the point has maximum of $d_p(v_i)$ and

associated with V_{i-1} without circle with **Lead**,

IF (Maximum $d_p(v_i)$ is not unique)

Then: Choose the peak has maximum $d_c(v_i)$ of V_i

End

Add V_i into **Lead**

Lead:= Lead has been added V_i

End

Fig. 4. The pseudo code of Lead Algorithm

If the names of required documents are fixed, the agent can directly get the name and remember it, achieve the HTTP method of those documents. However, the names are not fixed in many cases, so the URL should be surely dynamical. Thus, we can use some key words as the searching form of leading URL, and combine the lead and the keywords to get the method to actually express a serial of interested webs. This method can resolve the problem that caused by the changeable name of the document.

5 Structuring the Text Information

With the help of the lead order and document object model, the agent can transform the interested information into a form of pure-text, and analyze these texts by method---- concept node, which combines mechanical matching method (MMM) and characteristic dictionary method (CDM), and can be understood by natural language[8].

5.1 Mechanical Matching Method (MMM)

The basic thought of *MMM* is: building a dictionary includes all words in advance, segmenting the sub-string of *S* according to a certain confirmed principle for the designated non-segmentation characters strings *S*. and then if the sub-string matches with some lemma in the dictionary, then the sub-string is a word. Continue to segment the remained parts, until the rest is vacant. Otherwise the sub-string is not a word, then return to cutting the sub-string of *S* to match.

The data structure of *MMM* is always simple. Generally speaking, the dictionary can be divided into basic dictionary and professional dictionary. In order to improve efficiency, they can be subdivided into the single-character dictionaries, dual-word dictionaries, ternate-word dictionaries, four-word dictionaries and multi-word dictionaries etc. As to MMM, the lemma in each dictionary is very simple. It only need to record its inner expresses, and don't have to attach other information.

This paper makes use of *MMM* to analyze some phrases, and the practice shows that it is more effective to analyze the little character string *S* which has known the meaning of this method.

5.2 Characteristic Dictionary Method (CDM)

The basic thought of the *CDM* is: building a characteristic dictionary in advance, which includes various words with segmentation character; segmenting *S* into several sub-strings according to characteristic dictionary for the designated non-segmentation characters strings *S*; segmenting every sub-string by *MMM* separately. Since each sub-string is shorter than *S*, the last problem in *MMM* mentioned above can be resolved.

The theoretical foundation of the *CDM* is that: Though the modal symbol of Chinese is not as abundant as western languages such as English, there are still some symbols in Chinese. These symbols offer the important basis for segmenting Chinese, and they can be used to segment automatically. Generally speaking, various affixes (including prefix and suffix), functional words and overlap-words, etc. can be regarded as the segmentation character. Though their quantity is limited, it is feasible and effective to separate and dispose them at first because frequency of their utilization is commonly high.

Since different kinds of characteristic word often require different treatments, the lemmas of characteristic dictionary have to record not only their inner expressions, but also their types. Generally, the scale of characteristic dictionary is not large, so the dictionary can often be folded into memory once, and can be order by its utilization frequency. So the words are segmented according to descending order of frequency.

The basis of choosing characteristic word is word formation of Chinese grammar or sentence formation in concrete language environment, etc. However, there is also some exceptive phenomenon in Chinese. As to this, it should consider as comprehensive as possible while building the characteristic dictionary, that is to say, it should estimate various exceptive situations for special-purpose processing

Since each lemma of dictionary is often an abstract of several words, segmenting these words has no unitary disposal. As a result, there is no need to include these words in the dictionary of MMM, as which can not only economize the space but also accelerate the speed of searching.

A common character of the two kinds of segmenting methods provided above is considering the word's form alone. However, each word in Chinese also has morphological features and the meaning besides form. In addition, the morphological feature and the meaning of the adjoined vocabulary must be consistent; otherwise, it will not conform to the grammar or illogic. In other words, morphological features and the meaning of adjoined vocabulary must satisfy a certain restraint relationship. These restrained relationships are important basis to judge whether the automatic segmentation result is right or not, so it should be present in the segmenting method possibly.

6 Conclusion

In this paper, we have proposed some common questions for extracting information from websites. During dealing with these questions, we divided the process of extracting information from internet into three steps and design an agent. Then we research on the method to generate the Lead order based on HTTP Tree in detail, through which users can retrieve the required websites easily. We extract information with the method of DOM from retrieved websites, and finally we discuss how to structure the extracted information.

Acknowledgment

This work was supported in part by the Guangdong science fund under Grant No06300278 and Doctoral Subject point special fund for Guangdong University of Technology under grand 053019.

References

1. Maes P., Moukas A., Amalthaea: An Evolving Multi-Agent Information Filtering and Discovery System for the WWW, Autonomous Agents and Multi-Agent Systems, 1(1)1998.
2. Hamdi, M.S, Information extraction using multi-agents, International Conference on Internet Computing - IC'03, pt. 1, pp.77-82,Vol.1(2003).
3. Arpteg, Anders, Multi-page list extraction: An agent-oriented approach to user-driven information extraction, , 2005 International Conference on Integration of Knowledge Intensive Multi-Agent Systems, KIMAS'05: Modeling, Exploration, and Engineering, v 2005, 2005 International Conference on Integration of Knowledge Intensive Multi-Agent Systems, KIMAS'05: Modeling, Exploration, and Engineering, 2005, pp.431-437.
4. Vlahovic, N. , Application of information extraction using information management agent for Croatian financial markets, WSEAS Transactions on Business and Economics, v 3, n 5, May 2006, pp.434-441.
5. Freitag, D. (1998). Information extraction from HTML: Application of a general learning approach. In Proceedings of the 15th National Conference on Artificial Intelligence (AAAI-98). Menlo Park, CA: AAAI Press.
6. Kushmerick, N., Weld, D. S., & Doorenbos, R. B. (1997). Wrapper induction for information extraction. In Proceedings of the International Joint Conference on Artificial Intelligence (IJCAI'97),pp.729–737.
7. Kenneth H.Rosen.Discrete Mathematics and Its applications (4th edition), 2002.11 McGraw-Hill College,pp.473-479.
8. Grosz, Barbara. The Contexts of Collaboration. In K. Korta, E Sosa, eds. Cognition, Agency and Rationality, Dordrecht: Kluwer Press, 1999, pp.175-188.

Governmental Information Resources Management Base on metadata

Zhen Long Li [1], Xiao Ming Zhao [1 2]
1 Computer Science Department, Taizhou University, Linhai, P.R. C
li_zhenlong@163.com.
2 Information engineering institute, zhejiang Industrial University,
Hangzhou 310014, P.R. China
tzxyzxm@yahoo.com.cn

Abstract. The current popular methods of organizing and searching of governmental information resources was analyzed under the circumstance of building Practical e-government integrating website, in this paper, and its metadata was also discussed. In order to solve the problem of information segregate, the framework of e-governmental information resources management was proposed by using metadata. Furthermore, a prototype of governmental information resources registration and directory service system has been developed.

1 Introduction

All around the world, e-government is revolutionizing the concept of how government works and the quality of the services it delivers. Its essence is that the government use the information technology to transform tradition centralized management system and the multilayer operating structure in order to meets the digitized society's need [1].

With the development of society, governmental function will gradually transform from management to the service [2]. This trend makes the relative isolation management system to be changed and thereafter cooperation among government department to be realized fully. This should be done through the resources integration and realization of the cross region, cross department and concurrent government affairs processing.

However, at present the majority design of government website take the governmental function as the center. It is difficult to provide the cross department and integrated service for the social publics, as shown in the Fig.10. Because the

Please use the following format when citing this chapter:

Li, Z. L., Zhao, X. M., 2007, in IFIP International Federation for Information Processing, Volume 252, Integration and Innovation Orient to E-Society Volume 2, eds. Wang, W., (Boston: Springer), pp. 333-339.

information resource and business processes are separated by the function organization, "isolated Information Island" was produced, as a result of which the publics not only needs to know what they want to do (e.g., apply for business license), but also needs to know which department have the function which they wanted to utilize (e.g., commerce bureau, police station and tax affairs department etc). For the solution of question, they have to jump form one government department website to another. Meanwhile, the information which they filled in one department is usually unable to share with other ones.

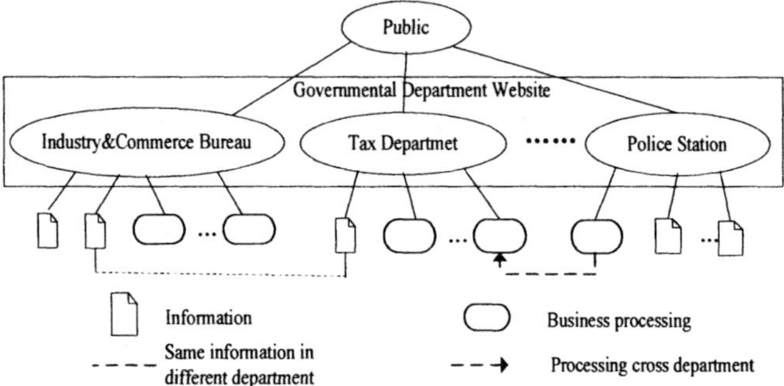

Fig. 1. Government department centered E-government system model.

2   Our Objective

Facing the massive separate government information resources, on the one hand, the government must research the technical means to organizes, control and manage information resource so as to provides the high efficiency and quality information service under the network environment. On the other hand, the users have to find the method to overcome the barrier which the multilayer of governmental structure lead up to them, and also to discover, obtain the valuable government information, it has become the very important issue to design the standard for the standardization description of government information resource, to realize the highly efficiency management using description standard, and to develop the new retrieval mechanism for the discovery and gain of government information resource.

In this paper, a service frame was proposed, in which the public convenience had been sufficiently considered and one-stop services were supplied, as shown in the Fig. 2. It has realized retrieval and management of government information resource in terms of the metadata and directory technology. It broke the information separation among government departments, supplied with integrated information resource and integrated information service, linked up the workflow between cooperative departments for the publics.

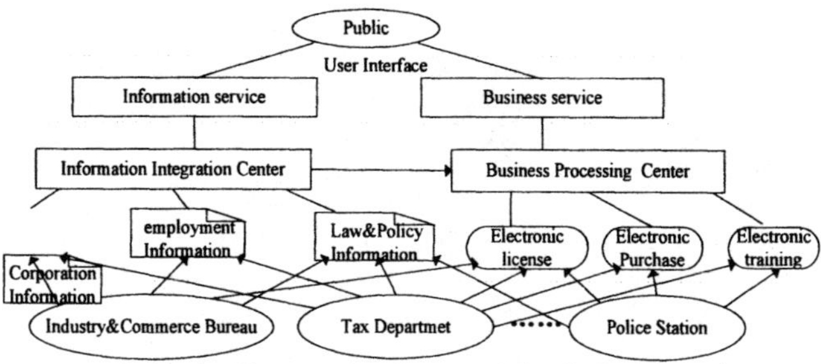

Fig. 2. public centered E-government system frame

3   The standard description of government information resource

In order to realize the integrated management and service of e-government information, we must find the method for the uniform description of information resource firstly. We here adopted the metadata technology for this purpose.

3.1   Metadata concept

The concept of metadata was first proposed by Myers in 1960. Its English meaning was interpreted as "structured data about data", also as "data which describes attributes of a resource" or as "information about data". Therefore, the metadata is called as structure data about the data content, quality, condition and other characteristic description data.

The metadata is one organizing way of information [3]; it not only offers a standardized method about information expression, but also provides a standard for definition, operation, exchange and the analysis of content in various levels of the information system as well as a tool for the computer intelligence recognition, processing, integration of information content, process and the system.

Because of unique characteristics with decentralization, changeability and multimode of the electronic information, the metadata have aroused more widespread concerns in publics. One of important research contents on metadata is the data description and the data management under the network environment.

3.2   Metadata expression of governmental information resource

The e-government information resource is those information which be used in the processing course of government affairs under the network environment[4]. It mainly includes the government decision information, the service information for the society, the feedback information and the intergovernmental exchange information.

At present the e-government metadata standard mainly has two systems. One is the standard which was developed by taking Dublin Core [5] as foundation, and another is the standard which was developed by taking American GILS (Government Information Locater Service) [6] as the foundation.

The metadata, according to its concrete function, generally can be divided into intellectual metadata, access control metadata and structural metadata and so on.

- **Intellectual metadata:** describe the principal part and the content characteristic of the information resource. It can be used as a tool for describing, discovering and distinguishing digital information object.
- **Access control metadata:** describe the usable condition, and deadline, intellectual property rights characteristic and usage jurisdiction of the digital information resource.
- **Structural metadata:** describe internal structure of the digital information resource.

Under the circumstance of construction of the local government affairs integrated website, we had constructed a metadata standard expression mode by referring to two standards mentioned above, as shown in the table 1.

In order to realize retrieval in the directory service according to the subject, profession and region, we pay attention to the attribute marked with bold words. For example, "**Publisher**" be used to point out the information resource URL, "**Coverage**" be used to point out administrative area ruled by document creators.

Table 1. Metadata and definition

Term name	Definition
Title	A name given to the resource.
Creator	An entity primarily responsible for making the resource
subject	The topic of the resource.
Description	An account of the resource
Publisher	An entity responsible for making the resource available
Contributor	An entity responsible for making contributions to the resource.
Date	A point or period of time associated with an event in the lifecycle of the resource
Type	The nature or genre of the resource
format	The file format, physical medium, or dimensions of the resource
Identifier	An unambiguous reference to the resource within a given context
Source	The resource from which the described resource is derived
Language	A language of the resource
Relation	A related resource
Coverage	The spatial or temporal topic of the resource, the spatial applicability of the resource, or the jurisdiction under which the resource is relevant
rights	Information about rights held in and over the resource

4 E-government information management Based on metadata

4.1 The search way of E-government information resource

Under the current e-government environment, the user has two basic ways to search and use the government information resource.

The first way: visiting related government website according to the government function. Because the government department mostly performs specific functions which had decided the content and property of the information resource in its website, the user may directly visit the related government website. if you, for instance, want to search the American education information, you may login the website of the American Ministry of Education (http://www.ed.gov). Similarly, one wants to search the Chinese law information, may land website of the Supreme people's Procuratorate of the People's Republic of China (http://www.spp.gov.cn) or website of the Supreme Court of the People's Republic of China (http://www.count.gov.cn). it is apparent fact that the information user must know the government function and its URL.

The second way: using the search engine tool. The search engine is an essential method to retrieves the information on internet. It is suitable for three kinds of situation: Firstly, One need visit some government website in order to know the related information, but unable to know the URL of this government website. Secondly, one has guessed the possible publisher of information, but unable to know for certain whether this information appeared in this government website. Next, one has known the specific names of some government information, and wants to search further its concrete content, but unable to know for certain its drawer and publisher.

With the exponential increase of WWW information, search engine technology based on robot has not been able to guarantee its recall and the accuracy. Therefore, it can not satisfy the people needs of searching government information resource at all.

4.2 Classified organization of e-government information resource

In order to satisfy user inquiry, we classified government information according to the category attribute in metadata. The information that has some common attributes is combined together, and establishes the directory separately.

The establishment of classification system is advantageous to realize the gathering, management, service, and sharing of government information resource, and to strengthen the protection and development of government information resource.

(1) The subject classification: classify according to the content of government information resources;

(2) The profession classification: according to the profession domain information of government information resource;

(3) The region classification: classify level by level according to the locus of creator of government information resource;

After classification, we may construct the service platform of government information resource in order to provide the many kinds of directory retrieval ways for the user.

4.3 The registration and directory service system based on metadata

The directory technology is refers to the technology of information resource classification, directory constitution, structure, storage, inquiry and so on [7].

The metadata has provided the structured description method of government information resource, so the metadata database can be established through metadata registration. Thereafter, the management, discovery and exchange system of government information resource can be developed using directory technology.

Using directory and metadata technology, we have constructed registration and directory service system of government information resource. Its overall frame as shown in the Fig. 3.

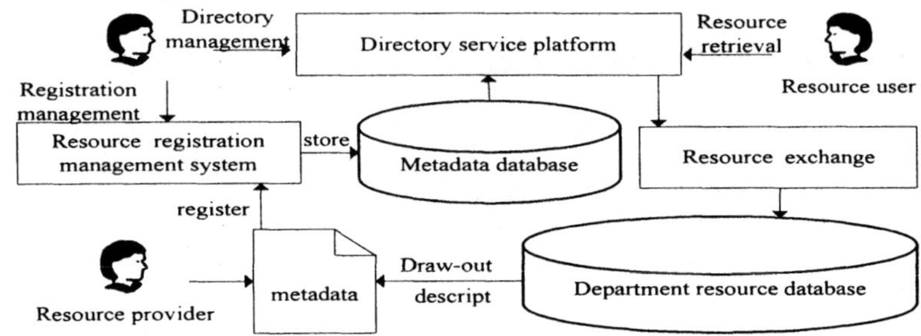

Fig. 3. Registration &directory service system of government information resources

There are resources provider, registration manager and resources user in the registration system. They deal with the resources submitting, resources registration management and the resources retrieval separately. Resources provider gathers the information resource from local department system, then catalog to form metadata which describe the resources. The registration manager will accept the metadata that come from resources provider and store it in the metadata database, then provides the searching service by create the resources directory using directory service platform. In the end, the resources user may query information using the directory service platform of the government information resource.

5 Conclusion

This research, under the circumstance of building effective local e-government integrated website, has developed the registration management and directory service system of the government information resources base on the metadata. The system already realized the retrieval of data resources and access of service through an integrated website. The service integration needs to be further studied. In the course of the system development, we realized deeply that in order to promote scaling property of the system, it is most important to make unified metadata standard referring to the division of national administrative area and the division of national economy profession.

Acknowledgements

The research was funded by the National Natural Science Foundation of China (No. 60473024) and by Zhejiang Province natural science foundation project (No.M603009).

References

1. W.L. Scherlis and J. Eisenberg, *IT Research Innovation and E-Government. Communication of ACM* 2003, 45(1), pp. 67-68.

2. C. Steven, E. William, The Future of E-Government, A Project of Potential Trends And Issues. *Proceedings of The 36th Hawaii International Conference on System Sciences*, 2003, pp.1-146.

3. L. Xiao, X.Y. Feng and Y.Y. Shen, *Study of Structure and Extended Rules in Descriptive Metada,* Digital library, 2004 (9), pp. 5-8.

4. H.C. Liu, Research on the Exploitation Tactics of E-government I Books Information *Knowledge nformation Resources,* 2005(4), pp. 58-62.

5. *Global Information Locator Service (GILS)* (May 31, 2005);http://www.gils.net/.

6. *Dublin Core Metadata Initiative (DCMI)* (December 18, 2006);http://dublincore.org/.

7. T. Roland and W. Maria, Directions in E-Government: Processes Portals, Knowledge. *Proceedings of The 12th International Workshop on Database And Expert Systems Applications*, IEEE Computer Society, 2001, pp. 313 -317.

Web Services Composition based on Domain Ontology and Discrete Particle Swarm Optimization

Zhenwu Wang[1] and Ming Chen[2]
Department of Computer Science and Technology, China
University of Petroleum, Beijing, China

Abstract. This paper proposes an approach for web services composition based on domain ontology and discrete particle swarm optimization (DPSO) algorithm. This method builds an optimized graph for service composition based on domain ontology and its reasoning capability, and then a discrete particle swarm optimization algorithm based on the graph is proposed to accomplish service composition. The simulation results show that it can produce good results, especially when the amount of web services is large.

The rapid development of web services shows that Internet software will be integrated following the service-oriented model (big granularity, loose coupling and dynamic banding) in the future. Single web service only provides the limited function, so web services composition is very important. Now most web services are composed by hand, so it is necessary to study web services composition based on semantic.

Literature [1] adopted the DOSCM method to study web services dynamic composition based on domain ontology, but it needs sort all the web services following the connection degrees among web services before composing them. Obviously it is very difficult to do so in the case of too many web services. In this paper, we adopt the discrete particle swarm optimization algorithm and domain ontology to compose web services dynamically based on literature [1],we can see that it has obvious effect when the service amount is large.

The remainder of this paper is organized as follows. Section 1 gives the description of web services composition based on domain ontology; Section 2 is the overview of the discrete particle swarm optimization (DPSO) algorithm; Section 3 details the proposed web services composition method which bases on DPSO and domain ontology (we called this method as DOPSO); Section 4 is the experimental result, and finally section 5 concludes this paper.

Please use the following format when citing this chapter:

Wang, Z., Chen, M., 2007, in IFIP International Federation for Information Processing, Volume 252, Integration and Innovation Orient to E-Society Volume 2, eds. Wang, W., (Boston: Springer), pp. 340-345.

1   The problem of web services composition based on domain ontology

The basic conceptions of domain ontology can refer to literature [1], on account of the paper's length,this paper will not discuss them. The problem of web services composition based on domain ontology can be described as follows.

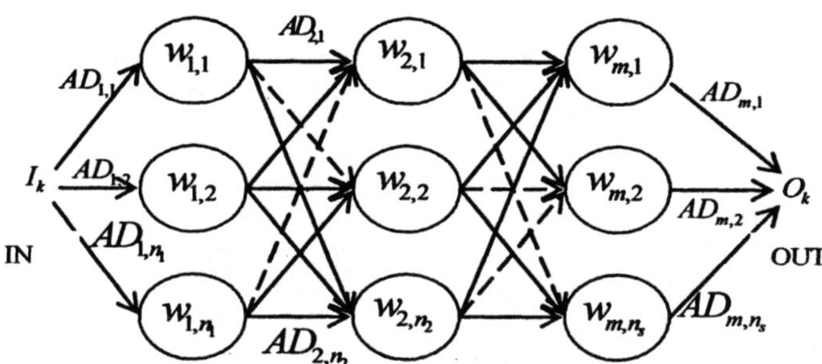

Fig. 1. WSC-Graph

The basic idea of DOPSO is that we can compute the connection degrees among web services based on conception similarity degrees and domain ontology to form an optimized web services composition graph (WSC-Graph), and then we can switch the web services composition problem to the problem that we find a path on the WSC-Graph which satisfies the users' requirement best. As described in figure 1,supposing composed service W has m basic web services, that is

$$W = (w_1, w_2, ..., w_m) \quad (1)$$

For the web service requirement $WSR_k(I_k, O_k)$, there are n_1 web services which have the semantic connection relationship(that is to say, w_1 has n_1 candidate web services), and these n_1 web service also have n_2 subsequent web services, the rest may be deduced by analogy, and W_m has n_s candidate web services, that is

$$I_k \bowtie I_{1,1} \quad I_{1,2} \bowtie .. \quad I_{1,n_1}, \; O_{1,1} \bowtie I_{2,1} \quad I_{2,n_2}, ..., \; O_{m,1} = O_{m,2} = ..O_{m,n_s} = O_k.$$ I_k in figure 1 presents the input of $WSR_k(I_k, O_k)$ and O_k is the output. The circles in figure 1 denote web services, the two web services which are connected by the directed edge have the signification of semantic connection, the broken lines in figure 1 show that the two web services connected by them have no signification of semantic connection, but for the simple aim, we still connect them and their semantic connection degrees are zero. Each path from I_k to O_k in WSC-Graph is a service composition result and the best one is the one which has the biggest web services composed satisfaction degree. The details of conceptions, such as the similarity degree between two domain ontology concepts, the semantic similarity degree between two conception sets and the formula about connection degree of two services, can refer to literature [1].

2   The discrete particle swarm optimization

Particle swarm optimization (PSO) is one of the evolutionary computational techniques. Suppose that the search space is D-dimensional, and the position of the ith particle of the swarm can be represented by a D-dimensional vector, $\overline{x_i} = \{x_{i,1}, x_{i,2}, ..., x_{i,D}\}$.The velocity (position change per generation) of the particle x_i can be represented by another D-dimensional vector, $\overline{v_i} = \{v_{i,1}, v_{i,2}, ..., v_{i,D}\}$.The best position previously visited by the ith particle is denoted as $PC_{i,best} = \{p_{i,1}, p_{i,2}, ..., p_{i,D}\}$ and its corresponding fitness value is denoted as $PL_{i,best}$.If the topology is defined such that all particles are assumed to be neighbors and g as the index of the particle visited the best position in the swarm, then $GL_{best} = \{p_{g,1}, p_{g,2}, ..., p_{g,D}\}$ becomes the best solution found so far and the responding fitness value is denoted as GC_{best}. The velocity of the particle and its new position will be determined according to the following two equations:

$$v_{i+1,d} = v_{i,d} + c_1 r_1 (p_{i,d} - x_{i,d}) + c_2 r_2 (p_{g,d} - x_{i,d}) \quad (2)$$

$$x_{i+1,d} = x_{i,d} + v_{i+1,d} \quad (3)$$

Where c_1 and c_2 are acceleration coefficients regulating the relative velocity toward global and local best, r_1 and r_2 are two random numbers in [0,1]. Popularly, set a maximal iterative number (such as n_{max}) as the concluding condition.

Usually, PSO has been applied to solve the continuous space optimization problems, and now some scholars used it to solve the discrete space optimization problems. In literature[5], Clerc proposed a discrete particle swarm optimization algorithm(DPSO) to solve the TSP problem, and some scholars used DPSO to handle QoS multicast routing problems in literature[6][7]. In literature [8], a hybrid particle swarm optimization algorithm (HPSO) has been described to solve the TSP problem, which combined genetic algorithm. Based on literature [5], literature [4] introduced repulsion operator and learning operator into DPSO to restrain the stagnant phenomena, and acquired good effects. In this paper, we propose an improved discrete particle swarm optimization algorithm to solve the problem of web services composition, which based on literature [4].In the next section; we will detail the improved algorithm.

2.1   Position and velocity of particles

As described in figure 1, the position X can be described by the basic services which are invoked by the composite service.

$$X = (x_1, x_2, ... x_i, ..., x_n), 1 \leq i \quad n, 1 \leq x_i \quad n_i, ..., 1 \leq x_n \quad n_s \quad (4)$$

Where x_i is the *ith* basic service, n is the amount of basic services which are invoked by the composite service. The dimension in X shows the composite sequence number of basic services. According to figure 1, x_i has n_i candidate web services.

The function of velocity is to change the positions of particles. Similar to the definition of position X, the velocity is defined as follows:

$$V = (v_1, v_2, ... v_i, ..., v_n), 1 \leq i \quad n, 1 \leq v_i \quad n_i, ..., 1 \leq v_n \quad n_s \quad (5)$$

Where the dimension in V shows the composite sequence number of basic services, and n is the amount of basic services which are invoked by the composite service. Each item in V has two meanings: if v_i equals 0, it means no operation, else means to modify the data in this item to v_i.

2.2   Operations about position and velocity

1 . Addition operation

The addition operation between the position and the velocity accomplishes the movement of the particle's position, and moves a particle to a new position. The formula is defined as follows:

$$X = X + V \quad (6)$$

Each data in the new position is defined by the formula (7):

$$\left[\begin{array}{l} x_i = v_i \quad \text{if } v_i \neq 0 \text{ or } v_i \neq x_i \\ \quad F \qquad \text{else} \end{array} \right. \quad (7)$$

When creating a new position X,   if v_i does not equal 0 or x_i, it means x_i equals v_i, else means no operation.

2. Subtraction operation

Two positions executing subtraction operation can produce a new velocity:

$V = X_2 - X_1$ (8)

Form the formula (8), we can see that the particle can move from position X_1 to X_2, if it has a velocity V. According to the formula (9), compared the data in each dimension between X_1 and X_2, if $x_{1,i}$ equals $x_{2,i}$, then v_i equals 0,else v_i equals $x_{2,i}$.

$$v_i = \begin{cases} 0 & if \quad x_{1,i} = x_{2,i} \\ x_{2,i} & else \end{cases} \quad (9)$$

3. Multiplication operation on velocity

Multiplication operation has the probability meanings, the formula is defined as follows:

$V_2 = c \times V_1, c \in [0,1]$ (10)

Where c is a constant, and it has the probability meanings. When computing V_2, we should produce a random number *randv*(*randv* $\in$ [0,1]) for each data $v_{1,i}$ in V_1. If *randv* is less than c, then $v_{2,i}$ equals $v_{1,i}$,else $v_{2,i}$ equals 0.The formula is defined as follows:

$$v_{2,i} = \begin{cases} v_{1,i} & if \quad randv < c \\ 0 & else \end{cases} \quad (11)$$

4. The addition operation between velocities

Executing addition operation between two velocities can produce a new velocity:

$V = V_1 + V_2$ (12)

Each data in V can be defined as follows:

$$v_i = \begin{cases} v_{2,i} & if \quad v_{2,i} \neq 0 \\ v_{1,i} & else \end{cases} \quad (13)$$

Generally, $V_1 + V_2 \neq V_2 + V_1$, and only if $V_1 = V_2$ we can conclude:

$V_1 + V_2 = V_2 + V_1$ (14)

2.3 The movement equation of particles

For the particularities of the discrete space optimization problems, we modified the movement equation, and canceled the first item in the formula (2) because it is insignificance for discrete space optimization problems. The equation is defined as follows:

$$V = c_1(X_{pbest} - X) + c_2(X_{gbest} - X), \quad (15)$$
$$X = X + V.$$

2.4 variation operator introduce

DPSO also has some disadvantages, for example, easy to stagnant. In this paper, we introduce variation operator to add the diversity of particles

Def 1: the position comparability $s_{i,j}$: $s_{i,j} = \frac{1}{m}\sum_{k=1}^{m} iif(s_{i,k} = s_{j,k}, 1, 0)$ (20)

Where m is the position dimension , and if $s_{i,j} = 1$,it implies that the two particles have the same position, else implies that the two particles have the different position absolutely, and $s_{i,j} \in [0,1]$.

Def 2: the particle diversity d_i:the similar degree of the current position *i*, the native best position *pbest* and the whole best position *gbest* for a certain particle:

$d_i = 1 - \frac{1}{3}(s_{i,pbest} + s_{i,gbest} + s_{pbest,gbest})$, $d_i \in [0,1]$ (21)

Def 3:the particle swarm diversity $\bar{d}_i$: $\bar{d}_i = \frac{1}{n}\sum_{i=1}^{size} d_i$ (22)

Where n is the swarm size. If $\bar{d}_i$ is less than a certain constant $c_{\bar{d}}$ (for example 0.2) , then start the variation operator to produce the diversity.

3   The DOPSO algorithm

The detailed algorithm can be described as follows:

1. Initialization: suppose the amount of particles is n, and the threshold of service satisfaction degree is x ,the probability constant in variation operation is $c_{\bar{d}}$, suppose the coefficients in the formula （15） are c_1,c_2 ;To produce the initial positions of particle swarm followed by the formula(4),that is $X_i,1 \# i \quad n$; To produce the initial velocity of each particle followed by the formula(6),that is $V_i,1 \# i \quad n$;To compute the fitness value for each particle, and according to the current position we can compute the fitness value $f_i,1 \# i \quad n$ followed by composition satisfaction degree which detailed in literature[1]; $PC_{i,best}=X_i$ and $PL_{i,best}=f_i;GL_{best}=PL_{i,best}$ if and only if $f_i=\max\{f_k\},1 \leqslant k \leqslant n;GC_{best}=PC_{i,best}$if and only if $GL_{best}=PL_{i,best}$;

2. To compare the current fitness value f_i with the fitness value $PL_{i,best},1 \# i \quad n$,which is its own best position $PC_{i,best},1 \# i \quad n$, if f_i is better than $PL_{i,best}$, $PL_{i,best}$ equals f_i;

3. To compare the current fitness value f_i with the fitness value GC_{best} ,which is the best position in the swarm GL_{best} . For each particle, if f_i is better than GC_{best} , then GC_{best} equals f_i ;

4. To compute the diversity of particles $\overline{d_i}$,and if $\overline{d_i}$ is less than $c_{\bar{d}}$,then it should start variation operator to produce a new velocity for all the particles;

5. To evolve the positions and velocities followed by the equation(15);

6. If the result does not reach to the threshold values, then return to the step (2).

4   Simulation experimentation

We compared the proposed method with the DOSCM method in literature [1], and for the justice aim, we adopt the same software and hardware environment. CPU is Intel Pentium IV 2.4GHz,memory is 1 GB ,operation system is XP professional ,the development language is java and the IDE is Eclipse3.1.The amount of particle swarm is 200, $c_1 = 0.2, c_2 = 0.3, c_{\bar{d}} = 0.2$,and the algorithm will run 50 times.

In this paper, we generate random data as connection degree data and used them in the experiment. We adopt five test data musters, the web services amount is 300,900,1500,2100,2700 respectively. The smallest services satisfaction degree threshold is 0.6 in the both methods

CASE 1 composition success probability

Table 1. DOPSO: DOSCM

Satisfaction degree / Services amount	DOPSO	DOSCM
300	0.80	0.81
900	0.82	0.83
1500	0.84	0.84
2100	0.85	0.84
2700	0.89	0.88

From the data in table 1, the DOPSO has unconspicuous effect when web services amount is little and with the increase of web services amount, we can see that the composition success probability of DOPSO is similar to that of DOSCM.

CASE 2 services composition efficiency

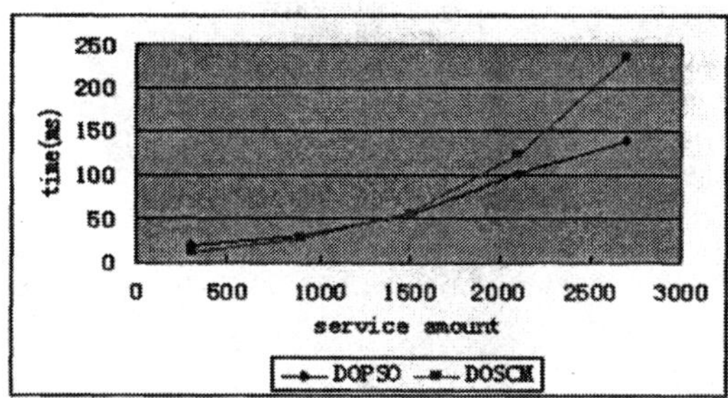

Fig .2. services composition efficiency

Figure 2 describes the relation between the services total amount and the composed time. We can see that DOPSO has an unconspicuous effect in the case of less web services, and with the increase of web services amount, the composed time which DOPSO used is less than that of DOSCM, it implies that DOPSO has an obvious effect when web services amount is large.

5   Conclusion

From the results of experiment we can see that the discrete particle swarm optimization algorithm has good application property to solve the problem of web services composition based on domain ontology, and it provides a new way to study web service composition. But at the same time, the particle swarm optimization algorithm also has some defaults, for example easy to stagnate. So the next work is to design better particle swarm optimization algorithm.

References

1. M. Li, D.Z. Wang, X.Y. Du, and S. Wang, "Dynamic Composition of Web Services based on Domain Ontology", *Chinese Journal of Computers*, 28(4),645-650(2005).

2. J. Wu, Z. h. Wu, Y. Li and S.G. Deng, "Web Service Discovery and Similarity of Words", *Chinese Journal of Computers*, 28(4), 596-602(2005).

3. J.F. Zhao, B. Xie, L. Zhang, F.q. Yang, "A Web Services Supporting DomainFeature", *Chinese Journal of Computers*, 28(4),732-738(2005).

4. Y.W. Zhong, J.g. Yang and Z.Y. Ning, "Discrete particle swarm optimization algorithm for TSP problem", *System Engineering −Theory & Practice*,6,89-93(2006).

5.M. Clerc, "Discrete particle swarm optimization",Onwubolu GC ,Babu BV, New Optimization Techniques in Engineering ,SpringerVerlag (2004).

6. D.R. Pan, "QoS Multicast Routing Optimization Algorithm Based on SCE Algorithm and Particle Swarm Optimization Algorithms", *Computer and Information Technology*, 14-18,(2006).

7. J. Qing, W.b. Xu and J. Sun, "QoS Multicast Routing Optimization Algorithm Based on Particle Swarm Optimization Algorithms", *Computer Engineering and Applications*, 27(1),106-108(2006).

8. S. Gao, B. Han, X.J. Wu, and J.Y. Yang, "Solving traveling salesman problem by hybrid particle swarm optimization algorithm", *Control and Decision,*,19(11), 1287-1289(2004).

Personal knowledge management based on social software
——From the explicit and tacit knowledge perspective

ChenglingZhao[1], Jianxia Cao[1], Xinhua Guo[2]
1 Educational technology Department Huazhong Normal University,
Wuhan, China
2 Administration Department, University Of shanghai for Science and
Technology, Shanghai, China)

Abstract. The emergence of information technology has provided a powerful hand for personal knowledge management, thus the personal knowledge management goes on more convenient and feasible. This paper gave the summary of personal knowledge management as well as social software, and then analyzed the characteristic of applying social software in personal knowledge management from the explicit and tacit knowledge perspective, finally gave a model of applying social software in personal knowledge management.

1 Personal Knowledge Management

1.1 The outline of personal knowledge management

The 21st century was a knowledge economy time, the knowledge capital already becomes an important resources and the core capital in the social life, along with the development of computer network, the importance of knowledge management highlighted day by day. The knowledge management is a process to create value using knowledge and intelligence of enterprise and individual. It divides into organization knowledge management and personal knowledge management, Professor Paul A.Dorsey, an expert on personal knowledge management research, said that personal knowledge management is the basis and origin of knowledge management. And we also hold the same opinion.

Please use the following format when citing this chapter:

Zhao, C., Cao, J., Guo, X., 2007, in IFIP International Federation for Information Processing, Volume 252, Integration and Innovation Orient to E-Society Volume 2, eds. Wang, W., (Boston: Springer), pp. 346-354.

Personal knowledge management is a conceptual framework to organize and integrate information that we, as individuals, feel is important so that it becomes part of our personal knowledge base. It provides a strategy for transforming what might be random pieces of information into something that can be systematically applied and that expands our personal knowledge [1].

Professor Eric tsui, the chief researcher in CSC Corporation and holds part-time jobs in Imperial Melbourne University of Science and Technology, pointed out that, "personal knowledge management is a continual process; individuals must do various works, such as gather, classification, collection, to ascend their personal knowledge in daily life. These activities not merely limit in the commercial and work, but also include individual interest, hobby, and leisure activity." [2]

Based on these, we may interpret personal knowledge management like this: under the information technology condition, individuals gain and process the information that they need, no matter where they are, and gradually establish their personal knowledge library, which is useful for the storage, use, communication, share and innovation of personal knowledge, at present and in future. In this process we should pay great attention to the share and innovation ability, which is the most important in personal knowledge management, so to explore individuals' maximum potential.

1.2 Necessary of personal knowledge management

"We live in the sea of network data material, but endured the thirsty and hunger of knowledge" this speech described the awkward situation vividly when the cyberspace main body faced the massive information on the Internet. The information overload in modern society causes us to exclaim at information's huge as well as leaved us in the situation of not knowing how to pick and choose the useful. We often slide into another subject homepage in carelessly that the material is irrelevant with which we search, which wasted time of normal study and work; When we need some material urgently, we couldn't think clearly where we place it before; we want to search some useful thing, but in fact, the "rubbish information" the Internet provides is much more than the useful, we have to take time and energy to identify, in the end we ourselves forgot what we want to find at first. Therefore it appears to be especially important how to pick the useful knowledge from the abundant information and how to transfer them into ourselves' personal knowledge. Moreover, the request of information literacy in e-learning times also demands us to grasp certain method on personal knowledge management. A person who has information literacy should be a knowledge manager first. Only if we learned to manage our personal knowledge effectively, absorb the beneficial knowledge, carry on the critical thinking, use professional technology proficiently, withdraw the knowledge form ourselves' knowledge library, share them with everybody, and share others' knowledge simultaneously, then can we learn to study, possess information literacy and become an independent lifelong learner.

Bill Gates had said: "the way of collecting, managing and using information, decided your victory", this speech gave a rather good annotation to the importance of personal knowledge management. Personal knowledge management can help individuals absorb the necessary knowledge pertinently, foster their habit and consciousness of lifelong learning, build the foundation for individuals' knowledge study and ability promotion, thus enhance individuals' specialized skill and competitive power.

2. Social Software

2.1 Definitions of social software

Scholars in and abroad have discussed the definitions of social software from different views. Stewart Butterfield defined it as a tool for people's communication, which has following traits: individuation, participation, Interpersonal relationship, bargaining and colony. LeeLe Fever believed that, the common software connects the human and computer as well as the network, but what the social software connect are people's thought, sentiment and viewpoint. [3] Stowe Boyd proposed that, the social software should meet with one or several premises, such as supporting interaction dialogue between individuals or among communities; supporting society feedback activity, for example, community can make appraisal on other people's contribution, then form "the digital prestige", supporting construction of society network, helping people establish and manage the new digitized interpersonal relationship. [4] Mao Xianghui (2003) pointed out that the social software meant "the individual brings the software to become a part of social network". Some researchers also expressed: "The social software is a tool helping people establish social network and automatic community or organization" and "social software pays more attention on the affiliation people established than the software technology itself". [5] It accorded with what SunirShah stressed, the correct definition needs to stress on a human's side, by no means a technical side. He believed that the fundamental rule on software originates from human's characteristic, not the area of technology. In fact, the social software stress the attribute "the society", it indicated society's individuals can construct social relations by software tool. The theory foundations of social software are "six degrees divisions" and "150 principles".

2.2 Connotations and characteristic of social software

There are three connotations of social software: First, it is individual software, a tool for individual network; second, what it constructs is the social network, including weak link, middle link and strong link; finally the social software is the unification of individuation and sociality. [6]

In the use process of social software, people pay more attention on social relations. Therefore, the characteristic of it includes: the software reflects the social network in the using process, both strong link and weak link have the intensity trust; form a team and a self-organization; individuals centered, user's status and trust can be manifested in the software; The software itself renews and self-develops unceasingly; Initiative participation into community. [7]

The social software took the realistic social relations as the foundation, simulated society's real interpersonal relationship network, brought a new pattern to social association, changed the way of knowledge disseminating, thus the gathering of knowledge and information became rather feasible and convenient. For example people may contact with each other promptly through IM, discover the network domain expert and what they pay attention to, or their research content through BLOG quickly, they may also promote the speed of information acquisition and renewal greatly by using the RSS news microreader. People can record fast, reorganize quickly and share simply on BLOG and WIKI, which favored the accumulation and sharing of knowledge; the social software may possibly become a kind of new media, form an interpersonal dissemination network. The social software perform the collection and fast dissemination of information through different participants, and the participants inform and are informed ,convince and are convinced through social software. [8]

3. Model design of social software applied in personal knowledge management

3.1 Present situation and characteristic of social software boosting personal knowledge management

Now the commonly used personal knowledge management tools include: iSpace Desktop (personal information management system), iNota (personal knowledge management), Mybase (documents resource management software), 360doc individual library (knowledge management and cooperation platform) and so on. The software have characteristic and function respectively, for example, the function modules iSpace Desktop provides include: Address book, documents management, knowledge classification, program record, program browsing and Blog and so on; The 360Doc personal library provides includes: knowledge management, association cooperation, and can produce the article abstract automatically, automatically establish the connection between content- correlation article, automatically recommends articles according to the cyberspace main body's collection interest, which used artificial intelligence technology based on the semantic understanding, These tools are serviceable, can satisfy the demand for personal carrying on the knowledge management.

The connotation of knowledge management includes: content, activity and value, its core is the knowledge activity, but the core of knowledge activity is knowledge process. Professor Ikujiro Nonaka and Tadeuchi, experts on knowledge manage in Japan thought that knowledge has formed a knowledge screw which grew unceasingly in the transformation of explicit knowledge and tacit knowledge; the knowledge will have the type transformation by processing socialization, externalization, combination and internalization. It is helpful for realizing the four processes by using social software.

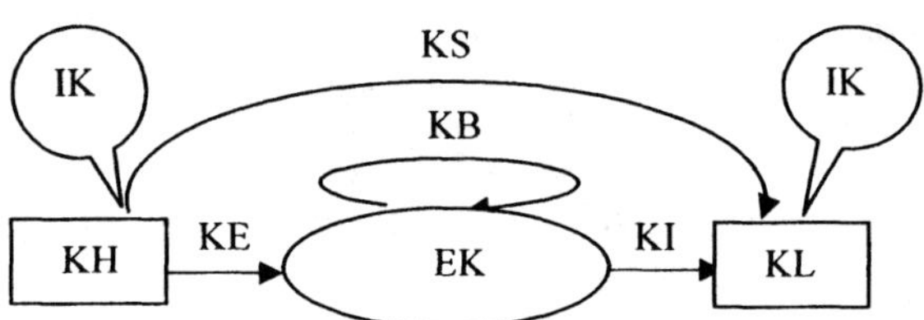

(EK= Explicit Knowledge   IK=Implicit Knowledge   KI=Knowledge Internalization KE=Knowledge Externalization KS=Knowledge Socialization
KB=Knowledge Combination KH=Knowledge Holder
KL=Knowledge Learner)
Fig 1. screwing theory of knowledge conversion

3.1.1 Knowledge Socialization

The knowledge socialization is a conversion process from tacit knowledge to tacit knowledge. Generally speaking people produced new tacit knowledge by sharing experience. The birth of social software enables the cyberspace main body to be able to establish virtual knowledge community, realize the knowledge socialization at a wider range. The individual can share the tacit knowledge by social software, and may pass them by observation, experience and practice. That Priest and disciple models, a new comer learn experience and skill from senior colleague, people make conversation or discussion about a main subject are all the typical way that individual shares tacit knowledge. Knowledge socialization is the beginning of knowledge creation, dissemination and sharing. People can share the experience that cyberspace main body accumulated among others by using social software, most of which is "only be possible to get an idea but cannot explain", they can communicate and discuss with each other freely, realize knowledge sharing and knowledge innovation.

3.1.2 Knowledge Externalization

Knowledge externalization is a conversion process from tacit knowledge to explicit knowledge. It mainly uses the method of analogy, metaphor and supposition, listening attentively as well as deep discussion to transform the tacit knowledge to an easily understanding form. The birth of social software, made this transformation more convenient, BBS, Blog and wiki can transform the knowledge that the individual accumulated for a long time and cannot be expressed by language, especially the knowledge that cannot be transferred at a large scale, to a principle and ordered knowledge that can be easily written down and easily learnt. We may save the different subject individual documents and information resource by classification in social software, build our knowledge library in practice, and may have inspiration and new understanding in the process of sharing and communication, thus realize knowledge innovation.

3.1.3 Knowledge Combination

Knowledge combination is a conversion process from explicit knowledge to explicit knowledge. It's a process of knowledge expansion, usually to make fragmentary explicit knowledge be further systematized and more complicated, form a huger explicit knowledge system. Combining the fragmentary knowledge, and expressing them with specialized language, is the combination process of knowledge. In the combination process, individual knowledge rise as collective knowledge, and may create value for more individuals. For instance we may collect, reorganize and learn knowledge from many origins, and find some new discoveries, thus obtain new knowledge. The main challenges in this process are: the massive knowledge is monopolized or hidden, it's difficult to search and integrate the knowledge existed in different medium. The social software may combine the knowledge by issuing, editing, estimating and discussing, causes knowledge to disseminate widely, achieves the goal of knowledge sharing, thus let the cyberspace main body form a higher value knowledge system.

3.1.4 Knowledge Internalization

Knowledge internalization is a conversion process from explicit knowledge to tacit knowledge. Internalization is a process the explicit knowledge are combined, assimilated by the individual, they use it in daily life and work or study, then transforms them to individual's new tacit knowledge, and presented it as the individual's ability. Enriching one's knowledge through reading massive books is a good example. Without doubt, social software provides a good supporting platform for knowledge internalization.

The knowledge process is climbing along the knowledge screw unceasingly, to achieve the goal of knowledge innovation. We can easily see it form the above analysis, using social software can promote knowledge gathering and processing, storing and accumulating, disseminating and sharing, expanding and innovating. The social software using process is a process that the explicit knowledge and tacit knowledge stimulate each other. Along with the unceasingly expansion of social group which established by social software, this process will move in circles, rise as screws, personnel's knowledge library will also be enriched and optimized unceasingly.

3.2 Model designing of social software applied in personal knowledge management

The construction learning theory believed that, learning is the process of meaning construction to exterior thing gradually when human interacts with them mutually. It emphasized on the students' initiative construction of knowledge, student's independence and innovation. The social software has provided exactly a very good platform for the construction learning way. The cyberspace main body will be able to integrate the study process and free communication through social software, gain each kind of dynamic informal knowledge quickly and conveniently.

The social software help people to establish the social network and the automatic organization and community, it can promote communication, exchange and cooperation between people's. After the influence software as QQ, email and BBS, Blog also grows like mushroom, according to the Xinhua News Agency reported ,up till now, the whole world Blog at present (network diary) reached 70,000,000; Every day increases about 120,000 equally, that is increasing 1.4 each second[9], the interpersonal network service Yiyou(www.yeeyoo.com) and Heiyou (www.heiyou.com) which based on the wireless correspondence and the Internet technology, rises rapidly and receives trillion web cam's favors. The social software has provided the friendly support for the study, it complements one another with the study occurrence and the knowledge transformation; It has opened up individuals' study space, brought more study resources and study channel, urges people to share the knowledge, stimulate knowledge innovation, raises the individual information-handling capacity and cooperation ability. The author has constructed personal knowledge management model based on social software as following.

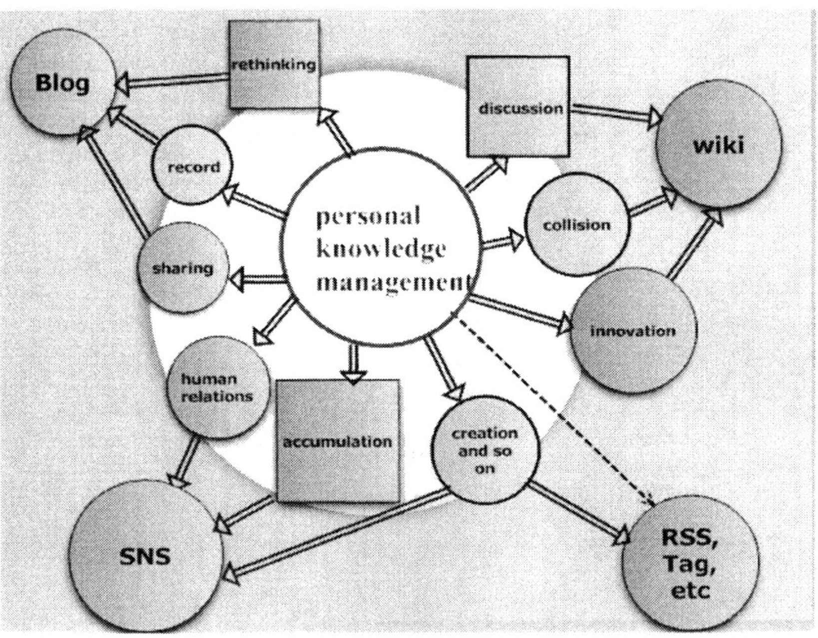

Fig 2. model of personal knowledge based on social software

Blog is a kind of running water recording form in the network, it can be easily used and quickly renewed, classify automatically and perform knowledge management;

its characteristic is sharing and interaction, spiritual sharing and communication demand is the two big backbones why Blog developed. Blog is the combination of individuation and sociality, so people can exhibit themselves and communicate with others freely. The realization of knowledge gaining, recording, sharing and reconsidering that personal knowledge management need may all get supported in Blog.

Wiki aims at the expansion and intensify on the identical subject; it mainly pursues the integrity, sufficiency and authority of information. Any cyberspace main body must comply with the subject wiki determined. The study individual may launch the discussion on some subject in wiki social group, by contrasting and analyzing the viewpoint of their own and other people, the original cognition structure of cyberspace main body will readjust and promote, and the individuals' knowledge will be supplemented and enriched, thus the new viewpoint will burgeon. In the process of collision and communication of thought, the cyberspace main body may carry on the management to their personal knowledge effectively.

SNS is a kind of social network service, mainly used for managing personal relationship. We generally thought the learning activity occurred only when going to school or taking regular training. In fact some experts' studies indicated that, in human's knowledge growth or the occurrence of learning activity, only 20% knowledge occurs in the formal study process, 80% occurs in the informal study process. Such as chatting with friends, watching movies, glancing over some homepages through the network and so on, all these are informal learning activities. The cyberspace main body can manage personal relationships through SNS, expand the knowledge origin, thus the occurrence of informal study will be more simple and frequent, and the individual knowledge library will also be enriched.

Except for these, we also may carry on knowledge storage and creation through other social software like RSS, Tag and so on. To summary, the social software enables the cyberspace main body to be able to participate in the study initiatively, extract the resources of specialized knowledge effectively, cooperate positively, obtain the newest information promptly; It can also promote the personality development, let them experience success, share joy, improve individual's learning capability and cognition ability better, it is apt to form the innovation thought, thus enhance the efficiency of personal knowledge management.

4 Epilogues

There are many successful cases that the social software used in personal knowledge management[11].The social software constructed a learning environment centered on individual. The cyberspace main body writes, records, thinks, enjoys, studies, creates through social software, they can have initiative participation, carry on cooperation learning with other people, integrate in the social group, become the master of learning, this initiative and enthusiastic learning process can promote personal knowledge management quite well. Of course, there are some challenges that we must face, such as how we can fast go to the appropriate information, how we can convert between study and practice; these are the tactic problems of personal knowledge management.

References:

1. J. Frand and C. Hixon, "Personal Knowledge Management: Who, What, Why, When, Where, How?" Dec.1999. Available in
http://www.anderson.ucla.edu/faculty/jason.frand/researcher/speeches/PKM.htm
2. K. Li, "Some fundamental concept on personal knowledge management", Available in [DB/OL].http://www.blogchina.com/new/display/15977.html,2003-11-09.
3. L.L. Fever. "Defining Social Software [EB/OL]", Available in
http://www.leelefever.com/archives/000143html,2003-06-04.
4. S. Boyd. "Are You Ready for Social Software?". *Darwinmagazine*,2003,(5).
5. X.L. Zhang, S.G. Liu,"Embrace2004 social software year".*China Educational Technology*,2004,(5).
6.7.8 "Blog science and technology channel special, How far is the spring of social software?" Available in http://tech.blogchina.com/special_topic/ss/2005-03-24/1111635795.html
9. "Dragon race alliance, forumsharing world"
 http://www.chinadforce.com/viewthread.php?tid=700136
10. "superiority analysis on knowledge management based on Blog",
http://www.360doc.com/showWeb/0/0/247893.aspx
11. "My personal knowledge management",
http://www.360doc.com/showWeb/0/0/390482.aspx
12. Q.W. Wang, B.C. Zhao, "Application research of Blog used in teachers' personal konwledge management", *Transaction of Yanbei normal school*,2006.5
13. P.F. Ma, J.J. Zhang, "Application explore of Blog used in personal knowledge management", Available in DB/OL].http://zcwbluesky.bokee.com/3021319.html,2005-09-24.
14. S.H. Hu, X.D. Wang , "Application explore of Blog used in educational teaching" .*Distance Education*,2004,(01):23-26.
15. Y.C. Gan, "Personal knowledge management in e-learning", *China Educational Technology*, 2003.6
16. Z.T. Zhu, *Make use of Internet educational resource*, higher education press, 2001
17. H.B. Zhang, Z.H. Shen, "On personal knowledge management", *Theory and practice of library*,2004.1
18. X.L. Zhuang, "How the social software change the way of learning and knowledge diffusing?"
Available in http://pkuer.net/wmkj/study2/SocialSoftware/3/13.htm

The Design And Implementing Of Collaborative Learning On Internet Curriculum Development

Chengling Zhao, Li Lin
Information Technology Department Central China Normal University,
Wuhan, Hubei, 430079
E-MAIL: zhcling@mail.ccnu.edu.cn
E-MAIL: linli_198288@163.com

Abstract: In the distant education, the learning of internet curriculum is widespread concerned by people. In order to promote internet curriculum learning, completing task cooperatively is the effective learning manner. In this article, writer expounds the concept of collaborative learning, and explains the implementing structural flow diagram of collaborative learning on internet curriculum. At last, writer analyzes the practice steps on collaborative learning concretely which are based on *The expanding of Junior middle school scientific curriculum*.

With the development of informational society, the core technique of modern distant education by multimedia and internet is the new mode of education, also is widespread accepted by people. When we talk about modern distant education, it's naturally to reflect internet education. The learning of internet curriculum also becomes the most important part of distant education. The superiority of internet is communication and interchange, and collaborative learning is just right embodying it. The writer just concisely expounds the collaborative learning on internet curriculum and analyzes the practice steps on collaborative learning concretely which is based on 《The expanding of Junior middle school scientific curriculum》 .

1 Collaborative learning and collaborative learning with internet environment

Constructivism theories of learning deem: learning is the process that learners initiatively construct innate psychology characteristic in the mutual mechanism of learners and environment. This theory puts emphasis on regarding learner as the

Please use the following format when citing this chapter:

Zhao, C., Lin, L., 2007, in IFIP International Federation for Information Processing, Volume 252, Integration and Innovation Orient to E-Society Volume 2, eds. Wang, W., (Boston: Springer), pp. 355-363.

centre, and thinks that "situation", "cooperate ", "conversation" and "resource" is the basic element and character in the constructivism learning environment. Moreover collaborative learning is developed at the base of this theory. [1]

1.1 Collaborative learning

In the information society, people have put forward higher requirement to quality. Constructivism is just the basic theory of collaborative learning. In the process of collaborative learning, the learners are just through interchange and communication with partners and teachers to obtain knowledge. In this way, they can achieve the further comprehension of question and knowledge, thus let the knowledge storage in the cerebrum long-term. Collaborative learning is a teaching method that some students finish the learning through group. Between the learners, they have the harmonious relationship, corporate attitude, and they share the information and resources, undertake to study the task together. Only in this way, they can achieve the common learning target. It can say: collaborative learning is the corporate process, also is the process to emerge the personal glamour.

1.2 Collaborative learning in the internet environment

Collaborative learning at the base of internet is the process. It uses computer internet, multimedia and other relative technique. In this process, most learners aim directly at the same learning task to interchange and cooperate with each other to attain the further understanding and grasping the teaching content. [2]

In the learning of internet curriculum, communication between teachers and learners, and learners with each other need internet. Now the roles of teachers are resources designers, teaching mentors and evaluator. Teaching tasks' allocation and clarification, and teaching processes' control can be supported by computer internet.

From the knowledge of collaborative learning and the view of learning, we can divide the collaborative learning on internet curriculum into four steps: analyzing learners' characteristic, grouping, processing of learning and evaluating. The mode of it also has: competition, cooperation, partner, designer and role playing. People who learn about internet curriculum are in the different direction. In order to finish the same learning task corporately, they can discuss and learn with groups at the environment of computer internet. In the process, the groups can share the information with other learners that they explore in the learning process.

2 Collaborative learning in the internet curriculum exploitation

The study of internet curriculum is mainly on individual learning. In order to attain good learning effect and grasp more knowledge, Internet curriculum can launch collaborative learning.

2.1 The character of internet curriculum

(1)Can't control by the time and space

Because the internet curriculum is on the Internet, and can be obtained whenever and wherever possible through the terminal station of the network, so the learners can study on time unrestrictedly. The learners who are in the different time and space can study with their own needing. Even if the internet curriculum is synchronous teaching, the learners are also free on space. Carrying on asynchronous teaching, the learner has the larger degree of freedom on the time and space.

(2) Resource sharing

Internet teaching resource is different from the traditional one. It takes books, newspapers and periodicals, tape, broadcast, TV, etc. as material carrier. Internet education resource is a kind of digitized resource taking electronic network as carriers and media of transmitting. These resources are suitable for network users' visiting at any time, and needn't be influenced by carrier quantity information like traditional education.

(3) Easy to cooperation

The study of internet curriculum may not be restricted by space-time to interchange and discuss. Also it can also utilize the appropriate software tool to support and create in coordination. A lot of online education platforms can support learners to carry on exchanging and information sharing.

(4) Multi-way interaction

Under this multi-way interactive, from the viewpoint of students, we can make use of the network resource to study and produce interaction on one hand; On the other hand can talk with teachers, companions, experts and produce interaction through the resources of network.

2.2 Collaborative learning in the internet curriculum exploitation

(1) Cultivating the habit of learning, and guaranteeing the teaching effect

Bring up the ability of students' study independently should run through all the study process. But, because of the influence by the long-term exam-oriented education, a lot of students in our country get used to studying passively, and get used to teachers' inculcating to study. When they enter into university, students can't adapt to the new network teaching form of study independently. And this situation has influenced the results of learning seriously. In order to help students to change this study method, collaborative learning plays a good transition role. It enables students to train the habit of independent study in the course of studying in coordination, and strengthen the ability of independent study progressively. [3]

(2) Breaching the limitation, and extruding interaction

For the single student, his learning ability, knowledge level has some limitation. When they meet the obstacle in the learning of internet curriculum, they'll spend a lot of time and energy on overcoming them even if they can work hard to overcome. But collaborative learning can just make up the limitation of individual study. Through collaborative learning, learners will cooperate with each other, learn from other's strong point to offset one's weakness, and interchange with each other to overcome the learning difficulty corporately. In this way, learners can learn more useful knowledge faster and finer. Even more, if let individual study as the unique learning method in the internet curriculum. On one hand, it can be short of communication with students and teachers, also, between students. As that situation, learners will be in their own thinking range long-term and won't obtain more information and train of thought extensively. On the other hand, individual study long-term may lead to learning tiredness, and now the request of learning target may not be finished on time and quality. In the environment of collaborative learning, students have more and more interchange and communicate with teachers also with each other. It makes the significance constructive coming true from easy to complicate in the learning as learners of the center. It promotes the learners to study finer. Not only cultivate the students' thinking ability, the ability of studying on one's own, also it is helpful to promote the corporate spirit of the students. It's useful to promote the development of students' high perception and the shaping of healthy sentiment.

3 The design and implementing of collaborative learning in the internet curriculum exploitation

3.1 Design of collaborative learning in the internet curriculum exploitation

According to the teaching requirement of implementing of collaborative learning on internet curriculum, I provide brief implementing flow diagram in coordination. The following Fig. 1 shows.

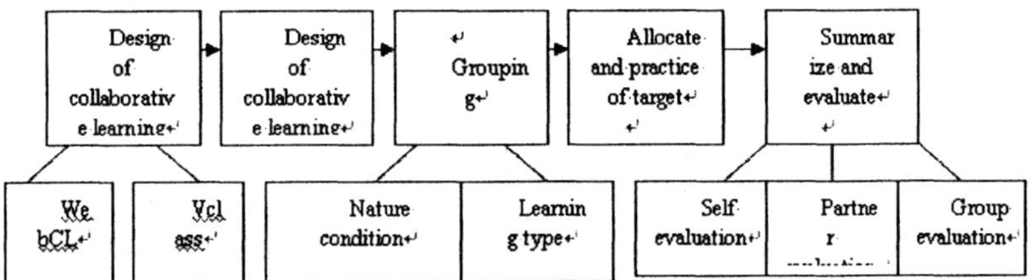

Fig. 1

In the near future, we have been finished the curriculum 《The expanding of junior middle school scientific curriculum》 .It can be the case of collaborative learning on internet curriculum. The purpose of this curriculum is to promote the teacher's lifetime study, and offer abundant resources for the teachers in the middle and primary schools of learning and teaching, and offer the theory and practice for the first line teachers who are engaged in teaching of course of 《Science》 .Through learning the resources of this curriculum, teachers can understand how to teach 《Science》 well and really grasp the teaching method of scientific knowledge. In this way, they can adapt to the teaching of 《Science》 as soon as possible, and improve self's specialization level. In order to implementing teaching in the 《Science》 , teachers, in the different area, have the necessity of launching collaborative learning.

This course has five units, analyze of curriculum standard and teaching material, expand of the life science field knowledge, expand of the matter science field knowledge, expand of the earth, the universe and space science field knowledge, and research of the science studies method.

The learning of this curriculum, (Fig. 2) we can adopt the scheme of individual learning. But in order to let teachers implement teaching quickly, collaborative learning can improve the target coming true.

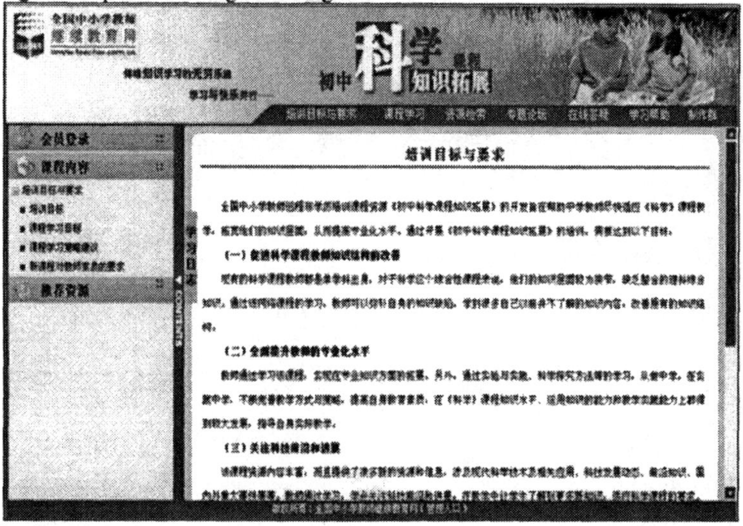

Fig. 2

3.2 The implementing of collaborative learning in the internet curriculum exploitation

Next, we will give the practice steps concretely and analyze briefly of collaborative learning which is based on 《The expanding of junior middle school scientific curriculum》.

（1）Design of collaborative learning

In order to collaborate to learn on internet curriculum, it needs the corporate learning environment based on network. Also it's the corporate environment that draw assistance from computer with distributing handling technique, multimedia technique, database technique, correspondence technique and network technique. The Web-based Cooperative learning that advanced by Ronghuai Huang in his doctor thesis of Beijing Normal University can be this environment. So it is Vclass. With the development of technology, it appears some assistant method to support interchange activity, for example, E-mail, BBS, ICQ. The fourth generation of interchanging method Blogging also becomes the good helper to launch collaborative learning.

In this course, the blogging(Fig.3) in the special subject forum provides a very good exchanging platform and material base for studying in coordination. It can be the bridge and passage of the exchanging between with students and teachers, also between students.

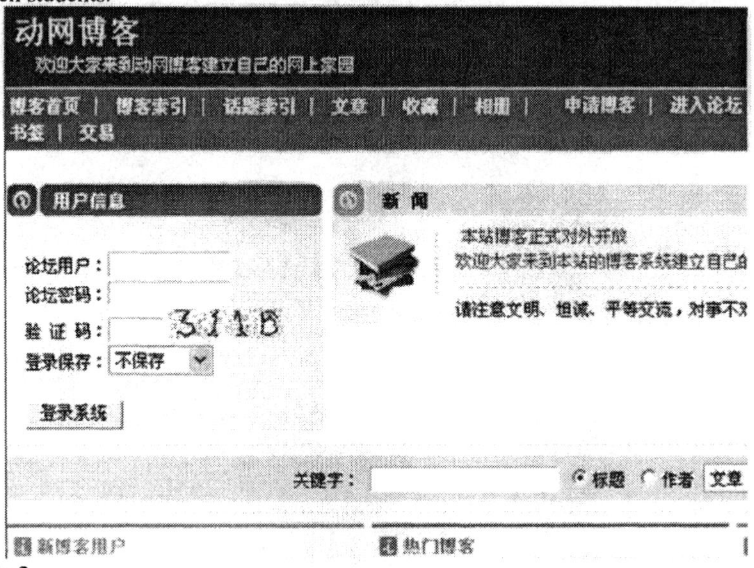

Fig.3

（2）Establish of learning target

Learning target is the prerequisite of learning, also is the navigation. Of course, not all of the internets curriculums are adapt to collaborate to learn. It needs teachers to choose some suitable contents, which depending on the teaching target and students' development situation to define the overall target. Then teachers resolve it and allocate the assignment to each student.

In the 《The expanding of Junior middle school scientific curriculum》, analyze of curriculum standard and teaching material, expand of the life science field knowledge, expand of the matter science field knowledge, expand of the earth, the universe and space science field knowledge, and research of the science studies method are the main composing of the special subject forum. Every thesis has small discussion topics.(Fig.4) In the training goal and requirement, we give the learning requirement concretely.

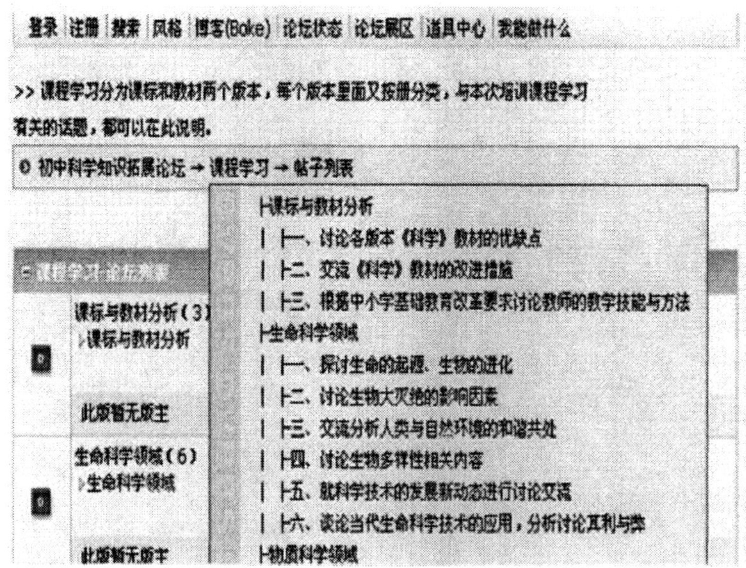

Fig.4

（3）Grouping

The process of grouping makes the learners the single condition into the corporate one .It has some restriction of group. Firstly, it depends on the character of nature condition. [4] Learners on the network have different from region, age, the structure of knowledge learning. Getting this information can through questionnaire, answer questions and so on. We can allocate reasonably as the learners have more difference, so that they can make progress together in the corporate discussing. Secondly, it depends on the character of learning type. [4] It means the learning habit and perception characteristic. In the group of collaborative learning, it can let the students with different type in the same learning group, that it's good for learners interchange and self-identity with each other. At the same time, grouping should base on learning content. Let the learners who are adapting to study the same learning content in the same group. This manner is helpful for them to grasp and absorb knowledge.

In the process of learning, teachers can go into the forums according to their own needing. So they can interchange and communicate with other learners, in order to reach the deeper understanding of the knowledge. Also they can be leaded with expert, and be grouped according to there area and their teaching subject.

（4）Allocate and practice of target

The allocation of corporate target should consider every members' characteristic, and bring into full play of their own good points. It needs for them to know their important in the grouping and increase their own feeling of responsibility. After allocating the target, the members should go their own way, and undertake their own learning target. They can search the documents through network, read, analyze, organization the date, then shape their own view and share with other members in the group. Through online to discuss and study to obtain knowledge.

When every teacher makes sure the group, they can choose the target according to their own predominance. It's also the learning target that the learners should be taken on and the knowledge that the learners should be interchanged and communicated with each other in the collaborative learning. In this process, all learners ought to realize the significance in the collaborative learning and give the practice steps according to the learning target. Then form self cognition and understanding of that part knowledge in the step-by-step accumulation. In this way, the learners can interchange and communicate with other learners.

（5）Summarize and evaluate

Evaluation is the important step of collaborative learning. The more evaluation has, the bigger progress will make. The content of evaluation is from the learning target's finishing situation and corporate situation of the learners on the collaborative learning. It should not only evaluate the results of learning, but also process of learning. In the group of collaborative learning, it can have self-evaluation, partner evaluation and group evaluation. Of course, the teachers should instruct the evaluation process. The evaluation of collaborative learning should from more directions. And performance of the personal task, behavior while cooperating, expression and discussing in the achievement showing should bring into the evaluation index system. [5]

Summarizing and evaluating are the most important part in the collaborative learning. In the learning of 《The expanding of Junior middle school scientific curriculum》, summarizing and evaluating are the important stage to promote the personal knowledge level and form the studying experience. Finishing the learning, the learners that are the teachers who learn the curriculum should self evaluate first. In the learning page, it has study daily record button rolling with the page. Clicking the mouse can see that button. (Fig.5)

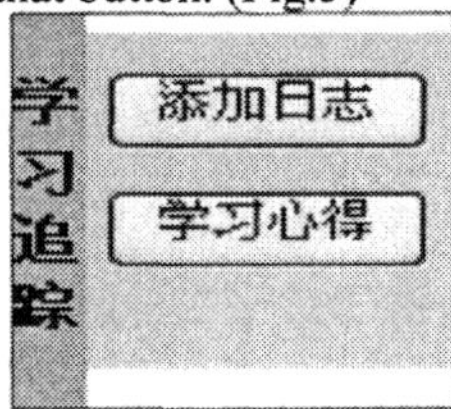

Fig.5

This part notes the learning situation of the learners. It can be the good basis and reference in the self evaluation. Next it's the partner evaluation. It's the communication with the partner after learning. It's helpful to absorb knowledge and accumulate experience for learners. Last, in the group of collaborative learning, there has the necessity to launch group evaluation. In this process, we usually consider the learners' contribution in the group and whether the learners can share the learning target with other learners or not. It's also the interchange and communication situation with the members. All the evaluation can be come true in the forum.

4 Conclusion

Modern distant education is the new teaching method in the informational society. Internet curriculum is the most important part in the distant education. Corporation in the internet curriculum becomes the effective learning method based on the character of internet curriculum. Collaborative learning in the internet curriculum exploitation is cultivating the habit of learning by oneself and guaranteeing the teaching effect. Also it offsets the shortage of individual study in the internet curriculum learning, and extrudes the interaction and communication. Writer gives the five steps implementing flow diagram, and analyze the implementing concretely based on the 《The expanding of junior middle school scientific curriculum》. It's useful for the actualization of collaborative learning on the internet curriculum. The students launching the learning on the internet are the process of exhibiting one's strong suit, also the process of promoting one's integration ability. So the implementing of collaborative learning on internet curriculum should be the focus for us.

References

1. Kekang He. *Instructional Technology*. Publishing house of Beijing Normal University (2002).
2. Yanping Wang. Design of the cooperating virtual learning environment of network . *Education technology guide*, 2006,(7).
3. Gang Peng. Individual learning and collaborative learning on network teaching . *Education technology guide*, 2006,(7).
4. Fei Dong. The collaborative learning research of adult studies based on network . *China's adult education*,2006, (6).
5. Qiuhong Geng. The discussion of collaborative learning environment based on network. *Science and Education Information*, 2006,(9).

eGovGrid: A Service-Grid-Based Framework for E-Government Interoperability

Dongju Yang, Yanbo Han, and Jinhua Xiong
Research Centre for Grid and Service Computing,
Institute of Computing Technology, Chinese Academy of Sciences,
100080 Beijing, China
{yangdongju, yhan, xjh}@ict.ac.cn
WWW home page: http://vega.ict.ac.cn

Abstract. Interoperability has been regarded as a major issue in implementing e-Government systems. In this paper, a service grid based framework for the interoperability – eGovGrid, is proposed, which facilitates "horizontal" resource sharing and interoperability among "vertical" e-Government subsystems. Key concepts and technologies include an ontology-based e-Government service metadata model, a service repository serving as a virtual pool of heterogeneous e-Government services, and corresponding architecture. The effectiveness of eGovGrid in constructing e-Government systems is demonstrated with a real case.

1   Introduction

Resource integration and interoperation among different government departments are of key importance for today's e-Government systems, in which information systems from different departments need to be integrated. There are two factors that hinder direct interconnection and interoperation. One is resource heterogeneity with diversity in resource formats, runtime environments, programming languages, interface contracts, etc. The other is semantic ambiguity, which results in misunderstanding among different information systems. Therefore, an e-government framework must be based on an open architecture, encapsulating heterogeneous resources with unified interface, logically centralizing and unified managing these resources, supporting interoperability based on semantic infrastructure, and let end-users use dynamic resources in secure, transparent, flexible and uniform environments.

Please use the following format when citing this chapter:

Yang, D., Han, Y., Xiong, J., 2007, in IFIP International Federation for Information Processing, Volume 252, Integration and Innovation Orient to E-Society Volume 2, eds. Wang, W., (Boston: Springer), pp. 364-372.

There are two kinds of approaches addressing e-government interoperability: one is based on semantic web or semantic driven [2,3,4,5], another one is based on cross-organizational workflow [6,7,8,9]. But most of the above works just provide basis or general ideas for the development of e-Government system, and are lack of operational instructions, a solid framework, related data models or software infrastructure to address the problems in an e-Government environment.

Service grid [11], a kind of combination of grid computing [10] and SOA technologies, helps to open up a new way for cross-organizational resources integrating and collaboration in e-government. Service grid technologies can be used to build the platform for resource sharing in e-government systems, and also bring new features of better reusability, flexibility and scalability.

Consequently we proposed a service-grid-based framework for e-government interoperability, named eGovGrid, which targets at facilitating resource sharing among "horizontal" organizations and interoperability among "vertical" e-Government subsystems. Hereinafter, "horizontal" means cross-organizational application, and "vertical" means information system within one organization. In eGovGrid, an ontology-based service metadata model is proposed. A service repository serving as a virtual pool of distributed e-Government services takes this model as basis. The key technologies are implemented and demonstrated in an e-government application of a city in southern China. As a result, seven departments, two counties and five companies have already been interconnected; then resource sharing and exchange are enabled. The preliminary result illustrates that: the eGovGrid framework enables interoperability among the above organizations; heterogeneous resources can be integrated dynamically and effectively.

2 Architecture of eGovGrid

The traditional pattern of "information center" adopts centralized data storage, which can not easily adapt to an open e-government environment due to non real-time update and high cost for management and maintenance of centralized data. Web services provide a loosely-coupled mechanism to encapsulate resources with standardized interfaces, which enables users to plug in/out resources dynamically. Users only need to use Web services, don't need to concern, manage, and maintain resource objects behind the Web services. However, there are several challenges needed to be addressed when using Web services. First, WSDL is used to describe implemental interface of Web services without semantic, which results in that the services are hard understood by end users, and interoperation between services are not easy to be achieved. So an end-user-understandable service metadata model is required. Second, UDDI severs as a discovery service for the WSDL descriptions. It can not work well with changing models.

Motivated by the above challenges, we proposed "business service" as an abstraction of Web services at business level. An ontology-based service metadata model is proposed to describe business services to achieve user-understandability and interoperability, and service repository serves as a virtual resource pool to enable resources physically distributed storage and logically centralized management. The service repository is responsible for creation, organization, and management of business services, and provides a unified service directory for service browsing and search. A service runtime environment is also provided for services discovery and invoking. The architecture of e-government applications is illustrated in Fig. 1.

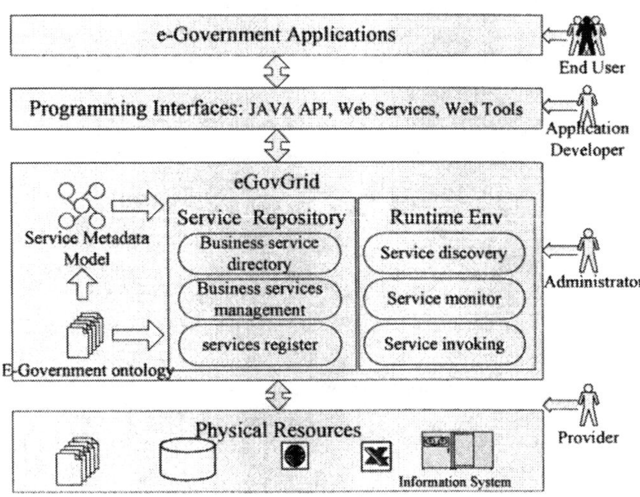

Fig. 1. Architecture of eGovGrid

2.1 Business service and its metadata model

Business service is the business-level abstraction of Web services to achieve user-centric understandability and interoperability. Business service needs to be browsed and searched by end users, support interoperability between applications, and be executed to access the behind physical resources. It is necessary to monitor services status and analyze their usage and quality to provide statistical data to users. Furthermore, appropriate authority is necessary in order to prevent misuse of services. And an extensible metadata model is helpful to build flexible and adaptable application.

OWL-S [12] and WSDL-S [13] are two notable service description languages to describe semantic Web services. However, OWL-S aims at automatic Web service composition and interoperation by describing the prerequisites and consequences of application of individual services, which makes it too complex to use; WSDL-S is an extension of WSDL, and its emphasis is still to describe implementation interface of services. So these two languages are not suitable for business service description. Another wide-used resource metadata model is Dublin Core Metadata Element Set [14], which is a set of vocabulary of fifteen properties used for resource property description. But DC focuses only on for information resources, such as a book in digital library, and not suitable for business services.

Motivated by the above requirements our service metadata model takes E-Government ontology as basis and comprises six facets, illustrated in Fig. 2. Hereinafter, e-Government ontology is described by OWL [1] and aims at normatively describing basic concepts, relationships between objects, and interfaces in e-Government application. It can provide the vocabulary base for referring to the terms in certain subject areas, and the logical statements [15]. E-Government ontology can define the metadata elements (leaf nodes in the model), define the value range of one metadata elements, and describe the relationships of metadata elements, so as to facilitate the metadata model more clear and accurate without misunderstanding, and support model evolution based on ontology reasoning.

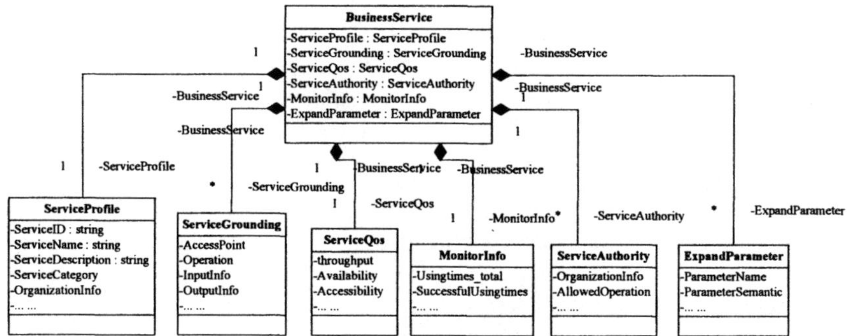

Fig. 2. Service metadata model

- ServiceProfile is to describe the basic properties of a service, such as service name, description, organization info (provider), service category, etc. which helps end users to know what it is.

- ServiceGrounding is to describe the implementation properties of a service, such as access point, operation, input, and output. The latter three items must be specified with semantic annotation to identify their relationships, so as to enable interconnection and interoperation of services. A BusinessService may have more than one ServiceGrounding, which indicates that many Web services can implement this business service. ServiceGrounding is used for service addressing and invoking.

- ServiceQos is to describe the QOS of a service, such as throughput, availability, accessibility, etc. which is used for service evaluation.

- MonitorInfo is to describe the usage of a service and give some statistical data, such as using times and successful using times within some periods, which is used for service evaluation.

- ServiceAuthority is to describe which organizations have authorities to use the service and which operations are allowed. Then manager of the organization can assign her/his authority to other users within organizations. So an authority chain is produced. ServiceAuthority is the important properties to prevent misuse of services.

- ExpandParameter is to describe the additional properties of services, which may be required in some contexts, such as price, available time, etc. ExpandParameter is used to achieve extensibility and adaptability.

The values of the above metadata elements may be filled out in three ways. The first is that providers describe some service properties during registration, such as ServiceProfile, ServiceQos, and ServiceAuthority. The second is that the information system automatically parses the WSDL file to fill out some properties, such as ServiceGrounding. The last one is that service runtime environment provides and modifies some properties by analyzing the usage of services, such as MonitorInfo and ServiceQos.

Compared with other existing service metadata model [12,13,16], the major contribution is that our service metadata model includes not only static but also dynamic properties, such as service usage and service quality. Authority property is also brought into model. All of these properties ensure integrity of the services information and make services use and management easy.

2.2 Service repository

Service repository aims at building a centralized services pool, to enable registration, unified management, and discovery of business services. It brings out a lot of challenges when adopting service repository to build application.

First, a service repository is taken as the basis to build various applications with different requirements. One unified metadata model may be not enough to describe all kinds of services clearly, so multiple service metadata models in one repository are necessary. We take the previous service metadata model as core metadata model. Each metadata model in service repository is an extension of core metadata model. Therefore, our service repository can satisfy requirements of different applications with extension mechanism, and enable interoperability among different services with core metadata and its ontology basis.

Second, when registering a service into the service repository, the provider should select the appropriate service metadata model and fill out each metadata element. It is a challenging task for the provider to associate proper semantic annotation to the value. How to quickly locate the proper ontology classes or properties from semantic database is the major issue. Our approach is to automatically recommend the proper ontology classes and properties according to the context based on initial recommendation mechanism.

Third, the effectively organizing and managing services are necessary to facilitate service browsing, querying and discovery. In service repository, an ontology-based taxonomy is built, so that services can be aligned with trees with many roots according to their categories and relationships defined in ontology base.

Finally, an end-user friendly tool is required for services browsing, querying and invoking. A service directory supports users to browse services from different views. Furthermore, service query language enables flexible query of services, which is similar to SQL in database. A runtime engine enables service parsing and addressing, and then submits the invoking requirements to runtime environment, and acquires the result in synchronous or asynchronous way.

Based on the service repository, cross-organizational e-government applications can be constructed to enable unified management of services, without concerning heterogeneous and distributed resources behind of services. The service repository also supports direct access to business services, which will be dynamically bound (interpret) to corresponding physical resources.

3 Applications

In recent years Chinese government are experiencing the transformation from management-oriented government to service-oriented government. In order to provide more convenient services to citizens and companies, government must effectively organize internal and external resources on-demand. eGovGrid took the real requirements from a southern China city, and has already been partly demonstrated in an e-Government system project of the city. The goal of this project is to build a virtual resource center to enable integration of all resources distributed in multiple departments and transparent access to these resources in a unified way.

Aiming at the above goal, a resources interoperation platform with virtual resource center is implemented. Seven departments, five companies, and two counties are taken as demonstration units to exchange economic information via this platform.

First, by analyzing business requirements, existed or new e-Government ontology is imported or created to build semantic infrastructure. There are two kinds of services related to economic information exchange. One is information retrieving service, which encapsulates information resources for retrieving, and another one is information transaction service, which encapsulates information system for more operations, such as updating, analyzing, etc. Accordingly, two kinds of service metadata models are designed. One is for information retrieving service and emphasizes on description of on-behind information resources; another is for information transaction service and emphasizes on description of service operation.

Second, over thirty information retrieving services and information transaction services are registered into the virtual resource center. The description contents are based on the above two service models.

Based on service directory, users can browse services in multiple views, or query services by service query language. They can submit their request for service invoking, so as to transparently access to physical resources.

Interoperability is easily achieved when constructing virtual resource center with eGovGrid. The following is a comparison of the processes of exchange information with and without eGovGrid support (Fig. 3). Without eGovGrid, the process could be divided into several steps: an end user brings forward requirements; a provider exports data from the original information system; the provider sends data to the end user; the end user checks the data; the end user imports the data to the target information system. If there are multiple exchange requirements, the process needs to be repeated multiple times. Now with eGovGrid support, the exchange information process is divided into two stages: "preparation state" and "exchange stage". In "preparation stage", end users and providers share their read and write interface of information system. When information needs to be exchanged, end user retrieves and connects two services (read interface from other system and write interface to own system) to form a process, and then invokes the process to finish information exchanging. If there are multiple exchange requirements only the second stage needs to be repeated.

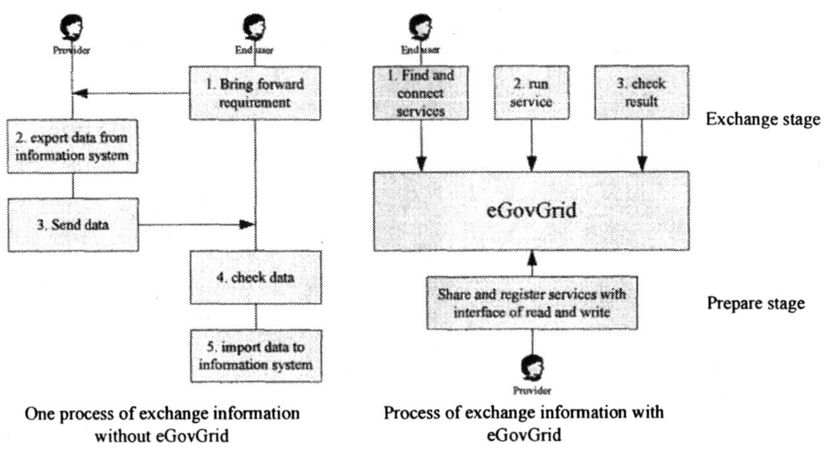

Fig. 3. Comparison of exchange information process, without and with eGovGrid support

Furthermore, resources are logically centralized management without changing physical storage and the maintenance is undertaken by each provider. Resource can be plug in/out dynamically. Extensibility is also achieved, including organization extension, user extension, services extension, service metadata model extension etc.

4 Conclusions

eGovGrid proposed in the paper is a useful trial. It facilitates "horizontal" resource sharing and interoperability among "vertical" e-Government subsystems. Key concepts and technologies include ontology-based e-Government service metadata model, a service repository, i.e. a virtual pool of heterogeneous e-Government services, and corresponding architecture. The effectiveness of eGovGrid in constructing e-Government systems is demonstrated with a real case in a southern China city.

Many important issues are still work-in-progress, which include how to deal with various loads of concurrent requests for service at peak times, how to deal with application change, how to build the appropriate ontology at runtime, how to deal with authority and security, etc.

Acknowledge

This paper is supported by the National Natural Science Foundation of China under Grant No. 70673098, National Basic Research Program of China (973 Program) under Grant No. 2007CB310805 and Open Funding of SKLSE of China under Grant No. SKLSE05-08.

References

1. OWL Web Ontology Language Guide, Michael K. Smith, Chris Welty, and Deborah L. McGuinness, Editors, W3C Recommendation, 10 February 2004, http://www.w3.org/TR/2004/REC-owl-guide-20040210/ . Latest version available at http://www.w3.org/TR/owl-guide/.
2. R. Klischewski. Semantic Web for e-Government. *Proceedings of EGOV* 2003.
3. Luis 'Alvarez Sabucedo and Luis Anido Rif'on, A Proposal for a Semantic-Driven eGovernment Service Architecture, EGOV 2005, LNCS 3591, pp. 237–248, 2005.
4. Witold Staniszkis, Edyta Kałka, Grzegorz Nittner, Eliza Staniszkis, and Jakub Strychowski, *Integration of Pre-existing Heterogeneous Information Sources in a Knowledge Management System*, EGOV 2004, LNCS 3183, pp. 507–514, 2004.
5. Matti Järvenpää, Maiju Virtanen, Airi Salminen, *Semantic Portal for Legislative Information.*, EGOV 2006, LNCS 4084, pp. 219-230, 2006
6. D. Gouscos, G. Mentzas & P. Georgiadis, PASSPORT : A Novel Architectural Model for the Provision of Seamless Cross-Border e-Government Services, 12th International Conference on Database and Expert Systems Applications (DEXA 2001), Munich, September 2001, *IEEE Computer Society Press*, pp. 318–322.
7. Giannis Verginadis, Dimitris Gouscos, Maria Legal, Gregoris Mentzas, An Architecture for Integrating. *Heterogeneous Administrative Services. into One-Stop e-Government, the eChallenges 2003 Conference, Bologna.*
8. Euripidis Loukis and Spyros Kokolakis, Computer Supported Collaboration in citizens Sector: The ICTE-PAN Project, EGOV 2003, LNCS 2739, pp. 181–186, 2003.
9. D. Gouscos, G. Laskaridis, D. Lioulias, G. Mentzas & P. Georgiadis, An Approach to Offering One-Stop e-Government Services: Available Technologies and Architectural Issues, e-Government: *State of the Art and Perspectives Conference* (EGOV 2002), Aix-en-Provence, September 2002.
10. Foster, I., C. Kesselman, and S. Tuecke, The Anatomy of the Grid: Enabling Scalable Virtual Departments. *International J. Supercomputer Applications*, 2001. 15(3)
11. Weissman, J.B. and B.-D. Lee, The Service Grid: Supporting Scalable Heterogeneous Services in Wide-Area Networks. In Proc. of Symp. *Applications and the Internet*, San Diego, CA, 2001: p. 95-104.

12. Coalition, O.S.: Owl-s: Semantic markup for Web services. Web available (2005)
http://www.daml.org/services/owl-s/1.1/.
13. Rama Akkiraju, Joel Farrell, John Miller, Meenakshi Nagarajan, Marc-Thomas Schmidt,
Amit Sheth, Kunal Verma, Web service Semantics - WSDL-S,
http://www.w3.org/Submission/WSDL-S/
14. Dublin Core Metadata Element Set, Version 1.1, http://dublincore.org/documents/dces/
15. Antoniou G, Harmelen F. A semantic web primer[M]. The MIT Press, 2004.
16. Broekstra, J., Ehrig, M., Haase, P., van Harmelen, F., Kampman, A., Sabou, M., Siebes, R.,
Staab, S., Stuckenschmidt, H., and Tempich, C. A metadata model for semantics-based peer-
to-peer systems. *In Proceedings of the 1st Workshop on Semantics in Peer-to-Peer and Grid
Computing at the 12th International World Wide Web Conference*. Budapest, Hungary. 2003.

Information Specificity Vulnerability: Comparison of Medication Information Flows in Different Health Care Units

Eeva Aarnio[1] and Reetta Raitoharju[2]

1 Turku School of Economics, Information Systems Science,
Rehtorinpellonkatu 3, FI-20500 Turku, Finland
eeva.aarnio@tse.fi

2 Turku School of Economics, Information Systems Science,
Rehtorinpellonkatu 3, FI-20500 Turku, Finland
reetta.raitoharju@tse.fi

Abstract. Information on patient's medication is often vital especially when patient's condition is critical. However, the information does not yet move freely between different health care units and organizations. Before reaching the point of putting into practice any system that makes the inter-organizational medication information transmission possible, some prerequisites and characteristics of the information in different user organization should be defined. There are for instance units with different level of urgency and data/information intensity (e.g. emergency department vs. medical floor). The higher the urgency level, the more vulnerable the medication information flow is to different discontinuation situations. As a conceptual framework, a scoring system based on the asset specificity in the transaction cost theory and previous literacy on information flows of different health care units is created to define the vulnerability of the information flows. As there is a national medication database under planning, the scoring system could be used to assess the prerequisites for the medication database in Finland.

1 Introduction

The success of patient care is dependent on the availability of the appropriate information when needed. To be able to provide successful patient care it is essential to understand what effects technologies and work practices have on movement of information [1]. There are differences between the different health care units when it comes to the information needs [2] and the urgency to acquire the information. For

Please use the following format when citing this chapter:

Aarnio, E., Raitoharju, R., 2007, in IFIP International Federation for Information Processing, Volume 252, Integration and Innovation Orient to E-Society Volume 2, eds. Wang, W., (Boston: Springer), pp. 373-381.

instance, the required information in an emergency department (ED) differs remarkably from the information required at a surgical-intensive care unit (SICU) [3].

The aim of using medications is to improve patients' health but sometimes there are also situations when medications cause injuries that could be preventable. The injuries could be caused for instance by the drug allergy of the patient, drug-drug interaction or wrong dosage. To prevent these errors, the patient data should be appropriately presented [4]. Without the appropriate movement of information between organizations, units and clinicians, the patient data including medication information could not be used to assure successful treatment of the patients. The movement of information is in this article called *information flow*. Reddy et al. [1, 229] use the term 'information flow' to describe patterns of information movement in a health care organization. According to them, the information flows are the ones that connect the different units of the hospital, but also units situated outside the hospital. In addition to the definition above, in this article the information flow also covers the flows inside the units.

Information could be bound to a particular site (e.g. incompatible computer system), time, person or knowledge and is therefore difficult or even impossible to move to another place and time [5]. The focus of this study is to explore the specificities present in different types of health care organizations and create a scoring system to define the most critical and vulnerable units in the context of medication information flow based on previous literature. Medication information is in this article defined as the generic and commercial name of the drug, the dosage, and the use indication.

The hospital districts in Finland are usually municipal federations consisting of one main hospital and several regional hospitals. In the same region, there are also various health centers owned by the municipalities and required by law to offer comprehensive primary health care services to the population of the municipality or other fixed area [6]. Almost all the health centers in Finland used an electronic patient record in 2006 but in the main and regional hospitals the electronic patient records were still in different implementation or development stages. There are many different electronic patient record systems in use but the national aim is to make it possible to move the patient information freely between different systems by the end of 2007. There are two possibilities for the extensive database: a centralized one, where all the organizations should have the same patient record system, and a decentralized base that is based on references which refer the place where the required information can be found. [7] However, the national database is still under planning and in the worst case it could take years before all the organizations could join in and use it efficiently [8]. Definition of the most vulnerable units is essential especially in the current situation of fragmented patient record systems and interfaces in Finland. The presented scoring system is based on the asset specificity in the transaction cost theory and previous literature on information flows of different health care units.

This paper is organized as follows: in the next section, information flows in the health care sector units are discussed. In chapter 3, specificities influencing health care sector units are presented based on previous research. Next, a conceptual framework for assessing the vulnerability of the medication information flow is provided. Finally, information flows in the context of medication information are discussed shortly.

2 Special Characteristics of Health Care Units' Information Flows

The information flow is dependent on the type of required information for instance in primary care [9]. As the required information varies, also the required information flow varies depending on the health care unit. The required information flow in each health care unit is different depending on for instance variables based on literature listed next, [e.g. 10]:
- Size of the clinic
- Purpose of the organization
- Depth of the physician-patient relationship
- Level of the specialization

Other variables affecting the flow are for example urgency of the operations performed at the unit, e.g. emergency department vs. surgical intensive care unit [3] and data intensity of the unit [e.g. 11]. The need for information technology solutions that guarantee the information to be available immediately is essential especially in the data-intensive, high-speed and heavily process-oriented areas such as emergency department (ED), the surgery area and the intensive care units (ICU) [11].

There are different types of intensive care units (ICU) (e.g. neonatal intensive care (NICU), surgical intensive care units (SICU)) and they all have in common the characteristic that all the possible medication-related risks should be minimized. The high intensity areas also differ from each other in data intensity. However, those areas are in any case a lot of more data-intensive than for instance medical/surgical floors in the inpatient hospitals [11]. In SICU or any intensive care units, the used medications are complex and extremely potent. The risks caused by medication errors are then also high. Information technology offers some possibilities to these situations. The requirements for the drug-related systems in the ICU are that they include patient-specific drug alerts, drug-drug interaction checking, recommended dosages and regime. Also the recognition of patients and drugs with a barcode are things that help in medication information use at the ICU. [12] In NICU the very tiny children are taken care of and even the smallest error can have significant impacts. Therefore patient's weight and age are especially essential information to have in the context of medication information. [13] Generally, surgery area is more data-intensive than ED or ICU. There is a lot of information needed and created during the surgery by many different people, e.g. anesthesiologist and nurses. [11].

In small offices or clinics there are usually paper-based patient record that are at hand easily [10]. Small organizations, such as small independent physician practices could, however, have problems related to finance and human resources when trying to acquire similar information technology than the big organizations [14]. Less technology is also required in less data intensive areas such as on a typical medical floor. For instance the vital signs of the patients on the floor do not need to be taken than once every hour to even eight hours whereas in the ICU the frequency could be even 5 or 10 minutes. Also the amount of clinicians is smaller on the floor [11].

The number of visits at the ED has multiplied and the complexity of the patients' illnesses has also increased. However, patients usually spend only a couple of hours at the ED [15]. The status of the patients is critical and they need to be treated as rapidly as possible. The ED is very information-intensive and collaborative in nature and the clinicians must find the accurate information fast, often from multiple resources. Patients' condition is often unknown when he/she is admitted to the ED and also the problems are not always clear. At the ED, the nursing staff usually has the best knowledge on patients' status and tasks performed, e.g. given medication. As in most of the units, one mistake can cause extreme consequences. When it comes to the medication given at the ED, patient's weight, pain rating, symptoms, and the location of the pain should be known before deciding the medication. In the intensive settings there are often also information that is not written down, for instance, medication is given but it is not written down to the patient record. [3] Engeström [6] has studied the medical cognition. He has categorized the objects of medical cognition that are presented modified in the figure 1.

	Domain is narrow and well constrained, cases are elective and foreseen operations	Domain is broad and poorly constrained, cases are unpredictable and/or at some level urgent
Cases are predominantly not serious or demanding in biomedical terms	E.g., cosmetic surgery	E.g., primary care general practice or family practices
Cases are predominantly serious or demanding in biomedical terms	E.g., oncology, neurosurgery	E.g., emergency room medicine

Fig. 1. A two-dimensional classification of objects of medical cognition (modified from Engeström [6, 398]).

Analyzing the figure 1 in the context of medication information, in the upper left hand category there are tasks that are usually foreseen and there is plenty of time to acquire the information on the patients' condition and medication before the operation. In the upper right hand side there are tasks where the patient's medication information can be easily acquired before the appointment because the patient probably goes to the same place frequently with a wide range of problems that are not usually urgent. In the lower left hand category there are physicians' tasks that are serious medical problems for the patients and also need strong knowledge from the physician but because of the seriousness of the patient's condition, medication has probably been seriously considered and is well known at the time of the operation. The fourth category represents the situations where there are possibly serious cases and the range of them is wide. In the cases of this category, efficient information flows are mostly required because patient's life could be dependent on his/her medication information.

As the data intensity is different in different units, also the systems that are ideal for each unit are different and many times there is a problem whether choose the ideal system or a system that compatible with other systems [11]. The focus of medical informatics (MI) research is to design IT applications that take into account the users (e.g. physicians, nurses, pharmacists). However, also only the change from the paper-based patient record has an effect on the communicative practices, the content and patterns of interdepartmental communication [14]. The paper records could be only viewed by one person at the time but with information systems many users can use it at the same time [15]. The individuals and institutions in healthcare settings familiarizing with new IT solutions are slow to change [16].

In Finland, only quite small number of patients moves from one organization to another. That is why the organizations should first fine-tune their own internal systems to match the expectations of the users [7]. For clinicians, the essential information on medication is the relevant patient history and data. To choose the right medication, they also require e.g. information on the dose forms, formulations and strengths the drug is available, appropriate clinical and dosage information. There could also be the information on which lab test results should be monitored or physical exams should be done. [13] The information flows in and between the units should provide this information taken into account the special characteristics of each unit.

3 Specificities Influencing Health Care Sector Information Flows

Asset specificity refers to the situation where assets are valuable in transactions between two certain partners. If the relationship between these two breaks, loss of value is caused by the break [17]. The concept of asset specificity is based on the transaction cost theory (TCT) that is an interdisciplinary approach joining economics, organization theory, and some aspects of contract law [18]. The different asset specificities classified by Williamson [18, 19] are human specificity, physical specificity, site specificity and dedicated assets. In the literature, also the specificities of time [20], procedural [21] and brand capital [e.g. 22] have been defined by different authors. Choudhury and Sampler [23] have studied the specificity of information and they add knowledge specificity in the list. In this article, the elaborated specificities are site, time, knowledge and human specificities. Human specificity is here understood as a specificity that refers to certain person possessing the asset and knowledge specificity refers to the specific knowledge of a professional. In noncommercial relationships transaction cost analysis cannot be realized completely but in those relationships there could be sacrifices of other valued objectives [18]. In this article, medication information is regarded as an asset. The costs could arise if the required medication information is not in the right time and place and, the patient cannot be treated correctly. The specificities could be seen consisting of hierarchically dependent layers so that the knowledge specificity is the strongest specificity, after that human, site and time specificities. In other words, if the information is knowledge specific, it is also human, site and time specific [5].

Human specificity appears in the context of medication information for instance in a situation, when the patient him/herself, a nurse or a physician, is the only one that has the information on taken/given medication. It could be, that the context why something was done is not written down and it is only in the minds of the individuals involved [24]. Wireless technology is one of the factors influencing strongly in the information flows of the health care sector and could also be one solution for the human specificity. The technologies enable the real-time notification of patient-care events and release human resources, especially physicians from less-critical issues [1].

Site specificity is present for instance when paper-based data such as medication chart is used. It means that the information is located only in one place and could not be easily moved to another. The same situation could also be caused by the incompatibility of electronic patient record systems. The problem of time specificity, also known as temporal specificity, is present when information must be acquired very shortly after it becomes available or when it losses value if not used very soon after becoming available [23]. An example in the context of medication information is that patient's allergic reaction caused by a drug could be documented only at the moment it happens. Also a blood sample taken earlier could loose its value if patient's condition changes rapidly.

Knowledge specificity is present when special knowledge is required to acquire and/or interpret the information [23]. Patient him/herself cannot often interpret, why a certain prescription was written to him/her by the physician because special knowledge on the issue is required.

4 Conceptual Framework for Analyzing the Information Flow in Different Health Care Units

In table 1 the specificities and different types of health care units discussed in this article are presented. The characteristics that change between different units are for instance urgency of the cases, the broadness of the domain and information/data intensity. The scoring presented next is not based on any empirical data but on literature discussed earlier. The more there are points (max. 4) the more vulnerable the flow of medication information and the more essential it is to treat the patient rapidly, and the more problems are caused if the information flow breaks down.

Table 1. Information flows and different health care units' information specificity vulnerability.

Type of Unit	Site Specificity	Time Specificity	Knowledge Specificity	Human Specificity	Score
ED	x	x	x	x	4
ICU	x	x	x	-	3
Medical Floor	x	-	-	-	1
Primary Care	x	-	-	-	1
Small Clinic	x	-	x	-	2

In the "high score" units like ED the medication information flow is affected easily and extreme problems are caused if the flow breaks down because of any specificity, for instance, a patient in critical condition is brought at the ED but his/her medication information is only in a paper-based patient record in some other unit (site specificity) or worse, he/she is the only one to tell the real medication (human specificity). The information should be acquired as soon as possible because of the critical condition (time specificity). Still, even if the medication information is acquired in the right place in the right time, a physician is required to interpret, what are the possible effects etc. the medication could cause during the treatment (knowledge specificity). In the primary care and medical floor units the knowledge is of course also required but the need for human resources, e.g. physicians or the treatment in general may not be that time specific than in the ED or ICU. At a small clinic the cases may not be that time specific either but the criticality is based on the fact that there could be only one physician at the clinic and without him/her the clinic cannot operate. The human specificity is present mostly in the ED because the patient may not be able to tell his/her medication information but in other units the patient is in the condition to tell the information or the information has been acquired earlier (e.g. medical floor or ICU). However, the table presents only the requiring side of the information flow. Small clinics, primary care or suchlike may not usually need medication information rapidly but are remarkable producers of the information. Therefore in a critical situation it should be essential that also above mentioned units could provide the medication information prescribed for the patient in their unit.

5 Discussion

After discussing the specificity vulnerability of the medication information flows, it should be assessed, how to guarantee the efficient flows between the units producing medication information and the units requiring the information in critical and less critical moments. In the case of Finnish medication data base solution, there should be considerations on how to integrate also the small, perhaps private organizations to the medication database at affordable price. The question to be asked is, would it be more secure that the units had their own medication records and the other units collected the required information based on the references, or that there was one national database where all the units should join in one way or another. The critical factors here are how to answer efficiently the requirements of urgency and data intensity of each unit and guarantee the information flow without any shortages. If there is only a small amount of patients moving from one organization to another [7] and if in most cases time is the critical factor in treating the patient, would it then be safer to have the decentralized databases if it was possible to read the information by using some references? Or, would one national medication database be the right choice to share the information? Further research should then focus on studying the risks of shortages related to the one national database compared to the amount of medication information required from other organizations' databases. If the need for information is minor than the risk of breaking the information flow completely, it should be carefully weighted, how to put into practice this process of getting rid of the fragmented medication information in Finland.

References

1. M.C. Reddy, et al., Technology, work, and information flows: Lessons from the implementation of a wireless alert pager system. *Journal of Biomedical Informatics*.**38**(3),229-238 (2005)

2. R.N. Jerome, et al., Information needs of clinical teams: analysis of questions received by the Clinical Informatics Consult Service. *Bulletin of the Medical Library Association*.**89**(2),177-185 (2001)

3. M.C. Reddy and P.R. Spence, Collaborative information seeking: A field study of a multidisciplinary patient care team. *Information Processing and Management*.**Article in press** (2007)

4. G.J. Kuperman, et al., Medication-related Clinical Decision Support in Computerized Provider Order Entry Systems: A Review. *Journal of the American Medical Informatics Association*.**14**(1),29-40 (2007)

5. E. Aarnio and R. Raitoharju. *Information specificity in the context of medication information: a conceptual analysis*. in *The 30th Information Systems Research Seminar in Scandinavia IRIS 2007*. 2007. Tampere, Finland.

6. Y. Engeström, Objects, contradictions and collaboration in medical cognition: an activity-theoretical perspective. *Artificial Intelligence in Medicine*.**7**(5),395-412 (1995)

7. K. Mäkelä, Terveydenhuollon tietotekniikka - Terveyden ja hyvinvoinnin sovellukset. 2006, Helsinki: Talentum.

8. J. Lahti, Potilastietoa uhkaa vuosien tietokatkokset. 2007: Digitoday, www.digittoday.fi.

9. N. Blackburn, Building bridges: towards integrated library and information services for mental health and social care. *Health Information and Libraries Journal*.**18**(4),203-212 (2001)

10. P.N. Gorman, Information Needs of Physicians. *Journal of the American Society for Information Science*.**46**(10),729-736 (1995)

11. M. Hagland, Intensive Care: The Next Level for IT. *Health Management Technology*.**19**(13) (1998)

12. M. Kaukonen, Lääkitysvirheet tehohoidossa. *Finnanest*.**39**(1),36-38 (2006)

13. K. Lillis, Automated Dosing. *Health Management Technology*.**24**(11),36-37 (2003)

14. M. Chiasson, et al., Expanding multi-disciplinary approaches to healthcare information technologies: What does information systems offer medical informatics? *International Journal of Medical Informatics*.**Corrected proof** (2006)

15. Anonymous, ED on Track With IT. *Health Management Technology*.**26**(8),28-31 (2005)

16. P.A. Gross and D.W. Bates, A Pragmatic Approach to Implementing Best Practices for Clinical Decision Support Systems in Computerized Provider Order

Entry Systems. *Journal of the American Medical Informatics Association*.**14**(1),25-28 (2007)
17. P.-O. Bjuggren, Competition for the Market in the Swedish Primary Health Care Sector. *International Review of Law and Economics*.**18**(4),529-541 (1998)
18. O. Williamson, The Economics of Organization: The Transaction Cost Approach. *American Journal of Sociology*.**87**(3),548-577 (1981)
19. O. Williamson, The Economic Institutions of Capitalism. 1985, New York: Free Press.
20. T.W. Malone, J. Yates, and R.I. Benjamin, Electronic markets and electronic hierarchies. *Communications of the ACM*.**30**(6),484-497 (1987)
21. A. Zaheer and N. Venkatraman, Determinants of Electronic Integration in the Insurance Industry: An Empirical Test. *Management Science*.**40**(5),549-566 (1994)
22. D. Lamminmaki, Why do hotels outsource? An investigation using asset specificity. *International Journal of Contemporary Hospitality Management*.**17**(6),516-528 (2005)
23. V. Choudhury and J.L. Sampler, Information Specificity and Environmental Scanning: An Economic Perspective. *MIS Quaterly*, (March 1997) (1997)
24. M.C. Reddy, et al. *Asking Questions: Information Needs in a Surgical Intensive Care Unit.* in *Proceedings of the American Medical Informatics Association Fall Symposiun AMIA'02.* 2002. San Antonio, TX.

Service quality of Early Childhood Education web portals in Finnish municipalities

Eija Koskivaara[1] and Päivi Pihlaja[2]
1 Turku School of Economics, Information System Science,
Rehtorinpellonkatu 3, 20500 Turku, Finland, eija.koskivaara@tse.fi,
WWW home page: http://www.tse.fi/tjt
2 University of Turku, Faculty of Education, Assistentinkatu 5, FI-
20014 Turku, ppihlaja@utu.fi,
WWW home page: http://www.utu.fi

Abstract. Increasing number of governmental organizations have transformed material on their web sites as a way of providing users with information about their products and services. In this paper, we apply Yang et al (2005) instrument for analyzing municipal early childhood education (ECE) web sites in Finland. The objective of the study was to find out the quality of ECE web portals as well as to give hints to improve their value from users' point of view. In general the five dimensions, usability, usefulness of content, adequacy of information, accessibility, and interaction, of the Yang et al model seems to be applicable also in the early childhood education environment.

1 Introduction

Increasing number of governmental organizations have set up material on their web sites as a way of providing users with information about their products and services. In this paper we are interesting of the quality of the early childhood education (ECE) information and service at the web sites, and what is the situation of the transformation of this information and service into virtual mode in Finland. The ECE in Finland is the state and municipality controlled public service, which every child have subjective right to have. The main objective of ECE in day care is to promote child's healthy growth, development and learning skills. The social task of ECE includes the promotion of child's social, intellectual and emotional development [2].

Day care should also support parents in raising their children [1,2]. Parents are seen more and more as partners. State is guiding municipalities by resources and information and for example the government determines the maximum price per month, which means that there is no price elasticity of the ECE service. According to Lee, Tan & Trimi [5], the value and quality of public services for citizens are essential of the e-governmental services. The rewards of virtual government-to-citizen (G2C) services are realized partially through well-design web sites, since nowadays they act as the primary contact with customer. Surfing the municipal ECE web sites reveals that the functionality and especially the content varies a lot.

The research of service quality of web portals is still an under-defined construct and heavily depends on the type of site. For example, Lightner [6] has proposed a list of 50 functional requirements to create more effective business-to-customer (B2C) sites. However, these requirements do not directly fit into the governmental services, which have no price elasticity. Hassan and Lee [4] have evaluated political web sites with benchmarking approach. In this paper, we apply the instrument developed by Yang, Cai, Zhou, and Zhou [7] for ECE web sites in Finland. The main selection criteria are that its focus is also on non-commercial web sites, built up by non-profit organizations. This instrument measures user perceived service quality of information presenting web sites. The instrument focuses on usability, usefulness of content, adequacy of information, accessibility, and interaction of the web site.

The research design is presented in section 2. The analysis of the ECE web sites is presented in the section 3 with the help of earlier mentioned five dimensions. Section 5 outlines our improvements proposals which are partly based on benchmarking and identifying the "best practices" of other municipalities' ECE web sites in Finland. Section 6 discusses the results against the measurement instrument and concludes the paper.

2   Research Design

The web sites and their texts are produced in socially organized ways [3]. Therefore, these sites are social productions, which are not transparent representations of organizations, or organizations values. This means, that it is very interesting to draw back "the curtain" and to examine the content of ECE web sites in Finnish municipalities. In order to do that, we are using content analyze to municipal ECE web sites.

Primary we analyze four different municipal ECE web sites. The municipals are Turku, Lieto, Salo, and Uusikaupunki. The number of children in the ECE service varies from 900 to 6000 in the municipalities. The biggest municipality has divided its' services in to ten services areas. These four municipalities were selected to our cases because they are taking part to a project which is aiming to developed ECE processes and services with the help of information technology. This study is a part of bigger ongoing research and development process.

3   Quality of ECE information

3.1   Usability

According to Yang et al. [7] studies, usability most significantly influences users' service quality perceptions of the web sites. Therefore, web sites should design so that its intended users are able to locate the needed information without difficulty. Therefore, we may say that in human-computer interaction usability refers to the elegance and clarity of the interaction. The usability of the case municipality ECE web sites are analyzed based on the following items: place and organization of ECE services, readability of the information, search facilities.

ECE services in Turku can be founded from the main page under the family- and social service menu, where they are the first service in the menu. The ECE services are organized based on the content of service. The main ECE menu also has link for frequently asked questions. The ECE services in Lieto can be founded from the main page under the social services, where ECE services were the first service in the menu. The ECE services in Lieto are also based on the content. In Salo the ECE services can be found under the service directory, where social services are one item. Under the social services all the services are presented in alphabetical order, where children's day care is again one item. The ECE services are organized based on the content. The ECE services in Uusikaupunki can be founded from the main page under the social- and health service menu, where all the services are presented in alphabetical order and the ECE services is one item. The ECE services are organized based on the content of service.

Readability of the information in Turku is good, which means that there is not too much text on the page and titles give a brief idea about the content. In Lieto the municipal main menu remains all the time on the left side of the page, which makes finding, reading and understanding the ECE content a little bit confused. Also, the layout of the Lieto ECE page is restless. The size of the letters and block capitals differ in disorder which makes the reading uneasy. The amount of the text in Salo ECE pages is at the moderate level, but some subtitles could help the reader. The amount and layout of the information per pages in Uusikaupunki ECE pages differs, which makes the reading uneasy.

Search facilities in Turku are always located at right-left corner of the page. Searching with the word "day care" gives 900 hints. Search facilities in Lieto are also located at the right-left corner the page. Searching with the word "day care" gives 13 hints. Search facilities in Salo are also located at the right-left corner the page, but new searching engine spring open after the search, which confused a little bit. Searching with the word "day care" gives 16 hints. Search facilities in Uusikaupunki are also located at the right-left corner the page, but again new searching engine spring open. This new searching machine searches either from all the pages or proposes precise pages. The searching with word "day care" gave 31 hint links organized by alphabetical order.

3.2 Usefulness of content

Usefulness of content refers to the relevant information to the customer and valuable tips on services, customized information presentation and up-to-date information. The relevant information is based on customers needs. Before parents are sending in an application for a day care place to their child, they have right to know what kind of day care services are available. The way how the text is taking parents' point of view in describing services and guiding parents what to choose is important. Furthermore, this means description about how does the ECE come true and how do children react to new context and how to ease child's adaptation process. Therefore, child-centered information is of a great value in ECE web sites. Therefore, this arise several question such as, is the text easily to approach, does it communicate or try to start a dialog with parents, and with whom co-operation is essential. The key words examining the content of web site text are: client centered information, useful information about different kind of day care, goals and implementation of ECE.

Children's point of view is not seen in these web sites. In Turku web sites are written in bureaucratic and organizational way. In Lieto and Uusikaupunki parents are seen more as partners: "We are about 150 day care professionals in Lieto. We want to offer the best we can, to ensure that your child should enjoy in Lieto".

The information about different kind of day care services is in superficial level in every municipal. Sides are not dealing with the differences of family day care, group family day care and day care centres. The strengths and weaknesses of these should be told to parents. Parents have right to know what kind of education the personal is implementing, what features are common to different kind of services.

Every municipal is dealing with preschool education little bit more and detailed. Finnish preschool is meant to children at 6 years old, only one year period before school start. Minister of Education is in charge of preschool education and Ministry of Social and Health of day care.

Goals of ECE are most explicit in sites of Uusikaupunki, even thought the web implementation is light.

3.3 Adequacy of information

Adequacy of information is related to completeness of information. The ECE web portals should provide information to facilitate families understanding of the whole content of the ECE services. Indeed, families need supplemental services, such as professional advice, club activity, social services, school system, research reports, and hyperlinks to relevant web sites. In here the most important items are: information about services to children and families organized by municipals and other providers such as non-profit or private organizations, sufficient information for potential and existing customers, and detailed contact information.

Every municipality has information about the structure of possible day care services: family day care and day care centers. In Turku there is also some information of other providers, very well about private providers, but worse about other activities for families (clubs etc). In Salo the content of day care services is quite informative: what does family day care means. But in Salo in web sites other providers are quite invisible. There is information about family center, but other organizations are not seen in these web sites. In Lieto the information about different day care systems are written in pedagogical way. "Our goal in Lieto is offer to families in our municipal different kind of day care services so, that families needs are taken care of. We want to offer different kind of day care places, and also offer to children who are taken care at their homes possibility to interact with other children in groups and get stimulating clubs". So in Lieto, we can see also the ground ideas of municipal ECE-services. There is not information of other providers in web sites, which can be seen as a shortage. But Lieto is offering clubs for children who are not in day care services, which are more than many other municipalities, can offer. In Uusikaupunki there is also two kind of information about possible day care services. Firstly, the information includes a description of the service content. Secondly, the information focuses on possible ways how families can organize their children's day care i.e. either in family day care or day care centers. Also in Uusikaupunki the emphasis is on children and families. "The aim of the day care is together with homes to contribute the growth of child's harmonious personality. Essential in the ECE is the interaction and educational partnership of parents, children, and day care personal."

Detailed content information is also important; it is some kind of visiting card of a person, who is in charge of this service. This is well taken care in Lieto, Salo, and Uusikaupunki. In Turku it is difficult for a client to know to whom to contact.

3.4 Accessibility

Accessibility of web site involves two aspects, namely availability and responsiveness. In this study we focus on easiness of web site access and speed of web page loading, which are also emphasized by Yang et al. [7]. In this analyze we count how many clicking a user needs from the municipal main page to find the ECE service and one day care center.

In Turku, user needs two clicking to open ECE service page, when the main page is the starting point. To find one day care center requires three more clicking. In Lieto, user needs two clicking to open ECE service page, when the main page is the starting point. To get contact information to a daycare center one more clicking is needed. In Uusikaupunki, user needs two clicking to open ECE service page, when the main page is the starting point. Also in Uusikaupunki one more clicking is needed to get contact information to a day care center. In Salo, user needs two clicking to open ECE service page, when the main page is the starting point. To find one day care center requires two more clicking.

The speed of loading of the ECE sites of Turku and Uusikaupunki are high, which means user view their content very quickly. With Lieto pages the user can see and sense the exchange of the pages. The uploading and exchange of some pages in Salo are slow, which means that it takes five to six seconds. However, this slowness is not valid in every loading.

3.5   Interaction

Yang et al. [7] argue that, web sites should satisfy users' information need by two interaction aspects. Firstly, interaction between users and web sites are needed, especially the possibility for inquiries is must. Secondly, users seek guidance, suggestions, and testimonies from peer users. In this study we look for the interaction the ECE web portals provide for user in the case municipalities.

All the case municipalities provide contact information, which also includes email address. Also digital application for ECE services can be downloaded via the web site. Besides, Lieto provides health inquiry application and Salo provides income inquiry application digitally. But, at the moment all the applications have to return manually. Turku ECE site keeps lists of frequently asked question about payment policy as well as some useful ECE links. Uusikaupunki and Salo have a link for the local community of the Mannerheim League for Child Welfare. None of the case companies has any peer services for the families.

4   Proposed Improvements for ECE portals

The following improvement focuses on the criteria mentioned earlier and emphasizes the users' point of view. In the Finnish public sector there is an aim to serve citizen from one point, therefore to find all the services from one place is attempting. This is where web portals really have advantage compared to other ways of providing informing about the services. Whether this one point of service really works with web portals is still a question, however at least Salo and e.g. Kirkkonummi have try to it. The next question is how to name the service so that users easily find the ECE services. Turku gives a nice example by emphasizing family point of view whereas other municipals strictly stick to social- and health services, which gives a little bit wrong view of the ECE service. Some of the municipals, like Kaarina, only present the services by alphabetical order, which hides the holistic view of the service content. E.g. in Tampere users have the possibility to select whether they want to see the service supply by alphabetical or content based order. By providing different kinds of ways to find the service really help citizens who certainly have different abilities to find and understand the messages.

Readability of the information in the ECE web sites really differs, and very often the picture is very restless. Therefore, guidelines as well as some training for the web writing are urgently needed. It seems that every municipal have search facilities in their web portals, but the improvement is needed to categorize the finding in a meaningful manner. For instance, some business intelligence could be embedded into the search engines.

Families demand valuable, reliable, up-to-date information from ECE web sites. Therefore, a formal policy of content development and information selection should be set. The main finding in this sector is that families can read something about day care, but there is too little information of the implementation of ECE and no information of how to adjust a child to new environment and child group. In these sites the information to parents is in organizational level and it does not give any empowerment for families. These sites could strengthen parenthood; give information of children and their development and especially how to support this phase of childhood. Transitions practices have a great value to an individual child, this process can be also supportive in new situation like this. Now-a-days parents are quite alone with this upbringing task and in a new situation when they are having a child. Migration and decrease of children in families are processes that bring generations apart of each others. Cultural legacy of care and upbringing is not so obvious what it was in agricultural Finnish society.

Day care is a service to families in Finland. In many other countries there is ECE services meant mainly to children, despite parents are at home or at work. It can be said that the pedagogical and developmental needs of children was ignored, and employment, adult-cantered factors were the main reason why this system was developed in Finland in 1970`s.. So we have a tradition that is emphasizing more adult centred values comparing this to child-centered values. These values are "written" to web sites by absence of this kind of information.

Every municipal has a task of organize day care that is based on the law. Information about this service that municipalities organize is coming true very clear. Service guidance is a task that every municipal should do, but at the moment it is not coming true very well. The information of all kind of services that families with small children should need is presented in way one can describe at random and partially. Web sites are quite new structures to inform and communicate, and municipal services are leaning on "old fashioned bureaucratic line organizations" which needs time to confront new demands of citizens and technology.

In "big" municipalities, like Turku is in Finland with 170 000 inhabitants, the way how a possible client get information to whom can contact is have great value to every people. Now municipalities over 100 000 inhabitants can be seen as a faceless and distant organizations. This should change, because organizer of these services should tempt new clients to communication and partnership. There should be a person who can answer to questions on municipal level and of course a person who knows the situation at day care provider level.

As long as the content of the ECE web sites is such that the interaction between families and day care provider is very minimal or it does not exist the accessibility is not the first factor of users' perceived quality. However, when the service is on the web customers expect them to be available at all the times; they also desire speedy log-on, access, and download of documents etc.

ECE service providers may increase the interaction by digitalization of ECE application procedures, which has been done, for instance, in Tampere and Espoo. The application procedure in Espoo differs from Tampere so that it requires identification of the parent before sending an e-application to the authorities. Also some day care centers such as Keinuhevonen in Orimattila already uses digital application procedures. So far, none of the services providers use digital forms for inquiring absence during summer, Christmas, or other holidays. This is astonishing because by integrating these procedures into the operational management systems of the municipals really could spare niche resources of ECE function and allocate them into promoting child's healthy growth, development, and learning skills.

5   Conclusions

The present paper analyses the municipal ECE web sites with the help of instrument. Families demand valuable, reliable, up-to-date information from ECE web sites. Therefore, a formal policy of content development and information selection should be set.

ECE services and implementation of ECE processes need further examination in Finland. The content of web sites of ECE services, implementation and its meaning to children has many weaknesses. One reason for this is that early childhood education and day care has a tradition of conflicting views in our society. One point of view is underlining the education and learning of small children. The other has long roots to social welfare and legislation brings out that *"social welfare means social services, social assistance, social allowance and related measures intended to promote and maintain the social security and functional ability of the individual, the family and the community"* [8]. One solution to create quality to ECE in national level can be the transition of the whole service system to the Ministry of Education.

In Finland were economical depression in 1990`s, when the services to children and child-families were diminished. Personal have many years of hard work behind and to create new quality and new information systems need both resources and enthusiasm. Attitudes and knowledge are going hand by hand, and therefore the IS competence of day care personal needs also some improvement.

As users at the moment do not conduct any online transactions, we have kept the security issues beyond the research scope. However, as municipals diversify their digital content of ECE services, web sites need strict security policies and have to use advanced security technologies.

References

1.Day care act 36(1973).
2.Day care act 117(1983).
3.N. Denzin and Y.S. Lincoln, *The Handbook of Qualitative Reserch.Thousand Oaks:Sage Publications,*2000.
4.S. Hassan and F. Li, "Evaluating the usability and content usefulness of web sites:a benchmarking approach, *Journal of Electronic commerce in Organizations ,*3(2005),46-47.
5. S.M. Lee, X. Tan and S. Trimi, "Current Practices of Leading e-Government Countries", *Communications of the ACM* 48, 99-104(2005).
6. N.J. Lightner, "Evaluating E-commerce functionality with a focus on customer service", *Communication of the ACM* 47,88-92 (2004).
7. Z. Yang, S. Cai, Z. Zhou and N. Zhou, "Development and validation of an instrument to measure user perceived service quality of information presenting Web portals", *Information & Management ,*42,575-589 (2005).
8. Social welfare act 1982.

Exploring the Intelligent and Collaborative control for E-Government System

Fangli Su [1], and Hongtao Zhu [2]
1 Zheng Zhou Institute of Aeronautical Industry Management, Zheng Zhou
450015, P.R.of China
Suli_2000@163.com
2 Zheng Zhou Institute of Aeronautical Industry Management, Zheng Zhou
450015, P.R.of China
pds_zhht@126.com

Abstract. This article embarked from the e-government affairs and the collaboration theory, has discussed the meaning of intelligent and collaborative control for E-government system, and proposed the intelligent and collaborative E-government system.

1   Introduction

The important feature of the network era is society and government's informationization， the main content of government's informationization is the implementation of e-government affairs, it has changed the official organization pattern and the government forms, and then has changed the government's management model. From the late 20th century to present, the human society has entered the information time, corresponding to the form of government is network government. organization is a complex system, the interaction between elements of the system has the driving force of innovation. the non-linear interaction of various essential factors in complex system interior is the inner impetus impelling the system to the order development. The collaboration effect is the interaction between various subsystems in the complex system, producing the effect beyond their effects alone, also is a whole greater than the sum of its parts.

1.1 E-government

Several recent investigations [2, 3, 5] indicate，E-government is the process of offering better government service to the public at a lower cost, improving the decision-making and investment environment, migrating the government's management, service, and the communication function to the internet. E-government is the means to modernize public administration and to achieve social participation. Among them, "electronic" is a method, and "the government affair" is the key. E-government has to do more with "government" than with the "e."

1.2 Collaboration theory

The synergetic was proposed in the sixties of the twentieth century by Germany's Professor Hermann Haken , which studies the rules of interaction between systems. It has been shown [1] that it contains two basic viewpoints:

1.2.1 Coordination effect
In complex systems, it exists the non-linear mutual function between various essential factors, when the outside control parameter achieved a certain value, the elements are interrelated, interconnected, replacing their relative independence, thus displays the coordination, cooperation, enhancing their overall effect, and the system moves towards the ordered state from the disordered state.

1.2.2 Self-organizing
Self-organization is a structure, forming through the systems' internal drive, which emphasizes achieving the coordination effect of a complex system. The formation of self-organizing system requires four conditions: The system must be open and be able to exchange material, energy, and information with the environment; the external function, through its internal mechanism to be effective; the non-linear interaction of elements within the system; Fluctuations as the catalyst. If the four conditions are met, the system will form self-organization in the absence of external directives.

2 the meaning of intelligent and collaborative control for E-government system

2.1 The transformation from information management to knowledge management.

The e-government affairs in our country has entered the third generation, its main goal is enhancing the government's decision-making ability by using knowledge management technology under government information environment, establishing Network-based distributed government structure, and providing trans-departmental government service through distributed "one-stop" service center. This stage of e-government affairs has not been limited in the information management or transaction processing, but to enhance the government departments' ability about knowledge collection, analysis, transmission and use, to integrate knowledge management closely with business processes, thus to enhanced the whole management level and efficiency of government.

2.2 personalization of E-service

In the public service, in view of the government offices are located in different locations, thus the office organization is dispersible, and the service window is multitudinous. Even for a simple business, need all the relevant agencies and department. The integrated use of various departments' public information resource is limited, difficult to play the best efficiency of automatic system. So it is emphasized that the government website must face the different types of user groups to provide the entire life information and the service and the integrated service resources.

2.3 performance optimization of collaborative system

The future collaborative information system will be more agile and real-time, manifesting the people-centered thinking, adapting to the government affairs' transformation from management to service. Through applications, processes and information departments of synergy, Collaborative government affairs greater play to the advantages. The collaborative government affairs are not only a better tool to do the similar matter, but also is a set tools which can handle the different or better matters, it is one brand-new way to provide services. The collaborative government affairs emphasize taking government staff's cooperation as the core, strengthening government information resource's sharing, optimizing the work flow, is the highest stage of current e-government affairs technology's application.

2.4 Deeply development of e-government application

With the development of e-government, application level has also been constantly rising. Some government departments' network which was completed at the early times began to expose some problems. First, as the government departments have their own original internal network, how can these heterogeneous network be interconnected is still a problem; Secondly, after the network linked, how can consolidate network resources, make full use of the department's original data; finally, how to protect the internal network resources. These problems have solutions now: Establishment of Intelligent and Collaborative e-government system.

3 Collaborative and intelligent e-government system

E-government need to satisfy government departments more in-depth application requirements, System should not always stay in the conventional business and business management, but shift to operational synergies and collaborative decision making.

E-government has pushed for a collaborative management model. It has been shown [4] that Collaborative management includes three aspects: First, the vertical separation of powers within the government collaborative management; Second, the government horizontal integration synergies; Third, the government and other manager's collaborative management.

The actual demand of government department, forced the building of e-government to the collaborative and intelligent direction. The so-called government intelligence is, to improve the effectiveness and coordination of transaction processing as well as the scientific and continuity of significant decision-making, a information system that constructed by using the information technology to be used for coordinating service and decision-making between the departments, namely government intelligent system.

3.1 The core content of government collaborative and intelligent system

Electron government collaborative and intelligent system is studied on the basis of collaborative theory, auto-adapted websites, and data mining. The basic technical construction is shown in figure 1.

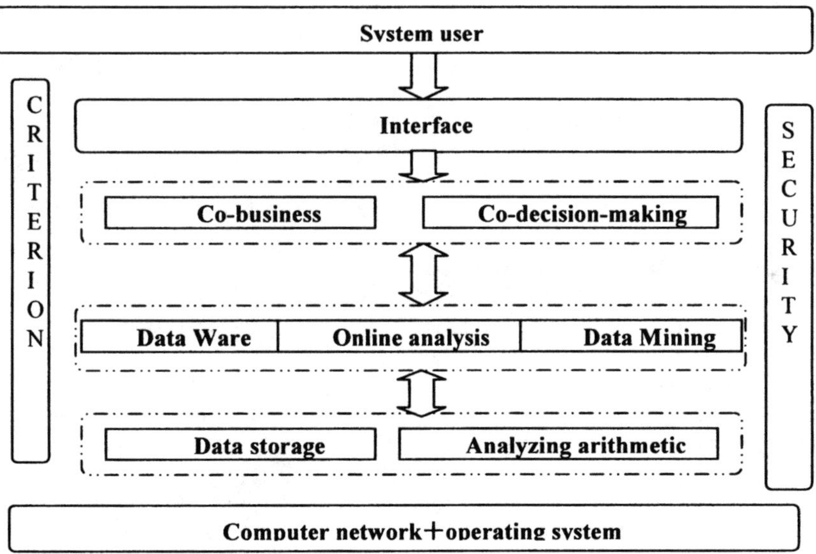

Fig. 1 The technical construction of government collaborative and intelligent system

Synthesizing its ideological sources, technical basis, existing tools and so on, the core content of the intelligent and collaborative government may approximately divide into following five aspects: 1) Data processing based on network communications, the data originates from many government departments, the use of network communication will enable information collection, transmission and digital storage more real-time; 2) Business collaboration Based on the message mechanism, the major goal to establish the intelligent and collaborative government system is strengthening the government departments with coordination; it should be clear about the single department work standard, and the basic principle which should be followed on exchanging and sharing information. Technically, based on the data exchange service coordination, the application integration or the flow coordination, they are using the system's message mechanism to trigger event, thus completing coordination mission. 3) The information management based on the subject analysis, the intelligent and collaborative government system is not merely technical, but also unceasingly establishes the business-oriented analysis subject. 4) Auxiliary decision-making based on the knowledge discovery. The auxiliary decision-making function of the intelligent and collaborative government system is to carry on the decision-making judgment using the new knowledge. 5) Administrative management based on the evaluation of the performance, the intelligent and collaborative government system should be able to evaluate the government's administrative capacity and performance. it is helpful to establish the reasonable drive mechanism.

3.2 Collaborative and Intelligent e-government model

3.2.1 Personalized and custom-made information services of the e-government system

As a public information service system, the problem that E-government needs urgently to solve is how to ease the strong contradictions caused by the contrast between the massive administrative information and the information control ability of users. in order to satisfy the users' usability requirements to the e-government system, what the personalized and custom-made information service present to users should be user-friendly and includes the information which the user be interest in.

In view of the above, proposes such a design concept: By analyzing the activities of users, the system automatically collects related information, transmits this information to user's desk promptly and regularly, helps users identify valuable information resources. This is a dynamic process; it can auto-adapted to user's interest and the change of information source.

Assume that add such a module to the e-government system, may be called the subject intelligence briefcase which based on personalized and custom-made information service. The module can automatically record each user's characteristics and establish the knowledge system, have good self-adaptive, learning and customized characteristics; According to the characteristics of users to filter the retrieved information, and push useful information to users, enable users to access their really wanted information accurately, direct and effectively. Its service model is shown in figure 2.

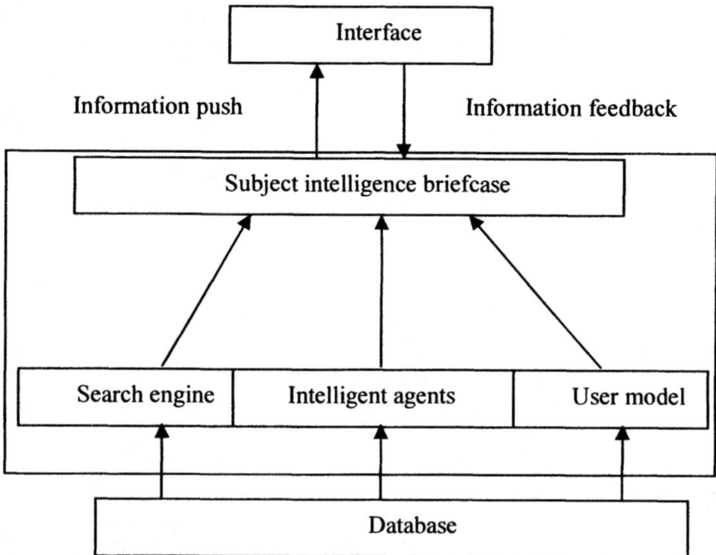

Fig. 2. The subject intelligence briefcase service model

3.2.2 Electronic documents intelligent retrieves of E-government system

Document includes the various information used in e-government, is an important component of e-government. How to find out the documentation which related to existing work from the rich e-government documents is an important task of e-government document intelligent retrieval. Several recent investigations [6, 7] indicate, in view of the lack of semantic retrieval, we can use the semantic e-government document retrieval. Combining the resources tagging of semantic web, according to the existing classification system and thesaurus in e-government, carries on the knowledge inference and the intelligent retrieval under the semantic net frame, enhances the accuracy of retrieval.

3.2.3 Intelligent network invasion examination of e-government system

The invasion examination technology is using the trace of the intruder, like the defeated records of attempting to land and so on, so can discover the illegal invasions which come from the external or internal. it takes survey and control as the technical essence, and Play a proactive role in the defense. In the invasion examination the functional technology includes: method based on neural network; method based on expert system; method based on model inference.

(1) Intrusion detection method based on neural network: This method has the study and auto-adapted function to the user behavior; it can process effectively according to the information of actual examination, and make judgment of possible invasion.

(2) Intrusion detection method based on expert system: according to the experience from analyzing suspicious behavior by the security expert, forms a set of

inference rules; and then establishes the expert system, so this expert system can automatically analyzes the behavior of invasion.

(3) Intrusion detection method based on model inference: According to the characteristics of certain behavior that executed by intruder, to establish an invasion behavior model, and according to this behavior model to judge whether user's operation belongs to intrusions.

4 conclusion

The network era need the collaborative management mode for government, and the E-government sped up the pace. With the increasing depth of e-government, the intelligent and collaborative government will be the future direction. In practical application we should strengthen the affairs management and information communication at administrative departments, pay attention to their professional background knowledge and work experience of the personnel. The application of intelligent and collaborative e-government needs some analysis software to support, but cannot excessively rely on the software tools. E-government has to do more with government than with the e .At the same time, the construction and execution of Openness in government affairs, exchange of information system is the fundamental guarantee to the service coordination.

References:
1. S. J. Han, S. Y. Nie,and W.Y. Zhao Remote-cooperative official business system design,*Journal of Dalian Institute of Light Industry*.(2), 149-151(2006).
2. Z.T, Yuan Q.Y, Zhang X, Wang and Y, Yang Research of CWE and its application in E-government,*Computer Engineering and Design*.(15), 2892-2894(2006)
3. W. Chen, G.Z. Yang Land L Chen S.M., IU Research of E-government Workflow Model Based Message Oriented Midelle Ware,*Science Technology and Engineer*.(14), 1021-1025(2005)
4. B. Xu –X.,Jia –B. Zhan,and Y. Liu – wen,Research on the Applying Patterns of Workflow Technology in Coordination of E - government Business,*Information Science*, (5), 742-745(2005)
5. J.Zhang 1,and KJ. Hu.,Study on Electronic Government Cooperation Work Model Based on Cooperative Unit,*Journal of Tongji University*,(10), 1380-1384(2005)
6. F. Yang,and Z.S. Yang ,E-Government document retrieval based on semantic Web,*Computer Applications*, (10), 2434-2436(2005)
7. Z.J Zhang, H.L Liu.,and J. Sun,Study on thematic and intelligent portfolio service in E-government system,*Journal of Northeast Normal University (Natural Science Edition)*, (4), 38-42(2005)

Evaluating the E-government Based on BSC

Jianjun Cheng[1], Sencheng Cheng[1], ,and Meiju Yang[2]
1 Management school, Wuhan University of Technology, 430070, Wuhan,
P.R. China
Chengjianjun007@153.com; chengsc@whut.edu.cn
2 College of Politics and Public Management, Jiujiang University, 332005,
Jiujiang, P.R. China
meijuyang@sina.com.cn

Abstract. The rapid development of information and communication technologies has given rise to the emerging of the e –government. Various approaches have been adopted to evaluate the e-government. This paper suggests the Balanced Scoreboard approach and attempts to devise a systematic evaluation framework.

1 Introduction

The rapid development of information and communication technologies has given rise to the emerging of the e -government. The United Nations (UN) and the American Society for Public Administration (ASPA) defined e-government as "utilizing the Internet for delivering government information and services to citizens" [1]. E-government is defined by the Organization for Economic Cooperation and Development [2] as the use of ICTs, and particularly the Internet, as a tool to achieve better government. At present e-government may refer to narrower or broader areas: in one, it is defined as online service delivery; and in the other, it entails the capacity to transform public administration using information and communication technologies (ICTs) to introduce the concept of e-governance.

The objectives of e-government are to: bring government closer to citizens by providing them with easier access to information through personal computers, telephones and other resources; modernize public services in which "joined-up government" institutions communicate and work more effectively and efficiently; increase and capture revenue more efficiently; increase mechanisms to create more accountability and transparency in the public sector. For these reasons, the governments all over the world are implementing their e-government projects and programs.

Please use the following format when citing this chapter:

Cheng, J., Cheng, S., Yang, M., 2007, in IFIP International Federation for Information Processing, Volume 252, Integration and Innovation Orient to E-Society Volume 2, eds. Wang, W., (Boston: Springer), pp. 397-403.

The governments throughout the world have invested hugely in e-governments, so they are confronted with the problem of evaluating the performance. Currently, there are a variety of e-government performance evaluation standards, but none is from the Balanced Scoreboard (BSC) perspective. This paper attempts to use BSC approach to the e-government evaluation in an effort to establish effective operational standards. The rest of the paper are structured as following: Section 2 analyzes the need to evaluate the e-government; Section 3 is an overview of the existing approaches to evaluating the e-government; Section 4 proposes a performance standards based on BSC, the final section concludes the paper.

2. The need to evaluate the e-government

2.1 The new model of e-government determines the need for performance evaluation

As a part of systematic evaluation, performance evaluation began in the 1930s. It is a managerial method which can assess quantitatively the input, short-term benefits and long-term effects. Since 1970s, the new public administration reform has prevailed across the world, and various techniques have been developed to evaluate the government's performance. In the United States, Britain, and other Western countries, performance has become one of the core elements to be evaluated regarding the government's achievements. E-government as a revolutionary change means not only technical change but also change in governance and structure. It requires totally new operation processes and performance evaluation standards compared with the traditional government. The evaluation results should be used to guide the development of e-government in the right direction and to enhance its efficiency.

2.2 Status quo of the e-government determines the need to implement a performance evaluation

At present e-government's overall efficiency is not high. According to the United Nations World Public Sector Report 2003 [3] " E -government at the Crossroads", there are there types of e-government: wasteful ones, that is, resources have been input but the government operations have not been optimized; pointless ones, that is, the operations of the government have been optimized, but have not been conducive to the social development goals; the meaningful ones, that is   the operations of the government have been optimized so that people can really participate in the political process and contribute to human development.   Most e-governments across the world belong to the first and the second type. 60% to 80% of e-government projects in the developing countries fail. They can be classified as wasteful e-governments. Only 15 countries can receive public comments on policy issues via internet. Only 33 countries allow people to submit form and pay the fines online.

3. Existing approaches to e-government evaluation

A large amount of research has already been carried out to evaluate the e-government. An overview of approaches shows that they cover different areas and aspects of e-government. They include various indicators that can be categorized in the following groups:
- E-readiness
- Back-office
- Front-office: Supply and demand
- Effects and impacts.

3.1 E-readiness

The existence and maturity of the right environment for launching and using e-government solutions in individual areas are two key elements in the successful development of e-government and, by measuring enabling factors for IT, indicate the readiness of individual players (government, citizens and businesses) to participate in the electronic world, i.e. e-readiness. On the government's side this is mainly an issue relating to strategies, policies and action plans for the introduction and development of e-government, IT use policies, the adoption and use of information infrastructure, IT training, awareness of the advantages and problems of e-government and issues relating to financing, motivation and obstacles for the development of e-government. External (citizens and businesses) aspects include primarily ownership, interests and the level of use of information infrastructure, reasons for their under-use and opinions on the development of e-government in general. These indicators partially overlap with the evaluation of the information society as a whole.

3.2 Front-office

The front-office area is studied from two complementary points of view: supply and demand. Supply-side approaches entail evaluating online supply, and only in individual cases does it also involve supply via other channels of communication such as digital television, mobile technologies, call centers, dedicated kiosks and so on. These approaches generally investigate availability, level of development, quality and other characteristics of individual websites, and portals as well as particular e-services and information content.

On the other side demand-side approaches study the field from the point of view of the users (citizens and businesses). This kind of research primarily involves investigating actual use of websites, portals, e-services, information content and other elements of supply, the level of interest in use and reasons for not using services as well as evaluations of the quality of services as perceived by the users and evaluation of their perceptions, requirements and needs.

3.3 Back-office

The research that has dealt with evaluating the back-offices has assessed the adoption and use of different information systems including data sharing and exchanging technologies (databases, document management, process and workflow management, data sharing and exchange between organizations, etc)

3.4 Effects and impacts

Approaches to effects and impact evaluation include assessments of the impact of e-government on economic, social and democratic processes, such as cost and benefit analyses, impact on organization, work methods, etc.

A detailed review of these approaches reveals that they are focused mostly on individual area or aspect of e-government, first of all on dealing with customers (front-office), evaluating the supply-side of e-government and something less demand-side, while largely neglecting the back-office and the impact and effects of e-government. This proves the opening supposition that current approaches do not support a comprehensive e-government assessment, but only partial evaluations that cannot give policy makers evaluation elements for their decisions, especially not in the direction of transformative government, characterized by integrated services development, where quality highly depends on back-office systems.

4. The BSC-based approaches to e-government

4.1 Introduction to BSC

The Balanced Scorecard is a multi-perspective approach aiming, on the one hand, at the "balance" of a strategy by considering various perspectives and on the other, on the operationalization of the corresponding strategic goals and their "translation" into a set of measurable targets [4]. Originally, the concept was developed for the business area and contained the financial, customer, business process and learning perspective. The perspectives are interrelated through cause and effect relationships showing the ability to realize the strategy and to monitor this relationship.

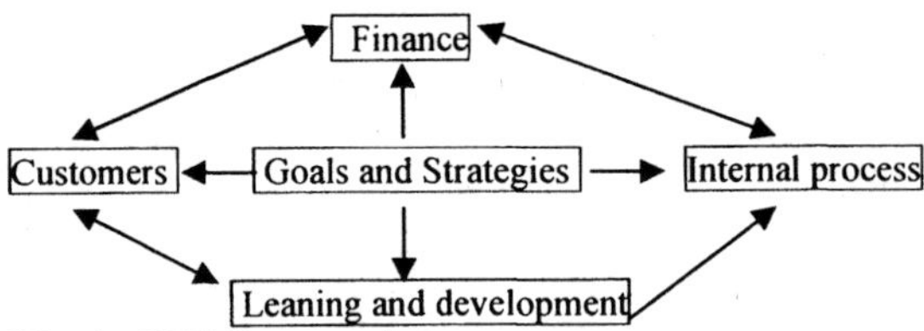

Fig. 1. BSC framework

4.2   E-government evaluation Based on BSC

4.2.1 Financial indicators
Governments belong to the non-profit sector, different from the general enterprises which set the economic benefits as the key of performance evaluation. The purposes

of the government are to manage the society, and provide services for people. But this does not mean that the government will have no financial targets, the government's budget scale and operating costs have been important criterion for evaluating government performance. As a new government management model, the e-government's establishing and operating costs are important indicators that can not be ignored. Financial indicators generally include three aspects, namely, income, costs and asset utilization ratio. The income indicator, if included in performance evaluation standards, is inconsistent with the strategic goal of the e-government-providing services. But in a sense, the saving by the adoption of the e-government over the traditional one can be regarded as income and can be ranked as income indicator. " For cost indicators, they can be divided into two categories: one category is the cost of establishing the governmental websites; the other is the cost of running including software upgrading and hardware maintenance. For utilization ratio of assets, because the governments are different from enterprises, the indicator here is ignored. In addition, as a public service sector, their evaluation should include social benefit indicators. This can be translated into the total amount of money involved in the website transaction.

4.2.2 Customer indicators

Core indicators to measure customer dimensions include five aspects: market share, customers retention, Customer acquisition, customer satisfaction and customer profitability. In evaluating the value of the enterprises, the customer usually judge from product / service attributes, customer relationships, image and reputation. Based on customer dimensions in enterprises and in the light of the characteristics government, the authors summarized the e-government customer dimensions as follows.

Different government departments function differently, so the competitive indicators such as market share and customer retention do not have corresponding ones in the government performance evaluation. But the e-governments do have some competitive indicators. Competitions do exist between the traditional and information processing of governmental transactions, which can be represented by transaction information processing rate (Re), that is, the rate of transactions(ne) handled by the government website in the total volume of departments transactions : $Re = ne/ n$. In addition, the number of people(hg) visiting the governmental websites in the total number of people(h) who have access to the internet can be another competitive indicator, that is $Rh = hg / h$.

As for e-government product / service attributes, they can be measured by the service effect indicators. Using information technology to provide the public with information and quality services is one of the main tasks of the electronic government. Therefore the indicators concerning service effect include: the number of hits on the website, the downloaded number of document, the volume of transaction through website, the number of online windows opened and closed, the visiting number of databases and the visiting frequency of the information stored in the databases.

In customer relationship, the main concerns are the connection between the people and governmental websites. Apart from the number of e-mail people sent to the website, the interaction between the public and the websites, citizen's comments online and the response to the online survey should all be assessed. In addition, connection with other departments and agencies should also be measured.

The image and reputation of e-government can be reflected by the people's satisfaction in the services provided by e-governments. Satisfaction and credibility can be surveyed online or in other general ways. As the public expects rapid and quality services, any error can damage their satisfaction. The complaining rate(Rt) on the website is also an effective measurement of e-government image and reputation. The complaining rate(Rt) can be expressed by (Qt)/Q, here Qt refers to the quantity of complaints, and Q represents the quantity of transactions.

4.2.3 Internal process indicators

Compared with the traditional performance evaluation approaches, the BSC is characterized by formulating goals and evaluation methods for the enterprise's internal operation. Unlike the enterprises, the internal processes of the e-government include: services provided, the maintenance, the security, collaboration with other departments and website and follow-up services. Indicators regarding internal process are based on the above.

Providing services is one of the main objectives of the e-government. Service attributes indicators are used to evaluating the services; one is the service content, the other the service quality, to be exact. Service content can be measured by the variety of services, the abundance of information provided and the craftsmanship of the web pages. Whether customized services are provided should also be considered.

The network serves as the platform the e-government. The maintenance and security are the prerequisites for improving the performance and can be summarized as technical attributes. For maintenance, it can be measured by the portal, bad(empty) link rate, the promptness of upgrading the software and etc. The security can be assessed by the resistance to virus and malicious invasion, and by the protection of privacy of those who log into the websites.

The e-government should be an island isolate from the outside. It should collaborate with other websites and department. Its influence can be measured by the links and the departments integrated together.

The sound follow-up services the enterprises can bring with them excellent images and quick development. In the same way, the e-governments need follow-up services for a better image and high public satisfaction. The follow-up services can measured by the time for the e-mails inquiry, the solution ratio to the complaints and etc.

4.2.4 Learning and developing indicators

The evaluation of the learning and developing capability lies in that it is a planning to implement finance, customer and internal operation procedures, in that it is a push to for the three to score. Evaluation in this aspect involves mainly human resource development and environmental building. The indicators include: employee quality, working environment, innovation and learning capability.

5. Conclusion

E-government evaluation is important in that it provides direction for development, for decision making and for improvement. But current approaches do not support a comprehensive e-government assessment, but only partial evaluations that cannot give policy makers evaluation elements for their decisions. This paper suggests the BSC approach, it combines technology and service, and it is more comprehensive and operational. Experimental research is needed to test its effectiveness.

References

1 . United Nations/American Society for Public Administration (UN/ASPA). 2002.*Benchmarking E-Government: A Global Perspective*. New York: UN/ASPA.

2 . Organization for Economic Co-operation and Development (OECD).. 2003. *The E-Government Imperative: Main Findings*. Paris: OECD.

3 . United Nations (UN). (2004). *UN Global E-Government Survey 2003*. New York: United Nations Online Network in Public Administration and Finance(UN/PAN).

4 . Robert S. Kaplan; David P. Norton: The balanced scorecard - translating strategy into action, Harvard Business School Press, Boston, 1996.

A New Multi-Agent Approach to Adaptive E-Education

Jing Chen and Peng Cheng
Department Of Computer Science, Huazhong Normal University, Wuhan,
430079, P.R.China
dancinglulu@sina.com

Abstract. Improving customer satisfaction degree is important in e-Education. This paper describes a new approach to adaptive e-Education taking into account the full spectrum of Web service techniques and activities. It presents a multi-agents architecture based on artificial psychology techniques, which makes the e-Education process both adaptable and dynamic, and hence up-to-date. Knowledge base techniques are used to support the e-Education process, and artificial psychology techniques to deal with user psychology, which makes the e-Education system more effective and satisfying.

1 Introduction

In the age of the new information and communication technology, it should be possible to learn not only by a locally available electronic support, i.e. an interactive CD-Rom, but even "far away" from the teaching source. One challenge for designers and HCI researchers is to develop software tools able to engage novice learners and to support their learning even at distance.

Usability is the vital role of e-Education systems [1]. But there are more works can be done. Customer satisfaction is going to be more and more important to e-Education. Computer Science, together with Psychology and Education, has been trying to refine teaching computational tools towards personalized self-learning [2,3, 4]. Every day, new approaches to the use of Computer and Education are bringing new perspectives to this area. The evolution of Computer and Education became computational teaching environments an excellent choice for Distance Learning, by bringing new vigor to this field of science.

Please use the following format when citing this chapter:

Chen, J., Cheng, P., 2007, in IFIP International Federation for Information Processing, Volume 252, Integration and Innovation Orient to E-Society Volume 2, eds. Wang, W., (Boston: Springer), pp. 404-411.

E-Education projects must take into consideration that there are different classes of users. A simple result can be: the non-cooperative, those who act in a passive way or even try to frustrate the program's objective; the cooperative, who follow orientations, but do not necessarily know where to go; and the pro-active students, who know very well their objective, and search for aid to relief the task burden [2]. Obviously this method is too cursory, especially to arts e-Education. Study about cognitive expansion of queries aims at the implementation of a knowledge-based query builder that allows complex query building in tight cooperation with the user. Due to the cognitive knowledge involved, these complex queries are expected to return more relevant results than traditional database queries or classifications [5], [6]. Besides advanced techniques in personalization (preference modeling, etc.) research issues will have to focus on results from sociology and psychology to include implicit knowledge about human behavior and social expectations in the retrieval process.

The teaching methodology employed in each case is different and there must have a clear concern by the technological environment on the profile of the user that will use the system. In order to reach this goal, cognitive student's modeling is required, and it must make a clear specification of him or hers, including his or her psychology. One main purpose of Artificial Psychology technologies is to imitate human psychology with computer, meanwhile, to provide some subjective evaluations for the objective things. This kind of research in e-Education is still at the beginning.

Section 2 implements a multi-agent architecture, based on the Java Agent framework for Distance learning Environments – JADE project, for approach to adaptive e-Education, in which a knowledge base is used to manage experimental knowledge of users. In Sections 3, the cycle of agents' adaptation, the adaptation of rules and the adaptation of psychology are illustrated respectively. The conclusions are stated in Section 4.

2   Multi-Agent Architecture for Adaptive E-Education System

The Java Agent framework for Distance learning Environments – JADE project [7] proposes an infrastructure of project, development and implementation of Distribute Intelligent Learning Environments – DILE, based on the approach of Multi-Agents architecture towards Distance Education, for multiple domains.

JADE architecture encompasses a Multi-Agent environment composed of an agent responsible for the system general control (Student's Model), and a Communication Manager (Manager agent) and other agents (Teacher agents), which are responsible for tasks related to their teaching tactics, where each agent may have its tasks specified according to its goal. All actions of student's data accessing are taken by the Student's Model, thus when a teacher agent is required to update the student's historic, this agent sends to the Student Model data to be updated, as well as any other change in the student's state of teaching. The tasks performed in teaching are decomposed and performed individually or in groups of agents. How the task will be decomposed is defined by the content of messages exchanged between agents. In our work, we aim at perceptual situations such as the e-Education of arts and put our emphases on the user satisfaction (see Fig. 1). The teacher agent dispensable and the student model agent cares more about the experimental knowledge than JADE, and one additional work of the browser agent is cognitive queries.

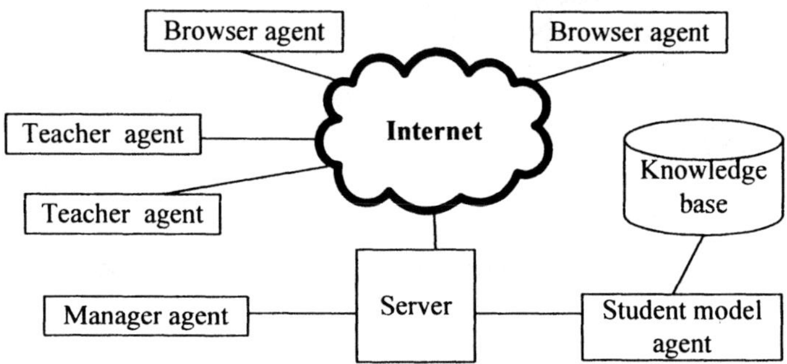

Fig.1. the multi-agent architecture for adaptive e-Education system.

The knowledge base plays an important role in adaptive e-Education systems. User psychology, a kind of implicit knowledge, is quantified in our work and a new cognitive model involving artificial psychology is presented in Fig. 2. The skills are the skills of the user it represents. It communicates by exchanging information about the knowledge base of the whole system. Beliefs are related to the description that an agent or user possesses about the others' and its own skills. And the psychology: the knowledge base should represent a student's psychology. Semantic beliefs are not enough to satisfy the user.

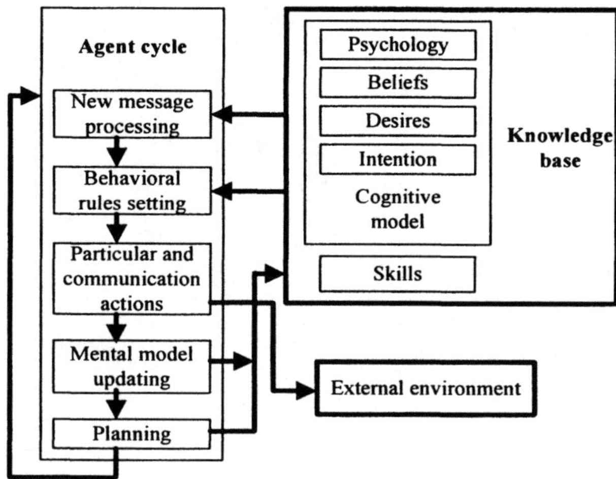

Fig. 2. The knowledge-based cycle of agents' adaptation or execution consists of five stages, and it is also a co-evolution process of the agents and the knowledge base.

3   The Knowledge Based Adaptation

3.1   The Agents' Adaptation Cycle

The cycle of agents' adaptation or execution, also shown in Fig. 2, consists of the following steps:(1) New messages processing: the task is decomposed;(2) Determination of which rules are suitable in the current situation: analysis of task and if necessary delegation of other agent(s) task;(3)Execution of actions specified for such rules: task execution;(4) Mental state update according to those rules: management of knowledge about the world, including the artificial psychology;(5) Planning: module that must develop plans that reach goals specified by agents intentions.

3.2   The Adaptation of Rules

The key point of this adaptive approach of e-Education is the adaptation of rules based on the adaptation of user psychology and the adaptation of beliefs, desires and intention. Figure 3 describes the determination of rules in our approach. The user profiles and the cognitive queries files built by the browser agent consists basic information about user usage and preference, from which beliefs, desires and intention can be draw as JADE does in [7]. And user's artificial psychology can also be build from them, which will appear in section 3.3. The belief technology is comparatively mature in e-Education system, so in view of both efficiency and effect, artificial psychology technology is applied to refine the suggestion results of beliefs, desires and intention. This process is dynamic, so the determination and the adaptation of rules are dynamic too.

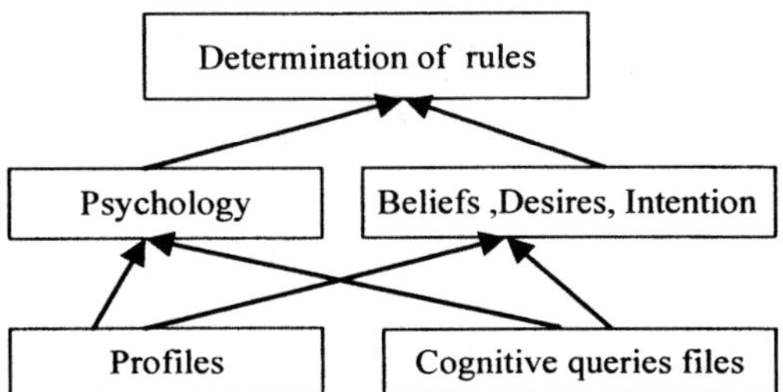

Fig. 3. Determination of rules based on the adaptation of user psychology and the adaptation of beliefs, desires and intention.

3.3   The Adaptation of Psychology

Aiming to maintain the Psychology, a cognitive expander is developed. Figure 4 shows the generalized architecture of cognitive expander.

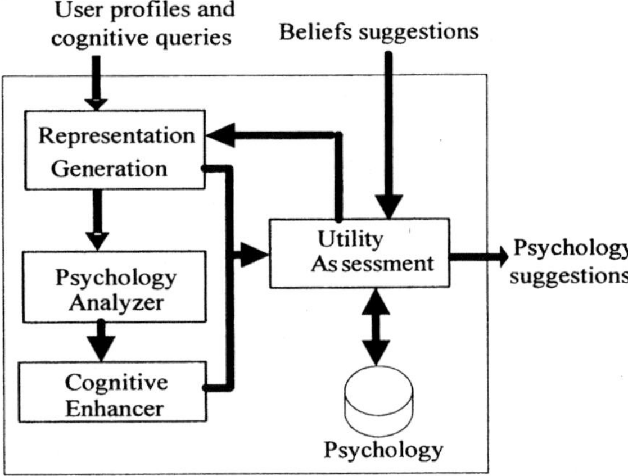

Fig.4. The cognitive expander to maintain the Psychology in the knowledge base using artificial psychology techniques.

Each user session in a user session file can be thought of in two ways; either as a single transaction of many page references, or a set of many transactions each consisting of a single page reference. The goal of transaction identification is to dynamically create meaningful clusters of references for each user. Based on an underlying model of the user's browsing behavior, each page reference can be categorized as a content reference, auxiliary (or navigational) reference, or hybrid. In this way different types of transactions can be obtained from the user session file. The details of methods for transaction identification are discussed in [10].

Based on the user model in [11] the user query and answer in user transaction file and user cognitive queries files is enhanced with cognitive psychology and the subjective expected utility is assigned. Considering the utilities for different combinations of preferences within a query a trade-off between query complexity or processing costs and an expected improvement of the query result has to be optimized. Comparing subjective expected utilities eventually leads to decisions about the retrieval strategy and an adequate query can be generated. This query is processed by the database retrieval system and the results are returned to the user. The essential component is the Psychology Analyzer that refines the transaction file and passes user psychology to the Cognitive Enhancer.

Cognitive expander aims at the implementation of a query builder based on psychology knowledge that allows complex query building in tight cooperation with the user accord with individual psychology preference. The Psychology Analyzer studies users' psychology using Artificial Psychology model. Cognitive Enhancer should remember the info (query and evaluation) of the former cases made by every user, and analysis the query and evaluation to gain experience about user Psychology. A repository is used to record the evaluation of former cases of one user. Psychology Analyzer use Artificial Psychology (AP) to analysis the preference of user. First, the Representation Generation collects the adjectives used by user to describe what he or she wants and whether he or she is satisfied with the service, such as "lovely-bothersome", "magnificent-plain". However, not all the adjectives pairs are necessary; some adjective pairs have close correlation. So the representative pairs should be abstracted by factor analysis. The repository will record the numeric evaluation value of every case corresponding to the adjective pair. Second, the user should fill a questionnaire to describe the service that he needs, which is a new query. At last, Cognitive Enhancer will build the appropriate query.

For example, a user want to find a picture or flash in the system, firstly, there is a user preference value correspondence with the adjacent pair, and we call them average of the representative pairs, such as table 1.

Table 1. Average of the representative pairs: user preference values correspondence with the adjacent pairs.

	Case 1	Case 2	Case 3	Case 4	Case 5
Expensive-cheap	0.3	0.6	0.8	0.1	0.5
Romantic-prim	0.5	0.7	0.9	0.4	0.3
Modern-outdated	0.1	0.8	0.3	0.7	0.2
...	...	...	...	...	...

We can get the value like this, for instance, for expensive-cheap, 0.1 represent cheapest, 0.5 represent not expensive and not cheap, 0.9 represent most expensive. Now we find out the numerical representations.

Then we select red, green, blue, lightness, cold or warm as the items. We measure the color value (0-255) by PHOTOSHOP; the value of lightness and the value (0-100) of cold or warm are obtained by the questionnaire. Table 2 gives the result:

Table 2.   Characters determination and numerical representation of the samples.

	sample 1	sample 2	sample 3	sample 4	sample 5
red	99	240	85	246	8
green	208	139	180	255	194
blue	37	74	23	10	234
lightness	60	50	80	10	40
cold or warm	50	80	40	70	20

The corresponding reactor matrix:

$$X = \begin{bmatrix} 99 & 208 & 37 & 60 & 50 \\ 240 & 139 & 74 & 50 & 80 \\ 85 & 180 & 23 & 80 & 40 \\ 246 & 255 & 10 & 10 & 70 \\ 8 & 194 & 234 & 40 & 20 \end{bmatrix} \tag{1}$$

With the help of Quantification Theory I , each case can be written in the form of reactor matrix. According to the formula of Quantification Theory I :

$$b = (X'X)^{-1}X'Y \tag{2}$$

We obtain the quantification relationship of the adjective pairs and the case, with Y is a column vector and its value is the average of the previously evaluation corresponding to an adjective pair, like table 2. X is the reactor matrix. All values of b correspond with the adjective pairs are obtained. By replacing b with its expression, we can calculate the evaluation Y of case with the help of the predictive formula

$$\hat{Y} = Xb \tag{3}$$

Then we calculate the sample multiple correlation coefficient of $\hat{Y}$ from formula 4 to checkout the validity of predictive results:

$$r_{\hat{y}y} = \sqrt{\frac{\sum_{i=1}^{n}(\hat{y}_i - \bar{y})^2}{\sum_{i=1}^{n}(y_i - \bar{y})^2}} \tag{4}$$

The quantification relationships $\{b\}$ are stored in the repository. When a query comes, the Cognitive Expander will depend on its repository to calculate the evaluation Y to refine the suggestions of beliefs; and from the user feedback and formula 4, the adaptation or recalculation can be trigged. Surely it is going to be more and more accurate over time. The consequence is an improving self-evolution process between users and the psychology.

4 Conclusions

In this paper, advanced e-Education approach using cognitive techniques and artificial psychology techniques is investigated. Usability of e-Education has been implemented basically. Customer satisfaction has aroused concerns in these fields. Thus systems should manage experimental knowledge of users to satisfy them and support them effectively.

In the process of the model construction, we synthesize data mining techniques and AP mathematics theories, and integrate them into cognitive theory to form the Architecture for Adaptive E-Education System.

The analysis of knowledge based adaptation and Cognitive Expander applying artificial psychology technology to refine the suggestion results of beliefs, desires and intention will lead to the adaptation of agents' cycle and e-Education. And the efficiency and convenience of this system will be our future works.

References

1. A. Carmelo, "Towards Guidelines for Usability of e-Learning Applications",*UI4All 2004, LNCS 3196*, 185–202(2004).
2. A.S. Ricardo and M. V. Rosa, "Improving Interactivity in e-Learning Systems with Multi-agent Architecture", *AH 2002, LNCS 2347*, 466–471(2002).
3. Q.M. He, "Design and Implementation of a J2EE-Based Platform for Network Teaching", *ICWL 2005, LNCS 3583*, 49–55(2005).
4. G. Lekakos, K. Chorianopoulos, D. Spinellis, "Information systems in the living room: A case study of personalized interactive TV design", *Proceedings of the 9th European Conference on Information Systems*. Moderna Organizacija: Kranj, 2001.
5. D. Emmanuel,"Dinosys: An Annotation Tool for Web-Based Learning", *ICWL 2004, LNCS 3143*, 59–66(2004).
6. D. Patrick and V.Q. Le, "A Question Answering Mining platform",*0-7803-8596-9/04/ 2004 IEEE.*
7. Silivira, A. Ricardo, Vicari and M. Rosa, "JADE - Java Agents for Distance Education Framework", *In: DEC 2001, 2001, Austin. DEC 2001. CD-ROM, 2001.*
8. L.N. Martin, "A Mixed XML-JavaBeans Approach to Developing T-learning Applications for the Multimedia Home Platform", *MIPS 2003, LNCS 2899*, 376–387(2003).
9. Q. Lu, "Web Personalization Based on Artificial Psychology", *WISE 2006 Workshops, LNCS 4256*, 223 – 229(2006).
10. B. Mobasher, H.H. Dai, T. Luo, N.A. Miki, Y.Q. Sun and W. Jim, "Discovery of Aggregate Usage Profiles for Web Personalization", *Proceedings of the Web mining for E-commerce Workshop,*Boston,2000
11. R. Cooley, B. Mobasher and J. Srivastava, "Data preparation for mining World Wide Web browsing patterns",*Journal of Knowledge and Information Systems*, (1) 1, 1999.
12. D.S. Statelov, "SMART EDU A new TV video enabled interactive e-learning platform",   *0-7803-7993-4/03*   *2003*   *IEEE.*

A Research on Issues Related to RFID Security and Privacy

Jongki Kim1, Chao Yang2, Jinhwan Jeon3
1 Division of Business Administration, College of Business,
Pusan National University, 30, GeumJeong-Gu, Busan,
609-735, Korea, E-mail: jkkim1@pusan.ac.kr
2 Department of Business Administration, Graduate School,
Pusan National University, 30, GeumJeong-Gu, Busan,
609-735, Korea, E-mail:nvhair0818@hanmail.net
3 Research and Education Institute of Banking, Security and
Derivatives, Pusan National University, 30, GeumJeong-Gu,
Busan, 609-735, Korea, E-mail: jeonjinhwan@pusan.ac.kr

Abstract: Radio Frequency Identification (RFID) is a technology for automated identification of objects and people. RFID systems have been gaining more popularity in areas especially in supply chain management and automated identification systems. However, there are many existing and potential problems in the RFID systems which could threat the technology's future. To successfully adopt RFID technology in various applications, we need to develop the solutions to protect the RFID system's data information. This study investigates important issues related to privacy and security of RFID based on the recent literature and suggests solutions to cope with the problem.

1 Introduction

Radio Frequency Identification (RFID) is a technology for identification of objects and people automatically, as a supplementary technology or replace traditional barcode technology to identify, track, and trace items automatically. RFID may be viewed as a means of explicitly labeling objects to facilitate their "perception"[1] by computing devices.

Please use the following format when citing this chapter:

Kim, J., Yang, C., Jeon, J., 2007, in IFIP International Federation for Information Processing, Volume 252, Integration and Innovation Orient to E-Society Volume 2, eds. Wang, W., (Boston: Springer), pp. 412-420.

RFID dates back to the 1940's. The British Air Force used RFID-like technology in World War II to identify whether planes belonged to them or not. The theory of RFID was first put forwarded in 1948 in a conference paper which entitled "Communication by Means of Reflected Power" by Stockman, and the first patent for RFID was filed by Charles Walton in 1973.

RFID system is composed of two core components, reader which is the central component of an RFID system and RFID-tag in which records the production's information and a unique ID. Moreover, antenna, middleware, and back database also play an important role in RFID system.

RFID-tag is small microchip designed for wireless data transmission. Tags have various forms and functional characteristics, and could be classified into active tags and passive tags. Active tags use the onboard power sources, like batteries, so can support more sophisticated electronics with increased data storage, long read/write range, sensor interfaces, and specialized functions. Passive tags designed without onboard power source, receive the power from the RFID reader devices, so the read/write range is shorter than active tags.

Thanks to the effort of large organizations, such as Wal-Mart, Procter and Gamble, and the U.S. Department of Defense, to deploy RFID as a tool for automated oversight of their supply chains, RFID has been paid more and more attention in the past years. RFID technologies could have been used in so many applications, the combination of dropping tag cost and forceful RFID standardization is an important reason.

However, RFID confronts many challenges, in order to accept this technology in broader fields, we need to develop the solution to secure and protect the human's privacy. Thus, we will review the attacks to the systems, reported privacy threats and some possible solutions.

2 Security and Privacy Issues

In the near future, RFID will become part of more high-profile applications. But at the mean time, more and more people worry that security and privacy problems would interfere the future of this technology, particularly as it is used for more critical purposes. Now, we review the issues related to RFID system first.

2.1 Risks in RFID Business Process

Many threats to RFID systems can be aroused by human or the environment in management and technical areas. Anybody can damage or destroy a tag mindfully or mindlessly, also can remove the tag from the item to which it was attached, or replace a tag with another one to meet some certain intentions.

The environment's changes also can influence the RFID systems' data. In the extreme heat, cold, moisture, vibration, shock, and radiation circumstance, the tag performance could be menaced because of the impacts, which include degradation of the tags and their performance, and separation of the tags from the associated items.

A mount of factors can influence the business risks in RFID systems, including the importance of the RFID-supported business processes to the mission of the organization, the robustness of business continuity planning or fallback procedures, the existence of adversaries with the motivation and the capability to perform RFID attacks, and the presence and effectiveness of RFID security controls.

NIST (2006) proposed some other factors that influence business intelligence risk, including the type of information stored on the tag, the usefulness or relevance of information available to the adversary, and the location of RFID components.

Externality risk is another important risk worth discussing in RFID system, which results from electromagnetic radiation. The main types of hazards from electromagnetic radiation are the hazards to ordnance which is evaluated by the U.S. military regulations, the hazards to fuel that is the danger of electromagnetic waves causing the sparking or arcing between two metals, the hazards to people which can heat living tissue and the hazards to other materials such as blood products, vaccines, and pharmaceuticals. Although each type has special characteristics, the influence factors are similar. Include RFID operating power and frequency, distance between RFID system components and object, and the complex cavity effects [2].

2.2 Attacks to RFID Tag

Since RFID tag computational resource is limited, the RFID environment connects everything, and an RFID tag can't identify authentic readers generally, so RFID system is vulnerable to suffer from variable attacks.

Denial-of-Service (DoS) Attacks Computer and Information Science Security Research Group at Edith Cowan University indicates that hackers could launch DoS attacks against some types of RFID systems [3].

Attacking and Modifying Tag Lukas Grunwald noted that hackers with the proper equipment could record data from a low-cost RFID chip and upload another data to it. He also said that some programs could access the Internet and become available to hackers. Specially, counterfeiting tags is an attack that consisted in modifying the identity of an item [3].

Traffic Analysis Traffic analysis is another kind of attacks that describes the process of intercepting and examining messages in order to extract information from patterns in communication [4].

Spoofing Spoofing tag can occur if an attacker is able to impersonate a legitimate tag successfully [4].

2.3 Privacy Threat

The biggest social issue centers on privacy concerns and threat of legislative oversight. Artifact LLC and BIG research recently found that more than 60% of consumers concerned on the privacy issues about the RFID [5].

RFID tags respond to reader interrogation without alerting their owners or bearers. Therefore, if the read range permits, it is possible to do the clandestine scanning of tag. Whoever carrying an RFID tag can broadcast a serial number to the nearby readers   effectively, so provides a good vehicle for clandestine physical tracking, even if the tag number is random and carries no intrinsic data [1]. The privacy threat will become serious if a tag number combines with personal information.

Location Threat Users who carry RFID tags can be monitored and then their location revealed. A tagged object's location may be unauthorized disclosure without thinking of who is carrying it [6].

Constellation Threat The tags form a unique RFID constellation around the person whether user's identity is associated with a tag set or not and adversaries can use this constellation to track people [7].

Transaction Threat Anyone who takes RFID reader can conjecture the transaction between users associated with the constellation when tagged objects change from one constellation to another. Tow typical threats of this threat are action threat that the individual's behavior is inferred by monitoring the action of a group of tags and the association threat that the individual's identity can be associated with the purchased items containing the RFID tag [8].

Preference Threat A tag uniquely identifies the manufacture, the product type, and the object's unique identity. This shows the customer preferences at a low cost. If the adversary can easily determine the item's monetary value, this threat can become a value threat [9].

Breadcrumb Threat This is a threat that the discarded breadcrumbs keep tagged items and identities associating with them, so they can be subject to be used to commit malicious act [7].

2.4 Other Risks

Besides those risks and threats mentioned above, there are some other issues, such as the risk of embedding virus into the RFID tags and the problem of cloning tags.

Viruses Researchers of Vrije University's Computer Systems Group said that hackers could create viruses and embed them in RFID tags. The viruses could exploit application vulnerabilities and cause a buffer overflow or some other problem that could infect a back-end system. Once the database is infected, RFID applications that access its information could write the mal-ware into other tags and thereby propagate the infection [3].

Cloning RFID Tag Johns Hopkins University's Information Security Institute and RSA Laboratories' researchers have demonstrated that hackers could clone implanted tags in the way that thieves steal RFID-protected vehicles [9]. Hackers could use cloners to intercept a tag's digital identity, and then crack the encryption and use a software radio simulate the legitimate tag, and then deceive the reader.

3. Solutions

In the following, we will describe several mechanisms have bee proposed to enhance the RFID's security and privacy. Effective mechanisms should provide protection against the risks mentioned. But at the meanwhile, the cost of the approaches should also be taken into account.

"Killing" and "Sleeping" Command EPC tags address users protect the privacy in the way of killing tags. When tagged objects are purchased, the EPC tag receives a "kill" command from a reader and then it deactivated itself permanently. Sleeping tag is an improved approach which is similar to killing tag, but the merit of it is that the deactivated tag can be activated by "wake" [10].

Tag Password Verifying PINs or passwords in basic RFID tags is a simple way to protect the information. The tags do not send out important information unless it receives the right password. Only if the reader knows the tag's identity, otherwise it can not know which password to transmit to a tag [11].

BlockingTag [10] proposed the blocker tag, which enhances RFID privacy in a different way. This scheme depends on the incorporation into tags of a modifiable bit called a privacy bit.

However, the blocking tags approach has some limitations. Such as, it may enable the store pickpocket to be possible to hide the stores' security check. Thus, the authors proposed the selective blocking tags in the same paper, and then Juels and Brainard [12] proposed another improved scheme-soft blocking, which are the schemes can protect against the preference threat.

Schemes Based on Hash Functions Weis et al. [13] proposed a Hash-Lock scheme to protect information privacy of RFID. In this approach, a tag's ID is saved in memory in two states: locked and unlocked. It is possible that using the ID to lock a tag to prevent revealing information, and use another key to unlock a locked tag. Then he designed another randomized Hash-Lock scheme to improve the temporarily unchanged meta-ID problem which existed in the Hash-Lock scheme. Ohkubo et al. [14] designed Hash-Chain scheme to satisfy the requirements that tag embeds two different hash functions and can generate one out-going value to response and new secret value quickly.

Regulating Tag Garfinkel [15] proposed RFID Bill of Rights that should be upheld when using RFID systems. The RFID Bill of Rights addresses privacy problems through regulation on consumers' knowledge of the RFID tags' existence, removal/deactivation on purchase, consumers' data and service accessibility, the time and location, and the tags accessing reasons.

Classic Cryptography Kinoshita et al. [16] proposed an anonymous-ID scheme based on rewritable memory. Concealing a tag's permanent ID, which has a rewritable memory contains a user-chosen private ID or assign a partial ID sequence to a user-assignable tag, so that users could control the uniqueness of IDs from local to global without revealing the relationship between the ID and the object.

Symmetric key encryption is another approach which was proposed by Feldhofer et al. [17] based on a simple two-way challenge-response algorithm. And an RFID protocol-yoking was proposed by Juels [18]. He pointed the cryptographic proof that two tags have been scanned simultaneously, and evidence that the tags were scanned in physical proximity to one another. This scheme is suitable for basic tags that require no computation virtually.

Public key encryption is also an approach that based on the cryptographic principle of re-encryption.

As the approach to protect information privacy, encryption is an effective method, but it dose have limits. First, the encrypted identifier itself is just another identifier. Second, there is the problem of key management in encryption scheme. Moreover, the problem of cost is the most important and it is difficult to apply them to low-cost tags.

Distance Measurement Signal-to-noise ratio of the reader signal in an RFID system provides a rough metric of the distance between a reader and a tag [19]. With some additional, low-cost circuitry tag might achieve rough measurement of the distance of an interrogating reader, and proposed that this distance can serve as a metric for trust.

Shielding Tag The faraday cage approach is one kind of shielding. It isolates RFID tags from any kind of electromagnetic waves by using a faraday cage which is a container made of metal mesh or foil that is impenetrably by radio signals. In addition, after products are taken out of the containers, they can still be scanned by unauthorized personal. Another approach of shielding tags is the active jamming approach which isolating from electromagnetic waves by disturbing the radio channel [11].

Proxy Approach It is possible that users carry their own privacy-enforcing devices for RFID instead of relying on public RFID readers to enforce privacy protection, like the mobile devices. RFID Guardian is a typical approach, which is a platform that offers centralized RFID security and privacy management for individual people which is meant for personal use. The consumers can protect their privacy through carrying a battery-powered mobile device that monitors and regulates their RFID usage. The heart of the RFID Guardian is that it integrates four previously separate security properties that include auditing, key management, access control, and authentication into a single device [20].

Tag Pseudonyms It is an approach that uses a small pseudonyms collection and rotates these pseudonyms as its identifier in every tag, release a different one on each reader query. The authorized readers share the full pseudonym set with tag in advance, so they can identify the tag. Since attackers are unable to correlate two different pseudonyms of the same tag, it would be more difficult for unauthorized tag to track [1].

Trusted Computing Molnar et al. [21] proposed an approach which relies on "privacy bits". They describe how equipped with trusted platform modules can internally enforce tag privacy policies. However, this scheme dose not solve the rogue readers' problem, it can be as a complement for other privacy protection (Juels, 2006).

Authentication Molar and Wagner [22] proposed a basic PRF private authentication scheme for mutual authentication between tags and readers. This protocol uses a shared secret and a Pseudo-Random Function (PRF) to protect the messages exchanged between the tag and the reader. In the same paper, the authors proposed a tree-based private authentication and delegation tree scheme to reduce the server's load which exists in the hash schemes.

Non-Cryptographic Primitives Vajda and Buttyan [6] proposed a set of extremely lightweight challenge-response authentication protocols which can be used for authenticating tags.

Human Protocols Weis [23] introduced the concept of human computer authentication protocol due to Hopper and Blum, adaptable to low-cost RFID.

Besides the mechanisms described above, the National Institute of Standards and Technology of U.S. drew up the guidance for securing RFID systems. This security controls divided into 3 groups that are management, operational and technical in which described the considerations and controls in detail. Besides these security controls, it also discusses the privacy considerations including the privacy principles, applicable privacy controls and some other recommendations [2].

In addition, the experts have been paying more attention to legal concerns over RFID data collection. For example, in 1998, the European Parliament enacted guidelines on information privacy called the "European Community Directive on Data Protection". Under the EU Directive, information can be collected and used only if in some certain purpose and conditions. To determine the lawfulness of a data processing operation, the Directive also sets out a number of principles. In the practical implementation of RFID systems, 6 golden rules have to be obeyed [24].

Not only European, many countries also have set up regulations to restrict RFID uses from tag production to data collection. Especially, Korea Ministry of

Information and Communication set up the privacy protection guardian to regulate every stage of the use of RFID.

The security loophole and the privacy threats are so complex, it is not possible to solve the problem by depending upon one measure alone, therefore it should evaluate each aspect of the question overall. Any single solution is not comprehensive, and it has the possibility to cause the RFID system to appear other security weakness and loophole. In order to guarantee the RFID system secure, the extendibility, administration and system expenses should be evaluated in overall.

4. Conclusion

RFID technology is universal, useful and convenient, and will be continued to develop quickly in the future. However, it brings many challenges in the implementation, especially on the security and privacy aspects.

This paper provides investigates the security risks and privacy threat in the RFID systems, and gives several approaches in which to solve the issues of RFID based on the recent literature.

With the development of the RFID technology, it will create more and complex problems. Since this technology will be used in more high level applications broadly in the future, the demands in security will also be higher.

References

1. A. Juels, RFID Security and Privacy: A Research Survey, *IEEE Journal on Selected Areas in Communications*, Vol. 24, NO.2, 2006, pp.381-394.
2. NIST. Guidance for Securing Radio Frequency Identification (RFID) Systems (Draft), Special Publication 800-98 (2006).
3. Sixto Ortiz Jr. How Secure Is RFID? IEEE COMPUTER SOCIETY, Computer Archive Vol. 39, 2006, pp.17-19.
4. P. Peris-Lopez, J. C. Hernandez-Castro, J. M. Estevez-Tapiador, and A. Ribagorda, RFID Systems: A Survey on Security Threats and Proposed Solutions, *The 11th IFIP International Conference on Personal Wireless Communications-PWC'06*, Vol. 4217, 2006, pp. 159-170.
5. L. Stegeman, *Who's Afraid of the Big Bad Wolf?* (Market Wire, 2004)
6. I. Vajda, and L. Buttyan, Lightweight Authentication Protocols for Low-Cost RFID Tags, *Proceedings of the 2nd Workshop on Security in Ubiquitous Computing*, 2003, pp. 1-10.
7. I. Kim, B. Lee, and H. Kim, Privacy Protection Based on User-defined Preferences in RFID System, *International Conference on Advanced Communication Technology-ICACT'06*, 2006, pp. 858-862.
8. H. Lee, and J. Kim, Privacy Threats and Issues in Mobile RFID, *Proceedings of the First International Conference on Availability, Reliability, and Security* (ARES' 2006). IEEE Computer Society (April, 2006).

9. S. L. Garfinkel, A. Juels, and R. Pappu, RFID Privacy: An Overview of Problems and Proposed Solutions, IEEE Security and Privacy, vol. 3, 2005, pp. 34-43.

10. A. Juels, R. L. Rivest, and M. Szydlo, The Blocker Tag: Selective Blocking of RFID Tags for Consumer Privacy, *Proceedings of the 8th ACM Conference on Computer and Communications Security*, 2003, pp. 103-111.

11. Y. Xiao, X. Shen, B. Sun, and L. Cai, Security and Privacy in RFID and Applications in Telemedicine, *IEEE Communications Magazine,* Vol. 44, No. 4, 2006, pp.64-72.

12. A. Juels, and J. Brainared, Soft blocking: Flexible Blocker Tags on the Cheap, *Proceedings of Workshop on Privacy in the Electronic Society(WPES04)*, 2004, pp. 1-7.

13. S. A. Weis, S. E. Sarma, L. Ronald Rivest, and W. Daiel Engels, Security and Privacy Aspects of Low-cost Radio Frequency Identification System, *Proceedings of the 1st International Conference on Security in Pervasive Computing,* 2003, pp. 201-212.

14. M. Ohkubo, K. Suzuki, and S. Kinoshita, Cryptographic Approach to Privacy-friendly Tags," RFID Privacy Workshop (2003): http://www.rfidprivacy.us/2003/agenda.php.

15. S. L. Garfinkel, An RFID Bill of Rights, *Technology Review,* 2002, p. 35.

16. S. Kinoshita, F. Hoshino, T. Komuro, A. Fujimura, and M. Ohkubo, Low-cost RFID Privacy Protection Scheme, *Journal of the International Planetarium Society,* Vol. 8, 2003, pp.2007-2021.

17. M. Feldhofer, S. Dominikus, and J. Wolkerstorfer, Strong Authentication for RFID Systems Using the AES Algorithm, *Proceedings of Cryptographic Hardware and Embedded Systems-CHES'04*, Vol. 3156 of LNCS, 2004, pp. 357-370.

18. A. Juels, Yoking-proof's for RFID Tags, *Proceedings of the 2nd IEEE Annual Conference on Pervasive Computing and Communications Workshops (PERCOMW04)*, 2004, pp.138-143.

19. C. Floerkemeier, R. Schneider, and M. Langheinrich, Scanning With Purpose-Supporting the Fair Information Principles in RFID Protocols, *Proceedings of the 2nd International Symposium on Ubiquitous Computing Systems,* 2004, pp. 1-9.

20. M. Rieback, C. Cripo, and A. Tanenbaum, RFID Guardian: A Battery-powered Mobile Device for RFID Privacy Management, *Proceedings of the 10th Australasian Conference on Information Security and Privacy (ACISP2005),* Vol. 3574 of LNCS, 2005, pp. 184-194.

21. D. Molnar, A. Soppera, and D. Wagner, Privacy for RFID through Trusted Computing, *Proceedings of Workshop on Privacy in the Electronic Society, 2005,* pp. 31-34.

22. D. Molnar, and D. Wagner, Privacy and Security in Library RFID: Issues, Practices, and Architectures, *Proceedings of the 11th ACM Conference on Computer and Communications Security,* 2004, pp. 210-219.

23. S. A. Weis, Security Parallels Between People and Pervasive Devices, *The 3rd IEEE Conference on Pervasive Computing and Communications Workshops-PERSEC'05,* 2005, pp. 105-109.

24. P. Van Eecke, and G. Skouma, RFID and Privacy: A Difficult Marriage? *Journal of Computer, Media and Telecommunications Law,* Vol. 3, 2005, pp. 84-90.

Business Models of E-Government: Research on Dynamic E-Government Based on Web Services

Li Yan[1,2], Jiumin Yang [3]
1 Department of Information Management, Huazhong Normal University,
2 Engineering Research Center of Education Information Technology,
Huazhong Normal University, Wuhan, China 430079
yanli@mail.ccnu.edu.cn
3 Department of Information Technology, Huazhong Normal University,
Wuhan, China 430079   yjm@mail.ccnu.edu.cn

Abstract. Government transcends all sectors in a society. It provides not only the legal, political and economic infrastructure to support other sectors, but also exerts significant influence on the social factors that contribute to their development. With its maturity of technologies and management, e-government will eventually enter into the time of 'one-stop' services. Among others, the technology of Web services is the major contributor to this achievement. Web services provides a new way of standard-based software technology, letting programmers combine existing computer system in new ways over the Internet within one business or across many, and would thereby bring about profound and far-reaching impacts on e-government. This paper introduced the business modes of e-government, architecture of dynamic e-government and its key technologies. Finally future prospect of dynamic e-government was also briefly discussed.

1 Introduction

In the past several years, improvement and modernization of services demanded by the public, the need for increased resource efficiency and the supply of advanced information and communication technologies have formed major agencies to drive contemporary governments to transform to electronic government (e-government). The e-government initially defined as the delivery and administration of government products and services over an information technology infrastructure, aiming at efficiency savings and a more effective administration and seeking to achieve an e-commerce styled public sector model. After that, more people realized the need for

Please use the following format when citing this chapter:

Yan, Li., Yang, J., 2007, in IFIP International Federation for Information Processing, Volume 252, Integration and Innovation Orient to E-Society Volume 2, eds. Wang, W., (Boston: Springer), pp. 421-428.

greater citizen participation in government. Since then, the democracy element was introduced into the concept of e-government, whereas the impacts of governance and government itself are equally emphasized. The informatization practice of countries all over the world has shown that the level of a government's informatization is one main factor that can affect its international competitive power [1]. Therefore, based on its maturity levels and transformation processes, e-government can be generally divided into three stages: information, transaction and transformation [2].

2 Web services architecture and technologies

2.1 Web services architecture

A typical web services architecture consists of three entities: service providers, service brokers and service requesters. They provide the three fundamental operations - publish, find and bind - respectively [3].

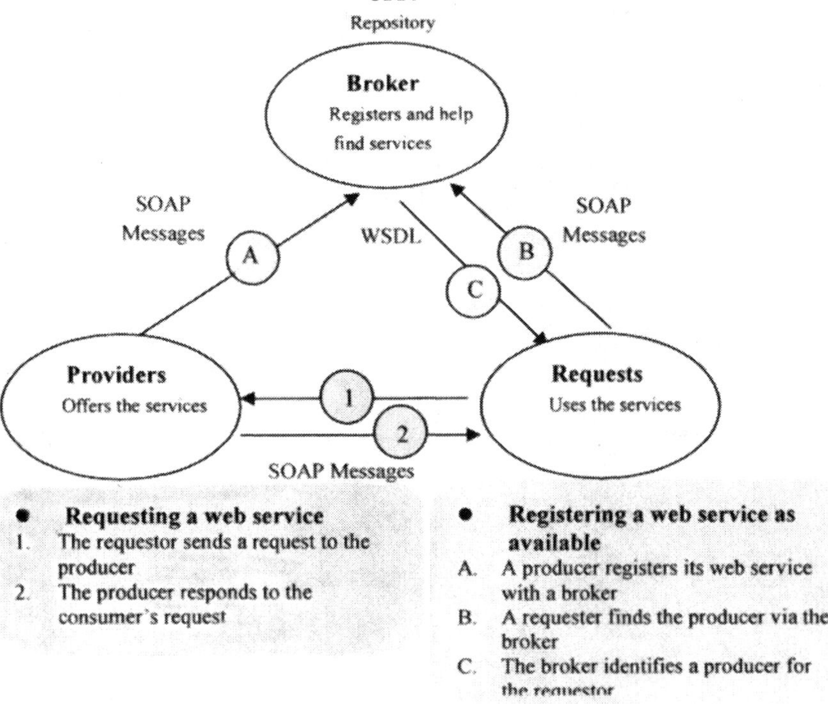

Fig.1. Interaction between service brokers, providers and requests

- Service providers create web services and publish them by registering the services with service brokers.
- Service brokers maintain a registry of published services.
- Service requesters find required services by searching the service broker's registry, and bind their applications to the service provider to use particular services.

The interaction between these three entities is shown in Figure 1.

2.2 Web services Technologies

Web Services Description Language (WSDL), Universal Description, Discovery and Integration (UDDI) and the Simple Object Access Protocol (SOAP) form the core technologies of web services. The roles of each technology in web services will be illustrated in turn [3,4].

- **WSDL**

The WSCL is an XML language used to describe the web services interfaces that are accessible from a wide variety of platforms and programming languages. The description includes such details as data type definitions, the operations supported by the services, input/output message formats, network address and protocol bindings. This means WSDL not only describes message contents, but also defines where the service is available and what communication protocol is used to talk to the service. In other words, WSDL file defines everything required to write a program to work with web services.

- **UDDI**

The UDDI specifies a mechanism to register and locate web services. It lets WS register their characteristics with a registry so that other applications can discover and integrate with them. Users can search for a company that offers the services needed, read about the services offered and contact the company for further information.

In web services, the description of a business and the services it offers are presented by UDDI directory entry. Typically an entry in the UDDI consists of three parts. The 'Yellow Pages' describes the companies offering the services. The information covers names, addresses, contacts, etc. The 'White Pages' includes industrial categories based on standard taxonomies. The 'Green Pages' describes the interface to the service in enough detail for users to write an application to use the web services.

Meanwhile, the UDDI directory provides several ways to let users search for the services they need to build their own applications. For instance, the search can be based on a specified geographic location or on business of a specified type. The UDDI directory will present information, contacts, links and technical data of each service to allow users to evaluate and choose from. Needless to say, such a function makes the search more flexible and efficient.

- **SOAP**

The SOAP lets a program working in one operating system communicate with a program working in another by using HTTP and XML as information-exchange mechanisms. It is therefore provides the means for communication between web services and client applications.

Taken them together, while WSDL defines how web services are described, UDDL describes how to find web services, and SOAP describes how to talk to web services. These technologies constitute a set of baseline specifications that provide the foundation for application integration and aggregation.

3 Dynamic e-government business models

Business model is an overall architecture reflecting the core business of an organization. Unlike the traditional governments, an e-government takes on a new look with its framework and operation mode more suitable for the contemporary era [1]. Since e-commerce and e-government are the two comprehensive guiding visions of e-business, e-government is akin to e-commerce in many aspects of business model. In efforts to use information and communication technologies for the civil and political conduct of government, many countries have begun supporting e-government initiatives. The ultimate goal is to improve government-citizen interactions through an infrastructure built around the "life experience" of citizens [5].

Based on the entities involved, e-government can be classified as G2C, G2B, G2G and G2E [6,7].

Based on its scope, e-government's architecture involves public network access to facilitate government-citizen interaction, intranets to support intra-governmental processes and extranets to support interactions between government and non-government organizations [7]. Figure 2 illustrates a general architectural model for e-government.

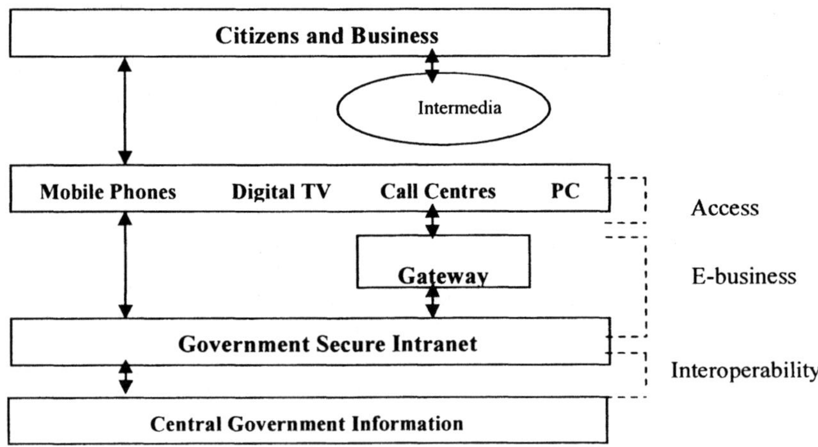

Fig. 2. Architectural model of dynamic e-government

4 Merits of web services to dynamic e-government

Web services produce significant benefits, mainly involving interoperability, flexibility, automatic integration and cost-effectiveness.
● Interoperability
As presented, the significant feature of web services is language-, platform- and location-independent. It provides a means for different organizations with different applications and platform to conduct dynamic e-government across a network, and in turn offering a new range of possibilities for organizations and their partners to develop business solutions.
● Flexibility
Using the traditional approaches to build business applications like in-house custom development software solution and electronic data interchange (EDI) software mentioned above, companies had to know the information such as who was using the applications, how, when, where and why. With WS, companies can build applications without having to know this information. More importantly, each company can have choices of becoming a provider or consumer of services. New revenue streams and new business models would be generated by using existing software assets and integrating them with other businesses.

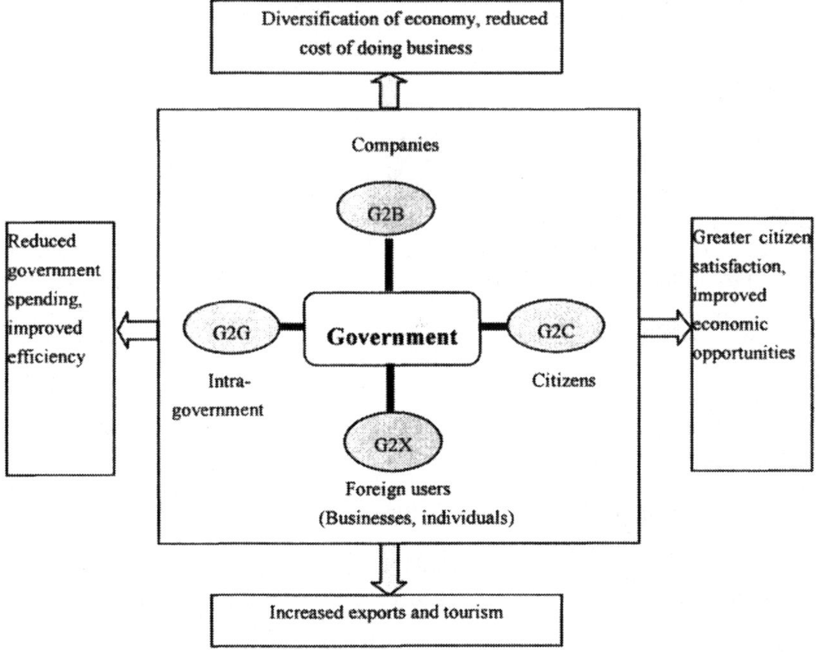

Fig.3. Benefits of dynamic e-government to key stakeholders

● Automatic integration

Since applications are written to the new standards, WS enable the applications to be automatically integrated regardless where they originate. This provides large potential benefits to the achievement of dynamic e-government.

- Cost-effectiveness

The flexibility of WS also benefits companies to switch to a different preferred supplier more swiftly and smoothly than has ever been possible without disrupting processes or requiring new investments. For this reason, web services are cost-effective.

From the standpoint of key stakeholders, the benefits generated by dynamic e-government are displayed in the Figure 3.

5 Challenges

E-government is facing a number of exceptional challenges because of its strict and commitment natures of relationships of G2C, G2G, G2B and G2E [4,8]. In spite of the considerable literature on e-government, we still do not have a comprehensive, holistic framework in place that assesses the potential of e-government by taking into consideration all the critical dimensions [4]. The major technological challenges include two aspects [9].

5.1 Equality of access

Productive, meaningful e-government means citizens must be able to access critical information and services through a variety of devices at their convenience. However, there is an obvious risk that government services and democratic processes will be more accessible to some than to others due to the problem of 'digital divide' of different kinds, between rich and poor countries or regions, between groups within one country differing on social or economic status, age, education level or cultural background and between urban and rural areas [7].

From managerial perspective, to mitigate the digital divide at local or national level is relatively easy to achieve. However, to achieve this goal at international level is a hardship task. Many issues, such as democracy, national development, international aid, local and international business, as well as binational and multinational cooperation program are on the table. With no intention to discuss the social policies that the government should boost to overcome the risk of digital divide, this paper introduces so-called 'Avatars' technology, which can diminish the digital divide to some degrees.

Avatars are animated humanlike characters in knowledge-based presentation systems. They are intelligent interface agents with varying degrees of conversational ability. Technically, they have modules for language processing, interaction management, manipulation interface output animation and so on. Avatars can be helpful in diminishing digital divide because users do not need to be trained in usage of the communication protocols. Every citizen has the skill to use them.

5.2 Security and privacy

The issues of security and privacy in e-government are vital to maintain the public trusts. Old government systems were difficult to access and often provided little in the way of useable data. But they were usually very secure. Only a handful of individuals could access them and security procedures were relatively easy to set and carry out. This situation is not so with web-based e-government systems. Given the reason that the technical solutions to security in e-commerce are transferable to and applicable in e-government, this section focuses on privacy issue.

Privacy is defined as 'the right of individuals to control the collection, use and dissemination of their person information that is held by others'. Also, it is widely understood as the ethical obligations associated with the collection and use of personal information. Its principles include transparency, fairness, access and security. However, recent surveys have found that while small percentage of government entities have accepted the practices for wide spread use, the evolving technologies (such as click streams, web bugs and cookies) have created a dramatic increase in the collection, use and movement of information and have in turn eroded the perception of personal privacy [4]. Thus it is not surprising that consumers and citizens rank the lack of privacy protection as the foremost deterrent for conducting online transactions.

In addition, some privacy experts contend that a privacy divide, much like the digital divide is developing. The contention is that lower income households have to face more risk of privacy exposure than the middle and upper income households, because they often have no privacy choice when receiving benefits from government or when they attain free services from a company. Certainly privacy divide is not directly related to e-government. However, if this issue does not well addressed, it will effect e-government development in the future.

Developing appropriate security and privacy policies while balance the demands of open public access is a great challenge. The 'holistic view' approach is often recommended, in which security and privacy requirements have to be specified and implemented for each lay of the strategy, process, interaction and data and information.

6 Conclusion

Nowadays, a majority of the world's government has Web sites that offer citizens basic information about government organizations, processes and programs, and the quality of these sites is improving at a rapid pace. Although for obvious reasons, e-government within the most economically developed nations (such as the US, UK, EU, Canada and Australia) has progressed faster than within developing countries, developing countries have started to apply new technologies to build their e-governments. At present, e-government construction is regarded as one of the most important tasks for the national economy and society informatization in China [1]. In our country, strategies and initiatives of e-government are underway. The national E-Government project is currently undertaking by the State Information Center [1].

With its maturity of technologies and management, e-government is moving towards and will eventually enter into the time of 'one-stop' services. Among others, the technology of Web service will be the major contributor to this achievement [11].

In conclusion, e-government gives rise to new kind of government model, which offers a remarkable set of opportunities to increase the transparency of government operations, improve access to government services and enhance efficiency of government administration [4]. Nevertheless, e-government is still in its evolution and is facing various technical and managerial challenges. It needs to be realized that success of e-government relies on three fundamental factors: business, technology and human.

References

1. J. J. Ning, "E-government in China: current status, strategies and practice, E-Commerce Technology for Dynamic E-Business", *IEEE International Conference*(2004) .

2. P. Mao, *E-Government Guide* ,Peking University Press, Beijing (2003).

3. B. Medjahed, A. Rezgui, A. Bouguettaya and M. Ouzzani, "Infrastructure for e-government Web services", *Internet Computing*, IEEE, V 7, 11, 58 – 65 (2003).

4. M. A. Usman, M. Nadeem, M. Z. A. Ansari, and S. Raza, "Multi-agent Based Semantic E-government Web Service Architecture Using Extended WSDL", Web Intelligence and International Agent Technology Workshops, WI-IAT 2006 Workshops. *2006 IEEE/WIC/ACM International Conference* on Dec. 2006 ,599- 604.

5. B. Medjahed, A. Rezgui, A. Bouguettaya.and M. Ouzzani, "Infrastructure for e-government Web services", *Internet Computing, IEEE*, Volume 7, Issue 1, 58 – 65(2003).

6. M. Ramaswamy,and A. N. Selian, "e-Government in Transition Countries: Prospects and Challenges System Sciences", *HICSS*, Annual Hawaii International Conference (Jan. 2007), 92(2006).

7. P. Salhofer and D. Ferbas, "A Business Process Engine Based E-Government Platform Internet and Web Applications and Services", *ICIW '07*. Second International Conference on 13-19 , 54[2007-5].

8. H. L. Liu, Z. J. Zhang and Z. F. Peng, *E-Government System Outline*, Posts&Telecom Press, Beijing (2005).

9. X. N. Su Xinning, *E-Government Technologies* , National Defense Industry Press (2003).

10. X. B. Ma and D.Y.Ye, *Software Platform and Middleware Technologies*, Xiamen University Press (2005).

11. B. Meneklis, A. Kaliontzoglou, C. Douligeris and D. Polemi, "Engineering and technology aspects of an e-government architecture based on Web services", *Third IEEE European Conference* ,2[2005-12].

Education for Digitization: A Case Studyon Sharing E-Information Resources inUniversity Library

Li-hong Zhu
Library of Huazhong Normal University,
Wuhan, Hubei 430079, P.R.China
E-mail:zlh_lib@mail.ccnu.edu.cn

Abstract: This paper reported an international survey of library, information science (LIS), computer science faculty and websites, regarding digital libraries courses and curriculum at our institutions. We concluded that few universities currently offer courses on digital libraries while many universities have not developed Digital Library (DL) courses, even they are aware of the need to develop curriculum in this growing area of research and practice. The major aim of the paper is to present results from a survey on the current state of digital library education (DLE) in academic institutions. Additionally we examine the rationale and orientation for digital library education. We suggest several models that have emerged in the teaching of DLE and in incorporation of relevant topics into various curricula.

1   Introduction

Information, especially digital information, is becoming an increasingly important component of modern life. More and more individuals rely upon the Internet for routine information gathering. It is particularly important for students: 88.4 percent of entering 2002 full-time freshmen reported using the Internet for homework during the year prior to beginning college, as compared with 84.5 percent in the fall of 2006[1]. Naturally, librarians are playing essential roles in making electronic information resources and services more widely available to the public.

Digital libraries (DLs) are emerging as an important area of research and education for information science, computer science and a number of other related disciplines. In this paper, our discussion is based on a recent worldwide survey of DL courses. What we conclude from our analysis is the urgent need for the development of DL education programs amidst a burgeoning growth of DL research and practice by librarians, and information and computer scientists.

Please use the following format when citing this chapter:

Zhu, L.-H., 2007, in IFIP International Federation for Information Processing, Volume 252, Integration and Innovation Orient to E-Society Volume 2, eds. Wang, W., (Boston: Springer), pp. 429-436.

Today's libraries are facing with the challenges of integrating traditional and emerging formats, balancing resource allocation between traditional and upcoming technologies and building new information management processes and procedures. As intermediaries between the challenging, multi-format, multi-media information domain and the ever demanding user community, librarians need to be proactive and concerned about the new information landscape. The four distinct categories of information discussed are popular information, scholarly information, digitization projects and Web resources. 'Popular information' is more or less trade and commercial in nature which comprises the print book and its electronic counterpart, the emerging print-on-demand (POD), journals and newspapers (print and online), and the audio/visual media (analogue and digital). The 'scholarly information' is academic and scientific in nature and consists of the print and electronic books, journals, scholarly articles, theses and dissertations, course management materials and e-print archives[2]. The 'digitization projects' mainly concern themselves with the vast number of worldwide initiatives on commercial, national, state and local digital library projects.

Digital libraries in China are seen as the systematic engineering of cross-institutions, professions, disciplines and regional boundaries. The Government realizes the importance of digital libraries in serving the country's goals. The construction of the national digital library is prioritized as one important component of its new national information infrastructure. Government departments involved include the Ministries of Culture, Education, Science and Technology, Finance, Communications, Information Industry, and the State Development and Planning Commission, among others.

Another characteristic of the Chinese digital libraries is the collaboration between government agencies and professional institutions/associations. China Digital Library was brought under the control of the Department of Ministry. It was also the key project, ``Project 863" of the State Council. Tsinghua University Digital Library was sponsored by the Ministry of Education. National Technological Library and The practical collaborative applications of the China Digital Library have advanced communications, information and knowledge power in the developing world. For example, In recent years, the storage capability of digital databases in HNUL(Huazhong Normal University Library) has greatly expanded and Multimedia resource has reached 1.5 TB, 7050 online E-books are subscribed. 43 Chinese and foreign language databases legally connected with HNUL have covered all main disciplines in HNU campus. Among them, there are 19 Chinese databases, 14 foreign ones, 8 trial databases, and 2 special databases created by its staff members of HNUL. The E-journal and E-book databases are popular with all kinds of patrons for their convenience. Besides the commercial databases, HNUL has been developing its own databases, "The database of Issues in the rural area of China" and "The database of thesis by HNU graduates" which are branches of China Academic Library & Information System (CALIS).This paper concentrated on the education for digital libraries such as interpretation of digital library, essential educational context, as well as perspective for choices and orientation. Classic educational questions regarding digital libraries arise in many institutions including:

What is the meaning of "digital library education"?
Which kinds of courses do we teach about in digital library?
How to teach the users in DL?

2. DLE Review

What is a "digital library"? The answer is not self-evident. Digital library as a concept and a reality is defined in a number of ways; at times it is even treated as a primitive, undefined concept. In other words, there is no agreed upon definition of digital libraries. We will reflect more about this in the review of definitions in the next section[3][4]. Currently, there is little systematic support for developing DL courses and curricula, and no coordinated effort in library and information science (LIS) or computer science to provide DL education. At present, we do not know much about good digital library education. We do not know what knowledge is required to produce information or computer professionals to work as digital librarians, digital developers, or in other job categories, or even what the job designations or requirements will be in the future. Computer scientists may be responsible for the technical development of digital libraries, with information scientists focusing on the content, organization, users, and retrieval of information. But just a decade later, by the start of 2000s, research, practical developments, and general interest in digital libraries has exploded globally. What a decade for digital libraries!

The emerging demand for digital librarians and digital libraries may warrant the restructuring of the library and information science, and the computer science curricula. In the United States, several universities have reorganized existing library schools to emphasize digital information and online services. Two notable examples are at Berkeley and Michigan. In addition, there are numerous specialized courses, ranging from creating web sites for computer scientists to seminars on intellectual property for lawyers. Nevertheless, the number of courses that are specifically on digital libraries is surprisingly small[5].

Several trends affected this digital library explosion.

First, advanced societies in the Western world kept evolving into a new form variously referred to as information, knowledge, or post-industrial society. Managing knowledge records became an ever more important part and problem of that evolving society, especially since the phenomenon of information explosion, the unabated growth of knowledge records of all kinds, kept accelerating.

Second, the digital and networked technology reached a certain level of maturity and spread rapidly, which provided for more involved, varied, and broader opportunities and problems at the same time.

Third, in most, if not all fields, the nature of scholarly communication changed drastically, creating problems and fueling exploration for new approaches for supporting and sustaining it.

Finally, substantive funding became available for research and for practical developments and explorations on a variety of solutions to these problems. Digital libraries have been embraced as one (but not the only one) of the more advanced and more encompassing conceptual and practical solutions.

The digital library education questions, we concern about teaching in such kind of these educational areas, and resolve the question the contents and methods of digital library education A scheduling instance consists of a set of n jobs $V = \{1,2,...,n\}$. With each job $j \in V$ we associate a (strictly) positive processing time p_j and a non-negative weight ω_j. In addition to the jobs, a number m of identical parallel machines will be given. The machines all run with the same speed and can process any job. Of course, at any point in time, each machine can process only one job and every job can only be processed by one machine. We will restrict to the non-preemptive case. Once a job is started on a certain machine, it will be finished on that machine without any interruption.

3. DLE Project

3.1 What kinds of course s do we teach about in digital library

The answer depends, to a large extent, on having a relatively clear idea about what are digital libraries. As mentioned, no agreed upon definition exists, which is fine, because the same constructs can be viewed from a number of viewpoints or perspectives. Let us explore some of these perspectives through definitions offered. Of course, a choice of a given perspective dictates the choice of the content.

Different perspectives about digital libraries, together with competing visions and associated definitions, come from several communities that are involved in digital library work. We are concentrating here on two communities: research and practice. While they work and proceed independently of each other, they can be considered on two ends of a spectrum, which as yet have not met in the middle. To use another metaphor: the research and practice communities are in the same planetary system, but one is on Mars, the other on Venus. The research community grounded mostly in computer science, on one end of the spectrum, asks research questions directed toward future vision or visions of digital libraries, or rather of their various technology oriented aspects and components, unrestricted by practice. On the other end of the spectrum, the practice community, grounded mostly in librarianship and information science, asks developmental, operational, and use questions in real-life economic and institutional contexts, restrictions, and possibilities, concentrating on applications on the use end of the spectrum.

In research, DLIs did not define 'digital library.' In order to incorporate a wide range of possible approaches and domains, the concept is treated broadly and vaguely. Thus, the projects, particularly in DLE, cover a wide range of topics, stretching the possible meaning of digital library to and even beyond the limit of what can be considered as being digital and at the same time recognizable as any kind of a library or a part thereof. This is perfectly acceptable for research -- frontiers need to be stretched. But at the same time, it makes choices for educational content diffuse and difficult.

Digital libraries are organizations that provide the resources, including the specialized staff, to select, structure, offer intellectual access to, interpret, distribute, preserve the integrity of, and ensure the persistence over time of collections of digital works so that they are readily and economically available for use by a defined community or set of communities.

3.2 Toward of Model of DLE

At this point in time, it is premature to suggest a fully developed curriculum, including courses, for digital library education. However, following the model of the ACM in their development of an undergraduate curriculum in Information Studies, we can suggest several curriculum areas and substantive topics that seem to be important in the further development and incorporation of digital libraries education into LIS. If we are to succeed in developing effective models for digital libraries education, we need to fashion a hybrid curriculum that brings together the complementary strengths from diverse departments such as computer science, psychology, policy studies, and library and information studies. Such interdisciplinary partnerships, while not new, often prove to be problematic in their implementation.

Our personal position is that digital libraries are first and foremost *libraries*, and, as such, any model curriculum should maintain a core set of courses that address the major functions and activities of libraries in general, in both digital and traditional forms. At the same time, courses explicitly focusing on technology for digital libraries should strive to connect specific technical applications to the library environment. Our suggested list of curriculum areas for digital libraries education takes into account the need for interdisciplinary collaboration.

Table1. Curriculum Areas and Suggested Topics for Digital Library Education

CURRICULUM AREAS:	TOPICS:
Theoretical and Historical Foundations	History of libraries; Human information behavior; Information retrieval theory; Development of digital collections and digital libraries
Technical Infrastructure of the Digital Library	Information retrieval engines; Database construction of digital libraries; Distributed collections; Multimedia formats and applications; Interoperability
Knowledge Organization in Digital Libraries	Metadata; Indexing; Classification; Database integration; Document formats
Collection Development and Maintenance	Digital archives; Digital conversion technology; Digital preservation
Information Access and Utilization of Digital Libraries	Users and uses of digital libraries; Usability and evaluation research; Information behavior in digital libraries
Social, Economic and Policy Issues	Electronic publishing; Scholarly communication; Copyright issues and intellectual property rights in digital libraries
Professional Issues	Roles and responsibilities of the digital librarian; Management of digital libraries; Bibliographic instruction

4. Training to use the Digital Resources in DL

University libraries are faced with the challenges of integrating traditional and emerging formats, balancing resource allocation between traditional and upcoming technologies and building new information management processes and procedures. Libraries today buy, subscribe, license and accumulate information in an unprecedented array of content categories or publication types, and in a rapidly proliferating mix of formats (digital as well as print).

As intermediaries between the challenging, multi-format, multi-media information domain and the ever demanding user community, DLE need to be proactive and concerned about the new information landscape. The four distinct categories of information discussed are popular information, scholarly information, digitization projects and Web resources. 'Popular information' is more or less trade and commercial in nature which comprises the print book and its electronic counterpart, the emerging print-on-demand (POD), journals and newspapers (print and online), and the audio/visual media (analogue and digital). The 'scholarly information' is academic and scientific in nature and consists of the print and electronic books, journals, scholarly articles, theses and dissertations, course management materials and e-print archives. The 'digitization projects' mainly concern themselves with the vast number of worldwide initiatives on commercial, national, state and local digital library projects. The 'Web resources' form an important stakeholder in the new genre of information resources, providing an array of challenges as well as opportunities to the information professional. The information available in the Web (WWW) could be categorized as surface Web (visible Web) resources and the deep Web (invisible Web) resources.

As the new information landscape, the DLE need to reform to profile of user behavior, and must teach use of electronic information services (EIS) , information skills, and the role of training and wider learning experiences in DL. DLE training project for user is including three aspects as follows.

4.1 Teaching users to known DL architecture in university library

A digital library is a complicated systematic engineering. It covers telecommunication infrastructure, computer hardware support systems, information

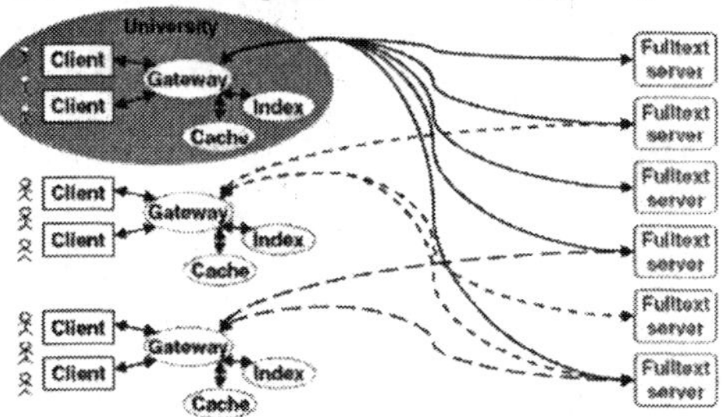

Fig. 1. Distributed Digital Library Architecture

retrieval, digital information processing, digital information storage, digital information exchange, digital information organization, and interface design from the technique perspective. The World Wide Web has changed the way research literature is accessed. Most publishers put their fulltext archive onto the web as DL containing downloadable files in the portable document format (PDF). Integrating multiple indexes of bibliographic data about the accessible documents into a single DL portal allows users to search all archives simultaneously. The result is the DL architecture shown in Figure. 1.

4.2 Teaching users to use CALIS information resources in university library

The China Academic Library & Information System (CALIS) is one of the two public service systems planned by the Chinese Higher Education Schema "211

Program" authorized by the State Council of China. CALIS organized the indexes/abstract (I/A) titles included Ei Village, Web of Science, INSPEC, Cambridge Science Abstracts (CSA), OCLC's First Search, ProQuest Digital Dissertations, BIOSIS Previews (BP), Current Contents, Chemistry Server, Derwent Innovation Index, Journal Citation Reports on the Web(JCR), CA on CD, and National Technical Information Service (NTIS), Full-text products included ScienceDirect OnSite, IEE/IEEE Electronic Library (IEL), International Digital Electronic Access Library (IDEAL), Springer-LINK, Kluwer Online, Academic Search Elite, Business Source Premier, ABI/INFORM Global, Academic Research Library, IOPP, Science Online, and Nature etc.

The duty of DLE is known to be able to render both active and individualized services to its users in imparting the knowledge and transmitting information. By means of literature service network, we can convey the information from periodicals and dissertations to readers, which will enable readers to share information embodied, And, we will collect the relevant information with regard to the latest publications, which will be sent to readers on the regular basis so as to enable readers to obtain information from various databases. Besides, we have also set such special columns as "Specific Information about Books" and "Online Consultation Activity".

4.3 Teaching users to use information retrieval system in university library

The content/information integration model adopted for the system is illustrated in Figure. 2. Information retrieval in the library portal has been made as user friendly as possible so that even people with less or no computer and Web background can get the best out of the vast treasure of information resources available at HNU.

Hyperlink buttons are provided for each and every significant information source or publication type. Simple pop-up and pull-down menus appear as and when these links are clicked. Users can select the service of their choice based on context relevance such as the library specific information and library rules/regulations, DL OF HNU onsite full-text /abstract/index databases, e-journals, online services such as Web-based databases (scholarly as well as corporate) and value added information products, popular and useful hyperlinks, online reference queries, Frequently Asked Questions (FAQs) on library services/activities, etc.

The Library Portal interface frame is shown in Figure. 3. DL do enable the creation of local content, strengthening the mechanisms and capacity of the library's information systems and services. They increase the portability, efficiency of access, flexibility, availability and preservation of content. Value added and pinpointed information at the click of the mouse has become a reality at DL of HNU and the library portal is now giving access to the invaluable collection hosted by the DL.

5. Conclusions and Further Research

An aggregated and integrated approach to the complex, yet challenging information education strategies to be adopted and practiced by the libraries for the 21st century is illustrated in this paper. Our state-of-the-art analysis of DL education, worldwide, was an initial foray into an important and expanding area of investigation. Ongoing research is required on a larger scale to gather data from every university of LIS and computer science in order to update and extend our findings. We need to develop good models of DL educational programs and courses, and a greater synergy between DL research and education. Finally, we need the resources to develop and sustain an expanding and far reaching program of DL education.

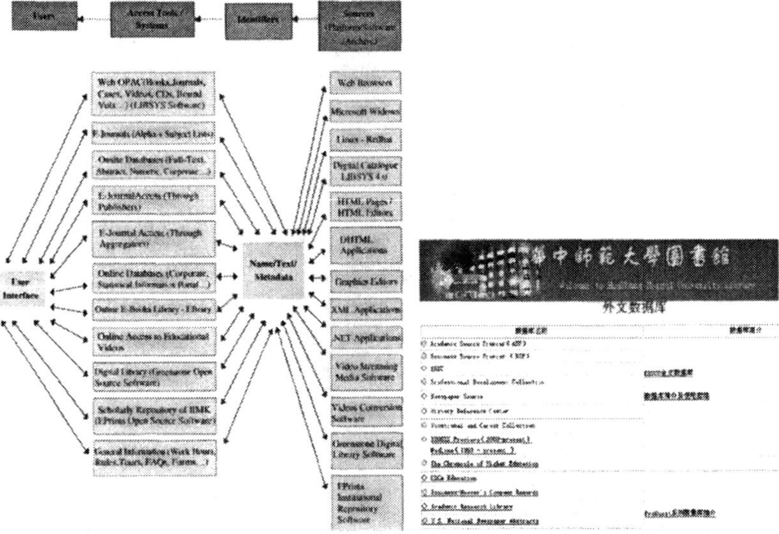

Fig2.   Content/information integration model of DL portal

Fig3.   Library Portal interface frame of DL HNU

References

1. Claudia A. Perry Education for Digitization: How Do We Prepare?, *Academic Librarianship*, Vol: 31(6), 523–532 (2005)
2. Peter Hernon Candy Schwartz , Library education and its accrediting body: An opportunity for partnerships, *Library & Information Science Research* ,Vol:26 , 1–4 (2004)
3. Jane T. Bradford, Barbara Costello, and Robert Lenholt, Reference Service in the Digital Age: An Analysis of Sources Used to Answer Reference Questions, *Academic Librarianship Available online 21* April, 263–272 (2005)
4. Jane M. Kathman and Michael D. Kathman, Training Student Employees for Quality Service , *Academic Librarianship*, Vol:26,(3), 176–182 (2004)
5 Natalia Donchenkoa,Irina Kerzumb, Between slump and hope: Library and information science education in Russia *The International Information & Library Review The International Information & Library Review* 38, 181–184 (2006)

Role-based Administration of User-role Assignment and Its Oracle Implementation

Lilong Han, Qingtan Liu, and Zongkai Yang
Department of Information and Technology&Engineer Research Center on
Education Infromation Technology,Huazhong Normal
University,Wuhan,China
Hanlilong2001@yahoo.com.cn
WWW home page: http://eitec.ccnu.edu.cn/

Abstract. In role-based access control (RBAC) permissions are associated with roles, and users are made members of appropriate roles thereby acquiring the roles' permissions. The principal motivation behind RBAC is to simplify administration. An appealing possibility is to use RBAC itself to manage RBAC, to further provide administrative convenience. In this paper we investigate one aspect of RBAC administration concerning assignment of users to roles. We define a role-based administrative model, called URA (User-Role Assignment), for this purpose and describe its implementation in the Oracle database management system. Although our model is quite different from that built into Oracle, we demonstrate how to use Oracle stored procedures to implement it.

1   Introduction

Role-based access control (RBAC) has recently received considerable attention as a promising alternative to traditional discretionary and mandatory access controls [1-3]. In RBAC permissions are associated with roles, and users are made members of appropriate roles thereby acquiring the roles' permissions. This greatly simplifies management of permissions. Roles are created for the various job functions in an organization and users are assigned roles based on their responsibilities and qualifications. Users can be easily reassigned from one role to another. Roles can be granted new permissions as new applications and systems are incorporated, and permissions can be revoked from roles as needed. Role–role relationships can be established to lay out broad policy objectives.

Figure 1 illustrates the most general model in this family. In Fig.1 a single headed arrow indicates a one to one relationship and a double headed arrow indicates a many to many relationship. For simplicity we overload the term RBAC to refer to the family of models as well as its most general member.

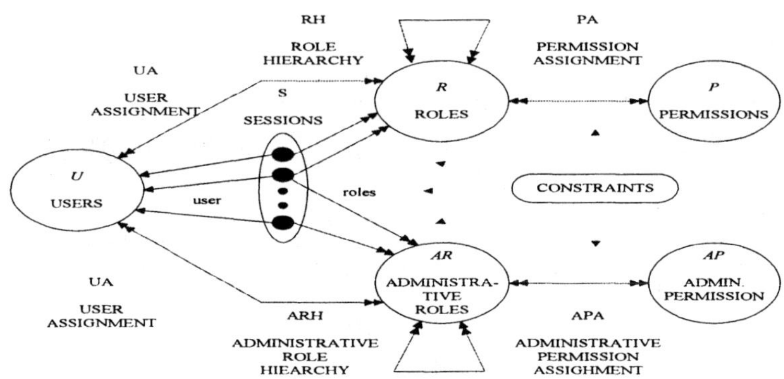

Fig. 1 RBAC model

In this paper we propose a model for the assignment of users to roles by means of administrative roles and permissions. For ease of reference we call this model as URA. URA imposes strict limits on individual administrators regarding which users can be assigned to which roles. We then describe an implementation of URA in the Oracle database management system [4-5]. Oracle's administrative model for user-role assignment is very different from URA. Nevertheless, we show how to use Oracle's stored procedures to implement URA.

2   URA Administrative Model

Administration of RBAC can be partitioned into several areas for which administrative models can be separately and independently developed to be later integrated. Our focus is exclusively on user-role assignment. As discussed in Section 1 this is likely to the first and most widely decentralized administrative task in RBAC.

2.1   URA Grant Model

In several systems, including Oracle, it is possible to designate a role, say, junior security officer (JSO) whose members have administrative control over one or more regular roles, say, A, B and C. Thus limited administrative authority is delegated to the JSO role. Unfortunately these systems typically allow the JSO role to have complete control over roles A, B and C. A member of JSO can not only add users to A, B and C but also delete users from these roles and add and delete permissions. Moreover, there is no control on which users can be added to the A, B and C roles by

JSO members. Finally, JSO members are allowed to assign A, B and C as junior to any role in the existing hierarchy (so long as this does not introduce a cycle). All this is consistent with classical discretionary thinking whereby member of JSO are effectively designated as "owners" of the A, B and C roles, and therefore are free to do whatever they want to these roles.

In URA our goal is to impose restrictions on which users can be added to a role by whom, as well as to clearly separate the ability to add and remove users from other operations on the role [6]. The notion of a prerequisite condition is a key part of URA.

Definition 1. A prerequisite condition is a boolean expression using the usual $\wedge$ and $\vee$ operators on terms of the form x and $\bar{x}$ where x is a regular role (i.e., $x \in R$). A prerequisite condition is evaluated for a user u by interpreting x to be true if $(\exists x' \geq x)(u, x') \in UA$ and $\bar{x}$ to be true if $(\forall x' \geq x)(u, x') \notin UA$. For a given set of roles R let CR denotes all possible prerequisite conditions that can be formed using the roles in R.

In the trivial case a prerequisite condition can be a tautology which is always true. The simplest non-trivial case of a prerequisite condition is test for membership in a single role, in which situation that single role is called a prerequisite role. User-role assignment is authorized in URA by the following relation.

Definition 2. The URA model controls user-role assignment by means of the relation $can\text{-}assign \subseteq AR \times CR \times 2^R$.

The meaning of $can\text{-}assign$(x, y, {a, b, c}) is that a member of the administrative role x (or a member of an administrative role that is senior to x) can assign a user whose current membership, or non-membership, in regular roles satisfies the prerequisite condition y to be a member of regular roles a, b or c.

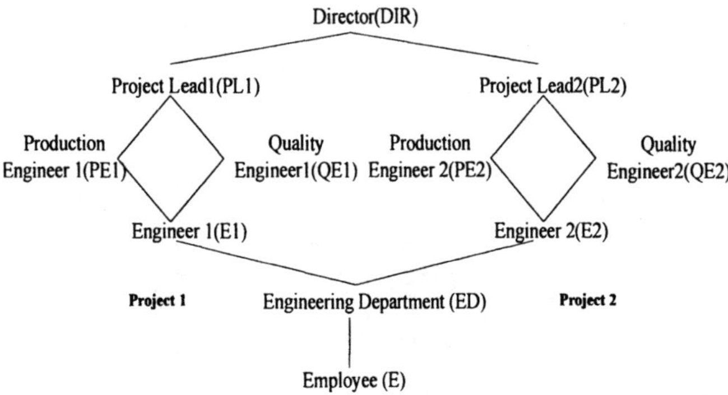

Fig. 2. An example role hierarchy

To appreciate the motivation behind the *can-assign* relation referring to the role hierarchy of Fig. 2 and the administrative role hierarchy of Fig. 3. Figure 2 shows the regular roles that exist in an engineering department. There is a junior-most role E to which all employees in the organization. Within the engineering department there is a junior-most role ED and senior-most role DIR. In between there are roles for two projects within the department, project 1 on the left and project 2 on the right. Each project has a senior-most project lead role (PL1 and PL2) and a junior-most engineer role (E1 and E2). In between each project has two incomparable roles, production engineer (PE1 and PE2) and quality engineer (QE1 and QE2).

Figure 2 suffices for our purpose but this structure can be extended to dozens and even hundreds of projects within the engineering department. Moreover, each project could have a different structure for its roles. The example can also be extended to multiple departments with different structure and policies applied to each department.

Figure 3 shows the administrative role hierarchy which co-exists with Fig. 2. The senior-most role is the senior security officer (SSO). Our main interest is in the administrative roles junior to SSO. These consist of two project security officer roles (PSO1 and PSO2) and a department security officer (DSO) role with the relationships illustrated in the figure.

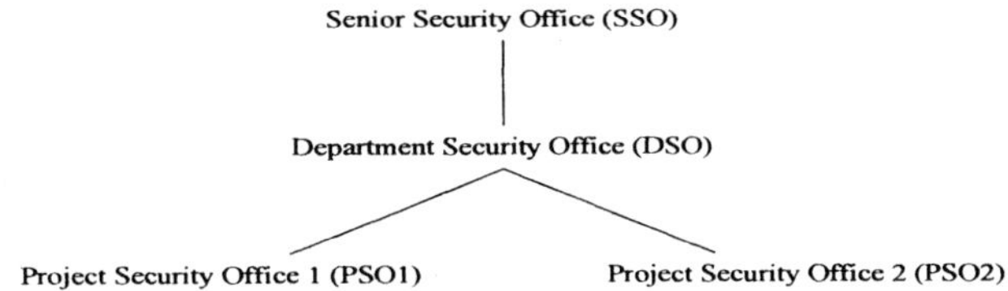

Fig. 3. An example administrative role hierarchy

The role structure shown in Fig. 2 becomes a project oriented if the users are assigned to roles in a single project. If the users are assigned to roles from multiple projects then the structure is of matrix-form and if the users are assigned to same functional role in different projects then the structure is of functional oriented.

2.2 Prerequisite Roles of URA

For sake of illustration we define the *can-assign* relation shown in Table 1. This example has the simplest prerequisite condition of testing membership in a single role known as the prerequisite role [7].

The PSO1 role has partial responsibility over project 1 roles. Let Alice be a member of the PSO1 role and Bob a member of the ED role. Alice can assign Bob to any of the E1, PE1 and QE1 roles, but not to the PL1 role. Also if Charlie is not a member of the ED role, then Alice cannot assign him to any project 1 role. Hence, Alice has authority to enroll users in the E1, PE1 and QE1 roles provided these users are already members of ED. Note that if Alice assigns Bob to PE1 he does not need to be explicitly assigned to E1, since E1 permissions will be inherited via the role hierarchy. The PSO2 role is similar to PSO1 but with respect to project 2. The DSO role inherits the authority of PSO1 and PSO2 roles but can further add users who are members of ED to the PL1 and PL2 roles. The SSO role can add users who are in the E role to the ED role, as well as add users who are in the ED role to the DIR role.

This ensures that even the SSO must first enroll a user in the ED role before that user is enrolled in a role senior to ED. This is a reasonable specification for *can-assign*. There are, of course, lots of other equally reasonable specifications in this context. This is a matter of policy decision and our model provides the necessary flexibility.

In general, one would expect that the role being assigned is senior to the role previously required of the user. That is, if we have *can-assign* (a, b, C) then b is junior to all roles $c \in C$. We believe this will usually be the case, but we do not require it in the model. This allows URA to be applicable to situations where there is no role hierarchy or where such a constraint may not be appropriate.

The notation of Table 1 has benefited from the administrative role hierarchy. Thus for the DSO we have specified the role set as {PL1, PL2} and the other values are inherited from PSO1 and PSO2. Similarly for the SSO. Nevertheless explicit enumeration of the role set is unwieldy, particularly if we were to scale up to dozens or hundreds of projects in the department. Moreover, explicit enumeration is not resilient with respect to changes in the role hierarchy. Suppose a third project is introduced in the department, with roles E3, PE3, QE3, PL3 and PSO3 analogous to corresponding roles for projects 1 and 2.

Table 1. Example of *can-assign* with prerequisite roles

Administrative role	Prerequisite role	Role set
PSO1	ED	{E1,PE1,QE1}
PSO2	ED	{E2,PE2,QE2}
DSO	ED	{PL1,PL2}
SSO	E	{ED}
SSO	ED	{DIR}

3 Oracle RBAC and Related Features

The Oracle database management [4-5] system provides support for RBAC including support for hierarchical roles. However, Oracle does not directly support the URA model. In particular, Oracle has a strong discretionary flavor to its administrative model for user-role assignment. We will see in the next section how it is possible to use Oracle's stored procedures to implement URA. In this section we briefly review relevant features of Oracle access control.

3.1 Privileges

Oracle has two kinds of privileges, system privileges and object privileges. System privileges authorize actions on a particular type of object for example create table, create user, etc. There are over 60 distinct system privileges. Object privileges authorize actions on a specific object (table, view, procedure, package, etc.). Typical examples of object privileges are select rows from a table, delete rows, execute procedures, etc.

Who can grant or revoke privileges from users or roles? The answer depends on various issues such as whether it is a system or an object privilege, and whether the object is owned by the user, etc. In order to grant or revoke a system privilege the user should have the admin option on that privilege or the user should have GRANT_ANY_PRIVILEGE system privilege. In order to grant or revoke an object privilege a user should own that particular object or the user should have grant option on the object if it is owned by someone else.

3.2 Roles in Oracle

Oracle provides roles (from Oracle 7.0 onwards) for ease of management of privilege assignment. System and object privileges can be granted to a role. A role can be granted to any other role (circular granting is not allowed). Any role can be granted to any user in the database. A role can either be enabled or disabled during a session. This includes both explicit and implicit roles that a user is a member of. Enabling a role will implicitly enable all the roles granted to it directly or transitively. The system privileges related to role management are CREATE_ROLE, GRANT_ANY_ROLE, DROP_ROLE, and DROP_ANY_ROLE. Information about privileges assigned to a role can be obtained from Oracle's built-in views ROLE_SYS_PRIVILEGES, ROLE_TAB_PRIVILEGES, and ROLE_ROLE_PRIVS. When a regular user performs query on these views these views only show information pertaining to the roles granted to that user. However, the Oracle internal user SYS will see information about all the roles through these views. The view SESSION_ROLES provides information about roles that are enabled in a session. The view ROLE_ROLE_PRIVS shows information about which roles are directly assigned to another role. Roles inherited transitively are not shown. For example, if role C was granted to role B and role B to role A the ROLE_ROLE_PRIVS view will show that B has been granted to A and C to B, but will not show the implied transitive C to A grant.

4　Implementing URA in Oracle

To implement URA we define Oracle relations which encode the *can-assign* URA. The *can-assign* relation of URA is implemented in Oracle as per the entity-relation diagram of Fig. 4. We assume that the prerequisite condition is converted into disjunctive normal form using standard techniques. Disjunctive normal form has the following structure [8-9].

$$(\cdots \wedge \cdots \wedge \cdots) \vee (\cdots \wedge \cdots \wedge \cdots) \vee \cdots \vee \cdots (\cdots \wedge \cdots \wedge \cdots)$$

Each $\cdots$ is a positive literal or a negated literal x. Each group $(\cdots \wedge \cdots \wedge \cdots)$ is called a disjunction. For a given prerequisite condition *can-assign2* has a tuple for each disjunction. All positive literals of a single disjunction are in *can-assign3*, while negated literals are in *can-assign4*.

The *can-assign, can-assign2, can-assign3* and *can-assign4* relations are owned by the DBA who also decides what their content should be. In addition we have three accompanying procedures and a package to support these. Execute privilege on these procedures is given to all administrative roles. We achieve this by introducing a junior-most administrative role, say GSO (generic security officer), and assigning it the permission to execute these procedures.

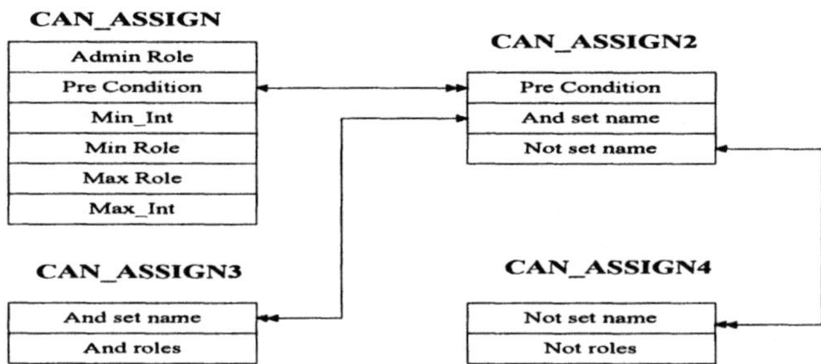

Fig. 4. Entity-relation diagram for *can-assign* relation

Oracle does not provide convenient primitives for testing whether or not a user is an implicit member of a particular role. Testing explicit membership is straightforward since explicit membership is encoded as a tuple in Oracle's system relations. To test implicit membership, however, we need to chase the role hierarchy.

In our implementation of URA a user invokes the stored procedure to grant a role from or to another user. The procedure calls are then as follows.

ASSIGN(user, trole, arole)

The parameters user and trole (target role) specify which user is to be added to trole. The arole parameter specifies which administrative role should be applied (with respect to the user who is invoking the URA procedure). The procedure code will check whether or not the user who calls the procedure has turned on the arole.

All the three procedures follow three basic steps.

1. If the user executing the procedure is an explicit or implicit member of arole then proceed to step 2, else stop execution and return an error message indicating this is not an authorized operation.

2. The tuple(s) from *can-assign* (for assign procedure) are obtained where AR role value equals or is junior to the arole parameter specified in the procedure call.

3. If trole is in the specified range for any one of the tuples selected in step 2, then assign the trole else return an appropriate error message. In case of ASSIGN also check whether the user being assigned to trole satisfies the prerequisite condition specified in the authorizing *can-assign* tuple or not.

Our implementation is convenient for the DBA since the stored procedures and packages we provide are generic and can be reused by other databases. The DBA only needs to define the roles and administrative roles, and configure the *can-assign* relations. Our implementation is available in the public domain for other researchers and practitioners to experiment with.

5   Conclusion

Authorization to assign to and from roles is controlled by administrative roles. The model requires users must previously satisfy a designated prerequisite condition before they can be enrolled via URA into additional roles. URA applies only to regular roles. Control of membership in administrative roles remains entirely in hands of the chief security officer.

The paper has also described an implementation of URA using Oracle stored procedures [10]. Oracle's built in primitives are cumbersome to use for determining indirect membership in roles. We have implemented suitable functions and packages to enable this conveniently. These should be of use to other researchers and practitioners and are available in the public domain.

Acknowledgement

This work was supported by doctor degree point in National Science Foundation under Grant No:20050511002 and supported by important project plan of education under Grant No:705038.

References

1. R.S. Sandhu, E.J. Coyne, H.L. Feinstein and C.E. Youman, Role-based access control models, IEEE Computer 29(2) (1996), 38–47.
2. S.H. von Solms and I. van der Merwe, The management of computer security profiles using a roleoriented approach, *Computers & Security* 13(8) (1994), 673–680.
3. C. Youman, E. Coyne and R. Sandhu, eds, *Proceedings of the 1st ACM Workshop on Role-Based Access Control,* Nov. 31–Dec. 1, 1995, ACM, 1997.
4. S. Feuerstein, Oracle PL/SQL Programming, O'Reilly & Associates, Inc., 1995.
5. G. Koch and K. Loney, *Oracle The Complete Reference*, Oracle Press, 1995.
6. L. Guiri and P. Iglio, A formal model for role-based access control with constraints, in: *Proceedings of IEEE* Computer Security Foundations Workshop 9, Kenmare, Ireland, June 1996, pp. 136–145.
7. R. Sandhu, Rationale for the RBAC96 family of access control models, in: *Proceedings of the 1st ACM Workshop on Role-Based Access Control, ACM,* 1997.
8. R.S. Sandhu, E.J. Coyne, H.L. Feinstein and C.E. Youman, Role-based access control models, IEEE Computer 29(2) (1996), 38–47.
9. C. Youman, E. Coyne and R. Sandhu, eds, *Proceedings of the 1st ACM Workshop on Role-Based Access Control, Nov.* 31–Dec. 1, 1995, ACM, 1997.
10. I. Mohammed and D.M. Dilts, Design for dynamic user-role-based security, Computers & Security 13(8) (1994), 661–671.

An Empirical Analysis of the Determinants of International Digital Divide

Liu Yun [1]

Business Department, Xiamen university of technology,
No 600,ligong Rd,Jimei District,Xiamen,P.R.China,FL:361024
Tel:13906036625;Email:liu.racky@gmail.com

Abstract. International Digital Divide is an imbalance state of ICT penetration between countries. This paper analyzes the current status and trends of international digital divide, adopts Gompertz technology diffusion model to verify the determinants of ICT penetration level and diffusion rate separately. Finally, China should use "policy levers" to strengthen international trade cooperation, improve the capability of independent innovation, and achieve Chinese goal of bridging digital divide.

1   Introduction

Digital divide is a new phenomenon emerging with the development of Information and communication technology (ICT). ICT creates a new group of leading technology, changing the technical foundation of the economic development, and eventually leads to a fundamental change in social economic production.

Rapid growth of ICT adoption in developed countries is raised the specter of international digital divide and marginalized developing countries. From a narrow view, the digital divide between different entities represents universal unbalanced state on the Internet and the proliferation of new ICT products. This paper analyzes the main ICT penetration and diffusion rate between countries, gives an objective description of the status quo and development trends of international digital divide. A Gompertz technology diffusion model is used to study the determinants of ICT penetration and diffusion empirically, focusing on Chinese proposals for bridging digital divide.

Please use the following format when citing this chapter:

Yun, L., 2007, in IFIP International Federation for Information Processing, Volume 252, Integration and Innovation Orient to E-Society Volume 2, eds. Wang, W., (Boston: Springer), pp. 445-452.

2   Status and Trends of the International Digital Divide

According to the data available, I choose a sample of 43 countries and regions to analyze the current situation and development trends of international digital divide.

Firstly, the global ICT penetration levels were rising during 1998-2004. The initial speed was relatively slow, but in 2000 proliferation was notably faster, with telephone and the Internet was most evident in the trend of changes in the basic S-type show, lots of literatures have proven rapid development of Internet in 2000 was the critical mass.

Secondly, in order to objectively observe changes in the level of ICT penetration, logarithmic ratio of four ICT products penetration level in 2000 and 2004 is used to show the ICT proliferation of diffusion rate. As shown in Fig 1, the diffusion rate of Internet users is faster than the telephone and personal computers. The proliferation of Internet hosts speed greater volatility and some countries of them have even negative growth. This shows that since 2000, the popularity of Internet users significantly raise. However, the Internet hosts might be influenced by more complex factors, show irregular variations.

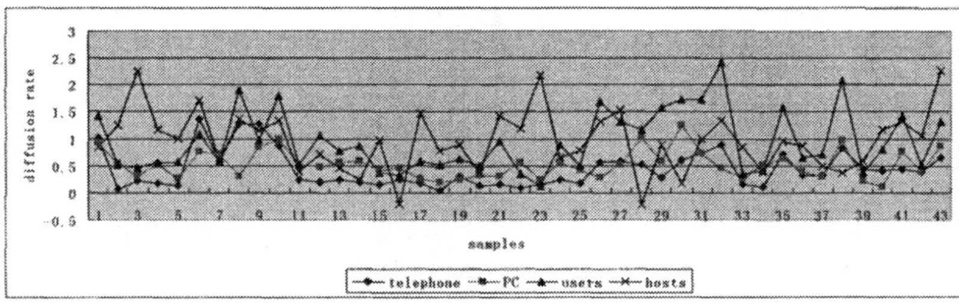

Fig.1. ICT diffusion rate in countries, 2000-2004

Finally, I choose average value, standard deviation and dispersion coefficient of global ICT penetration to describe the trend of changes in the international digital divide. The level of telephone penetration has increased and the standard deviation remains basically unchanged after 2000. Dispersion coefficient was decreased significantly from 2000. Judging from the trend of development, especially in 2000, global ICT penetration was in the narrow dispersion, and international digital divide was in narrowing trend. On this basis, I try to choose different econometric model, both in absolute and relative speed, to observe determinants of the ICT penetration level, to identify the root causes of the digital divide, to explain the factors that affect all countries. In order to make developing countries realize technical leapfrogging, the fundamental way should be used to catch up with developed countries.

3 Variable Selection

3.1 Dependent Variables

As mentioned above, this paper selects four ICT indicators as dependent variables, including telephones per 1,000 inhabitants, personal computers per 1,000 inhabitants, Internet hosts per 10,000 inhabitants and Internet users per 1,000 inhabitants. The data on the variables are for the period 2000-2004 and taken from the website of the International Telecommunication Union.

3.2 Independent Variables

(1) Income per capita. This paper assumes that there is a positive correlation between the level of income per capita and level of ICT diffusion rate. Countries with higher income per capita levels will invest more money in research and development, more access to use advanced ICT. In this paper, I adopt GDP per capita (PPP international dollars) as the proxy for variables.

(2) The Level of Urbanization. I hypothesize that the development of the Internet economy might allow a higher density of ICT community. On the other hand, the proportion of urban population in a certain city reflects a country's level of industrialization and the development of the service industry [1-2]. The greater proportion of the urban population, the higher the level of industrialization, and lower the level of agriculture.

(3) Education Level. Early researchers [3-4] believe that there is a significant positive correlation between the level of education and penetration of ICT, low level of education and literacy rates mean a lower level of a country's human capital, it's the main factors hindering the popularization of ICT. Higher level of education can promote ICT penetration, and gradually reduce the learning costs, increase the economic value of technology (Hargittai, 1999) [5]. Therefore, I assume that the level of education is an important factor and chose a country's higher education enrollment rate to represent it.

(4) Information Infrastructure. Information infrastructure is a prerequisite for the adoption of ICT. In this paper represent variables is the number of telephone lines per 1,000 inhabitants.

(5) Regulatory Standards. I assume the government's competition policy and regulatory system impact the ICT diffusion. It will also affect a country's supply and use density of ICT. This paper adopts the Government Regulatory Quality Index (promulgated by the World Bank Institute) as a variable, on behalf of a national government's work efficiency and the quality of economic operation of the regulatory system.

(6) Market Openness. "Imperfect information leads to reduction of trade" (Stiglitz, 1989) [6]. On the one hand, ICT can reduce the space of distance of global trade, thereby reduce information asymmetry. On the other hand, in the process of trade and technology transfer, knowledge and technology spills over. Therefore, I

assume that there is a positive correlation between a country's market openness and ICT diffusion rate, and choose trade proportion of GDP as a proxy variable.

(7) Technology Innovation. ICT products is not only consumer goods, but also a kind of investment products, therefore, I here join the indicator to reflect a country's level of scientific research. The proportion of total industrial exports of high-tech products used here as a representative of variables.

4 Empirical Models

In light of the current development of international digital divide, first of all, this paper at first adopts multiple linear regression equation for the static analysis of ICT penetration, which comes to the conclusion that the study results are consistent with previous studies, The level of education and Per capita income are most important factors affecting the level of ICT penetration. Therefore, this paper focuses on analysis of ICT diffusion from the dynamic approach.

A Gompertz technology diffusion model (Chow, 1983) [7] is adopted to study the determinants of ICT diffusion speed. The model assumes that the ICT diffusion rate (n) is proportional to the log difference between the current level and long-run equilibrium level (the latter is determined by a series of exogenous variables X_j).

$$n_t = \theta(\log n_t^* - \log n_t)$$

(1)

n_t means the speed of ICT diffusion during t period. To facilitate estimation, I use the following equation to approximate expressions (1):

$$\log n_t - \log n_{t-1} = \theta(\log n_t^* - \log n_{t-1})$$

(2)

Which

$$\log n_t^* = \beta_0 + \sum_{j=1}^{n} \beta_j \log X_{jt}$$

(3)

X_{jt} : the proliferation of explanatory variables affecting ICT

Through alternative and increased random errors, we have estimated the following equation:

$$\log n_t - \log n_{t-1} = \theta\beta_0 + \sum_{j=1}^{n} \theta\beta_j \log X_{jt} - \theta \log n_{t-1} + \varepsilon_t$$

(4)

In this paper, the cross section data of 43 national sample during 2000-2004 is used, aiming at telephones, PCs and Internet users and hosts. Based on different variables, the three models were used to estimate as following:

Model- I :

$$\log N_{04}^T - \log N_{00}^T = \theta\beta_0 - \theta \log N_{00}^T + \sum_{j=1}^{n} \theta\beta_j \log X_{j04} + \varepsilon_{04}$$

(5)

N_{04}^T And N_{00}^T represent four different ICT indicators expressed in the 2004 and 2000, which $T \in$ (phone, PC, Internet users, Internet hosts) ($j \geq 1 \ldots$ n), j is the value of the explanatory variable in 2004.

Model- II :

$$\log N_{04}^T - \log N_{00}^T = \theta\beta_0 - \theta \log N_{00}^T + \sum_{j=1}^{n} \theta\beta_j \log X_{j04} + \theta\gamma DD + \varepsilon_{04}$$

$$(6)$$

DD is a dummy variable reflects the overall state situation, 1 for the developed countries, 0 for developing countries.

Model-III:

$$\log N_{04}^T - \log N_{00}^T = \theta\beta_0 - \theta \log N_{00}^T + \sum_{j=1}^{n} \theta\beta_j \log X_{j04} + \sum_{k=1}^{m} \theta\gamma_k D_k + \varepsilon_{04}$$

$$(7)$$

D_k (k=1...m) is a dummy variable reflects regions of the virtual vector (D1 = 1: samples of specific Asian countries. D2 = 1: Eastern European transition countries, D3 = 1: Latin American and African countries).

5 Empirical Results

This paper use 43 countries cross-section data during 2000-2004, analyzes four ICT indicators. According to research result of Ben and Pohjola (2002) [7], technology diffusion changed with time. Model parameter θ depends on the time interval. As I select time interval 2000-2004, In view of the proliferation of the Internet in 2000 after the peak time of the web, the shorter time spans, the shorter time interval has little impact on diffusion speed. On the other hand, in the late 1990s, ICT diffusion speed went faster in the past five years, compared with the 20th century, the mid-1990s; the ICT diffusion rate may have significantly changed. ICT is in a period of rapid expansion. Although only a sample of 43 countries, the regression statistics are quite robust. Table 1 shows the empirical results associated with telephone diffusion, reflecting national and regional characteristics and features by adding the dummy variables. Different from the results of previous studies, the income per capita levels are negatively correlated with the telephone diffusion speed. I think that to some extent, the results in the initial spread of ICT products shows income per capita levels may be an important factor affecting the diffusion rate, but since 2000, with telephones and services continue to grow, ICT prices drop rapidly. The consumption level of products and services will no longer be bound by income level and educational skills.

Therefore, although telephone penetration rate is relatively low, it disseminates rapidly in many developing countries, even faster than the high-income developed countries. On the other hand, the proportions of telephone and urbanization rate also show a negative correlation with diffusion rate. This also shows that urban market has been gradually saturated; telephone consumption may have shifted to low-income rural groups. The empirical results are further proof of what we have seen in the analysis of the status quo: the increasing penetration level in developing countries.

Table 1. the Regression Results of Telephone Diffusion Speed
LOG (PHONE04)-LOG (PHONE00)

model	I	II	III
Sample	43	43	43
adjusted R^2	0.867686	0.869778	0.861478
F-test value	46.90435***	41.07527***	30.02225***
C	2.559346***	1.973846*	2.565862**
	(0.741878)	(1.026154)	(1.182722)
LOG(PHONE00)	-0.195873***	-0.196935***	0.224093***
	(0.062549)	(0.060726)	(0.069968)
LOG(INCOME)	-0.182133**	-0.123460	-0.152468
	(0.079832)	(0.081569)	(0.096107)
LOG(EDU)	0.243570	0.286688	0.218543
	(0.200328)	(0.209274)	(0.268839)
LOG(TRADE)	0.093047***	0.090834***	0.082587**
	(0.030106)	(0.028245)	(0.037379)
LOG(HTECH)	0.046882**	0.047906***	0.054580**
	(0.019887)	(0.020711)	(0.024225)
LOG(CITY)	-0.180776	-0.203195	-0.173752
	(0.130678)	(0.124585)	(0.174452)
DD		-0.102131	
		(0.085679)	
D1			-0.027402
			(0.077170)
D2			0.052103
			(0.081022)
D3			-0.029792
			(0.121575)

*, ** and *** indicate significance at 10%,5% and 1% respectively, standard errors in parentheses; White heteroskedasticity-consistent standard error and covariance estimates.

It is very notable that a country's market openness and the pace of proliferation of technology influence the phone diffusion speed, the diffusion rate of telephones would rise when the level of globalization and technological develops in a country, it shows that the importance of current trade and technology to the demand for phones and other ICT products. Virtual region and state variables in the model is not significant, but since the variables impact the income per capita level, actually shows the income differences between developed and developing countries and regions.

When the ICT indicator is personal computers, the estimates yield an insignificant model. However, the statistical model is still significant (significantly higher than the 1% level), which shows the income per capita, educational level, quality of government regulation and the openness of the market are still relevant factors affecting the proliferation of personal computers.

When the ICT indicator is personal computers, the result shows the main impact of the proliferation of Internet users during 2000-2004, the adjusted R^2 is 0.83.

Telephone mainlines per 1,000 inhabitants and Internet users are in the significant correlation (significantly higher than the 1% level), indicating that with the rapid development of the Internet, telephone dial-up access is still the main channel, infrastructure is an important factor affecting the rapid proliferation of the Internet.

Meanwhile, income per capita and level of education remain a negative correlation with Internet users, but it was not significant. I interpret the result from the following perspectives. Firstly, "Internet users" are inhabitants who take more than one hour a week online, it may overestimate the number of Internet users; secondly, most Internet users have no fixed source of income, including students. Although the number of Internet is growing faster, the use of the Internet is not clear verification purposes. This is further illustrated right that analysis the ICT only as a consumer goods, not a product.

However, the market openness, the level of urbanization and regulation quality index were positively correlated with the Internet diffusion speed, Although not very significant, but it also shows a certain degree of maturity on the Internet, For the Internet plays an important role in the proliferation of trade, trade can promote the proliferation of the Internet too. Meanwhile, the popularity of Internet was later than telephones, cities are mainly market of the Internet, popularization of the Internet plays an important positive impact and good government regulation of emerging Internet is more conducive to raise the speed.

From empirical results of the Internet hosts diffusion speed, we can see that the socio-economic variables and technology diffusion model can not reflect the determinants of Internet hosts diffusion. This explains the proliferation of Internet hosts differs from the general characteristics of telephones, Internet users and other infrastructure, but more emphasis on the production of capital goods as well as the use of economic value, hence it need further analysis in the future.

In short, in this paper, the Gompertz technology diffusion model is used to come with the empirical results which are very different from previous studies, possible reasons are as follows. Firstly, the basic indicators selected are not much different from previous studies, but the result was quite different. It shows that in the 20th century, especially in the late 1990s, the proliferation of high-speed universal ICT development period, the developing country get access to a fast rate of proliferation, to be more open and its capability of science and technology promoting the development of the market, rather than income per capita and level of education, it proves that a certain degree of economic convergence; Secondly, the selected proxy variables may not accurately reflect the true situation of the variables that affect the empirical results; Thirdly, during the annual rate of the proliferation may be influenced by the random events of the period; Finally, A national ICT diffusion rate and the current level of popularity may be different factors.

6 Conclusions

International digital divide is a particularly significant phenomenon between the developed and developing countries. From the overall growth trend, diffusion rate of four ICT products rapidly rises particularly in 2000. On the other hand, in developing countries, the diffusion rate is relatively faster than it in developed countries. However, there is still a great gap between the absolute level of penetration, according to the existing speed and trends; it's difficult for developing countries to catch up with developed countries in the near future.

Since 2000, the proliferation of telephones, personal computers and Internet users is different from the early trend, income per capita, the level of education are not important factors affecting ICT diffusion, but market openness, high-tech and the impact of the information infrastructure seemed to be speedy. This provides guidance and recommendations for developing countries to catch up.

The results show that if all countries adopted various "policy leverage" to promote market liberalization, technological innovations, and substantial investment in information infrastructure, the impact of international digital divide will reduce. If the developing countries wish to catch up with developed countries, they should strengthen cooperation in international trade and enhance independent innovation in science and technology, encouraging deregulation in the telecommunications services through a variety of approaches for universal access, from the export of technology to speed up the transfer of technology.

As far as China is concerned, firstly, combined with the balanced development strategy of China's inter-regional, China should emphasize the applicability of ICT, focus on the application of ICT in backward areas, and avoid the path of "individual pursuit of high technology indicators" partial road. Secondly, with respect to technology import, a flexible approach should be developed to a variety of technical trade through licensing trade, cooperative production, technical services, consultancy, import key equipment and complete sets of equipment and other means, find an independent innovation and development way to combine domestic and international technology transfer.

References

1. M. Granovetter, "The Strength of Weak Ties: A Network Theory Revisited", *Sociological Theory*, San Francisco: Jossey-Bass, 1983.
2. G8, "Digital Opportunities for All: Meeting the Challenge, Report of the Digital Opportunities Task Force", *including a proposal for a Genoa Plan of Action*, 2001.
3. P. Norris, *Digital Divide: Civic Engagement, Information Poverty, and the Internet Worldwide*, Cambridge University Press, 2001.
4. C. Shapiro, H. Varian., *Information Rules: A Strategic Guide to the Network Economy*, Cambridge, MA: Harvard Business School Press, 1999.
5. E. Hargittai, "Weaving the Western Web–Explaining Differences in Internet Connectivity among OECD Countries" [J]. *Telecommunications Policy*, 1999: 701-718.
6. Shengya, *Technology innovation diffusion and New Products Marketing*, China Development Publication, 2002.
7. S. Kiiski, and M. Pohjola. *Cross-country Diffusion of the Internet*, United Nations University, World Institute for Development Economic Research, 2001.

Integration of E-education and Knowledge Management

Liyong Wan[1], Chengling Zhao[2], and Wei Guo[2]
1 College of Humanity and Social Science, Wuhan University of Science
and Engineering ,Wuhan,China,wanliyongccnu@yahoo.com.cn
2 Department of Inforamtion Techonology,Central China Normal
Universtiy,Wuhan,China

Abstract. With the realization that knowledge is a core resource, organizations are now attempting to manage knowledge in a more systematic and more effective way. However, managing knowledge is not always an easy task. In particular contexts, such as online e-education, knowledge is distributed across both time and space and may be constrained by social, cultural and language differences. This paper demonstrated the common characters of knowledge management and e-education, and proposed the current potential problems in e-education. The authors tried to develop a set of guidelines to help overcome problems using tools and techniques from KM, they proposed three strategies: corporate explicit knowledge and tacit knowledge; use the theory of KM to guide e-education resource management; use the theory of KM to guide e-education resource management. These strategies will help us to develop a better e-education framework.

1 Introduction

The term "Knowledge Management" (KM) is used to describe everything from the application of new technology to the harnessing of the intellectual capital of an organization (Sallis and Jones, 2002). It is not one single discipline; rather, it is an integration of numerous endeavors and fields of study. In brief, KM is the management of processes that govern the creation, dissemination, and utilization of knowledge by merging technologies, organizational structures and people to create the most effective learning, problem solving, and decision-making in an organization [1, 2].

In the recent years a wide range of business techniques, including performance management, quality assurance and total quality management, have had a direct or indirect impact on education, and KM is set to do the same KM should have a

Please use the following format when citing this chapter:

Wan, L., Zhao, C., Guo, W., 2007, in IFIP International Federation for Information Processing, Volume 252, Integration and Innovation Orient to E-Society Volume 2, eds. Wang, W., (Boston: Springer), pp. 453-459.

resonance in education, as one major function of education is the imparting of knowledge. This implies that just as businesses attempt to improve the efficiency and effectiveness of their operations through KM, so educational institutions could use the potential of KM to enhance the learning of students. We can see that KM and online e-education share some common elements.

The first is community. From KM perspectives, the concept of communities is essential because knowledge in an organization is often built up and generated by small, informal, self-organizing network of practitioners. In e-education, community is regarded as the model for dynamic, productive knowledge creation and sharing in education. The second is collaboration. Most organizations realize that they will improve performance if their staffs work together. Tools such as e-mail and intranets are also used to encourage active collaboration among people in organization. Collaboration is one of the most critical issues in educational context, especially in online e-education where people and knowledge are distributed across time and space [2].

2   Knowledge Management strategies

An effective KM initiative requires the combination of the three strategies: the utilization of both explicit and tacit knowledge, the promotion of knowledge creation and sharing at all levels, and the application of the right mix of KM tools and techniques.

2.1   Knowledge Management Process

In some ways, educational systems are like knowledge management (KM) systems; both involve the creation of useful knowledge from information or data found in available resources. Knowledge management is a "system and managerial approach to collecting, processing and organizing enterprise-specific knowledge assets". Accenture views knowledge management functions as a six-step process: (1) acquire, (2) create, (3) synthesize, (4) share, (5) use to achieve organizational goals, and (6) establish an environment conducive to knowledge sharing. Ernst and Young promote a 4-phase KM approach: (1) knowledge generation, (2) knowledge representation, (3) knowledge codification, and (4) knowledge application. Not surprisingly, there are some similarities between Kuhlthau's information search process and these KM models.

2.2   Knowledge Conversion

According to Nonaka (1991), tacit and explicit knowledge are not totally separate but mutually complementary entities. They interact with each other in the creative activities of human beings. Nonaka calls the interaction of these two forms of knowledge, the "knowledge conversion" process. This conversion process is composed of four steps: socialization, externalization, combination, and internalization. The first step, "socialization", transfers tacit knowledge between individuals through observation, imitation and practice. In the next step, "externalization", triggered by dialogue or collective reflection, relies on analogy and metaphor to translate this collective tacit knowledge into documents and procedures. "Combination", consequently, reconfigures bodies of explicit knowledge through sorting, adding, combining, and categorizing processes, and spreads it throughout an organization. Lastly, "internalization" Translates explicit knowledge into individual tacit knowledge. [1, 2]

2.3   Combination of Tools and Technologies

Technology can support collaborative work and interaction among individuals within the community in which knowledge creation and sharing takes place. E-mail, groupware, and computer networks are commonly used to connect people with a need to share knowledge over a distance. However, while it is true that no modern organization can manage its knowledge without technology, it is only a part of the equation [2].

3   The Potential Problems in E-education

3.1   The Lack of Human Interaction

Learning tasks and activities are an important characteristic of good instructional design. Engaging learners and actively involving them in the learning process often increases motivation and learning gain.[3] To be successfully re-used for learning information chunks need to be embedded in interactive learning activities. In order to solve the problems, technologies such as video conferencing, MUDs and MOOs, have been used to create a 'telepresence' or a 'virtual presence'. [2]Nonetheless, people in so-called virtual teams still find that collaborative work is most effective when performed in face-to-face meetings where the issue of trust and ambiguity that surrounds identity in the virtual world are most easily overcome.

3.2   Problem of Trust

Trust is at the heart of collaboration. However, communication and social interaction in an online community can present a serious challenge to the existence of trust. From KM perspectives, personal contact and trust are intimately related. Good relations among people in community purge the process of distrust and fear, and break down personal and organizational barriers. Through well-established relationships, people develop the sense of trust, identity and commitment that allows them to create new knowledge and share that knowledge to other people in the community. [2]

3.3   Problem of Context Neglect

Situated learning approaches developed mainly at the end of the 1980s emphasize that a human's tasks always depend on the situation they are performed in, i.e., they are influenced by the characteristics and relationships of the context. Because of the relation between cognition and context, knowledge and the cognitive activities meant to create, adapt, and restructure the knowledge can't be seen as isolated psychological products – they all depend on the situation in which they take place. [3]

E-education solutions often do not consider that corporate learning takes place in an organizational context and that learning goals are based on real-world needs [3]. Secondly, many e-education approaches neglect the fact that the delivery of information chunks does not necessarily mean that the user acquires new knowledge. In particular, if the individual's context and characteristics are ignored, learning might not take place at all.

4   Integration of E-education and Knowledge Management

Based on the common characters of KM and e-education, we can use some theory and technique of KM to solve the potential problems in e-education, and can also optimize some aspects of e-education.

4.1   Corporate Explicit Knowledge and Tacit Knowledge

In e-education, knowledge can also be divided into explicit knowledge and tacit knowledge. Explicit knowledge refers to the knowledge which can be expressed by strict data, formula, axiom and text, easy to be stored and conveyed, such as subject knowledge. Tacit knowledge refers to the knowledge based on personal experiences and several invisible factors, such as personal faith, conception, intuition and power of observation. Tacit knowledge is a kind of knowledge which is hard to express, describe, communicate and share. Explicit knowledge can be delivered in the form of E-mail, CD-ROM and text, and can also be stored in knowledge libraries to be accessed and used in any time. Tacit knowledge can only be manifested by experience sharing among different individuals. We corporate the model of knowledge translation into e-education, the flow process is as follows: [1]

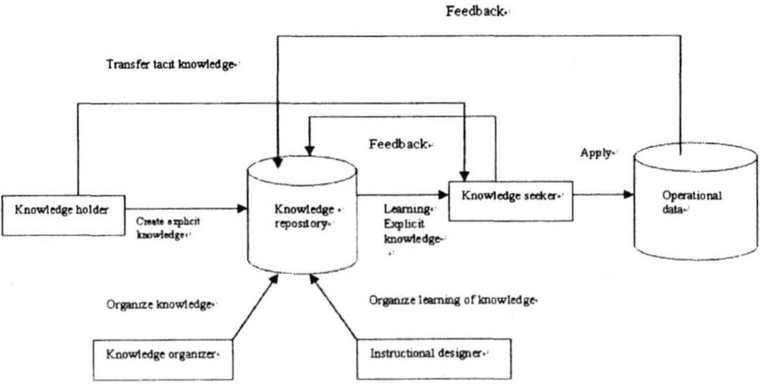

Fig. 1. Corporate knowledge conversion model into the e-education process

Figure 1 represents the knowledge management phases with e-Learning enhancements. In Figure 1, a Knowledge Holder can either transfer tacit knowledge to a Knowledge Seeker through socialization or create explicit knowledge and store it in a knowledge repository. The Knowledge Organizer in Figure 1 is a person (or software program) who relates the created knowledge to other knowledge in the repository or further refines the created knowledge. The Instructional Designer is a person (or software program) who organizes the learning of the knowledge by adding pre-assessments, additional learning aids, and post-assessments. The Knowledge Seeker then learns the explicit knowledge through an online guided learning experience. The Knowledge Seeker then uses the knowledge gained through socialization or internalization to make decisions and perform tasks in the enterprise. The performance of the Knowledge Seeker on these decisions and tasks is measured and returned to the knowledge repository as feedback that can be used to help determine if the skills have been learned and to suggest additional e-Learning experiences.[2, 4]

4.2   Apply Knowledge Tools and Techniques into E-education

In the four steps of knowledge translation, every process has the relevant information technology tools to support it. In the process of socialization , there are video meeting tools, network camera tools and virtual reality tools ; in the process of combination, there are systematic knowledge tools, collaborative tools, intranet, groupware, forum and practical databases; in the process of externalization ,there are peer-to-peer networks, expert system, data mining tools, intelligence agency and chat platforms; in the process of internalization, there are Notes databases, pattern recognition and neural network. Apply the knowledge tools into e-education can not only help the learners manage explicit knowledge, but also can lighten the pressure of time and space. For example, intranet and collaborative groupware can promote the acquisition and communication of knowledge in online learning communities; video meeting and chat rooms permit the learners to discuss simultaneously by interactive media. All of them can lighten the evidence of learners and conscious of identity, in order to create a more suitable e-education environment.

4.3   Use the theory of KM to Guide E-education Resource Management

E-education resources libraries include media library, exercise problem library, test paper library, instructional case library, literature library and Q&A library and so on. Education resource management includes index, check and retrieve. [3] Because resource repository is a kind of knowledge repository, a refined knowledge repository, we can use the theory of KM to guide the management of e-education resource management. In the process of resource management, we should consider what kind of resource can be stored in the library, how to access and organize the resources. [5, 6] According to the concepts of KM, firstly we must understand the framework of education resources and the tools to evaluate and control the resources;

secondly we must master the structure and component of the repository and know how to monitor the behaviors of the learners. We designed a resource management framework, the framework divided into six steps [7, 8], see figure 2:

Step 1: confirm the learners' request from the aspects of subject, search context, the type of resources, resource type and so on.

Step2: collect the learners' profiles, including their main interest, mater degree of knowledge, the expected status and learning styles.

Step 3: synthesis the learners' request and profiles.

Step 4: acquire the search results from local resource repositories, if the local resources can't satisfy the learner's request, start the global search mechanism to search more resources base on the user's restrict request.

Step 5: as soon as we have find the relative resource, we need to check and examine the resource. Subject expert system can pick up the expert knowledge to check the resource [8].

Step 6: the resources passed examination are organized and categorized again, then we store them into the local resource repository and provide the learner, they can also be used by other learners.

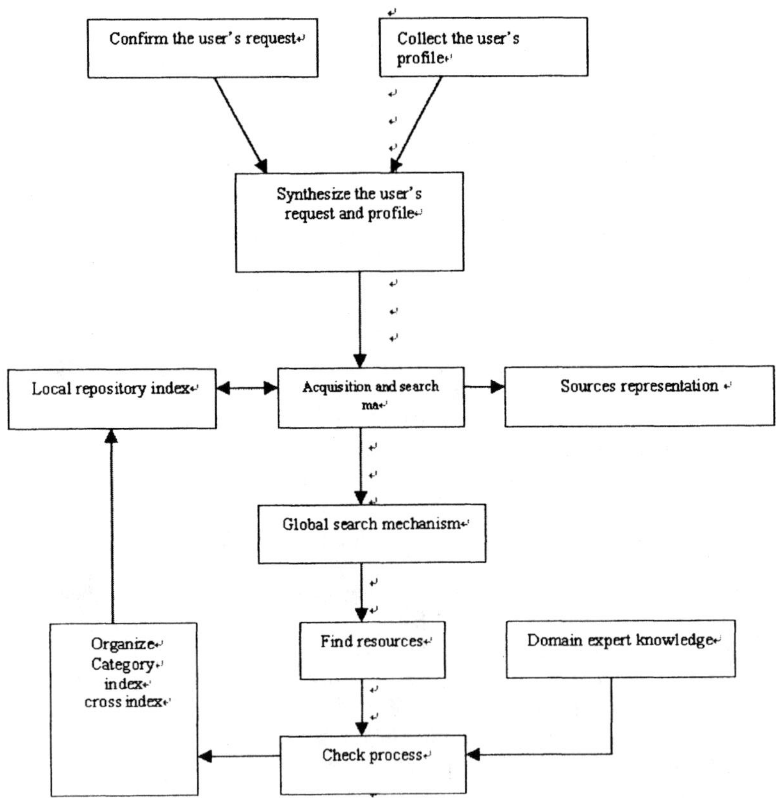

Fig. 2. The e-education resource management framework using knowledge management theory

5   Conclusions

Most organizations realize that "knowledge" is a strategic resource that gives them sustainable competitive advantage and helps them achieve long-term organizational goals. With the realization that knowledge is a core resource, organizations are now attempting to manage knowledge in a more systematic and more effective way. However, managing knowledge is not always an easy task. [6, 9, 10] In particular contexts, such as online e-education, knowledge is distributed across both time and space and may be constrained by social, cultural and language differences. This paper demonstrated the common characters of KM and e-education, and proposed the current potential problems in e-education .the authors tried to develop a set of guidelines to help overcome problems using tools and techniques from KM. We proposed three strategies: corporate explicit knowledge and tacit knowledge; Use the theory of KM to guide e-education resource management; Use the theory of KM to guide e-education resource management. These strategies will help us to develop a better e-education framework.

References

1. D.Woelk and S.Agarwal, Integration of e-Learning and Knowledge Management, http://dmc.ic2.org/publications/elearnkm.pdf.
2. A.N.Ubon and C.Kimble, Knowledge Management in Online Distance Education, *Proceedings of Networked Learning* 2002.
3. E.Ras, Integration of E-Learning and Knowledge Management – Barriers, Solutions and Future Issues, http://www.easy-hub.org/stephan/ras-postlokmol05.pdf.
4. Y.Zhang and Z.Zhu, Research on knowledge management and e-learning resource repository, *E-education Research.* 2003,(5).
5. H.Yang and L.Wang, Design and implementation of instructional case knowledge management system, *China e-education.* 2004,(10).
6. J.Mason, From elearning to e-knowledge, .*Knowledge management tools and techniques* 2005.
7. B.Marshall and Y.Zhang, Convergence of knowledge management and e-learning: the getsmart experience, http://www. ai.bpa.arizona.edu/go/intranet/Publication/JCDL-2003-Marshall.pdf.
8. A.Petrides, T.R.Nodine, Knowledge management in education: definition and landscape,http://www.iskme.org.
9. Y.N.Singh and S.N.Chabra, E-education and content development: an experience, http://home.iitk.ac.in/~ynsingh/papers/itedu.pdf.
10. J.J.Kidwell, M.V.Linde and S.L.Johnson, *Applying corporate knowledge management practices in higher education, Educause quarterly,*2000 (4),pp.28-33.

Spontaneous Group Learning in Ambient Learning Environments

Markus Bick[1], Achim Jughardt[2], Jan M. Pawlowski[2], Patrick Veith[2]

1   ESCP-EAP European School of Management, Business Information Systems, Heubnerweg 6, 14059 Berlin, markus.bick@escp-eap.de
WWW home page: http://www.escp-eap.de
2   University of Duisburg-Essen, Institute for Computer Science and Business Information Systems, Universitätsstraße 9, 45141 Essen, [achim.jughardt|jan.pawlowski|patrick.veith]@icb.uni-due.de
WWW home page: http://www.wip.uni-due.de

Abstract. Spontaneous Group Learning is a concept to form and facilitate face-to-face, ad-hoc learning groups in collaborative settings. We show how to use Ambient Intelligence to identify, support, and initiate group processes. Learners' positions are determined by widely used technologies, e.g., Bluetooth and WLAN. As a second step, learners' positions, tasks, and interests are visualized. Finally, a group process is initiated supported by relevant documents and services. Our solution is a starting point to develop new didactical solutions for collaborative processes.

1   Introduction

In this paper, we discuss the use of Ambient Intelligence to support learning and teaching processes to facilitate spontaneous groups in a university environment.

In the last years, collaborative scenarios have gained an increased importance in university settings [1]. New scenarios have been constructed and evaluated by using mobile and ambient technologies [2]. Consequently, we propose the concept of spontaneous group building using Ambient Intelligence in a university setting. After a short review of existing research in this field, we introduce a specific Ambient Learning framework. We show the potential for learners and teachers to build groups based on their location, tasks, and preferences, i.e., on their context. Our intended implementation makes use of Bluetooth in the classroom learning space as well as wireless local area network (WLAN) applications on the campus. Using such technologies, we offer the opportunity to create new communication and interaction processes and new didactic scenarios.

Please use the following format when citing this chapter:

Bick, M., Jughardt, A., Pawlowski, J. M., Veith, P., 2007, in IFIP International Federation for Information Processing, Volume 252, Integration and Innovation Orient to E-Society Volume 2, eds. Wang, W., (Boston: Springer), pp. 460-468.

2   Ambient Intelligence

Ambient Intelligence or Ubiquitous Computing applications denote the use of information and communication technologies (ICT) which are embedded in our natural surroundings, present whenever needed, and adaptive to the user [3]. In the context of e-Learning, this means that while the learners are moving with their mobile devices, the system dynamically supports their learning by communicating with embedded computers/systems in the environment [4], allowing for personalization and customization to their needs [5]. Consequently, Ambient Intelligence leads to Ambient Learning.

The main objective of an Ambient Learning Environment – contrary to typical more or less client-server oriented e-learning environments – is to provide answers to the following questions [4]: 1) Who has the same problem or knowledge?; 2) Who has a different view on the problem or knowledge?; And 3) ,who has the potential to assist in solving the problem? Accordingly, typical Ambient Learning services are device and network detection services, location tracking services, calendar and social activities services, or content access services [6]. Ambient Learning focuses on how to provide learners with the right information at the right time, delivered in the right way and to the right place, based on their context [4].

Ambient Learning Environments can be described by various key characteristics ([7, 8] cited by [4]): permanency, accessibility, immediacy, interactivity, and situating of instructional activities. These were extended by [9] with regard to the adaptability of Ambient Learning Environments, i.e., providing the right information at the right time and the right place. Accordingly, learners will be able to select the learning methods preferred by or suited to them [10].

Following the afore mentioned key characteristics [11] derived a framework for Ambient Knowledge & Learning Environments (ALKE). The ALKE-Framework provides the opportunity to approach this highly complex domain from six different perspectives (see Figure 1), i.e., knowledge management tasks, actors/competencies, ambient technologies, mobile technologies, cases, and context.

With in this framework the various perspectives are attached to typical knowledge management tasks. The knowledge identification, acquisition, development, distribution, preservation, or use – as a common subset provided by [12] – can be supported by various ambient and mobile technologies. These components of the framework define the technological aspects of the learning processes. [11] deliberately distinguish between mobile technologies which contain all technologies of adequate mobile devices and ambient technologies which are attached to a certain location (e.g., a certain position within a school or on a campus) or object (e.g., a machine). Consequently, learners can access learning processes depending on the context (e.g., external influences) and their profile. The context contains the main influence factors of such learning processes. Hence, Ambient Learning & Knowledge Environments are strongly dependent on the context, for example, in which context the actors demand specific learning materials. The ALKE offers a perspective of integrated professional experiences represented in various corresponding case studies. These cases increase the understanding of Ambient Intelligence and support the analysis of corresponding information. Besides, various characteristics of the learner (actor) must be analyzed, e.g., learning preferences, competencies, or experiences.

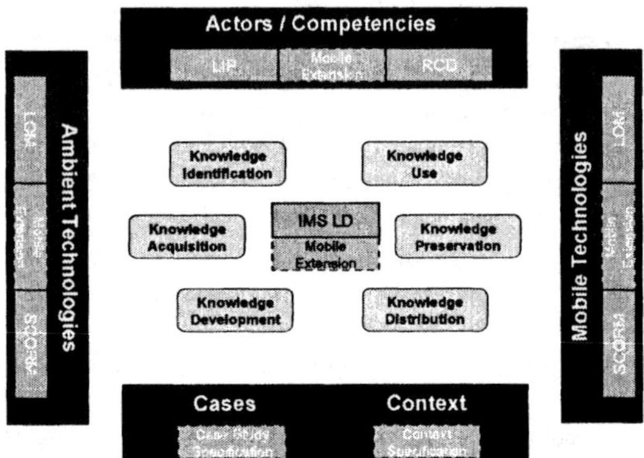

Fig. 1. ALKE-Framework [11]

To achieve a highly integrated and interoperable Ambient Learning & Knowledge Environment various standards have to be recognized on different levels of integration: devices, data, middleware, and application [12]. Ambient Intelligence standards thereby mainly focus on wireless networks and telecommunication between the various involved devices. The information transfer relies on wireless technology standards (e.g., Bluetooth), corresponding data exchange standards (e.g., Extensible Markup Language – XML) as well as specific middleware technologies (e.g., Web services). On the application level widely accepted learning standards should be used or adapted. However, not all aspects of ambient or mobile solutions are covered by the existing specifications [11, 12]. Figure 1 shows specifications which should be used/extended to implement an Ambient Learning & Knowledge Environment.

3   Spontaneous Group Learning

Learning in collaborative settings has been studied extensively in the last years [1]. Most reports focus on the facilitation of groups and/or teams either within classrooms [14] or in distributed environments [15, 16]. Spontaneous group building (also: ad hoc group building or spontaneous cooperation [15]) is one potentially successful method to initiate group (building) processes and social interaction for learning.

In extension to such methods for classrooms and internet-based environments, ambient and mobile technologies make possible new scenarios of interaction. For example, location-based messaging services are used to enhance presence and awareness of fellow learners [17, 18]. Furthermore, radio frequency identification

(RFID) networks are used to provide information on useful resources or persons [19]. Whereas in traditional approaches groups are usually formed by a tutor or agent [9], these new approaches enable learners to build their own networks based on there needs, requirements, and interests.

Our approach aims at supporting groups of learners in a campus environment: Spontaneous Group Learning (SGL). Students are enabled to form groups independently on the basis of their course, location, and user profile. This means that, for example, students in a certain course are able to form a group once they have the need to communicate and interact with others. As a second option, SGL can be used as a didactical concept by the teachers and tutors to form groups within a course on the basis of the user characteristics.

4   The Spontaneous Group Learning Environment

In the following, we describe our Spontaneous Group Learning (SGL) environment for students in Higher Education. The technical realization consists of three steps: 1) positioning, 2) visualizing fellow learners, and 3) initiating the group process. We focus on supporting students to build spontaneous groups by designing a learner awareness interface.

4.1   Infrastructure and Architecture

90% of the students in our study used common (mobile) devices: notebooks and cellular phones. We grounded our implementation on free or inexpensive network connections and widely available infrastructures, i.e., wired, wireless and Bluetooth networks. For the visualization, we aimed at developing an awareness component as a basis for collaborative processes. For further discussion cf. [20]. As Learning Management System (LMS) we used sTeam [21], a tool for cooperative knowledge management in learning groups. A specialized sTeam-client was developed to access the LMS with notebooks and Bluetooth enabled cellular phones.

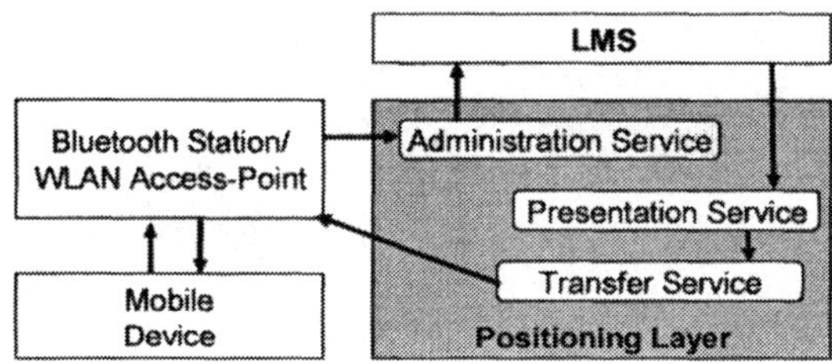

Fig. 2 Positioning layer architecture

Our architecture was based on the described ALKE-Framework (sec. 2). The positioning service was implemented on the software layer using routing data and

Bluetooth IDs to provide the positioning data for each learner to the LMS (Figure 2). The sTeam-client sent the corresponding login data, which was received by the positioning layer. For wireless and wired connections the IP-routing information was interpreted to identify the used access point and deduce which area the student was in. For Bluetooth connections the ID of the connected Bluetooth station was associated with an area and the end user device Bluetooth ID was used to identify the learner.

4.2   Positioning

As a first step, we identify the position of a student using both WLAN and Bluetooth positioning.

WLAN access points provide network access to larger areas. Thus, we use room identification numbers of campus buildings to provide a more accurate positioning. This was achieved by providing the server with a list of rooms with each access point covered. Using routing information of packages [22] sent to the positioning layer via IP-networks, we are able to identify which access point a client uses. Students who log into the system automatically get a list of rooms of their entry access point so that they can select their current position. Thus, the corresponding service can provide a fairly accurate position and enable students to conveniently contact their fellow students.

For a detailed positioning, we use Bluetooth technologies available on certain locations on campus. The Bluetooth positioning adds two features. It allows the learner already logged into the system to provide his exact position. Secondly, it gives the learner the possibility to show his interest in spontaneous group building without having his WLAN device available or in use.

A student can therefore have three states: 1) empty (the learner does not disclose his position or is outside the WLAN/Bluetooth range of the campus), 2) WLAN position (the object contains the description of the WLAN area the learner is connected with), or 3) Bluetooth position (the object contains the exact position of the learner based on the range of the Bluetooth access point).

As shown in the ALKE-Framework (sec 2), the status of the learner is stored as an extension to the Learner Information Package (LIP) [23]. This means that the characteristics of the learner are related to the position. To implement this feature – discovering and storing the position – the sTeam-client sends the local device Bluetooth ID to the positioning layer, which in turn adds the position to the LIP object in the LMS. In this way a student who logs into the network can automatically be assigned a position.

4.3   Visualization

Whereas the positioning is realized by network access point and Bluetooth IDs, the corresponding visualization of the students and their specific learning tasks is supported by a map of the campus and each of its buildings. Students using the client outside the campus network are depicted in a special off-campus area (Figure 3).

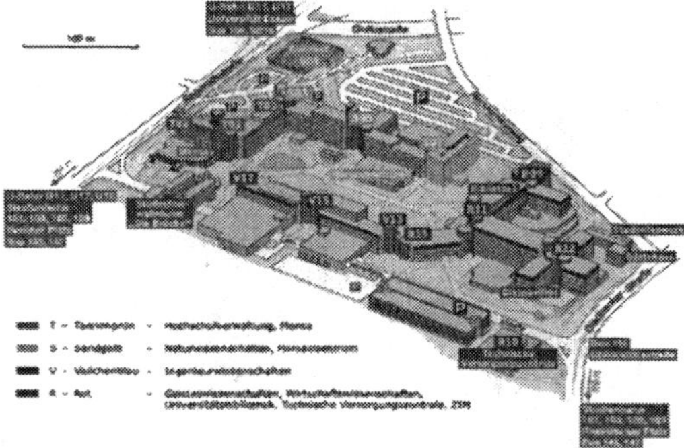

Fig. 3. Campus Map

Students are able to identify their fellow learners by selecting different attributes. In a first step, we use two attributes: 1) the current activity (e.g., self-study, performing an assessment), 2) a certain topic as part of a classification (e.g., course "E-Learning", topic "User Modeling", module "Stereotypes"). Furthermore, it is possible to select potential group partners based on their location. Figure 4 shows the visualization.

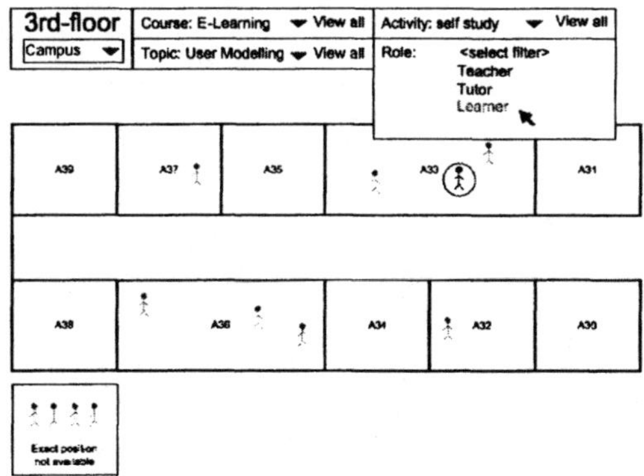

Fig. 4. Visualization

Applying this approach, the students will be positioned on the map (Figure 3) and add the positioning information to the LMS. Additionally, the actual learning activity the student is working on and the learning communities he is in will be retrieved from the LMS. The corresponding data is provided by the LMS and the position layer reformats the information for the end device(s) used.

4.4   Initiating the group process

The implemented selection process enables students to find fellow learners and to initiate a spontaneous learning session. To start a learning session, a group room is automatically generated in sTeam, providing a communication channel (via chat) and relevant documents. Since this is only the starting point for the face-to-face phase of the SGL, the chat is only used for the initiation. The following Figure 5 shows available information on fellow learners and corresponding documents in the initiation process.

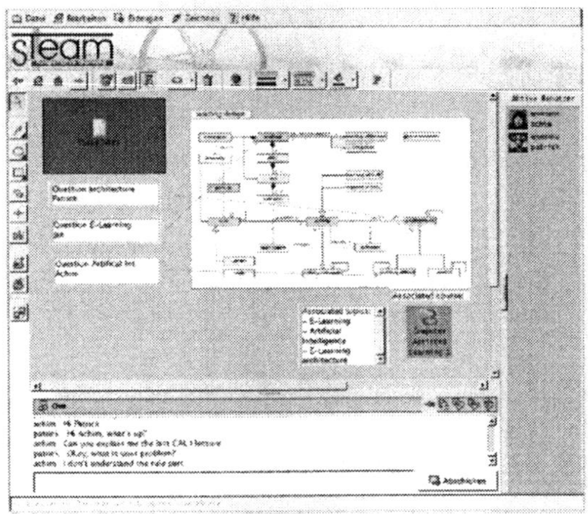

Fig. 5. Support Room

The presented SGL approach enables new possibilities for initiating spontaneous learning processes as a combination of electronic and presence cooperation. We provide new methods to initiate groups and corresponding learning processes. A main aspect is (independent) group building based on specific attributes, e.g., position or preferences. Our current attribute selection could be extended using further attributes, e.g., using LIP categories [23]. This can lead to new didactic scenarios and new scenarios based on widely used technologies.

5   Conclusion

We presented a technological solution to initiate and support Spontaneous Group Learning (SGL). Thereby, we have shown how to implement an SGL environment based on widely used and accepted technologies applying the ALKE-Framework. This solution enables new group building and learning processes. Using different attributes to select and contact fellow learners can also be helpful in other contexts, especially in the field of human-oriented knowledge management.

As a next step, we will evaluate the non-technological aspects of the approach, specifically the communication structure of electronic and face-to-face phases of the process.

By this promising approach we hope to create new creative learning processes and provide support mechanisms which can easily be implemented in current infrastructures.

References

1. J.W. Strijbos, P.A. Kirschner, and R.L. Martens, *What we know about CSCL and implementing it in higher education* , Kluwer Academic Publishers, Norwell, 2004.
2. H.-Y. So and B. Kim, in: Computer Supported Collaborative Learning 2005: "The Next 10 Years, *International Society of the Learning Sciences*, Taipei, 2005, pp. 607-616.
3. W. Weber, J. Rabaey, and E. Aarts, *in: Ambient Intelligence*, Springer, Berlin, 2005, pp. 1-2.
4. H. Ogata and Y. Yano, "Knowledge awareness for a computer-assisted language learning using handhelds", *International Journal of Continuous Engineering Education and Lifelong Learning* 14(4/5), 435-449 (2005).
5. V. Jones and J.H. Jo, Beyond the comfort zone: Proceedings of the 21st ASCILITE Conference. pp. 468-474. Perth, 2004
100. http://www.ascilite.org.au/conferences/perth04/procs/jones.pdf
6. S.J.H. Yang, "Context Aware Ubiquitous Learning Environments for Peer-to-Peer Collaborative Learning", *Educational Technology & Society* 9(1), 188-201 (2006).
7. Y.S. Chen, T.C. Kao, J.P. Sheu, and C.Y. Chiang, *WMTE '02: Proceedings IEEE International Workshop on Wireless and Mobile Technologies in Education*, IEEE Computer Society Press, Washington (2002), pp. 15-22.
8. M. Curtis, K. Luchini, W. Bobrowsky, C. Quintana, and E. Soloway, in: *WMTE '02: Proceedings IEEE International Workshop on Wireless and Mobile Technologies in Education*, IEEE Computer Society Press, Washington (2002) , pp. 23-30.
9. B. Bomsdorf, Mobile Computing and Ambient Intelligence: The Challenge of Multimedia, Dagstuhl (2005).
http://drops.dagstuhl.de/opus/volltexte/2005/371/pdf/05181.BomsdorfBirgit.Paper.371.pdf.
10. M. Yoshida, Towards Ubiquitous Learning and Education, Proc. of the 6th Distance Learning and the Internet Conference, Tokyo, Japan, 2006. [WWW Dokument] http://apru2006.dir.u-tokyo.ac.jp/pdf/1a-1.pdf (2 Nov. 2006).
11. M. Bick, J.M. Pawlowski, in: *4th Conference on Professional Knowledge Management - Experiences and Visions*, edited by N. Gronau (*GITO*-Verlag, Berlin, 2007), pp. 335-342.
12. G. Probst, K. Romhardt, *Building Blocks of Knowledge Management – A Practical Approach* (John Wiley & Sons, Hoboken, 2000).
13. M. Bick, T. Kummer, J.M. Pawlowski, and P. Veith, in: *MMS 2007: Mobilität und mobile Informationssysteme*, edited by B. König-Ries, F. Lehner, R. Malaka, C. Türker (Köllen Druck+Verlag GmbH, Bonn, 2007), pp. 103-114.
14. D.G. Oblinger, (January 29, 2007). http://www-cdn.educause.edu/ir/library/pdf/PUB7102.pdf.
15. M. Wessner and H.R. Pfister, "Group formation in computer-supported collaborative learning", *Proceedings of the 2001 International ACM SIGGROUP Conference on Supporting Group Work*, Boulder, 2001.
16. A.L. Soller, "Supporting Social Interaction in an Intelligent Collaborative Learning System", *International Journal of Artificial Intelligence in Education* 12, 40-62 (2001).

17. M. Eisenstadt, J. Komzak, and S.A. Cerri, in: Proceedings of the TelEduc04, 3rd International Symposium on Tele-Education and Lifelong Learning (http://kmi.open.ac.uk/people/marc/papers/eisenstadt-komzak-cerri-teleduc-04.doc, Havana, 2004).

18. J. Berghoff, M. Matthes, and O. Drobnik. in: *Proceedings of the Joint Conference of the 3rd World Multiconference on Systemics, Cybernetics and Informatics* (SCI '99) and *the 5th International Conference on Information Systems Analysis and Synthesis* (ISAS '99, Orlando, 1999).

19. M. Derntl, K.A. Hummel, in: *PERCOMW '05: Proceedings of the Third IEEE International Conference on Pervasive Computing and Communications Workshops* (IEEE Computer Society, Washington, 2005), pp. 337-342.

20. OPLC, (January 29, 2007); http://laptop.org/laptop/interface/principles.shtml

21. T. Hampel, *Virtuelle Wissenräume – Ein Ansatz für die kooperative Wissensorganisation* (Dissertation, University of Paderborn, 2002).

22. B. Augustssons, (January 29, 2007); http://www.dtek.chalmers.se/~d3august/xt/

23. C. Smythe, F. Tansey, and R. Robson, (January 31, 2007); http://www.imsproject.org/profiles/lipinfo01.html, 2001, (12. Oct. 2006)

Roadmapping Future E-Government Research
Government's role and responsibilities in the virtual world

Melanie Bicking
University of Koblenz-Landau, Institute for IS Research,
Research Group eGovernment
Universitaetsstr. 1, 56070 Koblenz, Germany
Tel: +49 261 287 2646, Fax: +49 261 287 100 2646
bicking@uni-koblenz.de
WWW home page: http://www.uni-
koblenz.de/FB4/Institutes/IWVI/AGVInf

Abstract: Global electronic markets, virtual organisations, virtual identities, virtual products and services, and Internet-related crime are growing in prominence and importance. In a world that is increasingly non-physical and borderless, what are government's roles, responsibilities and limitations? The Internet plays a central role within the transformation process from traditional governments towards modern and innovative government that the requirements of an Information Society. Based on the findings of the eGovRTD2020 project, that aims at identifying key research challenges and at implementing a model for a holistic government with horizon 2020, this paper explains the necessity to investigate and understand the Internet and in particular government's role and responsibilities in it. Furthermore, the paper provides a research roadmap that details how to address certain issue related research questions.

1 Introduction

Many countries, as well as the European Union, ranked the development of an Information Society very high at their agenda. Scanning existing strategic documents and policies, international and national strategies focus often on research issues related to trust and security aspects, as well as user acceptance. At the moment

Please use the following format when citing this chapter:

Bicking, M., 2007, in IFIP International Federation for Information Processing, Volume 252, Integration and Innovation Orient to E-Society Volume 2, eds. Wang, W., (Boston: Springer), pp. 469-480.

governments main interest in the virtual world is on how to deliver electronic public services secure through the Internet. Analysis of several strategic documents indicate a common awareness across Europe that people and business will only use online services if data transfer and transactions are secured and protected. Hence European governments fund research and development on security issues, e.g. Digital Rights Management (DRM). But the virtual world offers much more opportunities and threats than discovered by now. The Internet is a paradise not only for information search and customising but also for all kinds of criminals 00. Global electronic markets, virtual organisations, virtual identities, and virtual products and services are increasingly prominent. Governments all over the world have to face this growing new world. First problems and challenges appeared through increasing movie and music piracy via peer-to-peer systems established in the Internet. Existing legal frameworks, as well as law enforcement methods and tools were very high ranked in agendas of several governments. Following questions came up and needs still to be answered: How to regulate the Internet? What are government's role, responsibilities and limitations in a world that is increasingly non-physical and borderless?

Within the foci of the 6th Framework Programme of Information Society Technology (IST) that address "ICT research for innovative Government" and "Strengthening the Integration of the ICT research effort in an Enlarged Europe"0 the EC funded the project eGovRTD2020. This project is a specific support action in order to develop a research roadmap for eGovernment in 2020. It aims at identifying key research challenges and at implementing a model for a holistic government with horizon 2020. Key findings from the eGovRTD2020 project leads to insight that government's role and responsibilities in the virtual world are still unclear but it will be necessary for governments to become more proactive in the Internet. The following chapters introduce the methodology of eGovRTD2020 and point out those research themes and activities, as well as actors needed in order to investigate and define government's role and responsibilities in the virtual world.

2   Overall methodology to develop an eGovernment research roadmap

This chapter is about the underlying holistic reference framework of eGovRTD2020 (see Fig. 7). It introduces the overall methodology of the eGovRTD2020 project that is applied to develop research roadmap for eGovernment 2020.

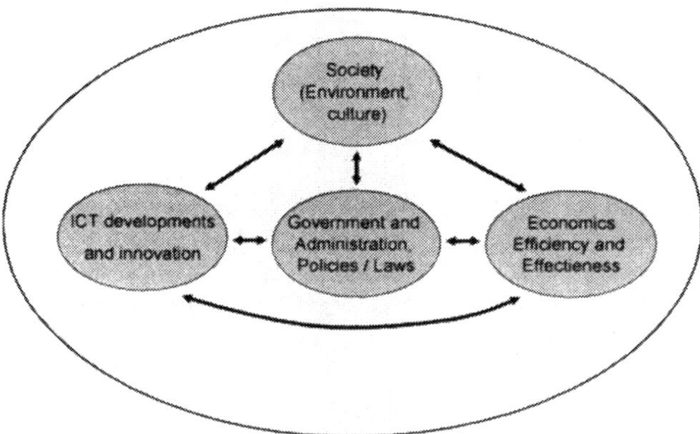

Fig. 7, Holistic reference framework of eGovRTD2020 0

According to the EC 00 "eGovernment is the use of information and communication technologies (ICT) in public administrations - combined with organisational change and new skills - to improve public services and democratic processes and to strengthen support to public policies." Besides, the United Nations (UN) 0 defines eGovernment as "a government that applies ICT to transform its internal and external relationships". Each of above mentioned definitions underscore the growing awareness that eGovernment should be based on considerations from technology, social, organisational, economic and legal areas that guided the investigations of the overall project methodology that is divided in four successive steps (see

2).

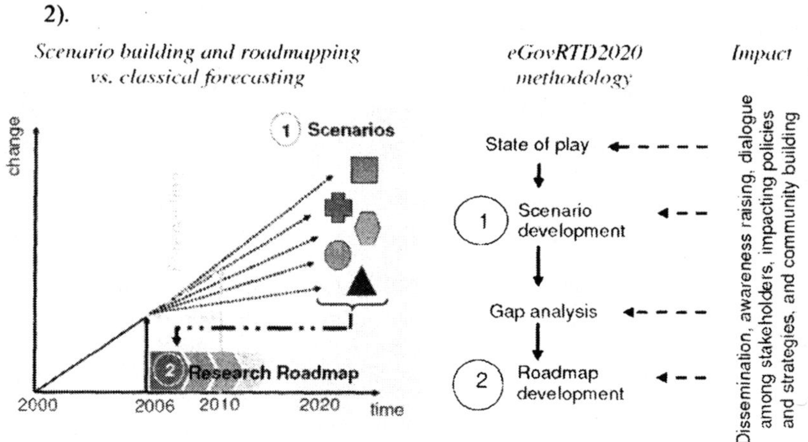

Fig. 2, eGovRTD2020 overall methodology to develop an eGovernment research roadmap for innovative Governments in 2020 0

The holistic framework of eGovRTD2020, depicted in Fig 1, bases on the above named definition of the EC. A key function within the project was to take the EC definition and breaks the broad definition down into a framework in order to make it easier to process the single aspects in the following steps.

In step 1 current status of eGovernment research and eGovernment strategies is given in order to outline trends related to design the current eGovernment transformation process through research (cf. 0). For instance, several strategies and research programmes focus on security issues. All eGovernment services are or will be delivered through the Internet face security issues, e.g. data protection. Consequently, many eGovernment strategies focus on research and development in order to develop a secure communication infrastructure. In this context the following topics of interest are mentioned several times, for example data protection, identity management, authentication, secure data and information transfer.

In step 2 different visions of the future were built up during a series of regional workshops in Europe, the USA and Australia. Experts from those regions develop scenarios about governments interacting with society and market through innovative ICT and thereby creating a certain public value (cf. 0). In the end 29 scenarios were carried out in seven workshops. In order to condense the scenario results and to provide a reasonable and manageable amount of input for the roadmapping workshops, the scenario analysis aims at identifying a minimal set of three key dimensions (contextual environment, trust in government and scope of government service provision) to classify the 29 scenarios and derive a final set of eight consolidated scenarios. The scenarios draw pictures of future eGovernment in which ICT penetrates every part of every day life. In this context ICT networking and convergences of ICT are often mentioned. Besides, expectations that governments all over the world will cooperate and collaborate through ICT networks and the Internet, in several scenarios internet crime and the loss of data privacy through the internet is pointed out. It follows from this that many experts are concerned about developments in the Internet.

Step 3, the gap analysis, extracts the major discontinuities, unknowns, and contrasts between the situation today and the alternative futures. The object of analysis might be classified as a problem 000 or as a gap 0. During analysis redundancies across the gap descriptions occurred and have lead to the insight that sometimes one or several gaps might be clustered or even merged. Hence the gap storylines were developed in order to show the interrelationships and interdependencies between the identified gaps. Gaps and gap storylines such as cyber wars and crimes, information access and transparency, crisis management, intellectual property, changing public values, virtual borders and citizenship, automatic monitoring and enforcement, competition among nations, rationalise the legal framework for eGovernment, standardisation of laws, regulations and taxes were identified in this step (cf. 0). They serve as foundation of the research theme "government's role in the virtual world" and of the corresponding roadmap (see Fig 3). Lastly on this basis, a research roadmap for the transformation process was developed within a second round of targeted workshops. The roadmapping effort was to examine the scenarios, gaps, and detailed underlying data from the international workshops in order to review scenarios, prioritise gaps, and propose and phase research themes and actions. The final outcome comprises thirteen recurring themes that cut across the current state, the future scenarios, and the gaps in current practice and knowledge. The following chapter traces the line of argumentation through related aspects of government's role in the virtual included in the state-of-play and the future scenarios to the gap analysis. It concludes with the final research themes and actions that should be addressed in future.

3 Government's role and responsibilities in the virtual world

Within the last years Internet related crime became more and more popular in media since music and movie industry have suffered high losses when people started to swap songs and movies at Internet exchange meets. Currently main research and development efforts to actively counteract this kind of Internet related crime are undertaken by affected industries, consumer protection agencies and other private parties. Although governments expend efforts in setting up a proper regular framework for Internet related crimes in general, they are not really able to enforce these laws. What is the best regulatory framework good for, if there is no way to execute and enforce it? In the physical world governments know their role including obligations and restrictions with regard to crime prevention and prosecution. They have proved methods and means for law enforcement. Every Nation found its own way not only to deal with crime but also balance freedom and security. They set up policies and laws to protect both within its borders. These physical borders ground the variety of different nation depended individual rights. In the course of globalisation authorities of the different countries negotiated responsibilities in cases of international crime and consequently international law enforcement. But within the virtual world national borders disappeared and with it the enforcement of any national law becomes not only extraordinarily complex in general but also impossible in particular cases. Government's protection got lost in majority of cases. International cooperation 0 is often pointed out as crucial in regard to eGovernment in Europe. According to the Maastricht Treaty 0 the European Union bases on the following three main pillars:
1.   European Community
2.   Common Foreign and Security Policy
3.   Police and Judicial Co-operation in Criminal Matters
The two last pillars are strongly related to government's role in the virtual world and substantiate previous argumentation for more cooperation in matters concerning the virtual world including Internet related crime.

However, several future scenarios mention that the trend of collecting more and more data is certain. But it is uncertain how these data will be used0. In addition several scenarios point out increasing competition between nations and global regions. In regard to government's role at regulating the Internet both leads to the question: What will happen if one or more governments extend efforts to strongly regulate the Internet? History is full of examples that changing balance of powers has been lead to strong reactions from affected people. Two fundamental principles of western societies will be threatened by such developments. On the one hand there is freedom of opinion and on the other hand there is the right to privacy. The definition and therewith the protection of both variegates from country to country and within the borders of one country the protection of corresponding law is more or less guaranteed. But within the virtual world there are no explicit borders that would protect the individual against violations of unauthorised third parties, both individuals and organisation, as well as governments themselves. Consequently research question 1 arises: *How to translate national law into the Internet?*

There is a need to investigate what is realisable and what are restrictions? Is it possible to build up national borders in the Internet and do we really want virtual borders? A further solution might be the development of an international legal framework and enforcement. If national law solution is preferred for whatever reasons, then research question 2 is: *How to generate national borders in the virtual world?* If international law solution (see 0 'The new eWorld order') is favoured, then research question 2 is: *Who will then execute the law? Who will watch the watchers?*

However, the Internet is the first medium that supports individual and mass, synchronic and asynchronic, supply- and demand-oriented, moderated and unmoderated, personalised and anonymous, open and encrypted communication at the same time 0. The virtual world is world of imagination, re-imagination where people can have multiple identities and change identity if necessary. For instance, if one identity is regulated by government, people will create a new one. From this it follows the question: *What kind of virtual citizenship might appear?* Many people are living a second life within the Internet. For instance they are working and/or 'living' within the Internet. Virtual companies are making huge revenues because they are not paying taxes. At present there is a lack of taxation for virtual companies in the Internet. One approach to monitor and control Internet taxation might be the regulation of cash flows through physical banks. However, question still keeps how to apply and execute national tax systems in the Internet? For governments in general the question should be interesting, *what money governments might extract from the virtual world by e.g. taxation?*

At the moment the virtual world is faster than any regulating mechanism can react. Governments are always in the pursuit mode. Coherence and appearance is mentioned as requirement in order to regulate the Internet. Institutions are trapped in structural models. Acceleration of the regulation process has its own way on the grounds of democracy. Consequently regulation needs its time at the moment. But in future the adaptation of regulating mechanism needs accelerated modifications. There are two ways to approach the problem.

1. *Slow down Internet dynamics:* What are the conditions for sustainability in the virtual world?

2. *Accelerate legislative reforms:* What are the conditions for anticipation and flexibility in legislative?

Present approaches to change institutions towards new environmental needs and restrictions call for the challenge to jump the quantum for research. But participants claimed enthusiasm for smoother changing of institutions instead of fast revolution. Governments should not wait until the situation escalates. Because of capacity restrictions, changes should be carried out not so quick if something happens.

Decentralisation as far as possible, and with it anarchy, is one of the fundamental structural attributes of the Internet 00. Hence self-regulation within the Internet is the most popular kind of regulation because governmental regulation is very hard and maybe impossible to transform *properly*. Future research should identify what cases of Internet crime, e.g. protection of intellectual property, minors, etc. need to regulate by national or international law and governments, and what cases are better self-regulated 0. Within the virtual world things changing so fast that learning to adjust ourselves are also needed. However, only self-regulation might lead to anarchy within the Internet. In the case of data and privacy protection, individual concerns might lead to living in an Internet free zone.

If an Internet crime is discovered, prosecution will be required. But challenge is how to prosecute a crime in the Internet without coherence and appearance? Consequently governments need to know what the conditions for sustainability are in the virtual world.

In summary the following key research questions need to be addressed in future:
- What are government's roles, responsibilities and limitations in a world that is increasingly non-physical and borderless?
- Is a different legislation needed for the cyberspace? What is needed if national laws are to be translated into the Internet, e.g. to generate virtual national borders or to set up global international legal framework? If new international laws are needed, who will define and who will implement the laws?
- Who will monitor the legislators of international cyber laws? Who could be in possession of the sovereign power? What will happen if only a few governments undertake efforts to strongly regulate the Internet?
- What kind of virtual citizenship will appear?

summarises the research questions needs to be addressed in future and assigns them to the actors involved and needed for investigating the research questions.

Table 1. Phased actions for the research theme "Government's role in the virtual world"

No.	Description	Means	Actors	Timeline

1	Studies to investigate a proper understanding of the nature of the internet and where these characteristics challenge Governments to intervene in terms of action, reaction, prevention, and legislation, including the
	    Identify current challenging trends in the Internet that require government action, intervention and regulation in order to prevent e.g. crimes
	    Identify currently existing internet activity monitoring and crime prevention detection
	    Linking trends with activities and actors, and assess the specific aspects that require government interaction (Privacy, data access, Intellectual property rights (IPR), criminal actions)
		Risk and trend analysis, desk research, SWOT analyses, surveys, comparative studies, establishment of international expert groups	Research with key players from Governments, Politics and civic sector representatives	2007 -> 2009

2	Perform futures analysis on the basis of critical trends and evolutions identified, with specific focus on:
	    Risks of cyber crime, cyber terrorism, spamming, spoofing, manipulation of the virtual world code of conduct, etc.
	    Usage of the Internet as a crucial platform of communication in cases of catastrophes and near-
	    What are the potential dangers and opportunities of internet, where government needs to clearly regulate the way and means as well as priorities of action in such scenarios
		SWOT analysis, Scenario building, Trend analysis, risk analysis, analysis of critical interdependencies and hazardous situations	Researchers, legal experts, Governments and ICT industry	2008 --> 2010

3	Develop mechanisms and framework in order to monitor activities and trends in the virtual world; and to assess these activities and changes in terms of how far governments will be required to regulate imbalanced internet activities of stakeholders	Change analysis, Trend analysis, surveillance and monitoring conceptual design, internet laws	Research with key players from governments and consulting	2008 -> 2012

4	Put needs of regulations, mechanisms and framework into action and implementation
	    How to properly adapt and enlarge a legal framework for eCrime
	    Mechanisms and tools for crime prevention and prosecution with regard to balance freedom and security
	    How to create sustainability in the internet?
	    Examples of virtual regulation areas: taxation; IPR, customs; trade; information sharing, data privacy, violence; cyber crimes; education, eHealth issues, virtual citizenship, etc.
		Legal drafting and implementation, reengineering of national laws, pilot projects; European directives	Governments, with support from research and consulting	2010 -> 2020

5	Training and education to prepare and empower people to handle the virtual world and make them aware of the challenges and implications of using the Internet
	    Introduction of awareness and education in primary schools and continuing till higher
	    Concepts for life-long learning, especially for newcomers in the Internet aera and parents which enable their kids unsupervised and unmonitored
		Curricula updates, development of training and education modules, Seminars and workshops for new internet users, pilot projects	Research and education, Government, Consulting	2010 -> 2020

6	Implementation and monitoring of impact of regulations and training	EU directives	Governments, Consulting, ICT Industry, Academia, Civic Society and NGO	2010 -> 2020

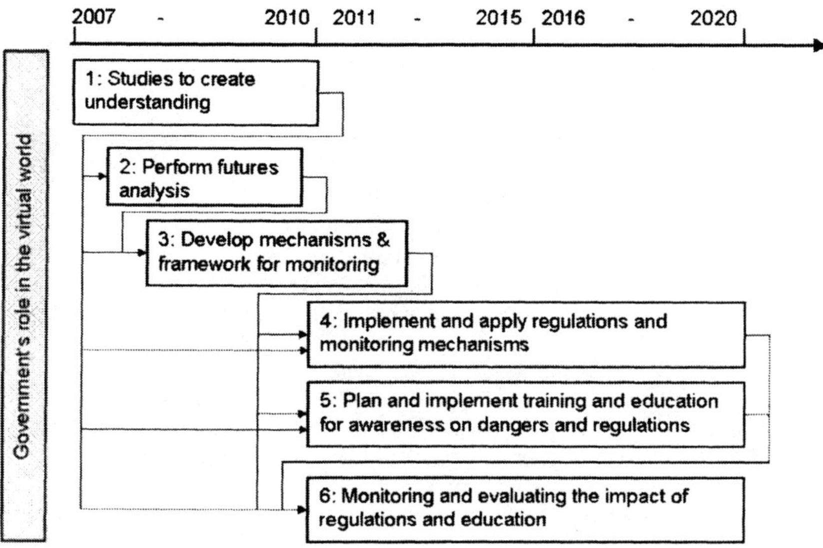

Fig 3, Phased actions for the research theme "Government's role in the virtual world"

In conclusion, although governments and private organisations already started to investigate the Internet, there is still a lack of effective laws, methods, measurements and technologies to enforce any law in the Internet. For instance the Centre for Socio-Legal Studies that is part of the Law Faculty of the University of Oxford discovered that existing laws, measurements and technologies are inappropriate to match the challenges of crime within the virtual world 0. However they pointed out that transparency of the Internet (e.g. standardisation of processes) is a key success factor for regulative interventions within the virtual world.

Concluding global electronic markets, virtual organisations, virtual identities, virtual products and services, and Internet-related crime are growing in prominence and importance. In a world that is increasingly non-physical and borderless, government's roles, responsibilities and limitations are currently not clear. Therefore research is absolutely necessary to discover the functional and structural basis of the Internet in general and to develop efficient and ethical correct laws and technologies to protect the individual, business and society. This task will be an essential part in order to create an information society. Participants of the Brussels workshop emphasised that doing nothing is the way to death. Now, the need for research about the virtual world is discovered, but governments still not react. Participants at the roadmapping workshops agreed that governments should not wait until the situation escalates. At this point more smooth changing of institutions is possible, instead of challenging institutions to jump the quantum for research towards a fast revolution later on. Governments need to identify their role in the new world. New power structures are coming up for younger people because they are growing up with the virtual world. In order to shape the future governments should understand what is next.

4 Conclusion

This paper shows that eGovernment, as a research discipline, is a complex and dynamic socio-technical system. Particularly, the question about government's role in the virtual world gives an idea about how complex and multifaceted eGovernment is. Also, the Internet itself is complex and dynamic system that serves for opportunities and threats whose extension we still not know. Chapter 3 depicts lacks of current eGovernment research regarding various Internet related issues concerning modern governments and in particular the Information Society. In future there is a particular need to focus research on the Internet and its impact related to governmental issues. At the moment governments main interest in the Internet is its deployment as a tool for service delivery but the eGovRTD2020 project finds out that the Internet's potential towards eGovernment is much more complex and extensive. Businesses both legal and criminal continue researching the potential of the Internet in order to find new fields of application useful for their business. From businesses findings about and business activities in the Internet, as well as from private activities a lot of areas of responsibility result for governments in the Internet. In future it will be absolutely necessary that government becomes more proactive in these relations. Laws, as well as law enforcement methods and tools are existing in the physical world do not meet the requirements of the virtual world.

However the chosen example, government's role and responsibilities in the virtual world, is just one research theme out of thirteen that is discovered by for 2020. The roadmapping methodology which is described in chapter 2 covers both transdisciplinary approach that resulted in broad field of investigation and a detailed analysis. Hence, the final roadmap comprises thirteen recurring themes that cut across the current state, the future scenarios, and the gaps in current practice and knowledge. Thereby each theme is the basis for a research roadmap. Chapter 2 introduces the research roadmap for government's role in the virtual world. But together with the twelve remaining research themes, the roadmaps cover the wide range of challenges needs to be addressed in future. Already years ago Alan Curtis Kay claimed that "the best way to predict the future is to invent it".

Acknowledgements

eGovRTD2020 (Roadmapping eGovernment research 2020, IST-2004-4-27139) is a specific support action co-funded by the European Commission under the 6th framework program of IST with the following partners: University of Koblenz-Landau (coordinator, DE), Delft University of Technology (NL), Center for Technology and Innovation Management (DE), Mykolas Romeris University (LT), University of Maribor (SI), European Institute of Public Administration (NL), Hautes Etudes Commerciales (FR), Australian National University, Center for applied philosophy (AU), Center for Technology in Government, University at Albany-SUNY (USA).

References

1. Bertelsmann Stiftung (2000) Selbstregulierung von Internet-Inhalten; http://www.bertelsmann-stiftung.de/cps/rde/xchg/SID-0A000F0A-C9914222/bst/hs.xsl/prj_8642_8650.htm

2. M. Bicking, M.A.Wimmer, *eGovernment research in Europe: findings from a recent state-of-play study.* In: Grönlund, A., Scholl, H.J., Andersen, K.V., Wimmer, M.A. (eds.). EGOV 2006 communications proceedings, Schriftenreihe Informatik # 18, Trauner Verlag, Linz, 2006, pp. 1-12

3. M. Bicking, M. Janssen, and M.A. Wimmer, *eGovernment 2020: Towards a Roadmap for future eGovernment research in Europe.* In: Cunningham, P., Cunningham, M. (eds.): Exploiting the knowledge Economy: Issues, Applications, Case Studies. Part 1, IOS Press, Amsterdam et al. (2006) 407-415

4. Capgemini (2005), Online Avaliability of Public Services: How is Europe Progressing? Web Based Survey on Electronic Public Services. Report of the Fifth Measurement Otober 2004. Online in the Internet; http://europa.eu.int/information_society/eeurope/2005/doc/all_about/egov_communication_de.pdf

5. Capgemini (2006), Online Avaliability of Public Services: How is Europe Progressing? Web Based Survey on Electronic Public Services. Report of the 6th Measurement June 2006. Online in the Internet; http://ec.europa.eu/information_society/eeurope/i2010/docs/benchmarking/online_availability_2006.pdf

6. Centre for Socio-Legal Studies (2004), Self-Regulation of Digital Media Converging on the Internet: Industry Codes of Conduct in Sectoral Analysis; http://pcmlp.socleg.ox.ac.uk/text/execsummary.pdf

7. CERT (2007), International Coordination for Cyber Crime and Terrorism in the 21st Century; http://www.cert.org/reports/stanford_whitepaper-V6.pdf

8. P. Checkland, *Systems Thinking, Systems Practice,* John Wiley & Sons, Chichester (1999)

9. Computer Crime Research Center, Fraud in the Internet (2005); http://www.crime-research.org/articles/Internet_fraud_0405/2

10. K. Dahmann, Überwachung oder Selbstregulierung? (2004); http://www.dw-world.de/dw/article/0,,1311400,00.html?mpb=de

11. eGovRTD2020 consortium, Deliverable D 3.1 – Gap Analysis Report (2006); http://www.egovrtd2020.org

12. eGovRTD2020 consortium, Deliverable D1.1 – State of Play report, (2006); http://www.egovrtd2020.org/

13. eGovRTD2020 consortium, Deliverable D 2.1 - Scenarios report (including regional workshops report), (2006); http://www.egovrtd2020.org

14. European Commission, Better Public Services, (2003); http://europa.eu.int/information_society/soccul/egov/index_en.htm

15. European Union, Treaty on European Union, (1992); http://europa.eu/eur-lex/en/treaties/dat/EU_treaty.html

16. R. Heeks, Most eGovernment-for-Development Projects Fail, IDPM, (2003). International Content Rating Association (ICRA 2006); http://www.icra.org/

17. IST, Fith Framework Programme. List of "key" actions, (2002); http://www.cordis.lu/fp5/src/key.htm (9th May 2006)

18. IST, A thematic priority for research and development under the specific programme "Integrating and strengthening the European research area" in the Community sixth framework programme, (Commission Decision C (2005) 5588 of 14 December 2005); ftp://ftp.cordis.lu/pub/ist/docs/wp_4th_update_en.pdf

19. G. Lenart, U. Hribar,, *Technology support for soft problem solving, Informatics and management*, ISBN 3-631-51869-2, Florjančič, J., Pütz, K. (eds.),P. Lang, Frankfurt am Main (2004).

20. M. K. Lottor, RFC 1296 Internet Growth (1981-1991). Menlo Park, CA, (1992); ftp://ftp.cs.tu-berlin.de/pub/doc/rfc/rfc1296.gz

21. S. Možina, R. Rozman, M.I. Tavčar, D. Pučko, Š. Ivanko, B. Lipičnik, J. Gričar, M. Glas, J. Kralj, M. Tekavčič, V. Dimovski, B. Kovač, *MANAGEMENT: nova znanja za uspeh*, (2002).

22. OECD, Glossary of e-Government Terms, (2007); http://webdomino1.oecd.org/COMNET/PUM/egovproweb.nsf/viewHtml/index/$FILE/glossary.htm Definition dates back to the year 2005

23. S. Stecklow, Computer Users Battle High Tech Marketers Over Soul of Internet. *Wall Street Journal*, (16.9.1994)

24. B. Sterling, A Short History of the Internet. THE MAGAZINE OF FANTASY AND SCIENCE FICTION, (1993); gopher://gopher.eff.org/00/Publications/Bruce_Sterling/FSF_columns/fsf5

25. B. Sterling, The Hacker Crackdown. *Literary Freeware*, (1994).

26. M.A. Wimmer, Approaching secure and trustful e-government applications: technology won't make it alone! In P. Cunningham, M. Cunningham, P. Fatelnig (Eds.), Building the Knowledge Economy: Issues, Applications, Case Studies. Part 1, *IOS Press*, Amsterdam et al, pp. 626 – 632 (2003).

27. M.A. Wimmer, "Integrated service modeling for online one-stop Government. EM – Electronic Markets", *special issue on e-Government*, Vol. 12, No. 3, pp. 1-8 (2002).

28. M. A. Wimmer, B. von Bredow, "Sicherheitskonzepte für e-Government. Technische versus ganzheitliche Ansätze". *In Datenschutz und Datensicherheit*, Vol. 26, 9/2002, pp. 536 – 541. (2002).

An E-education Framework Based on Semantic Web Agents

Ming Dong and Rong Rong
School of Information, Renmin University of China
59 Zhongguancun Ave, Beijing, 100872, P.R.China
dongming@ruc.edu.cn, rongbaba@msn.com

Abstract. The booming web technology stimulates computer-based e-education which is considered to be an appropriate lifelong education approach in this era due to the spatial and temporal convenience. In this paper we propose a service-oriented agent e-education framework based on the next generation web, viz. semantic web. Compared with the framework on which the e-education performs now, this new framework has many advanced properties due to the use of intelligent agents and is expected to perform an automated style for the future education.

1   Introduction

Nowadays, the lifelong education and re-training are considered as key aspects to both individuals and enterprises. Unfortunately, the traditional classroom education seems unsuitable today due to time, distance and cost limitations caused by modern intensive lifestyle [1, 2]. Moreover, in this new era, learners are supposed to get the specific knowledge corresponding to their own needs. E-education seems to be a proper approach for achieving the objects above, for its abilities to overcome the temporal, spatial and learning style problems. In [3] the author predicated much of companies training would shift to e-learning or other web based activities in the future and by the year 2010, the e-education market would reach $50billion. E-education allows teachers and students to finish the education activities in a virtual classroom via the booming development of the network technology. In this paper we propose an intelligent agents e-education framework based on the next generation web, the semantic web, to construct a better formed e-education system. This new framework makes education activities automated while optimizes the share of learning materials. So, it is supposed to be a promising framework for the future e-education.

Please use the following format when citing this chapter:

Dong, M., Rong, R., 2007, in IFIP International Federation for Information Processing, Volume 252, Integration and Innovation Orient to E-Society Volume 2, eds. Wang, W., (Boston: Springer), pp. 481-486.

2 Preliminaries

2.1 Semantic Web

E-education changes learning concepts in several aspects, it offers more personalized and adaptive learning style. Unfortunately, the current web based methods are not considered to be a suitable platform for implementing the e-education, because of many limitations, e.g. lack of intelligence. Semantic web which has higher capacities on information sharing, nonhuman autonomous implementing and communication supporting seems to be a proper platform to satisfy the requirement of e-education [4, 5].

In semantic web, contents are described by formal semantics. By means of this, resources on semantic web are much easier for machines to understand. Thus, an autonomous e-education system could be constructed well. The resources provider (teacher) prepares learning resources, and the consumer (student) describes his own situations and interests, his learning agent will search for learning materials of his own circumstance. This search is performed by semantic querying and navigation, which is considered more accurate compared to current technology.

In this paper, we propose an e-education framework on Semantic Web formed by intelligent agents. All the agents use commonly agreed service language. Thus, communication between agents is easy to achieve. Each agent has a specified function; it receives requests and matches them with semantic descriptions. At last, implements corresponding applications and acknowledges the request.

2.1 Agents

Agents are software-based autonomous systems made for specific functions to finish several tasks automatically in order to make the specific process much easier to users. Their functions could cover administrating process, fetching matched resources, triggering specified events, formalizing specifications etc. With the help of intelligent agents the whole process is transparent to learners and teachers.

In our proposed framework, intelligent agents are introduced to finish the granulated model functions. The learners/teachers only need to describe their own demands then the corresponding agents will finish the work and transport information to the correct applications, each agent also could call other agents for collaboration, e.g. these is no matched learning material on one server agent (will be introduced later). So, this Server agent calls other server agents to match the materials and transport them back.

3 Proposed Framework

3.1 Overview

In the following context, we will present our framework in detail. In the proposed framework, each user (students and teachers) will have a personal agent. These personal agents have their own knowledge bases which contain the formalized commands, interface protocols and user's profiles besides. Each personal agent receives demands and data from the user and generates commands corresponding to user's profiles and demand. Each server agent receives commands from other agents and sends feedbacks back to the enquirer. In [9, 10], similar frameworks are presented; but we supposed our framework is more efficient and convenient to build larger e-education systems due to two reasons. Firstly, in our framework, every agent generates formalized commands which could be recognized by other agents and every agent has the ability to communicate to other agents; these properties are highly advantaged to form an active e-education environment without adding so many burdens to the server. Secondly, server agents could be made heuristically; all these server agents could be distributed all around the world, we could use cascaded enquiry to get the corresponding materials. These cascaded server agents are much easier to maintain and modify, but still preserving easy entrance property. With the help of semantic web, all learning materials could be well annotated and shared; then an internet-liked e-education system will be built.

3.2   Framework Layout

Fig.1 describes the top-level view of our proposed framework. In this framework, we use the service-oriented model [7] to perform education activities. In service-oriented model, students control whole process, they describe their own demands and offer other relevant information (their situation etc.). Teachers provide learning materials and other educational services related to their courses under the specific description rules(such as LOM, ARIADNE, IMS, etc.). Student agents receive demands from students, finish their own functions and call Server agents to provide corresponding services. Sever agents receive orders sent by student agents and match descriptions with its own knowledge base then generate the relevant services and send these information back to students/teachers/other agents or trigger the corresponding applications.

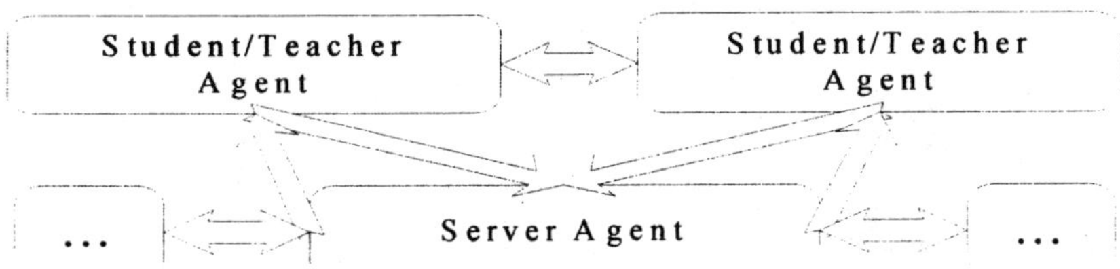

Fig. 1. Top level of the e-education framework

3.3   Infrastructure

The Students/Teacher Agents
In our framework, the students/teacher agent is composed of three main function blocks. Namely, application trigger, command generator and interface manager. Command generator is used to generate the required description which depicts the demands and situations of current user. Interface Manager contributes to formalization of the communication with sever agents. Both Command Generator

and Interface Manager search the knowledge base to match the relevant items and then generate results. Application trigger receives information from other agents and triggers corresponding applications to finish the e-education activities. E.g. if the sever agent decides to transport an educational video back to the student agent, the application trigger will accept this video and then initialize the video player.

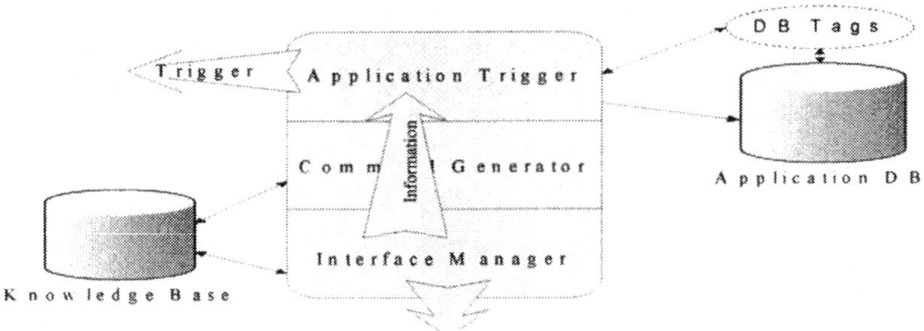

Fig. 2. The infrastructure of the Students/Teacher Agents

The Server Agents

The structure of server agent is represented in Fig.3. There are several sub-agents in this system to perform specific functions on the semantic web; all the sub-agents could communicate with other sever agents to derive relative information/resources.

In server agent, the first layer is portal. This portal waits for requests from other agents. After receiving a request from student, teacher or other agents, user's status will be checked by authentification&recognition process. Then different rights will be allocated for the following procedures. Meanwhile system reads the user's information from DB. E.g., for students the information could be: research directions, learning history, etc.

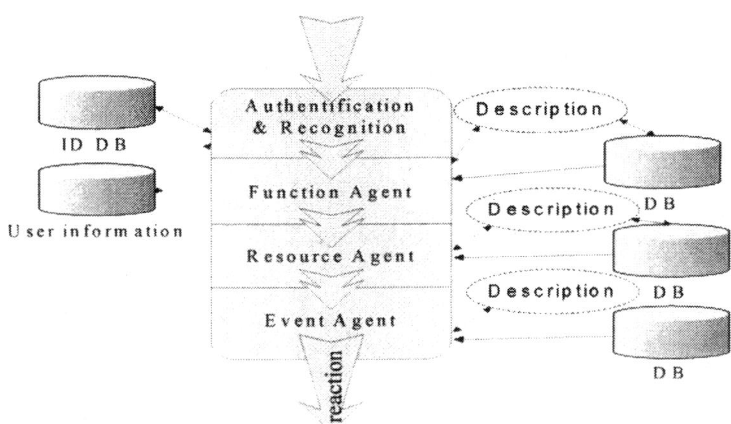

Fig. 3. The infrastructure of the Server Agents

After decoding received orders, server agent would generate corresponding responds. In the function agent layer, function agent matches the needed function with descriptions from the user. E.g. look at fig.4, we give a demonstration of the function matching. The inspiration is derived from[1].

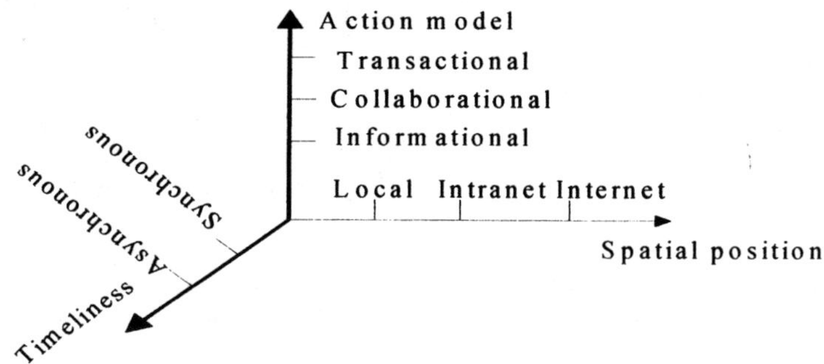

Fig. 4. Function Matching

Function space is divided into small cells; the granularity depends on agent designers. In this demonstration, the space is divided into 18 cells; agents categorize every function into these cells and match the functions with the user's status. E.g. a student wants to take a net-meeting with his teacher, if this student is not a full-time student in this university, then this demand will be classified into 'Internet, Collaborational, Synchronous' cell; after this the agent could match the demand with services belong to this cell.

After selecting correct function, resource agent and event agent will select correct resources to users and generate relative service events corresponds to user's preferred behaviors and results from pre-steps. After these steps the server agent will initial the selected events. These events could be a learning resource delivery from/to a teacher/student, triggering of connection between a teacher and a student, visiting another server agent for getting relevant resources, etc. Finally, after acknowledging the request, the sever agent will finish its jobs and student/teacher agent will carry on their further jobs depends on the resources and instructions received from the server agent.

4   Conclusion

We proposed an e-education framework based on semantic web agent. This framework is a service-oriented one. So, students are in the center of the education, all the agents and teachers are passive and collaborational, they only offer the services to students. This property maximizes the benefits of students; they could make their own plan corresponding to themselves. The semantic agent approach is a quite advanced method to perform the e-education based on the next generation web. Semantic standard could ultimately share and get the correct resources to a certain circumstance; meanwhile agent method could get more flexibility, modularity and customization. In all, it is an effective method to perform e-education with the emerging of new web technology.

References

1.L.F. Motiwalla, "An e-education framework for training in the next generationenterprises", *Research Challenges, 2000. Proceedings. Academia/Industry Working Conference* ,139-144(2000).

2.T.F. Stafford, "Understanding motivations for Internet use in distance education", *Education, IEEE Transaction,* 48(2),301-306 (2005).

3.K. Levis, "The Business of E-learning: A Revolution in Training and Education Markets". http://www.hrmguide.net/usa/hrd/e-learning_survey.htm.

4.http://www.aifb.uni-karlsruhe.de/WBS/Publ/2001/WebNet_1stsstrst_2001.pdf.

5.T. Anderson and D. Whitelock, "The educational semantic Web: visioning and racticing the future of education", *Journal of Interactive Media and Education* , 1, 2004.

6.N. Hussain and M.K. Khan, "Service-Oriented E-Learning Architecture Using Web Service-Based Intelligent Agents", *Information and Communication Technologies, 2005. ICICT 2005. First International Conference,* 137-143(2005).

7.R.D. Andreev and N.V. Troyanova, "E-learning Design: An Integrated Agent-Grid Service Architecture", *Modern Computing, 2006. JVA '06. IEEE John Vincent Atanasoff 2006 International Symposium,* 208-213(2006).

8.Z. Abbas, M. Umer, M. Odeh, R. McClatchey, A. Ali and A. Farooq, "**A** semantic grid-based e-learning framework (SELF)", *Cluster Computing and the Grid, 2005. CCGrid 2005. IEEE International Symposium,* 1, 11-18(2005).

9.P. Nilas, N. , Nilas and S. Mitatha, "A Dynamic Associative E-Learning Model based on a Spreading Activation Network", *Electrical and Computer Engineering, Canadian Conference* ,2472-2475(2006).

10. Y. Shang, H.C. Shi and S.S. Chen, "An Intelligent Distributed Environment for Active Learning", *Journal of Educational Resources in Computing,* 2001.

11. R. Koper, "Use of the Semantic Web to Solve Some Basic Problems in Education", *Journal of Interactive Media in Education,* 2004.

A Framework for Web Usage Mining in Electronic Government

Ping Zhou, Zhongjian Le
School of Information Management,
JiangXi University of Finance and Economic, NanChang ,China 330013
Zp_jx@126.com

Abstract. Web usage mining has been a major component of management strategy to enhance organizational analysis and decision. The literature on Web usage mining that deals with strategies and technologies for effectively employing Web usage mining is quite vast. In recent years, E-government has received much attention from researchers and practitioners. Huge amounts of user access data are produced in Electronic government Web site everyday. The role of these data in the success of government management cannot be overstated because they affect government analysis, prediction, strategies, tactical, operational planning and control. Web usage miming in E-government has an important role to play in setting government objectives, discovering citizen behavior, and determining future courses of actions. Web usage mining in E-government has not received adequate attention from researchers or practitioners. We developed a framework to promote a better understanding of the importance of Web usage mining in E-government. Using the current literature, we developed the framework presented herein, in hopes that it would stimulate more interest in this important area.

1 Introduction

The recent years have seen the flourishing of research in the area of Web usage mining from both the research and practice communities. With the rapid growth and development of electronic government as well as the ease and speed with which government affairs can be carried out over the Web, one of the important application fields of Web mining is electronic government systems. Electronic government is one of the most appropriate applications of data mining, that is because electronic government domain is very easy to suit the conditions of data mining: richest and the most common source of data, automatically generated data. The result of data mining

---

can be quickly converted into the government behavior, at the same time the policies of government derived from the mining can be evaluated in time.

Web Mining is that area of Data Mining, which deals with the extraction of hidden and interesting knowledge from the large volume of Web documents and records[1] . It is a comprehensively integrated technique, involving Internet, Artificial intelligence, Computer language, informatics, statistics etc. Web Mining can be broadly divided into three classes[2]: content mining, structure mining and usage mining. Web content mining is that part of Web Mining, which focuses on the raw information available on Web pages or the searched results(e.g. words); Web Structure Mining is that part of Web Mining, which focuses on the structure of Web site including intra-page structural information and inter-page structural information presented on Web pages(e.g., links to other pages).

Web Usage Mining is that part of Web mining, which deals with the extraction of knowledge on users' access patterns and user behavior from data collected from the main sources: Web servers, proxy servers, Web clients (including registration data and user profile information) using some kind of data mining techniques.

Web content mining and Web structure mining focus on the raw information on web pages. In Web usage mining, the focus is on data describing the usage pattern of Web pages, including: Web server side access log files, proxy side log files, client side log records, user registration information, user suggestions and user request information etc, which can be used to track the behavior, the goal and the motivation of users producing these data. Exploiting these usage data can largely help government to identify the citizen's or the business' needs, requests, requirements and behaviors etc and make corresponding policies. Hence in E-government, Web usage mining is the main Web mining. The remaining of this paper is organized as follows: Initially, in section 2 we propose a framework for Web usage mining in e-government. Then in section 3 some concrete applications of Web usage mining in e-government platform are presented. Finally, in section 4 the conclusions are drawn.

2   Web Usage Mining in Electronic Government

As shown in figure 1, a framework for Web Usage Mining in E-government is presented. There are four main tasks for performing Web Usage Mining in E-government. This section presents an overview of the tasks for each step.

2.1   Data Collection

Server (including Web server and proxy) side, client side and user registration information are the present main three sources of usage data on E-government Web site.

2.1.1 Server side

Web server side usage data mainly consist of: Web server log files, Cookies, submission data and the statistic information from the external third side, which all implicitly record the browsing behavior of site visitors.

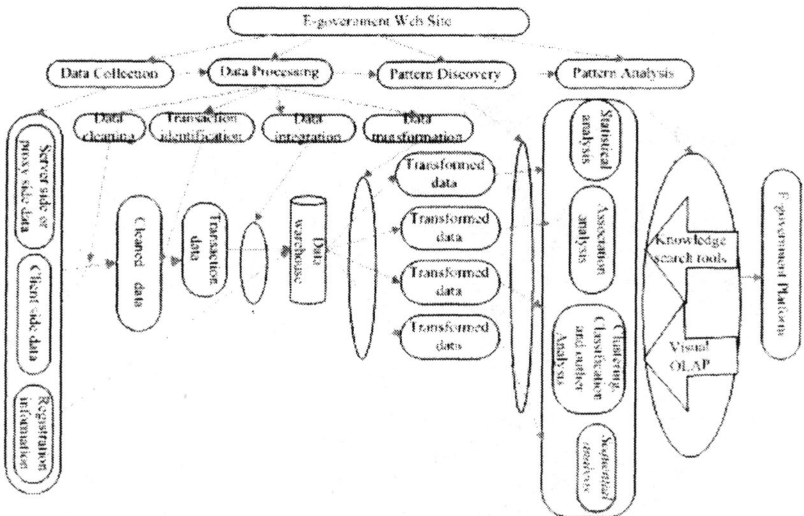

Fig. 1. Web usage mining in E-government framework

(1)Web server side log files: important sources of data for performing Web usage mining. The data recorded in server logs reflect the access of single server by multiple users. These log files can be stored in various formats such as common log or extended log formats.

(2) Cookies: Cookies are tokens generated by the Web server for individual client browser in order to automatically track the site visitor. When the user visits the same Web site again, she/he can be identified immediately.

(3)Submission data: various openly entered and submitted data by users, which basically reflect the user's interest and preferences, merged with the government Web site's structure, content, key words semantics and domain knowledge can perfectly discover the visitor's behavior and motivation.

(4) The statistic information: information on some users can be bought from external channels, for example, the third database.

Proxy side usage data: collecting navigation data at the proxy level in many respects is basically the same as collecting data at the server level. The main difference in this case is that proxy servers collect data of groups of users accessing huge groups of web servers, which help to reveal the visitors' behavior and action behind the proxy.

2.1.2 Client side

Usage data on client side, which records data of single user accessing groups of web servers, provide detailed information on actual user behavior [3]. The client side data are more credible than that of the server side, because it avoids the high caching and IP errors.

2.1.3 Registration information

Registration data refers to the relevant information submitted to the Web server through Web pages, including logon message, suggestion on Web etc., which must be integrated with all accessing log files in order to increase the accuracy of Web usage mining in E-government.

2.2   Data Processing

In practice, data in E-government systems provided by the data sources described above are usually inconsistent, incomplete, redundancy and obscure. Data processing means converting the data contained in the various available data sources in E-government Web site into the data necessary for useful pattern discovery. Only the clean, accuracy and simple abstract data can be used for mining analysis. Data processing usually comprises data cleaning, transaction identification, data integration and data transformation.

2.2.1 Data cleaning

Data cleaning refers to removing all the data tracked in Web logs that are invalid for web usage mining purposes [4,11,12,14]. We only want to keep the entries that carry relevant information. Therefore, data cleaning is used to eliminate the irrelevant entries from the log file, e.g. requests for graphical page content; requests for any other file which might be included into a web page. The data collected from Web servers or Proxy servers, which record the interactions between groups of users and multiple servers, usually need to be cleaned before use for mining. In contrast, data collected from client side are relevantly cleaner because of less user interference. Moreover, the data input by users should be confirmed, restructured and formatted for pattern discovery.

2.2.2 Transaction identification

Before performing Web usage mining in E-government, transaction should be predefined according to the characteristics of pattern mining. Usually, different user sessions analysis can produce different transaction to extract different useful information.

2.2.3 Data integration

Web usage data in E-government, which distributed over various sources of data as described above, are regularly localized or even personal and difficult to share. Only merging these data can it be applied to Web usage mining to extract the truly useful information for government.

2.2.4 Data transformation

Data transformation refers to mobilization and conversion of the existing integrated data for different analysis and decision making tools.

2.3   Pattern Discovery

Pattern discovery draws upon methods and algorithms developed from several fields such as statistics, data mining, machine learning and pattern recognition etc.

Methods developed from other fields must take into consideration the different kinds of data abstractions and prior knowledge available for Web Mining. For example, in association rule discovery, the notion of a transaction for market-basket analysis does not take into consideration the order in which items are selected. The following are common methods to extract knowledge about visitors to government Web sites.

2.3.1 Statistical Analysis

Statistical methods are the most common method to extract knowledge about visitors to a government Web site. By analyzing the session file, one can perform different kinds of descriptive statistical analysis (frequency, mean, median, etc.) on variables such as page views, viewing time and length of a navigational path. Despite lacking in the depth of its analysis, this type of knowledge can be potentially useful for improving the system performance, enhancing the security of the system, facilitating the site modification task, and providing support for government's decision making.

2.3.2 Association analysis

Association analysis can be used to relate pages that are most often referenced together in a single server session[4]. In the context of Web Usage Mining, association rules refer to sets of pages that are accessed together with a support value exceeding some specified threshold. These pages may not be directly connected to one another via hyperlinks. In actual government Web site design, applying these related pages can help Web designers to restructure their Web site so that it is easy for citizens to access their wanted pages. The association rules may also serve as a heuristic for pre-fetching documents in order to reduce user-perceived latency when loading a page from a remote site.

2.3.3 Clustering, Classification and outlier Analysis

Clustering is a technique to group together a set of items having similar characteristics[5]. Clustering of users tends to establish groups of users exhibiting similar browsing patterns. Such knowledge is especially useful for inferring user demographics in order to perform service segmentation in E-government applications or providing personalized Web content to the citizens. On the other hand, clustering of pages will discover groups of related Web pages. This information is useful for Internet search engines and Web service providers. In both applications, permanent or dynamic HTML pages can be created that suggest related hyperlinks to the user according to the user's query or past history of information needs[4].

Classification is the task of mapping a data item into one of several predefined classes [6]. In the Web domain, one is interested in developing a profile of users belonging to a particular class or category. This requires extraction and selection of features that best describe the properties of a given class or category.

Outlier refers to the data that do not comply with the general behavior or model of the data. Data mining in many fields often try to minimize the influence of outliers or eliminate them all together. This, however, would result in the loss of important information because the outliers may be of particular signal reflecting abnormal events, irregularities, such as the case of criminal activity, fraud etc. Outlier detection can reveal points that behave "anomalously" with respect to other observations. Examining such points can reveal clues to solve the problem at hand. In other cases, the sudden appearance of a large number of outliers can point to a change in the underlying process that is generating the data.

Thus, in E-government, outlier detection and analysis are a very important and interesting data miming task. Analyzing these outliers, government departments can take action accordingly in time, predict the trend of society development, consequently enhance the government service ability and the capability of reining the complicated events etc.

2.3.4 Sequential Patterns analysis

The technique of sequential pattern analysis attempts to find inter-session patterns such that the presence of a set of items is followed by another item in a time-ordered set of sessions or episodes[1]. By using this approach, government Web observers can predict future visit patterns which will be helpful in placing especial messages aimed at certain user groups. Other types of temporal analysis that can be performed on sequential patterns include trend analysis, change point detection or similarity analysis.

2.4   Pattern Analysis

Pattern analysis is the last step in the overall Web Usage mining process in E-government as described in Figure 1. The motivation behind pattern analysis is to filter out uninteresting rules or patterns from the set found in the pattern discovery phase. The exact analysis methodology is usually governed by the application for which Web mining is done. The most common form of pattern analysis consists of a knowledge query mechanism such as SQL. Another method is to load usage data into a data cube in order to perform OLAP operations. Visualization techniques, such as graphing patterns or assigning colors to different values, can often highlight overall patterns or trends in the data. Content and structure information can be used to filter out patterns containing pages of a certain usage type, content type, or pages that match a certain hyperlink structure.

2.5   Applying to E-government platform

The previous sections described how the knowledge on the public we have been discussing in this paper can be obtained.

Examples are:
- cleaning, tracking, browsing and discovering usage data,
- being alerted to abnormal outliers,
- knowledge visualization,
- querying knowledge in similar natural language.

To be really effective in every use, the end-user functionality needs to be integrated into, for example, desktop applications. We can also see these discovered knowledge as part of an organization, being integrated into more specific government applications and solutions. A few examples of the possibilities are given in the next section. This is by no means an exhaustive list.

3   Applications of Web usage mining in E-government

In this section we present the main applications of Web usage mining in E-government, as shown in Figure 2. The application of Web usage mining to E-government is a procedure which translates citizen or business' usage data on government Web site into valuable knowledge which can provide various decision supports in government affairs, such as: finding out the preferences/interests/desires of citizen and improving the citizen or business satisfaction; Restructuring the Government Web Site and Increasing the System Performance; enhancing the government planning and promoting government innovation; improving the analysis and decision making of government etc.

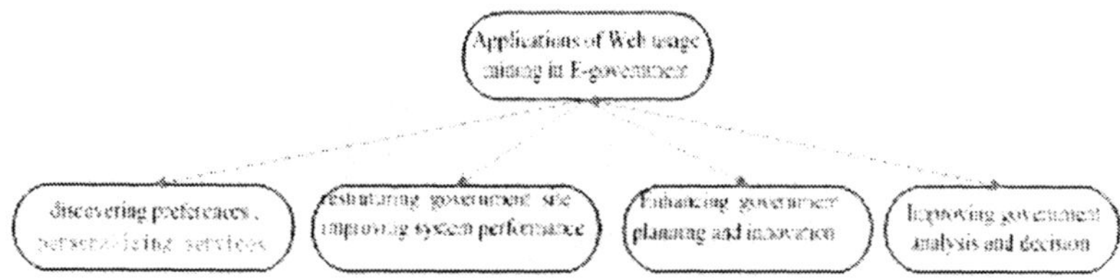

Fig.2. Application areas for Web Usage Mining in E-government

3.1   Discovering the Preferences/Interests of Citizens and Providing Personalization Services

User's actions can observe his/her behavior and derive his/her preferences/interests [7] [8]. For example, Where does he click, how long does she remain on certain pages, what words does he search for, from which websites did she come, interactions done with this website, and so on. A list of keywords from pages that a user has spent a significant amount of time viewing is compiled and presented to the user. Through feedback analysis of the keyword list and his profile, recommendations for other pages within the site are made. Personalizing the Web experience for a user is the holy grail of Web-based applications based on her/his registration data and usage behavior which were often used to discover clusters of users having similar access patterns and their respective preferences. Every user will be assigned to a single cluster based on their current traversal pattern. The links that are presented to a given user are dynamically selected based on what pages other users assigned to the same cluster have visited. Tracking a user as he or she browses the government Web site and identifying the links that are potentially interesting to the user are necessary for understanding citizen behavior, their preferences and desires and providing each citizen excellent and personalized services and corresponding management responding to their needs[14]. The whole process can be described in figure 3.

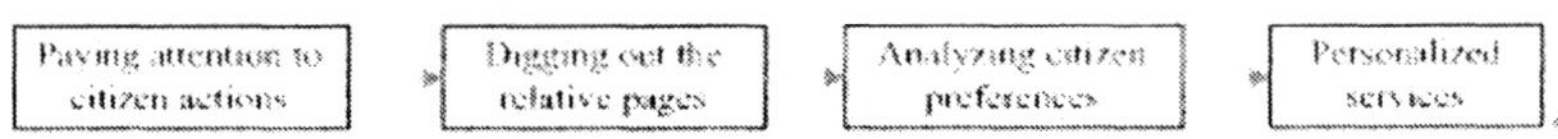

Fig.3. The process of providing personalization services

3.2   Restructuring the Government Web Site and Increasing the System Performance

The content and structure of a government Web site are not constant. The designers of a government Web site can not only completely rely on specialists in the field to design the structure of the Web site, they should dynamically restructure the structure and content of government Web site according to the result derived from Web usage mining in E-government in order to convenience the citizen and business access[9]. For example, you should restructure the Web site with respect to the frequent access paths of visitors, on the one hand, user access time is saved. On the other hand, expenditure of Web site is significantly economized.

The following three suggestions can be used to optimize the government Web site structure:

(1)Mining the Web log files can extract the related access pages, then new links are added between them to facilitate the visitors.

(2)Using the path analysis techniques to find out the most frequent access path and putting the important message over there will enhance the appetency of government to citizens and improve the service qualities.

(3)Mining the Web log files can discovery expected information position by citizens. If the expected access position frequency is higher than that of the actual, a navigation link can be established between them to optimize the structure of the Web site.

Web usage mining in E-government can effectively observe and analyze the users of government Web site and their behaviors and actions, which inscribe the knowledge in human or social domain essentially related to human action and benefit the system improvement, e.g., security is an important issue for government site, by tracking the users' access pattern and access paths, the hidden intrusion can be detected fleetly and easily.

3.3   Enhancing the Government Planning and Fostering Government Innovation

Through employing data mining technology, government can manage with reason the human resources, material resources and information resources to harmonize the relation between resources inside government and those outside government, such as, the whole process from program planning to program implementing can exchange and share the same data. OLAP(Online analysis and process) can optimize the project flow to best fit together the society resources, which will largely reduce the cost that social resources circulate and information transfers, promote the government planning to be more scientific, informational and intelligent. A scientific and effective government planning can be achieved by intensifying government's real time control and management with intelligent technology and visualization technology.

Mining Web usage data on government site can quickly obtain the information about government affairs to make the government grasp the society development trends in time, which at the same time make management and redeployment of society resources more systematic, macroscopical and dynamic to improve the government innovation capability.

Innovation, which does not only limit to administrative method and government affair process flow, and that including constituting government development strategies and public policies, is the basic requirement that change government from functional organization to service organization. Beside that, mining usage data on government site can significantly improve governmental responsiveness to all the issues, from day-to-day citizen request to paroxysmal events, also foster the government work innovation and personnel making increasing.

3.4   Improving the Government Analysis and Decisions

Mining and analyzing the vast quantities of usage data on government site are of great benefit to the government analysis and decisions. Government decisions making through analyzing information about citizens(e.g. suggestion, request, desire, etc) are more likely to be acceptable to the majority of people. Citizen usage data on government site provide a source of special insight, information, knowledge, and experience, which contributes to the soundness of government solutions to public problems[10]. Citizen participation in public affairs also serves to check and balance political activities. A cross section of citizen participation in the decision-making process reduces the likelihood of government leaders making self-serving decisions. Mining these citizen usage data on government Web site can also legitimize a program, its plans, actions, and leadership. Unsupported leaders often become discouraged and drop activities that are potentially beneficial to citizens. On the other hand, citizen's voluntary suggestion can reduce the cost of personnel needed to carry out many of the duties associated with community action. In a word, mining citizens' usage data can identify and extract the hidden important information to provide all levels government department with effective decision support[13]. For example, mining the client side log files can obtain the opinion of citizen and effectively assist government department to make scientific and rational adjustment to their desires.

4   Conclusions

In this paper, a framework for Web usage data in E-government was presented. This framework consists of five parts. We believe that this framework can provide a number of benefits to the different stakeholders within public authorities who need to capture the hidden and tacit knowledge on the citizens, businesses or other organizations. At the same time, important applications of Web usage mining in E-government platform were described, which provide analytical help for decision making, for monitoring or for revisions. Decision makers in government agencies should fully make use of these mined valuable information to modulate strategy and tactics accordingly, dynamically design government site to satisfy citizen and business and improve the government affair service efficiency.

References:

1. Jiawei Han and Micheline kamber, *Data Mining Concepts and Techniques*(second edition)(China Machine Press, Bei Jing, 2006).
2. Federico Michele Facca, Pier Luca Lanzi, Mining Interesting Knowledge from Weblogs: a survey, *Data & Knowledge Engineering (*53), 225 – 241(2005).
3. K.D. Fenstermacher, M. Ginsburg, Mining Client-side Activity for Personalization, *in: Fourth IEEE International Workshop on Advanced Issues of E-Commerce and Web-Based Information Systems* (WECWIS_02), 205 – 212(2002).
4. Jaideep Srivastava , Robert Cooley , Mukund Deshpande et al ,Web Usage Mining : Discovery and Applications of Usage Patterns from Web Data[J] . *SIGKDD Explorations* , 1 (2), 12 – 23(2000).
5. MOBASHER B, COOLEY R, SR IVASTAVA J, Creating Adaptive Web Sites Through Usage-based Clustering of URLs[C], *Proceedings of the 1999 IEEE Knowledge and Data Engineering Exchange Workshop* (KDEXp99) , 19 – 25(1999).
6.LIU JG, WU W P. Web Usage Mining for Electronic Business Applications [J], *Machine Learning and Cybernetics*(2) ,1314-1318(2004).
7. Mobasher B ,Cooly R. Srivastara J . Automatic Personalization Based on Web Usage Mining[J], *Communications of the ACM*, ,43 (8) ,142- 151(2000).
8. Przemysław Kazienko , Michał Adamski., AdROSA—Adaptive Personalization of Web Advertising. *Information Sciences* (177) ,2269 – 2295(*2007).
9.Elisabeth N. Bui, Brent L. Henderson and Karin Viergever, Knowledge Discovery from Models of Soil Properties Developed Through Data Mining, *Ecological Modeling* (5), 431-446(2006).
10. Milakovich, M. and Gordon, G. ,Public Administration in America (7th Ed.),Bedford/St. Martin's (New York, 2001).
11.C.R. Anderson, A Machine Learning Approach to Web Personalization, Ph.D. thesis, *University of Washington*(2002).
12. B. Diebold, M. Kaufmann, Usage-based Visualization of Web Localities, in: *Australian symposium on information visualization*, 159 – 164(2001).
13. Paul Beynon-Davies, Constructing Electronic Government: the case of the UK inland revenue, *International Journal of Information Management (*25),3 – 20(2005).
14.Haibin Liu, Vlado Keselj, Combined Mining of Web Server Logs and Web Contents for Classifying User Navigation Patterns and Predicting Users' Future Requests, *Data & Knowledge Engineering* (61), 304 – 330(2007).

A Theoretical Approach to Information Needs Across Different Healthcare Stakeholders

Reetta Raitoharju[1] and Eeva Aarnio[2]

1 Turku School of Economics, Information Systems Science
Rehtorinpellonkatu 3, 20500 Turku, Finland.
reetta.raitoharju@tse.fi

2 Turku School of Economics, Information Systems Science
Rehtorinpellonkatu 3, 20500 Turku, Finland.
eeva.aarnio@tse.fi

Abstract. Increased access to medical information can lead to information overload among both the employees in the healthcare sector as well as among healthcare consumers. Moreover, medical information can be hard to understand for consumers who have no prerequisites for interpreting and understanding it. Information systems (e.g. electronic patient records) are normally designed to meet the demands of one professional group, for instance those of physicians. Therefore, the same information in the same form is presented to all the users of the systems regardless of the actual need or prerequisites. The purpose of this article is to illustrate the differences in information needs across different stakeholders in healthcare. A literature review was conducted to collect examples of these different information needs. Based on the findings the role of more user specific information systems is discussed.

1 Introduction

Healthcare sector is an information intensive field and, therefore, information can be seen as the most important asset of the sector. However, despite the increased use of clinical information technology, healthcare professionals often have problems in finding the needed information [1]. This, obviously, is a problem since well-managed information is said to be one of the most important resources in clinical

Please use the following format when citing this chapter:

Raitoharju, R., Aarnio, E., 2007, in IFIP International Federation for Information Processing, Volume 252, Integration and Innovation Orient to E-Society Volume 2, eds. Wang, W., (Boston: Springer), pp. 497-504.

practice. The collection, transmission, storage, and retrieval of information are crucial for most healthcare activities and, therefore, access to information is a prerequisite for evidence-based practice and coordination of care. [2]

However, the increased access to medical information can lead to information overload among the clinicians [3] as well as among the healthcare consumers [4]. Health information is one of the most searched topic in Internet [5] and as there is an increasing interest in reaching healthcare consumers through different information systems for instance through Internet, a variety of applications have been launched. At its best information systems are cost-effective and timesaving. However, studies have found that the effects can also be negative such as doctors feeling threatened by the information the patient brings to the consultation [5].

Another problem related to medical information is that understanding medical information requires specific abilities that not everybody has. For instance, Internet users searching for medical information go to sites aimed at health professionals [5]. This is a problem since the medical information has been stated to be created for the professionals, not the public [6]. Health literacy – the ability to understand and act on health information has been addressed to be one of the most pressing issues in healthcare. Medical information is produced by and targeted to several categories of users and public consumers have found to have difficulties in finding, understanding and acting on health information due to their lack of domain knowledge [7]. The mediating role of language has been recognized and it is important for instance in development of medical artificial intelligence and terminologies and nomenclatures has been noticed [8]. Multidisciplinary organizations are essential part of healthcare and the medical treatment of a patient takes place often in multidisciplinary teams – consisting of physicians, nurses, pharmacists as well as non medical persons such as family or friends. Given such, it is very challenging to make the medical information understandable and accessible for all the parties without exposing them to an information overload or the risk of misinterpreting information.

In order to avoid the problems of information overload and challenges in understanding and interpreting medical information, it should be more specifically personalized to different users and filtered from unnecessary or even wrong information. Information systems designed to meet the needs of certain group of users may be of much less use to others. To maximize the benefits of the medical information, it should be easy to find and easy to understand. Therefore, in this article we illustrate the information needs in the healthcare setting across different healthcare stakeholders: physicians, nurses and healthcare consumers. By information need we understand *"an expression of missing information needed to perform a particular task"* [9 p. 247] The purpose of this article is to examine the previous studies about the information needs of different user groups in the medical treatment process. The study is conducted as a non-systematic literature review without an intention to be a meta-analysis. The aim is illustrate the main differences in the information needs in healthcare.

This article is structured as follows. First, the information needs perspective is presented. Then the different information needs of physicians, nurses and healthcare consumers are discussed based on previous literature. Finally, examples are presented to help understand the different information needs of different healthcare stakeholders. The purpose of this paper in short is to approach theoretically the different information needs of healthcare professionals and discuss how personalizing information systems could help to avoid current problems.

2 Information needs in the healthcare

There has not been an established way to identify existing information needs in the health care setting [10]. What has been widely noticed is that if the access to needed information is limited and communication is not efficient, errors are more probable to happen in-patient care [11]. However, decision making by healthcare professionals is often complicated by the need to integrate ill-structured, uncertain and conflicting information from various sources [12]. Besides the formal sources of information, the information needs can be often met by collaboration with other individuals, such as clinical team members [13]. To find the needed information, team members often search multiple resources and collaborate with different team members (e.g. physician asks the secretary to find the lab results). There are usually many different components of the information that need to be combined to treat the patient and choose the right medication such as medical condition of the patient, his/her weight, pain rating, symptoms and pain location)[14].

In team-oriented healthcare environments (e.g. intensive care unit) the information needs differ from those in other organizational settings [13] and the information needs are also unique in each clinical unit [15]. Besides the differences between the units, there are also variation in the use of information resources and information searching techniques on personal level, whereupon the way to meet the information needs could also be different within a unit. However, the required information resources should always be available when the clinician has identified the information need [16]. In the units where multidisciplinary information is needed, the information needs are more attached to the domain of the clinician whereas the information needs in narrowly constrained domains such as cardiology, could be from other domains [17]. In a study about an emergency department team's information needs were found to be most crucial when the professionals had fragmented information resources or when the information need was complex or when they were lacking expertise [14].

Based on other researchers' studies, Gorman [10, 732] has identified the states of information needs. According to him, there are unrecognized, recognized, pursued and satisfied needs. In the first case, information cannot be pursued because the need is not recognized [see also 17]. When the need is recognized, it may or may not be pursued. In the case of seeking the information, the seeking is not always successful. The information seeking could be unsuccessful for instance due to information flow breakdown. Three reasons for the information flow breakdown were identified by Reddy and Spence [18]: information was not available when it was supposed to be available, the information was incorrect or incomplete, and the information was delivered to a wrong person.

Besides the clinical staff, the patients also need health information and the differences between the needs are influenced by demographic factors. The information is extremely important for the patients themselves especially when they have got some serious illness e.g. cancer. When it comes to the patients the information needs vary for instance according to their age, education, and gender. [19] Patients can also be important sources of information for other patients because of their experience related to their illness and disease [20].

2.1   Information needs of physicians

Published studies of physicians' information needs have reported fluctuating results. In order to interpret and compare physicians information needs Gorman [10] build a framework based on a literature review for classification of the information that clinicians use when caring for patients (Table 2).

Table 1 Types of information used by clinicians [10 p. 730]

Type of information	Description	Examples
Patient data	Refers to a single person	Medical history, Physical exam, Laboratory data
Population statistics	Aggregate patient data	Recent patterns of illness, Public health data
Medical knowledge	Generalizable to many persons	Original research, Textbook descriptions, Common knowledge
Logic information	How to get the job done	Required form, Preferred consultant, Covered procedure
Social influences	How others get the job done	Local practice patterns

Patient data includes items of a patient's history, recent symptoms, and diagnostic test results. Population statistics refers to data about groups or populations of patients whereas medical knowledge refers to information that is understood to be generalizible to the care of all patients. Logistic Information includes local knowledge about how to get the job done and finally Social Influences refers to knowledge about expectations and beliefs of others such as colleagues and also family. [10]

2.2   Information needs of nurses

The main problem the nurses encounter when searching for information was using the databases, being unaware of the sources, lack of familiarity, accessing what they want and lack of time [21]. In a study about the demands of PDA the need to make the information in general richer was stated. Especially nurses expected access to information about the patients, knowledge resources and functions for their daily work. Some nurses addressed the problem that they had spent a lot of time searching for medical information in books and memos. [22]

The patient information that the nurses wanted was, for instance, schedule displaying the patients' stay, and test results. There was a need to easily know where the patient is located and what the needs are during the stay. It was important also to pass this information to the relatives' and answer their questions. [22].

The need for knowledge database was also expressed. This would optimally include reference books, dictionaries, practical handbooks and internal memos. Internal memos both from nurses' own ward and other wards are important to get information about procedures e.g. preparations before surgery. Especially access to an electronic pharmaceutical record with a handheld devices was named to be important [22]. It has also been seen as a problem that the rehabilitation information is not necessarily consistent coming from different surgeons in a day surgery to patients. Especially to nurses working on a busy day-unit where there are patients from different hospitals [23].

2.3   Information needs of healthcare consumers

Effective communication is said to be key to optimal health outcomes [24]. However, the research about the information needs of the healthcare consumers has mostly concentrated on information needs of the patients with a certain diagnosis [e.g. 25, 26, 27]. Although, this is obviously important a more general approach to estimate the specific information needs of the healthcare consumers should be taken. A review of research of information needs and sources among cancer patients found the most important information needs to be: cancer specific information, treatment-related information, prognosis information, rehabilitation information, surveillance and health information, coping information, interpersonal/social information, financial/legal information, medical system information and body image/sexuality information [24].

Cancer specific information consisted of information such as type of cancer, stage of disease, physical effects of disease and seeking second opinions. Treatment-related information was for instance, side effects of treatment, tests and procedures involved in treatment, alternative or complimentary treatments or referrals for treatment. Prognosis information included information like chance of cure, life span or survival rate or options if initial treatment fails. Rehabilitation information consisted of information such as self care issues or home care during recovery, nutrition during recovery or recovery time. Surveillance and health information was maintaining physical health or physical activity, prevention and early detection or health behavior and promotion. Coping information included information such as emotional reactions, support groups or community counseling or support. Interpersonal/social information was the effect on family, friends, or caregivers, effect on social life or leisure or effect on employment. Financial/legal information consist information like cost of treatment, insurance coverage, or other financial issues as well as advanced directives or writing a will. Medical system information is information about interactions with healthcare providers, health care systems or experience or qualifications of physician and medical staff. [24]

Nowadays, patients have less time to ask advice about the rehabilitation form their surgeons. It was also stated that the advice the patients feel they need may not necessarily be the same as those areas identified as important by professionals such as is it safe to vacuum clean or have sex after the surgery [23]. Problems identified with hospital post-operative information leaflets were according to Bradshaw et al. [23] the lack of precision, jargon and difficulties to read.

3   Comparisons of the information needs in healthcare

The development of information systems in the healthcare is often executed without consulting the personnel or the healthcare customers. Besides leading to systems that are not easy to use the systems can offer information that does not meet the needs of the different focus groups. In an evaluation of an electronic patient information system for children with amblyopia and their parents it appeared that the system was little used because of the needs of those people who actually would be using the system had never really been investigated [28]. It can be stated that the medical information systems often are designed from the perspective of the physicians information needs.

Table 2 below summarizes examples of different information needs found in previous literature.

Table2 Comparision of types of information needs in the healthcare

Type of information	Physicians (adapted from Gorman 1995)	Nurses	Healthcare consumers (adapted from Finney Rutten et al. 2005)
Patient data	Medical history, physical exam, laboratory data	Schedule displaying the patients' stay, location and needs during the stay and test results	Prognosis information, treatment information
Population statistics	Recent patterns of illness, public health data	n/a	Other patients' experiences or choices about treatment, Recovery times
Medical knowledge	Original research, textbook descriptions, common knowledge	Pharmaceutical record, reference books, dictionaries, practical handbooks and internal memos	Nature and effects of disease, information sources of disease
Logic information	Required form, preferred consultant, covered procedure	Functions for daily work	Cost of treatment or other financial issues, advance directives or writing a will, medical system information
Social influences	Local practice patterns	Information to the relatives' and answer their questions	Effect and risks on family, friends, caregivers, work life, social life, sex life
Rehabilitation information	n/a	Consistent information from surgeons	Self care issues, nutrition information

4   Discussion

The preliminary research review illustrates the different, and at the same time overlapping information needs of different healthcare stakeholders. As found in previous literature information needs at a meta-level are very similar. However, there are differences in scope of need and the form in which the information should be available to the stakeholders. For instance, the important logic information needed by a physician to treat a patient is to know the required form whereas to patient it can be the cost of treatment. Therefore, taking into consideration the different needs of different stakeholders when planning the information systems could enable more personalized inquiries of medical information.

REFERENCES

1. M.C. Reddy and W. Pratt, Asking questions: Information needs in a surgical intensive care unit. *American Medical Informatics Association Fall Symposium*, (2002)
2. A. Moen, A nursing perspective to design and implementation of electronic patient record systems. *Journal of Biomedical Informatics*. **36**,375-378 (2003)
3. R.E. Hunt and R.G. Newman, Medical knowledge overload: a disturbing trend for physicians. *Health Care Management Review*. **22**(1),70-75 (1997)
4. K. Ankem, Factors influencing information needs among cancer patients: A meta-analysis. *LIbrary & Information Scinece Research*. **28**,7-23 (2006)
5. M. McMullan, Patients using the Internet to obtain health information: How this affects the patient-health professional relationship. *Patient Education and Counseling*. **63**,24-28 (2006)
6. M. Kisilowska, Knowledge management prerequisites for building an information society in healthcare. *International Journal of Medical Informatics*. **75**,322-329 (2006)
7. Q.T. Zeng and T. Tse, Exploring and developing consumer health vocabularies. *Journal of the American Medical Informatics Association*. **13**(1),24-29 (2006)
8. T. Timpka, Situated clinical cognition. *Artificial Intelligence in Medicine*. **7**(5),387-394 (1995)
9. L.M.M. Braun, et al., Towards patient-related information needs. *International Journal of Medical Informatics*. **76**,246-251 (2007)
10. P.N. Gorman, Information needs of physicians. *Journal of the American Society for Information Science*. **46**(10),729-736 (1995)
11. E.A. Mendonca, et al., Approach to mobile information and communicatipn for health care. *International Journal of Medical Informatics*. **73**,631-638 (2004)
12. A.W. Kushniruk, Analysis of complex decision-making process in health care: Cognitive approaches to health informatics. *Journal of Biomedical Informatics*. **34**,365-376 (2001)
13. M.C. Reddy, et al. *Asking Questions: Information Needs in a Surgical Intensive Care Unit*. in *Proceedings of the American Medical Informatics Association Fall Symposiun AMIA'02*. 2002. San Antonio, TX.

14. M.C. Reddy and P.R. Spence, Collaborative information seeking: A field study of a multidisciplinary patient care team. *Information Processing and Management.* **Article in press** (2007)

15. R.N. Jerome, et al., Information needs of clinical teams: analysis of questions received by the Clinical Informatics Consult Service. *Bulletin of the Medical Library Association.* **89**(2),177-185 (2001)

16. K.A. McKibbon and D.B. Fridsma, Effectiveness of Clinician-selected Electronic Information resources for Answering primary care Physicians' Information Needs. *Journal of the American Medical Informatics Association.* **13**(6),653-659 (2006)

17. L.M.M. Braun, et al., Towards patient-related information needs. *International Journal of Medical Informatics.* **76**(2-3),246-251 (2007)

18. M.C. Reddy and P.R. Spence, Collaborative information seeking: A field study of a multidisciplinary patient care team. *Information processing & management.* **Article in press** (2007)

19. K. Ankem, Factors influencing information needs among cancer patients: A meta-analysis. *Library & Information Science Research.* **28**(1),7-23 (2006)

20. K.M. Åkesson, B.-I. Saveman, and G. Nilsson, Health care consumers' experiences of information communication technology - A summary of literature. *International Journal of Medical Informatics.* **Article in press.** (2006)

21. P.J. Stokes and D. Lewin, Information-seeking behaviour of nurse teachers in a school of health studies: a soft systems analysis. *Nurse Education Today.* **24**,47-54 (2004)

22. M. Berglund, et al., Nurses' adn nurse students' demands of functions and usability in a PDA. *International Journal of Medical Informatics.* **Article in press** (2006)

23. C. Bradshaw, et al., Information needs of general day surgery patients. *Ambulatory surgery.* **7**(39-44) (1999)

24. L.J. Finney Rutten, et al., Information needs and sources of information among cancer patiens: a systematic review of research (1980-2003). *Patient Education and Counseling.* **57**,250-261 (2005)

25. I. Mesters, et al., Measuring information needs among cancer patients. *Patient Education and Counseling.* **43**(3),255-264 (2001)

26. D. Casarett, et al., Obtaining informed consent for clinical pain research: patients' concerns and information needs. *Pain.* **92**(1-2),71-79 (2001)

27. S.F. Zarbock, Meeting the Information Needs of Patients with Metastatic Breast Cancer. *Home Care Provider.* **6**(1),37-40 (2001)

28. van't Riet Annemarie, et al., Meeting patients' needs with patient information systems: potential benefits of qualitative research methods. *International Journal of Medical Informatics.* **64**(1-14) (2001)

The Moderating Effect of Leader-member Exchange on the Job Insecurity-Organizational   Commitment Relationship

Sanman Hu, Bin Zuo
College of Psychology, Huazhong Normal University, Wuhan, China
430079, sanman_hu@yahoo.com.cn

Abstract. Job insecurity has become an important issue for society and organizations in the last decades due to uncertain economic conditions, global competition, and the advancement of information technology. As job insecurity have detrimental consequences for employees and organizations, it is vital to identify variables that could buffer against the negative effects of job insecurity. In this study, we examined the moderating effect of Leader-member exchange on the relation between job insecurity and organizational commitment. Data collected from 314 employees indicated that the negative relationship between qualitative insecurity and affective commitment was alleviated as Leader-member exchange increased. Furthermore, the positive relation between quantitative insecurity and continuance commitment decreased as Leader-member exchange increased.

1   Introduction

Working life has been subject to dramatic change over the past two decades as economic recessions, new information technology, industrial restructuring, and an accelerated global competition unceasingly have proved to be crucial and abiding factors influencing the nature of work and organization. In their struggle for survival, organizations are faced with the necessity of making their operations more effective with fewer resources, especially human resources. These unpredictable economic situation and tougher competitive standards have resulted in downsizing, mergers, acquisitions, and other types of structural change, all of which tend to produce increased feelings of insecurity among the workers, not only pertaining to their jobs but also about the future in general [1]. As a result, job insecurity has received growing recognition of researchers [2].

Please use the following format when citing this chapter:

Hu, S., Zuo, B., 2007, in IFIP International Federation for Information Processing, Volume 252, Integration and Innovation Orient to E-Society Volume 2, eds. Wang, W., (Boston: Springer), pp. 505-513.

2   Theoretical backgrounds and hypothesis

Job insecurity is a subjective phenomenon, in contrast to actual of job loss, it refers to the anticipation of this stressful event in such a way that the nature and continued existence of one's job are perceived to be at risk [3]. However, Greenhalgh and Rosenblatt [4], who were the first to introduce a multidimensional definition, noted: "Loss of valued job features is an important but often overlooked aspect of job insecurity". Later on, a number of researchers agreed with this opinion. For instance, Hellgren, Sverke, and Isaksson [2] made a distinction between quantitative job insecurity (worries about losing the job itself) and qualitative job insecurity (worries about losing important job features, including future career opportunities, stimulating job content, competence exertion, pay development).

In a meta-analysis of job insecurity, Sverke, Hellgren, & Naswall [1] summed up it's potential consequences. The results indicated that job insecurity has detrimental consequence for employees' job attitudes, organizational attitudes, health, and, to some extent, their behavioral relationship with the organization. Job insecurity has already been considered as an important stressor in work field at the present time [5]. Hence, the question of how to reduce these negative consequences is a high priority now. The answer of this question will deepen our understanding of mechanism of job insecurity's negative effect, and contribute to the solutions alleviating most impact of job insecurity.

Considerable research attention has been given to how job insecurity is related to organizational attitudes, such as commitment, which is a very important organizational attitude and also has received a lot of attention. In most of the studies, organizational commitment has been found to have a moderate negative association with job insecurity [1], so finding variables which can alleviate job insecurity's negative impact on commitment is in urgent need. On the other hand, some studies have reported a strong negative relationship or no significant relation at all [1]. Thus, because the strengths of correlations vary across studies, it is likely some other factors influence the relationships between job insecurity and organizational commitment. Owing to the above reasons, examining potential moderators between job insecurity and commitment is not only meaningful in practice, also essential for theoretical development.

The Leader-member exchange (LMX) model proposed by Graen and UhI-Bien explains that leaders develop unique one-on-one relationships with different subordinates. High-quality LMX, sometimes called "in-group", is characterized by increased levels of information exchange, mutual support, informal influence, professional trust, greater negotiating latitude, and input in decisions. Lower quality LMX, sometimes called "out-group", is characterized by more formal supervision, less support, and less trust and attention from the leader [6]. Perhaps the most important distinction between the differences in Leader-member relationships is the degree of emotional support and task challenge given to the member.

Joelson and Wahlquist [7] suggested that job insecurity is burdening because of prolonged uncertainty. While two factors: unpredictability and uncontrollability are considered the probable reasons in explaining the harmful impact of "uncertainty". First of all, job insecurity means unpredictability: what will happen in the future is unclear for those concerned. This makes it difficult to react appropriately. Besides, uncontrollability also plays a crucial role. The lack of control, or the feeling of powerlessness towards the threat, is considered by some authors to be the core of the phenomenon of job insecurity [8]. Given above mentioned nature and character of LMX, one can expect that favorable LMX will play a role in helping employees decrease unpredictability and increase controllability, also contributing to their level of commitment to the organization even though the level of job insecurity felt by employees is high, so the following two hypotheses are proposed.

H1: Leader-member exchange will moderate the relationship between quantitative job insecurity and organizational commitment. The negative relationship between quantitative job insecurity and organizational commitment will be stronger for employees with low LMX than those with high LMX.

H2: Leader-member exchange will moderate the relationship between qualitative job insecurity and organizational commitment. The negative relationship between qualitative job insecurity and organizational commitment will be stronger for employees with low LMX than those with high LMX.

3   Methods

3.1   Subjects

Participants were 400 full-time employees from 10 enterprises in Wuhan, Guangzhou, and Ningbo city in China. 314 questionnaires (response rate = 78.5%) were returned. The total group of respondents can be characterized as follows: 78 percent were men and 69 percent subjects below 30 years; 42 percent have high school diploma, 25 percent have junior college diploma, 24 percent have university diploma, 9 percent have master degree or above; 38 percent were staff member, 50 percent were supervisor, 12 percent were manager. 26 percent were from state-owned enterprise, 24 percent were form foreign-funded enterprise, 50 percent were from private enterprise.

3.2   Measures

Job insecurity. The two dimensions of job insecurity scale developed by Hellgren, Sverke, and Isaksson [2] were used, and scored on a 5-point Likert scale (1=strongly disagree; 5=strongly agree). Quantitative job insecurity was measured by three items, sample items include:" I am worried about having to leave my job before I would like to" and "I feel uneasy about losing my job in the near future". Qualitative job insecurity was measured by four items, sample items include:" My future career opportunities in the organization are favorable" (Reverse coded). The internal consistency reliability was satisfactory for both quantitative (alpha=0.68) and qualitative job insecurity (alpha=0.81).

Leader-member exchange. The LMX-7 scale, developed by Graen and Uhl-Bien (1995), was designed to measure the perception of quality of exchange relationships between the supervisor and the subordinate [6]. In our research, it also scored on a 5-

point Likert scale (1=strongly disagree; 5=strongly agree). Sample items include: "I know how satisfied my supervisor is with what I do". The internal consistency reliability was satisfactory (alpha=0.80).

   Organizational commitment. The three dimensions of organizational commitment scale developed by Meyer, Allen, and Smith [9] were used, and scored on a 5-point Likert scale (1=strongly disagree; 5=strongly agree). Affective commitment, normative commitment, and continuance commitment were measured by six items separately. The internal consistency reliability for these commitments were acceptable (alpha were 0.70, 0.64, and 0.69 accordingly).

3.3   Data Analysis

To test the hypothesized moderators, we conducted moderated regression analyses. Specially, we entered the control variables in the first step, followed by three independent variables (i.e. quantitative insecurity, qualitative insecurity, and leader-member exchange) in the second step, and all of the two-way interaction terms in the third step. Using this analysis, one would expect to find that the interaction effects of job insecurity and LMX explain an additional significant amount of the variance beyond their main effects. To reduce multicollinearity among the interaction terms, we centered the component scales and computed the interaction terms using the centered scores [10].

4   Results

4.1   Descriptive statistics and correlations

Descriptive statistics, correlation coefficients among the study variables are displayed in Table 1. This tale revealed several important points. First, quantitative job insecurity have significant correlations with normative and continuance commitment. Second, qualitative job insecurity have significant correlations with affective and normative commitment. Third, LMX also have significant correlations with affective commitment and normative commitment.

Table 1. Descriptive statistics and correlations among variables

variables	M	SD	1	2	3	4	5
1.Gender	1.22	.413	—				
2.Age	1.312	.464	-.164[**]	—			
3.Educational level	1.99	1.008	-.148[*]	-.104	—		
4.Position	1.75	.661	-.128[*]	.310[**]	.095	—	
5.Company type	2.24	.837	-.038[*]	-.135[*]	.054	.420	—
6.Quantitative insecurity	2.963	.839	-.111	.192[**]	-.185[**]	.250[**]	.014
7.Qualitative insecurity	2.754	.767	-.172[**]	-.133[*]	.054	.008	.106
8. Leader-member exchange	3.598	.609	-.043	.050	-.036	.027	-.078
9. Affective commitment	3.208	.587	-.073	-.044	-.097	-.056	.020

variables						
10.Normative commitment	3.001	.626	-.052	.033	-.102	.105	-.028
11.Continuance commitment	2.758	.629	-.038	.165**	-.067	.104	-.162**

variables	6	7	8	9	10	11
6.Quantitative insecurity	—					
7.Qualitative insecurity	-.251**	—				
8. Leader-member exchange	.111*	-.303**	—			
9. Affective commitment	.103	-.465**	.379**	—		
10.Normative commitment	.207**	-.501**	.285**	.480**	—	
11.Continuance commitment	.392**	-.036	.005	-.150**	.152**	

Note. *p<0.05,**p<0.01.

4.2 Moderating effects of Leader-member exchange between job insecurity and commitment

A summary of the results of moderated regression analyses is shown in Table 2. As shown in this table, after controlling some demographic variables, quantitative job insecurity was still a strong predictor of continuance commitment (β=0.324, t=5.437,p =0.000), and qualitative insecurity was a strong positive predictor of affective commitment and normative commitment(β=-0.400, t=-7.208,p =0.000; β=-0.451, t=-8.137,p =0.000).

Table 2 Results of moderated regression analyses

variables		Organizational commitment		
		Affective commitment	Normative commitment	Continuance commitment
Step1:	Gender	-0.095	-0.041	0.016
	Age	-0.020	-0.055	0.006
	Educational level	-0.128	-0.114	-0.011
	Position	-0.058	0.158*	0.141*
	foreign-funded enterprise	-0.028	-0.028	0.101
	private enterprise	-0.011	-0.136	-0.222**
R^2		0.024	0.036	0.097**
Step2:	Quantitative insecurity	-0.022	0.046	0.324**
	Qualitative insecurity	-0.400**	-0.451**	0.112
	Leader-member exchange	0.248**	0.128*	-0.021
$\triangle R^2$		0.258**	0.247**	0.090**
Step3:	Quantitative insecurity×LMX	-0.051	-0.032	0.111
	Qualitative insecurity ×LMX	0.138**	0.026	0.002
$\triangle R^2$		0.021*	0.002	0.011

Also as shown in table 2, after the interaction terms of two kinds of job insecurity and leader-member exchange entering the regression, the interaction effect of quantitative job insecurity and LMX on continuance commitment was nearly significant (β=0.111, t=1.947,p =0.053), and the interaction effect of qualitative insecurity and LMX on affective commitment was significant (β=0.138, t=2.582,p =0.010). These results indicated the relationship between quantitative job insecurity and continuance commitment, and the relationship between qualitative insecurity and affective commitment are all moderated by LMX. Furthermore, the amount of explained variance for each interaction term is above the range expected (.01-.03) for moderator effects in field studies [11], which means the nature of two interaction effect needs thorough theoretic analyze and also have practical implications.

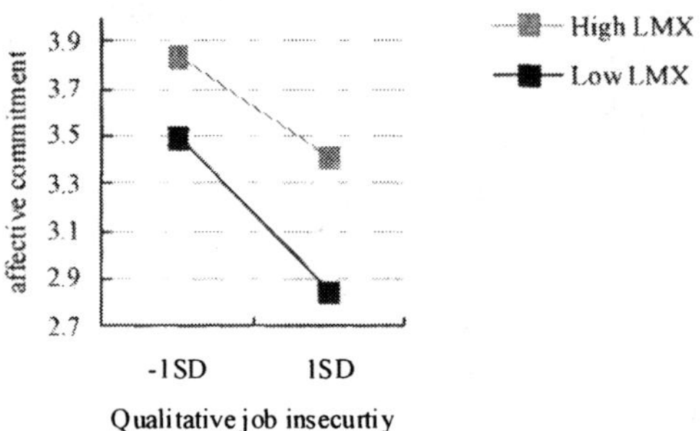

Figure. 1. Interactive effect of qualitative insecurity and LMX on affective commitment

We assessed the nature of above two interaction by plotting values of plus and minus on standard deviation from the means on two kinds of job insecurity and leader-member exchange. Figure 1 depicts graphically the interaction of LMX on the relationship between qualitative insecurity and affective commitment. As shown in the figure, the directions of the relationship were in line with Hypothesis 2 in that the slope of the regression line of affective commitment on qualitative insecurity for low LMX was steeper than the slope of the regression for high LMX. Thus, we conclude that the negative relationship between qualitative insecurity and affective commitment was stronger for those who perceived low LMX and weaker for those who perceived high LMX.

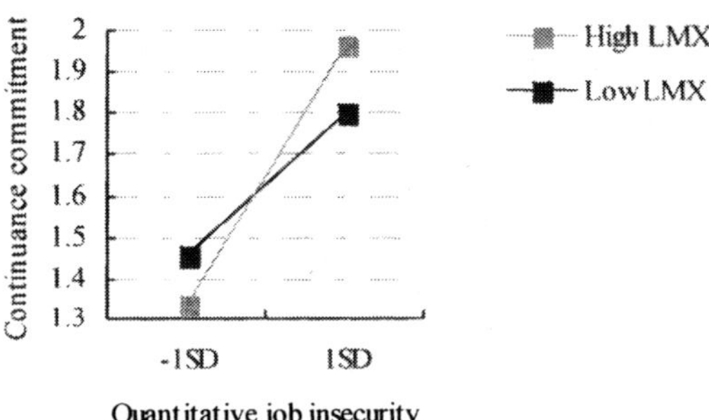

Figure 2. Interactive effect of quantitative job insecurity and LMX on continuance

commitment

Figure 2 revealed that, the most unexpected finding is, as the level of quantitative job insecurity increased, employee's continuance commitment also increased, and contrary to Hypothesis 1, the relationship between quantitative job insecurity and continuance commitment became weaker for those with low LMX.

5   Discussion

A perceived loss of continuity in a job situation can span the range from threats of imminent job loss to loss of important job features, these different aspects may evoke divergent reactions. To date, only a few studies report relationships of different job insecurity dimensions and outcomes [12, 13, 2]. Clearly, further research is needed to understand the potentially differential effects of various dimensions of job insecurity. Meanwhile, previous researches about job insecurity and commitment were also lack of more specific exploration toward different dimensions of commitment. Our results indicated that, quantitative job insecurity and qualitative job insecurity indeed have very different impact on different dimensions of commitment. Quantitative insecurity was a positive predictor of continuance commitment, while qualitative insecurity was a negative predictor of affective commitment and normative commitment.

Continuance commitment is based on an economic need to stay with an organization rather than an emotional attachment. Hence, to employees, it is reasonable that the more worries about job loss, the more continuance commitment toward organization. However the damage of employment quality, such as lack of career opportunities, stimulating job content, competence exertion, pay development et al., will definitely impair the relative strength of an individual's identification with and involvement in a particular organization, and the willingness of abiding organizational rules.

While researchers advocate the importance of effective leadership to enact and support change, previous studies have not focused on the moderating effects of leadership on the relationship between job insecurity and employee outcomes. Therefore, the main focus of the present study was to explore the role Leader-member exchange relationship plays as a buffer against the negative impact of job insecurity on employee's organizational commitment. Results of moderated regression analyses indicated that the negative relationship between qualitative insecurity and affective commitment was alleviated as Leader-member exchange increased, while the positive relationship between quantitative insecurity and continuance commitment decreased as Leader-member exchange increased.

At every stage of its development, with deterioration of employment quality, what organization urgently needs is all members' concerted effort. Obviously, low level of affective commitment will make it difficult for members to complete their task and accomplish their mission. Fortunately, our results, to some degree, identify that favorable LMX can help employees maintain affective commitment to the organization despite high level of job insecurity.

For developing and maintaining favorable Leader-member exchange relation with their supervisor, those "in-group" members pay harder working. Hence, their cost of dimission will be higher than those "out-group". Meanwhile, due to supervisors' special trust and support, "in-group" members will also attach greater importance to their jobs. As a result, "in-group" members with great concern about losing present job will have greater continuance commitment than ever. During developing and transforming stage, this kind of well-established LMX can have a great deal of positive effect, such as making member undisturbed and wishful for organizational change. However, the strength of continuance commitment in members with low LMX didn't significantly enhance. They may hold a fence-sitting attitude. Etzioni characterized these members with "alienative involvement" toward organization [14]. It could expect that this kind of low continuance commitment would probably not only destroy group's cohesive force and also reduce organizational efficiency.

References

1. M. Sverke, J. Hellgren, K. Naswall, No security: a meta-analysis and review of job insecurity and its consequences, *Journal of occupational health psychology*. 7(3), 242-264 (2002).
2. J. Hellgren, M. Sverke, K. Isaksson, A tow-dimensional approach to job insecurity: consequences for employee attitudes and well-being, *European Journal of Work and Organizational Psychology*. 8(2), 179-195 (1999).
3. M. Sverke, J. Hellgren, The nature of job insecurity: understanding employment uncertainty on the brink of a new millennium, *Applied psychology: an international review*. 51(1), 23-42, (2002).
4. L. Greenhalgh, Z. Rosenblatt, Job security: toward conceptual clarity, *Academy of Management Review*. 9(3), 438-448 (1984).
5. A. S. Mak, J. Mueller, Job insecurity ,coping resources and personality dispositions in occupational strain, *Work & Stress*. 14(4), 312-328, (2000).
6. A. Castanon, Managing traumatic change: the role of leadership as a buffer against the negative impact of job insecurity on employment outcomes, Alliant International University, Los Angeles, California. *Unpublished doctoral dissertation*. 2005,p.31.
7. L. Joelson, L. Wahlquist, The psychological meaning of job insecurity and job loss: results of a longitudinal study, *Social science and medicine*. 25(2), 179-182, (1987)
8. H. De Witte, Job insecurity and psychological well-being: review of the literature and exploration of some unresolved issues, *European Journal of Work and Organizational Psychology*. 8(2), 155-177 (1999).
9. J. P. Meyer, N. J. Allen, C. A. Smith, Commitment to organizations and occupations: extension and test of a three-component conceptualization, *Journal of Applied Psychology*. 78(4), 538-551 (1993)
10. M. C. Andrews, L. A. Witt, K. M. Kacmar, The interactive effects of organizational politics an exchange ideology on manager ratings of retention, *Journal of vocational behavior*. 62, 357-369 (2003).

11. Z. S. Byrne, C. Kacmar, J. Stoner, W. Hochwarter, The relationship between perceptions of politics and depressed mood at work: unique moderators across three levels, *Journal of Occupational Health Psychology*. 10(4), 330-343, (2005).
12. M. Sverke, J. Hellgren, K. Naswall, Job insecurity: a literature review, http//www. arbetslivsinstitutet.se/saltsa/2006/wlr2006_01.pdf
13. S. J. Ashford, C. Lee, P. Bobko, Content, causes, and consequences of job insecurity: a theory-based measure and substantive test, *Academy of Management Journal*. 32(4), 803-829 (1989).
14. A. Lord, J. Hartley, *Organizational commitment and job insecurity in a changing public service organization, European Journal of Work and Organizational Psychology*. 7(3), 341-354 (1999).

Trust-based Access Control in Virtual Learning Community

Shujuan Wang[1], Qingtang Liu[1,2]

1 Department of Information Technology,Huazhong Normal University,
Wuhan,Hubei.P.R.China, wsj_xgz@126.com
2 Engineering Research Center of Education Information Technology,
Huazhong Normal University,.Wuhan, Hubei.P.R.China
liuqtang@mail.ccnu.edu.cn

Abstract. The virtual learning community is an important application pattern of E-Learning. It emphasizes the cooperation of the members in the community, the members would like to share their learning resources, to exchange their experience and complete the study task together. This instructional mode has already been proved as an effective way to improve the quality and efficiency of instruction. At the present time, the virtual learning communities are mostly designed using static access control policy by which the access permission rights are authorized by the super administrator, the super administrator assigns different rights to different roles, but the virtual and social characteristics of virtual learning community make information sharing and collaboration a complex problem, the community realizes its instructional goal only if the members in it believe that others will offer the knowledge they owned and believe the knowledge others offered is well-meaning and worthy. This paper tries to constitute an effective trust mechanism, which could promise favorable interaction and lasting knowledge sharing.

1 Introduction

The access control and trust management both are key policies in the information security management, and the application of information technology such as computer technology and network technology in education is obvious to all, E-Learning is becoming a leading instructional mode. The virtual learning community is an important application pattern of E-Learning [4]. It emphasizes students' subjectivity and independency within learning activities, it also emphasizes the cooperation of the members (learners) in the community, the members would like to

---

Please use the following format when citing this chapter:

Wang, S., Liu, Q., 2007, in IFIP International Federation for Information Processing, Volume 252, Integration and Innovation Orient to E-Society Volume 2, eds. Wang, W., (Boston: Springer), pp. 514-520.

share their learning resources, to exchange their experience and complete the study task together. It has already been proved that the virtual learning community is an effective way to improve the quality and efficiency of instruction [4]. at the present time, the virtual learning community are designed using static access control policy by which the access permission rights are authorized by the super administrator, the super administrator assigns different rights to different roles, but the virtual and social feature of virtual learning community makes information sharing and collaboration a complex problem, in which an important aspect is whether the members trust others will offer the knowledge they owned. It could promise favorable interaction and lasting knowledge sharing by constituting an effective trust mechanism.

Access control is more applied in the field of computer security and network security, it is a method to allow or constraint the subject's access to the object through many ways, and it is also a key measure to confirm the system's security. As an open instruction system, the virtual learning community also should take apt access control policy to fulfill the needed security of the learning resource and instruction. The investigation indicated that the virtual learning community's authorization management is mostly based on static access control policy managed by the super administrator. Its basic idea is to grant the members certain rights to access and operate the learning resource.

The general roles in virtual learning community may include administrator, expert, teacher as well as student. The administrator's work is to manage the behaviors of other members, namely experts, teachers and students; the expert's work is to evaluate the resources in the community, to answer the difficult problems; the teacher's work is to organize instruction and learning activity, assign instruction task, supervise the students' study; the students participate in the instruction activity, the team discussion, advance questions, accomplish the task collaborated with others, as well as upload their own knowledge. Actually, there may be other roles in virtual learning community, just depends on the instructional requirement. Having registered as a member in virtual learning community, the user would act certain role and execute corresponding rights.

The members of virtual learning community are mostly quasi-permanent separated in space and time [5]; they contact each other by virtue of e-mail, BBS, community chat-room, and so forth; the anonymous feature of virtual status causes the feeling of strange and distrust. Separation in space and time as well as lack of face-to-face interaction makes mutual trust among members a complicated problem.

The virtual learning community presents some social characteristics [4]; in which trust between two parties is foundational, but the existing virtual learning communities adopt static role-based access control policy, ignoring the constitution and maintain of the trust relations among the individuals.

This paper presented a trust-based access control model in virtual learning community, and realized the access control decision-making based on the members' creditability through integrating trust component into the access control mechanism.

2   Trust-based Access Control Model

In the virtual learning community, embedding trust component into the existing role-based access control [1,2] offers a safeguard mechanism over the interaction among the members, the figure followed is a trust-based access control model which clarifies the relationship among the components.

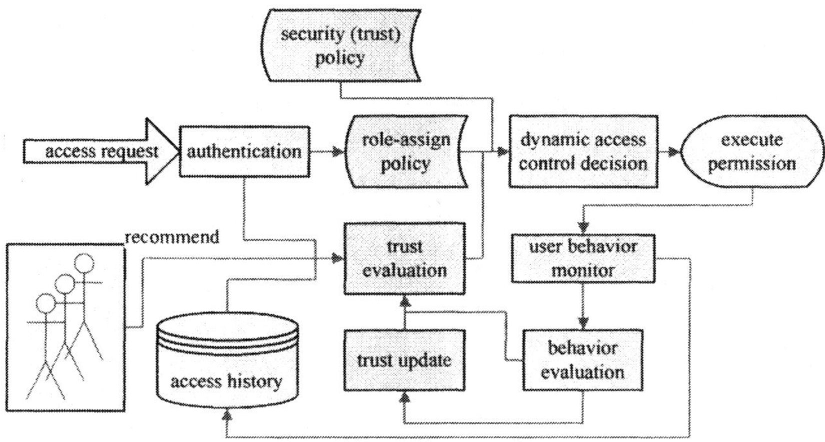

Fig. 1. Trust-based Access Control Model

In this figure, there are several points to be noticed.

(1). Authentication is the first step of access control [6] in virtual learning community, and the primary work is to make it clear that the user is registered member of this community or not, if the answer is yes, judge from the corresponding access history and the trust degree associated with the user's status identity.

(2). Behaviors monitoring includes logging and measuring the state and operative behaviors in virtual learning community. It provides information evidences for the calculation of trust degree, the things need to be monitored mainly include the user's participating degree, the resource's quantity and worthiness he contributed, and so forth. The realization of trust policy relies on corresponding trust mechanism, and behaviors monitor acts a significant role. After an access operation is finished, the access behaviors will be logged and the behaviors will be evaluated, the interaction production should be marked off different trust grade at least; sequentially influences the trust degree evaluation to the target member.

(3). We can analyze the target member's creditability and calculate his basic trust degree referring to his own access history, furthermore, we also have to collect the trust recommendations come from other members who have interacted with target member in this virtual learning community, then we can calculate the target member's reputation degree in virtual learning community, we get the weight sum of the two value, and name it final trust degree. In addition, as this accessing operation finished, target member's trust degree should be recalculated, overwritten and updated, if it is the first time the user access this virtual learning community and have no access history and no trust degree, we should put him an initial trust degree value in order to assign access rights to him.

(4). In the trust-based access control model, dynamic access control decision-making need to carry through various considerations according to the access request and his creditability.

This figure has clarified the relationships among components and the flow of authorization. Part 3 will explain trust-based authorization in detail.

3   Trust-based Authorization

Role-based access control (RBAC) [1, 2] is a popular mode at the present time, and most virtual learning communities are applying this kind of access control mechanism. In RBAC, the user could manage the access rights upon the resources he owned easily, and the administrator could realize flexible authorization by roles assignment [1, 2, 6], in view of the virtual learning community's social characteristics, we introduce trust into the existing role-based access control and form a trust- consolidated role assignment.

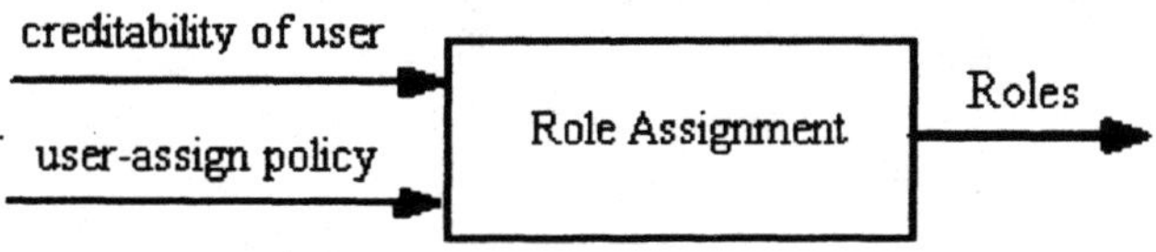

Fig. 2. Trust-consolidated role assignment in authorization

Trust is a complicated conception in interpersonal interaction network, and we could interpret it as the subject's approval to the object's reliability, honesty and ability. The degree of trust is defined as trust degree. Trust degree reflects subject's expectation to the object's to-be behaviors, and this expectation is related to the environment, it is the sum-up to the historical experience.

Trust has more subjectivity, and different people will make different conclusions to same object's trust degree. The judgment will be influenced by various parameters, and trust is content- correlative, trust to one aspect of object may not influence the distrust to another aspect of the same object, so trust only makes sense in certain context. Trust to object will change dynamically along with the update of trust information and the change of member's behaviors. Trust degree in virtual learning community is related to two aspects: the direct trust degree brought by target member's behaviors in the community and recommendations come from other members. The measure and calculation of trust as well as the Algorithm of the authorization will be explained in brief.

3.1 Measure of Trust Degree

The direct trust brought by target member's behaviors in the virtual learning community can be defined as basic trust degree. The influential factors mainly include the times of the member visited the community, initiated discussion, participated discussion, contributed resources (we need to notice that there will be two-faces: contributing valuable resources and offering useless even vicious resources. We augment the influential factor's value if the resource is valuable, otherwise reduce.), and so forth. The influential parameters set could be expressed as:

$F=\{ f1, f2, f3, f4\}$

The significations of the parameters are listed in table 1.

Table 1. Influential parameters sample for trust degree calculation

parameters	signification
f_1	the times of visiting the community
f_2	the times of initiating discussion
f_3	the times of participating discussion
f_4	the times of contributing resources

For the parameters listed in this table is just a sample to clarify the calculation process, it could be different which depends on the type and need of your system.

The basic trust degree is confirmed by virtue of calculating each influential factor, and expressed as:

$$T=\sum_{i=1}^{4} \lambda_i \cdot f_i \qquad (1)$$

λ_i is the weigh of influential factor i, f_i is the value of influential factor i, T is the basic trust degree of target member.

The community's general trust evaluation to the target member is defined as reputation, and it comes from the other members who have interacted with the target member. Generally speaking, except examining the target member's behaviors, his reputation should also be examined in virtual learning community in order to trust the target member. Other members take trust evaluation on target member according to their interaction histories with the target member. The value of reputation is decided by other members' trust recommendations, expressed as （**n** is amount of members in virtual learning community）:

$$R=\sum_{i=0}^{n} \omega_i \cdot r_i \qquad (2)$$

ω_i is the adoptive weight of member i, ω_i is related with the own trust degree of member i, r_i is trust recommendation values comes from member i, R is the final reputation value of target member.

So the final trust degree to target member, namely trust degree, can be expressed formally as:

$$T_{final}=\alpha \cdot T+(1-\alpha)\cdot R \qquad 0<\alpha<1 \qquad (3)$$

T_{final} is trust degree of target member, T is the basic trust degree brought by target member's behaviors in virtual learning community, R denotes the reputation value of the target member, α denotes the power of the basic trust value.

3.2   Trust-based Access Control Authorization Algorithm

The trust-based access control authorization could be described as the flow:
(1). Set roles: super administrator(SA), community administrator(A), expert E, teacher(T), student(S), visitor(V) (the super administrator is fixed, community administrator will inherit partial rights of the super administrator);
(2). Set rights: browse the community's resource(S1), participate in community's discussion(S2), upload resource(S3), download resource(S4);
(3). Set the trust degree threshold T*;
(4). Specify basic role(such as visitor), assign initial trust degree $T_{initial}$ to the role, the initial reputation value R is 0;
(5). Measure and calculate trust degree $T_{final}=\alpha \cdot T+(1-\alpha)\cdot R$
(6). If $T_{final}\geq T^*$, judge the role of the user, assign corresponding rights; Else, execute basic role's rights.

With this algorithm, we could set up trustworthy access control mechanism in virtual learning community. We have developed an archetypal module which could realize this authorization algorithm using C# as programming language, and inserted this module into existing virtual community, it works as we described.

4   Conclusion

In this paper, we integrated trust component into the existing access control mechanism, this is an attempt to bring behaviors-based trust management into E-Learning. We advanced a trust-based access control model in virtual learning community through research on the virtual learning communities and access control models existing at the present time, and described the calculation of the trust degree, bring forward trust-based access control authorization algorithm. This model did not depend on any idiographic trust model, for it may be suitable to other opening systems.

Many of these open issues and problems are intertwined and will require an integrated approach to be satisfactorily resolved, and this is the work we should make great efforts in the future.

Acknowledge

This paper is supported by NSFC of China (NO.60673010), partly supported by National Key Project of Scientific and Technical Supporting Programs Funded by Ministry of Science & Technology of China During the 11th Five-year Plan (NO 2006BAJ07B06）, and supported by the Cultivation Fund of the Key Scientific and Technical Innovation Project，Ministry of Education of China（NO705038）.

References

1. R. S. Sandhu, "Role-Based Access Control Models", *IEEE Computer*, 29(2):38-47,（Feb. 1996）

2. D. F.Ferraiolo and D.Richard Kuhn, "Ramaswamy Chandramouli", *Role-Based Access Control* (Artech House,2003), ISBN:1580533701

3. K. Aberer and Z. Despotovic, "Managing Trust in a Peer-2-Peer Information System", In: Proc. of the Tenth Intl. Conf. on. Information and Knowledge Management (*ACM CIKM'*01), 310~317(2001).

4. H .L. Ma, "sociological analyses of virtual learning community", *Distance Education in Chin* , 20-24(2006).

5. Z. K. Yang, H. B. Liu and Q. T. Liu, "Application Research for Role Based Access Control Technique in E-Learning", *Application Research of Computers*, 133-136（Oct. 2005).

6. S. Q. Zhang, D.X.Lu,Y.T.Yang, "Trust-Based Access Control in P2P Networks", *Computer Science*, vol.32 No.5, 31-33(2005)

7. E. Bertino, L. Khan, R. Sandhu and B. Thuraisingham, "Secure Knowledge Management: Confidentiality, Trust, and Privacy", *IEEE Transactions on Systems, Man and Cybernetics*, Part A: Systems and Humans, 36(3):429-438, (May 2006)

One Continuous Auditing Practice in China: Data-oriented Online Auditing(DOOA)

Wei Chen, Jin-cheng Zhang, and Yu-quan Jiang
Nanjing Audit University, Nanjing, Jiangsu 210029, China
chenweich@nau.edu.cn
WWW home page: http://info.nau.edu.cn

Abstract. Application of information technologies (IT) in the field of audit is worth studying. Continuous auditing (CA) is an active research domain in computer-assisted audit field. In this paper, the concept of continuous auditing is analyzed firstly. Then, based on analysis on research literatures of continuous auditing, technique realization methods are classified into embedded mode and separate mode. According to the condition of implementing online auditing in China, data-oriented online auditing (DOOA) used in China is also one of separate mode of continuous auditing. And the principle of DOOA is analyzed. Furthermore, the advantages and disadvantages of DOOA are also discussed. Finally, advices to implement DOOA in China are given, and the future research topics related to continuous auditing are also discussed.

1 Introduction

Auditing is a part of control process in organizations, which can be used to examine and observe the reliability of the accounts and that they give a true and fair view of the auditee's result of operations and financial position. Therefore, it is very important to a country. As computer technology has advanced, government organizations have become increasingly dependent on computerized information systems to carry out their business operations and service delivery and to process, maintain and report essential information.

In order to finish audit work in informationization environment, computer-assisted audit technologies [1-3] must be used. With the development of information technologies (IT), IT applications in audit area are also changing. The development of IT will make computer-assisted audit become continuous, dynamic and real-time.

Please use the following format when citing this chapter:

Chen, W., Zhang, J.-C., Jiang, Y.-Q., 2007, in IFIP International Federation for Information Processing, Volume 252, Integration and Innovation Orient to E-Society Volume 2, eds. Wang, W., (Boston: Springer), pp. 521-528.

Koskivaara[4] has developed five stages of information technology utilization in auditing. At stage one, standard software applications are used. At stage two, some databases, email, and graphics are also adapted. At stage three, several different external and internal databases, audit software applications, and company models are in use. At stage four, expert systems, decision support systems, and special audit software for continuous auditing are utilized. At the fifth stage, the software applications are based on advanced methods like ANNs (artificial neural networks), fuzzy logic, and genetic algorithms. These advanced methods could produce information for continuous monitoring and controlling. Therefore, continuous auditing becomes an important research trend in computer-assisted audit field. Although the thoughts of continuous auditing have been proposed for many years, the developments of IT recently make continuous auditing feasible. Continuous auditing has attracted a lot of attention from researchers, auditors and software developers over the past three decades. Continuous auditing research center was also founded in Rutgers, the state university of New Jersey, and the meeting on continuous auditing is held every year. As a consequence, Continuous auditing researches develop quickly.

In China, in order to meet the requirements of computer-assisted audit, some researches on continuous auditing were also done. In this paper, the researches on continuous auditing are analyzed firstly. Then, the realization methods of continuous auditing are summarized and classed. Finally, DOOA, one realization methods of continuous auditing in China are studies, the advantages and disadvantages of DOOA are also discussed, and advices to implement DOOA are given.

2   Concept and Category of Continuous Auditing

Continuous auditing was defined in some literatures. CICA (the Canadian Institute of Chartered Accountants) and AICPA (the American Institute of Certified Public Accountants) defined continuous auditing as "a methodology that enables the auditor to provide assurance on a subject matter simultaneously with, or very shortly after, the occurrence of events underlying the subject matter [5]." Alexander[6] thought that continuous auditing was defined here as a type of auditing that produces audit results simultaneously with, or a short period of time after, the occurrence of relevant events. According to this define, Alexander thought continuous auditing would be more accurate to call this type of auditing instant rather than continuous. Furthermore, Alexander also thought that the only known way to make continuous auditing feasible is to implement continuous auditing on an online computer system. So, continuous auditing can also be called continuous online auditing (COA). One realization method of off-site audit in informationization environment is researched [7]. This style of off-site audit is also one mode of continuous auditing.

In a word, researches of continuous auditing mainly concentrate on realization methods, theory analysis and key technologies. And most researches are about realization methods. The realization principle of continuous auditing is different in different periods and different technology conditions. According to [8], continuous auditing methodology can be categorized into two major streams: stand-alone systems that continuously monitor auditee systems, extract data from those systems, compare data patterns with standards, trigger alarms/report exceptions, and ultimately achieve the goal of auditing; and sub-systems or modules that must be embedded into auditee systems.

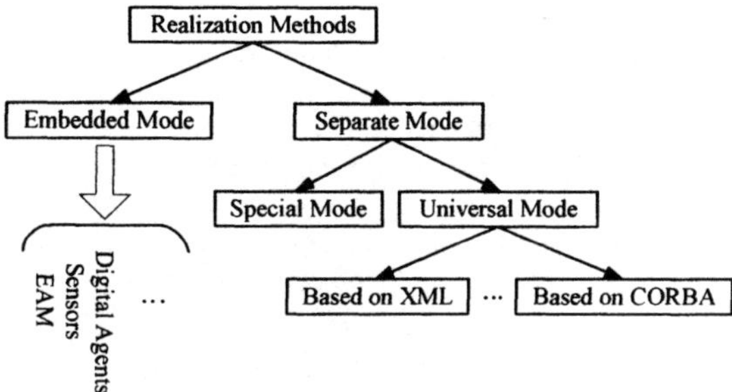

Fig. 1. The sorts of realization methods on continuous auditing

Based on analysis on research literatures of continuous auditing, realization methods of continuous auditing are classed as fig.1 in this paper. That is to say, realization methods of continuous auditing can be classed into two major kinds: embedded mode (such as [9,10]) and separate mode (such as [11,12]). Embedded mode is realized using EAM, sensors, digital agents, and so on. Separate mode is mainstream. According to the flexibility of continuous auditing system, realization methods of separate mode continuous auditing also can be classed into special mode and universal mode. Special mode is a realization method designed for one continuous auditing system, and cannot be used for another continuous auditing system. Universal mode is a realization method that is universal and can be used for many continuous auditing systems. The methods used in universal mode include methods based on XML, methods based on CORBA, and so on.

3   Data-oriented Online Auditing in China

The National Audit Office of China (CNAO) is dedicated in researching, realizing, popularizing and applying online auditing techniques and attempts to change the ways of audit work in recent years in China.

In China, in order to adapt the requirement of computer-assisted audit, the National Audit Office of China (CNAO) has implemented the first period of "Jin-shen Project" successfully. The "Jin-shen Project" is also means the "Golden Auditing Project", which is one of the 12 key IT business systems defined by the State Council under China's e-Government framework.

In a short, the "Jin-shen Project" is Chinese audit informationization. The main aim of the "Jin-shen Project" is to discovery the new audit mode; carry out a new online auditing model; and achieve three "transformations", which are to move from ex post audit to a combination of ex post audit and continuous audit; from static audit to a combination of static and dynamic audit; and from on-the-spot audit to a combination of on-the-spot and remote audit.

Through the first period of "Jin-shen Project", the infrastructures of audit departments, such as software and hardware, have been constructed; some audit software have been developed; and auditors have been trained to familiar with database, network, and so on.

Furthermore, in order to prepare for implementing the second period of "Jin-shen Project", the National Audit Office of China (CNAO) also has finished two research projects of the National High-Tech Research and Development Plan of China "data acquisition and process of IT audit". Through these two projects, online auditing technologies that adapt to Chinese condition are researched.

In China, online auditing is using network computer techniques to collect the auditee' data and transmit data to auditor' department. Then, auditors can process the auditee' data in their own department. And it is data-oriented. So, it is called data-oriented online auditing (DOOA). The principle of DOOA is shown in Fig.2. From Fig.2, we can see that the realization method of online auditing researched in China is also one mode of continuous auditing. It is one of separate mode of continuous auditing.

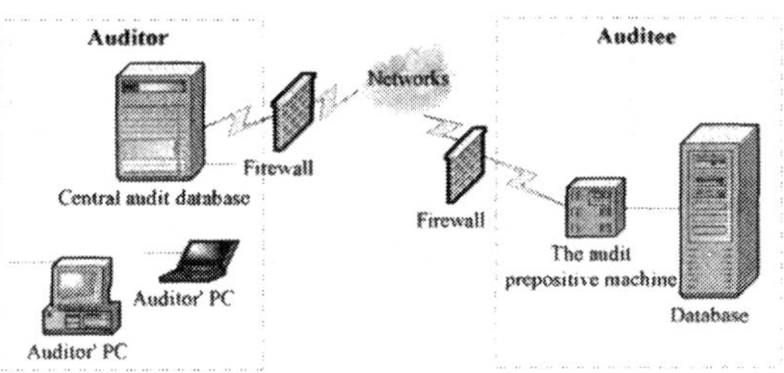

Fig. 2. The principle of continuous audit in China

Fig.2 shows that DOOA has 4 steps [13]:

(1) Audit data acquisition

In order to effectively implement the audit supervision in online auditing, it is necessary to collect the auditee' data timely. Auditors should not depend on monthly backup data, or yearly backup data of auditee. So, a PC server can be set at auditees, which is called audit prepositive machines, to collect the auditee' data according to the need of auditors. Through setting the audit prepositive machine appropriately, auditors can collect the auditee' data that auditors need and store in the audit prepositive machine.

(2) Audit data transmission

After finishing data acquisition, the audit prepositive machine will transmit the auditee' data to auditors' PC server through networks according to auditors' command.

(3) Audit data storage

Data collected from auditee increase massively under the condition of DOOA. It makes a good basis for mastering auditees' situations and also provides convenience to support other audit projects. To improve the efficiency of audit supervision, on-line storage and near-line storage are adopted in auditors' data storage. And data storage methods used in DOOA are researched in [14].

(4) Audit data processing

Audit data processing is an important step in DOOA. Through data processing, doubtful data can be found from the auditee' data.

Nowadays, in China, auditors usually use audit software, through using analysis methods such as browse, selection, comparison and check, sampling, statistics and gap, etc, to analyze data. And Audit Office (AO) is one of important audit software, which is developed by IT Center of CNAO. Audit Office is an integrated software, which integrates many data acquisition and analysis methods of other audit software.

However, the volume and complexity of accounting transactions in major organizations have increased dramatically. To audit such organizations, auditors frequently must deal with voluminous data with rather complicated data structure. Consequently, auditors can use technologies such as OLAP (On-Line Analytical Processing) to analyze the auditee' data. Rather, additional tools such as data mining techniques that can automatically extract information from a large amount of data might be very useful.

4 Advantages and Disadvantages of Implementing DOOA

In this section, we will discuss advantages and disadvantages of DOOA. According to analysis on DOOA above, we can see that advantages of implementing DOOA are as follows.

(1) Implementing DOOA can eliminate seven types of audit wastes.

Usually, there are seven types of audit wastes that can occur in the current audit domain, which are over auditing, waiting, time delays, the audit process, work-in-process, review process, errors and mistakes. DOOA is one mode of CA. So, these seven types of audit wastes can be eliminated through implementing DOOA.

(2) Implementing DOOA can reduce the audit cost.

If DOOA is implemented, the number of auditors will be reduced, so, the costs that spend on auditors will also be reduced. For some audit projects that are not in the same place with auditors, the outlay such as the cost of go on errands, the cost of hotel, and so on, will be reduced through implementing DOOA.

(3) Implementing DOOA can save the audit time and improve the efficiency of audit.

Because the condition of auditee is usually complicated, all problems cannot be found through one auditing in traditional audit mode. Through implementing DOOA, the auditee's data are collected and auditors can use the advanced audit methods, such as data mining, to analyze the auditee's data carefully. Therefore, the problems can be found roundly.

However, implementing DOOA also has some disadvantages. And disadvantages of DOOA are as follows.

(1) The cost of implementing DOOA is high.

The cost of implementing DOOA can be categorized into two kinds: one is one-off cost, and another is regular cost. One-off cost is investment of developing and implementing initially online audit system. Regular cost is investment of using and maintaining online auditing system in all life of online auditing system. Through the realization principle of DOOA, we can see that the cost of implementing DOOA is high.

(2) The techniques need of implementing DOOA is high.

DOOA is realized using information technologies in China. In order to ensure the progress of DOOA, auditors should understand each parts of DOOA, such as data acquisition, data transmission, data storage, and data process, which requires that auditors should familiar with software, hardware, network and databases.

(3) The audit risk of implementing DOOA is high.

The objects of auditing are electronic data that are collected from the auditee's information systems in DOOA. However, these electronic data needed to be ensured by internal control. If there are not efficient internal control systems to ensure the facticity of these electronic data, auditors will get wrong results from illusive electronic data, which will cause great audit risk.

Furthermore, DOOA system is also a complex system. Sometimes, some disasters will happen, which can cause DOOA system pause. The pauses of DOOA system will influent auditing work. So, the audit risk of implementing DOOA is high.

5   Advices on Implementing DOOA in China

According to the characters of DOOA implementing in China, some problems that should be paid attention are as follows:

(1) When choosing the auditees to implement DOOA, some aspects should be considered: ① For state audit, the auditees to implement DOOA should be important departments that are audited frequently, which can make DOOA more valuable. For internal audit in some large enterprises, DOOA also can be implemented if circumstance is feasible; ② In order to reduce audit risk, the internal control system of auditee should be perfect to ensure that actual data can be collected by DOOA system. ③ The degree of informationization in auditee should be higher, and finance software should be normative, which are basal condition to implement DOOA. ④ Under condition of safe network transmission, the cost of implementing DOOA between Auditor and auditee should be cheaper.

(2) Universal and portable DOOA software should be designed when DOOA system is developed. So, the audit implementing cost can be reduced. For example, it is important to research how to design universal audit data acquisition interface, such as interface based on XBRL, or how to design reconfigurable audit data acquisition system, which can make DOOA system universal.

(3) According to the condition of auditee, other proper methods also can be used when realization method presented in this paper is not feasible. For example, EAMs (Embedded Audit Modules) mode can be used for some ERP (Enterprise Resource Planning) systems in order to implement online auditing.

6   Conclusions

Continuous auditing is one new audit mode in informationization environment. Developments in information technology enabled continuous auditing feasible. In a words, implementing continuous auditing can improve the efficiency of auditing, reduce the audit cost, improve the quality of auditing, extend the scope of auditing, and make auditing work standardization. With developments in continuous auditing, traditional audit mode will be impacted, although continuous auditing cannot substitute traditional audit mode completely.

However, there are many problems on continuous auditing that need be studied deeply. For example, some researches are as follows:

(1) Research on key technologies of continuous auditing.

In order to implement continuous auditing, more technologies, such as data processing methods that are more efficient and adaptive to continuous auditing, should be researched.

(2) Research on how to make realization methods of continuous auditing universal and portable.

For example, for separate mode of continuous auditing, it is important to research how to design universal audit data acquisition interface, such as interface based on XBRL, or how to design reconfigurable audit data acquisition system, which can make continuous auditing system universal.

(3) Research on realization methods of continuous auditing for special trade.

For example, current versions of ERP systems neither include EAMs nor provide any real continuous auditing capability [15]. So, it is important to research realization methods of continuous auditing on ERP system.

Now, supported by the National High-Tech Research and Development Plan of China and China Postdoctoral Science Foundation, we are doing some researches on DOOA, and hope make some contributions to develop continuous auditing.

Acknowledgement

This work is supported by China Postdoctoral Science Foundation (No. 20060390281); the Natural Science Research Programs of college of Jiangsu Province (No. 05KJB520054); Jiangsu Planned Projects for Postdoctoral Research Funds (No. 0502023C); the National High-Tech Research and Development Plan of China (No. 2005AA1Z2140).

References

1. M. L. Linda. "Audit Technology and the Use of Computer Assisted Audit Techniques." *Journal of Information Systems* 4 (2), 60-68 (1990).

2. L. B. Robert, E. D. "Harold. Computer-assisted Audit Tools and Techniques: Analysis and Perspectives". *Managerial Auditing Journal* 18 (9), 725-731 (2003).

3. INTOSAI audit committee. Principles of Computer Assisted Audit Techniques - Student Notes, 2004, (unpublished).

4. E. Koskivaara. Artificial Neural Networks for Analytical Review in Auditing. Finland: Turku School of Economics and Business Admistration, (2004).

5. CICA/AICPA. Continuous Auditing Research Report. The Canadian Institute of Chartered Accountants, Toronto, Ontario, (1999).

6. K. Alexander, F. S. Ephraim, and A. V. Miklos. "Continuous Online Auditing: a Program of Research". *Journal of Information Systems* 13(2), 87-103 (1999).

7. Wang Huijin, Chen wei. Study on the realization method of off-site audit. Audit and Economy Research 20(3), 36-39 (2005).

8. H. Du, S. Roohani. A Framework for Independent Continuous Auditing of Financial Statements. In: American Accounting Association 2006 Annual Meeting. Washington, (2006).

9. S. M. Groomer, U. S. Murthy. "Continuous Auditing of Database Applications: An Embedded Audit Module Approach". *Journal of Information Systems* 3(2), 53-69 (1989).

10. R. S. Debreceny, G. L. Gray, J. Ng, et al. "Embedded Audit Modules in Enterprise Resource Planning Systems: Implementation and Functionality". *Journal of Information Systems*, 19(2), 7-27 (2005).

11. Z. Rezaee, A. Sharbatoghlie, and R. Elam, etc. "Continuous Auditing: Building Automated Auditing Capability". Auditing: *A Journal of Practice and Theory* 21(1), 147-163 (2002).

12. U. S. Murthy, S. M. Groomer." A Continuous Auditing Web Services Model for XML-based Accounting Systems". *International Journal of Accounting Information System* 5(2), 139-163 (2004).

13. Chen wei, Wang hao, Zhu Wenming. Study on Data-oriented IT Audit Used in China. In: Proceedings of the 11th Joint International Computer Conference. Singapore: World Scientific Publishing, pp. 666 – 669 (2005).

14. Wu Haiping, Yu Hongliang, Zheng Weimin, etc. "A Massive Data Storage and Management Strategy for Online Computer-assisted Audit System". *Chinese Journal of Computer* 29(4), 618-624 (2006).

15. M. G. Alles, A. Kogan, M. A. Vasarhelyi. "Feasibility and Economics of Continuous Assurance". Auditing: *A Journal of Theory and Practice* 21 (1), 125-138 (2002).

Research on the Status Quo and System Architecture of the Web Information Resource Evaluation

Wei Xu, Ji Liu, and Xiangxing Shen
School Information Management, Wuhan University, Wuhan 430072,
China
wilson_hu@126.com, sim@whu.edu.cn, x.shen@whu.edu.cn

Abstract. Web information resource evaluation (website evaluation) becomes more and more important, as the web information resources become larger and more complex. Thus, a lot of theory and methods have been developed to evaluate websites. In this paper, the author analyzes the primary methods applied currently in the evaluation of the web information resource and points out the main problems in this area from the perspectives of qualitative evaluation, quantitative evaluation, synthetic evaluation and automatic evaluation, after making an in-depth and comprehensive research of the literature and evaluation tools at home and abroad. Furthermore, the paper concludes that the evaluation of information resource on the Internet should take the internal and external characteristics into consideration, in the meantime, the paper puts forward a system architecture scheme of the automatic website evaluation based on the usability engineering.

1 Introduction

Internet, since its birth several decades ago, has published far more information than any traditional media. According to the 19th Survey Report [1] published in January, 2007, until December 31st, 2006, the number of computers accessed to the Internet in China mounts to 59,400,000, which is increased by 20.0% by comparing to the number last year; websites are altogether 843,000, increased by 21.4%.

The rapid development of the Internet on one hand stimulates the dramatic growth and accumulation of information. On the other hand, it brings about a large

Please use the following format when citing this chapter:

Xu, W., Liu, J., Shen, X., 2007, in IFIP International Federation for Information Processing, Volume 252, Integration and Innovation Orient to E-Society Volume 2, eds. Wang, W., (Boston: Springer), pp. 529-539.

amount of junk information and jam information, which results in serious information overload. A great many researches show searching for information is the main purpose for individuals to surf on line. However, in the searching period, about 60% of the time is wasted on futile work. For organizations, about 50% prospective users are lost because they cannot find the information they need. The common demand of individuals and organizations makes the digital information resource management [2], efficient search and evaluation imperative under the situation. Web information resource (websites), as the principal information carrier in cyberspace, plays a key role as the information node in the network. Therefore, the evaluation and method selection become more important than ever in the age of ever-accelerating information. Presently, foreign countries have set about the research on website evaluation; China also launches the projects too. But the large numbers of evaluation methods do not mean this area has become mature. The underlying reasons are due to the complexity of the websites themselves. The difference of website platform, implementing technology, positioning, contents and dimensions cause enormous obstacles for website analysis in reality. The large number of evaluation methods reveal the scarcity of the consistent theoretical guide and precise implementing frame. Confronting with the complicated network environment, without the uniform theoretical guide or scientific methodology, it will be difficult to collect and associate the separated problems of details, find out the crux and direction for improvement and ensure the accuracy and reliability of the analysis and evaluation results.

2   Researches on the Status Quo of Website Evaluation

2.1   Qualitative Evaluation

Qualitative evaluation mainly contains two methods: indexes system and questionnaire. Indexes system is to detect the quality of the website through setting a set of indexes. The indexes will vary according to the purpose, perspective and type of websites. An oversea scholar Betsy Richaman put forward 10C [3] principles; Harris Robert established four standards for website evaluation [4]; David Stoker and Alision Cooke raised 8 criteria [5] which are totally different from Harris's; Gemer L. Wilkinson, etc. compared and summarized the evaluation criteria brought by scholars in the thesis Index Listing of Evaluation Criteria and Quality. Based on the comprehensive analysis of the characteristics and attributes of websites, they concluded 125 qualitative website evaluation indexes in 11 categories [6]. Domestic scholars provided relevant index systems for websites of different types, for instance, the library website evaluation index system [7] and literature [8] discuss the synthetic evaluation index system from the angles of website design, contents and technology. Questionnaire makes best use of the users' recognition, perception and attitude to the websites to measure the impact they work on the users. This method is often carried out by evaluation organization or individual to know the serving capacity and operating effect of the website. They make a series of questionnaire, conducting the research, analyze the collected data and evaluate the website quality.

Qualitative evaluation can analyze the website quality roundly, make full use of the individual's perception of the website, and acquire direct and understandable results. But it still has following problems.

2.1.1 Some Problems Exit in Indexes System Method

- The index system doesn't cover all the main attributes. Website is a very complicated and enormous system. The evaluation indexes are complex too. Until now, the differences of index systems raised by scholars and evaluation institutes and the disagreement on this issue display this point clearly. As a matter of fact, few have not conducted comprehensive and synthetic observation of websites, nor have they engaged in objective unveiling of the internal and external attributes of the websites.
- Some of the indexes are not reasonable. The websites have many attributes. There are cause-and-effect relations between each of them. Some of the evaluation methods have not given scientific positioning for the indexes, for example, the relation between the quality of the information, website traffic, page views and connectivity is usually defined separately. Repetitions often occur in indexes, for example, although there are some differences in the expression of indexes, the essence meaning is quite the same or similar (e.g. credibility and accuracy). Some indexes are hard to understand, such as critical thinking. Some indexes seem reasonable, but the practical examination and application are really hard. They are not feasible. For example, the indexes such as justice and perception of the world can not be taken as the criteria to evaluate the website quality.
- Some indexes are aimed at ambiguous objects. The website is constituted by the framework as well as the information content. The evaluation indexes of webpage structure and information content are not properly distinguished. Some indexes are applicable for webpage evaluation, while some are applicable for information content. Blurring the boundary between them confuses the objects and makes them not scientific.

2.1.2 Some Problems Exit in Questionnaire Method

During the process of implementing questionnaire, the error is difficult to control, especially the validity and objectivity of the users' answers, which affects the accuracy of the quality research results.

Besides, due to the strong subjectivity of qualitative evaluation, the evaluation result is easy to be impact by the network environment, evaluation standard, as well as the qualification and emotion of the evaluation staff. This causes this method not so feasible. The reliability of the results is weakened too. Time, human endeavor, facility and money will be increased in this case. The cost is too high. It can hardly meet the demand of massive websites evaluation.

2.2   Quantitative Evaluation

Quantitative evaluation provides a series of scientific, normative and objective evaluation methods, illustrating and solving the problem by reliable figures. Originally, it evolved from the analysis of the basic elements such as connectivity, page views and so on, developed into a systematical quantitative evaluation method. The three typical quantitative evaluation methods applied abroad include Webometrics (Link Analysis), analytical hierarchy process and correspondence analysis.

2.2.1 Webometrics

Webometrics, adopting traditional citation analysis theories, is an efficient method applied in website evaluation. It is taken for granted that the more linkage a website has, the higher the quality is. Research shows the research of the relation between the webpage links is somewhat similar to that of the citation research of the published articles. But they still have some nuance. This is in accordance with Lotka effect [9]. When the linkage analysis is applied in research, some famous searching engines such as Google and Alta Vista are used. These engines can usually offer some special software interface and data searches method, which helps the users to find out the data they need.

2.2.2 Analytical Hierarchy

Analytical hierarchy process utilizes human's conventional thoughts to solve problems. It divides a complicated problem into several detailed problems, making full use of the analysis, judgment and integration capacities, and quantifies the complexity. This method makes the conception classification of website attributes, collecting and measuring the data by the experts' investigation. In this way, it evaluates the grades and ranks of websites, such as some literature [10] explores into the trains of thought and method of the application of analytic hierarchy process to university libraries websites evaluation.

2.2.3 Correspondence Analysis

Correspondence analysis (Relational Analysis) was originally raised by a French scientist and adopted in enterprise decision-making positioning analysis. The English professor Berthon applied correspondence analysis to evaluate 15 websites of the telecommunication company in the world in 2001 [11]. It was proved to be a breakthrough in this area. He pointed out correspondence analysis could solve the positioning problems of the website evaluation; distinguish the exact difference between the websites. This method can not only be helpful in telecommunication websites evaluation, but also websites of different kinds. The literature [12] used correspondence analysis to make an experimental evaluation of the media website in China. It established a mathematical model of this analysis through defining the basic attributes of the websites, collecting relevant data from Alexa [13] database and generating the correspondence positioning graph. This can be involved in decision-making positioning analysis and has great reference value.

Quantitative evaluation to some extent overcomes the problems of subjectivity and controllability in qualitative analysis. Whereas, it still has many problems too.

- The limitation of link analysis

As the research goes further, it is discovered that there are spectacular differences between literature citations and website connections. Many problems arise. For example, Stephen P. Harter and Charlotte E. Ford discover in their research, among the links to the e-print websites, nearly half of them are linked to themselves, which is helpless for the evaluation of literature academic value and research on academic communication; among the webpage linked to e-periodical websites, the percentage of the academic websites is lower than 8%. Thelwall [14] analyses the 100 webpage linked with the highest frequency by the English universities. The result also shows the linkage can not indicate the academic value of the websites. Currently the reached agreement is that the links of the webpage is substantially different from the citation. Although citation analysis can illuminate the linage research, considering the difference between them, the results concluded from it should be processed accordingly.

- The limitation of analytical hierarchy process

There are two limitations of the application of analytical hierarchy process to website evaluation. First, the process itself has some disadvantages. Secondly, the process still has some problems in adjusting with the website evaluation. The classification and measurement of analytical hierarchy process are carried out by human beings. So is the scoring procedure. The error control is enforced, but cannot avoid human subjectivity, which causes some deviation between the result and reality. The component elements of the websites are also interacted. Even if the relationships between the elements, the general and simple classification of the hierarchy worked out by the process still makes the results deviate the reality.

- The limitation of correspondence analysis

Since correspondence analysis only evaluates the information of website positioning and distinctions, it is not based on the integrity of the website. Therefore, it can hardly reflect the synthetic level of the website roundly and systematically. On the other hand, the data of the data warehouse also have defects. They can be modified easily and may have some errors in data check, which causes obstacles to the practical work of website evaluation.

Up to date, quantitative evaluation of websites adopts traditional theories and methods which provide a useful train of thought and consulting reference in website evaluation but result in the neglect of the characteristics of the websites themselves and further research aimed at the users. The scarcity of a scientific positioning of evaluation objects is also one of the disadvantages. It has not made any substantial development in evaluation, but still has the consulting value in academic research.

2.3   Synthetic Evaluation

Synthetic evaluation includes the synthetic method based on user research and quantity detecting, website evaluation based on Information Architecture (IA) theory and website framework evaluation.

2.3.1 Website Evaluation Based on IA Theory

This method conducts access analysis [15] from four systems: the classification, navigation, searching and labeling of the content of the IA. It is usually carried out from the angle of the user experience, evaluating the website by making the users define the application target and then checking their performance in practicing. By comparing with the qualitative evaluation, it is more systematical and scientific, belonging to the demonstrating analysis category.

2.3.2 Website Framework Evaluation

This method accords to the different profiles of the website, establishes a set of measuring standard, putting all the standard indexes in the structure frame and table, regarding the indexes as the criteria of website evaluation. This method can be described objectively and quantified by the quantitative criteria. The evaluation result is comprehensive. It is a compromise.

Since synthetic evaluation applies the merits of both qualitative and quantitative evaluation, it can obtain better results. But two questions should be coped with properly: how to decide the proportion of qualitative and quantitative evaluation. If it is taken randomly, error will occur in the evaluation system. While actually the efforts and costs spent on this method are far more than merely using qualitative or quantitative method.

2.4   Automatic Evaluation

Automatic evaluation sets about from the attributes and characteristics of the websites, utilizes digital, automatic and intelligentzed means to solve the problems. It develops relevant automatic detecting software or websites, makes them available for all websites testing and evaluation data automatic collecting, according to the established website evaluation model, conducts the Stat., analysis and calculation automatically, and then works out the evaluation result. The automatic testing takes counter, Cookies, cache memory and IP address as the basic analytic data, on the ground of the user's page view record analysis, applying the analysis on the Web sites and automatic analysis on the server log, etc. to evaluate the load and quality of the information on the website objectively. It is objective and credible [16].

Though automatic evaluation can detect some more relational mistakes, enhance the coverage of the analyzing features, reduce the experts' dissatisfaction and time consumption and fuse with usability interface (UI) design and analysis. But automatic analysis can only be taken as the standard analysis. Different techniques reveal raise different problems. The subjective evaluation on the user's satisfaction can not adopt automatic testing. Meanwhile, this area is still premature. The reason for the phenomenon lies in the complexity of the website itself. Users want to know and observe the data. But it is too complicated to be practicable. In this case, it can merely be regarded as the reference in website evaluation.

3   Architecture of Website Evaluation

3.1   Setting of the Evaluation Index System

Website evaluation must be implemented based on its own characteristics, under the guidance of the theories of this area. The existent research and practice have not distinguished the attributes of the websites properly, leading to the chaos of the setting of index system. The author believes, for a website, it has internal and external characteristics, reflecting its quality from different angles. Thus the evaluation should be carried out from these two standpoints.

3.1.1 Website Internal Characteristic

The internal characteristic of the website is decided by the component elements of the website entity. It mirrors the technological implementation of the website target. Newman and Landay's research [17] shows website is a multidimensional compound which covers content, navigation and appearance [18], just as what Figure 1 indicates.

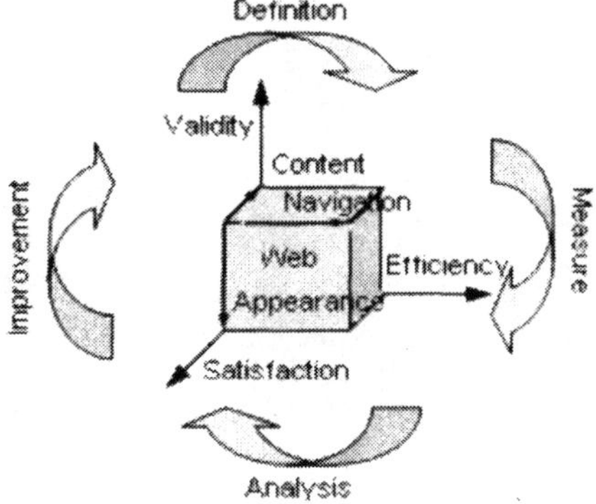

Fig. 1. Website internal evaluation objects

This distinction can avoid the interaction of the elements. Hence analytic hierarchy process may help to set scientific indexes. Content evaluation focuses on the information construction. In detail, it includes four aspects [19]: sorting system, search system, index system and information security system. Navigation evaluation needs to involve global navigation, local navigation, supplementary navigation and semantic navigation evaluation. The appearance evaluation judges the display and distribution, for example, the color collocation of the website, selection of multimedia materials and so on. This process researches the objective attributes such as content, navigation and appearance thoroughly. By applying the hierarchy analysis, the weight will be ascertained; the website internal characteristic evaluation index system will be established.

3.1.2 Website External Characteristic

Website external characteristic includes Web traffic, visit, Connectivity, Speed, Page Views, user's average page views and freshness as well as the number of the registered users and their website application frequency. The ultimate target is to serve the user. The users' degree of satisfaction and indexes related to the user experience are the core of the external characteristic. As it is showed in Figure 2, acquiring the data, adopting correspondence analysis to conduct cluster analysis and elaborating the distinctions of the websites in the network are a helpful supplementary factor in website evaluation [20].

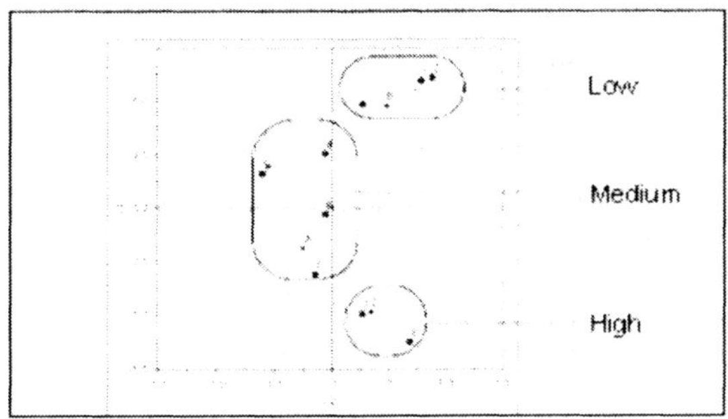

Fig. 2. Cluster analysis graph of correspondence analysis

The problems, such as ambiguous positioning still exist in the previous index system, index unable to reflect the website quality, defects and limits are found in the adaptability of analytic hierarchy process and correspondence analysis, can be revealed through the characteristic analysis of the websites. This will be helpful to form a series of indexes which are mainly supported by qualitative evaluation and assisted by quantitative evaluation.

3.2   Architecture of Automatic Evaluation System

The system adopts software fast prototype method, combining with the Object-Oriented Design methods. It is used to develop automatic website evaluation tool model system based on B/S model. The development process will involve Java or NET technology, UML, XML, Web Services, Intelligent Agent and Portal techniques, applying the multi-layer software structure grounded on J2EE and NET Framework. Maybe it can realize the expansibility and maintainability of the software platform as Figure 3 shows.

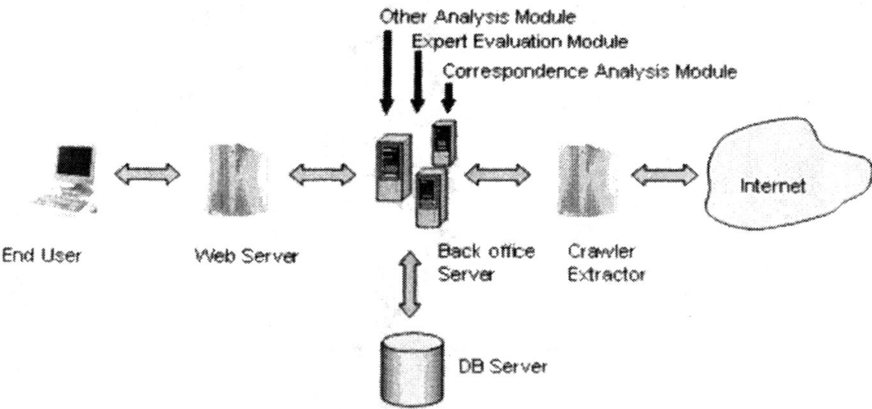

Fig. 3. Structure of the automatic website evaluation system

3.2.1 End User

Terminal user uses personal computer to visit all the Web Serves to get the evaluation (main information) of different websites and basic website development information (supplementary information).

3.2.2 Web Server

Web server provides Web browse service, applying program interface and component interface through distribution scheme to use the background server application module.

3.2.3 Back Office Server

Back office server is the critical and difficult part of the system development. The development is implemented on the basis of the development of the open software system of J2EE or NET Framework, etc to realize the dynamic increase and adjustment of the automatic website analysis tools. The main components include Profile developing tool, matrix calculating tool and analysis calculating tool, etc. The key is to establish a standard website characteristics corpus and an intelligent analytic comparing algorithm of the development. The website parameter standard characteristic corpus, such as the website information construction standard, color standard and navigation standard, etc., should vary according to the types of different websites in order to offer the reference to comparative analysis. The parameter standard corpus should include the weights of parameters raised by the experts. They should vary with the types of different websites too. Intelligent analysis tools can be functionally divided to three systems: relational analysis, comparative analysis and indirect measurement. Relational analysis system is applicable in website positioning and distinguishing to expel relevant interference factors. Comparative analysis system is used to compare the eigenvalues of the parameter standard corpus and websites [21]. It combines with the calculation and corresponding analytic matrix, and conducts an all-round analysis of all the components inside the website. Indirect measurement system is adapted to measure two comparatively subjective indexes of the user's degree of satisfaction and website practice experience. Meanwhile, it indirectly indicates the analysis of the characteristic parameters of the two indexes in order to evaluate the user's satisfaction degree and practice experience [22].

3.2.4 Crawler and Extractor

Crawler and extractor is the crucial component in collecting the objective website data [23]. It utilizes the well-shaped searching engines and the characteristics of the system itself, develops the extractor which is suitable for the system. Accords to the set index system, it provides objective data to the automatic website evaluation. The extractor observes the established requirement; captures the internal and external characteristics data of the website, converts them into needed forms and extracts the objective data of the demanding websites.

3.2.5 DB (Data-Base) Server

The data in the system is stored in the database. It includes the data of the benchmark website, data of the target website evaluation, matrix generated or analyzed in calculation and data of the users' page views. In practice, the system will apply distributed database to balance the load.

4   Conclusions

At present, applied website evaluation is rare. The methods raised until now cannot evaluate all the indexes of a website roundly. Therefore, on the base of a systematical conclusion and research of the achievements in the area home and abroad, it is necessary to explore the automatic website evaluation model and method grounded on usability engineering theories. It will be useful for the perfect of information resources web site evaluation indexes system، evaluation model and evaluation mechanism, optimizing the information web site configure, promoting the government function conversion for fulfilling the market supervision function and common management function.

Acknowledgment

This paper is the Major Project of Philosophical and Social Science of Ministry of Education, Management and Utility of Digital Information Resources (05JID00024).

References

1. China Internet Network Information Center, The 19th survey report (February 18, 2007); http://www.cnnic.net.cn/en//index/0O/02/index.htm.
2. W.C. Wu and J.Z. Zhang, "Study of network information standardization system", *Information Science.* **19**(1), 40-46 (2001).
3. J. Su, "Research on the network information resources evaluation", *Journal of Academic Libraries.* **23**(1), 7-13 (2005).

4. W.J. Chen and Y.S. Chen, "Commentary on evaluation of network information resources", *Journal of the Library Science Society of Sichuan.* **40**(1), 25-31 (2004).

5. J. Shen and Q.H. Zhu, "Current research on evaluation criteria of networked information resources in China and overseas", *Information Science.* **23**(7), 1104-1109 (2005).

6. J.L. Zhao and L.J. Chen, "Research summary on the network information resources evaluation overseas", *Library Work and study.* **18**(3), 24-26 (2005).

7. H.T. Zhang, "A study of indicators for the evaluation of library website", *Document Information & Knowledge.* **25**(2), 96-99 (2005).

8. D.M. Li, "Preliminary exploration of website integrative evaluation", *Information studies Theory & Application.* **28**(2), 303-306 (2005).

9. R. Rousseau, "Sitations: An exploratory study", *Cybernetics.* **1**(1), 1-9 (1997).

10. H.M. Wei, "Application of analytical hierarchy process in libraries webs evaluation", *New Technology Library and Information Service.* **29**(10), 74-83 (2005).

11. P. Berthon, "Positioning in Cyberspace: Evaluating Telecom Websites Using Correspondence Analysis", *Information Resources Management Journal.* **14**(1), 13-21 (2001).

12. X.S. Shen and D.M. Li, "Research on China network media websites evaluation: Using correspondence analysis", *China Soft Science.* **19**(1), 126-133 (2005).

13. "Alexa Internet Inc, Alexa Web Search Platform" (December 13, 2006); http://www.alexa.com/.

14. M. Thelwall, "An initial exploration of the link relationship between UK university Web sites", *Aslib Proceeding.* **52**(2), 118-126 (2002).

15. L. Gan, "Examination & analysis of information architecture of e-commerce website", *Information Studies Theory & Application.* **28**(6), 605-608 (2005).

16. D.M. Li, "The research on the automated website information evaluation", *Document Information & Knowledge.* **25**(1), 104-107 (2005).

17. M.W. Newman, and J.A. Landay, "Sitemaps, storyboards, and specifications: A sketch of web site design practice", *Proceedings of Designing Interactive Systems* (New York, 2000), pp. 263-274.

18. J.X. Hao and X.X. Shen, "Study on the framework for website analysis based on usability engineering", *Document Information & Knowledge.* **26**(2), 81-86 (2006).

19. Y.H. Rong and Z.P. Liang, "An approach to information architecture", *Journal of the China Society for Scientific and Technical Information.* **21**(2), 229-232 (2003).

20. X.X. Shen, et al, "Evaluating China's university library websites using correspondence analysis", *Journal of the American Society for Information Science and Technology.* **57**(4), 493-500 (2006).

21. Chi, Ed H, et al, "The bloodhound project: Automating Discovery of Web Usability Issues Using the Info Scent TM Simulator", *Proceedings of the Conference on Human Factors in Computing Systems* (ACM Press, New York, 2003), pp. 505-512.

22. B.J. Cockrell, Jayne, and E. Ahow, "Do I Find an Article? Insights from a Web Usability Study", *The Journal of Academic Librarianship.* **28**(2), 54-64 (2002).

23. J.I. Hong, et al, "Web Quilt: A proxy-based approach to remote web usability testing", *ACM Transactions on Information Systems.* (19), 263-285 (2001).

Citizen Engagement: Driving Force of E-Society Development

Xiaolin Qiu
School of Information Management Wuhan University, Wuhan, China
430072

Abstract. Starting from the belief that e-inclusion should be the strategic choice, and full engagement of every citizen is the key to the success and healthy development of e-society, this paper puts forward that "Information Commons" model can be applied to a larger target group: the disadvantaged citizens for their information rights and e-literacy education. Three IC applications: residents' community IC, public library IC, and government agency IC are discussed.

1 Introduction

This paper presents the views of the author in relation to e-inclusion as a very important strategy of e-society. The author believes e-inclusion will eliminate digital divide which checks the healthy development of e-government, e-commerce, and e-learning, significant indicators of e-society.

Research on e-inclusion shows that there has been a cry for information equality and great efforts have been made such as Open Access Movement, information literacy education, and e-learning initiatives. However, the research mainly remains in the academic community, higher education, high schools and a few primary schools. Research on grass roots citizens is scarce. To address this gap, this paper focuses on measures promoting ordinary citizens' information rights, information literacy education, and information usage leading to the full engagement into e-society.

The paper discusses, as specific measures of promoting citizen engagement into e-society, the information commons model at residents' community level, public library level, and government agent level. Next steps are briefly described.

Please use the following format when citing this chapter:

Qui, X., 2007, in IFIP International Federation for Information Processing, Volume 252, Integration and Innovation Orient to E-Society Volume 2, eds. Wang, W., (Boston: Springer), pp. 540-548.

2 Background

An information society, or knowledge-based economy, is one in which people's lives, business operations, and government decision makings etc. are greatly improved and impacted by quantity, quality and speed of their information aquiring, processing and using. With wide applications of ICT, e-government, e-commerce and e-learning are becoming important indicators of a country's comprehensive competitiveness and national strength. Information resources have become pillar resources for economic development. Information society is seen as the successor to industrial society and draws its growth from the forces of globalization (through its intensive investment forces, cultural influence and unification of the market), knowledge intensity (over 70% of the workers in the developed world are knowledge/information workers), connectivity (internet, mobile networks, advanced interactive applications) [1]

2.1 E-government an achievement of e-society

With ICT, and especially the Internet technology, governments around the world can deliver online government information and services to citizens, business, and other government agencies. Public sectors' performance is evaluated with indexes like "Efficiency, Effectiveness, Economy, and Equity". Up to now, more than 90% of local governments have established one-stop portals in China. [2] "Government Online Project", "The Golden Projects", "Business Online Project", and "Family Online Project" have made great achievements in promoting e-society's development. China e-government ranked the 12th in 2003 among 198 countries around the world. [3]

According to the study undertaken in AUG. 2000, which was sponsored by the Council for Excellence in Government about public attitudes toward and use of e-government in the US, more than two-thirds of adult e-government users gave public agencies high marks for their websites. 71% believed that the quality of government websites they had visited was excellent or good, 26% felt they were only fair, 2% rated them poor, and 1% was unsure. [4] Generally people think e-government makes government more accountable and more transparent, more efficient and cost-effective, provides greater access to government information, and makes government service more convenient.

2.2 "Digital divide" the greatest concern of e-society

Digital divide, the gap between the information-haves and information-have nots, is the major concern for each and every country in the world. The gap exists between rich people and poor ones in the traditional sense within a certain country, and it also does exist between developed and developing countries. Survey results show that more than half of the Internet users are young male with higher income and better education (also a result of being rich). A majority of non-users of the Internet are either poor being unable to afford a computer and access fees, or short of necessary Internet and information skills. Economic wealth and the level of

R&D spending were the best predictors of Internet usage (Pippa Norris). [5] Countries that were wealthy and had a competitive market structure feature higher levels of connectivity. (Eazter Hargittai) [6] Economic wealth and digital access costs mattered more than market structure or regulatory approach. (Sampsa Kiiski and Matti Pohjola) [7] Globally, special-needs populations are not receiving much help in terms of accessibility. [8]

Even in the US, one of the most advanced countries in e-government development, half to two-thirds of the adult population remain outside the world of digital government, [9] let alone the developing countries. The negative impact of the paucity of e-government users is the difficulty in reaching the economy of scale which lowers per-unit costs. Lack of engagement by most of the people widens the digital divide, causes potential conflicts and dissatisfaction among people. People's negative opinion about the technology limits the technological diffusion in government agencies. Lack of most citizen engagement loses the win-win benefit of e-government that makes government officials be more responsive to ordinary citizens, and the general public more supportive to the government. E-government will not produce a major transformation in citizen usage as long as most people do not access government websites.

3. Related Literature Review

3.1 Open Access Movement

Many initiatives have been made in academic community as far as equality in the access and use of research results is concerned. Budapest Open Access Initiative in 2002 starts the OA Movement, which has got a lot of supporting voices from OECD, IFLA, Wellcome Trust, UN, and ACRL etc. etc. [10] The most recent one comes in January, 2007, five leading European research institutions launched a petition that called on the European Commission to establish a new policy to require that all government-funded research be made available to the public shortly after publication. Within weeks, it garnered more than 20,000 signatures, including several Nobel Prize winners and more than 750 education, research, and cultural organizations from around the world. [11]

The open access principle is that the published output of scientific research should be available on the public Internet, without change, to EVERYONE, "not merely among those who can attend the daily lectures — but far and wide."(Daniel Coit Gilman). The Directory of Open Access Journals, a Swedish project that links to open access journals in all disciplines, currently lists more than 2,500 open access journals worldwide featuring over 127,000 articles. [12]

3.2 Information Literacy Education

Information literacy education has long been a great concern in developed countries like United States. They connect the inability to master and apply new technologies with "mediocrity that threatens our very future as a nation and a people" facing ever increasing competition in the global economy. [13] So, many initiatives concerning information literacy education and e-learning have been going on. Seven U. S. states such as Virginia, New Mexico, Louisiana, etc. have their own education programs. For instance, Pennsylvania received a $1.8 million grant from the U.S. Department of Education to study the impact of computers on student achievement. Arkansas' Environmental and Spatial Technology Initiative includes strong relationship between business, government and education, providing awareness and access to resources normally not available to educators. [14]

3.3 E-Learning

Since 2000, there has been an explosive growth in e-learning and virtual schools in America, making it possible for students at all levels to receive high quality supplemental or full courses of instructions personalized to their needs. In higher education, some 90 % of four-public institutions and more than half of four-year private institutions offer some form on online education, by providing every student access to e-learning, and by enabling every teacher to participate in e-learning training. A teacher from a small, rural Florida District said: "Online learning 'evens the playing field' for rural students." "No Child Left Behind Act" passed in 2001 was signed into law by U.S. President Bush in January 2002. The goals are to end the achievement gap between rich and poor and white and minority students, and improve the academic performance of all students by 2014. The US Department of Education is promoting the value of broadband and other technologies for lifelong learning. Broadband technologies have great educational value as well as far-reaching economic impact and on March 26, 2004, President Bush announced a major broadband initiative with the goal of connecting every home to broadband by 2007. [15]

4 Concept Basis and Research Focus

4.1 "E-inclusion" Choice of E-society

E-society consisting of e-governance, e-commerce, and e-learning forms the foundation of a nation's competitiveness. Social divide weakens a nation's competitive strength. Social divide is not a direct result of e-society, but a phenomenon that has long been preexisting. Poverty and backwardness caused by scarcity of natural resources, geographical limitations, different historical and cultural background, and unsuitable economic systems, etc. existed within one country as well as between countries. New forms of social divide we are facing today: "Digital divide" or "technological divide", which are directly relevant to the above factors though, are more serious and more strongly concerned by more and more people around the world. Because "Digital divide" can either deteriorate the already worse situation of polarization between the rich and the poor, or have it improved and eliminated. The choice of e-society for each and every country should be "e-inclusion" to turn the risk of a digital divide into "digital cohesion" and "digital opportunities", by bringing the benefit of the Information Society into all segments of the population, including: people who are disadvantaged due to education, ageing, limited resources, gender, ethnicity, people with disabilities, geographical digital divide. [16]

4.2 Research Focus

Embracing the strategy of e-inclusion and emphasizing "outreach" and "responsiveness" of e-government services, the paper focuses on the measures promoting grass-root citizens' information rights, information literacy education, and information usage leading to the full engagement into e-society. Specific target is those who are unable to access the Internet due to their inability to buy a computer or to pay for Internet access, or to know how to get information.

5   Discussion and Analysis

5.1 "Information Commons" Model

Information Commons Model is widely adopted by universities. "Information Commons" means a shared information resource for academic community. It is more than a library, more than a study space, more than an IT center, the whole is greater than the sum of the parts. [17] The Information Commons unites all the facts and figures of the world into a resource available to everyone. Through a massive peer-to-peer network, the Commons enables individuals, non-profits and government agencies to fuse their data together into one database, distributed across many different computers. Sharing data in the Commons is seamless between individuals and organizations, offering easy, flexible data integration and reuse. [18]

The central idea behind IC is the shift of the university mission from teaching to learning, and learning becomes the new organizing principle for the academic libraries. Information literacy reflects a new understanding of learning in which technology and information facilitate the process of learning and the creation of knowledge. The key features of an Information Commons are its external and internal relationships, sense of community, partnerships and collaborations. [19] In IC students have integrated access to printed and electronic information sources in the same place at the same time. The services co-provided by network technicians, librarians, and teachers are seamless creating an ideal condition for shared exploration and ownership of information literacy.

5.2 Different IC Applications

IC consists of three key elements in one place: broadband connected computers, information resources, and professionals. The essence is learning, or "learning by doing". Such places equipped with computers and broadband and professionals provide computers for people who can not afford computers, offer free broadband to those who can not afford Internet fees, and help educate those who lack ICT knowledge. Establishing IC at different organizations such as residents' communities, public libraries, and government agencies can have different characteristics, advantages and drawbacks.

5.2.1 Residents' Community IC

In China, residents' committee is the grass roots people's organization, which is closest to every citizen by contacting them day in and day out. The idea of "IC" at this level is a simplified one with the basic elements such as a room with a computer, broadband and one staff. The training and education of community IC focuses on:

- On-line paying of bills (property management, water, electricity, gas, phone and Internet, etc.)
  - Health care knowledge (health food, medical care etc.)
- Family management knowledge (marriage issues, children education, elderly caring, etc.)
  - Money management knowledge;
  - Residential environment protection knowledge
  - Domestic service information
  - Residential activity information (entertainment & sports, etc.)
  - Job information

5.2.2 Public Library IC

The advantages of establishing IC in public libraries are:

- Infrastructure guarantee (broadband, or wireless access to the Internet)
- Equipment guarantee (quantity and quality of computers)
- Software guarantee (free open-source software and e-learning solutions)
- Information resources guarantee (traditional printed materials and digital materials)
  - Expertise guarantee (librarians and information professionals)
  - Feeling of belonging (sense of community and collaborated learning)

The training and education of community IC focuses on:

- Kinds of information resources
- Library service information
- Knowledge of how to analyze one's information needs
- Knowledge of how to use information resources
- Knowledge of how to evaluate information resources
- Knowledge of how to use information to solve the problem
- Knowledge of how to innovate with information

5.2.3 Government Agency IC

Government agencies can create public access rooms in which citizens can visit government websites. This kind of IC focuses on equal access to e-government information and e-services for the purpose of citizen engagement into rule making. The training and education of community IC focuses on:

- Knowledge of how to use government portal website
- On-line government information
- Government e-service information
- On-line G2C interaction / communication
- E-democracy
- On-line shopping
- Restaurant and traveling information

5.3 Comparison and Analysis

A summary of the differences in software and hardware development degree and focus is shown in Table 1.

Table 1. RCIC x PLIC x GAIC

Topic of Comparison	Residents' Community IC	Public Library IC	Government Agency IC
Infrastructure	Low	High	High
Equipment	Low	High	High
Software	Low	High	Medium
Information Resources	Low	High	Medium
Expertise	Low	High	High
Feeling of Belonging	High	Medium	Low
Convenience	High	Medium	Low
Focus	E-life	E-learning	E-democracy

From the above comparison we can see that the three types are complementary meeting different needs. It's obvious that both hardware and software in residents' community are relatively inadequate and in a poor condition. But people choose the place to go for its vicinity and convenience, for its free atmosphere and familiarity. Several ways can be used to improve its condition. Government can provide regulatory and financial help. Large business in the community can offer funds or equipment. Hundreds of students in the community can work as volunteers to help teach people how to use computers, where to find information, and what decision to make like whether paying the bills online or by visiting an office improving quality of people's lives.

Comparatively, public libraries are the best both in software and hardware condition. However, there is much room for improvement. The highest priority should be given to marketing, promoting, and making full use of the expertise, equipment and information resources. With rich resources like e-learning solutions, open course databases and open access journals as well as expertise in public libraries, citizens can learn to teach themselves new knowledge and new skills, thus raising the employment rate, quality of workforce, innovation ability, strengthening the competitiveness of the whole nation.

Different from community or public library IC, government agency IC is more focused on e-government information resources and services, one of the most important parts of e-inclusion. But they have things in common such as Internet access, computers, information resources and information expertise. Priming test of U.S. e-government shows that with educational effort about the issue of e-government, citizen beliefs can be transformed in a direction positive for beliefs about government effectiveness. [20] With the help of public servants, citizen usage of e-government can be effectively increased, isolation reduced, digital divide bridged, citizen trust in government built up, citizen relationship with government improved, social injustice removed, governance reinforced, sustainable social development guaranteed, and society advanced.

5.4 Government's Role

Government, as the highest forum for policy making within its jurisdiction, is playing a vital role in e-inclusion society, and e-government development. It should take the responsibility for the full engagement of every citizen into information society by making appropriate decisions (policies, regulations, and laws), forming right strategies, and having them completely implemented. At the same time, government should control the process, collect, deploy, and disseminate best practices. For instance, at EU level e-Inclusion is part of the third pillar of the i2010 policy initiative, managed by Directorate-General for Information Society and Media of the European Commission. [21]

As far as the above mentioned IC model is concerned, the quickest and most effective way by government to encourage citizen engagement is

- Funding and investing in information infrastructure, providing computers and free Internet access in residents' communities, schools, libraries, and government agencies
- Issuing guiding principles for encouraging citizen's engagement
- Making detailed plans of information literacy education catering to ordinary citizens
- Making it a rule for public servants to take turns serving at residents' communities and government agencies as professional experts
- Guaranteeing the connecting to and free use of all available information resources
- Promoting participation;
- Supervising and evaluating process and outcome

6 Conclusion

This paper discusses the applications of "Information Commons" model in order to safeguard the information rights of the disadvantage group. The paper builds on a conceptual basis of e-inclusion which I believe should be the strategic choice of e-society. The success and advancement of e-society depend on full engagement of every citizen. By providing computers, Internet access, expertise, and all kinds of information resources to citizens, they can acquire information skills and become information literates. IC model meets all the requirements of helping the needy. Three complementary types of IC have different focuses and characteristics catering to different needs: e-life, e-learning, and e-democracy. Theoretically it is a program of practicality. I hope this paper encourages further empirical research on the operability and better solutions in the field.

References

1. http://www.e-society_org_mk-key Concepts.mht

2. it.sohu.com/20041104/n222838803.shtml 54K 2007-1-29

3. Darrel M. West, *Digital Government Technology and Public Sector Performance*,(Princeton University Press, Princeton and Oxford, 2005), pp.191-193.

4. Darrel M. West, *Digital Government Technology and Public Sector Performance*, (Princeton University Press, Princeton and Oxford, 2005), pp. 120.

5, 6, 7. Darrel M. West, *Digital Government Technology and Public Sector* Performance, (Princeton University Press, Princeton and Oxford, 2005), pp.141-142

8. Darrel M. West, *Digital Government Technology and Public Sector Performance*, (Princeton University Press, Princeton and Oxford, 2005), pp. 152

9. Darrel M. West, *Digital Government Technology and Public Sector Performance*, (Princeton University Press, Princeton and Oxford, 2005), pp. 124

10. http://www.arl.org/sc/models/oa.shtml

11, 12. Michael Geist, Open access: Reshaping rules of research (February 26,2007); http://www.thestar.com-sciencetech

13. National Commission on Excellence in Education, *A Nation at Risk* (Washington, DC: U.S. Department of Education, 1983); http://www.ed.gov/pubs/NatAtRisk/risk.html

14, 15. U.S. Department of Education, Office of Educational Technology, Toward A New Golden Age in American Education: How the Internet, the Law and Today's Students Are Revolutionizing Expectations (Washington, D. C., 2004); http://www.NationalEdTechPlan.org.

16. http://www.e-society_org_mk-key Concepts.mht

17. (http://www.shef.ac.uk/infocommons/

18. (http://www.maya.com/infocommons/

19. Melanie Remy, Information Literacy: *The Information Commons Connection*, Teaching & Learning with Technology Conference: *Enhancing the Learning Experience* (September 17, 2004); http://www.usc.edu/libraries/locations/leavey/news/conference/presentations/presentations_9-17/USC_Remy.pdf

20. Darrel M. West, *Digital Government Technology and Public Sector Performance*, (Princeton University Press, Princeton and Oxford, 2005), pp. 13621. http://www.e-society_org_mk-key Concepts.mht

The Personal Digital Library (PDL)-based e-learning: Using the PDL as an e-learning support tool

Xiaozhao Deng [1] , Jianhai Ruan [2]

1 Faculty of computer and information science
Southwest University, Chongqing, China, 400715
dxz@swu.edu.cn

2 Library, Southwest University, Chongqing, China, 400715
rjh@swu.edu.cn

Abstract. The paper describes a support tool for learners engaged in e-learning, the Personal Digital Library (PDL). The characteristics and functionality of the PDL are presented. Suggested steps for constructing and managing a PDL are outlined and discussed briefly. The authors believe that the PDL as a support tool of e-learning will be important and essential in the future.

1 Introduction

The development and popularization of Internet is changing our society, everyday life, work and the environments of learning. With the change of the learning environments, there arises a new way of learning——e-learning, which is now making great changes in the contents and methods of learning, and will bring about a revolution of learning. E-learning covers a wide set of applications and processes such as Web-based learning, computer-based learning, virtual classrooms, and digital collaboration. It is composed of four elements:

① A learner,

②An instructor,

③ Technology, including a computer and,

④ Information or skills to be learned.

E-learning is important to learners because it offers a new way to learn at anywhere and at anytime. Learners can get abundant resources of learning content via Internet, intranet/extranet (LAN/WAN), and CD-ROM, etc. in the digital

Please use the following format when citing this chapter:

Deng, X., Ruan, J., 2007, in IFIP International Federation for Information Processing, Volume 252, Integration and Innovation Orient to E-Society Volume 2, eds. Wang, W., (Boston: Springer), pp. 549-555.

environment of e-learning. As a self-directed learning, e-learning gives prominence to self-determination of learners and realizes the individualization of learning. Learners can obtain the information needed as much as possible via Internet according to one's own learning characteristic and the content of e-learning in the process of e-learning. The information needed for e-learning may includes multimedia data or files, learning materials, electronic textbooks, courseware, application programs, E-mail, BBS (Bulletin Board System), Usenet, Mailing-list, etc., which form the resources bank of learning and will be increasing day by day on the computer's hard drive till it becomes necessary and exigent for learners to manage and utilize them for proper and efficient e-learning. To construct the personal digital library (PDL) is just the effective solution for managing and utilizing the e-learning resources in digital environment.

We propose that using the personal digital library as e-learning support tool based on our experimenting with building a PDL and testing the functionality of the PDL. The research aim is to provide a support tool of e-Learning by managing and utilizing the e-learning resources in the PDL.

2 The necessity of constructing the PDL in e-learning

The personal digital library (PDL) refers to the digital library in which the digital information resources for purpose of e-learning are gathered and stored by individuals. It is the structured information aggregation for private utilization. Compared with the public-oriented digital libraries which abound on Internet, the PDL shows many distinguishing characteristics:

① The pertinence of information collection;
② The substantiality of data storage;
③ The convenience of information utilization;
④ The facility of information management;
⑤ The economy of structuring and maintaining PDL.

PDL is the purification and concretion of information resources on Internet. Also, it is the result of treating learning resources with individualization and the Supplement of the public- oriented digital library and Internet-based learning [1].

As e-learning is in vogue nowadays, it is inevitable and essential to construct the PDL for the following reasons:

(1) E-learning is distributed learning and advocates the self-directed learning. Learners can download files via Internet and store learning resources on the individual hard drive independently according to their own needs. When the learning resources on the individual hard drive are too miscellaneous to manage and utilize for learning, effective ways to organize, treat, safeguard, maintain, and manage these learning resources will be expected.

(2) E-learning is the process of individualized learning. The individualization of learning requires that the learning resources on the hard drive being hold and managed in the learner's own way.

(3) The effective e-learning is actually the process in which the learner chooses, organizes, manages, stores, and utilizes information to change his knowledge

structure. Relatively stable learning environments and information management tactics are needed to meet the individual's demand and the goal of e-learning in the formation of e-learning modes.

(4) The environment of e-learning still has the following limitations that require learners to take effective measures and methods to deal with.

• Internet bandwidth may not be robust enough to support the desired level of multimedia. The delivery speed of data on Internet is too slow to meet the need of e-learning so that learners have to obtain learning materials by other ways. In order to benefit fully from the learning resources, it is necessary to bring the learning resources to the learners' hard drive.

• The learning resources on Internet are unstable because of the constant renewal of learning contents and sometimes the disappearance of some learning contents from the web-sites. Therefore, the learners have to store these important learning data on the individual hard drive for e-learning at any time.

There are a lot of e-learning resources on the Internet [2]. E-Learning is the Internet-based learning. Learners should use the Internet as school [3].

In consideration of the reasons discussed above, learners should construct the PDL and using the PDL as e-learning support tool.

3   The process of constructing and using the PDL

In general, there are following main steps to construct and use the personal digital library:

① To determine the goal of structuring the personal digital library according to learners' needs;

② To select the application software of constructing the personal digital library;

③ Using the selected application software to structure the personal digital library;

④ To collect and download the learning materials for the personal digital library;

⑤ To manage the learning materials in the personal digital library;

⑥ To export or to use the learning materials from the personal digital library for e-learning, etc.

The flow chart of constructing and using the personal digital library is illustrated as follows:

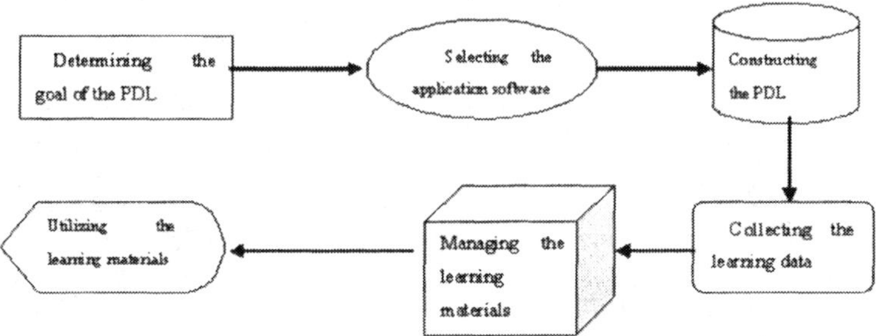

Fig. 1. The flow chart of constructing and using the Personal Digital Library

3.1   To determine the goal of structuring the PDL according to learners' needs

Each learner has his/her own goal of learning. At the first step, the learner should determine the goal of constructing the PDL according to his/her own needs. Generally speaking, the goal of constructing the PDL is to store, manage, and utilize the learning materials properly so as to improve the efficiency and the effect of e-learning.

3.2   To select the application software of structuring the PDL

The key of structuring the PDL is to select the proper application software. Different software has different functions. When learners select the application software to construct the PDL, they should consider the following parameter:
- Information organization methods
- Editing function
- File formats of supporting
- Import function
- Export function
- Searching function
- Supplementary functions, etc.

Generally speaking, the PDL that the learner constructs and uses for e-learning should possess the following functions:

• All learning contents can be organized and managed in the PDL regularly and scientifically.

• The PDL can organize and manage multi-format files.

The PDL can export the learning contents in the formats according to learners' needs.

• The PDL can keep the learning contents on individual hard drive steadily and substantially.

• The PDL should have the search function enabling learner to find out the learning materials conveniently and swiftly.

• The functions of the PDL should be powerful enough to meet the various needs of organizing and managing the learning contents for e-learning.

• The interface of the PDL should be friendly and the operation should be simple and easy.

• The maintenance and management of the PDL should be at low costs.

• The PDL can set up the security password, emphasize the protection of the reader's privacy, and the like.

We have evaluated and analyzed the full text database software suited for the PDL. Based on the evaluation and analysis of full text database software that can be used to construct the PDL, we consider that the application software suited for building the PDL including:

①Super-emanager V2.0 beta 5 (http:// emanager.yeah.net);

②Netcollect V2001 beta4 build1015 (http://www.cssc.com.cn/netcollect/);

③Textfriend V3.68 (http://ourbooks.yeah.com);

④eLib V2.01 (http://www.shijun.com);

⑤TRS personal information center V3.0 build1009;

⑥Tips manager V3.2.4.725 (http://tipsmanager.yeah.net);

⑦MYBASE V4.56 (http://junjiao.yeah.net);

⑧ASKSAM4 RTS DEMO V4.0 (http://www.asksam.com).

After the test, comparison and consideration of the application software, we prefer choosing Super-emanager V2.0 beta 5 to structure the PDL [4].

3.3   To construct the PDL

Taking Super-emanager V2.0 beta 5 as an example, the following is the concrete measure and method of structuring the personal digital library:

① Download, setup and run the Super-emanager V2.0 beta 5;

②Building the new database as "stack room" in Super-emanager V2.0 for storing learning contents.

3.4   To collect the learning contents for the PDL

There are two methods to collect the learning contents for the PDL.

① Importing files

Learners can import single file or multi-files to the PDL. The file formats that Super-emanager V2.0 supports to manage involve: zip, rar, mht, msg, eml, doc, htm, txt, rtf, mpg, mp3, mp2, dat, avi, wav, mid, mov, wma, wmv, asf, rm, ram, rpm, ra, swf, etc.

② Snatching homepages at Internet

Learners can snatch homepages on Internet by hitting the right- button of mouse on browser. Super-emanager V2.0 will save the selected homepage in the special files.

3.5   To manage the learning contents in the PDL

It is necessary to manage the learning materials in the PDL after the PDL is structured. The management of learning materials in the PDL embraces:
① To delete, rename, move, open and copy a file.
② To undelete the deleted file.
③ To set up the security password for system or for important files
④ To search and find the file that is needed by learners swiftly. Super-emanager V2.0 can do the full-text retrieval in the files of HTML and TXT.
⑤ To backup important learning materials.

3.6   To export and use the learning materials from the PDL

There are many manners to export the learning materials from the PDL.
① Exporting the learning materials in the form of "data package".

Super-emanager V2.0 can export the learning materials in the formats such as zip, mht, dex, chm, and xml. The learner can copy the exported file from one disk to another, or exchange the learning materials in the exported formats with other learners by E-mail.
② Exporting the learning materials in the form of "catalogue"

Super-emanager V2.0 can export the learning materials in the form of "catalogue". That is to say, it can export the selected learning materials to the special disk or special path in the original structure in the PDL.

After finishing the process above, the learner can construct and use the PDL for e-learning.

4   The functions of the PDL in e-learning

The PDL can play a heavy role in e-learning. Its advantages in e-learning are demonstrated as follows:

• The PDL can realize the integration of learning contents. The PDL is the data repository of various types of learning materials such as texts, homepages, e-books, e-journals, E-mail, software, pictures, Video files, audio files, and the files produced by learners themselves, etc. Based on the evaluation and test of software suited for building the Personal Digital Library, we find that the learning materials can be organized and managed in the PDL regularly and scientifically. The PDL can empower the organization and management of learning contents, enable learners to store and retrieve information and organize data pertinent to the focused topics. Besides, it can be used to improve the learning environment. In the PDL, information is stored on learners' machines rather than a central file server. The PDL could have a great impact on the way learners retrieve and act on information.

• The PDL can offer an effective condition and environment of e-learning for learners to obtain the strong support of learning contents in it conveniently. The learning contents in the PDL can be used repeatedly and the PDL provides links to other learning resources makes learners more comfortable and more efficient in e-learning. With its advantages set off by the PDL, e-learning can arouse learners' enthusiasm of learning, and will exert a profound influence on learners' personality and their capability of learning as well.

The research works of using the PDL as e-learning support tool have been done by researchers. The researcher has demonstrated that the usage the Full-text Searching function of the PDL system to implement the idea of "Learning words with a large amount of texts" [5]. It is identified that the PDL-based learning is important and essential. As a support tool of e-learning, the PDL can aid learning.

5   Conclusion

E-learning will be the mainstream of learning in the 21st century. The PDL will be the principal mode for learner to organize and manage information resources. As an e-learning support tool, the PDL provides a foundation for learner to build a more comfortable e-learning environment of the future. The PDL-based learning will be the next hot trend of e-learning, and will accelerate the pace of e-learning technology advances. The influence of the PDL will reach far beyond learners.

References

1. Chen, GZ. Ruan, JH & Zang, GQ, "On the Personal Digital Library", *Journal of Library Science in China*, 3, 34-38 (2002). (In Chinese)

2. E-learning resources on the Internet. (April 16, 2007) http://ekb.mwr.biz/eresources.htm.

3. J.H. Ruan & X.Z. Deng, "The Internet-Based Education: Using the Internet as School", *Global Education on the Net: Proceedings of ICCE'98 Vol.2. China High-Education Press, Springer -Verlag.* 434-437 (1998). (In English)

4. G.Q. Zang, "Evaluation and Analysis of Full Text Database Software Suited for Building Personal Digital Library", *Journal of the china society for scientific and technical information*, 1, 59-64 (2003). (In Chinese)

5. F.C. Kuo, "Learning Words with Personal Digital Library"(March 26, 2007) http://www.cis.scu.edu.tw/~kuo/pub-paper/p97-2.htm

Research on Methods of Processing Transit IC Card Information and Constructing Transit OD Matrix

Xiuhua Han[1], Jin Li[1], and Han Peng[2]

1 Transportation School, Jillin University, 5988 Renmin Street, Changchun, China, 130022, hxh1952@163.com; li_jin@jlu.edu.cn

2 North China Institute of Water Conservancy and Hydroelectric Power, 36 Beihuan Road, Zhengzhou, China, 450011, penghan20@yahoo.com.cn

Abstract. Transit OD matrix is of vital importance when planning urban transit system. Traditional transit OD matrix constructing method needs a large range of spot check survey. It is expensive and needs long cycle time to process information. Recently transit IC card charging systems have been widely applied in big cities. Being processed reasonably, transit passenger information stored in IC card database can turn into information resource. It will reduce survey cost a lot. The concept of transit trip chain is put forward in this paper. According to the characteristics of closed transit trip chain, it discusses how to process IC card information and construct transit OD matrix. It also points out that urban transit information platform and data warehouse should be constructed, and how to integrate IC card information.

1 Introduction

Developing urban transit is of vital importance in releasing urban congestion. Transit preference rule is universally acknowledged by various urban managing sectors. Recently, information technology is widely applied in urban transit field. Transit IC card charging systems are adopted in many cities. As aiming at charging and reckoning statistics information, transit IC card information management system is typically designed for information storing and processing, so lots of transit passenger flow and its space-time distributing information in database is deposited and cannot be applied reasonably.

Transit passenger flow OD（Origin-Destination）matrix is an important basis of planning urban transit system[1]. Traditional method of constructing OD matrix needs a large range of passenger trip spot check survey or transit passenger flow survey to achieve relative basic data. It requires a lot of manpower and expenditure.

Please use the following format when citing this chapter:

Han, X., Li, J., Peng, H., 2007, in IFIP International Federation for Information Processing, Volume 252, Integration and Innovation Orient to E-Society Volume 2, eds. Wang, W., (Boston: Springer), pp. 556-564.

The data processing needs heavy workload and long time. It is costliness to achieve data. So this kind of survey is merely done once after several years.

Nowadays, transit IC card is applied in various big cities. The cardholder percentage of office worker and student group is more than 90%. It is of practical sense to plan dynamic transit system, to improve quality of transit operating scheme , to reduce correlative survey cost by proper processing urban transit IC card information and to accumulate available transit passenger trip information.

2   Analyzing Transit IC Card Data

2.1   Time Distributing of Resident Transit trip

Transit passenger distributing is of obvious asymmetry. Hereinto passenger flow rhythm taking a day or a week as a cycle is most obvious. Thus passenger flow in holidays differentiates from that in workdays. Properly processing transit IC card data, we can find card-holders trip time distributing rule during transit operating period[2]. Transit trip time distributing status of all card-holders in a workday is illustrated in Figure 1. Card-holder trip periods distributing status of Changchun transit line 306 is illustrated in figure 2.

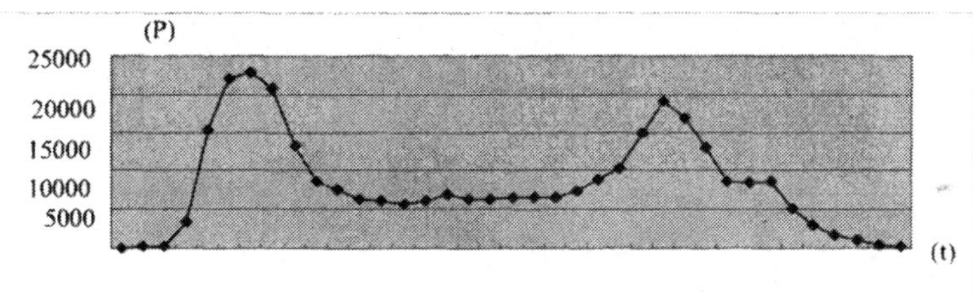

Fig. 1. Changchun Card-holder Trip Periods Distributing Status in a Whole Day

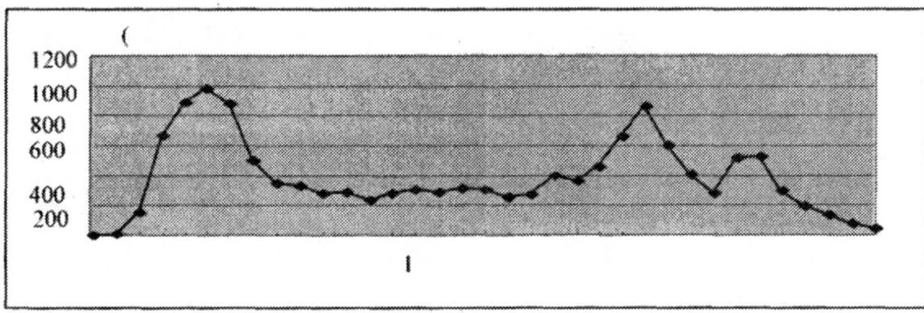

Fig. 2. Card-holder Trip Periods Distributing Status of Changchun Bus Line 306

The figures illustrate that transit passenger flow has obvious peak periods in the morning and evening. Passenger distributing is more concentrated in morning peak period. Evening peak period occurs during 16: 00 to 18: 00. It is as well off duty passenger rush hour. There is a sub peak period as to 19: 00, during which students leave school and people in service industry ring out to take bus. Transit passenger flow in rush hour accounts for a higher percentage in a whole day. The card-holder percentage during 6: 30 to 8: 30 accounts for 26% in whole day; the percentage of evening rush hour from 16: 00 to 18: 00 accounts for about 21%。

Since 2007, Changchun everyday card-scanning amount is as to 460 thousand person-time, accounting for about 38% of 1300 thousand person-time of all-day transit passenger flow. Morning and evening rush hours are card-holder centralized periods. The percentage of the periods ought to be higher than this value. According to the analysis of transit passenger spot check, the characteristics of card-holders and all passengers during transit trip periods are by and large consistent. Taking IC card data as swatch, the analysis can reflect the general characteristics of urban transit passenger flow time distributing.

2.2   Analyzing Transit IC Card Database Structure

Database structure of transit IC card charging system can be divided into two categories. One is when transit line is long and it is charged regarding various sections, a passenger scans his card severally when he gets into and gets off the bus to ensure passenger actual trip section and deduct the corresponding fare from IC card. The attributes of tuple in database table include passenger IC card number, line number, bus number, consuming date, stops and the time of getting on and off as well. Another category is when it uses a single fare in the whole journey, passenger scans IC card only when he gets into bus. Thus the tuple in database table doesn't include the attribute of getting off time. Beijing transit IC card system involves both circumstances. The database structure of transit IC card in many cities such as Changchun falls into the second category, the main attributes of tuple in database table are illustrated in Table 1.

Table 1. Status quo IC Card Database Structure

IC card NO.	Card-scanning time	line No.	Bus No.
249987	15:27:09	226	40445
394562	15:31:13	226	40445
179879	15:34:26	226	40445
394562	15:31:13	226	40445
......	......	......	......

Among the information needed to construct transit OD matrix, passenger ride OD information ought to include "getting into bus time", "getting off time", "stop of getting on", "stop of getting off", etc. But information such as stop of getting on and off is lack in today's most databases. In many cities where single fare is used in whole journey, card-scanning time of getting on is input in transit IC card database, whereas getting off time is lack, so it is very difficult to deduce the corresponding stops.

Moreover, information of transit line, relevant stops and transit scheduling of various lines is as well demanded to construct transit OD matrix.

2.3   Analyzing Transit Trip Chain of IC Card-holder

The transit trip chain here means the transit trip route originated from a passenger's first stop of getting on of his first trip, to the stop of getting off of his last trip in a day. Three factors of stop, time and route are encompassed in transit trip chain.

Transit passengers of morning and evening rush hours are mainly office workers and students. It can be generally called work trip. Card-holders account for a high percentage of these passengers. In workdays, the time and route of getting on is of obvious rule and symmetry. Thus the transit trip chain is simple and close. The getting on stop of first transit trip is the getting off stop of ultimate transit trip.

Close transit trip chains can be divided into following categories.

(1)invariable round trip chain

There is a unique through transit line between trip origin and destination. The transit stops are invariable. Nothing but two stops of same line are involved in a trip chain. Most passenger round trips fall into the simplest mode of transit trip chain.

(2)round trip chain of a choice of lines

There are at least two transit lines of same direction between trip origin and destination. Out and home trip are of different lines. But the stops of getting on and off are invariable. Nothing but two stops is as well involved in a trip chain.

(3)trip chain including midway transfer

There is not through lines between trip origin and destination. One or more midway transfer are demanded. At least 5 stops are involved in a round trip chain. The sections of the transit trip chain can be divided into two categories, i.e., invariable line and lines of choice. The midway transfer stops can be different. Transit trips in non-rush hours are typically occasional trips, such as trips for shopping, medical care as well.

Table 2 shows part of tuple in database table of card-scanning ranking by card number and card-scanning time in Changchun Transit IC Card Database.

Table 2. IC Card Record Ranking by Card Number and Time

Card number	Time	Route No.	Bus No.
1459	07:47:55	10	60017
1459	17:01:22	10	60007
21586	05:57:42	62	60017
21586	16:45:54	362	60071
312656	06:05:30	3	50008
312656	06:47:30	364	250009
312656	16:57:06	364	251020
312656	17:43:27	3	50022

3   Constructing Methods of Transits O-D Matrix

3.1   Determining Transit trip OD

Based on the above analysis, when transit O-D matrix is constructed, the key information is O-D stops of each trip, which is absent in IC card database. It should be estimated by characteristics of transit trip chain.

(1) In fixed line round trip chain and optional-route round trip chain table, only card-scanning time information of getting on is involved. Combined with transit schedules, direction and getting on stop can be inferred. As the transit chain is closed, the return stop of getting on is the foregoing stop of getting off. So judging stop of getting on of each record is all right.

(2) Midway-transfer transit trip chain is a little complex. But it is generally considered that the stop of getting off before transfer and the stop of getting on after transfer are of the same. Similarly, determining stop of getting on when card-scanning is enough. Constructing transit OD matrix need nothing but O-D stop information of each trip. Midway transfer can be neglected. Thus transfer information is meaningful to planning of transit transfer hub.

From the above discussion, because of the characteristics of closed transit trip chain, in order to construct OD matrix structure, we can determine the stop of getting off, depending on information of getting on stop of each trip.

3.2   Coordinating and Sorting Record

The original card-scanning record must be coordinated and sorted, which are usually collected by IC card management center, following charge statistics and reckoning. Main steps are as follows:

(1) Transmit all the intraday data into a central database, rank up and index them according to IC card number;

(2) Add a attribute "trip classification," to Database structure setting conditions to screen IC card records being ordered. According to the categories of transit trip chain, the field is given four different category values. Type 4 is the "other" category, which beyond the foregoing categories;

(3) Establish transit trip chain category database table. There is null attribute in the table, such as stops of getting on and get off, moving direction and so on. According to category number, records will be respectively to transmit into database tables of different types;

(4) Link category database tables to various vehicle Schedules in the same day, judge the trip direction and stop site of same vehicle number when cards are scanned. Fill its code into air field as illustrated by Table 3;

(5) After stops are determined, transmit the major fields into IC card historical database to preserve. The structure is shown by table 4.

Computerized management of Transit enterprise's vehicle scheduling information is very important. Now many urban transit enterprises have not done this, which causes difficulties to IC card data comprehensive utilization of.

Table 3. Transit Chain Categories Database Table

Card No.	Date	Route	Vehicle No.	Time	Direction	Get on Stop	Get off Stop	Trip Type
390712	20070423	361	020287	07:05:39	1	36103	36108	1
390712	20070423	361	020305	18:16:05	2	36108	36103	1
390718	20070423	306	040083	07:13:25	2	30601	30607	1
390718	20070423	306	040076	17:21:42	1	30607	30601	1

Table 4. IC Card Historical Information Database Table

Card No.	Date	Route	Time	Get on Stop	Get off Stop	Trip Type
390718	20070423	306	07:13:25	30601	30607	1
390718	20070423	306	17:21:42	30607	30601	1

3.3   Calibrating Vehicle Schedules

In bus management and operation, travel Schedules is the important basis for vehicle operation .It provides a vehicle for arrival time and leaving time, when it arrived at the flow along the site in each one-way trip and turnover trip. Vehicle Schedules normally are demarcated by different season, time, sections and the traffic situation around, and are tested by the vehicles actual operation. Nowadays urban traffic conditions are complicated, which disturb buses' running greatly. When traffic Schedules convicted passengers disembark stop, it is difficult to get totally accurate matching time, which is a fuzzy relationship. Certain time warp is allowed.

Fuzzy set is described by the membership function. Generally speaking, bus sends up at origin station. The time arrived at the site and stopping time are random variables. In order to simplify data processing, in terms of different directions and sections, on the basis of a detailed traffic Schedules calibration, membership function of each route can be established for operation time in peak and non-peak hour.

Trapezoidal curve can be used to express "stop" and "trip time" fuzzy relationship. Trapezoidal membership function allows a certain time range, which is vehicles arrival time and leaving time, to ensure the corresponding relation of card-scanning time and stop of getting on, shown in Figure 3. t_n means the time when a bus arrive at stop n , AB means stopping time, Some passengers might scan cards after drive, function is the non-isosceles trapezoid. At card-scanning moment fall on CD section, stop n-1 can be determined as the stop of getting on.

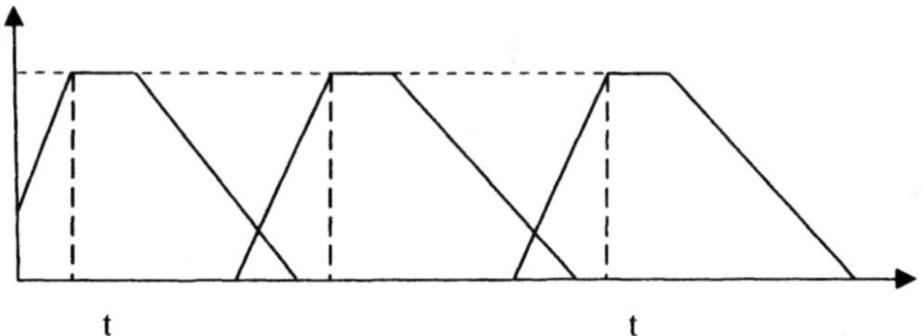

Fig. 3. Trapeziform curve of subjection degree function

3.4   Constructing Transit OD Matrix

(1)Line OD matrix

According to stop information of getting on and off of IC card record, passenger flow matrix of various transit stops OD matrix can be constructed of any transit line of whole day or different time periods. Take stops code of the transit line as "origin line" and "destination row". Take the line number as key character. Read the record in turn which takes in the same day's database table. Accumulates 1 in the corresponding matrix form, then the line OD matrix is generated. Line OD matrix may substitute for traditional passenger flow investigation. It can provide detailed passenger flow information at various stops along the route every day, to help schedule department reasonably disposition transportation resources.

(2) Net OD matrix

Net OD matrix involves all urban transit lines, the matrix dimension and all urban transit stops are of the same. The generating process is: The trip chain table of category 1 and 2 generates each line and row of OD matrix separately; for records of category 3, neglect the midway transfer process. Generate OD matrix between stops of various transit line. Net OD matrix is sum of the three categories, which can be generated according to the record of the entire day or various time periods.

The dimension of Net OD matrix is too large. The same stop of various lines uses same identical code. It can effectively reduce the dimension. Based on net OD matrix, the urban area transit OD matrix can be generated

(3) Urban area transit OD matrix

The urban area transit OD matrix takes inhabitant plot as trip OD points. From urban territory view, it can provide inhabitant transit trip information for transit planning and urban comprehensive transportation planning. For IC card information takes transit stops as trip OD, it is recommended that trip plot division method should be combined with kinds-gathering method on proximate stops by distance. Figure 4 illustrates the trip plot gravity center, merging 1,700 transit stops in Changchun. Based on trip plot, urban area transit OD matrix can be generated by merging transit net stops OD matrix.

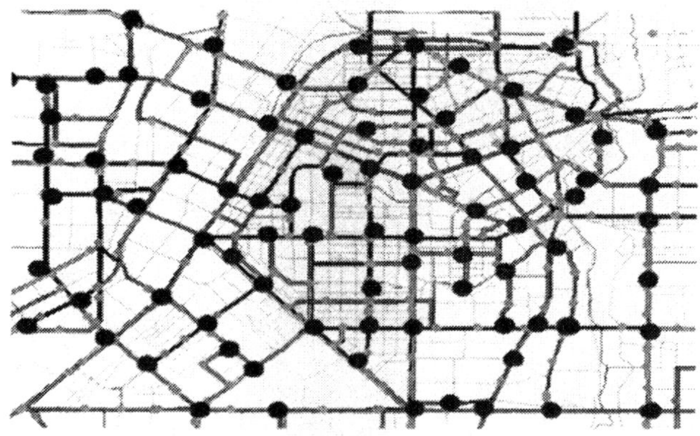

Fig. 4. gravity center sketch map after merging trip plots

4   Conclusions

It systematically researches on processing method and comprehensive application of transit IC card information. The concept of transit trip chain is proposed. Methods of information processing and transit OD matrix constructing are discussed, depending on existing IC card database structure. Main conclusions as follows:

(1)Transit trip time distribution characteristics of card holders and all passengers by spot checking are basically consistent. Taking IC card data as sample, we can analyze the overall time distribution characteristics, which can reflect to urban transit passenger flow.

(2) It introduces the concept of transit trip chain. The enclosed trip chain can be constructed according to the recording characteristics of card holder. We could only judge passengers' getting on stops to simplify IC card information processing.

(3)Use IC card information to structure public transportation OD matrix may save the cost of massive passenger flows investigation, and the data is reliable, timeliness. Transit line OD matrix can provide the real-time information for daily transit operation scheduling. The urban district public transportation OD matrix may provides the dynamic information for the usual public transportation line adjustment and for the regular public transportation system plan.

The current various urban transit IC card database is generally of different systems, which is viewed as information isolated island. Massive data leave unused. It cannot apply effectively in transit enterprise operation scheduling and transit planning, which means enormous waste of information resource. We should unify regular and rail transit to build urban transit information platform, and integrate transit IC card information with transit enterprise operation management information, the transit inquiry information, urban GIS information and the transit vehicles GPS information and so on, to construct transit data warehouse[3], to realize correlation information fusion, effectively utilize comprehensive IC card information.

References

1. W. Wang, X.M. Yang and X.W. Chen, *Planning Methods and Management Technologies of Urban Transit System*, Science Publication, 2002, p. 62.
2. F.M. Shi, "Research on Constructing Methods of Transit OD Matrix Based on IC Card Data", *Master's degree dissertation of Jilin University*, 2004, p. 15.
3. X. Dai, X.W. Chen and W.Y. Li, "Study of Data Mining Technique for Bus Intelligent Card Data Processing", *Computer and Communications*. 24(1), 40-42 (2006).

Research on Implementation of E-Government Integrated Information Services

Xuedong Wang[1], Xianli Shang[2], Kun Fan[3]

1 Department of Information Management, Hua Zhong Normal
University, 430079, Wuhan,China
wxd54@21cn.com
2 Department of Information Management, Hua Zhong Normal
University, 430079, Wuhan,China
Shangli3618@163.com
3 Department of Information Management, Hua Zhong Normal
University, 430079, Wuhan,China
Fankun389@163.com

Abstract. In order to meet the needs of developing E-government, E-government integrated information services are proposed in this paper. First, we define E-government integrated information services. Second, we explore E-government integrated information service patterns. Third, we construct an E-government integrated information service platform. Finally, we give some suggestions on developing E-government integrated information services. This paper enriches the notion of E-government integrated information services, improves E-government information services and provides a practical solution for government applications.

1 Introduction

In the five applications (E-commerce, E-government, Distance education, Telemedicine, E-entertainment) of "information superhighway", "E-government" was ranked number one. Development of E-government accelerates a major transition of government functions from management to services; however, one crucial thing is to provide efficient services. Hans Jochen Scholl indicated that, E-government is government specific in its various formats of government-to-citizen, government-to-business, government-to-government, and internal effectiveness and efficiency. And E-government provides citizens, businesses, and other government agencies with direct, every time access to government resources and services. [1] Citizens and

Please use the following format when citing this chapter:

Wang, X., Shang, X., Fan, K., 2007, in IFIP International Federation for Information Processing, Volume 252, Integration and Innovation Orient to E-Society Volume 2, eds. Wang, W., (Boston: Springer), pp. 565-573.

businesses alike face significant obstacles during interactions with public administrations and governments. However, the trends toward delivery of E-government information services and development of integrated customer-oriented administrative service offerings represent efforts to alleviate these problems. [2, 3] In the implementation of E-government applications, governments are seeking efficiency, effectiveness, and data quality improvement gains. [4] The public sector is one of the most primitive and predominant service domains in any community, with a wide array of governmental services catering to all aspects of society and economy. [5]

With the development of information technology "integration" is widely applied. In system integrations, integrations have brought people to a common level of understanding, namely system optimization through integrating subsystems or elements. [6] In the management, people air their views of integrations; however, they all emphasize transformations from combinations to integrations. [7] In the information services, integrations mean to promote information service effects. To a great extent E-government information services are public services, therefore, there are some obstacles, i.e. "information barriers", "information system isomerism", low standardization levels. Actually, it makes a requirement of integrated information services, and at the same time flings down new challenges to integrated information services.

2   The definition of E-government Integrated Information Services

In academic circles some thought that integrations are a process, which aim at optimum system state through integrating the elements. Some thought that integrations are a target. Directed at the particular target it organizes and manages information, and integrates information. By different standards integrations of information services are classified into the following five categories:

① Corresponding to object scopes it includes information integrations, technology integrations, application integrations, management integrations, staff integrations and institution integrations;

②Corresponding to degrees of optimization it includes contact integrations, joint integrations, communication integrations, and shared integrations;

③Corresponding to degrees of affinity it includes collaboration integrations, coordination integrations and harmony integrations;

④Corresponding to integration properties it includes logical integrations and physical integrations;

⑤Corresponding to priorities of the task it includes information integrations, process integrations and institution integrations.

E-government integrated information services we introduced are users-oriented information services, and they are integrations of resources, platforms and services according to integrated information service patterns. Therefore, E-government integrated information services are an entire and dynamic process, which is based on classifications and integrations of information resources, aims at the needs of specific users or organizations, and is realized by combinations of service integrations, cooperations, technologies integrations. And users obtain "one-stop" information services, that is, users can access information resources of all levels of governments from one government web. The characteristics of E-government integrated information services are as following:

①Integrations. It means not only integrations of information resources, but also integrations of all levels of E-government platforms, so that it forms into a structured, coordinated and complementary whole, and performs the overall function of E-government.

② Cooperations. E-government integrated information services rely on cooperations, i.e. standard cooperations, information integration cooperations, and platform cooperations.

③Dynamics. E-government information services are constantly developing and changing. Therefore, information resources, government system integrations, etc., are increasingly improving with changes of goals and external environments.

④Relative independences. E-government integrated information services require interactivities among all levels of government platforms; however, all levels of E-government platforms have relative independences to ensure safeties, flexibilities and personalities.

⑤ "one stop " services. Based on full integrations, users can access all government information through an interface, and it exemplifies the concept that governments center on users.

3   Construction of E-government Integrated Information Service Patterns

E-government information services include a wide range of contents, including almost all traditional government services. According to international E-government development and E-government practices in our country, E-government information services are divided into the following six patterns: governments and governments-oriented information services, internal affairs of a government-oriented information services, rural-oriented information services, education-oriented information services, business-oriented information services, and public-oriented information services. The six patterns embody user-oriented features fully, however, all the service patterns are not isolated, and they are associated, which is shown in **Fig. 1.**

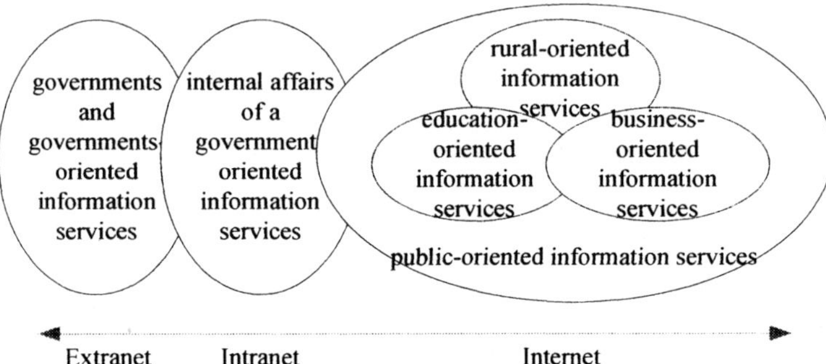

Fig. 1. E-government integrated information service patterns and relations

3.1   Governments and Governments-oriented Information Services

This pattern focuses on governments, and links up higher and lower governments, which provides office work and professional services. Specifically, the work and services include three aspects. First, it collects and processes requisite national and local information, i.e. population information, geographic information, and resources information. Second, it collects and processes information that is required in affairs among governments, i.e. planned management, economic management, socio-economic statistics, and national security. Third, it provides communication systems, which deal with affairs among governments, i.e. announcements in an emergency, measures in an emergency, etc.

3.2   Internal Affairs of a Government-oriented Information Services

Internal affairs of a government, namely, internal information of a government, is occult information, which is required in internal management or internal affairs, is used to adopt important decisions, or is related to classified documents. Such information is only shared in internal systems or Intranet.

3.3   Rural-oriented Information Services

The governments should guide and promote agricultural information services actively. On the one hand, they integrate agricultural information resources, establish and improve agricultural information services; on the other hand, they optimize distribution of resources and establish sharing mechanisms. While they provide guidance information for farmers, they coordinate operations of all information service providers, and provide "one stop" service, namely, policies, science, and market information, for farmers, and realize industrialization and socialization of agricultural information services. [8]

3.4   Education-oriented Information Services

Education informationization is an important part of government information services. Sharing knowledge resources, Network education and tele-education are important ways to raise the quality of people, and they are also foundations to construct knowledge-based society, learning society and innovation-oriented country.

3.5   Business-oriented Information Services

Enterprises are an important component in the national economy, and are important service target for governments. Governments increase working efficiency, provide services for enterprises fast, lighten the burden on enterprises and promote enterprise development through using information technology and streamlining management business processes. In 2005 Chinese governments at all levels applied macro-control, market supervision and management means, achieved remarkable success in administrative justice, administrative approval, taxation, and special funds control, and created good market conditions for the development of enterprises and improved the quality and efficiency of services.

3.6   Public-oriented Information Services

It refers to making government affairs public, that is, through portal website governments provide relevant policies and regulations, latest advances of government affairs, industry development, economic development, information related to people's livelihood, and so on.

4   Construction of E-government Integrated Information Service Platform

E-government integrated information service platform, from a structural perspective, is a platform integrated by interface structures, technical architectures, logic structures, organizational structures and standards, and it can be described by "portal website and database"; from a specific content perspective, it is a comprehensive information service platform including agriculture, commerce, government, education and scientific research and the public. It mainly provides user-oriented information services; and from a social benefit perspective, it is the key to realize information integrations. It raises office efficiency, accelerates economic, cultural and technological development, and improves efficiency of various sectors.

Based on E-government integrated information service patterns, we can see that different users need different information services. And the core is integrations in construction of E-government integrated information service platform, namely, it constructs information service platform by integrating resources, technologies and services. And the support of E-government integrated information service platform is illustrated in Fig.2. To some extent resource integrations depend on resource acquisitions. However, various governments have their own E-government system, and they provide information services independently. So we need use technology integrations to realize government resource exchanges. Service integrations are that, governments provide different service platforms according to E-government integrated information service patterns. Governments deal with internal affairs through Intranet, serve the public through Internet, and communicate with other governments through Extranet.

Service integrations	Network service platform integrated by Intranet, Extranet, Internet	E-government standard and security system
Technology integrations	Data mining, multi-data source integration, Web intelligent management technology, heterogeneous web platform exchange technology and isomeric web management technology	
Resource integrations	Data integration layer: data conversions, extraction, integration, filtering, classification, clustering, categorization Resource layer: government data center, namely, data warehouse	

Fig.2. Support of E-government integrated information service platform

5   Suggestions on Developing E-government Integrated Information Services

5.1   Promote Integration Capabilities of E-government Information Services through Knowledge Management

Information is the raw material of knowledge, and knowledge is the reorganization and distillation. Only through identification, analysis, synthesis, extraction, etc. information is converted into knowledge. Through accelerating the flow of knowledge by use of networks and information technologies we actualize the true value of information resources. And this process is knowledge management. E-government should adopt knowledge management to identify key information, extract and mine information, and form special knowledge to support corresponding information services in E-government.

5.2 Unify E-government Standards and Form a Unified Platform for Information Announcements

Standardization is groundwork in E-government constructions, is a premise that E-government system realizes sharing information, cooperations and interactions, and information security, but also is a guarantee to integrate E-government information. China National Committee of Standardization for E-government has produced E-government Standardization Guide, Six E-government Standards, and E-government References, however, these standards and references are not specific enough. We should unify E-government infrastructure components, and then on this basis, develop coordinated government system platforms, information announcement platforms, workflow platforms and data exchange platforms. In this way, we will not have any difficulties in sharing information resources. Also, with unified standards, E-government will break the isolated islands of information, so that the free flow of information is available to form a complete information flow.

5.3 Promote Information Process Reengineering (IPR) in E-government

Traditional E-government information process design is grounded on division of functions and hierarchical theory, and the result is dispersed, clumsy, closed and unpowered E-government information process. So, E-government information resources can not flow freely, and E-government information services are not achieved effectively. Therefore, IPR is needed. In order to achieve complete information processes and integrated information services, we should promote IPR and integrate information exchange models.

5.4 Establish Mechanisms of Open and Shared Government Information Resources

In a free market economy, governments have been transformed from economy superintendents into economy servers. Under the circumstances, non-confidential information governments grasp should be open to the public and shared with the public without pay. Therefore, we should break monopoly of governments at all levels on information resources, vigorously release and use government information resources, and strengthen the exploitation and utilization of public information resources, market information resources and other areas of information resources. Specific practices can be learnt from other countries, or we can formulate laws and regulations to ensure open and shared government information resources.

5.5   Adopt Personalized Information Services

E-government personalized information services mean that governments take the initiative in providing information services, which is based on users' interest. While governments choose content and format of information announcements, they should consider the related information users. First, governments analyze and classify information users to identify different service groups, such as businessmen, farmers, intellectuals, etc, and then summarize the characteristics of various service groups, i.e. knowledge structures, psychological orientations, historical experiences and behavior characteristics. Based on this, governments expand personalized information services to meet the needs of different users.

5.6   Foster a Good and Healthy Service Concept——"Customer Relationship Management" (CRM)

CRM is an important means for enterprises to impress customers and maintain customer loyalty. By nature, CRM is a new service concept, which adapts to knowledge economy and information social, and it is a new management mechanism to provide quality services for customers. The core of "new public administration" theory is to reform governments by "enterprise managerial spirit", and its purpose is to pursue "economy, efficiency, and effectiveness", namely, the goal of 3E. In this circumstance, administrative scholars introduce CRM into government management, and they compare service objects to customers and compare governments to product or service suppliers. They believe that governments should proceed from the needs of customers, and that customer satisfaction is a measure of public services. The connotation of E-government and the concept of CRM have the same point. They both emphasize services. In E-government, CRM is realized through self-service portal web. So it is required to understand the needs of users, to establish efficient service standards, and to set up a winning service team, and they provide value-added services through inspecting, monitoring, feed backing and improving services.

6   Conclusion

Development of E-government has accelerates a major transition of government functions from management to services. However, wide and relatively centralized users, extensive content, etc. are characteristics of E-government. Therefore, in order to provide efficient services, integrations are very crucial. In this paper, we adopt one key perspective based on integrations. And according to E-government information service patterns, they are integrations of resources, platforms and services. According to international E-government development and E-government practices in our country, we proposed six E-government information service patterns. Each pattern faces specific users. We also construct an integrated information service platform from the perspective of services, technologies and resources. Finally, we give some suggestions on developing E-government integrated information services.

However, there are many issues and challenges in implementation of E-government integrated information services that need to be further addressed, including information gulf issues among governments, security problems, individual privacy and data and technology standardization, etc., which is included in our future work.

References

1. Hans Jochen Scholl, "Electronic government: Information management capacity, organizational capabilities, and the sourcing mix", *Government Information Quarterly* 23 (2006) 73-96.
2. Http://www.worldbank.org/publicsector/egov/definition.htm (2005-06-15)
3. M. Sprecher, "Racing to e-Government: Using the Internet for citizen service delivery", *Government Finance Review* (2000) 21-22.
4. J. N. Danziger and K. V. Andersen, "Impacts of IT on politics and the public sector", Methodological, epistemological, and substantive evidence from the "Golden Age" of transformation, *International Journal of Public Administration* (2002) 591-627.
5. L. P. Shan, C. W. Tan and E.T.K. Lim, "Customer relationship management (CRM) in E-government: a relational perspective", *Decision Support Systems* (2006) 237-250.
6. F. Wei, "Commentary on integrated information services and comprehensive information integration", *Gansu Science and Technology* (2002) 22-24.
7. Q. Bi and H. Y. Shi, "Commentary on web information integrated services", *Intelligence Theory and Practice* (2004)20-24.
8. F. Li and D.Wang, "Commentary on farmers-oriented market information services", *JiangXi Library Journal* (2004) 49-51.
9. J. C. Zhou and J. Gao, "E-government Information Resources Integration Based on Knowledge Management", *Information Science* (2006) 1657-1661.

The E-learning system used in the civil servants' job-training

Rui Yang, Jianhai Ruan

College of Computer & Information Science ,Southwest University,
Tian Shengqiao Road 2, Chongqing 400715, P.R.of China
Email:yr1026@163.com
Email: rjh@swu.edu.cn

Abstract. The Chinese government is pursuing e-learning policies which makes job-training with a knowledge-based society. To explain more fully the important role of the e-learning environment, this article undertakes some typical examples of the governments' job-training under e-learning environment. The main problems in servants' job-training in China are the low quantity in the servants' training, short of restriction, the uniform manner in the training and less fairness and availability of opportunities for educational training. In order to develop the e-learning system, the civil servant's job-training policies are provided and the measures of the effective e-learning system are designed.

1 Introduction

In the knowledge-based society, the sharing and expansion of knowledge and information are the key factors for social development. Many nations around the world have created key policies for developing e-learning police; e-learning has emerged as a new alternative in job-training. The initiative to develop civil servants through e-learning has been widely adapted by the China government as e-learning overcome the limits of time and space and contributes to knowledge expansion through interaction.

Of all the educational technologies that have exhibited great potential, e-learning appears to be the most promising. Essentially, the e-learning system predominantly provides information, not instruction or other pedagogical supports for learning [1, 2]. What is e-learning? E-learning can be defined as the most recent evolution for distance learning [3]. In its broadest definition, e-learning includes instruction delivered via all electronic media, including the Internets, intranets, extranets, satellite broadcasts, audio/video tapes, interactive TV, and CD-ROM[4]. E-learning has been introduced into governments and other public sectors as a new learning and training mode in many countries and regions.

2   Execution and background of e-learning in China

The conception of "e-learning" was introduced into China only several years. There are few successful examples for the e-learning in China, except the multinationals which full of experience on e-learning. In a word, there is a big development potential in our home market, but it is still a long way to go. As the pioneer of the modernization, the government should create a better environment for the e-learning technology.

E-learning is a very useful way for job-training especially the basic training. Now many governments establish government universities on line. For instance the Shanghai official on-line(http://www.shgb.gov.cn/); and the e-learning project of Yunnan province. After fulfilling the e-learning of e-government in Yunnan, the system will give the training for civil servants from 53 departments. The main technologies of the system are Linux or Unix/windows server, java language; and the databases are oracle or SQL-server.

There are some other cases of the civil servants' job-trainings under the online environments in China:
- China e-government
  (http://www.e-gov.org.cn/peixun/) It provides some information about the job-training. This isn't a real e-learning, though it also lists some course such as spoken-English training, java script and senior system engineer, etc...
- Party school of the central committee of the Party
  (http://www.ccps.gov.cn/index.jsp)The web-learning provide the contents as follow: Graduate student education, distance education, scientific research of the party school, informatization , campus management
- The servants' on-line learning of Ningbo
  (http://www.nbstudy.gov.cn/)The main job-training settings of this e-learning environment are required courses, elective courses, public speech and self tests. All the servants need a learning ID and password to enter in.

3   The underutilization of the e-learning used in the governmental job-training

Internet communication training has had a positive influence in promoting the growth of e-learning within civil servants. This development can also be evaluated as an important result of the Internet communication training policy. However, despite the notable success in promoting government e-learning, there are still problems within the existing system that have to be addressed. These problems within government e-learning, however, cannot be said to originate in the Internet communication training system itself. Rather, the problems seem to lie in the fact that no systematic and varied efforts have been made to overcome and compensate for some of the present limitations in government e-learning.

3.1 Lower quality of the civil servants' training

Compared with the west countries, the government training in China remains room to develop. Not surprisingly, "course quality" is the most important concern in this e-learning environment. Course content should be carefully designed and presented sparingly [5]. The problems are (a) governments don't take the servants' training seriously. On the governments' side, they didn't take the training as the one important way of the human resource management. On the other hand, because of the lack of the publicizing, the servants didn't pay enough attention to the civil servants' training either. (b) Some of the courses are out of data, so they can't be satisfied with every servant's need. (c) Because of the fund of the civil servants' training is limited, many of the training can't provide profound education materials. All the problems above lead a lower quantity of the servants' job training in China.

3.2 Ineffective motive mechanism

In order to resolve the problems like lower motivation, lower enthusiasm of the job training, the government must complete the motivation mechanism. The government should consider the training grade as the civil servants' job achievements, and the government also should list the grade in the servants' archives. Those who don' take part in the training with no reasonable excuse and who don't get enough marks should be evaluated eligible and should not be prompted until they make up a missed lesson. So generally speaking, unless the governments build the effective motive mechanism, the servants won't inspire a strong learning volition and won't take part in the job training actively.

3.3 The uniform manner of training

The problem of uniform can be said to be magnified. More specifically, the problems arise from the fact that many of the Internet communication training courses prepared for government educational training are uniform in terms of their fields of knowledge, types of training, target users, levels, and development methods. Not only are the same courses being developed and taught, so they overlap, but they also tend either to be too theory-oriented or concentrated in only certain easy fields. Development methods also tend to be uniform, unable to fulfill the diverse and specialized needs of governments.

3.4 Disproportion in the fairness and availability of opportunities for educational training

There are also problems in terms of fairness and balance in educational training opportunities. Currently, the main beneficiaries of Internet communication training systems tend to be the office administrative staff of governments. When governments administered their own training programs, it was fount that all the courses, with the exception of one, were being targeted at leaders.

4 E-learning system used as job-training tools

Today, governments are making great effort to properly adjust to the change learning environment to enhance their competitiveness. In step with the development of information technology and the Internet, many governments are replacing traditional vocational training with e-learning.

The Interment and World Wide Web have provided opportunities of developing e-learning systems. The goal of introducing a training program is to increase task ability with advanced trainees' knowledge, technology and attitude.

4.1 To reform the training policy

The measurements of reforming the training policy are as follow:

4.1.1 To promotion by the result of the job-training

According to the report during the Eleventh Five-Year Plan period, all the civil servants will be examined comprehensively. The goal of examination is to improve all the servants' political thinking and the vocation abilities. What's more, the government will launch a principle which will take the servants' learning grade as one of the conditions of prompting.
(http://www.gmw.cn/content/2007-02/26/content_558387.htm)

4.1.2 To take work efficiency into count

The goal of the e-learning system is to improve the efficiency of the human resource. Task-related content directly affect trainee's learning performance. So if the government wants to improve the work efficiency by using e-learning, they must induce the e-learning into the every day's work. For instance, for the servants who need more practice, the e-learning should help them practice the work skillfully. For the other servants whose works on the datum, document and information management .etc, e-learning should help them how to deal with such work efficiently. Of course, all these above need a completive plan of e-learning.

4.1.3 To build a better learning environment

In order to remove the negativity from the servants, the governments and other public sectors should build a well learning environment inside the organizations. The civil servants should realize that "work" and "learning" are not opposite, but the two sides of one thing. Learning is the core of work, and the process of work is a process which is a kind of self-training and learning among all the staff. So if the governments want to build a well learning environment they must (a) The civil servants' e-learning must be supported by the office administrative staff of governments. The government leader themselves should take part in the e-learning and admit the new thinking and learning methods. (b) Harmonize the e-learning and other learning methods. Build a proper learning system, and create a completive learning environment step by step. (c) An effective motivation mechanism can help us build a good learning environment.

4.1.4 To reform the training methods

The civil servants' learning must turn from the traditional education methods to modern education methods. We must develop some scientific methods and use the web technology such as the www, E-mail and computer conference also can be combined with print materials. On the other hand, the e-learning can also choose a flexible timetable such as long-term learning, short-term learning and work-study program. In one word, in order to deal with the contradiction between work and trainings, the time problem must be well-handled.

4.1.5 To evaluate the training

Reaction and learning are studied as major indicators of training outcomes; however, these variables are not the appropriate indicators of the final desired outcome of training programs—transference of learning to the job. An appropriate evaluation of training outcomes is made by measuring changes in job performance and relating it to measurements of achievement of learning goals [6].

Evaluation is conducted after completing of a course or program. It shows the degree of accomplishment of program objectives. And of course program evaluation procedures can improve instruction significantly and also can serve as justification for continued effort or support in civil servants' lifelong learning. Evaluation is important because the outcomes of the evaluation can be used for more up-to date, more effective, and more efficient instruction in the future. The advantages of a web-based system will become easier because updates in web-courses are easier and faster to implement than with traditional education.

4.2   To design an effective system

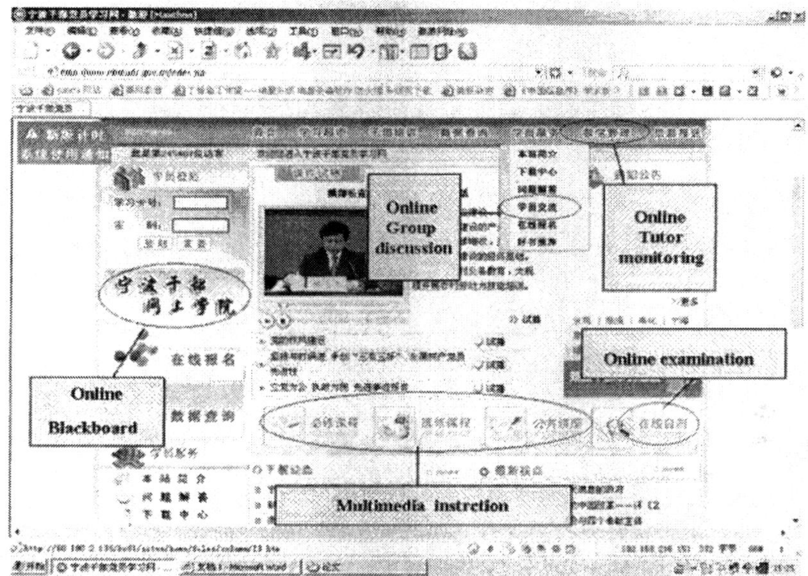

Fig. 1. The e-learning system

In general, e-learning refers to the use of Internet technologies to deliver a broad array of solutions that enhance knowledge and performance [7]. In other words, when an online site is designed, the site's ease of use should be considered important factors.

The e-learning system is a web-based system. Thus, it can be plugged into web browsers when civil servants use it as a learning assisted tool. The major functions of the e-learning system include: [8] multimedia instructional content, group discussion function, blackboard function, tutor monitoring function and e-learning system. First, based on the e-learning system, it supports nonlinear networks to access information, and instructional formats are ill-structured and networked. Secondly, it offers a multimedia environment where instructional contents are driven by multimedia. Third, it supports interactive communication and random-access network, thus activities are performed cooperatively and collaboratively. Fourth, based on the system, it provides a cross-platform environment. And fifth, it support interactive communication and cross-platform environments that accommodate learning activities. Fig1 shows such e-learning system.

The governments will create better online courses that ensure servants have access to high-quality course content, interaction among small groups of servants and colleagues. In my opinion an e-learning environments should be build and maintained as follow:

- Technology will be used to incorporate active and collaborative, resource-centered learning into general government courses.
- Key courses will be easily shared among governments or departments, civil servants from many departments into a single learning community.
- Traditional face-to-face courses will routinely include on-line elements as part of courses, and let every servants take part in.
- Enable members within a unit will be able to share online learning objects efficiently across individual courses in training and to ensure consistent quality in the presentation of content at all locations where a course is taught.
- Enable members will be able to store, access, and re-purpose digital course contents.
- Some government programs will be extended outside its own city and share through all the cities around China by using the e-learning environment.
- All faculty servants will have the opportunity to incorporate some level of on-line learning in their courses.
- All the civil servants, regardless of post and rank, will have the opportunity to participate as active producers, not just consumers, of web-based knowledge.

In order to realize this vision, the government requires an e-learning environment that integrates four elements of on-line learning. It refers to the distance education of pedagogic [9]:

① ***Creation of course modules:*** The quality of the e-learning experience follows from the quality of the course modules and of the interactions among trainers and servants that make up online courses. The faculty members, servants, and instructional staff who design and produce on-line course modules need access to powerful tools and reliable training strategies.

② ***Management of course modules:*** Innovative database management practices are required to facilitate efficient revision and re-purposing of course modules and to foster sharing of modules among servants and programs. Responsibility for this element is shared among departments, local governments support facilities

③ ***Delivery of courses:*** At the core of the common e-learning environment is a delivery system that makes course modules available on-line, mediates interactions between the government and the servants, and helps the government to efficiently manage servants' records.

④ ***Delivery of support services:*** All the civil servants---in government or off---deserve access to technical support, digital library resources and other key aspects of the government experience. A common e-learning environment will help facilitate this access.

The following considerations are also crucial in designing e-learning environment: keeping up servants' motivation and providing reinforcement, making direct assistance available, providing ongoing technical services, assuring easy access to computer and modem, ensuring that the network software system is appropriate for the application and available for the duration and extent required, and assuring the servants are at the appropriate level of computer usage.

5   Conclusion

E-learning in the civil servants' job-training is attracting interest not simply as a tool for innovating the civil servants' job-training and developing education system, but also for prompting social cohesion , actualizing educational welfare and encouraging international cooperation. Online learning is an alternative to traditional face-to-face education. Many governments are going to use e-learning to meet servants' needs, especially those of non-traditional servants with full time jobs. Since e-learning is conducted using the Internet and World Wide Web, the learning environment becomes more complicated. Servants' initial perceived satisfaction with technology-based e-learning will determine whether they will use the system continually.

Even though the e-learning's execution currently has a growth potential in China, the overall degree of social use is still low in China. Institution measures that take into consideration the needs of users are especially weak. Accordingly, in addition to fully reforming the job-training of the governments, legal systems, e-learning systems and the proper mechanism related to educational informatization and e-learning must be established in China.

References

1. S.S. Liaw andH. M. Huang, "Enhancing interactivity in Web-based instruction: A review of the literature", *Educational Technology* ,40(3), 41–45(2000).
2. S. Vosniadou, "Toward a revised cognitive psychology for new advances in learning and instruction", *Learning and Instruction,* 6(2), 95–109(1996).
3. R.T. Raab andW.W. Ellis and B.R. Abdon, "Multisectoral partnerships in e-learning: a potential force for improved human capital development in the Asia Pacific", *Internet and Higher Education* ,4 (3–4), 217–229 (2002).
4. T. Govindasamy, "Successful implementation of E-learning: pedagogical considerations", *Internet and Higher Education,* 4 (3–4), 287–299(2002).
5. P.C. Sun, J. Ray , Tsai and F. Glenn, "What drives a successful e-learning? An empirival investigation of the critical factors influencing learner satisfaction", *Computers&education* , 2007,1-20 (2006).
6. K. Kreiger, J. K. Ford and E. Salas, "Application of cognitive, skill-based, and affective theories of learning outcomes to new methods of training evaluation", *Journal of Applied Psycholog,y* 78, 311–328(1993).
7. M.J. Rosenberg, *E-learning, strategies for delivering knowledge in the digital age,* New York: McGraw Hill (2001).
8. S.S. Liaw, H.M. Huang and G.D. Chen, "An activity-theoretical approach to investigate learners' factors toward e-learning systems", *Computers in Human Behavior* 23(2006).
9. Hohn T Harwood.
http://www.web.psu.edu/archive/e-learning%2orepart%20051310.pdf.

Evaluate E-loyalty of sales website: a Fuzzy mathematics method

Ying Yi [1],Zhen-yu Liu[2] , Ying-zi Xiong[3]
1 School of Management, Xiamen University , Xiamen,361005,P.R.China
yidiandian99@sina.com
2 School of Management, Xiamen University,Xiamen,361005,P.R.China
freiman@sina.com
3 School of Management, Xiamen University,Xiamen,361005,P.R.China
xyingzi@xmu.edu.cn

Abstract. The study about online consumer loyalty is limited, but how to evaluate the customers' E-loyalty to a sales website is always a noticeable question. By using some methods of fuzzy mathematics, we provide a more accurate way to evaluate E-loyalty of sales website. Moreover, this method can differentiate level and degree of each factor that influences E-loyalty.

1   Introduction

With the development of electronic commerce, more and more companies have conducted online sales in their website. Generally, customers' switching costs of sales website is very low. For customer, jumping from one website to other alternative websites that offer similar products or services is very easy, just a click of mouse. Therefore a company must take some measures to retain their online customers. First of all, a company needs to know the customers' E-loyalty to their sales website. By evaluating the website E-loyalty degree, a company can find defects, then take action to improve customers' E-loyalty.

In this paper, website E-loyalty means online customers' loyalty to sales website. We know that costs associated with acquiring new customers is five times the costs of retaining customers[1]. In electronic commerce, research has revealed that keeping and attracting customers is so expensive and switching online is so easy[2]. This is why E-loyalty is so important to retailer online. Loyal customers would often visit your website and purchase merchandise. Loyal customers want to be associated with your website, and tell other people about your website. Loyal customers don't even want to consider the competition's offers. E-loyalty means that you can get a much bigger piece of each customer's lifetime value. Consequently, your profits would increase, and your stock prices would get higher.

Anyway, retailer online should evaluate its customers' E-loyalty and try to improve it. However evaluating E-loyalty is difficult because too many factors would influence E-loyalty, and the effect of each factor is different. Existing evaluating method usually don't differentiate effect of each factor, and factors are too miscellaneous. This reduces accuracy and usability of E-loyalty evaluating result.

In this paper, we provide a more accurate way to evaluate E-loyalty of sales website. We use some methods of fuzzy mathematics to evaluate E-loyalty. Using these methods we can differentiate effect of each factor.

2 Four-layer comprehensive evaluation index system

Many scholars have investigated online customer's switching behaviors. Some people study the difference of online customers. They analyze online customers' behavioral patterns, attitudes, demographic characteristics, and so on. They try to find out character and discriminate factors between stayers and switchers[3,4,5].

To establish evaluation index of E-loyalty, we are more interested in studies that investigate impact factors of E-loyalty. Based on conventional theory of consumer behavior, research has showed that customer loyalty and retention lie on customer satisfaction and switching barriers[6,7,8].Chen and Hitt found that customer demographic characteristics have little effect on switching online, but that systems usage measures and systems quality are associated with reduced switching[9]. Based on relationship marketing theory, commitment and trust are the main reasons for customer to stay with a business. The effects of these social and psychological factors are very important for customer retention.

Actually, the customers' E-loyalty to a sales website comes from many aspects. As we describe above, most studies show that these factors include customer satisfaction, switching barriers, commitment, trust and so on. To describe directly all these factors using quantitative index is almost impossible. However we find that these factors lie on the quality, service , action of website ultimately. So we adopt an indirect method to deal with this problem. We can describe the customers' E-loyalty to a sales website by a series of website evaluating index.

Indeed, a single index can't reflect all factors. In order to provide an effective evaluation, it is necessary to establish a systematic comprehensive index system. In order to distinguish so many factors, we should classify these factors in terms of characteristic of the factors. So we introduce a four-layer comprehensive evaluation index system by settling correlative study results.

According to existing correlative study and our analysis, we think the E-loyalty comes from customer satisfaction, switching costs and trust. Research has indicated that satisfaction have significant effect on online customer loyalty[6,8]. But customer satisfaction is a necessary condition of E-loyalty, not a sufficient condition . Online customers are likely to switch to other sales websites and select other E-retailers even though they are very satisfied with your online sales. In fact, switching costs is the actual reason preventing customer from switching. Switching costs is all expenses when customer switches to other suppliers which includes two kinds of costs. One can be scaled by currency while another can't be scaled by currency. In the later kind of switching costs, the most important representation is trust. So the factors effecting customers' E-loyalty are classified as three sorts, that is, customer satisfaction, switching costs and trust . Each sort needs to be subdivided. In the end, we establish a four-layer comprehensive evaluation index system.

We think E-loyalty comes from three aspects. Each aspects is influenced by many factors, we subdivide and conclude a hierarchy of primary factors(see Table 1).The analysis is chiefly based on existing study results[5,9,10,11].

So the E-loyalty is determined by three combined index, i.e.$O=f(U_1,U_2,U_3)$. Combined index U_1 is determined by combined $U_{11},U_{12},U_{13},U_{14},U_{15}$, and combined index U_{jj} is determined terminal index U_{ijk} . The index, U_2 and U_3 , are similar. The value of terminal index can be given by experts and customers.

Table 1. the four-layer comprehensive evaluation index system

First layer	Second layer	Third layer	Fourth layer
O: E-loyalty	U_1: Customer satisfaction	U_{11}: laying out merchandise	U_{111}: convenient navigation
			U_{112}: variety of merchandise
			U_{113}: update speed
		U_{12}: usability of website	U_{121}: speed of download
			U_{122}: variety information format
			U_{123}: security
			U_{124}: stability
			U_{125}: accessibility
		U_{13}: transaction process	U_{131} :choose and buy
			U_{132} :deal with order
			U_{133} : payment
			U_{134} :delivery
		U_{14}: support and service	U_{141}: various service and support mode
			U_{142}: responding speed of service and support
			U_{143}: conformity of online and offline
		U_{15}: provision of information and tool	U_{151}: search engine
			U_{152}: other helpful information
			U_{153}: tools of analysis and comparison
	U_2: Switching costs	U_{21} : renege on the contract	U_{211}: renege compensation
			U_{212}: bargaining costs
		U_{22} : repetitive purchase discount	
		U_{23} : profit from loyal plan	

		U_{31}:communication with customers	U_{311}: responding speed to reasonable customer demand and advice
			U_{312}: frequency of communicating with customer
			U_{313}: variety of communication mode
			U_{314}: effect of measure in customer relation maintenance
	U_3 Trust	U_{32}: treat with of customer complain	U_{321}: responding speed to customer complaint
			U_{322}: usefulness of customer complaint treatment
		U_{33}: privacy	U_{331}: customer privacy protection policy
			U_{332}: customer privacy protection technique
			U_{333}: transparency of private information collection

3 Fuzzy comprehensive evaluation model

Comprehensive evaluation includes three elements: evaluation index, evaluation value and evaluation result. For each evaluation index , we can acquire a evaluation value, and this evaluation value forms a evaluation result. In fuzzy comprehensive evaluation [12], evaluation index is a set of index , and evaluation value is a set of remarks. For example, the evaluation value is V={very satisfied, satisfied , appreciably satisfied, not satisfied}. Assuming evaluation index as set $U=\{u_1,u_2,...u_n\}$, evaluation value as set $V=\{v_1,v_2,...v_m\}$, the evaluation result is a fuzzy mapping:

$$f : U \rightarrow F(V)$$

the fuzzy mapping f forms a fuzzy relation R, R is a matrix:

$$R = \begin{bmatrix} r_{11}, r_{12}, ...r_{1m} \\ r_{21}, r_{22}, ...r_{2m} \\ .... \\ r_{n1}, r_{n2}, ...r_{nm} \end{bmatrix} \qquad (1)$$

Because weightiness of each evaluation index is different, we should distribute each evaluation index a weighting coefficient. Assuming the weighting coefficient set as

$$A = \left(a_1, a_2, ...a_n\right) \qquad (2)$$

Then fuzzy comprehensive evaluation is calculated as follows:

$$B = \left(b_1, b_2, ...b_m\right) = A \circ R \qquad (3)$$

$$b_i = \sum_j (a_j \times r_{ji}) \tag{4}$$

in Eq.(4), we use "+" and "x " operators instead of Zadeh operators(max and min)in order to get a normalization result.

Our evaluation index system has four-layer, so the comprehensive evaluation is calculated as follows:

$$O = A \circ B = A \circ \begin{bmatrix} B_1 \\ B_2 \\ B_3 \end{bmatrix} = A \circ \begin{bmatrix} A_1 \circ C_1 \\ A_2 \circ C_2 \\ A_3 \circ C_3 \end{bmatrix} \tag{5}$$

$$C_1 = \begin{bmatrix} C_{11} \\ C_{12} \\ C_{13} \\ C_{14} \\ C_{15} \end{bmatrix} = \begin{bmatrix} A_{11} \circ R_{11} \\ A_{12} \circ R_{12} \\ A_{13} \circ R_{13} \\ A_{14} \circ R_{14} \\ A_{15} \circ R_{15} \end{bmatrix} \tag{6}$$

$$C_2 = \begin{bmatrix} C_{21} \\ R_{22} \\ R_{23} \end{bmatrix} = \begin{bmatrix} A_{21} \circ R_{21} \\ R_{22} \circ R_{22} \\ R_{23} \circ R_{23} \end{bmatrix} \tag{7}$$

$$C_3 = \begin{bmatrix} C_{31} \\ C_{32} \\ C_{33} \end{bmatrix} = \begin{bmatrix} A_{31} \circ R_{31} \\ A_{32} \circ R_{32} \\ A_{33} \circ R_{33} \end{bmatrix} \tag{8}$$

where vector A denotes the weighting coefficients of second layer index U_1, U_2, U_3. Similarly, vector A_1, A_2, A_3 and A_{ij} are the weighting coefficients of third layer index and fourth layer index.

$$A = (a_1, a_2, a_3) \tag{9}$$

$$A_1 = (a_{11}, a_{12}, a_{13}, a_{14}, a_{15}) \tag{10}$$

$$A_{11} = (a_{111}, a_{112}, a_{113}) \tag{11}$$

$$A_{12} = (a_{121}, a_{122}, a_{123}, a_{124}, a_{125}) \tag{12}$$

$$A_{13} = (a_{131}, a_{132}, a_{133}, a_{134}) \tag{13}$$

$$A_{14} = (a_{141}, a_{142}, a_{143}) \tag{14}$$

$$A_{15} = (a_{151}, a_{152}, a_{153}) \tag{15}$$

$$A_2 = (a_{21}, a_{22}, a_{23}) \tag{16}$$

$$A_{21} = (a_{211}, a_{212}) \tag{17}$$

$$A_3 = (a_{31}, a_{32}, a_{33}) \tag{18}$$

$$A_{31} = (a_{311}, a_{312}, a_{313}, a_{314}) \tag{19}$$

$$A_{32} = (a_{321}, a_{322}) \tag{20}$$

$$A_{33} = (a_{331}, a_{332}, a_{333}) \tag{21}$$

Matrix R_{ij} is evaluation result, determined by fuzzy mapping:

$$f_{ij}: U_{ij} \text{->} F(V)$$

Rij can be obtained from experts' grade or/and customers inquiry . The process of obtaining these data is very simple. A company merely needs to send questionnaire to experts and customers through Internet, and call back questionnaire. In e-commerce circumstance, it is easy and low-cost. Certainly, the company should use right manner and means so that customers are willing to accept survey. In this way, the company could achieve high ratio of questionnaire callback. The evaluation result based on enough data is effective .

4 Determining weighting coefficients of the comprehensive evaluation model

There are many factors that influence E-loyalty. We differentiate these factors by classification, and establish fourth-layer index system. The effect of each index is different, so each index is distributed a weighting coefficient. But how to determine weighting coefficients is more accurate? There are many methods that we can choose to determine weighting coefficients. These methods are the Delphi method, the comparative matrix method, the analytical hierarchy process (AHP) and so on. When we implement fuzzy comprehensive evaluation, we can select an appropriate method according to convenience of data collection and decision environment. If the weighting coefficients can be directly determined, we can choose the Delphi method. If the data can be compared in pairs, we can choose the comparative matrix method. If the relative importance of index can be estimated, we can choose AHP.

Usually, weighting coefficients should conform to consistency, so we should make consistency test. If weighting coefficients can't conform to consistency, we should determine weighting coefficients once again. In the end, we should make weighting coefficients normalization to obtain final weighting coefficients.

The process of determining weighting coefficients is indicated in Fig.1.

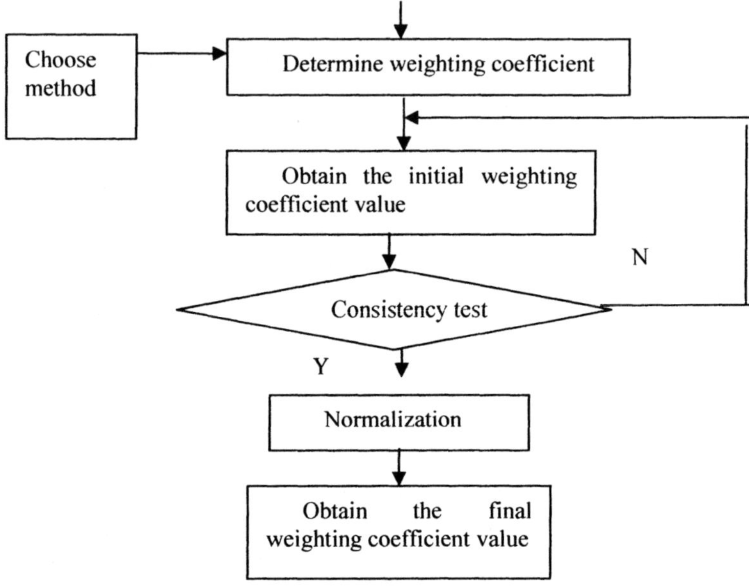

Fig. 1. the process of determining weighting coefficients

5 Conclusion

In this paper, we propose a four-layer evaluation index system and a fuzzy comprehensive evaluation model for evaluating E-loyalty of sales website. The main advantage of this method is that those factors affecting E-loyalty of sales website can be classified by four layers, and different effect of each factor can be differentiated by weighting coefficient. Moreover, the evaluation process, including data collection and calculation, is simple and feasible.

This model can be implemented conveniently on microcomputer using computer programming language and a relational database. For a sales website, evaluating its E-loyalty frequently, discovering existing disadvantage and improving E-loyalty is very important in fierce market competition.

References

1. S.M. Keaveney, "Customer switching behavior in service industries: An exploratory study", *Journal of Marketing*, 59,71-82 (1995).

2. F.F. Reichheld and P. Schefter, "E-loyalty: Your secret weapon on the Web", *Havard Business Review*,78(4),105-113(2000).

3. S.M. Keaveney and M. Parthasarathy, "Customers switching behavior in online services: An exploratory study of the role of selected attitudinal, behavioral , and demographic factors", *Journal of the Academy of Marketing Science*,29(4), 374-390(2001).

4. D. Gefen , E. Karahanna , and D. Straub, "Trust and TAM in online shopping: An integrated model", *MIS Quarterly*,27(1), 51-90(2003).

5. D.H .Li, G.J. Browne, and J.C. Wetherbe, "Online consumers' Switching behavior: A Buyer-Seller Relationship Perspective", *Journal of Electronic Commerce in Organizations*,5(1), 30-42(2007).

6. A. Bhattacherjee, "Understanding information systems continuance: An expectation confirmation model", *MIS Quarterly*,25(3), 351-370(2001).

7. C. Flavian, M. Guinaliu , and R. Gurrea, "The role played by perceived usability , satisfaction and consumer trust on Website loyalty", *Information & Management*,43(1), 1-14(2006).

8. C. Park and Y. Kim, "The effect of information satisfaction and relational benefit on consumers' online shopping site commitments", *Journal of Electronic Commerce in Organizations*,4(1) ,70-90(2006).

9. P.Y. Chen and L.M. Hitt, "Measuring Switching costs and Their Determinants in Internet-Enabled Businesses : A Study of the Online Brokerage Industry", *Information System Research*, 13(3),255-274(2002).

10.N. Sharma and P. Patterson, "Switching costs, alternative attractiveness and experience as moderators of relational commitment in professional consumer services", *International Journal of Service Industry Management*, 11(5),470-482(2000).

11.J.E. Collier and C.C. Bienstock, "How Do Customers Judge Quailty in a E-tailer?" ,*MITSloan Management Review*,48(1),35-40(2006).

12.L.B. Yang and Y.Y. Gao, *Fuzzy mathematics: theory and application*(South China University of Technology Press, Guangzhou,2001).

CSPMS supported by information technology

Hudan Zhang[1], Heng Wu[2]
1 School of information management, Wuhan University,
430072 Wuhan,China, tigertibet@163.com
2 School of economics and management, Wuhan University,
430072 Wuhan,China, carol_2002124@263.net

Abstract. This paper will propose a whole new viewpoint about building a CSPMS(Coal-mine Safety Production Management System) by means of information technology. This system whose core part is a four-grade automatic triggered warning system achieves the goal that information transmission will be smooth, nondestructive and in time. At the same time, the system provides a comprehensive and collective technology platform for various Public Management Organizations and coal-mine production units to deal with safety management, advance warning, unexpected incidents, preplan implementation, and resource deployment at different levels. The database of this system will support national related industry's resource control, plan, statistics, tax and the construction of laws and regulations effectively.

1 Introduction

The issue of coal-mine safety production is a rigorous society problem confronted by world wide countries especially by developing countries like China. Many countries invest a large number of labor power, material resources and financial strength to solve this problem, however recurring mine accidents cause huge losses to society. Nowadays, with the fast-speed development of information technology, it is a significant research topic to construct the new Coal-mine Safety Production Management System (CSPMS) using achievements of information technology wisely. Among systems that have been developing or have been put into practice presently, most of them depend on production units, searching and processing the production site information to proceed the purpose of warning and supervision.

This paper will describe an idea that putting all levels of production units and government management organizations into a collective platform, adopting the four-grade automatic triggered warning system, ultimately accomplish the goal that information transmission will be smooth and in time to the maximum extent. This system can truly attain informatization of coal-mine safety

Please use the following format when citing this chapter:

Zhang, H., Wu, H., 2007, in IFIP International Federation for Information Processing, Volume 252, Integration and Innovation Orient to E-Society Volume 2, eds. Wang, W., (Boston: Springer), pp. 590-596.

management, supervision and Administrative &law enforcement work, provide a new solution for government and various mines to handle things such as real-time accident prediction, eliminating hidden dangers, safety production trend analysis, dealing with serious unexpected incidents.

2 Basic structure of the CSPMS

The CSPMS consists of following parts: Data Acquisition, Database and Data Analysis System, and Four-grade automatic triggered mechanism.

2.1 Data Acquisition

Data acquisition, which mainly includes: all kinds of safety monitoring indicators on coal-mine production site, production and management data (such as underground safety production and monitoring data, mining volume, inventory, etc.) , is the basis of the whole system's ordinarily running. And the veracity of data directly influences the system's accuracy of advance warning and decision-making. All application data of system is collected in the field of coal-mine production site, using two different collect methods: automatic collection and artificial acquisition. Automatic collection refers to the collection that is done by acquisition instrument which has been tested and approved by production units, and automatic collected data will be input to system. Artificial acquisition is done by qualified individuals on the production site and then input the data to system in time.

To protect the originality and accuracy of data, responsibilities had to be signed to specific staff, and all data can not be updated and revised once they entered system. Time will be automatically recorded by systems, necessary changes will be proceeded by the way without covering the original data.

2.2 Database and Data Analysis System

Database is made up of production site collected data, comparative data and various preplans. Comparative data mainly come from all kinds of laws, regulations, technology standards, safety indicators system, and production units' characteristic safety production data in the actual production. Preplans are constituted by relevant government department based on laws and different situation in different area.

Data analysis system analyzes all kinds of real-time data on the production site according to the comparative data. Based on each grade's trigger point that has been pre-set, system will react different warning up to different grades and activate the preplans. Data analysis can also analyzes original data request to demands, to fulfill the government's demands of resource controlling, deployment, statistic, planning, etc.

2.3 Four-grade automatic triggered mechanism

Based on the demand of coal-mine safety production management and the actual situation of our country's present system, this system adopted four-grade automatic triggered mechanism. System pre-set the four automatic trigger points in accordance with comparative data, and when the real-time data has been input into the system, data analysis system will analyze at the very time: (1) Once production site has troubles, data anomalies activate first-grade trigger; (2) Once data analysis suggest approaching the risk critical point, second-grade trigger will be activated; (3) when common accident happened, third-grade trigger will be activated; (4) when serious accident happened, fourth-grade trigger will be activated.

When the first-grade trigger is activated, which means unusual situation of the production site, main managers of the production unit are informed, then they will activate preplan and deal with the situation immediately, until trouble is solved and system is back to the normal condition; When the second-grade trigger is activated, which means the risk critical point is approaching, the managers of production unit and managers in the high level (county, city level) of safety supervision and government's safety production management department should be informed at the same time, preplan will be activated and executed by the managers of higher level of safety supervision and government's safety production management department. The two kinds of trigger point is used for eliminating hidden danger and advance warning, and most problems generated in the actual production can be handled by using them.

When the third-trigger is activated, which means common accidents happened, at this time, Ministry of Supervision, relevant Ministries and Commissions Directly under the State Council and lower level government departments are informed at the same time, preplans will be activated and executed by province government or by departments of Ministry of Supervision that are at the same level with province government.

When the fourth-trigger is activated, which means sudden serious accidents happened, Ministry of Supervision, relevant Ministries and Commissions Directly under the State Council and lower department should be informed at the same time, preplan will be activated and executed by Ministry of Supervision and relevant Ministries and Commissions Directly under the State Council.

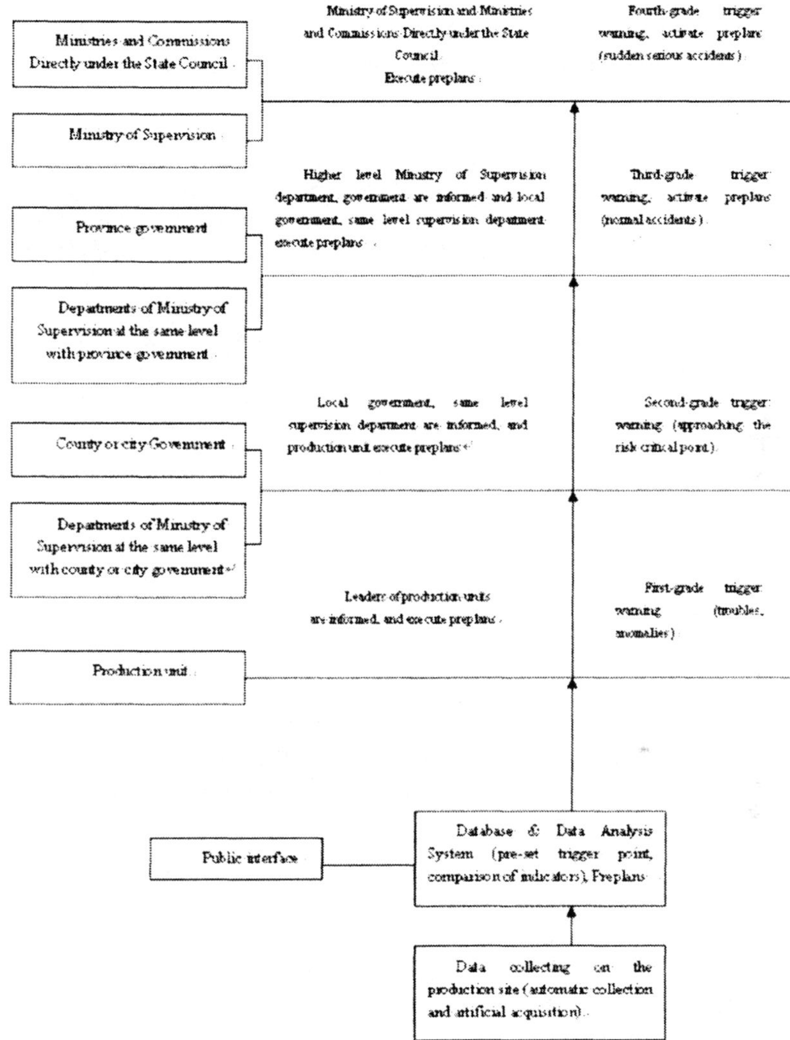

Fig 1. Four-grade automatic triggered mechanism

The third and fourth grade triggered points are used for advance warning and activating or implementing emergency preplans

All conditions and data of execution of preplan after the activation of four-grade automatic trigger mechanism will be recorded in the system in time.

The whole system adopts downward-compatible set of vertical authority, supervisors can monitor the condition of subordinate departments and production units.

3 Characteristics of the CSPMS

3.1 The accuracy of system information and smooth, nondestructive information transmission

Measures that are taken when acquiring information from the source, ensure the authenticity of the original information. Four-grade automatic trigger mechanism on the collective platform ensures that all levels of government departments and production units can be informed at the same time, and the mechanism greatly enhance the ability of supervision and security execution, make safety management and advance warning be more effective. As a result, phenomena that information has been concealed, omitted, misstated, deferred are avoid drastically.

3.2 Improve the handling accidents efficiency & Guarantee the implementation of preplans

When accidents---especially serious accidents---happen, because all related departments are informed at the same time, repeated communication is avoid and the efficiency and ability of accidents handling are improved. The constitution process of preplan makes all relevant departments doing their own jobs: relevant departments of Ministry of Supervision and coal-mine sectors rescue the injured and take care of accidents' consequence; local governments deploy police, medical and other social resources and public relations and crisis. The accuracy of information and the smooth of information transmission can ensure all kinds of preplans be implemented successfully and ensure that resource allocation can attain a maximum point during the accidents handling, finally, to achieve good results.

3.3 Easy to clarify responsibilities

Stringent control methods and constitution of various preplans in system that have been done on the production site where information is collected, has one of the main characteristics of which is to break down each work and responsibilities to individuals. And system has complete records on the work implementation. So it can trace the specific responsibilities to individuals when the problems arise. Then the situations that nobody or collectivity takes responsibility to the problems will no longer appear.

3.4 Easy for Implementation

This system can be immensely implemented and operated in reality. It is mainly reflected in two aspects:

Firstly, this system has a strong relevance with the existing system of China. In China's current system, the government departments are setting classified in accordance with the State Council ministries, provinces, cities and counties. All grades of institutions below the State Administration of Work Safety Supervision are also setting according to classification. Meanwhile governments at all levels are responsible for the safe production and positions setting. It is the system that putting production units and all grades of governments, control safety agencies on a common platform. Connect regulatory powers and responsibilities of relevant departments at all levels with one another through the 4 classes trigger mechanism. Thus the system can fully operate normally in our existing institutional framework.

Secondly, the implementation of the system can effectively utilize all existing inputs in information building of all production units and management departments. At present, the information building of all production units and management departments mainly fasten on the hardware, management and the building of locale security indicators monitoring system. This even provides a good foundation for the data acquisition of system.

4 Application and expansion of the CSPMS

The CSPMS is a management system of putting production units and management departments on the same management platform. Therefore, it can not only start implementation from a single mine, but also implement within the big scope. It can add new production units easily. The application is very flexible and convenient.

In the expansion of system functions, we can find the data collection and analysis system for database can provide a powerful function extension: 1) Comprehensive production data collection and analysis can provide the most authentic statistics for national statistics offices. 2) Can provide informative reference for national plan departments, and realize production control and capacity allocation in exceptional circumstances. 3) Can provide authentic reference for national resources control and protect. 4) Can effectively realize the sharing of resources with external management system, such as taxation, environmental protection. 5) Can provide reference materials for relevant industry laws and regulations.

What is more important is that the system is not limited to the application of coal security production management. By changing the source of data and the contrast indexes system of database, the system can be applied to all types of mine production safety production management.

5 Conclusion

Coal-mine safety production has become a very important issue of countries for a long time. Currently, the developed countries represented by Britain and the United States have solved such problems to a large extent, by increasing security funding, enacting complicated regulations and implementing them. However, it also brings increased costs and other practical problems. But limited to the shortage of funds and differences of social conditions, most developing countries represented by China are unable to apply the methods mechanically of Britain and the United States and other countries. The establishment of CSPMS integrates the management advantage of government agencies and production units. It can meet safety production requirements in a more effective way in the case of limited inputs and achieve a good result.

Acknowledge

This paper is supported by the grand research fund of State's Key research base of humanities and social sciences of China (Project No. 05JJD870159)

References

1. Z. J. Li, "Integral evaluation of operating quality and the deciding of management strategy in productive coal mines", *Journal of coal science & engineering,* 6: 91-96(2004)
2. L. A. Kong and W. Y. Zhang, "Analysis on safety production in coal mines henna Province", *Journal of coal science & engineering.* 6: 82-85(2006)
3. H. X. Li , S. C. Tian , Z. M. Yu, Y. G. Chen, "Research on safety management shell in coal mine", *Journal of Coal Science & Engineering.* 10(1) : 49-52(2004)
4. Y. D. Zhen, Y. X. Huang, "CSMS safety management system of coal mining enterprises", Journal of Liaoning Technical University (Social Science Edition). 8(6):608-610 (2006)
5. L. S. Shao, "The problem and solution of Coal mine management informationization", *Technology Economics.*9:94-96(2005)

An Exploratory Discuss of New Ways for Competitive Intelligence on WEB2.0

Zhonghua Deng, Ling Luo
School of Information Management, Wuhan University.
Wuhan, China
hellowdzh@126.com, luolinghuashi@163.com
WWW home page: http://www.whu.edu.cn

Abstract. Competitive Intelligence (CI) plays an increasingly important role in the strategic management and decision-making of enterprises. Adequate and timely information is the necessity of CI which makes the gathering information very import activities in CI. Web2.0 introduced many new types of applications for users to express their thoughts easily and quickly. In the view of CI, Web2.0 paved new ways and channels for gathering information. This article surveys the applications of Web2.0 relative to CI, and explores approaches of gathering information for CI through Web2.0. Four of applications of Web2.0 (Blog, Wiki, SNS, and RSS) are discussed for CI use in detail.

1 Introduction

Since the end of the Cold War, Competitive Intelligence (CI) once widely used in the military has rapidly infiltrated in business competition. According to statistics, in the top 500 enterprises of the world, over 90% of the enterprises have established CI systems, and the fast development speed exceeding the other business sectors, shows a strong vitality and vigorous development momentum. The quality and effectiveness of CI work has maintained close relations with the data collection. Information gathering is the basis and key of CI, therefore, whether or not to collect adequate valuable information determines the success or failure of CI. Elie Zakaria Cagliari Secretary, the senior intelligence analyst of U.S., has pointed out: 95% of the intelligence material from the public, 4% from the semi-public material, only 1% or less from the confidential material [1]. Network information on Internet is also important to public resources, so it is one of the main tasks for CI to collect information from the network.

Now, the new applications of Web2.0 provide new opportunities and channels for CI. Such as the liveliness Web Blogs (blog) which are created by thousands upon thousands individuals, the Wikipedia (wiki) which allow public jointly creating, the technology of RSS which using XML to classify and organize the information, makes the network information more clarity, and etc. All of them bring convenience for CI especially in collecting information. So researching the gathering strategy CI under the new environment is necessary

Please use the following format when citing this chapter:

Deng, Z., Luo, L., in IFIP International Federation for Information Processing, Volume 252, Integration and Innovation Orient to E-Society Volume 2, eds. Wang, W., (Boston: Springer), pp. 597-604.

and meaningful. Based on the analysis of the domestic and international researches on CI and Web2.0 study, we summed up some new approaches of gathering information for CI under the new environment. It is hoped that it is useful to the company engaged in a CI; meanwhile, it is also wished that more and more to study how to gather CI better in the environment of Web2.0.

2   Research Situation

From the essays the domestic and abroad scholars' works, there are many articles on the study of Web2.0 and CI gathering, but the study of combining the two is few. Through analysis, the key elements are as follows.

2.1   Web2.0

Web 2.0 is first raised by O'Reilly, the president and CEO of O'Reilly's media Company. He pointed that the important principle of Web2.0 is: The more users, the better the service. But the fact is that, at present, the IT sector did not reach a consensus for the right Web2.0 definition.

Some people say that WEB2.0 is the collective appellation of the new Internet applications against WEB1.0 and a revolution of application from the core content to the external application. It is a change from simply browse HTML pages through browser (Web1.0 mode) to being of a more enriched content, stronger interactive connectivity and more powerful tool (Web2.0 mode), which has become the new development trend of Internet [2]. Zhudeli[3] pointed out that the change from WEB1.0 to WEB2.0, specifically, is from simply "reading" to "write" and "jointly build" development on the model.

China Internet Association gave Web2.0 a definition: "Web2.0 is a concept of the Internet and the ideological system's upgrade, changed from the top-down Internet system which were concentrated controlled by the few resource holders into the bottom-up Internet-driven system leaded by the general Users wisdom and strength" [5].

In short, the summaries of Web2.0 concept are endless, but the essence of Web2.0 they all embodying is the same, that is, the public network will tap into the Internet resources in construction through a variety of technologies and services. Information is no longer a single expert, or the government and other authoritative bodies. Any person, as long as he has thinking, wanting disseminate information on the Internet, can own a piece of the sky on the Internet. Therefore, Web2.0 has its unique features: personality emphasized users' demand, interaction reflected the users' participation, information based on micro-content.

2.2 The main services of Web2.0

2.2.1 Blog

The most common definition of blog is that blog is a web log which can express one's thoughts, whose contents display according to chronological account, and updates constantly [5]. The ideas can quickly be issued on the blog, exchanging with others and engaging in other activities can be also conducted on the blog. All this is free, what's more, it is easy to operate, not needing professionals. As long as they are able to type, the people can speak freely on the blog.

Shin-ichi Todorlki, Tomoya Konishi. Satoru Inoue point out that [6], the blog has the following functional characteristics:

(1) The contents are ordered by the chronological;

(2) The users need the date, theme and keywords to arrange the special content;

(3) Registering new editorial content, including images, multimedia and linking to other resources, such as the past blog contents, website, the machine data files, remote databases and so on;

(4) All of these functions are achieved through the Web browser without the additional knowledge.

It is thought that the blog represents "the media version 3.0": The old media → new media → we media. So the research on the blog and the media will be more.

Huang Peng [7]: comparing to the other network communication tools, the blog's advantages is not only of a distinctive personal nature, he also has public nature that the media must have because of the face-to-face dissemination way.

Wu Xiaoming [8] pointed out that blog also has grass-roots nature, becoming an important source of news media; blog is of the property of removing center and sharing value; blog news is not subject to various political, economic and cultural taboos, often creating sensational news, as a supplement and innovation of the traditional news media.

There are many other aspects on blog. For example, Lance V.Porter, Kaye D.Sweetser Trammell and Deborah Chung, Kim pointed out that the persons who frequently use blog are prone to own rights in their company. The rights include structure rights, experts rights, priority rights, etc.. [9]; Kaye D.Trammel [10] even research on the mutual slander between Kerry and Bush on blog during the election campaign. Visibility, at this stage, the public relations impact and the interpersonal impact blog plays on is so large.

2.2.2 Wiki

Wiki site can be shared and maintained by many people, and everyone can express their views or expanse and explore the common theme. Many scholars believe that wiki has the following characteristics:(1)Easy to use, mainly in the fast maintenance, simple format, and convenient link and looked naming;(2)Organized, mainly in the function of self-organization and the effectiveness clustering;(3)Growth characteristics, mainly in that the link goals reflected in the pages have not yet exist; pages can be created through clicking on the link, which makes the system grew; and the various versions of pages can be access the revision history of pages;(4)Open, the community members can arbitrarily create, modify, delete pages and page changes of the system can be observed by visitors.

Wiki has been the best platform for academic exchanges and enterprises interpersonal communication. ZHU Chunlei [11] thought that, as wiki's openness, quickness, direct nature and storage, as well as correcting residual timely nature on the information dissemination, it is better than the other forms of communication in the aspects of key information accuracy and completeness.

As Google's founders Lari Pec said: "the convenience painted and alerted changes on wiki are much fitted for staff exchanges in the modern management system. Wiki can break the internal layers' barriers, making those managers, who rely on repressive measures to conduct management, inundated by the groups' command." Obviously, wiki site provides the internal staff for a reliable and practical exchange platform, strengthening the exchanges and knowledge and views sharing between the staffs.

2.2.3 SNS

The theoretical basis of SNS is the Six Separation Theory which founded by the Harvard University psychology professor Stanley Milgram in 1967, "interval persons between you and any strangers are no more than six." In other words, you will be able to recognize any strangers through less than six individuals. According to Six Separation Theory, each individual's social circles will continue to enlarge through SNS, and finally become a major social network [12]. SNS is a member of Web2.0, the abbreviation of Social Networking Service, services through providing the digital Internet to imitate the reality physical network of social, making the network more social, linking with the real world more easily. SNS provides to each person the opportunities to establish their own associations of friends. We all can use SNS establish our own societies, bringing together like-minded friends. The interpersonal networks will be broader than the real world through SNS.

2.2.4 RSS

RSS is the abbreviation of "RDF (Resource Description Framework) Site Summary ", "rich site summary ". It adopts the simple XML format, realizing contents sharing and polymerization among sites. It is a technology platform which lets publishers provide the fragment piecemeal content to the third parties and thereby makes the individual sites or individuals able to collect various materials to a single page; it is a technology that the web sites send the messages to the users' desktop directly. Users can subscribe to their interested contents by RSS. When the web content updates, users can also read the titles and summaries of the new information, and read the transcript [13].

The reader supports the web contents output from RSS without open the web site content pages, greatly saving time. For users, RSS is a subscription mechanism, as subscribe to the newspapers, magazines. Through this subscription mechanism, you can subscribe to any favorite content such as portal news, blog, forums and other articles. While for the content providers, RSS is technology that can send the latest new of the designated site to users directly. In a short RSS makes the content providers and users mutually beneficial.

2.3 The Gathering Information for CI

There are two information sources, one is public and the other is non-public.Wang Yu [14] explored the collection of enterprise CI under the network environment and thought that we can use the patent, search tools, professional institute's sites, Professional databases and the logged data of Internet site.

Yang Guirong [15] also researched on it and raised several principles about gathering data on network environment for CI, that are the bottom line, the maximum, minimum, average; Meanwhile, They also put forward strategy using network to collect the rivals' information.

The research on the gathering CI in environment Web2.0 is little. The research is just separately study the Web2.0 or collection of CI. However, Yang Guirong and other scholars (mentioned above) had referred to often visiting the BBS forum, it will be surprises, which has reflected the thinking of been CI gathering in Web2.0 environment. Michael Chau and Jennifer Xu [16] have also studied Blog Mining and researched the network hatred organizations and the relationship between them, with a very good Blog Network Information Mining thinking.

3. The New Channels for CI on Web2.0

3.1 Through the Blog

As blog is a good platform for expressing self-feelings and views, consequentially, we can mine vast amounts of information for our CI from blog. For example, employees who have a pleasant mood because of promotion will write their own experience how to fight for the promotion opportunities. We will be able to know which kinds of talents the company focuses, and then analyze the important development points, core products and other details through their blogs.

As mentioned above, many academics proved blog as a function of the new media, being added to the traditional media or even the prosperity of traditional news media reports. January 18th, 1998, Mart Dradge issued President Bill Clinton's sex scandal, becoming the first man to report the matter in the world. And the following half year, it leads the American public opinion, the traditional media are being followed up.

Generally, enterprises' CI is difficult to meet the objects of truth, fastness and actability, if it is only based on literature resources. It must need a substantial the "virtual soft" information [17]. Many astute entrepreneurs have the instinct catching "virtual soft" information early. Please look at the story of a few hundred years ago Napoleonic period, the European banker took close attention to the Napoleon-British war progress, for which he layout a thorough intelligence network. When Napoleon who swept across the entire Europe was defeated by Wellington Duke at British Waterloo, the intelligencer of Nafeimo used the intelligence carrier pigeon -- the equivalent of today's e-mail, and promptly notified the bank headquarters, then Nafeimo soled the stock and bonds timely. When the news that Napoleon was defeated reached Europe, as a "real tough" message, stocks and bonds nosedived. Since Nafeimo use the "virtual soft" information to decide timely, his bank made a big profit. Visibly, "virtual soft" plays an important role in CI, therefore, companies need to take advantage of new technologies to capture the "virtual soft" information. The blog news of Web2.0environmental is the very important channel of "virtual soft" information. Using a blog to acquire CI plays a very important role in the companies' strategic decision-making.

3.2 Through the Wiki

Wiki is a collaborative writing system, such a system most suitable to encyclopedias, knowledge base. Wiki technology has well been used in encyclopedias, manuals/FAQ prepared, subject knowledge base. Editing on the wiki, if there is a mistake, the persons who land to the wiki system later will prompt revision thus ensuring the knowledge's validity and accuracy. It is precisely because Wiki system provides everyone platform to display one's self-caliber that knowledge is enable to pooled into enormous knowledge base rapidly. It can save a lot of time to identify the needed information and knowledge on Wiki system, moreover, the information can be also more comprehensive.

In an experiment, we captured Microsoft's specific information from wiki. In the Wikipedia system, the keyword "Microsoft" is typed into the "Tieba". In a very short period of time, Microsoft's specific situation immediately appeared before my face; including Microsoft's development history, famous persons and the other Microsoft details including the pictures that someone went to Microsoft to conduct an inspection, and so on. At this point, if your company is in need of going to investigate in the competitive company, it is able to search their information in the simple way of using Wiki system; meanwhile you can save a lot of investigating expenses. Why not use this method to collect CI? Isn't it saving labors and money? And why should use the Wiki systems other than use the search engines directly to conduct the same operation? Main reasons are: first, search engine is not so successfully in relevance match. Although the matching results showed on the browser are many, the results of real value are just a few pages before. It is not always successful each time searching. While Wiki sites are of a higher degree of relevance, so some irrelevant information has been excluded when matching, and easier to search; Secondly, the another advantage of wiki is that because of many editors' editing and updating, the integrity and authority of the information are their goals, so it can ensure the information accuracy to some extent.

3.3 Through the SNS

In order to obtain competitor's information, Enterprises commonly let its staffs establish links with the staff of competitors, such as being the members of the same club, being the members of a society, being neighbors each other and so on, accessing to the competitor's information inadvertently in the exchanges of each other. But it does have some limitations. For example, the company and his competitors are not in the same city or region, so there is no way to obtain information through interpersonal contacts. However the majority competitors are not at the region.

In the Web2.0 environment, SNS breakthrough this bottleneck, making persons at different areas is also able to establish good interpersonal relationship. Through previous research and analysis, SNS contribute to the links between the virtual world and physical world, and to enable the interpersonal relationships more wide. Therefore, we can use SNS to achieve interpersonal networks that unable to achieve through the physical world, letting the staffs and the competitors' staffs to establish good interpersonal relationships, access to key information of competitors within mutual exchanges, as competitors recent strategic plan, development objectives, product research goals and development orientation of the company which are very valuable information. According to Six Separation Theory, through SNS, we can almost establish good relationships with every competitors' staffs. Thereby, we expand the scope comparing to traditional methods, and improve success rate of gaining CI from the staffs of competitors.

3.4 Through the RSS

For users, RSS is a subscription mechanism as subscribing to newspapers, magazines. Through this subscription mechanism, you can subscribe to any favorite content. For example: Portal news blog, forums and other articles. Due to the complex and confusion of network information, we spend a great deal of time to collect information and but often the information gathered is worthless. What makes us have a headache is that numbers of information providers will take the initiative to push the information without much significance to us to our desktop. Now we use RSS to subscribe to the information we need, and those messages we do not need will no longer be on the browser, lessening the burden of filtering information. For CI workers, they can subscribe to industry news, the development of the industry dynamic information blogs of competitors, the competitors' product advertisements through RSS. As long as there is the latest news, RSS readers will be quick to push these messages to the CI workers' desktop, thereby reducing the time cost of their using search engines to search and filter information, and also reducing a lot of useless information's interference, so CI workers more efficiently.

4 Summaries

CI gathering is not only the foundation of CI, but also the basis of strategic decisions for enterprises. CI gathering in the new network environment opens up a new path for CI work, also develops a new sky for CI research. Web2.0 provides rich application forms, and a convenient way for expressing ideas and the dissemination of information, as well as new channels for CI gathering. The four application forms blog, wiki, SNS, RSS can be used directly in CI gathering.

Of course, there are inherent shortcomings of Web2.0 such as the data random, the diverse expression, changes irregularity, so data mining, analysis of the valuable intelligence from them is the theme of the next step. Meanwhile, Web2.0 also raised another issue, that it provides new ways and means in the gathering intelligence, at the same time; it also brings new difficulties to implement the anti-CI. How to prevent the leakage of information, and how to strengthen the enterprise staffs' binding is also one of the themes following up. It is hoped that there will be more academics attention and research in this field.

Acknowledgments

This research was supported in part by the Ministry of Education under Social Science Major Research Project Fund under Grant NO.06JZD0032.

References

1. Y.Q Wang and Aroop Zutshi, Intelligence winning (Science Press, Beijing, 2004), pp. 520-531.
2. H. Meng, "Where is Web2.0 added to 1.0"., *E-commerce Times.* 2006 (2-3), 47-48.

3. D.L Zhu, "Web2.0 and Ideas for Information Transmission". China *information preview*. 2005 (11), 59-61.

4. Blogger Don. The Interpretation of WEB2.0 Concept (April 19, 2007); http://z.sohu.com/ detail-103208.html

5. X.M Wen, "The Information Services under WEB2.0 Environment". *Journal of Xiangtan Normal University*: 28 (6), 212-214(2006).

6. Shin-ichi Todoroki, Tomoya Konishi and Satoru Inoue, Blog-based Research Notebook: Personal Informatics Workbench for High-throughput Experimentation, *Applied Surface Science*, 252 (7), 2640-2645(2006).

7. H. Peng, "Blog: we media or public media", *Journal of Hebei University* (Philosophy and Social Science), 31(1), 47-48(2006).

8. X.M Wu, "The information dissemination of blog news at the WEB2.0 times", *Journal of Xuzhou Normal University* (Philosophy and Social Sciences Edition), 32(3), 130-137(2003).

9. Lance V. Porter, Kaye D. Sweetser Trammell, Deborah Chung and Eunseong Kim, Blog Power, Examining the effects of Practitioner blog Use on Power in Public Relations, *Public Relations Review*, 33(1), 92-95(2007).

10. Kaye D.Trammell, Blog offensive: An Exploratory Analysis of Attacks Published on Campaign Blog Posts from a Political Public Relations Perspective, *Public Relations Review*, 32 (4), 402-406 (2006).

11. C.L Zhu, "Wiki Begins to Show Excellence in Enterprise Information Application", *Experience Information*. 2006 (10), 73-75.

12. X.G Neng, "SNS : Return to the Reality of Interpersonal Networks Transmission. " *Journal of Hebei University* (Philosophy and Social Science). 31(2), 130-131 (2006).

13. J.H Shen, The Future of RSS Information Integration Dissemination, *Journal of Hebei University* (Philosophy and Social Science). 31 (2), 133-135 (2006).

14. Y. Wang, The Strategy for Enterprise Competitive Intelligence Gathering under Network Environment, Document, *Information & Knowledge*: 2001 (3), 37-38.

15. G.R Yang, G.M Mao and P.S Zhang . "The Strategy for Competitive Intelligence Based on the Network Conditions". *Library Tribune*, 25(6),235-237(2005)

16. Michael Chau and Jennifer Xu." Mining Communities and Their relationships in blogs: A Study of Online Hate Groups". *International Journal of Human-Computer Studies*. 65(1),57-70(2007).

17. F. Chen, Z.P Liang : "The concept of "Information sclerosis" and its guiding significance in Competitive Intelligence". Journal of the China *Society for Scientific and Technical Information*: 2003, 22 (3), 375-379.